Washingtoniana

PHOTOGRAPHS

OCT. 18. 1894.

Levin C. Handy. A view of the interior of the dome in
the Main Reading Room during construction of the
Library of Congress (Jefferson Building), October 18,
1894. Library of Congress Construction Photographs,
Lot 12365.

LC-USL5-572

Washingtoniana

PHOTOGRAPHS

COLLECTIONS IN THE PRINTS
AND PHOTOGRAPHS DIVISION
OF THE LIBRARY OF CONGRESS

KATHLEEN COLLINS

Library of Congress   Washington   1989

This book and the Washingtoniana project in the
Prints and Photographs Division of the Library of Congress
were made possible by a generous grant
from The Morris and Gwendolyn Cafritz Foundation.

Library of Congress Cataloging-in-Publication Data

Library of Congress. Prints and Photographs Division.
  Washingtoniana: photographs.

  Supt. of Docs. no.: LC25.8/2:W27
  Bibliography: p.
  Includes indexes.
  1. Washington (D.C.)—Description—Views—Catalogs.
2. Washington (D.C.)—History—Pictorial works—Catalogs.
3. Photograph collections—Washington (D.C.)—Catalogs.
4. Library of Congress. Prints and Photographs Division—
Catalogs.   I. Collins, Kathleen.   II. Title.
F195.L66   1988   016.779'99753   87–600421
ISBN 0–8444–0588–4 (alk. paper)

∞   The paper used in this publication meets the requirements for permanence
established by the American National Standard for Information Sciences
''Permanence of Paper for Printed Library Materials'' (ANSI Z39.48-1984).

The text is set in Meridien type. Display type is ITC Fenice Regular.

Design: ADRIANNE ONDERDONK DUDDEN

For sale by the Superintendent of Documents,
U.S. Government Printing Office, Washington, D.C. 20402

In the spring of 1983 the Library of Congress received a generous grant from The Morris and Gwendolyn Cafritz Foundation to support the preparation and publication of *Washingtoniana: Photographs.*

The grant allowed the Prints and Photographs Division to engage a project director and three library technicians, who concentrated on the physical processing and arranging of photographs, film negatives, and original glass negatives of Washington, D.C. The library technicians were well trained in archival and museum practices. During the project they found permanent positions outside the Library and thus these support positions had to be refilled more than once. Altogether nine library technicians, two work/study students, and three academic interns worked at different periods on the Washingtoniana project.

During the first six months of the project, the vast Washington, D.C., holdings of the division were carefully surveyed and an inventory of the materials was done. It became obvious that the unprocessed and uncataloged photographs could not be brought under control within a year. Accordingly, the Library applied for a supplementary grant from The Morris and Gwendolyn Cafritz Foundation, and this was received in the summer of 1984. The continuation of the processing of photographs and negatives was thus assured, and the physical arrangement of the 750,000 images was completed by the end of September 1985.

The project director, Dr. Kathleen Collins, supervised the work of the library technicians throughout the processing of the collections. She devised several innovative shortcuts for the transfer of negatives from deteriorating paper sleeves to archival jackets. Use of a photocopier to transfer information from old jackets to new ones saved weeks of tedious typing. Labels and lists were produced using word processors, which speeded work on these basic tasks.

The Washingtoniana project has allowed the Prints and Photographs Division to test new approaches to the sometimes seemingly impossible task of bringing hundreds of thousands of photographs under efficient control and into the hands of researchers. The experience gained during this intense two-year period can be applied to future projects in the Prints and Photographs Division as well as to projects in other large photograph repositories.

During the two-year project, virtually all staff members of the Prints and Photographs Division contributed their knowledge to this venture. Barbara Orbach helped in developing processing plans and provided up-to-date cataloging records for the 350,000 photographs newly processed by the project staff. Jackie Dooley did extensive recataloging, using additional information discovered by the project staff. Elisabeth Betz Parker advised on policies, procedures, and techniques of picture processing and cataloging.

Division curators Beverly Brannan, George Hobart, and C. Ford Peatross shared their knowledge of unprocessed collections and their subject expertise. The reading room reference staff advised on readers' needs and interests. Robert Lisbeth and Carol Johnson aided in choosing and ordering archival preservation supplies.

The Prints and Photographs Division is grateful to The Morris and Gwendolyn Cafritz Foundation for the support that made possible the processing of the Washingtoniana photographs and the preparation and publication of the guide that will open these valuable collections to research use.

Renata V. Shaw
Prints and Photographs Division

Levin C. Handy. Sculpture uncrated in the Main Reading Room during construction of the Library of Congress (Jefferson Building). Library of Congress Construction Photographs, Lot 12365.
LC-USL5-849

TUNNEL, AUG. 16, 1895,

Levin C. Handy. *Workers digging the tunnel between the Library of Congress (Jefferson Building) and the Capitol, August 16, 1895. Library of Congress Construction Photographs, Lot 12365.*

LC-USL5-600

Major Sources

The civil rights march on Washington, viewed from the top of the Lincoln Memorial, August 28, 1963. U.S. News & World Report Collection.

LC-U9-10365-20

Joseph Allen. Vermont Avenue and Fourteenth Street NW (Thomas Circle), since demolished. June 18, 1950. Allen Collection, Lot 11661–9.

LC-A7-5844

Contents

The Southwest Washington redevelopment area, March 26, 1959. U.S. News & World Report *Collection.*

LC-U9-2210-36

Harris & Ewing. "Elderly Mrs. Katie Marks, 4100 block of K Street NW, being rescued from flood waters." October 16, 1942. Harris & Ewing Collection.
LC-H231-4457

Other Sources

Browsing Files

Back Matter

Harris & Ewing. Banner carrier at the Congressional Union for Woman Suffrage. Harris & Ewing Collection.

LC-H25-912

Larz Anderson House (Society of the Cincinnati headquarters), 2118 Massachusetts Avenue NW, 1976. Historic American Buildings Survey.
HABS D.C. WASH 255-15; 1983 (HABS):176

Levin C. Handy. "Test load on east end of octagon
basement floor arch adjoining south stack . . . 4625
bricks in load = 55437 pounds . . . 1075 pounds
per square foot. No sign of crack or crushing . . .
duration of load 6 days." June 19, 1890. Library of
Congress Construction Photographs, Lot 12365.
LC-USL5-119

The Prints and Photographs Division holds about twelve million pictorial items, including political cartoons, posters, historical and fine prints, drawings, and architectural records, as well as documentary and master photographs, illustrated books, and a variety of printed items and ephemera. An estimated 80 percent of the division's holdings are photographic images, and about 8 percent of those photographs relate to the social, political, and architectural history of the capital and its environs, its citizens, and its visitors. These photographs are not housed in a single collection but may be found in hundreds of appropriate groups and storage locations within the Prints and Photographs Division.

As a result of The Morris and Gwendolyn Cafritz Foundation grant, from 1983 to 1985 library technicians with the Washingtoniana project processed for the first time about 350,000 photographs that had been in storage and unavailable, and they improved the arrangement and physical housing of hundreds of thousands of images that had been heavily used but were relatively unprotected and therefore subject to damage. Certain large collections of special interest to researchers are now processed and cataloged, including the Washington-based National Photo Company Collection (about 80,000 items), the lifework of a remarkable Washington photographer, Frances Benjamin Johnston (about 70,000 items), and the glass plate negatives (about 30,000) from the C. M. Bell studio, the most fashionable portrait studio in the capital in the last quarter of the nineteenth century. Photographs from Library of Congress Manuscript Division collections of the papers of important nineteenth- and twentieth-century Washingtonians have been newly processed and cataloged, including material relating to Montgomery Meigs, Benjamin Brown French, Asaph Hall, Nannie Helen Burroughs, and Harold Ickes. The popular Washington, D.C., Geographical File, containing familiar single images of the capital, was reorganized and expanded to about twice its original number of items.

The Washingtoniana project staff (listed below) developed efficient and innovative processing and preservation methods to arrange and protect this material and make it available to researchers. They instituted special marking and storage methods to increase the protection of the materials against theft, mishandling, and misfiling, and standardized names and subject headings, to make searches more effective. Xerographic technology was used to transfer extensive news agency photo caption information from old, acidic, and crumbling paper jackets to new archival sleeves. New microfilming methods made positive reference copies of glass and film negatives, with their accompanying caption information, available to researchers at a fraction of the cost of making photographic prints on paper. Dozens of new and more appropriate archival sleeves, folders, and storage containers for photographs were designed and obtained from manufacturers. These products were used to improve the protection of about 800 older groups of Washington pictures (about 300,000 items), which were processed before such archival materials were available.

Harris & Ewing. Oliver Wendell Holmes house; view of the first study on the second floor. Oliver Wendell Holmes Papers, Manuscript Division, Lot 10304.
LC-USZ62-1452

The Washingtoniana project staff acquired a basic knowledge of Washington history, through reading, tours of important Washington buildings, and neighborhood walking tours, to enable them to identify photographs of particular buildings or neighborhoods. Using word-processing equipment, they produced hundreds of thousands of caption labels for previously unidentified photographs and generated index cards for the Prints and Photographs Division biographical, geographical, and architectural indexes to individual images.

Throughout the project, the Washingtoniana staff put their knowledge of the collections to work in assisting researchers interested in historical photographs of particular buildings or houses, neighborhoods, organizations, or citizens. Research demand for particular subjects and collections shaped the processing priorities of the project and determined to a large extent the kind and degree of intellectual access given to particular subjects in large and small collections. Prints and Photographs Division catalogers worked closely with the Washingtoniana project to provide state-of-the-art bibliographic access to the collections, and to make that access a priority in the division. The Washingtoniana project staff met with curators and archivists from other Washington institutions and collections to share information about processing and preservation methods for collections of Washington photographs and subject access to them. Because of the work of this staff, the Library is able today to make available tens of thousands of individual photographs that were inaccessible to researchers before this time.

Haines Photo Company (Conneaut, Ohio). Panoramic view of downtown (Northwest) Washington and Georgetown, taken from the Washington Monument. Copyright 1912. Panoramic Photographs of Washington, Lot 12333-1.

LC-USZ62-92793   *LC-USZ62-92794*

LC-USZ62-87305   *LC-USZ62-92790*

PROJECT DIRECTOR

Kathleen Collins

LIBRARY TECHNICIANS

Carole Bianchi, September 1983–March 1984
Michael Costello, June 1985–September 1985
Jerrold Davis, August 1985–September 1985
Deborah Klochko, September 1984–February 1985
Inez McDermott, June 1985–September 1985
Druscilla Null, September 1983–June 1984
Phillip Seitz, June 1985–September 1985
Mary Wassermann, September 1983–July 1985
Victoria Westover, May 1984–March 1985

WORK/STUDY STUDENTS

Lisa Berger, November 1984–September 1985
Tanya Chiaravalle, October 1984–August 1985

ACADEMIC INTERNS

Jim Bado
Jim Oliver
Victoria Westover

LC-USZ62-92795

LC-USZ62-92796

LC-USZ62-92791

LC-USZ62-92792

Acknowledgments

The Washingtoniana project preceded and made possible the preparation of this book. Thanks go first and foremost to The Morris and Gwendolyn Cafritz Foundation, which funded both the project and this book.

During the Washingtoniana project, the most essential help was given by the highly competent and efficient processing staff members, who surveyed, sorted, arranged, captioned, preserved, and provided preliminary descriptions for about half of the photographs and collections included in this book. Those staff members are listed above. I am especially grateful to Mary Wassermann, who provided continuity by her long tenure on the project, and to Vickie Westover, who processed the enormous National Photo Company Collection practically single-handedly. Jim Oliver, an intern in the Prints and Photographs Division, has worked closely with the Harris & Ewing Collection for more than three years, from the beginning stages of sorting negatives and xerographically retrieving caption information to the current final stage of preparing a shelflist for use in microfilming the negatives. During the preparation of the manuscript for this book, he provided most of the information about the subjects documented in that collection.

The staff of the Prints and Photographs Division offered valuable support for tasks large and small. The reference staff was particularly helpful in directing the project staff to Washingtoniana sources and collections that might otherwise have been overlooked, and in answering questions about the provenance and processing history of older collections. I wish to thank Mary Ison, in particular, for her help with the architectural holdings, as well as Maja Felaco, Jerald Maddox, Jerry Kearns, and Milton Kaplan. Lacy Dick and Elaine Mills helped to process the Frances Benjamin Johnston Collection while stationed at the reception desk in the division. Annette Melville provided invaluable help by suggesting strategies and resources used by her in the preparation of *Special Collections in the Library of Congress*.

Prints and Photographs Division curators were closely involved with the project and were called upon often to provide information about collections under their care. George Hobart, curator of documentary photography, distinguished himself by an enthusiastic commitment of his time to the Washingtoniana project, particularly in regard to the Frances Benjamin Johnston, National Photo Company, and Harris & Ewing collections. Bernard Reilly, curator of popular and applied graphic art, shared the results of his work surveying and inventorying the entire holdings of the Prints and Photographs Division, information that facilitated our search for Washington, D.C., photographs. In addition, he was forthcoming with ideas and solutions for the physical and bibliographic control of collections.

Carol Johnson, preservation technician, oversaw the microfilming of glass negatives, the ordering of preservation supplies, and the re-housing of older groups of photographs. (The actual microfilming methods were developed and carried out by Myron Chace and James Postell in the Library's Photoduplication Service.)

The catalogers, Barbara Orbach and Jackie Dooley, helped with the processing of collections and provided formal descriptions for hundreds of newly processed groups of photographs, which formed the basis for many of the descriptions in this book. In addition, Barbara Orbach provided introductory information about the Frances Benjamin Johnston Collection and the Nannie Helen Burroughs photographs. Elisabeth Betz Parker provided guidance in the creation of those descriptions and in the arrangement of collections.

Prints and Photographs Division administrators Stephen Ostrow, Renata Shaw, and Oliver Jensen applied for the funding that made this project possible and provided support along the way. Robert Lisbeth and Doris Lee facilitated the considerable paperwork that enabled the processing work to go forward without delays.

Thanks go also to Joyce Nalewajk, who helped to select illustrations and pro-

Theodor Horydczak. Library of Congress Annex (John Adams Building). Horydczak Collection, Lot 12100-23.

LC-H8-L3-69

vided captions for the section on the HABS/HAER collections. Jacqueline Leclerc, Kermit Klouser, and Marita Stamey handled photoduplication orders for the hundreds of illustrations used in the book. Helena Zinkham searched the videodisk database for FSA-OWI Washington subjects. Elisabeth Betz Parker and Renata Shaw carefully read the manuscript.

Other Library of Congress divisions played a role in the preparation of this publication. The Manuscript Division staff searched for information about collections in their custody, for which I am particularly grateful to Mary Wolfskill, Charles Kelly, and John Hackett. Staff members in the Exchange and Gift Division and the Order Division helped trace the sources of several Washingtoniana collections. Carl Fleischhauer of the American Folklife Center shared the result of his research on the Farm Security Administration. John Cole, executive director of the Center for the Book, provided background on the history of the Library of Congress.

Contributions to the project and to the manuscript came from outside of the Library as well. Shirley Green, author of *Pictorial Resources in the Washington, D.C., Area,* shared her experiences in the preparation of that descriptive guide, and her considerable knowledge of the Prints and Photographs Division's Washington, D.C., holdings. Marilyn Wandrus of the National Park Service helped to identify photographs. Florian Thayne, head of the Art and Reference Division of the Office of the Architect of the Capitol, helped to process and identify thousands of photographs. James Glenn, deputy director and archivist, National Anthropological Archives, Smithsonian Institution, provided much of the background information about the C. M. Bell studio. James Goode was called upon frequently for his knowledge of Washington, D.C., architecture and outdoor sculpture. Betty Monkman, curator at the White House, gave the project staff a lengthy tour that aided in the identification of nineteenth- and twentieth-century photographs of that building. Ann Peterson contributed her knowledge of the Frances Benjamin Johnston Collection. Elizabeth Miller of the Columbia Historical Society and Roxanna Deane and Mary Ternes of the Washingtoniana Division of the Martin Luther King Memorial Library all provided help in tracing the identification and history of Washington photographs and photographers. Howard Gillette, from the Center for Washington Area Studies at George Washington University, offered information and encouragement throughout the project. Betty Hill of the National Archives and Records Administration shared her idea for photocopying old captions onto new negative jackets.

Thanks are due to Maurice Sanders, automation planning specialist in Special Collections, for his help with the word-processing and microcomputer indexing systems used in writing this book. My sister, Nancy Ellen Collins, helped to prepare the illustrations. The book designer, Adrianne Onderdonk Dudden, provided imaginative and attractive solutions to make this book a pleasure to use. Dana Pratt, director of publishing at the Library of Congress, contributed his wisdom and experience with the vicissitudes of book publication. Finally, Evelyn Sinclair, my editor in the Publishing Office, provided enthusiastic support for more than four years, from the halcyon days of idea-gathering through the grueling process of text-editing. Her meticulous scrutiny, her small and large efforts to correct, reword, and polish, improved this book immeasurably.

A stone carver at work at the National Cathedral in Washington, June 25, 1965. U.S. News & World Report *Collection.*

LC-U9-14100-5A

A. J. Russell. "U.S. Fire Department, Alexandria, Va., with Steam Fire Engines." July 1863. Lot 4336.

LC-B8184-10408

Detroit Publishing Company. Library of Congress, Main Reading Room rotunda in the Jefferson Building. Copyright 1904. Detroit Publishing Company Collection, Lot 9072–E.

Without ever intending to become a repository for local history materials, the Library of Congress has become the foremost research center for the study of the history of Washington, D.C., with the richest and most varied collections in existence. The Prints and Photographs Division of the Library of Congress holds numerous images of the capital, its buildings, its citizens and visitors, its events, and its environs within its total holdings, which number about twelve million items. The Library of Congress holds extensive resources for the study of Washington in its other special collections divisions as well—the Manuscript, Rare Book and Special Collections, Geography and Map, Motion Picture, Broadcasting, and Recorded Sound, and Music Divisions, to name only some of the broadest areas for exploration beyond the Library's general collections.

This guide describes a part of the Washingtoniana material held by the Prints and Photographs Division, concentrating specifically on photographs. The survey includes some 750,000 photographs that relate to Washington, D.C., or that concern historically important surrounding communities such as Alexandria, Arlington, Chevy Chase, Silver Spring, Bladensburg, and Anacostia and nearby Civil War forts and battlefields. These images of Washington and vicinity account for one in twelve of the photographs held in the division as a whole.

Harris & Ewing. National Theatre, Washington, D.C. Harris & Ewing Collection.

LC-H25-2383.

The nature of the capital city itself is partly responsible for the accumulation of photographs relating to its history. Not only has Washington been the hometown of its permanent citizens but it has been a mecca for those with causes to promote, messages to deliver, statements to make, and policies to influence. Wars, disasters, political movements, and social causes that occur anywhere in the world may have repercussions in Washington as well, through the activities of military, government, and private organizations based in the city, through official and unofficial visits by famous and infamous people, through the varied investigatory activities carried on by Congress and other government bodies and agencies, and through the presence of a large diplomatic community with its accompanying activities and events. The wealthy and powerful and their residences, their glittering banquets and balls and their ornate offices; ordinary citizens at work in the federal bureaucracy or shopping on F Street; citizens in the poorest neighborhoods and at public swimming beaches—all have been documented with a camera at various times. Various discoveries, inventions and technological developments, standards and regulations, social reforms, and political expressions have either originated in Washington or emanated from it, and along the way pictures have been made. Documentary surveys have produced copious record photographs of buildings, neighborhoods, living conditions, and life-styles.

Important people from around the world have visited Washington and had portraits done in its photographic studios, as have those temporarily in the city to serve as U.S. presidents, congressmen, judges, chairmen of boards, and agency chiefs. Ordinary citizens have acquired and collected family portraits and snapshots as well, and influential people portraits of their friends, colleagues, and acquaintances. Some of these collections have been acquired by the Library of Congress. Entire lifetimes of work by various commercial and artistic photographers have been donated to the Library or purchased for addition to the collections.

Washington Post staff photographer. The Palace Theatre, Washington's first motion picture theater, ca. 1900. James Goode Collection, Lot 12013–NN–1.

LC-G7-1229

Because of the ubiquity of the camera and the photographic record resulting from its use, particularly in the twentieth century since the development of portable, miniature cameras and high-speed films, scholars can be assured of finding in the Library's collections some photographs that relate to almost every newsworthy issue and public event and portraits of many of those in the public eye from about the 1860s on.

The Library presents local history scholars with a wealth of primary and secondary sources that complement those held in other research institutions, such as the Columbia Historical Society and the Washingtoniana Division of the Martin Luther King Memorial Library, or in the collections of Gallaudet College and George Washington, Georgetown, and Howard Universities. Also to be consulted in Washington are the many collections maintained by private and government institutions, including the Smithsonian Institution, the National Archives and Records Administration, the National Park Service, the Office of the Architect of the Capitol, the White House, the U.S. Naval Observatory, the American Institute of Architects, various District of Columbia agencies, the photo archives of the *Washington Post,* and numerous other organizations. A detailed listing may be found in *Pictorial Resources in the Washington, D.C., Area,* compiled by Shirley L. Green, with the assistance of Diane Hamilton, for the Federal Library Committee (Washington: Library of Congress, 1976).

The Prints and Photographs Division of the Library of Congress acquired the estimated 750,000 photographs of Washington, D.C., primarily through copyright deposit from 1870 on and through gifts and purchases of important collections and single items. Many of the photographs used by Washington researchers came to the Library as part of the personal papers and records of men, women, organizations, and institutions that planned, shaped, or otherwise influenced political and social events, architectural structures, and geographical areas and communities in Washington. These photographs have been transferred from the Manuscript Division, where the papers or records are housed, to the Prints and Photographs Division for processing, cataloging, and archival storage. The Washingtoniana photograph collections now include about 350,000 items that were previously unavailable to researchers, because they were unprocessed or uncataloged.

C. M. Bell. Portrait of Mrs. F. Lathers. C. M. Bell Collection.

LC-B5-34889

The Prints and Photographs Division Catalog lists hundreds of small and large groups and collections of material relevant to Washington but cataloged before the development of standardized methods for picture cataloging. Because the early catalog descriptions provide insufficient information, it was necessary to inspect each group or collection that contained pictures related to Washington, D.C., in preparing this guide. The descriptions in this book augment those found in the division's catalog and in the Library's online bibliographic data base, providing thorough and detailed descriptions of Washington subjects represented. Naturally, a collection of 70,000 items cannot be described in the same detail as can a group of 40 images, but every attempt has been made to list major subjects represented, so that researchers using the guide's index can find all of the sources of, say, photographs of the Washington Monument or the Grand Army of the Republic parades. Portraits of important and recognizable people in Washington history have been listed, as well, where space allowed.

Cataloged collections or groups of photographs are divided into smaller subject-, provenance-, or format-related groups that are intellectually and physically manageable for purposes of cataloging, storage, and retrieval. These groups are called *lots.* Each lot is assigned a unique shelf number, and some of them are parts of larger formal collections.

Because photographs have come to the Library from such a wide variety of sources and over the course of more than a century, and because some are badly faded, unidentified, or only marginally useful, an attempt has been made in this book to guide researchers who will need to set priorities for their searches as they confront the enormous quantities of material held by the Library. Therefore, the most rare as well as the most frequently requested collections and subjects are listed in the first, alphabetical section of the book (Major Sources), and miscellaneous single lots are listed in the second section in numerical order. This arrangement, however, in no way indicates that the lots listed under Other Sources contain material that is unimportant.

An extensive subject index provides a unifying access to the specific contents of

C. M. Bell. Portrait of W. H. Dorkins. C. M. Bell Collection.

LC-B5-38474

lots. By searching under "Washington Monument," or "Grand Army of the Republic," for example, researchers should be able to find all of the lots that contain images specifically of that building or that group. Researchers must develop strategies that enable them to find incidental photographs of particular neighborhoods. A search under "Pennsylvania Avenue" may yield additional photographs of the Washington Monument, where that building is not the main subject of a picture but is nevertheless visible. Similarly, a search for particular buildings on Pennsylvania Avenue might be aided by looking at collections that contain photographs of inaugural parades or other parades or military reviews along the traditional route. Those searching for photographs of segregation, civil rights activities, and the broader subject of black history in Washington should search under Civil War subjects, the names of major twentieth-century protest marches, subjects related to schools and housing, and the names of institutions and people important to those issues and events, such as Howard University, Nannie Helen Burroughs, Harold Ickes, and Mary Church Terrell.

In addition to cataloged collections, the Prints and Photographs Division maintains open-ended self-indexing files of pictures, more commonly called *browsing files,* which contain hundreds of thousands of pictures of potential use to local history researchers. The browsing files are described in this guide after the cataloged collections and lots. The contents of these large files are represented in the index only under general terms, such as "portraits" or "residential buildings."

Jack E. Boucher. Christian Heurich Mansion (Columbia Historical Society), 1307 New Hampshire Avenue NW. Historic American Buildings Survey. HABS D. C. WASH 292-4; 1983 (HABS):176

This book is designed to be used to plan research strategies before visiting the Library of Congress Prints and Photographs Division. Except for occasional and specific queries, the Prints and Photographs Division cannot respond to requests to search for general subjects or particular images that may be found among the twelve million items housed there. (The staff can, however, provide a list of professional picture researchers who carry out such searches for a fee.) In most cases researchers will need to spend time in the Prints and Photographs Division. A researcher who knows the copy negative number of a particular picture and wishes merely to request a copy photoprint may do so by mail. (See "How to Order Reproductions.") Requests for copy photographs, slides, and copy negatives are handled through the Photoduplication Service of the Library of Congress. Information about the cost of various kinds of reproductions (including microfilm copies of certain collections) may be obtained from the Prints and Photographs reference staff or from the Photoduplication Service. Researchers are responsible for determining the copyright status and reproduction restrictions that may apply to particular images. Anyone may use the collections in the Prints and Photographs Division, and appointments are required only in those few cases where curators must approve the use of rare, fragile, or physically cumbersome materials. Readers must register in the division and sign an agreement to abide by the rules that apply to physical handling of the materials.

The Prints and Photographs Division holds large numbers of nonphotographic Washington-related items, such as historical prints and political cartoons, architectural drawings, illustrated books and periodicals, posters, fine prints, and graphic materials, including copies of plans and reproductions of sketches and artwork for public buildings. Cataloged nonphotographic Washingtoniana may be found in the Prints and Photographs Division Catalog, located in the division's reading room. These materials do not fall within the scope of this guide.

It is the Library's hope that through its illustrations—many showing photographs that have never before been reproduced—its descriptions, and its indexes, this guide will stimulate new research interest in subjects related to Washington, D.C.

Levin C. Handy. Card Division, Library of Congress, ca. 1900s. Lot 9788.

ILLUSTRATIONS AND ILLUSTRATION CAPTIONS: Name of photographer and subject and date of the photograph are provided in brief captions wherever that information is readily available in catalog descriptions. For architectural subjects, the fact that a building has been demolished since the picture was taken is sometimes noted, but the absence of such a statement does not imply that a building necessarily still stands. With the exception of photographs reproduced on the endpapers or section openings, illustrations show entire uncropped photographs as they exist in the collections and never at a size larger than the original (though in the case of large-format photographs such as panoramas, they may be greatly reduced). No attempt has been made to retouch or enhance photographs that show effects of deterioration or other damage. To order copies of illustrations, please see ''How to Order Reproductions'' at the back of the book.

Brief paragraphs or longer essays introduce all Major Sources of Washingtoniana photographs. This introductory section provides, where relevant, biographical information, the history of the collection, an indication of its scope, and a brief description of related holdings in the Manuscript Division of the Library of Congress.

The entries themselves are not formal catalog descriptions but are designed to provide concise information about groups of photographs.

LOT: A *lot* is a group of photographs related by donor, subject, geographical area, or some other unifying factor. The Prints and Photographs Division assigns a shelf number to each "lotted" group of photographs. The divisional catalog includes a shelflist arranged numerically by lot number that indicates the storage format. Both the lot number and the storage format must be indicated on requests to examine a group of cataloged photographs.

COLLECTION NAME: Certain formal collections (for instance, the Frances Benjamin Johnston Collection, James Goode Collection, or National Photo Company Collection) consist of one or more lots or groups of related photographs. A group of lotted photographs is not always part of a formal collection.

Some photographs have been transferred from collections in the Manuscript Division of the Library of Congress; and for these the manuscript collection name is provided here.

SUBJECTS: Lots included in this book contain one or more photographs related to Washington, D.C., or its history. The description provided here features those Washington images. These lots may also include non-Washington materials, for which the description may not be complete or detailed. The Prints and Photographs Division Catalog contains the most current descriptions of subjects represented in a particular lot.

NOTE: Certain additional information of possible use to researchers is provided in the note, particularly information concerning related negatives held by the Library or the published use or provenance of certain images and information found on covers or title pages of albums.

BIOGRAPHICAL NOTE: Some collections of photographs held in the Prints and Photographs Division were transferred from Manuscript Division holdings of papers and records of people and organizations important to Washington's history. For these, short biographical summaries are often provided along with brief descriptions of related Manuscript Division material. In other cases, a brief description provides information about the donor or collector of a group of photographs.

DATE: Dates indicate when an event pictured in a photograph occurred or when a portrait was made. Because of the vast numbers of items involved, the exact date on which particular photographs were made was not always ascertainable. Copyright deposits that bear a date of copyright often provide clues to the approximate date a particular photograph was taken, but photographic prints can be produced years after a negative is first created and copy photographs of original images can be copyrighted long after the original image was produced. Dates are often given as approximations (ca. 1876-ca. 1900; ca. 1900-1930), indicating that either part or all of the date range is uncertain.

PHOTOGRAPHERS: Only for clearly or readily identifiable photographers are names provided. In most cases, only Washington, D.C., photographers or those

Frances Benjamin Johnston. Buckets of ink in the Bureau of Engraving and Printing. Frances Benjamin Johnston Collection, Lot 8861.

LC-J687-41

operating in the Washington vicinity have been listed, although the work of other artists or studios may be clearly identified in the collection. Exceptions have been made where particularly important non-Washington photographers are represented in collections. (Many photographs, in fact, carry no identification as to photographer or studio.)

PUBLISHER: Information related to a publisher is provided only where a lot consists of a published book or pamphlet. No attempt has been made to ascertain where particular photographs may have been published. Articles published about a particular collection are listed as references in collection introductions or given in the note, when that information would be helpful to researchers.

PHYSICAL DESCRIPTION: The number of items, size range of the materials, and photographic and graphic processes represented in a particular lot are listed here. In some cases, only approximations are provided. Size ranges are given in centimeters. For negatives in standard sizes, equivalent dimensions in both inches and centimeters are provided.

ARRANGEMENT: Some large groups of photographs are subdivided for convenience of access and to spare the images unnecessary handling. The arrangement is described here.

SOURCE: The acquisition source is given here, with the date of acquisition, where known. Collections acquired long ago by the Library may lack complete acquisition information.

RESTRICTIONS: The commercial or noncommercial use of individual images, groups of photographs, or entire collections may be restricted because of copyright or donor stipulations or for other reasons. A few collections or images require that researchers obtain the permission of the donor or photographer or pay a use fee. Where these restrictions are known, and when they apply to all of the images in a particular lot, such restrictions are mentioned here. The Library does not assume responsibility for determining whether particular images are currently protected by copyright. The lack of notice of such restrictions in this book or in catalog records in the Prints and Photographs Division does not indicate that particular items are free from such legal restrictions.

Some individual images or albums of photographs are restricted because of the fragility of the item or its relative rarity. In most such cases, the Prints and Photographs Division provides a surrogate microfilm or copy photographs of such material. Researchers must consult these reference copies unless special permission has been obtained for use of the original items.

The earliest panoramic view of Washington in the Library's collections consists of five albumen prints from glass negatives that form a detailed view of nineteenth-century Washington, taken from the Smithsonian Building, 1874. Panoramic Photographs of Washington, Lot 12361.

LC-USZ62-90246   *LC-USZ62-90247*   *LC-USZ62-90248*

Shaw, *A Century*	Renata V. Shaw, comp. *A Century of Photographs, 1846-1946.* Washington: Library of Congress, 1980.
Vanderbilt	Paul Vanderbilt, comp. *Guide to the Special Collections of Prints and Photographs in the Library of Congress.* Washington: Library of Congress, 1955.
LCIB	*Library of Congress Information Bulletin*
Melville	Annette Melville, comp. *Special Collections in the Library of Congress.* Washington: Library of Congress, 1980.
QJLC	*Quarterly Journal of the Library of Congress*
Viewpoints	*Viewpoints: The Library of Congress Selection of Pictorial Treasures.* Compiled by Alan Fern, Milton Kaplan, and the Staff of the Prints and Photographs Division. Washington: Library of Congress, 1975. Reprint edition, New York: Arno Press, 1976.

C. M. Bell. Harold Crump with a toy. C. M. Bell Collection.

LC-B5-40671

LC-USZ62-90249   *LC-USZ62-90250*

Major Sources

Both large collections that contain significant numbers of images relating to Washington, D.C., and smaller collections that are well known to researchers as especially valuable sources for the study of local history and architecture are considered major sources for research. This section also describes some very small collections that contain particularly rare images and features groups of photographs related to the capital that have been transferred to the Prints and Photographs Division from Manuscript Division collections of papers of people important to Washington's history.

These formal and informal collections are listed alphabetically by collection title. For any very large collection, only particular lots within it with material relating to Washington are described here. Researchers should consult the Prints and Photographs Division catalog for a full, comprehensive description of subject content for large collections.

Levin Handy. Second story stucco shop, showing artisans at work on decorations for the interior of the Library of Congress (Jefferson Building). July 19, 1894. Library of Congress Construction Photographs. Lot 12365.

LC-USL5-555

N.C. 2ND STORY, STUCCO SHOP,
JULY 19.1894,

Joseph S. Allen Collection

After thirty-two years of service to the Library of Congress, Joseph S. Allen retired as editor in the Subject Cataloging Division. At that time, he presented to the Library his collection of 11,427 photographs (with corresponding negatives) of churches, colleges, county courthouses, government buildings, residential structures, and historic monuments in twenty-seven eastern and midwestern states. The Washington, D.C., coverage is the most comprehensive regional survey in the collection and includes 289 monumental structures, 148 public outdoor sculptures, 289 government buildings, 558 churches, 111 embassies and chanceries, and 283 schools and colleges, as well as libraries, fire and police stations, office buildings, banks, department stores, hotels, apartment houses, private residences, hospitals, theaters, association headquarters, clubs, and bridges. The collection also includes photographs of suburban Maryland and Virginia. All of the pictures were taken with a 1935 Jiffy Kodak camera. Joseph Allen's project ended when he could no longer obtain the film and processing necessary to maintain the uniformity of his collection.

REFERENCES

"Former Employee Gives Architectural Photographs to LC," *LCIB* 37 (October 6, 1978): 607–8. Melville, p. 5.

Joseph Allen. Carnegie Institution of Washington, Department of Terrestrial Magnetism, 5241 Broad Branch Road NW, July 2, 1950. Allen Collection, Lot 11661–9.

LC-A7-4308

LOT 11661

COLLECTION NAME: Joseph S. Allen Collection

SUBJECTS: Buildings, especially county courthouses, as well as other government buildings, churches, educational and residential buildings, historic monuments, and outdoor sculpture in twenty-seven eastern and midwestern states; includes extensive coverage of Washington, D.C., structures, as well as structures in suburban Virginia and Maryland.

NOTE: Corresponding negatives are found in series LC-A7.

DATE: 1935–67 (Washington, D.C., portion covers 1945–57)

PHOTOGRAPHERS: Joseph S. Allen.

PHYSICAL DESCRIPTION: 37 albums (11,427 silver gelatin photoprints, 8 × 6 cm, of which 2,371 pertain to Washington, D.C.).

ARRANGEMENT: By state and city or town, with similar types of buildings grouped together. Each image is numbered and has a corresponding index card that provides full caption information. The Washington, D.C., portion of the collection is found in seven albums (9A through 9G), in Lot 11661–9, which contain prints no. 3862 through no. 6232. Cards with information identifying each image are available in the Prints and Photographs Reading Room (architectural indexes); one set of cards is arranged by photo number and another set by state, city, and building name. To identify photographs of buildings in the Joseph Allen Collection, take the number of any image in the albums to the Allen Collection negative/positive shelflist in the Prints and Photographs Reading Room. The card bearing that number will provide caption information. Search the second set of Allen Collection cards under "Washington, D.C." and name or type of building to find image numbers for particular buildings. District of Columbia photographs in Lot 11661–9 are grouped in the following order:

Government and monumental buildings
Associations, clubs
Historic events
Statues
Embassies and chanceries
Houses
Bridges and nature scenes
Churches
Universities, colleges
Secondary, elementary, and
    special schools
Commercial and office buildings
Department stores
Banks
Theaters, restaurants
Utility buildings
Hotels
Apartment houses
Retirement homes
Hospitals

Joseph Allen. Christian Heurich Brewing Company, Twenty-Sixth and D Streets NW, since demolished. April 1948. Allen Collection, Lot 11661–9.

LC-A7-5908

Joseph Allen. Commercial buildings on Pennsylvania Avenue, north side, between Ninth and Tenth Streets NW, since demolished. April 6, 1950. Allen Collection, Lot 11661–9.

LC-A7-5916

Joseph Allen. Water Gate Inn restaurant, 2700 F Street NW, since demolished. June 1949. Allen Collection, Lot 11661–9.

LC-A7-6009

Joseph Allen. Sedgwick Gardens apartments, 3726 Connecticut Avenue NW, July 2, 1950. Allen Collection, Lot 11661–9.

LC-A7-6122

Joseph Allen. Raleigh Hotel, Pennsylvania Avenue and Twelfth Street NW (northeast corner), since demolished. March 1948. Allen Collection, Lot 11661–9.

LC-A7-6054

Joseph Allen. Crossman Methodist Church, 384 North Washington Street, Falls Church, Virginia, since demolished. September 1948. Allen Collection, Lot 11661–10.

LC-A7-6373

Joseph Allen. 4813 Massachusetts Avenue NW, since demolished. July 1, 1950. Allen Collection, Lot 11661–9.

LC-A7-5989

Joseph Allen. Arlington County Courthouse, 1400 North Court House Road, Arlington, Virginia, since demolished. October 4, 1952. Allen Collection, Lot 11661–10.

LC-A7-6302

Joseph Allen. Belle Haven Apartments, 515 North Washington Street, Alexandria, Virginia, August 1948. Allen Collection, Lot 11661–10.

LC-A7-6364

Joseph Allen. Saint Agnes Episcopal School for Girls, Alexandria, Virginia, July 25, 1953. Allen Collection, Lot 11661–10.

LC-A7-6335

Joseph Allen. D.C. Police Station, Harbor Station, Maine Avenue and M Street SW, since demolished. May 27, 1950. Allen Collection, Lot 11661–9.

LC-A7-4201

Architect of the Capitol Photographs

The Architect of the Capitol oversees all construction, repair, and maintenance of buildings relating to the U.S. Capitol and its grounds, including the Library of Congress, the House and Senate office buildings, the Botanic Garden, various auxiliary buildings physically separate from the Capitol grounds, and the subway and tunnel systems that connect the Capitol with the Library and congressional office buildings. Photographs related to the construction and renovation of these structures and grounds are maintained by the Office of the Architect of the Capitol. Over the years, the Prints and Photographs Division has received prints from negatives produced by the Architect's staff. These images have been dispersed into appropriate browsing files, including the Washington, D.C., Geographical File. Several hundred historically and architecturally important documentary photographs, relating primarily to the U.S. Capitol, the House and Senate office buildings, the construction of the Library of Congress Madison Building and the Rayburn House Office Building, and the prior use of Capitol Hill sites on which these buildings were constructed are described below.

U.S. Capitol, East Front extension. The individual stones having been numbered, the arches are removed from their piers under the east portico floor, February 2, 1959. Architect of the Capitol Collection, Lot 12555–3.

LC-USA7-14208

Mason's mark in the stone jamb of a south window on the main east wall of the old House wing, second floor, U.S. Capitol. March 29, 1961. Architect of the Capitol Collection, Lot 12555–4.

LC-USA7-19905

LOT 12555

COLLECTION NAME: Architect of the Capitol Collection

SUBJECTS: Capitol, East Front extension and views. Includes 1959 cornerstone-laying ceremony officiated by President Eisenhower, Architect of the Capitol J. George Stewart, and Masons in formal dress. Construction workers, some posed for a portrait; stone carvers at work on sculpture; architectural elements and artwork undergoing restoration in the Capitol; grounds and street lamps. Construction machinery and materials; quarry at Barre, Vermont, and stoneyard at T Street.

NOTE: Accompanied by a brochure, "United States Capitol." Corresponding copy negatives are found in series LC-A7. Original negatives are held by the Architect of the Capitol. Photos are captioned and Architect of the Capitol numbers appear on versos.

DATE: 1955–56

PHOTOGRAPHERS: Harry L. Burnett, Jr., Mark V. Blair, George R. Holmes, and other Office of the Architect of the Capitol staff.

PHYSICAL DESCRIPTION: 520 silver gelatin photoprints, 20 × 25 cm.

ARRANGEMENT: *Lot 12555–1:* Architectural drawings and plans; *Lot 12555–2:* Ceremonies and events; *Lot 12555–3:* Construction; *Lot 12555–4:* Cornerstones and historical artifacts; *Lot 12555–5:* Exterior; *Lot 12555–6:* Interior. A finding aid is available in the Prints and Photographs Reading Room.

SOURCE: Transfer of copy negatives and copy photoprints by arrangement with the Architect of the Capitol, 1955–83.

LOT 12556

COLLECTION NAME: Architect of the Capitol Collection

SUBJECTS: Rayburn House Office Building construction and dedication. Includes site before construction; demolition of Wonders Court, apartment houses, commercial and government buildings, and garages. Construction activities and surveyor at work. Cornerstone dedication ceremony with congressmen, including Speaker John W. McCormack, and Architect of the Capitol J. George Stewart, attending; John F. Kennedy addressing crowd. Interiors, including unoccupied offices and committee rooms; architectural details and sculpture; view of surrounding area from roof. Parking lots.

NOTE: Corresponding copy negatives are found in series LC-A7. Original negatives are held by the Architect of the Capitol. Photos captioned. Architect of the Capitol numbers noted. Accompanied by a map of properties under jurisdiction of the Architect of the Capitol and a key identifying prominent individuals in three photographs.

DATE: 1955–65

PHOTOGRAPHERS: Harry L. Burnett, Jr., Mark M. Blair, George R. Holmes, and other Office of the Architect of the Capitol staff.

PHYSICAL DESCRIPTION: 197 silver gelatin and dye gelatin photoprints, 20 × 25 cm.

ARRANGEMENT: Finding aid available in the Prints and Photographs Reading Room.

SOURCE: Transfer of copy prints and copy negatives by arrangement with the Architect of the Capitol, 1955–83.

Statue of Freedom on the U.S. Capitol dome, December 15, 1964. Architect of the Capitol Collection, Lot 12555–5C.

LC-USA7-27751

Rayburn House Office Building site, looking west from roof of 247 Delaware Avenue, showing rear of rowhouses on C Street and Wonders Court (before demolition). December 13, 1955. Architect of the Capitol Collection, Lot 12556–5C.

LC-USA7-10044

Excavation at Capitol's East Front steps for the subway tunnel, November 3, 1959. Architect of the Capitol Collection, Lot 12557–15.

LC-USA7-15956

Two of six platinum-tipped lightning points on the feathered headpiece of the statue of Freedom on the U.S. Capitol dome, January 28, 1960. Architect of the Capitol Collection, Lot 12555–5C.

LC-USA7-17032

View of building fronts on Independence Avenue before their demolition for construction of the Library of Congress Madison Building. May 8, 1962. Architect of the Capitol Collection, Lot 12557–14–B.

LC-USA7-22263

LOT 12557

COLLECTION NAME: Architect of the Capitol Collection

SUBJECTS: Capitol Hill, Washington, D.C. Includes renovation, repair, and construction of Dirksen, Hart, and Russell office buildings and the Bartholdi fountain. Interiors of Cannon and Longworth buildings, including post office, snack bar, barbershop, and maintenance facilities. Capitol Hill structures, including George Washington Inn, dwellings, and two warehouses undergoing demolition, and alleys and streets with automobiles on sites where office buildings were to be erected. Library of Congress Jefferson Building being cleaned; site of Madison Memorial Building before and after demolition of previous structures and Madison Building interiors before offices were occupied; area around the Library taken from Capitol and Jefferson Building domes. Installation of steam heat distribution system. Construction of Capitol subway system, including two architectural drawings. Parking lots.

NOTE: Corresponding copy negatives are found in series LC-A7. Original negatives held by the Architect of the Capitol. Photos captioned. Architect of the Capitol numbers noted. Accompanied by a map showing properties under jurisdiction of the Architect of the Capitol.

DATE: 1931–79

PHOTOGRAPHERS: Harry L. Burnett, Jr., Mark M. Blair, George R. Holmes, and other Office of the Architect of the Capitol staff.

PHYSICAL DESCRIPTION: 519 silver gelatin photoprints, 20 × 25 cm.

ARRANGEMENT: Finding aid available in Prints and Photographs Reading Room.

SOURCE: Transfer of copy photoprints and copy negatives by arrangement with the Architect of the Capitol, ca. 1960–83.

Louis Fabian Bachrach, Photographer

The Bachrach studios in Washington, D.C., and Baltimore, Maryland, were visited by leading citizens of the day. In 1944, Louis Fabian Bachrach gave to the Library about 80 elegant photographs of such well-known figures as Albert Einstein, the composer Serge Koussevitsky, tennis star Helen Wills, Bishop Fulton J. Sheen, television executive William S. Paley, and photographic manufacturer George Eastman, among many others.

LOT 11823

COLLECTION NAME: Louis Fabian Bachrach Photographs

SUBJECTS: Leading political, social, and cultural figures of the period. Franklin D. Roosevelt and Eleanor Roosevelt, presidential candidates, cabinet members, diplomats, foreign leaders, religious leaders, political commentators, artists, scientists, authors, musicians, explorers, U.S. Supreme Court justices, and senators.

DATE: ca. 1939–42

PHOTOGRAPHERS: Louis Fabian Bachrach

PHYSICAL DESCRIPTION: 78 silver gelatin photoprints, images 28 × 36 cm, on mounts 36 × 44 cm.

ARRANGEMENT: The portraits are arranged alphabetically. A list of portrait subjects is available in the Prints and Photographs Reading Room. Indexed in the Biographical Index (see Biographical File).

SOURCE: Gift of Louis Fabian Bachrach, 1944.

RESTRICTIONS: No restrictions.

Fabian Bachrach. William O. Douglas, associate justice of the U.S. Supreme Court, 1939. Lot 11823.
LC-USZ62-77521

Fabian Bachrach. Frank B. Noyes, owner of the Washington Star. *Lot 11823.*
LC-USZ62-92754

Fabian Bachrach. Vice President Henry A. Wallace, 1941. Lot 11823.
LC-USZ62-77523

Fabian Bachrach. Eleanor Roosevelt (Mrs. Franklin D. Roosevelt), 1940. Lot 11823.
LC-USZ62-77526

Fabian Bachrach. Oliver Wendell Holmes. Lot 11823.
LC-USZ62-92753

In 1948, four years after George Bain's death, the Library of Congress purchased (from D. J. Culver of New York) Bain's collection of an estimated 120,000 glass plate negatives and tens of thousands of corresponding photoprints. The Bain News Service, founded in 1898, was located in New York City and is considered to have been the first news picture agency in the United States. George Bain was a news reporter himself, formerly affiliated with the (old) United Press, and was stationed for a time in Washington, D.C. He contributed to the *Century, Harper's, Frank Leslie's Illustrated Magazine, Munsey's Magazine,* and the *Strand Magazine.* He sent his own photographs to these magazines, along with his stories, and found the editors more interested in the pictures than the stories. When improvements in the technology of photomechanical reproductions made the publication of photographs feasible in the late 1890s, he founded his agencies, the Bain News Service and the Montauk Photo Concern.

White House State Dining Room, 1903. Bain Collection, Lot 8636.

LC-USZ62-17207

The majority of images in this collection pertain to New York City news events, but some cover other events in the eastern United States and elsewhere. The Bain News Service distributed its own pictures and those it purchased from other photographers (including Frances Benjamin Johnston) and commercial agencies to about a hundred newspapers, providing coverage of local sports events, theater shows, celebrities, crime, disasters, political activities, conventions, labor struggles, and public celebrations. Bain was fortunate to have made friends with William McKinley when he was a congressman from Ohio, and McKinley later granted him special access to the White House and invited him to ride along on his train to the Omaha Exposition of 1898.

The earliest Bain photographs were destroyed in a company fire at his office in the Parker Building in New York in 1908. Documentation is nearly complete from the 1910s on, however, with photographs grouped by subject and described in the Prints and Photographs Division catalog. A collection of portrait photographs from the Bain News Service has been incorporated in the Biographical File in the Prints and Photographs Division.

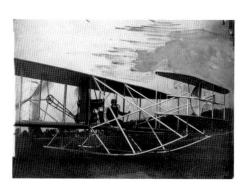

Orville Wright at the beginning of a flight, Fort Myer, Virginia, June 29, 1909. Retouched photograph. Bain Collection, Lot 10965–1.

LC-USZ62-91462

The Library has custody of Bain's extensive card indexes, arranged by several alphabetical schemes: American personalities; Foreign personalities; Artists; New York City; Sports; General. This index has been microfilmed. Negatives numbered by Bain in a chronological sequence provide a means of estimating the dates of most images in the collection. The Bain negatives, primarily 4 × 5 inch (11 × 13 cm) and 5 × 7 inch (13 × 18 cm) glass plate negatives, are in series LC-B2 and LC-B22. Much of the material is captioned. The Washington, D.C., coverage is limited to the photographs described below.

REFERENCES

Cushing, Charles Phelps. "Topics of the Times: Pictures of Everything." *New York Times*, May 11, 1953.
Little, Emma H. "The Father of News Photography, George Grantham Bain." *Picturescope* 20 (Autumn 1972), pp. 125–32.
Melville, p. 33.
Vanderbilt, no. 43, p. 11.

Orville Wright flying at Fort Myer, Virginia, July 1, 1909. Bain Collection, Lot 10965–1.

LC-USZ62-91463

LOT 8636

COLLECTION NAME: George Grantham Bain Collection

SUBJECTS: White House interiors. Views of the State Dining Room; Red, Green, and East rooms; hallway, entryway, fireplace, and tea service.

DATE: 1903

PHOTOGRAPHERS: George Grantham Bain and staff of Bain News Service (New York).

PHYSICAL DESCRIPTION: 17 silver gelatin photoprints, 13 × 18 cm.

SOURCE: Copyright deposit by George Bain, January 5, 1903.

LOT 10965

COLLECTION NAME: George Grantham Bain Collection

SUBJECTS: News photos of aviation activities of Orville and Wilbur Wright. Photographs taken in the Washington area (34 items, all captioned) are in Lot 10965–1 and include pictures of Orville Wright at army endurance tests for his airplane at Fort Myer, Virginia; winning a government prize; and testing his airplane in Washington in August and September 1908 and June and July 1909. Includes photographs of congressmen attending these events.

DATE: 1908–17

PHOTOGRAPHERS: George Grantham Bain and staff of Bain News Service (New York) and Harris & Ewing.

PHYSICAL DESCRIPTION: ca. 100 silver gelatin photoprints, 13 × 18 cm or smaller.

ARRANGEMENT: Lot 10965–1: Orville Wright's tests at Fort Myer, Virginia, 1908–9; Lot 10965–2: Wilbur Wright's flights over New York harbor, 1909; Lot 10965–3: Portraits, planes, trophies, and miscellaneous subjects, 1908–17; funeral of Wilbur Wright in 1912.

SOURCE: Purchase from D. J. Culver, 1948.

LOT 11052

COLLECTION NAME: George Grantham Bain Collection

SUBJECTS: News photos of women's suffrage activities in the United States, most taken in New York City. Washington, D.C., photographs (36 captioned photos in Lot 11052–2) include a March 1913 parade, with floats and contingents from Australia and New Zealand, Sweden, and the "Bible Lands"; American nurses and homemakers; and women who hiked from New York to Washington for the parade. Includes a tableau in front of the Treasury Building, women with banners protesting, and White House picketers.

NOTE: Includes a list of related unprinted glass negatives from series LC-B2.

DATE: 1905–17

PHOTOGRAPHERS: George Grantham Bain and staff of Bain News Service (New York).

PHYSICAL DESCRIPTION: Ca. 310 silver gelatin photoprints, 21 × 36 cm or smaller.

ARRANGEMENT: Lot 11052–1: Activities, 1905–12; Lot 11052–2: Activities in Washington, D.C., 1913–17; Lot 11052–3: Activities, 1913–14; Lot 11052–4: Activities, 1915–17; Lot 11052–5: Individual and group portraits, 1905–17.

SOURCE: Purchase from D. J. Culver, 1948.

LOT 12522

COLLECTION NAME: George Grantham Bain Collection

SUBJECTS: Events and sites in Washington, D.C. Suffrage parade, March 15, 1913, on Pennsylvania Avenue; New Year's crowd at the White House (1909); the tube and trolley between the Senate and annex.

DATE: 1909–13

PHOTOGRAPHERS: George Grantham Bain and staff of Bain News Service.

PHYSICAL DESCRIPTION: 4 silver gelatin photoprints, 13 × 18 cm or smaller.

SOURCE: Purchase from D. J. Culver, 1948.

Head of suffragette parade on Pennsylvania Avenue, March 3, 1913. Bain Collection, Lot 11052–2.
LC-USZ62-22262

Suffragettes picketing in front of the White House, 1917. Bain Collection, Lot 11052–2.
LC-B2-4103-6

Suffragette hikers on the way to Washington from New York, February 1913. Bain Collection, Lot 11052–2.
LC-USZ62-26806

Ray Stannard Baker (1870–1946) was a journalist, an author, and Woodrow Wilson's official biographer. He wrote for the *Chicago Record* and *American Magazine* and was at one time associate editor of *McClure's Magazine*. The Ray Stannard Baker Papers (30,000 items) span the years 1836–1947; they are housed in the Manuscript Division of the Library of Congress. Materials relating to Coxey's Army and Woodrow Wilson, among many other subjects, may be consulted there, along with a bibliography of Baker's publications on these subjects. The papers are available on 97 reels of microfilm (*The Papers of Ray Stannard Baker,* C-379). The photographs from the Baker Papers were transferred to the Prints and Photographs Division; those pictures relevant to Washington, D.C., are described below.

Woodrow Wilson before he ran for the presidency. Ray Stannard Baker Papers, Lot 2587.

LC-USZ62-92474

LOT 2587

COLLECTION NAME: Ray Stannard Baker Papers, Manuscript Division

SUBJECTS: Portraits of Woodrow Wilson, formal and informal. Wilson as student and professor at Princeton University, governor of New Jersey, and president of the United States. Members of his family, school friends, teachers, political supporters. Faculty members at Harvard University and Johns Hopkins University. Congressmen, cabinet members, and other government officials. Views of Princeton University buildings, the New Jersey State Capitol, and homes occupied by the Wilsons. A few reproductions of newspaper caricatures. Includes portraits of Wilson's first and second wives, William Howard Taft, Theodore Roosevelt, and William Jennings Bryan.

DATE: 1879–1919

PHYSICAL DESCRIPTION: Ca. 250 silver gelatin photoprints, many copy photos, 20 × 25 cm or smaller.

SOURCE: Bequest of Ray Stannard Baker, 1948. Transfer from the Manuscript Division.

LOT 4067

COLLECTION NAME: Ray Stannard Baker Papers

SUBJECTS: Coxey's Army somewhere between Massillon, Ohio, and Washington, D.C. Gatherings in protest of rising unemployment, speaker on platform, men on horseback, makeshift shelter, men traveling by canal barge, leader of parade with flag, and citizens in a small town watching the procession pass through on the way to Washington.

NOTE: Negatives are found in series LC–B31–27 through –B31–54. All photos are captioned. Some used in a publication by Ray Stannard Baker about Coxey's Army.

DATE: April 1894

PHOTOGRAPHERS: Ray Stannard Baker and others.

PHYSICAL DESCRIPTION: 28 silver gelatin photoprints, 21 × 26 cm or smaller. Most are modern prints made by the Library from Baker's nitrate negatives.

SOURCE: Gift of James Stannard Baker, 1949.

Arnold Genthe (New York). Edith Bolling Galt Wilson, second wife of Woodrow Wilson. Ray Stannard Baker Papers, Lot 2587.

LC-USZ62-92476

Coxey's Army on the C&O Canal, passing a Consolidated Coal Company barge, 1894. Ray Stannard Baker Papers, Lot 4067.

LC-USZ62-92477

Ray Stannard Baker. Jesse Coxey in marching trim, 1894. Ray Stannard Baker Papers, Lot 4067.

LC-USZ62-26146

Keystone View Company. Woodrow Wilson, governor of New Jersey, receiving telegrams congratulating him on his election to the presidency, 1912. Ray Stannard Baker Papers, Lot 2587.

LC-USZ62-92475

John Barrett (1866–1938) was a journalist in California, Oregon, and Washington State and a diplomat assigned as U.S. minister to Siam, Argentina, Colombia, and Panama. He served as director general of the Pan American Union, traveled in the Far East, and served as special adviser to Adm. George Dewey during the Philippine insurrection. He was involved in the Venezuelan boundary dispute and the Panama Canal and was active in the general area of relations between the United States and Latin America. His papers, found in the Manuscript Division, are supplemented by a finding aid and card index; they span the years 1861–1943 (chiefly 1907–33) and number 50,000 items. The papers are a gift of Mr. and Mrs. John Walton Barrett, 1939–64. Photographs from the papers were transferred to the Prints and Photographs Division, and those related to Washington, D.C., are described below.

LOT 8950

COLLECTION NAME: John Barrett Papers, Manuscript Division

SUBJECTS: Portraits of John Barrett by U.S. and foreign photographers. Includes pictures made while Barrett was in college, while he was minister to Siam, and while he was director general of the Pan American Union.

DATE: Ca. 1880–ca. 1938

PHOTOGRAPHERS: Underwood & Underwood, Harris & Ewing, Clinedinst, George Prince, Bachrach, Moffett, Bain News Service, and American Press Association.

PHYSICAL DESCRIPTION: Ca. 200 albumen, platinum, and silver gelatin photoprints (including cartes de visite and cabinet cards), 28 × 36 cm or smaller.

SOURCE: Transfer from the Manuscript Division, 1961.

LOT 8965

COLLECTION NAME: John Barrett Papers, Manuscript Division

SUBJECTS: Autographed portraits of Presidents Cleveland, Coolidge, Harding, Theodore Roosevelt, Taft, and Wilson. Portrait of Mrs. Coolidge.

DATE: Ca. 1885–ca. 1923

PHOTOGRAPHERS: C. M. Bell, Harris & Ewing, Underwood & Underwood, Clinedinst, Pach Brothers (New York), and B. J. Falk (New York).

PHYSICAL DESCRIPTION: 21 albumen and silver gelatin photoprints, 41 × 51 cm or smaller.

SOURCE: Transfer from the Manuscript Division, 1961.

Fabian Bachrach. John Barrett. John Barrett Papers, Lot 8950.
LC-USZ62-92747

American Press Association (New York). John Barrett, director general of the Pan American Union, in his office. John Barrett Papers, Lot 8950.
LC-USZ62-92745

Ernest L. Crandall. Pan American Union Building, stairway and foyer. John Barrett Papers, Lot 8971.
LC-USZ62-92749

LOT 8971

COLLECTION NAME: John Barrett Papers, Manuscript Division

SUBJECTS: The Pan American Union, Washington, D.C. General exterior views; gardens; fountain and other architectural details; library. Distinguished visitors; events attended by Presidents Wilson, Roosevelt, and Taft. Banquets and other social functions; group portraits of the governing board and of building staff and architect. Snapshots of the doorman, maids, and gardeners. The building under construction. Architectural models and drawings showing aerial views of various proposed redesigns of the Mall, Washington Monument grounds, and downtown Washington. Views of Washington taken from the Pan American Union Building, and of wartime buildings being constructed on the Mall.

DATE: Ca. 1915–ca. 1930

PHOTOGRAPHERS: Taylor, Ernest L. Crandall, Harris & Ewing, Taylor & Helm, Washington Photo Company, William Rau, T. S. Munson (Pittsburgh), and the Detroit Photographic Company.

PHYSICAL DESCRIPTION: 157 silver gelatin photoprints, 28 × 36 cm or smaller.

SOURCE: Transfer from the Manuscript Division, 1961.

LOT 8975

COLLECTION NAME: John Barrett Papers, Manuscript Division

SUBJECTS: Group portraits made at banquets, rallies, expositions, beauty contests, ground-breaking ceremonies, diplomatic functions, association meetings, and international congresses. Includes banquet photographs that show the interior of the Willard Hotel and photos of a dinner for debutantes (January 1920).

DATE: Ca. 1890–ca. 1930

PHOTOGRAPHERS: Harris & Ewing, Waldon Fawcett, Schütz, Underwood & Underwood, and the National Press Association.

PHYSICAL DESCRIPTION: Ca. 100 silver gelatin photoprints, 28 × 36 cm or smaller.

SOURCE: Transfer from the Manuscript Division, 1961.

Dedication of Pan American Union Building. Group portrait includes: far left, *John Barrett;* fifth from left, *Andrew Carnegie;* center, *President William Howard Taft;* fifth from right, *Elihu Root; and,* fourth from right, *Cardinal James Gibbons. John Barrett Papers, Lot 8971.*

LC-USZ62-59174

Pan American Union. Director John Barrett with administrators, architect, and messenger and building staff, August 1920. John Barrett Papers, Lot 8971.

LC-USZ62-92750

Pan American Union Building garden being constructed. John Barrett Papers, Lot 8971.

LC-USZ62-58823

Pan American Union Building ballroom. John Barrett Papers, Lot 8971.

LC-USZ62-17817

Clara Barton Papers

Clara Harlowe Barton (1821–1912) was a philanthropist, nurse, teacher, and lecturer, who founded the American Association of the Red Cross (now the American Red Cross). She made her home in Glen Echo, Maryland. Her correspondence, diaries, lectures, scrapbooks, and biographical and other material are held in the Manuscript Division of the Library of Congress. The papers number 70,000 items, ranging from 1834 to 1918. They were presented by Rena Hubbell of Glen Echo, Maryland, in 1940, and by Hermann P. Riccius, in 1959. Photographs from the Barton Papers were transferred to the Prints and Photographs Division. Those groups of pictures that contain materials that relate to Washington, D.C., are described below.

Carte-de-visite portrait of Clara Barton. From Frederick H. Meserve's collection of Americana. Ca. 1865. Clara Barton Papers, Lot 8494.
LC-USZ62-92528

LOT 6750

COLLECTION NAME: Clara Barton Papers, Manuscript Division

SUBJECTS: Nineteenth-century portraits, mainly of Clara Barton's associates and friends. Includes portraits of A. J. Solomons (vice president of the Red Cross in Washington), H. V. and Helen Boynton, G. Kennan, Antoinette Margot, Alexander Kent (pastor, Peoples Church), Dr. Lucy Hull-Brown, Edward Whitaker, Paul V. DeGraw, and Joseph E. Holmes, among other colleagues and friends from Washington and elsewhere.

DATE: Ca. 1857–ca. 1890s

PHOTOGRAPHERS: C. M. Bell, Bell's Photo Art Gallery, I. M. Boyce, Mathew Brady studio, Paul Tralles, Sarony (New York), Rockwood (New York), and Mumler (Boston).

PHYSICAL DESCRIPTION: 36 albumen and silver gelatin photoprints, and some copies of prints and paintings, 20 × 25 cm or smaller, including cartes de visite and cabinet card photographs.

SOURCE: Transfer from the Manuscript Division, 1955.

LOT 6751

COLLECTION NAME: Clara Barton Papers, Manuscript Division

SUBJECTS: Displays of medals and other awards presented to Clara Barton; commemorative stamp. Display of funeral flowers in her home in Glen Echo, Maryland.

DATE: Ca. 1912

PHOTOGRAPHERS: Graeme.

PHYSICAL DESCRIPTION: 11 silver gelatin photoprints and drawings, 20 × 25 cm or smaller.

SOURCE: Transfer from the Manuscript Division, 1955.

LOT 6759

COLLECTION NAME: Clara Barton Papers, Manuscript Division

SUBJECTS: Clara Barton's Red Cross activities and other subjects. Grand Army of the Republic encampment in Washington, D.C.; ambulance in Allegheny, Pennsylvania, 1889; Boer War soldiers. Includes one view of Arlington Cemetery.

DATE: 1863–1946

PHOTOGRAPHERS: H. A. Farnham.

PHYSICAL DESCRIPTION: 21 albumen, cyanotype, and silver gelatin photoprints, 20 × 25 cm or smaller.

SOURCE: Transfer from the Manuscript Division, 1955.

LOT 8533

COLLECTION NAME: Clara Barton Papers, Manuscript Division

SUBJECTS: Clara Barton's homes. Birthplace and homes in Dansville, New York, and Glen Echo, Maryland. Schools in which she taught. Barton family plot in North Oxford, Massachusetts. Relics of Andersonville Prison. Includes one photo of the stone tower near the entrance to Glen Echo Park, a photo labeled "Glen Echo—Chataqua," and a photomechanical reproduction of the National Red Cross Headquarters at Seventeenth and F Streets NW (General Grant's Mansion).

PHOTOGRAPHERS: Mathew Brady studio, Fassett, and Clara Barton Drew.

PHYSICAL DESCRIPTION: 117 albumen and silver gelatin photoprints (including one carte de visite), postcards, and photomechanical prints, 20 × 25 cm or smaller.

SOURCE: Gift of Hermann P. Riccius, 1959. Transfer from the Manuscript Division, 1959.

H. J. Reed (Worcester, Massachusetts). Carte-de-visite portrait of, left, Clara Barton, and her sister, ca. 1860s. Clara Barton Papers, Lot 8497.
LC-USZ62-39267

LOT 8493

COLLECTION NAME: Clara Barton Papers, Manuscript Division

SUBJECTS: Members of the Barton, Bigelow, Dennis, Hale, Monroe, Stout, Tufts, Vassell, Voris, Westfall, and Wilson families

NOTE: Some portraits are unidentified.

DATE: Ca. 1865

PHYSICAL DESCRIPTION: 1 album (30 cartes de visite and tintypes), 16 × 12 cm.

SOURCE: Gift of Hermann P. Riccius, 1959. Transfer from the Manuscript Division, 1959.

LOT 8494

COLLECTION NAME: Clara Barton Papers, Manuscript Division

SUBJECTS: Clara Barton's parents, brothers, sisters, cousins, and other relatives. Includes one carte-de-visite copy of a portrait of Clara Barton, with verso stamped, "Collection of Americana Frederick H. Meserve . . . ."

DATE: Ca. 1865

PHYSICAL DESCRIPTION: 1 album (41 cartes de visite and silhouettes), 16 × 13 cm.

SOURCE: Gift of Hermann P. Riccius, 1959. Transfer from the Manuscript Division, 1959.

LOT 8495

COLLECTION NAME: Clara Barton Papers, Manuscript Division

SUBJECTS: Members of the Barton, Atwater, Blodgett, Starr, Tarbell, and Tyler families. Includes some portraits of men in Civil War uniforms.

DATE: Ca. 1865

PHYSICAL DESCRIPTION: 1 album (14 cartes de visite and tintypes), 16 × 12 cm.

SOURCE: Gift of Hermann P. Riccius, 1959. Transfer from the Manuscript Division, 1959.

LOT 8496

COLLECTION NAME: Clara Barton Papers, Manuscript Division

SUBJECTS: Members of the Barton, Bigelow, Bullard, Buswell, Childs, Gage, Gibson, Golay, Hall, Lamb, Larned, and Pierce families. Includes portraits identified as "William M. Evarts, Sec'y of State during Civil War" and "V.P. Henry Wilson," in addition to portraits of Civil War officers.

NOTE: Some portraits are unidentified.

DATE: Ca. 1865

PHOTOGRAPHERS: Mathew Brady studio and others.

PHYSICAL DESCRIPTION: 1 album (50 cartes de visite), 16 × 13 cm.

SOURCE: Gift of Hermann P. Riccius, 1959. Transfer from the Manuscript Division, 1959.

LOT 8497

COLLECTION NAME: Clara Barton Papers, Manuscript Division

SUBJECTS: Portraits of unidentified men, women, and children. Includes portraits of emancipated slave children and a portrait of Sybil Swinnerton, an aged black woman. One portrait is tentatively identified as Clara Barton and her sister.

DATE: Ca. 1865

PHYSICAL DESCRIPTION: 1 album (26 cartes de visite and tintypes), 14 × 11 cm.

SOURCE: Gift of Hermann P. Riccius, 1959. Transfer from the Manuscript Division, 1959.

Clara Barton residence in Glen Echo, Maryland. Clara Barton Papers, Lot 8533.

C. M. Bell Studio Collection

HISTORY OF THE PHOTOGRAPHIC STUDIO, WASHINGTON, D.C., 1873–1909

Charles Milton Bell (1848–1893) was one of Washington's leading portrait photographers during the last quarter of the nineteenth century. He began work in photography as the youngest member of a family of photographers who operated a studio in the capital from about 1860 to 1874. Thomas and thirteen-year-old Nephi Bell, two sons of Francis Hamilton Bell, a gunsmith, first became photographers in the late 1850s, after the family moved to Washington from Fredericksburg, Virginia. In the early 1860s, Thomas and Nephi operated the Turner and Company studio on Pennsylvania Avenue and specialized in ambrotypes. The name was changed to Bell and Brother (Bell & Bro.) in 1862, and this studio eventually also provided employment to three other brothers and their father. Francis and his sons William Hamilton, Jackson Wood, and Charles Milton operated the studio in various combinations during its decade and a half of existence. The firm was known as Bell and Hall during parts of 1866 and 1867, Allen F. Hall being the husband of Francis Bell's only daughter. In addition to portraits, Bell and Brother produced many carte-de-visite and stereograph views of Washington and operated a sales stand at the Smithsonian Institution, perhaps in exchange for photographic services provided to the Smithsonian. C. M. Bell and two brothers also started a photolithographic firm called Bell Brothers, a company established to take advantage of the presence of the Patent Office in Washington. (To complicate matters, there was a photographer in the city named William Bell, not a relative, who is remembered today for his work at the Army Medical Museum and on western survey teams after the Civil War.) The Bell and Brother studio had competition from James McClees, Mathew Brady, and Alexander Gardner, and so remained a minor establishment. Bell and Brother's attempts to deal in photographic equipment were unsuccessful.

C. M. Bell studio logo (enlarged), from verso of a cabinet card in Lot 12270. Ca. 1870s.
LC-USZ62-92534

Charles Milton Bell became a photographer at Bell and Brother in 1867, at the age of nineteen. In late 1873, C. M. Bell—as he was to be known professionally—left that studio and established his own business nearby on Pennsylvania Avenue. The two businesses overlapped for a time, but the success of C. M. Bell eventually eclipsed that of his father and brothers, who closed Bell and Brother about a year later. Francis and some of his sons worked for the C. M. Bell studio during its busiest years.

C. M. Bell became known as the photographer who had the largest collection of images of Washington notables, including politicians, and leading businessmen. He photographed embassy officials and distinguished visitors from other countries, black ministers and church leaders, members of Washington's educated and cultured black middle class, and leading educators and citizens, with familiar names like Gallaudet, Frederick Douglass, Helen Keller, Anne Sullivan, Susan B. Anthony, Dr. Mary Walker, Edith Bolling, Mrs. Grover Cleveland, and Mr. and Mrs. Alexander Graham Bell. The photographer had come a long way since 1864, when President Abraham Lincoln had declined an invitation for a portrait sitting.

Bell also photographed Washington baseball players, actors, and comedians. He provided photographic copies of documents, works of art, and other photographs. A large number of amputees posed for Bell's camera, for before-and-after advertising and documentary photographs used by the local J. E. Hanger artificial limb company (which is still in existence). Architectural interiors and exteriors were photographed, primarily in the 21 × 26 cm (8 × 10 inch) and larger formats, and include major public buildings and residences, schools, churches, and some street scenes. He also photographed public events, such as openings of Congress, treaty signings, and parades. Bell enjoyed a congenial business relationship with the Grover Cleveland administration and made many portraits of the president's bride after their marriage. His portraits of the second Cleveland inauguration were published in the New York press. He managed to gain access with his camera to presidential assassin Charles Julius Guiteau in the District of Columbia Jail. He made scenic photographs along the Piedmont route of the Richmond and Danbury Railroad which were shown at the New Orleans Exposition in 1884–85. Those images that were commercially popular were deposited for copyright by C. M. Bell in the Library of Congress after 1870, and examples of these photographs may be found under the photographer's name in the Library's cataloged collections. They are described below.

C. M. Bell, photographer. C. M. Bell Collection,
LC-B5-62515

The studio had at the time a reputation equaling that of Plumb's, Whitehurst's, or

C. M. Bell. Frederick Douglass. C. M. Bell Collection.
LC-B51-21528

C. M. Bell. Helen Keller and Anne Sullivan. C. M. Bell Collection.
LC-B5-39969

C. M. Bell. Susan B. Anthony. C. M. Bell Collection.
LC-B5-36193

Mathew Brady's establishments. From the beginning, it was known as one of the most fashionable and best equipped photographic studios on the continent. Charles in fact occupied the rooms that had been the Washington studio of Jesse Whitehurst, the capital's most fashionable studio during the 1850s. From there, Bell expanded rather quickly until his studio occupied four street numbers between 459 and 465 Pennsylvania Avenue NW, with an additional "West End Branch" at 701 Fifteenth Street NW, not far from the White House. The Pennsylvania Avenue studio was very elegant. Its salon was forty by sixty feet, with frescoed walls and a high-arched ceiling. Lace curtains covered broad windows that looked out over Washington's main thoroughfare. Its appointments included gilded cornices, a particularly large glass chandelier, and comfortably upholstered furniture. There were, of course, examples of some of the best of Bell's photographic work on the walls. The studio's operating room was equipped with two skylights of clear French plate glass. After 1876, it also boasted a camera that had been specially made by E. and H. T. Anthony for exhibition at the Centennial Exposition in Philadelphia, a camera that some have claimed was the finest in the country.

C. M. Bell may be best known today for his photographs of Native Americans, which he began to produce in 1873, when Ferdinand V. Hayden, director of the United States Geological Survey of the Territories, turned to him for continuation of a project that had begun several years earlier. The assignment was to photograph as many of the Indian visitors to the capital as possible, during this period of intense treaty negotiations. A trip to the photographer's studio was apparently a reward accorded to cooperative chiefs. Hayden had employed photographers for the project from the studios of Washington photographers Alexander Gardner, A. Zeno Shindler, and Julius and Henry Ulke. In 1879, when Hayden's collection of negatives was turned over to the Smithsonian's Bureau of American Ethnology, Bell continued to be of service. For the Smithsonian, he made the photographs used as the basis for some of the illustrations of Garrick Mallery's classic work, "Sign Language among North American Indians," published in the first annual report of the Bureau of American Ethnology, 1879–80.

Bell's Indian photographs have often been attributed to the survey photographer William Henry Jackson. It seems clear, however, that Bell did most of the Hayden survey's

C. M. Bell. Dr. Mary Walker. C. M. Bell Collection.
LC-B5-950306

studio photography of Indians in Washington and also made prints for the survey. It is estimated that Bell produced about six hundred Indian portraits. Jackson seems to have limited his involvement to interviewing the Indians for information he incorporated into the catalog of the survey's collection. Although Jackson may also have helped pose Bell's Indian subjects on occasion, it seems likely that he was too busy printing and cataloging his own field photographs, preparing models and exhibits for the Centennial Exposition, and working on publications of the survey to do much original photography during the short winter seasons when he was in the capital.

From the end of the Hayden survey in 1879 until the 1890s, Bell also made photographs of Indians for the Department of the Interior and the Bureau of American Ethnology. In some cases, he also seems to have taken photographs of Indians entirely for his own purposes. Bell photographed many of the most prominent Indian leaders of his day in both individual and group portraits. Chief Joseph, Spotted Tail, Red Cloud, Medicine Crow, and Eskimizin were some of his well-known subjects. Stylistically, his Indian portraits fall into two broad groups. Those made for the Hayden survey and later for the Bureau of American Ethnology were simple busts of individuals seated in distinctly Victorian chairs. The backgrounds are plain. Generally two shots were made of each person—a fairly direct front view and a side view. The second type of photograph, perhaps intended more often for Bell's own use, places the Indians amid the romantic properties of a late Victorian studio, the backdrops showing bucolic scenes, sometimes mixed with architectural balustrades and columns, with a choice of the usual assortment of papier–mâché rocks, Victorian furniture, and ubiquitous twining ivy.

C. M. Bell. Portrait of Standing on the Prairie. C. M. Bell Collection.

LC-B5-46117

In time, the work of photographing the Indian visitors was undertaken by Smithsonian photographers, including John K. Hillers, William Dinwiddie, and De Lancey W. Gill. The Hayden Survey/Bureau of American Ethnology Collection, now in the Smithsonian's National Anthropological Archives, includes several hundred images by C. M. Bell, and some by the earlier Bell and Brother studio. Some of the negatives for these Indian portraits may be found in the Library of Congress collection of C. M. Bell studio negatives now on microfilm.

In the spring of 1893, while observing a naval review in Hampton Roads off Fort Monroe in Virginia, Charles Milton Bell suddenly became ill, and he died on May 12. (A notation about his death may be found in the studio logbooks on that date. See Lot 12250.) His wife, née Annie E. Colley, a native Washingtonian and daughter of the owner of the Windsor Hotel, took over the day-to-day operation of the studio, at times assisted by her two young sons. Annie Bell had difficulty keeping this large operation going and so closed the West End (White House vicinity) branch. Gradually the buildings occupied by the main studio were reduced to one, and around the turn of the century the business was sold to new proprietors, Atha and Cunningham, although Bell's name was retained. In 1907, the studio was moved to 1321 G Street NW, an effort to remain close to fashionable trade that had moved away from Pennsylvania Avenue. In 1909, however, the studio closed, having kept the C. M. Bell name and negative inventory until the end.

C. M. Bell. Cabinet card portrait of Big Road, ca. 1880s. Lot 12567.

LC-USZ62-74583

The negatives were then sold to another Washington photographer, I. M. Boyce. In 1916, Boyce pulled many of the Indian negatives out of the main collection and tried to sell them to the Bureau of American Ethnology. (The sale was finally made in the 1950s by a son of Boyce's.) After various attempts to sell the remaining studio negatives, Boyce sold most of the collection to Alexander Graham Bell (no family relation to C. M. Bell), who was involved with the study of human heredity and saw in this collection not only important documentation of Washington's social and political history but a great source for photographs of generations of the same families, ideal material for studying inherited physical traits. For a time, Alexander Graham Bell stored the negatives in the basement of his Volta Bureau in Georgetown. They were then donated to the American Genetic Association in Washington, which transferred the collection to several successive storage locations, including a basement and various farm buildings. The Library of Congress acquired the collection in 1975 from the American Genetic Association.

(NOTE: Background information about Charles Milton Bell and his portrait studio was provided by James Glenn, deputy director and archivist, National Anthropological Archives, Smithsonian Institution, Washington, D.C.)

PROCESSING HISTORY, ARRANGEMENT, AND USE OF THE COLLECTION

The original C. M. Bell studio numbers and identification of sitter, customer, or subject were written on strips of paper, which were then glued to the edge of each plate. Unfortunately, during the five or six decades in which the collection was in storage, before the Library took custody of it, many of these caption strips became detached or suffered water damage that made the information unreadable. The nineteenth-century handwriting on surviving strips is often difficult to decipher and the transcription provided for the negative jacket may occasionally be wrong. Some remaining original caption strips on the negatives are readable on the microfilm of the negative collection (Lot 12552) and may be consulted to verify the spelling of a name or an original negative number. Researchers should remember that the name on the label is often not the name of the sitter but the name of the person or organization who ordered the photographs (for instance, a child's parent or the J. E. Hanger artificial limb company). Other numbers and abbreviations on these caption strips (for example, "doz," "Mau," "cab," "plat," "6-Aristo") refer to the size, style, and quantity of images ordered by the customer.

Numbers 800,000 and above in any of the five negative series (LC−B5, −B51, −B52, −B53, and −B54) have been assigned by the Library in the absence of a studio-assigned number for particular negatives, and these images do not necessarily fall within their proper chronological order. The Library has also added letter suffixes to studio-assigned numbers that had been used for more than one negative or more than one sitter (e.g., LC−B5−72006C).

A small percentage of the C. M. Bell negatives were so badly deteriorated that no recognizable image remained and other negatives were badly broken while in transit from one location to another during the decades after the studio closed. Images (and fragments of negatives) that could be neither restored nor microfilmed were disposed of by the Library. Many negatives that were broken into two or three pieces were saved and microfilmed, however.

Fortunately, several studio logbooks and alphabetical client registers were found among the crates of C. M. Bell negatives (see Lot 12250). These "finding aids" enable researchers to (1) check a (roughly) alphabetical list of sitters or customers (covering the period from September 1893 to about 1904) for their corresponding negative numbers and (2) check a negative number for the name of the sitter, the customer's address, the quantity of photographs ordered, and the price of the order. Each negative number was assigned chronologically and listed under a specific day's work in the studio. This information enables researchers to date precisely particular images and to supply either missing names or negative numbers, where one piece of information is known. Unfortunately, no logbooks were found for the early part of the C. M. Bell studio's history, so negatives with numbers below 35,838 (January 1, 1891) cannot be searched in this way. The collection contains negatives numbered above 58,572, the number assigned for January 18, 1909, the last date for which logbook entries exist. Presumably, some of these images were made and added to the collection after I. M. Boyce bought the C. M. Bell negatives in 1909.

In 1965, an NBC production made use of modern photoprints made from these negatives, which were then in the custody of the American Genetic Association. About 550 of these modern photoprints were given to the Library by the association in 1985 and are available for study, although most are unidentified and bear no negative number. These prints may be found in Lots 12261, 12262, 12276, 12277, and 12278, described below.

Additional lotted C. M. Bell photographs, obtained through copyright deposit and other sources, may be found by searching under the photographer's name in the Prints and Photographs Division catalog. Some groups consisting entirely or mainly of C. M. Bell or Bell and Brother photographs are described below.

In addition to the collection's value as a source of portraits and topics, researchers interested in the evolution of dress styles and hairstyles or in the portrait studio props used in a particular period may find it interesting to simply browse through the microfilm reels in their numerical (chronological) order for each of the five formats, 5 × 7 inch (13 × 18 cm) to 18 × 22 inch (46 × 56 cm) glass plates (in negative series LC−B5, −B51, −B52, −B53, and −B54).

C. M. Bell. Portrait, commissioned by the J.E. Hanger artificial limb company, of G. L. Burnette wearing an artificial limb. C. M. Bell Collection.
LC-B5-50861

C. M. Bell. Portrait, commissioned by J.E. Hanger artificial limb company, of an unidentified amputee with his new artificial limbs. C. M. Bell Collection.
LC-B51-55577

C. M. Bell. Mrs. Grover Cleveland. C. M. Bell Collection.

LC-B5-11598

C. M. Bell. Mr. and Mrs. Alexander Graham Bell. C. M. Bell Collection.

LC-B5-42849

SELECTED PORTRAITS AND SUBJECTS

LOT 12552 (microfilm reels 1 and 2)

In the course of cleaning and re-jacketing the deteriorating studio negatives of C. M. Bell, Washingtoniana project staff members selected portraits of members of various ethnic groups as well as particularly interesting images from among the wide range of subjects C. M. Bell photographed to provide easier access to these examples. Among the highlights of the collection are photographs of particularly famous people in Washington (including C. M. Bell himself), sitters from Washington embassies, some buildings, and charming examples of period costumes, hairstyles, toys, studio props, and poses. Some medical and advertising photographs have been included in this selection as well.

These selected negatives are by no means the complete collection of portraits of blacks, Asians, Indians, or famous people in Washington. Serious researchers will search the entire collection in numerical (chronological) order by negative number, within each of the five formats. The negatives in this selection have also been filmed in their proper numerical order within the entire collection.

LOT 12552 (microfilm)

COLLECTION NAME: C. M. Bell Studio Collection

SUBJECTS: Collection of glass plate negatives from the C. M. Bell photographic studio, Washington, D.C. Portraits, including diplomats, cabinet members, congressmen, First Ladies, Supreme Court justices; black ministers and citizens, North American Indian chiefs and tribe members who visited Washington, members of various other ethnic groups; baseball players, entertainers (especially musicians), inventors with their inventions, U.S. Capitol Police, Pullman Car porters, office workers; children; amputees who were customers of J.E. Hanger artificial limb company; visitors to Washington, D.C.; postmortem photos. Portraits also record contemporary fashions and studio props. Also includes the White House, churches, restaurants, and government, commercial, educational, and residential buildings in Washington and such events as the openings of Congress, treaty signing, weddings. Organizations in Washington, including St. Ann's Infant Asylum, clubs. Medical and agricultural specimens. Copies of documents and works of art. Some images have original captions.

NOTE: Microfilm reproduces negatives in series LC-B5, -B51, -B52, -B53, and

-B54. Some negatives are badly deteriorated or broken. Some modern photoprints from these negatives are found in Lots 12261, 12262, 12276, 12277, 12278, and 12561. Some negatives made after C. M. Bell's death in 1893 may have been produced under the direction of Atha and Cunningham; some images with negative numbers above 58,572 may have been produced by I. M. Boyce. Explanatory materials about the collection are available on the microfilm and in the Prints and Photographs Reading Room.

DATE: 1873-ca. 1916

PHOTOGRAPHERS: C. M. Bell and employees.

PHYSICAL DESCRIPTION: Ca. 30,050 collodion and silver gelatin dry plate negatives, 46 × 56 cm or smaller.

ARRANGEMENT: Microfilmed in original negative number order, by size of negative (indicated by series code). *Reel 1*: Selected portraits of C. M. Bell and family, and selected portraits of blacks in Washington; *Reel 2*: Selected portraits of North American Indians, selected portraits of Asians, and selected miscellaneous subjects. Selected images filmed in reels 1 and 2 were filmed again in their proper numerical sequence within the entire collection, which is arranged in negative number order, by the following sizes. *Reels 3 to end*: Series LC-B5 includes 13 × 18 cm (5 × 7 inch) glass plate negatives (ca. 26,000 items). Series LC-B51 includes 20 × 25 cm (8 × 10 inch) glass plate negatives (ca. 3,100 items). Series LC-B52 includes 28 × 36 cm (11 × 14 inch) glass plate negatives (ca. 100 items). Series LC-B53 includes 36 × 44 cm (14 × 17 inch) glass plate negatives (ca. 700 items). Series LC-B54 includes 46 × 56 cm (18 × 22 inch) glass plate negatives (ca. 150 items). Studio logbooks and alphabetical client registers are available on microfilm in Lot 12250.

SOURCE: Gift of the American Genetic Association, 1975.

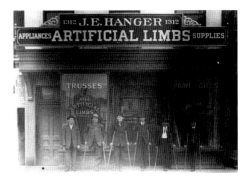

C. M. Bell. J.E. Hanger storefront with a group of amputees. C. M. Bell Collection.

LC-B51-57735

LOT 12250 (microfilm)

COLLECTION NAME: Logbooks of the C. M. Bell Studio Collection

SUBJECTS: Alphabetical client registers and logbooks listing portraits and other photographs made by the C. M. Bell studio in Washington, D.C.

NOTE: Glass negatives listed in logbooks are in series LC−B5, −B51, −B52, −B53, and −B54. Logbooks and alphabetical registers are in very poor condition; pages are brittle, loose, and dirty and bindings are broken. Use microfilm copy instead of original volumes.

DATE: 1887−1909

PHYSICAL DESCRIPTION: 8 vols. of studio logbooks and alphabetical client registers, 39 × 27 cm or smaller.

ARRANGEMENT: *Vols. 1−2:* Alphabetical listing of clients, 1887−1904; *vols. 3−8:* Chronological listing of negative numbers and subjects, 35,838 (January 1, 1891) to 58,572 (January 28, 1909).

SOURCE: Gift of the American Genetic Association, 1975.

LOT 4149 (stereographs)

SUBJECTS: Stereographic views of Washington scenes and buildings in the following subject subdivisions: 1) U.S. Capitol; 2) Botanic Gardens; 3) Smithsonian; 4) Patent Office; 5) White House; 6) Agriculture Building; 7) Treasury Building; 8) Arsenal; 9) Post Office; 10) Navy Yard; 11) Miscellaneous buildings, including the Franklin School, War Department, Corcoran Gallery, Navy Department, Ford's Theater, Soldier's Home, Washington Monument, and Naval Observatory; 12) Aqueduct and Long Bridges; 13) Statues of Jackson and Washington; 14) Maryland and Virginia views, including Great Falls, National Cemetery, Washington's Tomb at Mount Vernon, and Arlington House.

DATE: Ca. 1867−69

PHOTOGRAPHERS: Bell & Bro.

PHYSICAL DESCRIPTION: 116 albumen stereographs.

SOURCE: Copyright deposit by Bell & Bro., Washington, D.C., 1867−69.

LOT 12261

COLLECTION NAME: C. M. Bell Collection

SUBJECTS: Selected portraits. Includes diplomats, U.S. presidents, cabinet members, congressmen, Supreme Court justices, government officials, and businessmen. Groups from Washington, D.C., area military schools, colleges, and clubs. People near the Capitol and working in offices; amputees ice-skating.

NOTE: All but three photographs are modern prints made from original glass negatives in series LC−B5, −B51, and −B52; these and other C. M. Bell images may be viewed on microfilm in Lot 12552.

DATE: 1873−ca. 1916

PHOTOGRAPHERS: C. M. Bell and employees.

PHYSICAL DESCRIPTION: 260 modern silver gelatin photoprints, 35 × 28 cm or smaller.

ARRANGEMENT: *Lot 12261−1:* Men; *Lot 12261−2:* Women; *Lot 12261−3:* Children and couples; *Lot 12261−4:* Groups; *Lot 12261−5:* Blacks; *Lot 12261−6:* Asians; *Lot 12261−7:* Informal situations; *Lot 12261−8:* Postmortem portraits; *Lot 12261−9:* Oversize. Finding aid available in Prints and Photographs Reading Room.

SOURCE: Gift of the American Genetic Association, 1984.

C. M. Bell. An artificial limb recipient ice-skating near the Washington Monument. Photograph commissioned by the J.E. Hanger artificial limb company. C. M. Bell Collection.

LC-B5-820926

C. M. Bell. J. W. Mays, Pullman car porter. C. M. Bell Collection.

LC-B5-44843

C. M. Bell. Portrait of Bishop Arnett. C. M. Bell Collection.

LC-B5-465

C. M. Bell. Portrait of Chinese minister's sons. C. M. Bell Collection.

LC-B51-50469

LOT 12262

COLLECTION NAME: C. M. Bell Collection

SUBJECTS: Portraits of North American Indians, including Whitehorse and Deroin, as well as a group of Nez Perce.

NOTE: Photos are modern prints made from original glass negatives in series LC–B5 and –B51. Those negatives may be viewed on microfilm in Lot 12552.

DATE: 1873–92

PHOTOGRAPHERS: C. M. Bell and employees.

PHYSICAL DESCRIPTION: 9 modern silver gelatin photoprints, 20 × 25 cm or smaller.

SOURCE: Gift of the American Genetic Association, 1984.

LOT 12276

COLLECTION NAME: C. M. Bell Collection

SUBJECTS: Architecture in the Washington, D.C., region. Includes government buildings, churches, educational buildings, hotels, and restaurants. Interiors of offices and the Capitol, including art and sculpture.

NOTE: Photos are modern prints made from original glass negatives that may be viewed on microfilm in Lot 12552.

DATE: 1873–ca. 1916

PHOTOGRAPHERS: C. M. Bell and employees.

PHYSICAL DESCRIPTION: 199 modern silver gelatin photoprints, 20 × 25 cm or smaller.

ARRANGEMENT: Lot 12276–1: Public buildings and street views; Lot 12276–2: Businesses and commercial establishments; Lot 12276–3: Residences; Lot 12276–4: Interiors; Lot 12276–5: U.S. Capitol; Lot 12276–6: White House; Lot 12276–7: Library of Congress Thomas Jefferson Building. Finding aid available in the Prints and Photographs Reading Room.

SOURCE: Gift of the American Genetic Association, 1984

LOT 12277

COLLECTION NAME: C. M. Bell Collection

SUBJECTS: Views of the Washington, D.C., region. Parks include National Zoological Park. McKinley inauguration and arrival of his casket at the Capitol. Theodore Roosevelt dedicating Pan American Union Building. Funeral memorials, wreaths, and decorations. Some sites in Maryland or Virginia.

NOTE: Photos are modern prints made from original glass negatives that may be viewed on microfilm in Lot 12552.

DATE: 1873–ca. 1916

PHOTOGRAPHERS: C. M. Bell and employees.

PHYSICAL DESCRIPTION: 49 modern silver gelatin photoprints, 20 × 25 cm or smaller.

ARRANGEMENT: Lot 12277–1: Parks, landscapes, and rivers; Lot 12277–2: Public monuments and statues; Lot 12277–3: Ceremonies and parades; Lot 12277–4: Cemeteries and funerals.

SOURCE: Gift of the American Genetic Association, 1984.

LOT 12278

COLLECTION NAME: C. M. Bell Collection

SUBJECTS: Copy work. Photos of architectural renderings, designs for inventions, correspondence, advertisements, and paintings and drawings of presidents, including Abraham Lincoln, and First Ladies.

NOTE: Photos are modern prints made from original glass negatives that may be viewed on microfilm in Lot 12552.

DATE: 1873–ca. 1916

PHOTOGRAPHERS: C. M. Bell and employees.

PHYSICAL DESCRIPTION: 27 modern silver gelatin photoprints, 20 × 25 cm or smaller.

SOURCE: Gift of the American Genetic Association, 1984.

LOT 12380

COLLECTION NAME: C. M. Bell Collection

SUBJECTS: Portraits of C. M. Bell and his family, printed from C. M. Bell studio negatives. Includes portraits of C. M. Bell, Charlie Bell, Colley Bell, May and Gertie Bell, Miss S. Bell, Mrs. M. J. Bell, E. Bell, Nannie Bell, and others.

NOTE: Corresponding negatives in series LC–B5 and –B51.

DATE: Ca. 1863–ca. 1916

PHOTOGRAPHERS: C. M. Bell and employees.

PHYSICAL DESCRIPTION: 27 modern silver gelatin photoprints, 20 × 25 cm.

SOURCE: Received with the Grosvenor Collection of Photographs of Alexander Graham Bell.

C. M. Bell. Portrait of an unidentified U.S. Capitol Police officer. C. M. Bell Collection.

LC-B5-950055

C. M. Bell. Portrait of an unidentified child with blocks. C. M. Bell Collection.

LC-B5-57728

C. M. Bell. Portrait of an unidentified infant from St. Ann's Asylum. C. M. Bell Collection.

LC-B5-40589

C. M. Bell. The photographer Arthur McCurdy with his EBEDEC (daylight film) developing tank, patented in 1906 and named after a Nova Scotia town with the early Indian name of Baddeck. Arthur McCurdy was Alexander Graham Bell's assistant and secretary. C. M. Bell Collection.

LC-B5-46357

LOT 12527

COLLECTION NAME: C. M. Bell Collection

SUBJECTS: The Presidential Train, with some views of the B&P Railroad Depot in Washington, D.C.

DATE: 1887

PHOTOGRAPHERS: C. M. Bell and employees.

PHYSICAL DESCRIPTION: 4 albumen photoprints, 35 × 53 cm or smaller.

SOURCE: Copyright deposit by C. M. Bell, 1887.

LOT 12528

COLLECTION NAME: C. M. Bell Collection

SUBJECTS: Portraits of Bishops P. L. Chapelle and J. B. Salprints (1892); the War Investigating Commission (1898); the delegates to the International Congress, Washington, D.C. (1889).

DATE: 1889–98

PHOTOGRAPHERS: C. M. Bell and employees.

PHYSICAL DESCRIPTION: 3 albumen and silver gelatin photoprints, 34 × 41 cm or smaller.

SOURCE: Copyright deposit by C. M. Bell, 1889–98.

C. M. Bell. Portrait of the actor William Bramwell. C. M. Bell Collection.

LC-B5-43994

C. M. Bell. Portrait of Stocksdale, a Washington baseball player. C. M. Bell Collection.

LC-B5-41643.

C. M. Bell. Konrat Okou, sailor. C. M. Bell Collection.

LC-B5-46128

Bell & Bro. Half of a stereograph pair showing the uncompleted Washington Monument, ca. 1867. Lot 4149-1.

LC-USZ62-27822

C. M. Bell. "U.S. Commissioners and Delegations of Sioux Chiefs Visiting Washington, October 15, 1888." Copyright 1889. Lot 12566.

LC-USZ62-92959

LOT 12529

COLLECTION NAME: C. M. Bell Collection

SUBJECTS: Events in Washington, D.C. President Theodore Roosevelt inauguration at the Capitol, March 25, 1901; President Benjamin Harrison inauguration, March 4, 1889; the Knights Templars' Twenty-fourth Triennial Conclave parade down Pennsylvania Avenue, October 8, 1889.

DATE: 1889–1901

PHOTOGRAPHERS: C. M. Bell and employees.

PHYSICAL DESCRIPTION: 5 albumen and silver gelatin photoprints, 42 × 54 cm or smaller.

SOURCE: Copyright deposit by C. M. Bell, 1889–1901.

LOT 12530

COLLECTION NAME: C. M. Bell Collection

SUBJECTS: Buildings in Washington, D.C. Includes views of the Equitable Co-operative Building Association building (1887); the B&P Railroad Depot, draped after President Garfield's assassination there (1881); and interior views of the White House laundry and kitchen (1901).

DATE: 1881–1901

PHOTOGRAPHERS: C. M. Bell and employees.

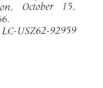

C. M. Bell. "The Fox Indians." Copyright 1890. Lot 12566.

LC-USZ62-92960

PHYSICAL DESCRIPTION: 6 albumen and silver gelatin photoprints, 36 × 31 cm or smaller.

SOURCE: Copyright deposit by C. M. Bell, 1881–1901.

LOT 12566

COLLECTION NAME: C. M. Bell Collection

SUBJECTS: Portraits of North American Indians, Indian tribes, and tribal leaders who visited Washington, D.C., to negotiate treaties with the U.S. government. Titles of portraits include "U.S. Commissioners and Delegations of Sioux Chiefs Visiting Washington," shown on the Capitol steps, October 15, 1888; "Sioux Delegation," February 1891; "The Fox Indians," January 1890; "Seven Sioux Warriors," February 1891; "The Delegation of Sioux Chiefs to Ratify the Sale of Lands in Dakota to the U.S. Government," December 1899; "Full Delegation of Sioux Indians," February 1891.

NOTE: Photo mounts bear full captions with tribe name and name of each Indian pictured.

DATE: 1888–91

PHOTOGRAPHERS: C. M. Bell.

PHYSICAL DESCRIPTION: 7 albumen photoprints on mounts, 45 × 54 cm or smaller.

SOURCE: Copyright deposit by C. M. Bell, 1889–91.

LOT 12567

COLLECTION NAME: C. M. Bell Collection

SUBJECTS: Portraits of Sioux Indians. Includes Big Road, High Hawk, Two Strike, Spotted Elk, Young-Man-Afraid-of-His-Horses, Fire Lightning, and Little Wound.

NOTE: Some mounts carry imprint, "Indian Photographs by C. M. Bell."

DATE: 1891

PHOTOGRAPHERS: C. M. Bell.

PHYSICAL DESCRIPTION: 7 albumen photoprints on cabinet card mounts, 12 × 17 cm.

SOURCE: Copyright deposit by C. M. Bell, 1891.

The Blair Family Papers, spanning 1830–1968 (chiefly 1841–83), are held in the Manuscript Division. They number 12,000 items and are accompanied by a finding aid. The holdings include lectures, printed matter, speeches, military and financial papers, and biographical and genealogical data. Family members represented include the families of Francis Preston Blair, Sr., Francis Preston Blair, Jr., Gist Blair, and Montgomery Blair. Papers relate to the publication of the *Washington Globe,* the Civil War and reconstruction period, the Dred Scott case, and Montgomery Blair's activities as postmaster general in Lincoln's cabinet. The Blair Family Papers were presented to the Manuscript Division as a gift from the Blair family and others, 1928–74. The photographs were transferred to the Prints and Photographs Division.

E. Anthony (New York), from a Mathew Brady negative. Carte-de-visite portrait of Montgomery Blair at the time he was postmaster general of the United States, ca. 1860s. Papers of the Blair Family, Lot 9946.

LC-USZ61-2036

LOT 9946

COLLECTION NAME: Blair Family Papers, Manuscript Division

SUBJECTS: Portraits of Francis Preston Blair and his wife (née Violet Gist); Francis P. Blair, Jr.; Mr. and Mrs. Montgomery Blair; Edith, Minna, and Montgomery Blair II as children (1898). Blair residences in Silver Spring, Maryland, Washington, D.C., and Portsmouth, New York. Includes a carte-de-visite view of the remnants of Montgomery Blair's house at Silver Spring, burned by the Confederate Army under the direction of Gen. Jubal Early; view of Francis Preston Blair house in Silver Spring; carte-de-visite portraits of Montgomery Blair while postmaster general during the Lincoln administration, Mrs. Montgomery Blair, and Francis P. Blair, Jr.; a carte-de-visite copy of a portrait of Mrs. Jefferson Davis. Interior of Lowery Home, 1000 Vermont Avenue and K Street, NW. Portrait of some Blair family members as tourists at Niagara Falls.

DATE: Ca. 1850s–ca. 1890s

PHOTOGRAPHERS: Alexander Gardner, Rice, Mathew Brady studio, J. Goldin, E. Anthony (New York), and Samuel J. Mason (Niagara Falls).

PHYSICAL DESCRIPTION: 34 albumen and silver gelatin photoprints, including some cartes de visite, cabinet cards, and copy photographs, 28 × 36 cm or smaller.

SOURCE: Transfer from the Manuscript Division, 1963.

Carte-de-visite portrait of Mrs. Montgomery Blair, 1867. Papers of the Blair Family, Lot 9946.
LC-USZ61-2037

Silver Spring residence of Francis Preston Blair. Papers of the Blair Family, Lot 9946.
LC-USZ62-23884

J. Goldin. Carte-de-visite photograph of the ruins of Montgomery Blair's house in Silver Spring, burned by Confederate soldiers under the command of Gen. Jubal Early. Papers of the Blair Family, Lot 9946.
LC-USZ62-23883

MATHEW B. BRADY COLLECTION

Mathew Brady (1823–1896) first established himself as a ''Daguerrean Artist'' in New York City in 1844. He had begun his photographic experiments in 1842, only two years after Daguerre's invention had been announced to the world and introduced in this country by Samuel F. B. Morse. Despite bad eyesight, Brady developed a reputation as a fashionable portrait daguerreotypist.

To achieve his ambition to preserve the likenesses of noteworthy citizens, the young Brady opened a gallery in Washington, D.C., early in 1849. He photographed President James K. Polk in his office in the White House on February 14, 1849, and President Zachary Taylor, who had just assumed office, in his gallery on May 5. The Washington gallery, called the National Photographic Art Gallery and located at what is now 625–627 Pennsylvania Avenue, was not highly profitable, however, and remained open only a few months before Brady returned to New York.

Ten years later, he opened another Washington gallery. By that time, the invention of the wet collodion and albumen processes had made it possible to make reproducible photographs and even common folks could afford to have their portraits taken. This seemed to guarantee the success of a Washington portrait studio. So, in 1858, Mathew Brady hired a Scottish photographer, Alexander Gardner, an expert in the wet collodion process, to manage his new gallery at Pennsylvania Avenue and Seventh Street NW. Brady himself maintained his residence in New York City until 1873, paying only occasional visits to Washington and relying heavily on his manager and operators to run the Washington business. By 1860, Brady had opened a lavishly appointed establishment in New York, the National Portrait Gallery. From Washington, he was able to obtain photographs of every member of the Thirty-sixth Congress. In February 1861, he photographed president-elect Abraham Lincoln, who had sat for Brady once before.

At the height of his success as a portrait photographer, Brady launched a project that he fully expected would make him rich and even more famous. He would document with cameras the events of the Civil War, the photographs to be sold to a patriotic public, government and military leaders, and discharged soldiers. He purchased supplies on credit from E. and H. T. Anthony and Company in New York, to equip at times more than twenty teams of photographers in the field, including D. B. Woodbury, S. R. Siebert, W. Morris Smith, C. Chester, J. F. Coonley, Fowx, David Knox, William R. Pywell, and J. Reekie. Brady also acquired photographs and negatives from other photographers of the Civil War. Thus, when reference is made to Mathew Brady's Civil War views, it is important to remember that although he himself produced a portion of the studio portraits—primarily those made in New York City—he left the more challenging and dangerous work in camp and field to his hired operators, who rarely saw their names imprinted on views distributed by Brady or subsequent owners of the Brady negatives.

Meanwhile, his Washington studio foundered under the new management of James F. Gibson, hired after Alexander Gardner left Brady's operation to join Gen. George B. McClellan and the Army of the Potomac as an official army photographer. Gardner returned to Washington a few years later, after General McClellan was relieved of his command. In 1863, Gardner established a studio at 511 Seventh Street NW, with his brothers James and John, taking with him Brady's former operators Timothy O'Sullivan and Egbert Guy Fox, and he became one of Brady's chief competitors. (See ''Alexander Gardner Photographs.'')

By 1869, owing to lack of interest in his war views and the confluence of several other business misfortunes, Brady was forced to close his New York establishment, and he appealed to the U.S. government to buy his collection of photographic views of the Civil War. (See ''Civil War Views.'') Only in March 1871 did the Joint Committee on the Library recommend to the House of Representatives that Brady's collection be purchased, and then Congress failed to act on the recommendation. Brady was forced to close his Washington studio in bankruptcy, and the firm of Burgess and Company took over the studio. Andrew Burgess had been hired by Brady in 1870, after the failure of the Brady establishment under James Gibson's management.

Brady had been forced to turn over a set of about 7,000 negatives, portraits, and views of the Civil War to E. and H. T. Anthony and Company, as attachments to satisfy his debts to

Mathew Brady. Portrait of Andrew Carnegie, from an album of portraits of delegates to the International American Conference, held in 1899–1900, Washington, D.C. Lot 3206.

LC-USZ62-93031

Mathew Brady. Portrait of General Sherman, from a two-album set of autographed cabinet card portraits of members of the Senate, Forty-first Congress, their wives, and a few prominent Civil War military leaders, ca. 1869–71. Lot 3583.

LC-USZ62-10509

this photographic supplier. (During healthier financial periods, Brady had contracted with the Anthony Company to publish large numbers of carte-de-visite portraits of famous Americans and Civil War heroes, to satisfy public demand that exceeded the capabilities of his Washington establishment.) He placed another set of 6,000 negatives in storage in Washington, D.C. In 1874, the Washington, D.C., set was sold at auction for $2,840 to the U.S. government, to satisfy the unpaid storage bill, and the War Department took custody of those negatives. In 1875, Congress finally voted to pay Brady the sum of $25,000 for this collection. It is sadly ironic that a single album of portraits of members of the Fiftieth Congress, produced by Mathew Brady and Levin C. Handy as the prototype for a book that was never published, was recently advertised for $25,000 by an antiquarian book dealer.

Brady was able to regain his Washington studio but not his former fashionable reputation. His Washington business finally closed in November 1881, and he worked in partnership with other Washington photographers, including his nephew Levin C. Handy, until his death on January 15, 1896. He was buried in an unmarked grave in the Handy plot in the Congressional Cemetery in Washington, D.C. A stone was placed on the grave in the early twentieth century, after the publication of Brady's accumulation of war views in the illustrated histories of the Civil War published by Eaton's Patriot Publishing Company.

In 1920, the U.S. Army War College transferred about 350 daguerreotype plates to the Library of Congress, from among the items that the War Department had purchased at auction. (See "Daguerreotype Collection.") The remaining glass negatives, many in formats ranging from 11 × 14 inches (28 × 36 cm) to 17 × 22 inches (43 × 56 cm), were transferred to the U.S. Signal Corps in 1928 and finally to the National Archives in the 1930s.

Meanwhile, the 7,000 negatives attached by Anthony and Company were changing hands. The Library of Congress would eventually acquire this collection of 8 × 10 inch (20 × 25 cm) or smaller negatives, embellished with additions along the way, as well as a collection of Civil War photographs from these negatives and other sources. (See "Civil War Views.") After E. and H. T. Anthony and Company had printed and sold images from Brady's negatives for a number of years, they sold the negatives to Col. Arnold A. Rand of Boston and Gen. Albert Ordway of Washington sometime in the 1870s. The two Civil War veterans wished to compile a record of the Civil War. Ordway and Rand also acquired 2,000 Civil War negatives made by Alexander Gardner.

John C. Taylor of Hartford, Connecticut, another Civil War veteran, bought the negatives after Ordway and Rand had printed them for their use. As Taylor and Huntington and the War Photograph and Exhibition Company, Taylor sold stereographic prints and lantern slides during the 1880s (see Lot 11448, described below). Taylor lent the negatives to the

Mathew Brady. Portrait of Edward Miner Gallaudet and his family, ca. 1860s–1870s. Lot 9291.
LC-USZ62-67629

Mathew Brady. Portrait of Ulysses S. Grant, U.S. president, 1869–77. Ca. 1860s–1870s. Lot 5896.
LC-USZ62-5894

Mathew Brady. Portrait of Edwin McMaster Stanton, secretary of war under Lincoln. Ca. 1860s–1870s. Lot 5896.

LC-USZ62-68702

Navy Department for printing, and the Library of Congress obtained a set of prints in 1905 as well.

John Taylor placed the negatives in storage until the publisher Edward B. Eaton of Hartford, Connecticut, bought them in 1907. Eaton's Patriot Publishing Company advertised itself as "Publishers and Specialists in War Photographs. Sole Owners of Famous Brady Collection of 7,000 Original Negatives Taken on the Battlefields During the Civil War." During the next six years, Eaton used Brady's negatives in six different publications, of which the best known is Francis Trevelyan Miller's ten-volume work *The Photographic History of the Civil War* (1911–12), published by the Review of Reviews in New York. The negatives were stored again until 1916, in a basement at the Phelps Publishing Company, where they suffered extensive damage. In 1919, the storage fee was unpaid. In 1926, Eaton's Patriot Publishing Company went out of business. The new owners of the Phelps Publishing Company retained the negatives as a dead asset, the nature of which they were evidently unaware.

At about the time of Eaton's death in 1942, a railroad historian investigating an illustration that had appeared in a Phelps publication was allowed to look around the company's basement in his search of the company's records, and there he found the crates of Brady negatives. The Library of Congress learned of their existence and purchased the negatives at cost (equivalent to the unpaid storage fees) from Phelps Publishing in 1943, after an auction. The prints his father had acquired from these negatives were purchased from Col. Albert Ordway's son in 1948 and are now part of the Anthony-Taylor-Rand-Ordway-Eaton Collection, popularly known as the Civil War Views collection in the Prints and Photographs Division.

Levin C. Handy. Bookstacks and pneumatic tubes in the Library of Congress (Jefferson Building), ca. 1895–97. Lot 4760.

LC-USZ62-90208

REFERENCES

Civil War Photographs, 1861–1865; A Catalog of Copy Negatives Made from Originals Selected from the Mathew B. Brady Collection in the Prints and Photographs Division of the Library of Congress. Compiled by Hirst D. Milhollen and Donald H. Mugridge. Washington: Library of Congress, 1961.

Cobb, Josephine. "Mathew B. Brady's Photographic Gallery in Washington." *Records of the Columbia Historical Society,* vols. 53-56 (1959).

Milhollen, Hirst. "The Mathew B. Brady Collection." In Shaw, *A Century,* pp. 30-36.

Vanderbilt, nos. 77-80, pp. 18-25.

THE BRADY-HANDY COLLECTION

In the 1850s, Mathew Brady married Julia Handy, who would be his loving partner and wife for nearly forty years. Her brother, Samuel S. Handy, worked as Brady's assistant in the Washington gallery during the 1860s. Samuel's son Levin C. Handy (ca. 1856–1932), began his apprenticeship in the gallery with his father and uncle at the age of twelve and became an "operator" by the age of fifteen. The Brady establishment would later be mortgaged to Samuel and Levin Handy. Levin Handy eventually established his own portrait business, in partnership with Samuel Chester (located in 1882 at 494 Maryland Avenue SW and in 1893 at 919 F Street NW) and with Chester and Brady (in operation in 1883 at 1113 Pennsylvania Avenue NW). The Maryland Avenue location was the most permanent and the place where Levin Handy resided at his death in 1932. Brady himself had worked and lived at the Maryland Avenue address for the last two years of his life.

Levin C. Handy. President Wilson delivering his inaugural address, 1917. Lot 4990.

LC-USZ62-50731

Those few thousand photographic negatives, daguerreotypes, furniture, equipment, business papers, and other materials that Brady had not sent to E. and H. T. Anthony and Company in New York or put in storage in Washington, and which had remained in Brady's studio at 627 Pennsylvania Avenue, were inherited by Levin Handy upon Brady's death and were transferred to Handy's Maryland Avenue studio. The Library of Congress acquired these Brady images and work by L. C. Handy, spanning the period from the 1840s to 1932, from Handy's daughters, Mrs. George W. Evans and Mrs. Edgar C. Cox, in September 1954. Brady's work was intermixed with Handy's negatives. Of the 10,000 images acquired by the Library, about 1,300 were the work of Levin Handy and the remaining plates are attributed to Brady's studio. The Brady work includes about 1,300 duplicate negatives and about 4,000 original wet collodion plates. The remaining plates include copy negatives made for customers by Brady and Handy of various photographs, prints, and paintings. Twenty-four daguerreotypes were included, portraits of famous Americans like Edwin Booth, Stephen Douglas, Daniel Webster, Brigham Young, and Mathew Brady himself (see "Daguerreotype Collection"). The Library also acquired a single volume of "M. B. Brady's Register," with entries dated from June 2, 1870, to January 1876 (see Lot 11446). This group of Brady and Handy negatives was sorted by the Library into various series by subject and type of negative, and a description of the contents of each was published (see Hirst D. Milhollen, "The Brady-Handy Collection," in Shaw, *A Century*, pp. 38-50).

The Library of Congress printed many of these Brady-Handy negatives. Washington views were incorporated into the Washington, D.C., Geographical File, and are identifiable by the "LC-BH" prefix that precedes the negative number in the picture caption. Some views of Washington, believed to have been made by Brady at the beginning of the Civil War, are among the earliest pictures of the capital in the Prints and Photographs Division. Some groups of Washington subjects were cataloged and are described below, as are other cataloged materials that came with the Brady-Handy acquisition. The Brady-Handy negatives included a large group of original negatives of members of Congress and other prominent people, dating from about 1855 to 1890. These portrait negatives were printed by the Library and incorporated in the Prints and Photographs Division Biographical File. In addition to well-known buildings and monuments, these photographs picture such events as inaugurations, Labor Day parades, Coxey's Army marching on Washington, and the flood of 1889.

Levin C. Handy. View of F Street NW taken from Seventh Street at the General Post Office, looking toward the Treasury Building, ca. 1885. Brady-Handy Collection, Lot 8894.

LC-USZ62-92206

Levin C. Handy had a special relationship with the Library of Congress, providing the Library's first photoduplication service. His studio made copies of material in the collections when requested by Library staff. He often brought his copy equipment to the Print Division. He did similar photographic work for other government agencies.

More importantly, perhaps, L. C. Handy was hired to document the construction of the Jefferson Building of the Library of Congress. Between 1880 and 1896, he photographed the progress on a regular basis of all the various stages of construction, from the clearing of the original site to the laying of the foundations and from the construction of the various floors to the decorative finishing work by the stone carvers. His collection of glass negatives of the Jefferson Building construction was turned over to the Library (see "Library of Congress Construction Photographs"). He also photographed staff members at work in the newly completed Jefferson Building, and he was allowed to set up a stand on the basement floor of the Library to sell his views to the public.

Cataloged photographs and related material by Mathew Brady, Levin C. Handy, and the two photographers together are described below. Some Brady and Handy photographs and materials have come from other sources, including gifts and copyright deposits, and are not technically part of the Brady or Brady-Handy Collections.

REFERENCES

Cobb, Josephine. "Mathew B. Brady's Photographic Gallery in Washington."*Records of the Columbia Historical Society*, vols. 53–56 (1959).
Melville, no. 34, p. 48.
Milhollen, Hirst. "The Brady-Handy Collection." In Shaw, *A Century*, pp. 38–50.
Vanderbilt, no. 80A, pp. 25–26.

CATALOG OF BRADY CIVIL WAR PHOTOGRAPHS

Original Mathew B. Brady Collection Civil War negatives were printed by the Library and film copy negatives were produced from these prints for use in subsequent printings, to preserve the original glass negatives. A catalog of 1,047 of the best and most interesting views of the Civil War was produced, describing each negative. *Civil War Photographs, 1861–1865; A Catalog of Copy Negatives Made from Originals Selected from the Mathew B. Brady Collection in the Prints and Photographs Division of the Library of Congress*, compiled by Hirst D. Milhollen and Donald H. Mugridge (Wash-

ington: Library of Congress, 1961), is divided into five sections: *Part 1:* "The Main Eastern Theater of War," by campaign or location, with an approximately chronological arrangement; *Part 2:* "The Federal Navy, and Seaborne Expeditions against the Atlantic Coast of the Confederacy," by location; *Part 3:* "The War in the West," by campaign or location, with an approximately chronological arrangement; *Part 4:* "Washington Views, 1862–1865," by subject (for instance, hospitals, defenses of Washington, execution of Captain Henry Wirz); and *Part 5:* "Portraits," arranged by government or military department, both Union and Confederate. The booklet in-

cludes an index of identified photographers, an index of general subjects, and an index of specific subjects and people.

The prints from the original Brady negatives, which were subsequently copied to produce the 8 × 10 inch (20 × 25 cm) copy negatives listed in the catalog, were microfilmed and are available for purchase in that form. Microfilm Lot 12020 includes a complete caption list and provides copy negative numbers and indexes of photographers and subjects. The archival prints from which the microfilm was produced are maintained in the Prints and Photographs Division for staff use only. Research access is limited to use of the microfilm.

LOT 2822 (microfilm)

SUBJECTS: "House of Representatives of the United States. 1864." Portraits of President Lincoln, Vice-President Johnson, cabinet members, senators, the clerk of the House, Speaker Colfax, and members of the House of Representatives, 1864. Supreme Court Justice Nelson, Montgomery Blair (postmaster general), Secretary of War Edwin Stanton, and Generals Grant, Hooker and Meade.

NOTE: The majority are vignette portraits and bear original autographs at the bottom of the card mount. The remaining images are identified in pencil by the collector. Some portraits are missing. In a contemporary album, stamped in gold leaf on the cover.

DATE: 1864

PHOTOGRAPHERS: Mathew Brady studio and C. D. Fredricks (New York).

PHYSICAL DESCRIPTION: 1 album (cartes de visite).

ARRANGEMENT: Arranged in alphabetical order.

SOURCE: Purchase from Mrs. John Nixon, 1949.

LOT 3206

SUBJECTS: Album of three-quarter-length portrait photographs of South American, Central American, and U.S. delegates to the International American Conference. The Wallach Mansion in Washington, where the conference was held, is also pic-

tured. Includes James G. Blaine, Cornelius N. Bliss, Clement Studebaker, T. Jefferson Coolidge, Andrew Carnegie, and William E. Curtis, among the American representatives.

NOTE: Cover of album carries embossed title: "Album of Delegates to the International American Conference. Washington, D.C. 1889–1900. Presented by the Government of the United States. Photographed by M. B. Brady." Inside title page carries additional note: "Designed and Photographed by M. B. Brady." All photographs bear handwritten captions.

DATE: 1889–90

PHOTOGRAPHERS: Mathew B. Brady.

PHYSICAL DESCRIPTION: 1 album (40 albumen "Imperial" cabinet card photographs), 21 × 18 cm.

ARRANGEMENT: Inside cover of album provides table of contents and titles for each person.

SOURCE: Gift of the International Bureau of American Republics, 1899.

LOT 3583

SUBJECTS: Portraits of the members of the Senate of the Forty-first Congress, their wives, and a few prominent Civil War military leaders. Includes Generals Terry, Hancock, Grant, and Sherman; Admirals Dahlgren and Porter; Simon Cameron, Surgeon General Barnes, Postmaster General Creswell, Secretaries Fish and Belknap, and Attorney General Hoar. Wives include Mrs. U. S. Grant and Mrs. Schuyler Colfax.

NOTE: All portraits are autographed and carry the Brady Studio imprint "Brady's National Photographic Portrait Galleries."

DATE: 1869–71

PHOTOGRAPHERS: Mathew Brady Studio.

PHYSICAL DESCRIPTION: 2 albums (ca. 100 albumen cabinet card photographs).

SOURCE: Gift of Mrs. Harold C. Bales, 1945.

LOT 4760

SUBJECTS: Library of Congress Jefferson Building exterior and interior views, just before its official opening. Main gallery, grand staircase, various reading rooms, bookstacks, halls, and statuary.

DATE: 1895–97

PHOTOGRAPHERS: L. C. Handy Studio.

PHYSICAL DESCRIPTION: 33 silver gelatin photoprints on mounts, 19 × 20 cm.

SOURCE: Purchase from Mrs. Pauline Spofford, 1950.

LOT 4771

SUBJECTS: Portraits of Union and Confederate military officers of the Civil War, some unidentified.

DATE: Ca. 1861–ca. 1865

PHOTOGRAPHERS: J. D. Rice, Merritt, Antrim, Alex. Hesler (Chicago), Gutekunst (Philadelphia), Chandler & Scheetz (Philadelphia), Edward Draper (Philadelphia), J. Notman (Boston), Sarony (New York), A. A. Turner [Appleton] (New York), A. Bogardus (New York), Rockwood (New York), and E. Anthony (New York).

PHYSICAL DESCRIPTION: Ca. 300 albumen, platinum, and silver gelatin photoprints, copy photos of paintings and engravings, and photomechanical prints, 28 × 18 cm or smaller, most cabinet cards and cartes de visite, most unmounted.

SOURCE: Part of the Ordway Collection, supplement to Lots 4192, 4193, and 4194. See "Civil War Views."

LOT 4990

SUBJECTS: Presidential inaugurations, ca. 1789–1933. Ceremonies at the Capitol, inaugural balls, parades on Pennsylvania Avenue, a White House reception, the U.S. Senate Chamber in 1859. Portraits of Presidents Lincoln, Grant, T. Roosevelt, Wilson, Hoover, and F. D. Roosevelt.

DATE: Before 1933.

PHOTOGRAPHERS: Mathew Brady and L. C. Handy.

PHYSICAL DESCRIPTION: 42 silver gelatin photoprints of photographs, prints, and photomechanical prints on mounts, 41 × 51 cm.

SOURCE: Transfer from the National Archives, 1944. And other sources.

LOT 5703

SUBJECTS: Reproductions of Civil War photographs by Mathew Brady. Advertising matter for Francis Trevelyan Miller, *Photographic History of the Civil War* and *Portrait Life of Lincoln*, in which the Brady images were used.

DATE: Ca. 1861–ca.1865

PHOTOGRAPHERS: Mathew B. Brady.

PHYSICAL DESCRIPTION: Ca. 30 sheets (ca. 150 pictures) halftone photomechanical prints.

SOURCE: Received with the E. B. Eaton Collection.

LOT 5896

SUBJECTS: Portraits, including Mme Catacazy, wife of the minister plenipotentiary of the emperor of Russia to the United States; William Pitt Fessenden, secretary of the treasury; Hamilton Fish, secretary of state; Edwin McMaster Stanton, secretary of war; Ulysses S. Grant; Winfield Scott Hancock; John Alexander Logan and his family; Ebenezer Rockwood Hoar; "Mrs. Shaffer"; and an unidentified woman.

NOTE: In 1949, George L. Andrews, former district attorney of Tioga County, New York, discovered forty-four plates in his Owego barn, wrapped in Washington, D.C., newspapers of 1866 and 1874. His mother had acquired the glass plate negatives from the widow of Andrew Burgess, a gunsmith who bought out one of Brady's Washington studios. Andrews sold the

plates to the Ansco Division of General Aniline & Film Corporation (GAF), Binghamton, New York, the country's oldest photographic manufacturer. Ansco and its predecessor, Edward Anthony & Co., and E. & H. T. Anthony & Co. had supplied Brady with the bulk of his materials. Prints were made by Ansco from glass plate negatives formerly the property of Mathew B. Brady. See also Lot 9291.

DATE: Ca. 1860s–ca. 1870s

PHOTOGRAPHERS: Mathew B. Brady.

PHYSICAL DESCRIPTION: 11 silver gelatin photoprints, 42 × 33 cm or smaller, mounted for exhibition.

SOURCE: Gift of Gen. U. S. Grant III, 1952.

LOT 7467

SUBJECTS: Newspaper accounts illustrated with photographs by Mathew B. Brady, describing the Anthony-Taylor-Rand-Ordway-Eaton and Brady-Handy Collections.

DATE: 1907–21

PHOTOGRAPHERS: Illustrations after Mathew Brady photographs.

PUBLISHER: Various newspapers.

PHYSICAL DESCRIPTION: 1 album (19 newspaper clippings).

Levin C. Handy. Left section of a three-part panoramic view of Washington, showing downtown area in vicinity of Fifteenth Street NW and Pennsylvania Avenue, ca. 1902. Brady-Handy Collection, Lot 8894.

LC-BH85-33

Levin C. Handy. Center section of a three-part panoramic view of Washington, showing the newly completed Post Office Department Building at Twelfth Street and Pennsylvania Avenue NW, and the building trades warehouses and Mall along B Street NW (now Constitution Avenue), the Pension Building, and the downtown area, ca. 1902. Brady-Handy Collection, Lot 8894.

LC-BH85-34

Levin C. Handy. Right-hand section of a three-part panoramic view of Washington, showing the Capitol (top left corner), the Mall and Smithsonian buildings, and Southwest Washington, ca. 1902. Brady-Handy Collection, Lot 8894.

LC-BH85-32

LOT 8894

COLLECTION NAME: Brady-Handy Collection.

SUBJECTS: Views of Washington, D.C. Includes a three-section panoramic view of Northwest Washington (ca. 1899), showing the Old Post Office, Pennsylvania Avenue, Constitution Avenue, Center Market, the B&O Railway station, the Mall, the old Department of Agriculture building; the U. S. Capitol and southeast Washington, the Pension Building, the Smithsonian Institution buildings, and southwest Washington. Also includes views of the Library of Congress from the Capitol dome (ca. 1897), the Senate Chamber, the Supreme Court under construction, the C&O Canal, Coxey's Army on Pennsylvania Avenue near the Capitol, and the Southern Railroad tracks; nineteenth-century bird's-eye views that include the Smithsonian Institution, Department of Agriculture, and downtown business establishments; street scenes at Ninth and F Streets NW; a view of F Street from the General Post Office and Seventh Street, looking toward the Treasury building (ca. 1885). Includes a photographic copy of a painting by Carl Gunther of Robert E. Lee.

DATE: Ca. 1880s–ca. 1929.

PHOTOGRAPHERS: Levin C. Handy studio.

PHYSICAL DESCRIPTION: 16 modern silver gelatin photoprints from original negatives, 28 × 36 cm or smaller.

LOT 9017

SUBJECTS: A wooden glass plate negative box, used to store or transport negatives.

DATE: Ca. 1850s–1870s.

PHYSICAL DESCRIPTIONS: 1 wooden box with cover and iron handle, 26 × 32 × 18 cm.

LOT 9291

SUBJECTS: Studio portraits of men, women, and children, many unidentified. Includes Edward Miner Gallaudet and his family; and Mme Catacazy.

NOTE: Accompanied by a 1949 news story telling how the negatives of these pictures were found in a barn in Owego, New York. Prints made by Ansco from original glass plate negatives. See also Lot 5896.

DATE: Ca. 1860s–ca. 1870s

PHOTOGRAPHERS: Mathew B. Brady.

PHYSICAL DESCRIPTION: 13 silver gelatin photoprints, 20 × 25 cm.

SOURCE: Gift of Ansco, 1961.

Lot 9737

COLLECTION NAME: Brady-Handy Collection

SUBJECTS: Snapshot photographs of historic buildings, monuments and markers, natural wonders, and tourist activities, many in or near Washington, D.C. Includes views of the Pan American Union under construction; the Old Stone House in Georgetown; views of Pennsylvania Avenue from the Capitol and from the Treasury Building; the C&O Canal; the Pension Office; Mount Vernon; Decatur House; the Key Mansion; Arlington Cemetery and the Custis Lee Mansion; the Octagon House; interior and exterior views of the Capitol and Capitol dome; copies of paintings in the Capitol; the St. Gaudens' *Grief* statue (the Clover Adams tomb) in Rock Creek Cemetery; the Corcoran home; view of Fifteenth Street and Pennsylvania Avenue; Bulfinch's Unitarian Church; Ford's Theater, Webster House (Sixth and D Streets), and Surratt House; the Van Ness Mansion; the S. Chase Home; a home at Twentieth Street and Massachusetts Avenue; the Bartholdi fountain; the Old Soldiers' Home; the Smithsonian Institution, including museum interiors; the Mall; Union Station; the Potomac River; and views of the Theodore Roosevelt inaugural parade stands. Includes one view of the McKinley funeral procession passing down Pennsylvania Avenue, in front of the C. M. Bell portrait studio. Also includes rural and city scenes, revolutionary and Civil War sites, historic buildings, monuments, gravestones, residences, and other scenes in Massachusetts, Florida, Virginia, Pennsylvania, Maryland, South Carolina, and Missouri.

NOTE: Album bears embossed title: "Aids to Memory." It was compiled by George W. Hall. Some photos lack captions.

DATE: Ca. 1890s–1900s.

PHOTOGRAPHERS: George W. Hall.

PHYSICAL DESCRIPTION: 1 album (593 silver gelatin photoprints, 11 × 13 cm or smaller).

SOURCE: Transfer, with materials from the Brady-Handy Collection.

LOT 9788

SUBJECTS: Interior views of the Library of Congress. Main Reading Room and dome, Great Hall, stack areas. Employees at work cataloging books, filing cards in the Card Division, and setting type in the Print Shop. Map room; Documents Division. Exhibit in the Library, featuring portraits of George Washington. Pictures of the old Library of Congress in the Capitol. Includes one view of the Smithsonian stacks.

NOTE: Prints made for an exhibition. Some photographs are heavily retouched.

DATE: Ca. 1884–1926

PHOTOGRAPHERS: Levin C. Handy.

PHYSICAL DESCRIPTION: 17 silver gelatin photoprints, 61 × 49 cm, mounted for an exhibition.

SOURCE: Transfer.

LOT 10285

COLLECTION NAME: Charles W. Reed Papers, Manuscript Division

SUBJECTS: Sample pages and illustrations from F. T. Miller, *Photographic History of the Civil War* (New York, 1911), which was illustrated with Mathew Brady photographs. Includes materials prepared to advertise Miller's work.

DATE: 1911

PHOTOGRAPHERS: Illustrations after photographs by Mathew B. Brady.

PUBLISHER: Review of Reviews Co.

PHYSICAL DESCRIPTION: 1 folder (22 halftone photomechanical prints and printed copy).

SOURCE: Transfer from the Manuscript Division, 1965.

LOT 11446

COLLECTION NAME: Brady-Handy Collection

SUBJECTS: Studio register of customers at Brady's Washington, D.C., establishment. Register gives sitters' names, dates, negative numbers, the styles and numbers of pictures ordered, the prices and dates of payment, notes on the complexion and hair and eye color of sitters, for use by studio colorists and retouchers, and indications of "complimentary" work. Register contains comments such as "Did not sit. Too late"; "[portrait] not approved"; "Would not pay."

NOTE: Incomplete record. The Library owns only this single volume and may not have corresponding Brady negatives for every photograph recorded therein.

DATE: June 1870–December 1875

PHOTOGRAPHERS: Mathew Brady studio.

PHYSICAL DESCRIPTION: 1 album.

ARRANGEMENT: Entries are chronological.

SOURCE: Transfer with the Brady-Handy Collection.

LOT 11448

SUBJECTS: Civil War scenes, from Brady negatives, most of which are represented in the Civil War Views collection in the Prints and Photographs Division. Includes views of Professor Lowe's military reconnaissance balloon; the Marshall House and a slave pen in Alexandria, Virginia; Battery Rodgers; a group of black soldiers at Fort Sedgwick. One slide shows Sam A. Cooley ("U.S. Photographer, Department of the South") with his camera and equipment wagon. Also includes a copy of a drawing by E. B. Thompson, Washington, of "President Lincoln at Fort Stevens, July 12, 1864."

DATE: Ca. 1861–ca. 1865

PHOTOGRAPHERS: Mathew B. Brady.

PUBLISHER: Original War Views (company) and Taylor & Huntington (Hartford, Connecticut).

PHYSICAL DESCRIPTION: 37 glass lantern slides (stereograph-half format).

LOT 12020 (microfilm)

SUBJECTS: Selection of Civil War images from original negatives made by Mathew Brady and others.

NOTE: Microfilm made from archival prints (produced by the Library from original glass negatives). The original archival prints are for staff use only. Microfilm serves as a reference copy.

DATE: Ca. 1861–ca. 1865

President McKinley's funeral parade on Pennsylvania Avenue, passing in front of the C.M. Bell photography studio. From "Aids to Memory," an album compiled by George W. Hall. 1901. Brady-Handy Collection, Lot 9737.

LC-USZ6-1303

PHOTOGRAPHERS: Mathew B. Brady and others.

PUBLISHER: *Civil War Photographs, 1861–1865: A Catalog of Copy Negatives Made from Originals Selected from the Mathew B. Brady Collection in the Prints and Photographs Division of the Library of Congress*, compiled by Hirst D. Milhollen and Donald H. Mugridge (Washington: Library of Congress, 1961).

PHYSICAL DESCRIPTION: 2 reels of microfilm (1,047 modern photoprints).

ARRANGEMENT: Includes copy negative numbers and indexes of photographers and subjects.

SOURCE: Microfilmed by the Library of Congress, 1961.

LOT 12562

SUBJECTS: Library of Congress Jefferson Building. Portrait of "Jury of Seven that Condemned the Library site June 30, 1886." Views of the Library of Congress in the U.S. Capitol. Detailed views of the book conveyor apparatus in the Library of Congress; hot water heaters, furnaces, and steam heating system and pipes in basement of Library; bookstacks; exhibit hall; Main Reading Room and dome; Newspaper and Current Periodicals Reading Room; Bindery; Map Division; Print Shop; unidentified offices and reading rooms; view of inside courtyard; high view of Jefferson Building.

DATE: Ca. 1880s–ca.1900s

PHOTOGRAPHERS: Levin C. Handy.

PHYSICAL DESCRIPTION: 31 silver gelatin photoprints, 19 × 24 cm or smaller.

LOT 12577

SUBJECTS: Construction of the Jefferson Building, Library of Congress. Architectural details and decorative elements. Includes statues, newly uncrated; architectural models of the Main Reading Room and dome; reading room furniture; plaster models of ethnographic heads; scaffolding in place for mural work; interiors under construction and rooms near completion; stone carvers at work; view of north side of building; view of East Capitol Street from the Library of Congress dome; construction workers on the grounds; horse-drawn construction wagons; street-paving crews.

NOTE: Corresponding negatives in series LC-USL5 and –USL51. Related material in microfilm Lot 12365.

DATE: Ca. 1880–96

PHOTOGRAPHERS: Levin C. Handy.

PHYSICAL DESCRIPTION: 13 albumen photoprints, mounted, 25 × 30 cm or smaller.

LOT 12578

SUBJECTS: Library of Congress. Carved plaster decorative elements for the Jefferson Building.

NOTE: Corresponding negatives in series LC-USL5. Related material in Microfilm Lot 12365.

DATE: Ca. 1880–96

PHOTOGRAPHERS: Levin C. Handy.

PHYSICAL DESCRIPTION: 2 silver gelatin photoprints, 36 × 44 cm or smaller.

Wilhelmus Bogart Bryan (1854–1938) was a historian and the author of *A History of the National Capital*, 2 vols. (New York: Macmillan Co., 1914–16). The Manuscript Division holds his notes (numbering 3,500 items) relating to the history of the District of Columbia, 1789–1888, including extracts from newspapers in the District, Maryland, and Virginia.

St. Vincent's Orphan Asylum at the southwest corner of Tenth and G Streets NW, Autumn 1901. Wilhelmus Bryan Collection, Lot 7077.

LC-USZ62-92417

LOT 7077

COLLECTION NAME: Wilhelmus Bogart Bryan Collection

SUBJECTS: Washington, D.C. Includes extensive coverage of downtown Washington, (NW and NE) streets and commercial buildings in the nineteenth and early twentieth centuries. The U. S. Capitol under construction, flood of 1889, historic homes, views of Pennsylvania Avenue, business establishments, railroad stations, Rock Creek Park. Includes views of the drinking fountain on the Capitol grounds and general views of the grounds; aerial views of East Potomac Park (1918) and panoramic view north from the Washington Monument; Long Bridge; War Department Building (ca. 1873); B&O Railroad station, Pennsylvania Railroad station, Union Station; St. Patrick's, St. Matthew's, Old Foundry, and First Congregational churches; ruins of the tower of the Church of the Covenant (1888); YMCA (burned in 1885); St. Vincent's Orphan Asylum (1901, at southwest corner of Tenth and G Streets NW); Riggs Bank (ca. 1890s, at Ninth and F Streets NW), and Palais Royale; Richmond Hotel, Willard's Hotel and Hall (1899), St. James Hotel, and Brock's Congressional Hotels; ruins of Lincoln Hall building fire and fire at Cable Power house; Old Medical College (Tenth and E Streets NW) and Columbian Law School building (416 Fifth Street NW); present site of Martin Luther King Memorial Library, as seen in 1913; old slave "prison" between Four-and-a-half and Sixth Streets NW, rear of lot on north side of G Street (removed in 1899); Lincoln Park and Emancipation statue (1918); Alexander Shepherd home, Corcoran house, Tudor Place, Carroll house (1886), David Burnes cottage (1886, site of Pan American Union Building), "Stewart's Folly" (1901, at Massachusetts and Connecticut Avenues NW); Old Metropolitan Club (later burned); flooded Pennsylvania Avenue at Ninth Street NW; Fourth of July parade (1903, at Pennsylvania Avenue and Eleventh Street NW).

DATE: Ca. 1860–ca. 1918

PHOTOGRAPHERS: National Photo Company and A. G. Gedney.

PHYSICAL DESCRIPTION: Ca. 250 albumen and silver gelatin photoprints and photomechanical prints, 20 × 25 cm or smaller, mounted on paper.

SOURCE: Gift of Wilhelmus Bogart Bryan, 1934.

Willard Hotel and Hall, southwest corner of Fourteenth and F Streets NW, December 1899. Wilhelmus Bryan Collection, Lot 7077.

LC-USZ62-20727

View from the Capitol roof, House side, of Southeast Washington and Independence Avenue SE, showing Providence Hospital in the upper left of image. January 1904. Wilhelmus Bryan Collection, Lot 7077.

LC-USZ62-44921

Temporary holding prison for slaves being transported to Richmond and elsewhere in Virginia. The building, demolished March 8, 1899, was located at the rear of a lot on the north side of G Street between Four-and-a-half and Sixth Streets NW. Ca. 1890s. Wilhelmus Bryan Collection, Lot 7077.

LC-USZ62-13786

Ninth and G Streets NW, northwest corner (present site of the Martin Luther King Memorial Library), showing Patent Office fence. Ca. 1913. Wilhelmus Bryan Collection, Lot 7077.

LC-USZ62-10280

Library of Congress site (Carroll Row), seen from Capitol Plaza, 1886. Wilhelmus Bryan Collection, Lot 7077.

LC-USZ62-9540

Flooded Pennsylvania Avenue at Ninth Street NW, 1889. Wilhelmus Bryan Collection, Lot 7077.

LC-USZ62-29608

Nannie Helen Burroughs (1883–1961) was a black educator and religious leader. In 1909, she founded the National Training School for Women and Girls (later the National Trade and Professional School for Women and Girls) in Lincoln Heights, Washington, D.C., to provide practical skills for black women. Her papers, numbering 110,000 items and spanning the years 1900–1963 (chiefly 1928–60), are held in the Manuscript Division. They are described by a finding aid. The papers consist of correspondence, financial records, memoranda, notebooks, speeches and writings, subscription and literature orders, student records, and printed matter and pertain to the National Training School and to Nannie Helen Burroughs's activities with the Woman's Convention Auxiliary to the National Baptist Convention and their publication, the *Worker*. The papers also include material relating to the National League of Republican Colored Women, the National Association of Wage Earners, the 1931 President's Conference on Home Building and Home Ownership, missionary activities in Africa, Cooperative Industries (a community self-help program in northeast Washington), and the Frederick Douglass Memorial and Historical Association. Correspondents include Mary McLeod Bethune, Margery Gaillard, Henrietta Gibbs, Una Roberts Lawrence, Adam Clayton Powell, Jr., and Powell, Sr., Anson Phelps Stokes, and many others. The papers were acquired through the gift of Aurelia H. Downey and the Nannie H. Burroughs School, 1976–77. The photographs were transferred to the Prints and Photographs Division.

The Rotograph Company, New York. Nannie Helen Burroughs, 1909. Papers of Nannie Helen Burroughs, Lot 12572.
LC-USZ62-79903

LOT 12569

COLLECTION NAME: Nannie Helen Burroughs Papers, Manuscript Division

SUBJECTS: Snapshot photographs of schoolmates at the National Trade and Professional School, some with their home cities and states identified; parents, school pets, teachers and administrators, some Liberian students, campus buildings and scenes; outings to the Washington Zoo; the Easter Monday egg roll at the school. Includes one photo of Althea Gibson as a young girl on the Sparrow's Point black swimming beach in Washington, D.C., on a Tabernacle School outing. Also includes photographs at the National Baptist Convention in Philadelphia (September 1939) and a group photo of the National Trade and Professional School Summer Institute (July 1959).

NOTE: Photograph album compiled by Alice Smith, a student at the National Trade and Professional School in Lincoln Heights, Washington, D.C. Most photographs are captioned.

DATE: Ca. 1930s–1959

PHOTOGRAPHERS: Alice Smith and others.

PHYSICAL DESCRIPTION: 1 album (80 silver gelatin photoprints, 20 × 25 cm or smaller).

SOURCE: Transfer from the Manuscript Division, 1980.

RESTRICTIONS: Album extremely brittle; must be handled with care.

Washington Photo Company. School buildings at Lincoln Heights, National Training School for Women and Girls, Washington, D.C., ca. 1910–30. Papers of Nannie Helen Burroughs, Lot 12571.
LC-USZ62-92834

Cooking class, National Training School for Women and Girls, Washington, D.C., ca. 1910. Papers of Nannie Helen Burroughs, Lot 12571.
LC-USZ62-92835

Cosby's Studio. Clerical training class, National Training School for Women and Girls, ca. 1910–20s. Papers of Nannie Helen Burroughs, Lot 12571.
LC-USZ62-92859

Cosby's Studio. Clerical training class, National Training School for Women and Girls, ca. 1910–20s. Papers of Nannie Helen Burroughs, Lot 12571.
LC-USZ62-92859

LOT 12571

COLLECTION NAME: Nannie Helen Burroughs Papers, Manuscript Division

SUBJECTS: Photographs of the National Training School for Women and Girls in Lincoln Heights, Washington, D.C. School buildings; group portraits of students and faculty with Nannie Helen Burroughs in front of school buildings; group portraits of faculty with Burroughs; group portraits of the Missionary Training Department; group portrait of younger and older students with faculty; first commencement exercises, June 9, 1911, held outdoors on the school grounds; the girls' basketball team; classrooms; the school office; classes in crafts, sewing, typing and dictation, cooking, Bible studies; gardening; students milking cows; elementary school children being taught; other student activities; building interiors, including dining room, printing shop, parlor, student bedroom. Group portrait of Nannie Helen Burroughs with students and staff at the commercial laundry on the school grounds; interior views of laundry, with students at work. Includes three unidentified photographs of shacks.

DATE; Ca. 1905–ca. 1940s

PHOTOGRAPHERS: Addison N. Scurlock, Scurlock Studio, Cosby's Studio, D. Freeman, Washington Photo Company, and National Photo Company.

PHYSICAL DESCRIPTION: Ca. 150 silver gelatin photoprints, 20 × 25 cm or smaller, some mounted and captioned for an exhibit.

SOURCE: Transfer from the Manuscript Division, 1980.

Scurlock Studio. Student group portrait, National Training School for Women and Girls, ca. 1910–20. Papers of Nannie Helen Burroughs, Lot 12571.
LC-USZ62-92858

LOT 12572

COLLECTION NAME: Nannie Helen Burroughs Papers, Manuscript Division.

SUBJECTS: Portraits and snapshots of Nannie Helen Burroughs, her relatives, students, colleagues, and associates. Includes some photographs of activities at the National Training School for Women and Girls in Lincoln Heights, Washington, D.C.

PHOTOGRAPHERS: Scurlock, D. Freeman, Kets Kemethy, and studios in Louisville, Kentucky.

PHYSICAL DESCRIPTION: Ca. 250 silver gelatin and albumen photoprints and halftone photomechanical prints, 21 × 25 cm or smaller.

SOURCE: Transfer from the Manuscript Division, 1980.

LOT 12574

COLLECTION NAME: Nannie Helen Burroughs Papers, Manuscript Division

SUBJECTS: Large photographs and portraits relating to Nannie Helen Burroughs and the National Training School for Women and Girls in Lincoln Heights, Washington, D.C. Includes banquet camera images of campus buildings and student body groups, portraits of Burroughs's colleagues, students, friends, relatives, and acquaintances. Also includes one halftone photomechanical print of the headquarters of the National Association of Wage Earners at 1115 Rhode Island Avenue, Washington, D.C.

DATE: Ca. 1907–ca. 1930

PHOTOGRAPHERS: Cosby's Studio.

PHYSICAL DESCRIPTION: Ca. 25 silver gelatin and albumen photoprints and halftone and other photomechanical prints, some in color, 49 × 64 cm or smaller.

SOURCE: Transfer from the Manuscript Division, 1980.

Scurlock Studio. Group portrait of faculty members at the National Training School for Women and Girls. Nannie Helen Burroughs, president, is seated at the far right. Ca. 1910–15. Papers of Nannie Helen Burroughs, Lot 12571.
LC-USZ62-92857

Frank Carpenter (1855–1924) was a journalist and traveler, remembered today for his geography textbooks, including Carpenter's Geographic Readers, which were used in schools for decades. The books were illustrated with pictures that showed agriculture, industry, religious practices, transportation, housing, national customs, and schools. He and his daughter Frances Carpenter (Mrs. W. Chapin Huntington) traveled together and took many of the pictures in his collections; others were purchased from commercial sources.

Their collection of travel photographs of the early twentieth century was presented to the Library in 1951 by Frances Carpenter Huntington, who continued to donate materials until her death in 1972. The Carpenter Collection includes approximately 20,000 loose and mounted photographs, albums of pictures, and negatives. The photographs cover a range of subjects on nearly every continent, including Europe, the Near and Far East, Africa, and North and South America. Washington, D.C., photographs have been cataloged and are described below.

The Manuscript Division holds related material, including some letters, and papers related to the book *Carp's Washington* (1960), which Frances Carpenter edited.

Policewoman and a child, Washington, D.C., ca. 1927. Frank and Frances Carpenter Collection, Lot 12560.

LC-USZ62-91903

REFERENCES

Kaplan, Milton. "Africa through the Eye of a Camera: The Carpenter Collection." In Shaw, *A Century*, pp. 96–108.
Melville, no. 40, p. 55.
Vanderbilt, no. 114, pp. 31–32.
Vanderbilt, Paul. "Carpenter's World Travels." *LCIB* 10 (April 23, 1951).
Viewpoints, no. 43–45.

LOT 12560

COLLECTION NAME: Frank G. Carpenter Collection

SUBJECTS: Views of Washington, D.C., and vicinity. Buildings, including interior of the U.S. Capitol and House of Representatives in session; interiors and architectural details of the Library of Congress and White House; activities of U.S. Weather Bureau and Treasury Department employees. Bridges, monuments, churches, streetcars, and scenes such as policewomen at work, children's activities. Aerial views and photos of documents relating to Carpenter's trips. One photo of the aftermath of a fire in the Willard Hotel ballroom.

DATE: 1897–1947

PHOTOGRAPHERS: Harris & Ewing, L. C. Handy, Ernest L. Crandall, Underwood & Underwood, Detroit Publishing Co., and International.

PHYSICAL DESCRIPTION: 113 silver gelatin photoprints and photomechanical prints, 21 × 29 cm or smaller, most mounted on cardboard, sometimes several to a mount.

SOURCE: Gift of Frances Carpenter, 1951.

C&O Canal near the Cabin John Bridge, ca. 1927. Frank and Frances Carpenter Collection, Lot 12560.

LC-USZ62-91904

Central High School, Washington, D.C., ca. 1926. Frank and Frances Carpenter Collection, Lot 12560.

LC-USZ62-91905

The Prints and Photographs Division maintains a collection of views of the Civil War, cataloged by subject, formally called the "Anthony-Taylor-Rand-Ordway-Eaton Collection." This collection comprises Civil War photographs obtained from various sources, including some from the Brady-Handy Collection and some printed from the Library of Congress collection of Mathew Brady negatives. (See "Mathew B. Brady and Brady-Handy Collections" and "Alexander Gardner, Photographer.")

To understand the history and contents of the Library's Civil War Views, it is necessary to know something of Mathew Brady's financial problems after the war and the break-up of his collection of negatives. The provenance of the Civil War Views begins with an arrangement whereby the photographic supply firm of E. and H. T. Anthony and Company, which had supplied Brady's team of photographers in the field, gained a judgment and an attachment on negatives of the Civil War from the Brady studios, which were stored in New York, to satisfy Brady's outstanding debts to the company. Anthony and Company printed and published them for several years, and then put them into storage.

Two collectors, Col. Arnold A. Rand of Boston and Gen. Albert Ordway of Washington, both Civil War veterans, purchased Anthony and Company's collection of Brady negatives sometime in the 1870s. They were interested in the Civil War subjects, rather than the general portraits and views that Brady had made in his studios. They added to this Brady material about 2,000 negatives made by Alexander Gardner after he had left Brady's staff early in the Civil War. General Ordway had albumen prints made from the negatives and added prints obtained from other sources. These photographs were mounted by Ordway, who provided captions and numbering that corresponds to some extent to that found on the negatives.

Eventually, Ordway and Rand sold the negatives, having obtained prints from the subjects that interested them. They first tried to sell them to the government but were unsuccessful. Eventually John C. Taylor (formerly commander of Post No. 50, Grand Army of the Republic) bought them, with the hope of exploiting their commercial value. As Taylor and Huntington (2 State Street, Hartford, Connecticut) and as The War Photograph and Exhibition Company (21 Linden Street), he sold stereographic prints and lantern slides during the 1880s. In 1890, Taylor published a catalog and agents' booklet.

The U.S. Navy borrowed the entire collection of negatives to supplement the government's collection of photographs of the Civil War. While the negatives were in storage at 920 E Street NW in Washington, the Library of Congress in 1905 ordered a full set of prints for its use also, and these prints would eventually be added to the Civil War Views.

Mathew Brady. Pontoon Bridge in Georgetown across the Potomac River to Analostan (now Theodore Roosevelt) Island, June 1865. Civil War Views, Lot 4161-F.

LC-B8184-7866

Mathew Brady. View of Georgetown from the Virginia side of the Potomac River, ca. 1863. Civil War Views, Lot 4161-G.

LC-B8171-7894

Mathew Brady. Bridge across the Eastern Branch of the Potomac River (now the Anacostia River), April 1865. Civil War Views, Lot 4161-F.

LC-B8184-40466-ZA

Mathew Brady. Battery Rodgers, on the banks of the Potomac River near Alexandria, ca. 1863. Civil War Views, Lot 4166-H.

LC-B8184-143

The negatives were returned to Taylor, were placed in storage again, and were acquired in 1907 by Edward B. Eaton of Hartford, Connecticut, who was at the time president of the *Connecticut Magazine.* He hoped to publish the views in book form. He advertised the existence of his collection of "7,000 actual photographic negatives of Civil War Scenes" and set about to publish them. Between the time Eaton acquired the negatives and 1913, he oversaw six different publications from the set, the best-known being *The Photographic History of the Civil War,* ten volumes, edited by Francis Trevelyan Miller and others (New York, Review of Reviews Co., 1911–12; reprinted in five volumes by T. Yoseloff, New York, 1957). In 1916, the negative collection went into storage again, this time in a basement vault where it incurred considerable damage.

In 1943, the Library of Congress purchased this collection of Mathew Brady negatives for the cost of the unpaid storage in the basement vault. (A separate collection was acquired by the War Department in 1874 and is now in the custody of the National Archives.) The Library received 7,500 original wet collodion glass plates and some 2,500 copy negatives on both glass and film, which yielded about 3,750 different views and about 2,650 different portraits. This negative collection is known as the Mathew B. Brady Collection and is described separately herein.

Mathew Brady. One hundred pound Parrott gun at Fort Totten, August 1865. Civil War Views, Lot 4166-H.

LC-B8184-7249

In 1948, General Ordway's son, Col. Godwin Ordway of Washington, D.C., presented the Ordway-Rand Collection to the Library of Congress, in return for payment of certain expenses, and it became the core of the Civil War Views collection. To this collection, the Library added the 1905 prints made from the 7,000 Brady negatives that had passed from Anthony to Taylor.

To complicate the provenance further, in 1905 the Library purchased from the L. C. Handy Studio (Levin C. Handy being Mathew Brady's nephew and his assistant and business partner) an apparently complete set of proofs from the Anthony-Taylor-Eaton negatives, which were mounted and numbered and which the Library also interfiled with the Ordway-Rand prints.

In 1954, the Library acquired from the heirs of L. C. Handy the Brady-Handy Collection, consisting of about 3,000 original glass plate negatives. Some prints produced by the Library from this collection have also been added to fill in subject gaps in the Civil War Views collection.

Mathew Brady. Fort Stevens, Company F, Third Massachusetts Artillery, ca. 1863. Civil War Views, Lot 4166-H.

LC-8184-7917

The publication *Civil War Photographs, 1861–1865: A Catalog of Copy Negatives Made from Originals Selected from the Mathew B. Brady Collection in the Prints and Photographs Division of the Library of Congress,* compiled by Hirst D. Milhollen and Donald H. Mugridge (Washington: Library of Congress, 1961), describes a microfilm copy of 1,047 Brady images of the Civil War. (See ''Mathew B. Brady and Brady-Handy Collections.'')

Finally, Civil War stereographs acquired from various sources were cataloged by subjects corresponding to those defined for the Civil War Views. The catalog record for each lot of Civil War Views indicates the existence of a related group of stereographs stored under the same lot number with the Stereograph Collection in the Prints and Photographs Reading Room.

Many people equate Civil War photography with Mathew Brady, and may refer to the ''Mathew Brady negatives'' for the sake of brevity and convenience. However, by the time Brady began his speculative venture to produce views of Civil War forts, battlefields, casualties, officers, soldiers, weapons, and other subjects—with the confident expectation that the sale of these views would make him a rich man—his eyesight was failing badly. Although he may well have produced many of the studio portraits done during that period, only a tiny percentage of the output of Brady's operation in the field was actually photographed by Brady. Rather, those twenty or more cameramen employed by Brady, whose names are now lost from specific views in most cases, were responsible for creating this unparalleled record of the Civil War. The best and largest portion of the work in the Library's collections was done by Alexander Gardner, who left Brady's operation to join Gen. George B. McClellan as photographer to the Army of the Potomac and as the official photographer of the Army Secret Service. (See ''Alexander Gardner Photographs''.) Timothy O'Sullivan, John F. Gibson, and Thomas C. Roche produced another large portion of the views, as did George Barnard, working independently. (Barnard was attached to the office of the chief engineer of the Military Division of the Mississippi.) Other photographers on Brady's team included D. B. Woodbury, S. R. Siebert, W. Morris Smith, C. Chester, J. F. Coonley, Fowx, David Knox, William R. Pywell, and J. Reekie. Brady also acquired photographs and negatives from other photographers of the Civil War. Thus, when reference is made to Mathew Brady's Civil War views, it is important to remember that although he himself produced a portion of the studio portraits—primarily those made in New York City—he left the more challenging and dangerous work in camp and field to his hired operators, who rarely saw their names imprinted on views distributed by Brady or subsequent owners of the Brady negatives.

The Civil War Views, which comprise the combined holdings of Anthony-Taylor-Rand-Ordway-Eaton, some Brady-Handy prints, and a few xerographic and thermographic copies of Civil War subjects found elsewhere in the Library's collections, are available as a cataloged browsing file in the Prints and Photographs Reading Room. The lots are grouped by subject and geographical location and are indexed in the Prints and Photographs Division Catalog by subject.

The coverage of the Civil War is encyclopedic, including streets, ruins, buildings, and bridges in major Civil War cities like Washington, Richmond, and Charleston, as well as views and sites in other cities associated with battlefields. Fortifications, war casualties, military camps and field headquarters, supply services, engineering operations, pontoon bridges, railroad operations and equipment, hospitals and medical personnel, repair shops, U.S. Sanitary Commission activities, prisons, and naval vessels were photographed. The collection includes many group and individual portraits of companies, officers, civilians, news reporters, and the conspirators in the assassination of President Lincoln, as well as coverage of the Grand Review of the Grand Army of the Republic. There are views by Confederate photographers, portraits of Confederate officers, and photographic copies of drawings by John R. Key and other Confederate officers. In addition, the Civil War Views collection contains some reproductions that appeared in F. T. Miller's ten-volume *Photographic History of the Civil War.* Washington subjects are found throughout these cataloged materials. As the war dragged on, Washington became the center of activities related to the administration of the war effort, as well as a large depot for materials, weapons, and transportation, and a hospital center that served armies along the eastern part of the United States. Most of the Washington views were taken in the latter half of the war. In addition, the capital was encircled by a chain of forts and gun emplacements that were photographed. Alexandria is also well covered, having been under federal occupation from May 24, 1861.

Cataloged lots pertaining in any way to Washington-area subjects are described below. The specific photographers whose work may be represented in a particular group of photographs cannot be thoroughly identified or credited today, however.

Mathew Brady. Camp of the Thirty-first Pennsylvania Infantry at Queen's Farm near Washington, D.C., ca. 1861–62. Civil War Views, Lot 4172.
LC-B811-2405

Mathew Brady. Quartermaster's Wharf, Alexandria, Virginia, ca. 1863. Civil War Views, Lot 4179.
LC-B8184-440

REFERENCES

Civil War Photographs, 1861–1865: A Catalog of Copy Negatives Made from Originals Selected from the Mathew B. Brady Collection in the Prints and Photographs Division of the Library of Congress. Compiled by Hirst D. Milhollen and Donald H. Mugridge. Washington: Library of Congress, 1961.

Cobb, Josephine. "Mathew B. Brady's Photographic Gallery in Washington." *Records of the Columbia Historical Society,* vols. 53–56 (1959).

Kaplan, Milton. "The Case of the Disappearing Photographers." In Shaw, *A Century,* pp. 51–57.

Melville, no. 48, p. 67.

Milhollen, Hirst D. "The Mathew B. Brady Collection." In Shaw, *A Century,* pp. 30–37.

Miller, Francis Trevelyan et al., editors. *The Photographic History of the Civil War.* 10 vols. New York: Review of Reviews Co., 1911–12.

Vanderbilt, no. 557, pp. 120–121; nos 79–80, pp. 19–25; and no. 317, pp. 71–72.

Mathew Brady. Armory Square Hospital, Washington, D.C., ca. 1863. Civil War Views, Lot 4180.
LC-B8184-5215

LOT 4161 (includes stereographs)

COLLECTION NAME: Civil War Views

SUBJECTS: City views of Washington, D.C., and vicinity. Potomac River bridges, hospital installations, residences of the military, cemeteries. *Lot 4161–A:* Washington—general views. Troops at Camp Fry (Washington, D.C.), Washington Arsenal, Seventh Street market, Pennsylvania Avenue, ox team with cannon on Pennsylvania Avenue, the Capitol Mall, Smithsonian building, Soldier's Cemetery in Alexandria, oxen grazing on the Mall, Long Bridge, Cabin John Bridge, Old Capitol Prison, house near Fort Stevens showing effects of shot during General Jubal Early's attack, the "great fire," a view from Georgetown Heights, the C&O Canal and Aqueduct Bridge. *Lot 4161–B:* Washington Arsenal. Pack of Wiard guns at Washington Arsenal (now Fort McNair), view of arsenal from shore, arsenal yard. *Lot 4161–C:* Washington—Christian Commission and Sanitary Commission. Storehouse of U.S. Christian Commission in Washington, Sanitary Commission office with sign "Lodge for Invalid Soldiers," Sanitary Commission storehouse at F and Fifteenth Streets, central office of the Sanitary Commission on F Street. *Lot 4161–D:* Washington—miscellaneous warehouses and headquarters. Headquarters of Gen. M. D. Hardin; quartermaster's warehouses; brigade headquarters at Fort Lincoln; government bakery, plumber's shop, stables, mess houses, and Medical Department; headquarters of the Signal Corps; Quartermaster's Office on the Seventh Street SW wharf. *Lot 4161–E:* Washington—miscellaneous buildings and houses. Provost Marshall's office, Old State Department Building at Fifteenth Street and Pennsylvania Avenue, soldier's cemetery at Fort Stevens, Gen. Alfred Pleasonton's quarters, Old Capitol Prison, U.S. Capitol, Old Navy Department Building, Pateller's House, Office of Commissary General of Prisoners, Gen. W. F. Bartlett's headquarters, U.S. Naval Observatory, U.S. Clothing Department building, Seventy-first New York State Militia at the Washington Navy Yard. *Lot 4161–F:* Bridges and river views.

Blockhouse for defense of Aqueduct Bridge, views of Aqueduct Bridge from Georgetown, Aqueduct Bridge and C&O Canal, Georgetown Ferry, Pimmit Run Bridge, Chain Bridge, Pontoon Bridge to Analostan Island. *Lot 4161–G:* Views of Georgetown. Foxhall Foundry and Georgetown University, Aqueduct Bridge, and sailing ships at Georgetown wharves, all viewed from the Virginia side of the Potomac River. *Lot 4161–H:* Virginia. Freedman's Barracks, Alexandria; Great Falls on Potomac River; slave pen in Alexandria at 1300 Duke Street, with sign reading, "Price, Birch & Co., Dealers in Slaves"; Mansion House in Alexandria, on the east side of Fairfax Street between King Street and Cameron Street; Quartermaster's wharf, Alexandria; men building stockades in Alexandria; Hunting Creek Bridge near Alexandria; camp of Forty-fourth New York Infantry near Alexandria; Marshall House in Alexandria and portrait of Col. E. E. Ellsworth of the New York Fire Zouaves, killed there on May 21, 1861, the first conspicuous casualty of the war; Falls Church, Virginia; military cemetery in Alexandria; Pohick Church in Lorton; Fort Ellsworth, Alexandria; Christ Church, Alexandria; Fairfax Seminary (Virginia Theological Seminary), Fairfax Church, and Fairfax Courthouse; Stone Church in Centreville; Taylor's Tavern near Falls Church; Sanitary Commission Headquarters and Lodge; Arlington House; general view of Alexandria. *Lot 4161–Stereographs:* two images by E. & H. T. Anthony (New York), a view of the west entrance to the Treasury Building, ca. 1870, and one of the East Front of the Capitol, showing the statue of Freedom on the dome, surrounded by scaffolding.

DATE: Ca. 1861–70 (mainly April, May, and August 1865)

PHOTOGRAPHERS: Mathew Brady, his field staff, A. J. Russell, George Barnard, and Timothy O'Sullivan.

PHYSICAL DESCRIPTION: Ca. 125 mounts (some carry more than one image) supporting albumen and modern silver gelatin photoprints, 20 × 25 or smaller.

ARRANGEMENT: *Lot 4161–A:* Washington—general views; *Lot 4161–B:* Washington Arsenal; *Lot 4161–C:* Washington—Christian Commission and Sanitary Commission; *Lot 4161–D:* Washington—miscellaneous warehouses, headquarters, mess halls, other military buildings, and corps; *Lot 4161–E:* Washington—miscellaneous buildings, houses, and offices; *Lot 4161–F:* Bridges and river views; *Lot 4161–G:* Views of Georgetown; *Lot 4161–H:* Virginia; *Lot 4161–Stereographs.*

SOURCE: Anthony-Taylor-Rand-Ordway-Eaton Collection and other sources.

LOT 4164 (includes stereographs)

COLLECTION NAME: Civil War Views

SUBJECTS: Views in various cities: Manassas, Harper's Ferry, Yorktown, and other locations. Overall views, occasional street scenes, camps, levees, and caves. Includes Bailey's Cross Roads, Warrenton, and Petersburg, Virginia.

DATE: Ca. 1861–ca. 1865

PHOTOGRAPHERS: Mathew Brady and his field staff.

PHYSICAL DESCRIPTION: 75 mounts (227 albumen and silver gelatin photoprints), 28 × 36 cm or smaller.

ARRANGEMENT: By name of city.

SOURCE: Anthony-Taylor-Rand-Ordway-Eaton Collection and other sources.

LOT 4165 (includes stereographs)

COLLECTION NAME: Civil War Views

SUBJECTS: Specific historical buildings throughout the Civil War area, principally those associated with battles. Maryland section (8 items) includes view of Emmitsburg and the Agricultural College near Bladensburg, Maryland. Virginia section (63 items) includes views of Arlington and Centreville.

DATE: Ca. 1861–ca. 1865

PHOTOGRAPHERS: Mathew Brady and his field staff.

PHYSICAL DESCRIPTION: Ca. 100 mounts (some carry more than one image) supporting albumen and silver gelatin photoprints, 28 × 36 cm or smaller.

ARRANGEMENT: By state.

SOURCE: Anthony-Taylor-Rand-Ordway-Eaton Collection and other sources.

LOT 4166 (includes stereographs)

COLLECTION NAME: Civil War Views

SUBJECTS: Views of fortifications, gun emplacements, breastworks, with and without personnel. *Lot 4166–H:* Fortifications—D.C. and vicinity (60 items). Includes views of Fort Stevens, and a house near Fort Stevens that shows the effect of cannon fire; Fort Slemmer, Arlington Heights; Fort Richardson; Battery Rodgers, Potomac River, near Alexandria; Fort Ellsworth, near Alexandria; Fort Richardson, near Fair Oaks Station, Virginia; Fort Gaines; Fort Totten, near the Soldiers' Home in Washington; Fort Corcoran; Fort Woodbury; Fort Whipple, Virginia; Fort C. F. Smith; Fort Carroll; Fort Lincoln; the Battery at Chain Bridge; and the Washington Arsenal.

DATE: Ca. 1861–ca. 1865

PHOTOGRAPHERS: Mathew Brady and his field staff.

PHYSICAL DESCRIPTION: Ca. 175 mounts (some carry more than one image) supporting albumen and silver gelatin photoprints, 28 × 36 cm or smaller.

ARRANGEMENT: By geographical area.

SOURCE: Anthony-Taylor-Rand-Ordway-Eaton Collection and other sources.

LOT 4168 (includes stereographs)

COLLECTION NAME: Civil War Views

SUBJECTS: Casualties on the field of battle; Union and Confederate dead; interment crews at work; an embalmer. Two relevant stereographs include views of abandoned Union dead at Gaines Mills, Virginia, published by the War Photograph & Exhibition Company, Hartford, Connecticut.

DATE: Ca. 1861–ca. 1865

PHOTOGRAPHERS: Mathew Brady and his field staff.

PHYSICAL DESCRIPTION: Ca. 35 mounts (some carry more than one image) supporting albumen and silver gelatin photoprints, 28 × 36 cm or smaller.

SOURCE: Anthony-Taylor-Rand-Ordway-Eaton Collection and other sources.

LOT 4169 (includes stereographs)

COLLECTION NAME: Civil War Views

SUBJECTS: Overall views of military camps. Wooden structures and tents. Four Washington-area images include views of the camp of the Forty-fourth New York Infantry near Alexandria, Virginia; the camp of the Fifty-fifth New York Infantry, near Tenallytown (Tenleytown), Washington, D.C.; and the camp of the Thirteenth New York Cavalry on Prospect Hill, near Washington.

DATE: Ca. 1861–ca. 1865

PHOTOGRAPHERS: Mathew Brady and his field staff.

PHYSICAL DESCRIPTION: Ca. 25 albumen and silver gelatin photoprints, 28 × 36 cm or smaller.

SOURCE: Anthony-Taylor-Rand-Ordway-Eaton Collection and other sources.

LOT 4170 (includes stereographs)

COLLECTION NAME: Civil War Views

SUBJECTS: Views of headquarters in the field. Permanent buildings with or without surrounding temporary structures. Occasional distant groups of personnel. Includes views of the Headquarters of Defenses of Washington, south of the Potomac River; headquarters of Gen. W. F. Bartlett, near Washington; officer's quarters at Signal Corps Camp, near Georgetown; headquarters at Fort Slocum; headquarters of General M. D. Hardin at Fort Slocum; and headquarters of Lowell's Cavalry Brigade, in Vienna, Virginia. Most of these views are dated February 1864 and summer 1865.

DATE: Ca. 1861–ca. 1865

PHOTOGRAPHERS: Mathew Brady and his field staff.

PHYSICAL DESCRIPTION: Ca. 75, albumen or silver gelatin photoprints, 28 × 36 cm or smaller.

SOURCE: Anthony-Taylor-Rand-Ordway-Eaton Collection and other sources.

LOT 4172 (includes stereographs)

COLLECTION NAME: Civil War Views

SUBJECTS: Miscellaneous views and landscapes. Varied activities not specifically covered elsewhere in this collection. Ruins, camp incidents. Professor Lowe's military balloon "Intrepid," near Gaines Mill, Virginia (used in the battle of Fair Oaks, Virginia); photograph of Professor Lowe "observing the battle of Fair Oaks"; Bealeton, Virginia; White House Landing, Virginia; Fort Smith, near Washington; Camp of Thirty-first Pennsylvania Infantry near Washington; Camp of Thirteenth New York Cavalry on Prospect Hill, near Washington; Brigade Headquarters at Fort Lincoln; Signal Corps officers of the Army of the Potomac, near Washington; Fort Monroe, Virginia; Fort Brady, Virginia; Belle Plains, Virginia; Signal Corps camp in Georgetown.

DATE: Ca. 1861–ca. 1865

PHOTOGRAPHERS: Mathew Brady and his field staff.

PHYSICAL DESCRIPTION: Ca. 125 albumen and silver gelatin photoprints, 28 × 36 cm or smaller.

SOURCE: Anthony-Taylor-Rand-Ordway-Eaton Collection and other sources.

LOT 4173 (includes stereographs)

COLLECTION NAME: Civil War Views

SUBJECTS: Large formal military groups and entire units in review. Views of the Twenty-sixth New York Infantry, Fort Lyon, Virginia; Thirteenth New York Cavalry on inspection, on Prospect Hill, near Washington; the Second Rhode Island Infantry at Camp Jameson, near Washington; Seventh New York Cavalry camp near Washington, Gen. I. N. Palmer and staff in foreground; troops drilling near Washington.

DATE: Ca. 1861–ca. 1865

PHOTOGRAPHERS: Mathew Brady and his field staff.

PHYSICAL DESCRIPTION: Ca. 60 albumen or silver gelatin photoprints, 28 × 36 cm or smaller.

SOURCE: Anthony-Taylor-Rand-Ordway-Eaton Collection and other sources.

LOT 4174 (includes stereographs)

COLLECTION NAME: Civil War Views

SUBJECTS: Field artillery installations, mainly group photographs. Two batteries in action. Details of ordnance. Fort Sumner, Fair Oaks, Virginia; Gibson's Battery of the Horse Artillery, near Fair Oaks; Seventeenth New York Battery Artillery Depot, Camp Barry, near Washington; First New York Artillery Battalion, and Benson's and Robertson's Horse Battery, near Fair Oaks; Wiard guns at the Washington Arsenal; troops drilling near Washington. Officers, Battery C, Third U.S. Artillery; officers, Battery A, Second U.S. Artillery; and officers, Battery B, Second U.S. Artillery; all near Fair Oaks, Virginia.

DATE: Ca. 1861–ca. 1865

PHOTOGRAPHERS: Mathew Brady, his field staff, and James F. Gibson.

PHYSICAL DESCRIPTION: Ca. 25 items (albumen and silver gelatin photoprints), 28 × 36 cm or smaller.

SOURCE: Anthony-Taylor-Rand-Ordway-Eaton Collection and other sources.

LOT 4177 (includes stereographs)

COLLECTION NAME: Civil War Views

SUBJECTS: Railroad locomotives, railroad operations, and railroad bridges and equipment. Includes views of various locations of the Orange & Alexandria Railroad, including Devereux Station and Union Mills, and crews repairing tracks. Long Bridge, Washington; Potomac Creek Bridge for Acquia Creek Railroad; outskirts of Alexandria, Virginia; and Bull Run Bridge.

DATE: Ca. 1861–ca. 1865

PHOTOGRAPHERS: Mathew Brady, his field staff, A. J. Russell, and Timothy O'Sullivan.

PHYSICAL DESCRIPTION: Ca. 65 albumen and silver gelatin photoprints, 28 × 36 cm or smaller.

SOURCE: Anthony-Taylor-Rand-Ordway-Eaton Collection and other sources.

LOT 4179

COLLECTION NAME: Civil War Views

SUBJECTS: Quartermaster Corps workshops. Groups of craftsmen and workers. Includes quartermaster office at Seventh Street SW wharf, ambulance shop, Office of Repair shops, carpenter shop, paint shop, repair shops, blacksmith's shop, and wheelwright's shop, Washington. Quartermaster's wharf in Alexandria; quartermas-

ter's corral, near Alexandria; and horseshoeing shop.

DATE: Ca. 1861–ca. 1865

PHOTOGRAPHERS: Mathew Brady and his field staff.

PHYSICAL DESCRIPTION: Ca. 40 albumen and silver gelatin photoprints, 28 × 36 cm or smaller.

SOURCE: Anthony-Taylor-Rand-Ordway-Eaton Collection and other sources.

LOT 4180 (includes stereographs)

COLLECTION NAME: Civil War Views

SUBJECTS: Exterior and interior views of hospitals. Ambulance trains and Medical Corps work. Work of the U.S. Sanitary Commission. Includes wards and exterior views of Armory Square Hospital, Campbell Army Hospital, Mt. Pleasant Hospital, Harewood Hospital and ambulance train, surgeons and hospital stewards, Sanitary Commission Lodge, Soldier's Rest, in the square of North Capitol, Delaware Avenue, and C and D Streets NE; Stanton Hospital, tent hospital at Randall Green, Quartermaster's Hospital, Douglas Hospital, and Kalorama Hospital, in Washington. Seminary Hospital, Georgetown. Slough Hospital, Sanitary Commission at Convalescent Hospital, exterior views and kitchen of Soldier's Rest, and Mansion House Hospital, in Alexandria.

DATE: Ca. 1861–ca. 1865

PHOTOGRAPHERS: Mathew Brady and his field staff.

PHYSICAL DESCRIPTION: Ca. 110 albumen and silver gelatin photoprints, 28 × 36 cm or smaller.

SOURCE: Anthony-Taylor-Rand-Ordway-Eaton Collection and other sources.

LOT 4181 (includes stereographs)

COLLECTION NAME: Civil War Views

SUBJECTS: Prisoners of war and prison camps. Examination of released emaciated soldiers. Copies of overall views of Andersonville prison, probably by a Southern photographer. Execution by hanging of Capt. Henry Wirtz, C.S.A., in Washington; newspaper reporters viewing execution.

DATE: Ca. 1861–ca. 1865

PHOTOGRAPHERS: Mathew Brady and his field staff.

PHYSICAL DESCRIPTION: Ca. 35 albumen and silver gelatin photoprints, 20 × 25 cm or smaller.

SOURCE: Anthony-Taylor-Rand-Ordway-Eaton Collection and other sources.

LOT 4182 (includes stereographs)

COLLECTION NAME: Civil War Views

SUBJECTS: Naval vessels and naval personnel groups. Includes views of a Brazilian steam frigate at the Washington Navy Yard (January 1863); U.S. Steam Sloop of War *Pensacola* (eighteen guns) off Alexandria, Virginia; and U.S.S. *Polaris*, at the Washington Navy Yard. One stereograph by Bell and Brother of the rebel ram *Stonewall*, probably in the Potomac River, copyright by F. Bell in 1867.

DATE: Ca. 1861–67

PHOTOGRAPHERS: Bell & Bro., Mathew Brady, and Brady's field staff.

PHYSICAL DESCRIPTION: Ca. 150 albumen and silver gelatin photoprints, 28 × 36 cm or smaller.

SOURCE: Anthony-Taylor-Rand-Ordway-Eaton Collection and other sources.

Mathew Brady. Headquarters of the U.S. Christian Commission, Washington, D.C., ca. 1863. Civil War Views, Lot 4188.

LC-B8171-7720

LOT 4186 (includes stereographs)

COLLECTION NAME: Civil War Views

SUBJECTS: Group portraits of generals with their staffs in the field. Occasional informal groups with civilian visitors. Includes portraits of Gen. A. McD. McCook and staff, Brightwood, Washington; Maj. Gen. C. C. Augur and staff, Washington; Brig. Gen. William Hawley and staff, Washington; Brig. Gen. M. D. Hardin and staff at Fort Slocum, Washington; Brig. Maj. Gen. W. Hoffman at Office of Commissary General of Prisons; Gen. S. P. Heintzelman and group at convalescent camp near Alexandria and with staff at Arlington House.

DATE: Ca. 1861–ca. 1865

PHOTOGRAPHERS: Mathew Brady and his field staff.

PHYSICAL DESCRIPTION: Ca. 200 albumen and silver gelatin photoprints, 28 × 36 cm or smaller.

SOURCE: Anthony-Taylor-Rand-Ordway-Eaton Collection and other sources.

LOT 4187

COLLECTION NAME: Civil War Views

SUBJECTS: Officer groups in the field. Formal groups. Camp life and incidents. Includes officers and noncommissioned staff of Thirteenth New York Cavalry on Prospect Hill, near Washington; Maj. H. W. Sawyer and staff at Camp Stoneman, Washington. Officer groups of the Thirty-third New York Infantry, Camp Granger, near Washington; Fourth U.S. Colored Infantry, Fort Slocum, Washington; Eighth New York State Militia, Arlington; Fourth New York Heavy Artillery, Fort Corcoran, Virginia; Fifth U.S. Cavalry, near Washington; 3d Massachusetts Artillery, Fort Totten; Company F and Company K, Third Massachusetts Artillery, Fort Stevens; First Battalion, New York Light Artillery, Fort Duncan, near Washington; Sixty-ninth New York State Militia, Fort Corcoran, Virginia. Officers' quarters, with officers, at Fort Lincoln.

DATE: Ca. 1861–ca. 1865

PHOTOGRAPHERS: Mathew Brady, his field staff, and others.

PHYSICAL DESCRIPTION: Ca. 300 albumen and silver gelatin photoprints, 28 × 36 cm or smaller.

SOURCE: Anthony-Taylor-Rand-Ordway-Eaton Collection and other sources.

LOT 4188

COLLECTION NAME: Civil War Views

SUBJECTS: Group portraits of civilians, telegraph operators, postal clerks, newsmen, intelligence "scouts," and other miscellaneous groups. Includes groups photographed at Alexandria Seminary and in Washington at quartermaster general's office (now the Renwick Gallery); at the War Department, at the Quartermaster's Depot, at the Signal Corps Headquarters, at the Central Signal Station, Washington; at the U.S. Christian Commission, and at the Mess House at government stables. Groups at Camp Stoneman, Giesboro (Giesborough) Maryland. Generals Card, Thomas, and Wise and groups at Quartermaster's Depot, Washington; quartermaster's employees; Col. B. F. Fisher and officers at the Signal Corps, Washington; military band and quarters at the Cavalry Depot; Captain Tompkins and group at the quartermaster's office, Washington; officers of Company F, Second New York Heavy Artillery, Fort C. F. Smith, near Washington; officers of the Ninth Veteran Reserve Corps, Washington; Ninth Massachusetts Infantry Camp, near Washington; First U.S. Veteran Volunteer Infantry, on F Street NW, and a group at the Sanitary Commission Lodge in Washington.

DATE: Ca. 1861–ca. 1865

PHOTOGRAPHERS: Mathew Brady and his field staff.

PHYSICAL DESCRIPTION: Ca. 300 albumen and silver gelatin photoprints, 28 × 36 cm or smaller.

SOURCE: Anthony-Taylor-Rand-Ordway-Eaton Collection and other sources.

LOT 4189

COLLECTION NAME: Civil War Views

SUBJECTS: Mostly posed groups and individuals identified only by military units. Includes numerous portraits of the Seventh New York Militia at Camp Cameron, Washington.

DATE: Ca. 1861–ca. 1865

PHOTOGRAPHERS: Mathew Brady and his field staff.

PHYSICAL DESCRIPTION: Ca. 200 albumen and silver gelatin photoprints (half-stereograph), 20 × 25 cm or smaller.

SOURCE: Anthony-Taylor-Rand-Ordway-Eaton Collection and other sources.

LOT 4190

COLLECTION NAME: Civil War Views

SUBJECTS: Company group portraits, mainly formal arrangements. Noncommissioned officers of Companies H, A, C, K, E, and I, Tenth Veterans Reserve Corps, Washington; Band and Drum Corps of Ninth and Tenth Veterans Reserve Corps, Washington. Camp Fry, at Washington Circle, on Pennsylvania Avenue. Company K, Third Massachusetts Artillery at Fort Stevens; Third Connecticut Infantry, Camp Douglas; group and Battalion of Marine Corps at Washington Navy Yard. Group portrait of Company A, Engineer Company, Drum Corps, and Band of the Eighth New York State Militia, Arlington; Companies L and F, Second New York Artillery, at Fort C. J. Smith. Company E, Fourth U.S. Colored Infantry, at Fort Lincoln; guardhouse, guard, and band of the 107th U.S. Colored Infantry at Fort Corcoran, near Washington.

DATE: Ca. 1861–ca. 1865

PHOTOGRAPHERS: Mathew Brady and his field staff.

PHYSICAL DESCRIPTION: Ca. 200 albumen and silver gelatin photoprints, 28 × 36 cm or smaller.

SOURCE: Anthony-Taylor-Rand-Ordway-Eaton Collection and other sources.

LOT 4191 (includes stereographs)

COLLECTION NAME: Civil War Views

SUBJECTS: Portraits of individual officers and occasional groups. Field visits by President Lincoln. Includes one portrait of Captain Sellars and his wife at Fort Totten. Stereograph images include one portrait of Edwin S. Stanton, Lincoln's secretary of war (published by the War Photograph & Exhibition Company, Hartford, Connecticut).

DATE: Ca. 1861–ca. 1865

PHOTOGRAPHERS: Mathew Brady and his field staff.

PHYSICAL DESCRIPTION: Ca. 100 items (albumen and silver gelatin photoprints), 28 × 36 cm or smaller.

ARRANGEMENT: Alphabetical by name.

SOURCE: Anthony-Taylor-Rand-Ordway-Eaton Collection and other sources.

Mathew Brady. Company E, Fourth U.S. Colored Infantry, Fort Lincoln, defenses of Washington, ca. 1863. Civil War Views, Lot 4190.
LC-B8171-7890

Mathew Brady. Crowd watching the hanging of the Lincoln assassination conspirators, Washington, D.C., 1865. Civil War Views, Lot 4195.
LC-B8171-7755

Mathew Brady. Crowd gathered for the hanging of the Lincoln assassination conspirators, Washington, D.C., 1865. Civil War Views, Lot 4195.
LC-B8171-7798

LOT 4192

COLLECTION NAME: Civil War Views

SUBJECTS: Formal portraits, including occasional engravings, of Union army officers.

DATE: Ca. 1861–ca. 1865

PHOTOGRAPHERS: Mathew Brady and his studio and field staffs.

PHYSICAL DESCRIPTION: Ca. 1,000 albumen and silver gelatin photoprints, and engravings, 20 × 25 cm or smaller.

ARRANGEMENT: Roughly alphabetical.

SOURCE: Anthony-Taylor-Rand-Ordway-Eaton Collection and other sources.

LOT 4193

COLLECTION NAME: Civil War Views

SUBJECTS: Union naval officers of the Civil War period.

DATE: Ca. 1861–ca. 1865

PHOTOGRAPHERS: Mathew Brady and his studio and field staffs.

PHYSICAL DESCRIPTION: Ca. 180 albumen and silver gelatin photoprints and engravings, 20 × 25 cm or smaller.

SOURCE: Anthony-Taylor-Rand-Ordway-Eaton Collection and other sources.

LOT 4195

COLLECTION NAME: Civil War Views

SUBJECTS: Photographs relating to the assassination of Abraham Lincoln. Portraits of John Wilkes Booth, Lewis Paine, George A. Atzerodt, Edward Spangler, Samuel Arnold, David E. Herold, Michael O'Laughlin, Richter Hartman (arrested on suspicion), Celestino (Portuguese ship captain), apparently made at the time of their arrest. Portraits of Isaac Surratt and Sgt. Boston Corbett (the soldier who killed Booth). Portrait of the board that tried the Lincoln assassination conspirators. Prisoners looking belligerent and wearing disheveled clothing. Scenes at the execution, which was held at the Washington Arsenal (now Fort McNair); the scaffold and hanging of the conspirators, reporters viewing the hanging; graves of the conspirators. Murray's Hotel in Bryantown, Maryland; J. C. Howard livery stable at which Booth hired the horse on which he escaped; Ford's Theater.

DATE: Ca. 1865–ca. 1867

PHOTOGRAPHERS: Alexander Gardner, Mathew Brady, and his field staff.

PHYSICAL DESCRIPTION: Ca. 40 albumen and silver gelatin photoprints, 20 × 25 cm or smaller.

SOURCE: Part acquired from Col. Godwin Ordway, 1948, part printed to order by the Handy Studio, 1905, and other sources.

LOT 4198 (includes stereographs)

COLLECTION NAME: Civil War Views

SUBJECTS: The Grand Review of the Union army held in Washington, D.C. Crowds of spectators, some with umbrellas; large groups of mounted soldiers; troops and presidential reviewing stands on Pennsylvania Avenue; the Capitol festooned with crepe and with its flag at half-mast. Includes nine stereographs by E. & H. T. Anthony from Brady negatives.

DATE: May 1865

PHOTOGRAPHERS: Mathew Brady and his studio staff, and E. & H. T. Anthony.

PHYSICAL DESCRIPTION: Ca. 65 albumen and silver gelatin photoprints, 20 × 25 cm or smaller.

SOURCE: Made to order by the Handy Studio in 1905.

LOT 4213

COLLECTION NAME: Civil War Views

SUBJECTS: Miscellaneous Confederate portraits relating to the Civil War. Confederate officers.

DATE: Ca. 1861–ca. 1865

PHOTOGRAPHERS: Mathew Brady and his field staff.

PHYSICAL DESCRIPTION: Ca. 150 items (albumen and silver gelatin photoprints and engravings), 20 × 25 cm or smaller.

ARRANGEMENT: Generally in alphabetical order.

SOURCE: Anthony-Taylor-Rand-Ordway-Eaton Collection and other sources.

Maurice Constant, a commander in the U.S. Navy, pursued his photographic portrait work during and after World War II, and he produced a large collection of formal portraits of Allied military and political leaders of that period. His portrait collection was presented to the Library of Congress in 1946 and is unrestricted.

LOT 11822

COLLECTION NAME: Maurice Constant Collection

SUBJECTS: Formal portraits of Allied military and political leaders of the World War II period. Includes American and foreign leaders and public officials, including ministers, cabinet officers, and U.S. Supreme Court justices. William Bankhead, Hugo Black, Leon Blum, Gen. Omar Bradley, Harold Burton, Winston Churchill, Tom Connally, Elmer Davis, Lt. Gen. James Doolittle, William O. Douglas, Anthony Eden, Dwight D. Eisenhower, James Farley, James Forrestal, Felix Frankfurter, Andrei Gromyko, J. Edgar Hoover, Harry Hopkins, Cordell Hull, Harold Ickes, Hiram Johnson, Jesse Jones, Frank Knox, Archibald MacLeish, Philip Murray, Frances Perkins, Gen. John J. Pershing, Franklin D. Roosevelt, Harold Stassen, Henry Stimson, Harlan Stone, Harry S. Truman, and Henry Wallace are among those represented.

DATE: 1939–45

PHOTOGRAPHERS: Maurice Constant.

PHYSICAL DESCRIPTION: 323 silver gelatin photoprints, 41 × 51 cm or smaller.

ARRANGEMENT: Alphabetical by name of sitter. A finding aid listing the contents of the collection is available in the Prints and Photographs Reading Room.

SOURCE: Gift of Comdr. Maurice Constant, USNR Retired, 1946.

RESTRICTIONS: No restrictions. Credit line for Maurice Constant requested.

Maurice Constant. Supreme Court Justice Felix Frankfurter, ca. 1939–45. Maurice Constant Collection, Lot 11822.
LC-USZ62-92853

Maurice Constant. Secretary of Labor Frances Perkins, ca. 1939–45. Maurice Constant Collection, Lot 11822.
LC-USZ62-92855

Maurice Constant. Harry S. Truman, ca. 1939–45. Maurice Constant Collection, Lot 11822.
LC-USZ62-53084

Maurice Constant. Gen. Omar N. Bradley, ca. 1939-45. Maurice Constant Collection, Lot 11822.
LC-USZ62-92854

Maurice Constant. William F. Bankhead, Speaker of the House, ca. 1939–45. Maurice Constant Collection, Lot 11822.
LC-USZ62-92851

George Creel (1876–1953) was an author, editor, and U.S. government official. He chaired the U.S. Committee on Public Information and he was the Washington correspondent for *Collier's Weekly*. The George Creel Papers in the Manuscript Division (500 items) span the years 1896–1953 and are accompanied by a finding aid. They were a gift from George Creel and others, 1943–54. Much of the material is in scrapbooks and bound volumes, and it relates in part to Woodrow Wilson and the U.S. Committee on Public Information. The photographs were transferred to the Prints and Photographs Division. Those pictures related to Washington, D.C., are described below.

LOT 6946

COLLECTION NAME: George Creel Papers, Manuscript Division

SUBJECTS: Portraits of George Creel. Snapshots, studio portraits, caricatures and sketches, showing Creel as a young man, with college groups, and at various stages in his career.

DATE: 1899–ca. 1950s

PHOTOGRAPHERS: Harris & Ewing.

PHYSICAL DESCRIPTION: 45 silver gelatin photoprints, 28 × 36 cm or smaller.

SOURCE: Transfer from the Manuscript Division, 1955.

LOT 6949

COLLECTION NAME: George Creel Papers, Manuscript Division

SUBJECTS: "Photos [of] some of my dearest friends past and present." Includes Frances Starr, Mary Roberts Rinehart, Lionel Moses, William L. Chenery, Edwin Markham, Eleanor Wilson McAdoo, and Gladys Shaw Erskine.

DATE: Ca. 1890s–ca. 1950s

PHYSICAL DESCRIPTION: 1 album (90 silver gelatin photoprints, 20 × 25 cm or smaller).

SOURCE: Gift of George Creel, Jr., 1954. Transfer from the Manuscript Division, 1955.

LOT 6951

COLLECTION NAME: George Creel Papers, Manuscript Division

SUBJECTS: Individual and group portraits. George Creel with Presidents Wilson, Hoover, and Roosevelt; David Belasco, George Dewey, James A. Farley, and others.

NOTE: Some photos are unidentified.

DATE: 1918–48

PHOTOGRAPHERS: Clinedinst.

PHYSICAL DESCRIPTION: 18 silver gelatin photoprints, 1 etching, and 1 cartoon, 28 × 36 cm or smaller.

SOURCE: Gift of George Creel, Jr., 1953. Transfer from the Manuscript Division.

George Creel with President and Mrs. Woodrow Wilson at Mount Vernon, July 4, 1918. Papers of George Creel, Lot 6951.

LC-USZ62-21702

Portrait of George Creel. Papers of George Creel, Lot 6946.

LC-USZ62-92526

The Prints and Photographs Division holds the largest collection of Mathew Brady daguerreotypes in existence, numbering about 350 items, most probably made in Brady's New York City studio (which opened in 1844), before he established his Washington, D.C., studio in 1858. In addition, the division holds over sixty cased images (daguerreotypes, ambrotypes, and tintypes) from the Frances Benjamin Johnston Collection and the Gilbert Grosvenor Collection of Photographs of Alexander Graham Bell, and about eighty-five cased images from various other collections and acquisition sources.

Consisting almost entirely of portrait subjects, these images are, in many cases, the earliest known photographic representations of important mid-nineteenth-century political and social figures, artists, musicians, scientists, philosophers, and writers, some of whom lived or worked in Washington, D.C. The faces of ordinary people as well appear on these plates.

A checklist of names and descriptions of images is available in the Prints and Photographs Reading Room.

REFERENCES

Vanderbilt, no. 77, p. 18.

Nicholas H. Shepherd (Springfield, Illinois). Quarter-plate daguerreotype portrait of Abraham Lincoln, ca. 1846–47. Daguerreotype Collection.
LC-USZ62-12457

Mathew Brady. Whole-plate daguerreotype portrait of President James K. Polk, February 17, 1849. Daguerreotype Collection, no. 391.
LC-USZ62-9062

Nicholas H. Shepherd (Springfield, Illinois). Quarter-plate daguerreotype portrait of Mary Todd Lincoln, ca. 1846–47. Daguerreotype Collection.
LC-USZ62-12458

Mathew Brady. Half-plate daguerreotype portrait of Dolley Madison, ca. 1849. Daguerreotype Collection.
LC-BH834-35

Mathew Brady. Whole-plate daguerreotype portrait of President Franklin Pierce, ca. 1853–55. Daguerreotype Collection, no. 390.
LC-USZ62-9059

Josephus Daniels (1862–1948) was a journalist, U.S. secretary of the navy during the Woodrow Wilson administration, and ambassador to Mexico. The Manuscript Division holds his papers (330,000 items), which span the years 1806–1948 and are described in a published register. Daniels's interests included prohibition, public health and welfare, naval aviation, and radio communication. The photographs were transferred to the Prints and Photographs Division.

National Newspaper Service (Chicago). Josephus Daniels in his office in the Navy Department with war chiefs (advisory council). Franklin D. Roosevelt, assistant secretary of the navy, stands behind Daniels. Papers of Josephus Daniels, Lot 5421.
LC-USZ62-92536

Seven-inch tractor-mount Mark V gun with limber, designed by the U.S. Naval Gun Factory, Washington Navy Yard. Ca. 1917–18. Papers of Josephus Daniels, Lot 5375.
LC-USZ62-92804

LOT 5363

COLLECTION NAME: Josephus Daniels Papers, Manuscript Division

SUBJECTS: Fourteen-inch naval railway battery MK.I., designed by the U.S. Naval Gun Factory, Washington, D.C. These guns were sent to France and used outside of Paris and north of Verdun during World War I. Several images show the gun inside the factory at the Washington Navy Yard. Other subjects include Franklin D. Roosevelt, assistant secretary of the navy, on an inspection tour at St. Nazaire; a copy of a map of the French railway lines over which the batteries were transported; a typical camouflaged installation; an ammunition car; construction car with crane, anti-aircraft railway mount; high-side gondola; berthing car; naval barracks and unloading activities at St. Nazaire.

NOTE: All photographs are captioned.

DATE: Ca. April 1918

PHYSICAL DESCRIPTION: 1 album (52 silver gelatin photoprints), 15 × 23 cm.

SOURCE: Gift of the heirs of Josephus Daniels, 1948. Transfer from the Manuscript Division.

LOT 5367

COLLECTION NAME: Josephus Daniels Papers, Manuscript Division

Washington Post staff photographer. Mrs. Franklin D. Roosevelt and Mrs. Woodrow Wilson chatting with Josephus Daniels, 1945. Papers of Josephus Daniels, Lot 5404. Reproduced with permission.

SUBJECTS: Executives and groups of office workers at their desks, probably in government or law offices in Washington, D.C. Images show furniture, fireplaces, desk accoutrements. Buildings include the Patent Office; interiors and exteriors in the Pension Office; the White House; the U.S. Capitol, the fresco inside the Capitol dome, the House Chamber, the Senate Chamber; and the Department of Agriculture grounds.

NOTE: Photographs mostly uncaptioned. Inside of album stamped "Capital City View Co."

DATE: 1893–95

PHOTOGRAPHERS: Possibly Capital City View Company.

PHYSICAL DESCRIPTION: 1 album (23 silver gelatin photoprints), 16 × 21 cm.

SOURCE: Gift of the heirs of Josephus Daniels, 1948. Transfer from the Manuscript Division.

LOT 5375

COLLECTION NAME: Josephus Daniels Papers, Manuscript Division

SUBJECTS: The seven-inch tractor-mount Mark V gun, designed by the U.S. Naval Gun Factory, Washington, D.C. Views of the counter-recoil cylinders, tractor axle and trail, and limber. Proof-firing of the gun. One photo shows the gun on the grounds in front of buildings at the Washington Navy Yard.

DATE: Ca. 1917–ca. 1918

PHYSICAL DESCRIPTION: 1 album (17 silver gelatin photoprints), 15 × 23 cm.

SOURCE: Gift of the heirs of Josephus Daniels, 1948. Transfer from the Manuscript Division.

LOT 5383

COLLECTION NAME: Josephus Daniels Papers, Manuscript Division

SUBJECTS: Portraits of women, some autographed for presentation to Daniels. Subjects include Mary Custis Lee (daughter of Robert E. Lee), G. Louise Kelsey, Margaret Stith, Frances Hull, Eleanor Roosevelt, Mildred McLean (Mrs. George) Dewey, Mary Tau, Edith Bolling Galt (Mrs. Woodrow) Wilson, Mrs. Charles R. Marshall (wife of the vice president), Ilo Wallace, Eleanor Randolph Wilson (President Wilson's first wife), Mrs. Grover Cleveland, Hughes Cornell, Jeanette Rankin, Helen Gardiner (first U.S. civil service commissioner) and others.

DATE: Ca. 1880–ca. 1948

PHOTOGRAPHERS: Harris & Ewing, Underwood & Underwood, Bachrach, Clinedinst, and G. V. Buck.

PHYSICAL DESCRIPTION: Ca. 65 silver gelatin and platinum photoprints, 28 × 36 cm or smaller.

SOURCE: Gift of the heirs of Josephus Daniels, 1948. Transfer from the Manuscript Division.

LOT 5384

COLLECTION NAME: Josephus Daniels Papers, Manuscript Division

SUBJECTS: Formal portraits of Woodrow Wilson and other Wilsoniana. News photographs made on shipboard and in various parts of Europe; Wilson at home; portraits of Wilson's contemporaries; views of Princeton.

DATE: Ca. 1912–ca. 1920

PHOTOGRAPHERS: Harris & Ewing, Underwood & Underwood, and Pach Bros. (New York).

PHYSICAL DESCRIPTION: Ca. 100 silver gelatin photoprints and photomechanical prints, 28 × 36 cm or smaller.

SOURCE: Gift of the heirs of Josephus Daniels, 1948. Transfer from the Manuscript Division.

LOT 5389

COLLECTION NAME: Josephus Daniels Papers, Manuscript Division

SUBJECTS: Single Oak and other residences occupied by the Daniels family, and scenes in the vicinity of Washington, D.C. Includes views of the Capitol and grounds after a snowstorm, the Washington Navy Yard, the White House, the old Willard House, the Edison Laboratory, Single Oak in Woodley (Park) in 1913, the library in the Daniels home. Also includes one photo of a store window display of World War I maps, posters, and portraits of soldiers.

DATE: Ca. 1910–ca. 1948

PHYSICAL DESCRIPTION: Ca. 60 silver gelatin photoprints, 28 × 36 cm or smaller.

SOURCE: Gift of the heirs of Josephus Daniels, 1948. Transfer from the Manuscript Division.

LOT 5401

COLLECTION NAME: Josephus Daniels Papers, Manuscript Division

SUBJECTS: Portraits of men, most autographed for presentation to Daniels. Includes Bernard M. Baruch, William Braisted (surgeon general, U.S. Navy), William Jennings Bryan, Winston Churchill (1921), Andrew Crinkley, Homer Cummings, Adm. George Dewey, Thomas A. Edison, James Farley, Percy

Wright Foote (commander, U.S. Navy), John N. Garner, Hollis Godfrey, Samuel Gompers, Herbert Hoover, Cordell Hull, John Wilbur Jenkins, B. R. Lacy, Maj.-Gen. John A. Lejeune, William G. McAdoo, Thomas R. Marshall, E. Meredith, Gen. John J. Pershing (1921), Julius Rosenwald, Charles M. Schwab, William ("Billy") Sunday, Henry A. Wallace, Daniel Willard, Rear Adm. A. G. Winterhalter, Robert Wickliffe Wooley, and others, especially U.S. and foreign military leaders. Includes one copy of a caricature.

DATE: Ca. 1910–ca. 1948

PHOTOGRAPHERS: Harris & Ewing, Bachrach, Modelle, Clinedinst, Edmonston, and Sarony (New York).

PHYSICAL DESCRIPTION: Ca. 150 silver gelatin photoprints, 31 × 46 cm or smaller.

SOURCE: Gift of the heirs of Josephus Daniels, 1948. Transfer from the Manuscript Division.

LOT 5404

COLLECTION NAME: Josephus Daniels Papers, Manuscript Division

SUBJECTS: News photographs made at various public functions attended by Josephus Daniels. Informal group and single portraits of naval officers, Shriners, newspapermen, and presidential parties. Subjects include the U.S. Navy Band on the grounds of the White House; Eleanor and Franklin D. Roosevelt on board navy ships; Josephus Daniels with Eleanor Roosevelt and Mrs. Woodrow Wilson; Franklin D. Roosevelt at the Democratic National Convention in Philadelphia (1936); the XPB2Y plane at Anacostia, after the plane flew nonstop from San Diego in thirteen hours (October 27, 1938). Two photographs show Eleanor Roosevelt and Josephus Daniels listening to Franklin D. Roosevelt speaking to Congress, vetoing the $2.2 million Patman (Soldier) Bonus Bill (May 22, 1935).

DATE: Ca. 1930–ca. 1948

PHYSICAL DESCRIPTION: Ca. 200 silver gelatin photoprints, 20 × 25 cm or smaller.

SOURCE: Gift of the heirs of Josephus Daniels, 1948. Transfer from the Manuscript Division.

LOT 5411

COLLECTION NAME: Josephus Daniels Papers, Manuscript Division

Office of Josephus Daniels, secretary of the navy, in the Navy Department Building. Papers of Josephus Daniels, Lot 5421.
LC-USZ62-92805

SUBJECTS: Family snapshots and other photographs related to the career of Josephus Daniels and the history of the Daniels family.

NOTE: Many photos lack captions or identifying information. Some are badly faded.

DATE: Ca. 1880–ca. 1948

PHYSICAL DESCRIPTION: Ca. 1,000 albumen and silver gelatin photoprints, 13 × 18 cm or smaller.

SOURCE: Gift of the heirs of Josephus Daniels, 1948. Transfer from the Manuscript Division.

LOT 5421

COLLECTION NAME: Josephus Daniels Papers, Manuscript Division

SUBJECTS: Photographs of the office of the secretary of the navy in the Navy Department (in the State, War, and Navy Building, now Old Executive Office Building). Portraits of Josephus Daniels with office staff and messengers, some black. Entry door to office, and interior of office shown in great detail. Some show Daniels with Franklin D. Roosevelt (assistant secretary of the navy) and other administrators. Also includes group of navy officials at the U.S. Naval Gun Factory, Washington Navy Yard.

DATE: Ca. 1913–21

PHOTOGRAPHERS: Harris & Ewing, Underwood & Underwood, and U.S. Naval Air Service.

PHYSICAL DESCRIPTION: Ca. 40 silver gelatin photoprints, 28 × 36 cm or smaller.

SOURCE: Gift of the heirs of Josephus Daniels, 1948. Transfer from the Manuscript Division.

The famous survey and landscape photographer William Henry Jackson (1843–1942), founder of the Jackson Photo Company of Denver, Colorado, formed the Detroit Photographic Company—more popularly called the Detroit Publishing Company after 1905—of Detroit, Michigan, in partnership with William A. Livingstone, founder of the Photochrom Company. Livingstone owned the American rights to the Swiss "AAC" process, by which color was lithographically added to prints from black-and-white negatives. This enterprise responded to the considerable demand from libraries, publishers, advertisers, and ordinary citizens who wanted black-and-white and color pictures of cities, small towns, resorts and parks, natural landmarks, buildings, monuments, industries, sports activities, cruise ships, street scenes, local events, and ethnic types from around the world. The company produced photographic and photolithographic copies of works of art from major museums. One of the largest American publishers of travel views, it provided large views, postcards, souvenir booklets, and panoramic photographs, and supplied tourist sites with such images for sale as souvenirs.

Jackson contributed to the company's stock file of negatives and pictures his own photographic negatives. They are dated from 1879 on and most carry Jackson's original negative numbers. Other negatives and prints were purchased by the Detroit Publishing Company from other photographers or commercial studios and republished under the Detroit Publishing Company name. Most Detroit Publishing Company images carry captions and negative numbers from hand-lettered inscriptions on the negatives.

Detroit Publishing Company. Assembled gun, Washington Navy Yard, ca. 1905. Detroit Publishing Company Collection, Lot 3000–R.

LC-D4-21322

In 1924, as a result of difficulty obtaining supplies and decreased demand for their products during World War I, the Detroit Publishing Company went into receivership, finally liquidating its assets in 1932. An attempt to revive the company in 1934 failed. In 1936, Jackson gave the entire collection of negatives, company albums, and some records to the Edison Institute, of Dearborn, Michigan. In 1949, the Edison Institute turned the negatives and duplicate prints over to the Colorado Historical Society. The Colorado Historical Society retained some company records and those negatives made west of the Mississippi River. The negatives and some duplicate prints made east of the Mississippi were transferred to the Library of Congress. (The original Hayden survey negatives made by Jackson in 1870–78 are held with the records of the U.S. Geological Survey by the National Archives and Records Administration.)

The Prints and Photographs Division holds over 22,000 photoprints, most obtained as copyright deposits, and about 25,000 original glass negatives in this collection. Photoprints and albums are cataloged in subject groupings, most on the basis of geographical location, with extensive coverage of the United States and some views of Europe, Africa, and Asia. Extensive coverage exists for foreign naval vessels and views and events in Havana, Cuba, during the Spanish-American War (1898–99). The division's negative holdings are filed by original Detroit Publishing Company number, according to size and type of negative. The Library holds some published advertising catalogs from the company, which provide listings of views and corresponding negative numbers and which may help to date particular images. Most copyright deposit pictures carry a copyright date, not always, however, a reliable indication of when the picture was made.

Detroit Publishing Company. The Key Mansion, Washington, D.C. Copyright 1908. Detroit Publishing Company Collection, Lot 9072–A.

LC-D4-71075

Through 1908, William Henry Jackson devoted most of his time in the company to photographing in the field, traveling across the United States in a comfortably equipped railroad car, complete with photographic studio and darkroom. One of the volumes of his diary, in the Manuscript Division of the New York Public Library, describes in detail the making of views in Washington, D.C. (His autobiography, *Time Exposure*, deals mainly with his early work, before his association with the Detroit Publishing Company.) Washington, D.C., views are cataloged, as are pictures made in Virginia and Maryland, and are described below.

As part of the Library of Congress Non-Print Optical Disk Pilot Program in the Prints and Photographs Division, Detroit Publishing Company "AAC" process color photo albums, large "AAC" color photoprints, glass plate negatives, and glass transparencies were copied and transferred to a videodisk. The Washington, D.C., subjects on videodisk are described below. Instructions for searching the videodisk and its accompanying computer data base of caption information are available in the Prints and Photographs Reading Room.

Detroit Publishing Company. Capt. Norman von Heldenreich Farquhar at his desk in the Bureau of Yards and Docks, ca. 1900–1905. Detroit Publishing Company Collection, Lot 3000–J.

LC-D4-21446

REFERENCES

Burdick, Jefferson R. *The Handbook of Detroit Publishing Company Post Cards.* Syracuse? N.Y., 1954.
Jackson, William Henry. *Time Exposure.* New York: Putnam, 1940.
Lowe, James L., and Ben Papell. *Detroit Publishing Company Collectors' Guide.* Newton Square, Pennsylvania: Deltiologists of America, 1975.
Melville, no. 60, p. 87.
Newhall, Beaumont, and Diane E. Edkins. *William H. Jackson.* Dobbs Ferry, N.Y.: Morgan & Morgan, 1974.
"Prints and Photographs." *Quarterly Journal of Current Acquisitions* 7 (November 1949), p. 45.
Read, Cynthia. "Detroit's Lens to the World." *Herald* (Greenfield Village and Henry Ford Museum, Dearborn, Michigan) 7, no. 4 (Fall 1978), pp. 4–9.
Vanderbilt, nos. 186–89, pp. 47–48.
Vanderbilt, Paul. "William Henry Jackson in the East." *U.S. Camera* 12 (May 1949), pp. 44–47.
Viewpoint, nos. 125, 130, and 155.

SUBJECTS ON VIDEODISK

Glass Photonegatives

Primarily photographic views of the United States, ca. 1898–1912. Includes copies of other photographs and reproductions of paintings. Approximately 25,000 glass negatives, 16 × 21 cm (6 × 8 inch) to 28 × 36 cm (11 × 14 inch), which are displayed as positives on the videodisk. Arranged by Prints and Photographs Division filing series (that is, by negative size, primarily). Material is in the public domain. In some cases, the Prints and Photographs Division holds original photoprints for these negatives; these are cataloged in lots.

Washington, D.C., subjects: Cabin John Bridge; Arlington National Cemetery; Arlington House and the Temple of Fame; Sheridan Gate, Arlington National Cemetery; President Theodore Roosevelt at Chevy Chase, Maryland; Lenox Street, Chevy Chase, Maryland; White House, State Dining Room; interior and exterior

Detroit Publishing Company. Carnegie Library, Washington, D.C. Copyright 1906. Detroit Publishing Company Collection, Lot 9072–B.

LC-D4-19144

views of the Library of Congress, including the Main Reading Room and rotunda, statues and artwork; U.S. Capitol, exterior views and Statuary Hall; Corcoran Gallery; Mount Vernon (including some panoramic views), the mansion and main hall, the kitchen, flower gardens and grounds, an old English coach, and Washington's Tomb; Great Falls on the Potomac River; Willard's Hotel; Washington Monument; a copy of a drawing by Jules Guérin of "The Future Washington Monument and Gardens" (ca. 1900–1906); Riggs Library, Georgetown University; Connecticut Avenue; Dutch Reform Church (Grace Reformed Church); Carnegie Library; Rock Creek Road and zoo; Washington Navy Yard gun foundry and administrators; portrait of Assistant Navy Secretary Soley; Pennsylvania Avenue from the Treasury Building and west from Eleventh Street; the State, War, and Navy Building; St. Gaudens's *Grief* statue on the Adams grave, Rock Creek Cemetery; Union Station, exteriors, interiors, and switchyards; the

Detroit Publishing Company. The fords in Rock Creek Park, Washington, D.C. Copyright 1906. Detroit Publishing Company Collection, Lot 9072–F.

LC-D401-19151

Logan monument; Pan American Union Building; night views of Washington; Bureau of Engraving and Printing; Post Office Department (Old Post Office Building); Jackson statue; Lafayette Monument; Thomas statue; Garfield monument; naval monument; Smithsonian Institution; Old Soldiers' Home; U.S. Treasury Building; Emancipation statue; and high views of Washington from the Capitol dome.

Glass Transparencies

Primarily photographic views of the United States, ca. 1898–1912. Also includes reproductions of paintings. Approximately 2,900 glass transparencies (positive images), 16 × 21 cm (6 × 8 inch) to 28 × 36 cm (11 × 14 inch). The collection is arranged by Prints and Photographs Division filing series (that is, by negative size, primarily). Material is in the public domain. In some cases, original photoprints corresponding to these transparencies are held by the Prints and Photographs Division; original photoprints are cataloged in lots.

Detroit Publishing Company. Statue of Brig. Gen. Count Casimir Pulaski, Revolutionary War hero, at Pennsylvania Avenue and Thirteenth Street NW. Copyright 1911. Detroit Publishing Company Collection, Lot 9072–G.

LC-D4-72223

Detroit Publishing Company. Currency wagon at the U.S. Treasury Department. Copyright 1906. Detroit Publishing Company Collection, Lot 9072–H.
LC-D4-19148

Washington, D.C., subjects: Custis-Lee Mansion in Arlington (ca. 1890–1906); views of Mount Vernon and Washington's Tomb (ca. 1890–1920); Library of Congress, Neptune Fountain, and C. S. Pearce mural "Labor" (ca. 1897–1910); White House (section of a panorama), Red Room, and President's Office (ca. 1890–1905); U.S. Capitol, Statuary Hall (ca. 1880–1904); Corcoran Gallery sculpture hall (ca. 1897–1920); and a copy of the Rembrandt Peale portrait of George Washington (ca. 1900–1912).

Large Color Photographs

Photographic views of the United States and Mexico, copyright 1896–1905, taken by William Henry Jackson. Fifty-eight "AAC" color photoprints, larger than 21 × 28 cm, made by adding color lithographically to prints from black-and-white negatives. The photoprints are arranged by Prints and Photographs Division lot number, covering (1) the United States and Mexico, (2) Niagara Falls, and (3) Western States. Material is in the public domain.

Washington, D.C., subjects: View of the old mill on the Potomac River, Maryland (1899), and one of the Capitol (1898).

LOT 3000

COLLECTION NAME: Detroit Publishing Company Collection

SUBJECTS: Extensive photographic survey of the U.S. Navy, 1890–1900. Many views of all classes of ships at sea or in dry dock. Mechanical and gun installations. Group

photographs of officers and men; informal groups on duty and at play, resting, eating, sleeping. Living quarters on ships and in various navy yards. Portraits of officers on their ships and naval officers at their desks. Some copy photographs of Spanish-American War naval battles; some foreign ships.

Washington, D.C., subjects include: *Lot 3000–J:* Portraits of high-ranking naval personnel, most made in Washington, D.C., offices, ca. 1895–1900. Includes Admiral Walker; Admiral Sampson and family in front of residence; Assistant Secretaries of the Navy Soley, Allen, and Tracy. Some portraits made inside State, War, and Navy Building (now Old Executive Office Building). Some copy photographs of portraits made by other photographers. *Lot 3000–R:* Navy yards and shore installations in or near Washington, D.C., Charlestown, West Virginia, Hampton Roads, Virginia, Newport, Rhode Island, Philadelphia, Pennsylvania, and Pensacola, Florida. Ships at anchor or in dry dock, boarding and landing parties, U.S. Marine guards, carrier pigeons, anchor and shoe park, gun and other shops, Naval Reserve units. Includes twelve photographs of the U.S. Gun Shops in the Washington Navy Yard, including views of workers rifling a gun, the lathe room, gun carriage shop, shrinking pit, and an assembled gun.

NOTE: Most photographs identified.

DATE: Ca. 1890–ca. 1900

PHOTOGRAPHERS: William Henry Jackson and others.

PUBLISHER: Detroit Publishing Company

LC-D401-15616-L

PHYSICAL DESCRIPTION: Ca. 2,500 (*Lot 3000–J,* 34 items; *Lot 3000–R,* 94 items) silver gelatin photoprints, 21 × 28 cm.

ARRANGEMENT: Lot subdivided into subject categories.

SOURCE: Gift of the Colorado Historical Society, 1949.

LOT 9072

COLLECTION NAME: Detroit Publishing Company

SUBJECTS: *Lot 9072–A:* Miscellaneous buildings. Forty photographs show Union Station and switchyard; the Pan American Union Building; the Daughters of the American Revolution Building and Constitution Hall; the Senate Office Building; the General Post Office; Ford's Theater and the House Where Lincoln Died; the Key Mansion; the Treasury Building; the Auditor's Building and Bureau of Engraving and Printing; the Government Printing Office; Tudor Place, the Cannon House Office Building; St. John's Church; the Nourse House in Tennally Town (Tenleytown); the Willard Hotel; the Ebbitt House; Washington Navy Yard interiors; the Dutch Reform Church; the Patent Office; the Pension Building; the Old Soldiers' Home; the Post Office Department Building (now the Old Post Office); and the State, War, and Navy Department Building (now Old Executive Office Building). Includes one panoramic view. *Lot 9072–B:* Museums, galleries, Georgetown University. Seventeen photographs show the Carnegie Library; the Smithsonian Institution Building ("Cas-

tle"), Natural History Museum, and Arts and Industries Building; the new Corcoran Gallery of Art (interior and exterior views); and the Georgetown University and chapel. *Lot 9072–C:* U.S. Capitol. Thirty photographs show the Capitol in high views, and in views of the West and East Fronts; view of the Capitol from Union Station; the "Marble Room"; a scale model of the Capitol by Thomas U. Walter; model of Liberty (statue of Freedom, atop the Capitol dome); the President's Room; photographic copies of architect's renderings of proposed pools and gardens on the Mall below the West Front of the Capitol; the Rogers Doors; Statuary Hall and individual statues; the Senate Chamber; the House of Representatives; the Supreme Court Room; a copy of "Battle of Lake Erie," by Powell; the Bartholdi fountain; and the Botanic Garden. *Lot 9072–D:* The White House. Twenty-six photographs (including two panoramic photographs) show the Presidential Office; Green Room; State Dining Room; Blue Room; East Room; Cabinet Room; Red Room; North Front entrance; South Front and grounds; White House and grounds viewed from the War Building; east terrace viewed from the north lawn; east entrance; and lobby at the south entrance. *Lot 9072–E:* Library of Congress. Fifteen photographs show the entrance and pavilion; west front; Main Reading Room; copies of murals and mosaics; second story and stairway of the Great Hall; north staircase of the Great Hall; entrances to the south and north hall; gallery of the rotunda; north curtain corridor; stairway from the east corridor; Neptune Fountain; and high views of the Library from the west (Capitol) side. *Lot 9072–F:* Rock Creek Park and zoo. Ten photographs show scenes in Rock Creek

Detroit Publishing Company. Cabin John Bridge. Copyright 1900. Detroit Publishing Company Collection, Lot 9072–I.

LC-D4-13028

Detroit Publishing Company. Panoramic view of switchyards, Union Station, Washington, D.C. Copyright 1908. Detroit Publishing Company Collection, Lot 9072–A.

LC-D401-15616-C

LC-D401-15616-R

LC-USZ62-52254

LC-USZ62-52255

Detroit Publishing Company. Panoramic view of Washington, D.C., taken from the Washington Monument. Copyright 1911. Detroit Publishing Company Collection, Lot 9072–H.

LC-USZ62-52257

Park and the National Zoo, including the fords (creek crossing) in the park; pathways; Rock Creek Road; a bridge over Rock Creek; and camels and elk in the National Zoo. *Lot 9072–G:* Monuments and memorials. Twenty-eight photographs show the Washington Monument and Tidal Basin; the Emancipation statue; Sheridan statue; Farragut statue; Sherman Memorial; Sheridan Gate (Arlington Cemetery); Winfield Scott statue; Thomas statue; Pulaski statue and the National Theater; Kosciuszko statue; Jackson statue; Bartholdi fountain; and artists' renderings of proposed redesign of the Washington Monument, with added gardens and terrace. *Lot 9072–H:* Street scenes. Twenty-three photographs (including one panoramic view) show Washington, D.C., from the Washington Monument; views of Pennsylvania Avenue from the Capitol and Treasury Building; high views of the city

from the Smithsonian Institution Building, showing the Capitol and Post Office Department Building (now the Old Post Office); the capital skyline and Potomac River from Arlington; Connecticut Avenue at L Street NW (including the Stoneleigh Apartment House); Rhode Island Avenue; Connecticut Avenue and N Street NW and the Connecticut Avenue Bridge; Connecticut Avenue at Columbia Road; the Dupont Circle neighborhood; Thomas Circle; F Street NW and downtown scenes; the Department of Agriculture Building on the Mall; a U.S. Treasury currency wagon; President Theodore Roosevelt and family walking in Chevy Chase (1904); and an artist's rendering of a proposed redesign for the Mall and gardens around the Washington Monument. *Lot 9072–I:* Marine scenes, canal, and bridges. Five photographs show Cabin John Bridge; the C&O Canal towpath; Great Falls on the Potomac River;

sunset on the Potomac near Washington, with canal boats; and the swimming pool at Monument Park.

NOTE: Corresponding negatives are found in series LC–D4.

DATE: Ca. 1890s–ca. 1920s

PHOTOGRAPHERS: William Henry Jackson and others.

PUBLISHER: Detroit Publishing Company.

PHYSICAL DESCRIPTION: Ca. 250 silver gelatin and cyanotype photoprints and AAC process prints, 18 × 66 cm or smaller; most 18 × 23 cm.

ARRANGEMENT: Subdivided into nine subject groups.

LC-USZ62-52256

LC-D401-15676-E

LC-D401-15676-F

SOURCE: Copyright deposit by Detroit Publishing Company, 1901–12.

LOT 9075

COLLECTION NAME: Detroit Publishing Company Collection

SUBJECTS: Washington, D.C. Capitol and grounds; 1898 views of the Library of Congress interiors, exteriors, and Neptune Fountain; the Peace Monument; Smithsonian Institution Building (the "Castle"); White House; Washington Monument; Treasury Building; and Jackson and Lafayette statues in Lafayette Park.

DATE: 1898–1914

PHOTOGRAPHERS: William Henry Jackson and others.

PUBLISHER: Detroit Publishing Company.

PHYSICAL DESCRIPTION: 17 AAC color process prints and silver gelatin photoprints, 18 × 23 cm or smaller.

SOURCE: Copyright deposit, 1898–1902, and gift.

LOT 9097

COLLECTION NAME: Detroit Publishing Company Collection

SUBJECTS: Maryland views. Cabin John Bridge; the Chesapeake and Ohio Canal; Great Falls, Maryland; Hanging Rock on the South Branch of the Potomac; fishermen and boaters on the Potomac River; churches, the Maryland State Capitol, his-

toric homes, post office, Governor's Mansion, Court House, and old Treasury Building in Annapolis; springs, chapel, paths, in Pen-Mar Park. High views of the Potomac River at Williamsport; the State Senate Chamber in which George Washington surrendered his commission. Includes five panoramic views.

DATE: 1898–1914

PHOTOGRAPHERS: William Henry Jackson and others.

PUBLISHER: Detroit Publishing Company.

PHYSICAL DESCRIPTION: 44 silver gelatin and cyanotype photoprints, 18 × 44 cm or smaller.

SOURCE: Gift of the Colorado Historical Society, 1949.

Detroit Publishing Company. The family dining room at Mount Vernon, Virginia. Copyright 1912. Detroit Publishing Company Collection, Lot 9204–A.
LC-USZ62-91649

Detroit Publishing Company. The U.S. Capitol. Copyright 1905. Detroit Publishing Company Collection, Lot 12674.

LOT 9203

COLLECTION NAME: Detroit Publishing Company Collection

SUBJECTS: Virginia views. Hotel, Christ Church, Confederate Monument, Fairfax House, Braddock House, Carlyle House, North Fairfax and Cameron Streets, Theological Seminary, in Alexandria; Temple of Fame, Monument to the Unknown Soldier, Sheridan's Gate (National Cemetery), and Custis-Lee Mansion in Arlington. Lighthouses at Cape Henry. Monticello and University of Virginia in Charlottesville. The Homestead Hotel in Hot Springs. President Roosevelt reviewing the fleet at Hampton Roads. Includes two panoramic views.

DATE: 1898–1914

PHOTOGRAPHERS: William Henry Jackson and others.

PUBLISHER: Detroit Publishing Company.

PHYSICAL DESCRIPTION: 64 silver gelatin photoprints, 19 × 61 cm or smaller.

SOURCE: Gift of the Colorado Historical Society, 1949.

LOT 9204

COLLECTION NAME: Detroit Publishing Company Collection

SUBJECTS: Virginia views. Washington-area photographs in *Lot 9204–A:* Mount Vernon. Subjects include interior views of George Washington's bedroom and Martha Washington's bedroom; the Lafayette bedroom; River Room; Nellie Custis Room; family dining room; music room;

Martha's kitchen; the library; main hall; sitting room; west parlor; spinning house; bowling green; summer house; old tomb; flower gardens and grounds; the servants' quarters and barns; steamboat landing at Mount Vernon; views of the Potomac River; and the Mount Vernon trolley station and lunchroom. Includes one panoramic view.

DATE: 1898–1914

PHOTOGRAPHERS: William Henry Jackson and others.

PUBLISHER: Detroit Publishing Company.

PHYSICAL DESCRIPTION: 183 (*Lot 9204–A,* 50 items) silver gelatin photoprints, 18 × 27 cm.

ARRANGEMENT: Subdivided into seven groups by subject: *Lot 9204–A:* Mount Vernon; *Lot 9204–B:* Westover, Lower Brandon, Shirley; *Lot 9204–C:* Fort Monroe, Old Point Comfort; *Lot 9204–D:* Newport News; *Lot 9204–E:* Norfolk; *Lot 9204–F:* Jamestown, Williamsburg, Yorktown, Petersburg, Portsmouth; *Lot 9204–G:* Natural Bridge, Pine Beach, White Sulphur Springs, Magnesia Spring.

SOURCE: Gift of the Colorado Historical Society, 1949.

LOT 9756

COLLECTION NAME: Detroit Publishing Company Collection

SUBJECTS: Washington subjects include three interior views of the U.S. Gun Shops at the Washington Navy Yard. Other subjects include sailors or marines aboard the *Atlanta, Boston, Enterprise, New Hampshire,*

LC-USZ62-92784

LC-USZ62-92785

LC-USZ62-92786

San Francisco, and *Trenton.* Land drill in Brooklyn, New York; hospital, Engineering Department, and a reception room at the Naval Academy; and personnel training carrier pigeons near Newport, Rhode Island.

NOTE: Printed by the Library's Photo-duplication Service in 1963 from nitrate negatives subsequently destroyed.

DATE: Ca. 1895–ca. 1910

PHOTOGRAPHERS: William Henry Jackson and others.

PHYSICAL DESCRIPTION: 29 silver gelatin photoprints, 20 × 25 cm.

LOT 9757

COLLECTION NAME: Detroit Publishing Company Collection

SUBJECTS: City views. Washington subjects include one view of the Smithsonian Institution. Other subjects include the Detroit skyline, business district, Livingston Memorial, and Ambassador Bridge, between Windsor, Ontario, and Detroit; the Triumphal Arch, Lennox Lyceum exhibit, and Hell Gate Bridge in New York City.

NOTE: Printed by the Library's Photo-duplication Service in 1963 from nitrate negatives subsequently destroyed.

DATE: Ca. 1900–ca. 1910

PHOTOGRAPHERS: William Henry Jackson and others.

PHYSICAL DESCRIPTION: 14 silver gelatin photoprints, 20 × 25 cm.

LOT 12659

COLLECTION NAME: Detroit Publishing Company Collection

SUBJECTS: U.S. Capitol, Library of Congress, and vicinity. Great Hall of the Library of Congress; high views of the Library of Congress from the Capitol dome; views of the Capitol from the Library of Congress dome (1902); the Rogers Doors to the Capitol (1904); architectural renderings of proposed landscaping design for the Mall and Washington Monument.

DATE: 1902–4

PHOTOGRAPHERS: William H. Jackson and others.

Detroit Publishing Company. Theological Seminary, Alexandria, Virginia. Copyright 1906. Detroit Publishing Company Collection, Lot 9203.
LC-USZ62-91648

PHYSICAL DESCRIPTION: 10 silver gelatin and cyanotype photoprints and AAC color prints, 42 × 53 cm or smaller.

SOURCE: Copyright deposit by the Detroit Publishing Company, 1902–4.

LOT 12674

COLLECTION NAME: Detroit Publishing Company Collection

SUBJECTS: Wide-angle views of Union Station and tracks (1908); Mount Vernon and grounds (1901); the White House and gardens (1901); Arlington Cemetery, the Temple of Fame, Sheridan Memorial, and Lee Mansion (1900–1903); and the U.S. Capitol, East Front (1902). Color photolithograph panorama of Washington from Washington Monument (1914).

DATE: 1900–1914

PHOTOGRAPHERS: William H. Jackson and others.

PHYSICAL DESCRIPTION: 11 silver gelatin photoprints and color AAC process prints, 25 × 121 cm or smaller.

SOURCE: Copyright deposit by the Detroit Publishing Company, and gift.

Detroit Publishing Company. Mount Vernon trolley station and restaurant, ca. 1912. Detroit Publishing Company Collection, Lot 9204–A.
LC-D4-72839

Dunlap Society Microfiche Collection of Architecture of Washington, D.C.

The Dunlap Society was founded in 1974 to broaden and encourage the study and awareness of American art. It has as its goal the establishment of a visual archive where researchers can acquire from a single source microfiche, slides, and photographs. The preparation of *The Architecture of Washington, D.C.*, edited by Bates Lowry, in 2 volumes (Washington: Dunlap Society, 1976–79) was the pilot project for this archive. Documentation of eighteen Washington, D.C., buildings, groups of buildings, and monumental structures, totaling over 3,500 images, relied heavily on the visual collections of the Library of Congress.

The illustrations were reproduced from the collections of numerous (mostly local) repositories and provide researchers with the convenience of sampling materials held in dozens of institutions. The microfiche reproduces historical photographs, architectural drawings, reproductions, and recently commissioned photographs to document the Washington buildings listed below. The microfiche carries a maximum of forty-five images per sheet and can be scanned without the use of a microfiche viewer if necessary. Microfiche illustration captions bear information about the collection, storage location, catalog number, or copy negative number of the image reproduced, when that information was available at the time of publication. Copies of most images can be obtained from the Dunlap Society. Alternately, researchers can obtain copies directly from the custodial institution that holds a particular item.

The accompanying text provides extensive information about the history, location, design, construction, alteration, renovation, and restoration dates for each building. Lists of building materials, building costs, and building and room dimensions are provided as well.

View of the east and north sides of ''Old State,'' adjacent to the colonnade designed by Robert Mills for the U.S. Treasury Building, ca. 1860. Reproduced in the Dunlap Society microfiche The Architecture of Washington, D.C., *volume 1, chapter 6, fiche B9. (Original in Lot 5341,' Prints and Photographs Division.)*

LC-USZ62-15248

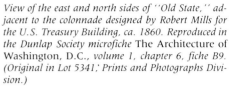

Front view of the Octagon House (now the headquarters of the American Institute of Architects). Reproduced in the Dunlap Society microfiche The Architecture of Washington, D.C., *volume 1, chapter 2, fiche 1. (From the Washington, D.C., Geographical File, Prints and Photographs Division.)*

LC-USZ62-25367

CONTENTS:

The Farm Security Administration (FSA)-Office of War Information (OWI) Collection is perhaps the most well-known and most popular collection in the Prints and Photographs Division. The photographic products of two distinct offices and projects, the collections are stored together in the division, with the source of individual photographs or projects identifiable by photographer, date, and negative series code. In some cases where the OWI reproduced FSA material or where full caption information is absent, it is difficult to tell which agency was responsible for what work.

Roy E. Stryker, an economics instructor at Columbia University, was hired in 1935 to direct a project that would document American life in the Great Depression of the 1930s, under the auspices of the Resettlement Administration. A year later, that agency became the Farm Security Administration, with Stryker still in a directorial role. Some of the most famous names in documentary photography were hired by the FSA, including Walker Evans, Ben Shahn, Arthur Rothstein, Marion Post Wolcott, Russell Lee, Dorothea Lange, John Vachon, Carl Mydans, and Jack Delano. Agricultural subjects, sharecroppers, and migrant workers were the primary interest of the photographers, but they photographed other aspects of rural life as well as living conditions in urban areas. Once the United States entered World War II, the focus turned to the impact of war on domestic life and military preparedness activities. In 1942, a new agency, the Office of War Information, was formed to serve the specific photographic propaganda needs of the wartime government. Approximately 164,000 negatives and 75,000 photoprints, along with color transparencies and FSA assignment files and correspondence, were transferred to the OWI.

In 1942 there was a clear shift in the content and tone of the photographs produced by government photographers, some of whom had been hired under the FSA. Instead of picturing a people surviving under the desperate living conditions brought by the Depression, they presented a picture of a strong and optimistic America, unified by its wartime efforts and willing to sacrifice for victory. Many new photographers were hired, and photographs were purchased from and contributed by commercial, industrial, and government sources for use in OWI publications, exhibits, and filmstrips. Soldiers on leave and in training, government workers and their temporary housing and office buildings, progress made to integrate blacks into the war effort, educational efforts, improved housing and living conditions, shipbuilding, trucking, and railroads—all were presented in a spirit of patriotism and American pride. Between 1944 and 1947, the OWI transferred to the Library of Congress much of its collections, including photographs, sound recordings, and some research materials. In addition to original and copy negatives and photoprints held in the Prints and Photographs Division, 50,000 foreign and domestic radio broadcasts are held in the Motion Picture, Broadcasting, and Recorded Sound Division. Related material may be found in the Library of Congress in the Manuscript Division and the American Folklife Center.

ORGANIZATION OF THE FSA-OWI COLLECTION

Mounted and captioned photographs were cataloged in related groups, usually on the basis of geographical location, photographer, and subject. Most of these lots were microfilmed, and the microfilmed images provide the only direct access by photographer or specific geographical area. The photoprints are available as a browsing file in the Prints and Photographs Reading Room, arranged first by geographical section of the country (for instance, northwest or northeast) and within that section, by broad subject categories (for instance, housing, social activities, or hospitals). This browsing file arrangement provides access to single subjects (such as churches) under a broad geographical location (for instance, churches in the southeast United States), or provides the means to compare the work of many different photographers on many different assignments in a broad geographical location (for example, all the work done in the southern United States). Negative numbers carry codes or suffixes that help to identify the work as either FSA or OWI photographs.

For the purposes of identifying the Washington, D.C., and some nearby Virginia and Maryland subjects, descriptions of the photographs cataloged as lots (and available on microfilm) follow. Because FSA-OWI staff members believed captions played an important role in conveying the meaning of these photographs, their language has often been retained here in describing the subject matter.

Reginald Hotchkiss. ''Farm Security Administration (later Office of War Information) photograph laboratory in the Auditor's Building, Washington, D.C.'' View of chemical mixing room, January 1941. FSA-OWI Collection, Lot 2212.

LC-USZ62-92478

FARM SECURITY ADMINISTRATION TEXTUAL RECORDS

Farm Security Administration: A Guide to Textual Records in the Library of Congress (Washington: Library of Congress, 1985), prepared by Annette Melville of the Prints and Photographs Division on the occasion of the fiftieth anniversary of the FSA, accompanies twenty-three reels of microfilm copies of these textual records. This pamphlet provides a chronology of the FSA and OWI and describes the scope and contents of the extensive collection of correspondence between Roy Stryker and his photographers in the field, as well as office files, captions, supplementary reference files that provide background on particular assignments; and scrapbooks kept by the agency. The guide notes the contents of specific boxes of records and their corresponding microfilm reels and gives bibliographic information about other published guides to materials in other repositories of FSA-OWI textual records.

REFERENCES

A list of books about the Farm Security Administration, books about individual photographers who worked for the FSA, and books illustrated with FSA photographs is available in the Prints and Photographs Reading Room. Similar bibliographic information is provided in Melville, no. 76, pp. 107–8.

Vanderbilt, no. 219, pp. 54–55, and nos. 553–55, pp. 117–20.

Melville, no. 76, pp. 107–9, and no. 177, pp. 260–61.

Marjorie Collins. "At 7 A.M., on June 21st, the day before stricter gas rationing was enforced, cars were pouring into this gas station on upper Wisconsin [Avenue NW]." July 1942. FSA-OWI Collection, Lot 6. LC-USF34-100563-E

COLOR TRANSPARENCIES ON VIDEODISK

The Library of Congress Non-Print Optical Disk Pilot Program in the Prints and Photographs Division includes videodisk copies of color transparencies produced by FSA and OWI photographers. The Washington, D.C., subjects are described below. Instructions for searching the videodisk and its accompanying computer data base of caption information are available in the Prints and Photographs Reading Room.

Farm Security Administration Color Transparencies

From a total collection of about 645 color slides and transparencies in 35 mm to 11 × 13 cm (4 × 5 inch) formats, fewer than ten are Washington subjects, all made in 1941–42. They include Royden Dixon's photographs of black troops at the 1942 Memorial Day parade; and Louise Rosskam's photographs of row houses in Southwest Washington, children playing in the streets, Shulman's market in southwest Washington, a laundry, barbershop, and store, and other residences in the city. An unidentified photographer took pictures of children aiming sticks as guns.

Office of War Information Color Transparencies

From a total collection of about 965 color slides and transparencies in 35 mm to 11 × 13 cm (4 × 5 inch) formats, about fifty photographs made in Washington and the nearby metropolitan area between 1941 and about 1945 include John Collier's pictures of a sailor and girl at the Tomb of the Unknown Soldier in Arlington Cemetery and his photographs of the Pan American Union Building. John Rous photographed black, white, and Chinese Boy Scouts in front of the Capitol and the visit of the sons of King Ibn Saud of Saudi Arabia to the city, after a tour of irrigation projects in the United States. Photographs unidentified as to photographer include the National Gallery of Art; Union Station, the Columbus Statue, and people in a nearby park; a soldier and woman in a park near the Senate Office Building; the War Department Building at Twenty-first Street and Virginia Avenue NW; Memorial Bridge, looking toward the Lincoln Memorial from Virginia; the U.S. Supreme Court Building; construction of the Department of Health, Education, and Welfare building; and a Color Guard of black engineers at Fort Belvoir, Virginia, and soldiers in training there.

LOT 1 (microfilm)

COLLECTION NAME: FSA-OWI Collection

SUBJECTS: Fort Belvoir, Virginia. The induction and training in the U.S. Army of George Camblair of Washington, D.C. Physical exam and other routines. Issuing of equipment, training, and drilling. Driving a tank, working on KP duty. Recreation, playing piano, on furlough with his family and his girlfriend.

DATE: September 1942

PHOTOGRAPHERS: Jack Delano.

SOURCE: Office of War Information.

LOT 5 (microfilm)

COLLECTION NAME: FSA-OWI Collection

SUBJECTS: Washington, D.C. Fish market and stores on waterfront, including workers and detail shots of seafood.

DATE: March 1942

PHOTOGRAPHERS: John Ferrell, Arthur Rothstein, and Reginald Hotchkiss.

SOURCE: Farm Security Administration.

LOT 6 (microfilm)

COLLECTION NAME: FSA-OWI Collection

SUBJECTS: Washington, D.C. Public and commercial reaction to the automobile, gasoline, and tire shortage immediately before and after rationing was initiated. Service stations, automobile sales rooms, repair shops, parking facilities. Changing tires and oil; tire inspection, repair, retreading, "vulcanizing." Car repair. Mechanics, service station attendant, car owners.

DATE: May 1942

PHOTOGRAPHERS: John Collier, Jr., and Marjory Collins.

SOURCE: Farm Security Administration.

LOT 24 (microfilm)

COLLECTION NAME: FSA-OWI Collection

SUBJECTS: Washington, D.C. Rubber, metal, and paper salvage campaign. Wholesale junk yard, scrap materials, workers "cleaning" metal, mechanically baling paper, pressing, collecting, and transferring metal to freight cars. Detail of junk company, children making door-to-door canvas. Official salvage depot. Detail of salvaged articles. Portraits.

DATE: May 1942

PHOTOGRAPHERS: Marjory Collins.

SOURCE: Farm Security Administration.

LOT 29 (microfilm)

COLLECTION NAME: FSA-OWI Collection

SUBJECTS: Washington, D.C. Photographs of textures for use as backgrounds for filmstrip and motion picture titles. Veined leaves, dried mud patterns, flagstone paving, stucco and pebbled stucco, stone and stone-and-concrete walls, a variety of tree barks, brick, metal concrete reinforcements, woven straw and reed, corrugated board and clouds.

DATE: September 1942

PHOTOGRAPHERS: John Ferrell.

SOURCE: Farm Security Administration.

LOT 33 (microfilm)

COLLECTION NAME: FSA-OWI Collection

SUBJECTS: Washington, D.C. Activities that indicate something of the scope and function of a self-help exchange. Men and women working for scrip to buy clothing and other necessities before seeking employment. Unloading salvaged materials. Bakery, kitchen, cafeteria, sewing room, shoe, radio, paint and print shops, salesroom. Members being interviewed, given physical examinations, buying clothes.

DATE: January 1942

PHOTOGRAPHERS: John Collier, Jr.

SOURCE: Farm Security Administration.

LOT 35 (microfilm)

COLLECTION NAME: FSA-OWI Collection

SUBJECTS: Washington, D.C. Swedish journalists on tour in the United States attending Secretary of State Hull's press conference and at the embassy with the Swedish ambassador.

DATE: July 1942

PHOTOGRAPHERS: John Vachon.

SOURCE: Office of War Information.

LOT 66 (microfilm)

COLLECTION NAME: FSA-OWI Collection

SUBJECTS: Miscellaneous Washington views made throughout the year in snowy, rainy, and fair weather. Public and private buildings, theaters, parks, transportation. Indoor and outdoor recreation and sports, national folk festival, dancing, walkathon, sightseeing. Scrap salvage rally, Memorial Day parade, Easter Sunday. Street scenes, shoppers, signs. Portraits.

DATE: 1942

PHOTOGRAPHERS: John Ferrell.

SOURCE: Farm Security Administration.

John Ferrell. Interior of a drugstore on Fourteenth Street NW. March 1942. FSA-OWI Collection, Lot 66.

LC-USF34-11473-D

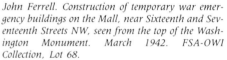

John Ferrell. Construction of temporary war emergency buildings on the Mall, near Sixteenth and Seventeenth Streets NW, seen from the top of the Washington Monument. March 1942. FSA-OWI Collection, Lot 68.

LC-USF34-11450-D

LOT 68 (microfilm)

COLLECTION NAME: FSA-OWI Collection

SUBJECTS: Washington, D.C. Construction of temporary emergency office space for the federal government on the Mall and in the downtown area. Clearing away earth and pavement, removing a tree to be transplanted, mixing and pouring concrete, nailing up walls. Asbestos siding, cast-iron pipe, nails, concrete forms, wire, cement, bricks, lumber. Power shovel, concrete mixer, tractor, and earth mover. Laborers and skilled workers on the job and at lunchtime.

DATE: February 1942

PHOTOGRAPHERS: John Collier, Jr., and John Ferrell.

SOURCE: Farm Security Administration.

LOT 72 (microfilm)

COLLECTION NAME: FSA-OWI Collection

SUBJECTS: Arlington, Virginia. Developing a subdivision for middle income groups. Exteriors of unfinished and completed houses. Neighborhood views.

DATE: May 1942

PHOTOGRAPHERS: John Collier, Jr.

SOURCE: Farm Security Administration.

LOT 73 (microfilm)

COLLECTION NAME: FSA-OWI Collection

SUBJECTS: Naval and Armored Force personnel. Portraits of a lieutenant made at the Naval Air Station, Anacostia, and of a tank driver at Fort Belvoir, Virginia. Binoculars, protective helmet, goggles.

DATE: August 1942

PHOTOGRAPHERS: John Collier, Jr.

SOURCE: Farm Security Administration.

LOT 77 (microfilm)

COLLECTION NAME: FSA-OWI Collection

SUBJECTS: Washington, D.C. Christmas evening in the home of an army doctor in Anacostia. Dinner table at the end of the meal, guests singing around the piano, dancing, mother preparing baby for bed.

DATE: December 1941

PHOTOGRAPHERS: John Collier, Jr.

SOURCE: Farm Security Administration.

LOT 81 (microfilm)

COLLECTION NAME: FSA-OWI Collection

SUBJECTS: Falls Church, Virginia. The living room at Christmastime in the home of a federal employee who works in Washington. Decorations and tree, guests, family, dogs. Children playing with new toys. Dolls and carriage, stuffed animals, books, games, blackboard, bicycle, tricycle, airplane, tank. Little girl trying to play piano.

DATE: December 1941

PHOTOGRAPHERS: John Collier, Jr.

SOURCE: Farm Security Administration.

LOT 83 (microfilm)

COLLECTION NAME: FSA-OWI Collection

SUBJECTS: Washington, D.C. National Airport at Gravelly Point. The runway and field. Administration building, lobby, waiting room, observation tower, telegraph desk, ticket office, visitors, passengers, airplanes. Tucking baggage and freight on a small carrier. Signaling a plane in.

DATE: July 1941

PHOTOGRAPHERS: Jack Delano.

SOURCE: Farm Security Administration.

LOT 85 (microfilm)

COLLECTION NAME: FSA-OWI Collection

SUBJECTS: Washington, D.C. Red Cross personnel and activities. Portraits of Otto Lund, director of the District of Columbia Red Cross, at his desk. Instructing taxi drivers on use of cabs for emergency ambulance service, nurse's aide at children's hospital, Norwegian volunteer unit wrapping bandages.

DATE: June 1942

PHOTOGRAPHERS: Marjory Collins.

SOURCE: Foreign Information Service, U.S. Office of the Coordinator of Information.

LOT 86 (microfilm)

COLLECTION NAME: FSA-OWI Collection

SUBJECTS: Washington, D.C. Children, adults, and servicemen Christmas shopping in Woolworth's five-and-ten-cent store. Toy, card, stationery, wrapping paper, and decoration counters. Saleswomen.

DATE: December 1941

PHOTOGRAPHERS: John Collier, Jr.

SOURCE: Farm Security Administration.

LOT 91 (microfilm)

COLLECTION NAME: FSA-OWI Collection

SUBJECTS: Christmas rush in the Greyhound bus terminal. Black and white servicemen and civilians. Ticket window, waiting room, telegraph offices, lockers, loading and unloading bus. Portraits.

DATE: December 1941

PHOTOGRAPHERS: John Collier, Jr., and John Vachon.

SOURCE: Farm Security Administration.

LOT 100 (microfilm)

COLLECTION NAME: FSA-OWI Collection

SUBJECTS: Washington, D.C. Registration for wartime sugar rationing at a public school. School teachers serving as volunteer registrars securing necessary information and explaining Office of Price Administration (OPA) regulations to black and white citizens making applications. Detail of war ration book, one showing stamps.

DATE: May 1942

PHOTOGRAPHERS: Marjory Collins.

SOURCE: Farm Security Administration.

LOT 102 (microfilm)

COLLECTION NAME: FSA-OWI Collection

SUBJECTS: Greenbelt, Maryland. Federal housing project in a planned community. Apartments and houses, cooperative stores, theater, school and community building, library, recreational facilities. Garden, health clinic, church services, parking facilities, underpass. Cooking demonstration, sewing, getting out a community paper. Residents commuting to Washington in a car pool.

DATE: 1940–42

PHOTOGRAPHERS: Marjory Collins and John Vachon.

SOURCE: Farm Security Administration and the Foreign Information Service, U.S. Office of the Coordinator of Information.

LOT 119 (microfilm)

COLLECTION NAME: FSA-OWI Collection

SUBJECTS: Washington, D.C. Wartime construction in vicinity of federal government buildings. Construction of bridge and road near Washington Monument. Bulldozer, pile driver, transit concrete mixer, air hammer, hoppers, forms, stakes, piles, welded steel reinforcements. Finishing curbs and road surface. Engineer, workmen, stonecutter.

DATE: February–May 1942

PHOTOGRAPHERS: John Ferrell.

SOURCE: Farm Security Administration.

LOT 155 (microfilm)

COLLECTION NAME: FSA-OWI Collection

SUBJECTS: Washington, D.C. Frederick Douglass housing project for blacks in Anacostia. Aerial views. Boys playing, little girls' dancing class. Babies napping in sun. Interior of home, mother preparing dinner, washing daughter, saying grace at table.

DATE: July 1942

PHOTOGRAPHERS: Gordon Parks.

SOURCE: Farm Security Administration.

LOT 156 (microfilm)

COLLECTION NAME: FSA-OWI Collection

SUBJECTS: Story of Ella Watson, black government charwoman for twenty-six years, and miscellaneous scenes in a black neighborhood. Going to work at 5:30 P.M. Cleaning offices, halls, toilets, and returning home at 2:30 A.M. At home with three grandchildren and adopted daughter she supports on salary of $1,080 per year (minus war bond and other deductions). Neighborhood stores. Attending service at St. Martin's spiritual church during special ceremonies.

DATE: August 1942

PHOTOGRAPHERS: Gordon Parks.

SOURCE: Farm Security Administration.

Gordon Parks. ''Government charwoman,'' Mrs. Ella Watson. August 1942. FSA-OWI Collection, Lot 156.

LC-USF34-13407-C

Gordon Parks. ''Negro woman in her bedroom, southwest Washington.'' November 1942. FSA-OWI Collection, Lot 160.

LC-USW3-11047-C

Gordon Parks. ''Two Negro boys shooting marbles in front of their homes [in] Washington, southwest section.'' November 1942. FSA-OWI Collection, Lot 160.

LC-USW3-11064-C

Gordon Parks. ''A family that lives in the southwest area.'' June 1942. FSA-OWI Collection, Lot 160.

LC-USF34-13302-C

Marjorie Collins. ''Occidental Hotel restaurant, on Pennsylvania Avenue, at noon. The board lists shows in town.'' July 1943. FSA-OWI Collection, Lot 186.
LC-USF34-100639-E

Marjorie Collins. ''Customers in the Giant food shopping center on Wisconsin Avenue.'' June–July 1942. FSA-OWI Collection, Lot 185.
LC-USF34-100322-E

Marjorie Collins. ''Line outside Scholl's cafeteria on Connecticut Avenue at 6 P.M. Over 100 people stand in line and are served at the rate of one every minute.'' August 1942. FSA-OWI Collection, Lot 186.
LC-USW3-6821-D

LOT 157 (microfilm)

COLLECTION NAME: FSA-OWI Collection

SUBJECTS: Washington, D.C. Civilian defense activities among blacks in the nation's capital. Meetings of auxiliary police and air raid wardens. Portrait of a junior air raid warden at the Frederick Douglass housing project.

DATE: July–August 1942

PHOTOGRAPHERS: Gordon Parks.

SOURCE: Farm Security Administration.

LOT 158 (microfilm)

COLLECTION NAME: FSA-OWI Collection

SUBJECTS: Washington, D.C. Demolition of private property along Independence Avenue opposite the Smithsonian Institution, predominantly a government area, to make way for government housing. Exteriors and interiors of houses, church. Construction materials, personal belongings left behind. Children playing in debris. Black wrecking crew.

DATE: June 1942

PHOTOGRAPHERS: Gordon Parks.

SOURCE: Farm Security Administration.

LOT 159 (microfilm)

COLLECTION NAME: FSA-OWI Collection

SUBJECTS: Washington, D.C. Russian War Anniversary Benefit at Watergate. Chorus and Paul Robeson on stage. Audience in amphitheater and in canoes on Potomac River. Paul Robeson backstage with autograph hunters, wife of Russian ambassador, Melvyn Douglas, and conductor and soloist of balalaika orchestra.

DATE: June 1942

PHOTOGRAPHERS: Gordon Parks.

SOURCE: Farm Security Administration.

LOT 160 (microfilm)

COLLECTION NAME: FSA-OWI Collection

SUBJECTS: Washington, D.C. Housing accommodations for low-income blacks in the nation's capital. Row houses, wooden structures, and shacks, many with no inside plumbing, gas, or electricity. Drawing water in yard, lighting oil lamps, preparing meals on dilapidated stoves. Outside privies. Children playing in alleys, yards piled with rubbish and debris, child ill after rat bite. Children's birthday party, aged peanut vendor. Portraits.

DATE: June–November 1942

PHOTOGRAPHERS: Gordon Parks.

SOURCE: Office of War Information.

LOT 163 (microfilm)

COLLECTION NAME: FSA-OWI Collection

SUBJECTS: Washington, D.C. International student assembly. Delegates from England, Egypt, Sweden, India, the Netherlands, East Indies, Africa, Free France, Canada, USSR, Philippines, Czechoslovakia, Poland, Australia, Turkey, Afghanistan, Iran, New Zealand, Scotland, Korea, Syria, Haiti, Iceland, and South America. In plenary and general sessions. Having lunch at American University, at Chinese Embassy, leaving White House. Eleanor Roosevelt, Robert R. Jackson, William L. Batt, Walter Nash.

DATE: September 1942

PHOTOGRAPHERS: Jack Delano and Gordon Parks.

SOURCE: Office of War Information.

LOT 166 (microfilm)

COLLECTION NAME: FSA-OWI Collection

SUBJECTS: Washington, D.C. Howard University. Aerial view of campus. Students changing class. Library, Douglass Hall. Male students lounging on dormitory steps. Thanksgiving dinner in home of university president. Commencement.

DATE: 1942

PHOTOGRAPHERS: Gordon Parks and John Collier, Jr.

SOURCE: Farm Security Administration, U.S. Office of the Coordinator of Information, and Office of War Information.

LOT 183 (microfilm)

COLLECTION NAME: FSA-OWI Collection

SUBJECTS: Washington, D.C. District Grocery Store (DGS) warehouse, in an area easily accessible to railroad, river, and truck transportation. Unloading into warehouse, filling orders for the 200 member stores. Meat cutting, candling eggs, grading fresh fruit and vegetables, checking merchandise, ripening bananas. Fish. U.S. inspector grading meat. Engineer and refrigerator plant.

DATE: July 1942

PHOTOGRAPHERS: Marjory Collins.

SOURCE: Farm Security Administration.

LOT 184 (microfilm)

COLLECTION NAME: FSA-OWI Collection

SUBJECTS: Washington, D.C. Farmers' market. Unloading produce. Vendors' stands. Preparing vegetables for sale. Melons, peppers, tomatoes, peaches, lima beans.

DATE: July 1942

PHOTOGRAPHERS: Marjory Collins.

SOURCE: Farm Security Administration.

LOT 185 (microfilm)

COLLECTION NAME: FSA-OWI Collection

SUBJECTS: Washington, D.C. Giant Food Store, a chain, self-service market, handling all types of food and household appliances. Individuals and families shopping with war ration book no. 1. Sales clerks and checkers. Fresh fruit and vegetables, canned and bottled products, cereals, crackers, poultry and seafood. Ceiling prices, go-cart shopping baskets. Customers on ramp, loading automobiles.

DATE: June–July 1942

PHOTOGRAPHERS: Marjory Collins.

SOURCE: Farm Security Administration.

LOT 186 (microfilm)

COLLECTION NAME: FSA-OWI Collection

SUBJECTS: Washington, D.C. Lunchtime in the wartime capital. Black and white government workers eating on Washington Monument grounds near Department of Agriculture. Coca Cola stand. Servicemen and civilians in S&W Cafeteria, People's Drug Store, Occidental Hotel. Cashier, waiter, hat rack.

DATE: July 1942

PHOTOGRAPHERS: Marjory Collins.

SOURCE: Farm Security Administration.

LOT 187 (microfilm)

COLLECTION NAME: FSA-OWI Collection

SUBJECTS: Washington, D.C. Various recreational activities of servicemen and black and white civilians. Amateur baseball on the Ellipse. Wading and picnicking in Rock Creek Park. Swimming, sunbathing at municipal pool and Hains Point. Horseback riding, cycling, playing tennis, fishing, taking pictures. Washington Monument. White House, Capitol, and Lincoln Memorial in background.

DATE: June–July 1942

PHOTOGRAPHERS: Marjory Collins.

SOURCE: Farm Security Administration.

LOT 188 (microfilm)

COLLECTION NAME: FSA-OWI Collection

SUBJECTS: Washington, D.C. Tourist homes and boardinghouses in Washington and just across the District line in Maryland. Highway from Montgomery County, Maryland. Tourist signs, lawns, exteriors of homes. Proprietress. Residence club, formerly a private mansion. Mail in the hall, parking space and refuse in rear. Dilapidated bathroom. Women going to work through park. Night views.

DATE: June–July 1942

PHOTOGRAPHERS: Marjory Collins.

SOURCE: Farm Security Administration.

LOT 194 (microfilm)

COLLECTION NAME: FSA-OWI Collection

SUBJECTS: Washington, D.C. Red Cross activities directly related to the war effort. Student nurses being admitted to the Red Cross Reserve Corps. Volunteers translating in the Foreign Inquiry section, working with soldiers in the Family Service Division, sorting and preparing wool to be reprocessed. Conducting first aid class aboard a Potomac River boat. Carrying civilian employees to the U.S. Army adjutant general's office.

DATE: June 1942

PHOTOGRAPHERS: Marjory Collins.

SOURCE: Foreign Information Service, U.S. Office of the Coordinator of Information.

LOT 195 (microfilm)

COLLECTION NAME: FSA-OWI Collection

SUBJECTS: Washington, D.C. Shortwave broadcasts from the International Student Assembly. Norwegian, Italian, French, Chinese, Australian, Peruvian, Cuban, Polish, Chilean, and Colombian delegates recording short talks in their native language to be broadcast after censorship to Nazi-held territory. Governor of East Java speaking.

DATE: September 1942

PHOTOGRAPHERS: Gordon Parks and Dan Nichols.

SOURCE: Foreign Information Service, U.S. Office of the Coordinator of Information.

LOT 198 (microfilm)

COLLECTION NAME: FSA-OWI Collection

SUBJECTS: Washington, D.C. U.S. legations of Australia, Turkey, the Netherlands, Iceland, Egypt, the Union of South Africa, Ireland, and Switzerland. Ministers and their families at home and in chanceries with staffs.

DATE: March–July 1942

PHOTOGRAPHERS: Marjory Collins.

SOURCE: Office of War Information.

LOT 204 (microfilm)

COLLECTION NAME: FSA-OWI Collection

SUBJECTS: Arlington, Virginia. Farm Security Administration trailer camp project for blacks. Trailer exteriors and interiors and expansible units. Bed, kitchen, dining and living rooms. Sanitary and laundry facilities in community building. Occupant working in tiny victory garden. Children playing. Project manager and secretary. Overall views showing adjacent school and houses.

DATE: April 1942

PHOTOGRAPHERS: Marjory Collins.

SOURCE: Farm Security Administration.

LOT 207 (microfilm)

COLLECTION NAME: FSA-OWI Collection

SUBJECTS: Library of Congress, Washington, D.C. Asiatic and Photostatic Divisions. Chief of Asiatic Division and staff of Chinese and American white and black employees. Views of stacks and open volumes. Microfilming Chinese documents. Comparing reproduction with original. Microfilm reader.

DATE: June 1942

PHOTOGRAPHERS: Royden Dixon.

SOURCE: Foreign Information Service, U.S. Office of the Coordinator of Information.

LOT 216 (microfilm)

COLLECTION NAME: FSA-OWI Collection

SUBJECTS: Washington, D.C. Activities in black elementary, junior high, and technical high schools. Classes in reading, science, sewing, cooking, drafting, machine shop, car repairs, bricklaying, gym, and dancing. Making airplane models, listening to radio broadcast on South America, collecting scrap metal and newspapers, buying war stamps. First aid, student council, free lunch. Recreational activities in school vicinity. One of the teachers in the classroom and at home with her family.

DATE: March 1942

PHOTOGRAPHERS: Marjory Collins.

SOURCE: U.S. Office of the Coordinator of Information.

LOT 233 (microfilm)

COLLECTION NAME: FSA-OWI Collection

SUBJECTS: Washington, D.C., and vicinity. Turkish journalists visiting America as guests of the OWI during the October 29, 1942, celebration of the nineteenth anniversary of the Turkish proclamation. At Tomb of the Unknown Soldier in Arlington, Virginia, and at the home of George Washington at Mount Vernon, Virginia. With Col. William Donovan, head of the Office of Strategic Services, in front of his home.

DATE: October 1942

PHOTOGRAPHERS: Gordon Parks.

SOURCE: Office of War Information.

LOT 234 (microfilm)

COLLECTION NAME: FSA-OWI Collection

SUBJECTS: Washington, D.C. Portraits of Col. A. D. Ennis, chief of the U.S. Army Air Corps, Office of Public Relations, at his desk in the Munitions Building.

DATE: April 1942

PHOTOGRAPHERS: Marjory Collins.

SOURCE: Farm Security Administration.

LOT 235 (microfilm)

COLLECTION NAME: FSA-OWI Collection

SUBJECTS: Washington, D.C. High school students visit the nation's capital under the auspices of the Bureau of University Travel and the National Capital School Visitor's Council. On the U.S. Capitol grounds, calling on congressmen, at the Library of Congress, U.S. Supreme Court, National Gallery of Art, and U.S. Maritime Commission. Attending a hearing of the Naval Affairs Committee. With Mrs. Roosevelt in the White House, at the Pan American Union, and at a party at American University.

DATE: February 1942

PHOTOGRAPHERS: Marjory Collins.

SOURCE: Office of War Information.

LOT 238 (microfilm)

COLLECTION NAME: FSA-OWI Collection

SUBJECTS: Washington, D.C. Wartime activities of blacks and miscellaneous views. Two second lieutenants recruiting for the Women's Army Auxiliary Corps (WAAC). First aid class sponsored by Civilian Defense neighborhood group, official salvage collector, waterboy on construction job. A family living in an ADA housing project. Gas station, attendant and coal truckers. Boys reading funny papers. Workers and loafers around the waterfront and seafood restaurants.

DATE: October–November 1942

PHOTOGRAPHERS: Gordon Parks.

SOURCE: Office of War Information.

LOT 253 (microfilm)

COLLECTION NAME: FSA-OWI Collection

SUBJECTS: Montgomery County, Olney, and Silver Spring, Maryland. Election day in suburbs of Washington, D.C. Outside the polls, inside Election Board office. Voting booths, waiting lines, instructing black citizen in the use of a voting machine. Farmers sharing trucks and cars on market day.

DATE: November 1942

PHOTOGRAPHERS: Marjory Collins.

SOURCE: Office of War Information.

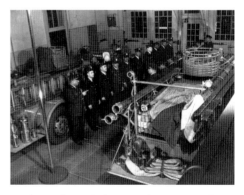

Gordon Parks. "Fire house station No. 4. Each evening, firemen from the oncoming platoon and the one going off duty line up and receive instructions for the day and the rest of the week from Lt. Mills." The station had an all-black platoon. January 1943. FSA-OWI Collection, Lot 270. LC-USW3-13615-C

LOT 269 (microfilm)

COLLECTION NAME: FSA-OWI Collection

SUBJECTS: Washington, D.C. Activities of black civic groups. Delegation of labor leaders and ministers on their way to the Capitol to protest the filibuster against the poll tax reform. Mass meeting of black and white citizens held in church to protest action of Capital Transit Company, which refused to hire blacks as operators on public carriers. Audience and speakers. Priority Ramblers, singers from the United Federal Workers of America (UFWA), an affiliate of the Congress of Industrial Organizations (CIO), entertaining.

DATE: November 1942

PHOTOGRAPHERS: Gordon Parks.

SOURCE: Office of War Information.

LOT 270 (microfilm)

COLLECTION NAME: FSA-OWI Collection

SUBJECTS: Washington, D.C. Fire Engine House No. 4, one of the separate black units in the District of Columbia. Lineup for instruction and orders, receiving alarm, watching control board for alarm location. Probationary fireman being questioned by lieutenant and learning use of equipment. Firemen awaiting calls, taking a nap, preparing lunch, playing cards. Firemen at fires, handling trucks and hoses, and making a rescue.

DATE: January 1943

PHOTOGRAPHERS: Gordon Parks.

SOURCE: Office of War Information.

LOT 275 (microfilm)

COLLECTION NAME: FSA-OWI Collection

SUBJECTS: Washington, D.C. Service of the Church of God in Christ. Members of the congregation. Pastor in pulpit and deacon's corner. Choir, and members playing piano, guitar, tambourine. Young converts, welcoming new members, taking collection.

DATE: November 1942

PHOTOGRAPHERS: Gordon Parks.

SOURCE: Office of War Information.

LOT 277 (microfilm)

COLLECTION NAME: FSA-OWI Collection

SUBJECTS: Union Station, Washington, D.C. Crowd of servicemen and civilians waiting to board trains. Information desks, ticket window, waiting rooms. Entrance to servicemen's lounge. War poster. Soldier and sailor kissing girlfriends goodbye. Stationmaster's office. Soldiers aboard a troop train. High views.

DATE: November 1942

PHOTOGRAPHERS: Gordon Parks.

SOURCE: Office of War Information.

LOT 295 (microfilm)

COLLECTION NAME: FSA-OWI Collection

SUBJECTS: Washington, D.C. Special Skills Division of the U.S. Resettlement Administration. Spray painting, modeling, weaving, sculptors and lithographers at work. Paintings, watercolors, wood carvings, poster.

DATE: 1935–38

PHOTOGRAPHERS: Arthur Rothstein and others.

SOURCE: Farm Security Administration.

Gordon Parks. "Interior of the Union Station with an OWI banner in the background." November 1942. FSA-OWI Collection, Lot 277.
LC-USW3-12129-C

LOT 296 (microfilm)

COLLECTION NAME: FSA-OWI Collection

SUBJECTS: Washington, D.C. Jewel Mazique, black federal worker employed by the Library of Congress. At work, eating lunch in cafeteria, going home. Shopping with husband. Reading to and playing piano with nieces. Attending union meetings. Giving blood for Red Cross blood bank. Speaking in church.

DATE: March 1943

PHOTOGRAPHERS: John Collier, Jr.

SOURCE: U.S. Office of the Coordinator of Information.

LOT 677 (microfilm)

COLLECTION NAME: FSA-OWI Collection

SUBJECTS: Washington, D.C. Capt. "Eddie" Rickenbacker at a press conference, with officials of the U.S. Office of Education, and with high school students.

DATE: February 1943

PHOTOGRAPHERS: John Vachon.

SOURCE: Office of War Information.

J. A. Horne. "A resident of the southwest section and her Victory garden." June 1943. FSA-OWI Collection, Lot 678.
LC-USW3-36865

LOT 678 (microfilm)

COLLECTION NAME: FSA-OWI Collection

SUBJECTS: Washington, D.C. Victory garden sites on Fairlawn Avenue SE. Land before clearing. Plowing and initial preparations. Gardeners at work. Detail shots of successful vegetables. Small sidewalk gardens in Southwest Washington. Strawberry plants in a barrel. Vice President Henry Wallace working in his victory garden.

DATE: April 1943

PHOTOGRAPHERS: Joseph A. Horne and John Vachon.

SOURCE: Office of War Information.

LOT 690 (microfilm)

COLLECTION NAME: FSA-OWI Collection

SUBJECTS: Washington, D.C. Servicemen in Greyhound bus terminal on a Sunday night. Soldiers and sailors buying tickets, bidding family and friends goodbye, waiting for special bus. Boarding buses, getting a last look at Washington. Portraits of servicemen, other travelers, and employees.

DATE: April 1943

PHOTOGRAPHERS: Esther Bubley.

SOURCE: Office of War Information.

LOT 691 (microfilm)

COLLECTION NAME: FSA-OWI Collection

SUBJECTS: Washington, D.C. Servicemen on leave and miscellaneous scenes in Washington. Sightseeing, taking pictures in the vicinity of the Capitol, Jefferson Memorial, Tidal Basin, Washington Monument, National Gallery of Art. Streetcar passengers in transit. Bowling alley, and Glen Echo amusement park. Club for federal workers and the Sea Gull, a tavern popular with servicemen.

DATE: March–April 1943

PHOTOGRAPHERS: Esther Bubley.

SOURCE: Office of War Information.

LOT 693 (microfilm)

COLLECTION NAME: FSA-OWI Collection

SUBJECTS: Washington, D.C. First Wesleyan Methodist Church. Minister preaching Sunday morning service in sackcloth. Worshippers and church orchestra. Servicemen, and children in Sunday school. Rehearsing for afternoon radio program. Leaving church at conclusion of service. Home and family of one of the members.

DATE: March 1943

PHOTOGRAPHERS: Esther Bubley.

SOURCE: Office of War Information.

LOT 696 (microfilm)

COLLECTION NAME: FSA-OWI Collection

SUBJECTS: Washington, D.C. Wartime repercussions in civilian life. Women grocery checkers, butcher, and fish clerks. Shoe store crowds on the last day that war ration coupon no. 17 was valid.

DATE: June 1943

PHOTOGRAPHERS: Esther Bubley.

SOURCE: Office of War Information.

LOT 703 (microfilm)

COLLECTION NAME: FSA-OWI Collection

SUBJECTS: Washington, D.C. Various phases of restorative and preventive medicine and surgery carried out at the Army Medical Center. Army professional schools, including those for the Medical Corps, Dental Corps, and Veterinary Corps. Walter Reed General Hospital, laboratories for testing all army food, shops where artificial limbs are made, laboratories for preparation of blood plasma, vaccines, and plastics, and other activities under the jurisdiction of the Army Medical Department.

NOTE: Microfilm made from photographs supplied by the U.S. Army.

DATE: May 1943

PHOTOGRAPHERS: U.S. Army photographers.

LOT 706 (microfilm)

COLLECTION NAME: FSA-OWI Collection

SUBJECTS: Washington, D.C. Women employees at the Western Union Telegraph Company. Telephoning, filing, routing, switching, pasting up, checking messages. Messengers and PBX operators. Pneumatic tube system.

DATE: June 1943

PHOTOGRAPHERS: Esther Bubley.

SOURCE: Office of War Information.

Esther Bubley. "Pin boy at a bowling alley." April 1943. FSA-OWI Collection, Lot 691.
LC-USW3-22787-E

Esther Bubley. "An instructor of the Capital Transit Company teaching a woman to operate a one-man streetcar." June 1943. FSA-OWI Collection, Lot 696.
LC-USW3-32187-E

LOT 711 (microfilm)

COLLECTION NAME: FSA-OWI Collection

SUBJECTS: Arlington, Virginia. Memorial Day services in Arlington National Cemetery. Amphitheater, speakers' platform, reserved boxes, and crowd. Singing "Star Spangled Banner," watching wreath-laying ceremony, Tomb of the Unknown Soldier. Boy Scouts, Legionnaires, WAVEs, servicemen, civilians. Decorating graves in black section of cemetery.

DATE: May 1943

PHOTOGRAPHERS: Esther Bubley.

SOURCE: Office of War Information.

LOT 746

COLLECTION NAME: FSA-OWI Collection

SUBJECTS: Washington, D.C. Theater Guild production of *The Russian People,* written by Konstantin Simonov and adapted by Clifford Odets, at the National Theater. Individuals and groups of the cast in costume, on the stage, with sets, in various scenes of the play.

NOTE: See *Washington Post,* December 15, 1942, p. 10B.

DATE: December 1942

PHOTOGRAPHERS: Royden Dixon, John Vachon, and John Collier, Jr.

SOURCE: Office of War Information.

LOT 747 (microfilm)

COLLECTION NAME: FSA-OWI Collection

SUBJECTS: Washington, D.C. U.S. Office of Civilian Defense workers called out to help in a temporary emergency caused by rising flood waters. Helping soldiers and firemen move people in a boat; roping off area. Canteen set up to take care of people driven from their homes.

DATE: October 1942

PHOTOGRAPHERS: Gordon Parks.

SOURCE: Office of War Information.

LOT 748 (microfilm)

COLLECTION NAME: FSA-OWI Collection

SUBJECTS: Washington, D.C. A day nursery for ten preschool children of mothers who are engaged in war work, operated under the supervision of the District of Columbia Health Department, by Mrs. Leroy Bonbrest at her home, 1144 Branch Avenue SE. Play groups indoors and out, yard; children with picture books, sleeping on cots, eating. Maid laundering. Portraits.

DATE: May 1943

PHOTOGRAPHERS: Carlton Smith.

SOURCE: Office of War Information.

LOT 750 (microfilm)

COLLECTION NAME: FSA-OWI Collection

SUBJECTS: Washington, D.C. Pan-American and United Nations exhibits in the OWI library, U.S. Information Center (Temporary V building). Flags of the United Nations, coats-of-arms of the American republics. Maps, pamphlets, and books on South American countries. Caricatures of primitive South American dancers. Menu covers featuring Mexican portraits and scenes. Foreign-language material distributed by the overseas branch of the U.S. Office of War Information.

DATE: April–June 1943

PHOTOGRAPHERS: John Collier, Jr.

SOURCE: Office of War Information.

LOT 763 (microfilm)

COLLECTION NAME: FSA-OWI Collection

SUBJECTS: Arlington, Virginia. Arlington Farms, a war-duration residence project in the vicinity of Washington for women government workers. Grounds and exterior. Heating plant. Bedrooms, showers, laundry, service shop, desk, lounge, date booths, card rooms. Residents writing letters, chatting, sunbathing, dating civilians and servicemen. Biweekly dance. Playing cards. Portraits.

DATE: June 1943

PHOTOGRAPHERS: Esther Bubley.

SOURCE: Office of War Information.

Arthur Rothstein. *"Handling Christmas packages at the main Post Office."* 1938. FSA-OWI Collection, Lot 776.

LC-USF34-12941-D

LOT 767 (microfilm)

COLLECTION NAME: FSA-OWI Collection

SUBJECTS: Washington, D.C. Presentation and dedication of an ambulance given by federal government workers to the U.S. Army. Medical officer accepting gift. Crowds at ceremony, inspecting car.

DATE: Summer 1943

PHOTOGRAPHERS: John Collier.

SOURCE: Office of War Information.

LOT 776 (microfilm)

COLLECTION NAME: FSA-OWI Collection

SUBJECTS: Washington, D.C. U.S. Post Office, main building, and railway mail operations. Exterior views, scenes in lobby, workrooms, loading platforms. Loading and unloading, sorting, canceling, handling Christmas mail. Receiving and sorting mail aboard railway mail car. Printing, gumming, perforating, examining, counting, and coiling postage stamps at the Bureau of Engraving and Printing. Bond, currency, and stamp designer. Storage vault.

DATE: 1938

PHOTOGRAPHERS: Arthur Rothstein.

SOURCE: Farm Security Administration.

LOT 784

COLLECTION NAME: FSA-OWI Collection

SUBJECTS: Washington, D.C. Group of Turkish journalists visiting in the United States. Group portraits, journalists in conversation, at luncheon, with Elmer Davis, with other U.S. government officials.

DATE: October 1942

PHOTOGRAPHERS: Jack Delano.

SOURCE: Office of War Information.

LOT 817 (microfilm)

COLLECTION NAME: FSA-OWI Collection

SUBJECTS: Washington, D.C. U.S. Army Band concert on the Capitol grounds. Musicians on temporary platform erected in driveway. Guests of all ages seated on the Capitol steps and lawn, standing to salute during the playing of the National Anthem.

DATE: June 1943

PHOTOGRAPHERS: Esther Bubley.

SOURCE: Office of War Information.

LOT 820 (microfilm)

COLLECTION NAME: FSA-OWI Collection

SUBJECTS: Miscellaneous U.S. photographs. Training nurses at Walter Reed Hospital and Johns Hopkins Hospital. Italian-American workers in bomber plant. Exhibition of wartime art by high school students. Temporary V building. Bank of America, Los Angeles. Sister Aquinas, the flying nun. Blood donor center. Conservation and "stay at home" posters.

DATE: Spring–Summer 1943

PHOTOGRAPHERS: Ann Rosener.

SOURCE: Office of War Information.

LOT 833 (microfilm)

COLLECTION NAME: FSA-OWI Collection

SUBJECTS: Nurses at Walter Reed and Johns Hopkins Hospitals. Students in anatomy class, and on duty in the pediatrics ward. Capping a student nurse. Operating room scenes (re-enacted). Frances Bullock packing, preparing to leave home and enter training. Portrait, as a graduate nurse on duty as a second lieutenant, Army Nurse Corps. With a patient in traction. Nurses' dance at Walter Reed Hospital.

DATE: May 1943

PHOTOGRAPHERS: Ann Rosener.

SOURCE: Office of War Information.

LOT 836 (microfilm)

COLLECTION NAME: FSA-OWI Collection

SUBJECTS: Washington, D.C. Weather forecasting at the U.S. Weather Bureau. Examining reports, checking data. Putting data on coding tape. Transmitting information in military and civilian war centers by teletype. Plotting data on sectional manuscript maps, assembling sectional maps. Preparation of analyses and auxiliary weather maps.

DATE: July 1943

PHOTOGRAPHERS: Esther Bubley.

SOURCE: Office of War Information.

LOT 842 (microfilm)

COLLECTION NAME: FSA-OWI Collection

SUBJECTS: Greyhound bus terminal. Waiting room crowded with civilians and servicemen. Boarding bus. Stewardess renting pillows, ticket lines, ticket checkers. Military Police and Shore Patrol on duty.

DATE: April 1942

PHOTOGRAPHERS: John Collier, Jr.

SOURCE: Office of War Information.

LOT 849 (microfilm)

COLLECTION NAME: FSA-OWI Collection

SUBJECTS: Washington, D.C. Street flower vendors at Eastertime. Black salesmen, civilian and serviceman customers. Crowds outside church after Easter service.

DATE: April 1943

PHOTOGRAPHERS: John Collier, Jr.

SOURCE: Office of War Information.

LOT 856 (microfilm)

COLLECTION NAME: FSA-OWI Collection

SUBJECTS: Washington, D.C. Parade to recruit Civilian Defense volunteers. Spectators along the line of march. Close-up photographs of facial expressions and attitudes, especially of children. Units in the parade. Black fife and drum corps. Man selling flags and button souvenirs. People watching parade from around base of Gen. Winfield Scott Hancock Monument.

DATE: July 1943

PHOTOGRAPHERS: Esther Bubley.

SOURCE: Office of War Information.

LOT 858 (microfilm)

COLLECTION NAME: FSA-OWI Collection

SUBJECTS: Washington, D.C. Victory gardens in the Northwest section. Displays of tools in hardware store, purchasing tools and seed. Girls with tools going to work in park plots. Overall views of gardens in parks with groups and families working. Breaking ground with plow and tractor. Seedlings started at home in paper cups. Planting, setting out seedlings, cultivating in early stages. Garden bulletin board.

DATE: May 1943

PHOTOGRAPHERS: Louise Rosskam.

SOURCE: Office of War Information.

LOT 880 (microfilm)

COLLECTION NAME: FSA-OWI Collection

SUBJECTS: Rockville, Maryland (vicinity). Furlough spent by Pfc. Harvey Horton, A.U.S., at the dairy farm of N. C. Stiles. Looking over farm and dairy barns. Watching cows being milked. Splitting wood, for exercise. Dinner with the family.

DATE: July 1943

PHOTOGRAPHERS: Ann Rosener.

SOURCE: Office of War Information.

LOT 882 (microfilm)

COLLECTION NAME: FSA-OWI Collection

SUBJECTS: Bus trip from Washington, D.C., to Columbus, Ohio. A Greyhound bus on the road to Pittsburgh. Scenery, passengers, waiting room in terminal. Baggage room and checkers. Drivers' quarters. Driver "protecting" his run (waiting in case a second section has to be made up). Servicing a bus.

DATE: September 1943

PHOTOGRAPHERS: Esther Bubley.

SOURCE: Office of War Information.

LOT 885 (microfilm)

COLLECTION NAME: FSA-OWI Collection

SUBJECTS: Bus trip to Louisville and Memphis and back to Washington, D.C. Local passengers hailing bus along highway. Travelers' Aid desk in Memphis terminal. Servicemen passengers and military policemen on duty. School boys working as baggage clerks, from 4:00 P.M. to midnight. Loading baggage on top of bus. Woman nursing infant at Chattanooga bus station. Sign labeling waiting room for blacks. Female baggage agent. Pillow saleswomen. Servicing a bus at Knoxville.

DATE: September 1943

PHOTOGRAPHERS: Esther Bubley.

SOURCE: Office of War Information.

LOT 887

COLLECTION NAME: FSA-OWI Collection

SUBJECTS: Washington, D.C. Storage of photographs and other materials for the Copyright Division in the basement of the Library of Congress, and quarters for sorting them in the attic. Dusty, disarranged shelves. Sheet music, bundles of photographs stored by copyright number. Old Kinetoscope reel and paper prints of motion picture film. Spiral stairway leading to attic.

DATE: October 1943

PHOTOGRAPHERS: J. A. Horne, for the Library of Congress.

SOURCE: Office of War Information.

Esther Bubley. "In a boarding house room." January 1943. FSA-OWI Collection, Lot 939.
LC-USW3-38335-E

LOT 888 (microfilm)

COLLECTION NAME: FSA-OWI Collection

SUBJECTS: Washington, D.C. Chevy Chase Ice Palace, an indoor skating rink. Young people purchasing tickets. Girls polishing skates. Couples skating, returning rented skates.

DATE: November 1941

PHOTOGRAPHERS: Edwin Rosskam.

SOURCE: Farm Security Administration.

LOT 900 (microfilm)

COLLECTION NAME: FSA-OWI Collection

SUBJECTS: Washington, D.C. William Hastie, adviser to Undersecretary of War Patterson. Portraits with Patterson.

DATE: April 1942

PHOTOGRAPHERS: Marjory Collins.

SOURCE: U.S. Office of the Coordinator of Information.

LOT 902

COLLECTION NAME: FSA-OWI Collection

SUBJECTS: Posters dealing with war objectives submitted by various artists to an exhibition at the National Gallery of Art, Washington, D.C. Posters on such themes as "Deliver us from evil," "Loose talk sinks ships," "Work to keep free," "Slave world or free world," "Someone talked," and "Buy more war bonds and stamps."

DATE: February 1943

PHOTOGRAPHERS: Howard Hollem.

SOURCE: Office of War Information.

LOT 910 (microfilm)

COLLECTION NAME: FSA-OWI Collection

SUBJECTS: Washington, D.C. The District's U.S. Weather Bureau Station at National Airport. Instrument panels in airplanes. Communications systems. Plotting charts and preparing maps. Wind vanes, anemometers, radio sonde balloons, theodolites, and other instruments in use.

DATE: October 1943

PHOTOGRAPHERS: Norman Driscoll.

SOURCE: Office of War Information.

LOT 928

COLLECTION NAME: FSA-OWI Collection

SUBJECTS: Washington, D.C. Leon Henderson and other U.S. Office of Price Administration officials at a luncheon meeting of regional administrators held in Washington on October 17, 1942.

DATE: October 1942

SOURCE: Transfer from the Office of War Information, 1944.

LOT 935

COLLECTION NAME: FSA-OWI Collection

SUBJECTS: Washington, D.C. Street scenes, interiors and exteriors of government buildings. Glen Echo amusement park.

DATE: 1939

PHOTOGRAPHERS: David Myers.

SOURCE: Farm Security Administration.

LOT 939 (microfilm)

COLLECTION NAME: FSA-OWI Collection

SUBJECTS: Washington, D.C. A boarding-house, exterior and interior views. Portrait of the landlady. Tenants playing a game of bridge, reading, looking at pictures, listening to the radio, and "visiting." Dinner. Waiting in line to use the bathroom.

DATE: January 1943

PHOTOGRAPHERS: Esther Bubley.

SOURCE: Office of War Information.

LOT 940 (microfilm)

COLLECTION NAME: FSA-OWI Collection

SUBJECTS: Washington, D.C. Woodrow Wilson High School students. Girls and boys entering building, changing classes. Principal instructing student fire marshals before a fire drill. Female students eating lunch outdoors. Current high school fashions: "sloppy Joe" or "box" sweaters, long ropes of beads, and moccasin-type shoes, with or without ankle socks. Groups, couples, portraits.

DATE: October 1943

PHOTOGRAPHERS: Esther Bubley.

SOURCE: Office of War Information.

LOT 941 (microfilm)

COLLECTION NAME: FSA-OWI Collection

SUBJECTS: Washington, D.C. Woodrow Wilson High School activities. Annual health examination. Dental hygienist examining students' teeth. Infirmary, library, and cafeteria. Meeting of student council. Tea for sorority members' mothers. School orchestra rehearsing. Returning June graduate, now in the navy, on his first leave. Faculty members and principal. Students at home of English instructor. High School Cadet Corps Regimental Ball. Faculty members serving as chaperones.

DATE: October 1943

PHOTOGRAPHERS: Esther Bubley.

SOURCE: Office of War Information.

LOT 942 (microfilm)

COLLECTION NAME: FSA-OWI Collection

SUBJECTS: Washington, D.C. Woodrow Wilson High School classes. Students in classes in home economics, science, mathematics, and office procedure. Boys' class in nutrition. Chemistry and biology laboratory tests. Art classes, clay modeling, mechanical drawing, and building model rooms. Health education. Manual training and printing. Geography.

DATE: October 1943

PHOTOGRAPHERS: Esther Bubley.

SOURCE: Office of War Information.

LOT 943 (microfilm)

COLLECTION NAME: FSA-OWI Collection

SUBJECTS: Washington, D.C. Woodrow Wilson High School athletics and physical education. Pep rally before a football game. Team coming onto the field. Football game, cheerleaders, boys and girls watching the game. Spectators outside the fence. Girls playing basketball and exercising in the gymnasium. Tennis, soccer, and hockey games.

DATE: October 1943

PHOTOGRAPHERS: Esther Bubley.

SOURCE: Office of War Information.

LOT 944 (microfilm)

COLLECTION NAME: FSA-OWI Collection

SUBJECTS: Washington, D.C. Walter Spangenberg, a student at Woodrow Wilson High School. As captain in the school corps of cadets, drilling his company. Demonstrating the manual of arms. With the rifle team. In classes and at the library. Building model planes and working on his model railroad at home in his attic workshop. At the Cadet Corps Regimental Ball, with his date.

DATE: October 1943

PHOTOGRAPHERS: Esther Bubley.

SOURCE: Office of War Information.

LOT 945 (microfilm)

COLLECTION NAME: FSA-OWI Collection

SUBJECTS: Frederick, Maryland. Walter Spangenberg, a student at Woodrow Wilson High School in Washington, D.C., at Stevens Airport. Waiting to fly, after a fifty-mile bus trip. Recording his trip in his pilot's logbook. In uniform of the Civil Air Patrol. Examining planes, and watching a mechanic make repairs. "Greaseball," the airport mascot.

DATE: October 1943

PHOTOGRAPHERS: Esther Bubley.

SOURCE: Office of War Information.

LOT 946 (microfilm)

COLLECTION NAME: FSA-OWI Collection

SUBJECTS: Washington, D.C. Sally Dessez, a student at Woodrow Wilson High School. Eating lunch outdoors. Attending class. Playing tennis and field hockey. Editing the school yearbook. Singing in the church choir. At home, with her father, a captain in the U.S. Navy, and her aunt. Studying. Ordering vegetables from a huckster. Assisting in the distribution of Office of Price Administration ration book no. 4.

DATE: October 1943

PHOTOGRAPHERS: Esther Bubley.

SOURCE: Office of War Information.

LOT 947 (microfilm)

COLLECTION NAME: FSA-OWI Collection

SUBJECTS: Washington, D.C. Woodrow Wilson High School faculty and students assisting in the registration for U.S. Office of Price Administration ration book no. 4. Filling in the application form. Directing people through the school building after they have received their ration books.

DATE: October 1943

PHOTOGRAPHERS: Esther Bubley.

SOURCE: Office of War Information.

LOT 948 (microfilm)

COLLECTION NAME: FSA-OWI Collection

SUBJECTS: Washington, D.C. Woodrow Wilson High School students serving as nurses' aides. On duty at Emergency Hospital. Learning to make a bed according to hospital requirements. Taking a temperature. Bedside care of patients. Checking supplies.

DATE: October 1943

PHOTOGRAPHERS: Esther Bubley.

SOURCE: Office of War Information.

LOT 953 (microfilm)

COLLECTION NAME: FSA-OWI Collection

SUBJECTS: Photographs of black Americans and their activities and occupations, drawn from various government agency files. Blacks in agriculture, growing sugar cane, tobacco, and cotton; as government employees; in war industries; in National Youth Training programs; in the armed forces. Black children in camp, eating school lunches, on playgrounds. Black personalities. Participants in Red Cross and other programs. Slossfield community project.

DATE: ca. 1940

SOURCE: Office of War Information.

LOT 976

COLLECTION NAME: FSA-OWI Collection

SUBJECTS: Washington, D.C. Record portraits of George Barnes, assistant director of the U.S. Office of War Information.

DATE: October 1943

SOURCE: Office of War Information.

LOT 979 (microfilm)

COLLECTION NAME: FSA-OWI Collection

SUBJECTS: Washington, D.C. The United Nations Service Center for the convenience of servicemen traveling through the capital. Reception desk, lounge, shower and dressing rooms, laundry, bedrooms, telephones, library. Servicemen playing games, hostesses, canteen. Nursery where day care is given to children of servicemen. Accommodations for servicewomen.

DATE: December 1943

PHOTOGRAPHERS: Esther Bubley.

SOURCE: Office of War Information.

LOT 980 (microfilm)

COLLECTION NAME: FSA-OWI Collection

SUBJECTS: Washington, D.C. The arrival in Washington of Hugh Massman, his wife, and their infant son. He is a second class petty officer in the navy, a student at the Naval Air Station, in the last month of training before sea duty. Telephoning to the United Nations Service Center. Baby being cared for at the nursery while parents see the sights and look for a place to live. Eating in cafeteria. Visiting public buildings.

DATE: December 1943

PHOTOGRAPHERS: Esther Bubley.

SOURCE: Office of War Information.

LOT 981 (microfilm)

COLLECTION NAME: FSA-OWI Collection

SUBJECTS: Washington, D.C. The home life of Hugh Massman, a second class petty officer in the navy and student at the Naval Air Station, his wife, and their infant son. He is studying for the last month before being assigned to sea duty. Mrs. Massman doing household tasks, shopping, taking care of baby. Portraits.

DATE: December 1943

PHOTOGRAPHERS: Esther Bubley.

SOURCE: Office of War Information.

LOT 982 (microfilm)

COLLECTION NAME: FSA-OWI Collection

SUBJECTS: Washington, D.C. A miscellany of scenes in the capital. Buildings, statues, Museum of Natural History, exhibits, children playing, feeding pigeons in a park.

DATE: December 1943

PHOTOGRAPHERS: Esther Bubley.

SOURCE: Office of War Information.

LOT 986

COLLECTION NAME: FSA-OWI Collection

SUBJECTS: Washington, D.C. Political and religious speakers in Franklin Park. Catholic Evidence Guild; Bethel Pentecostal Tabernacle; Ivo Capet, who proposes himself as postwar king of France. Banners and diagrams, musicians, audience reactions.

DATE: July 1943

PHOTOGRAPHERS: J. A. Horne.

SOURCE: Office of War Information.

LOT 989 (microfilm)

COLLECTION NAME: FSA-OWI Collection

SUBJECTS: College Park, Maryland. United Nations Relief and Rehabilitation Administration Training Center, University of Maryland. Classes and discussion groups in progress. Dr. Frank Munk, director of the school. Student appointees studying in their dormitory rooms, eating in cafeteria, reading in library.

DATE: May 1944

PHOTOGRAPHERS: John Collier, Jr.

SOURCE: Office of War Information.

LOT 990

COLLECTION NAME: FSA-OWI Collection

SUBJECTS: Washington, D.C. Visit of an Arabian princess. Informal groups at a reception.

DATE: November 1943

PHOTOGRAPHERS: Esther Bubley.

SOURCE: Office of War Information.

LOT 992

COLLECTION NAME: FSA-OWI Collection

SUBJECTS: Washington, D.C. Monuments, headstones, and grave markers in Congressional and Mt. Olivet Cemeteries. Children's corner in Congressional Cemetery. Mary and Child, angel, little girl, and broken column monuments. Grave covered with seashells.

DATE: Spring 1944

PHOTOGRAPHERS: J. A. Horne.

SOURCE: Office of War Information.

LOT 1363 (microfilm)

COLLECTION NAME: FSA-OWI Collection

SUBJECTS: Washington, D.C., Baltimore, Maryland, and vicinity. U.S. Highway No. 1. Washington suburbs. Signs and advertising, souvenir stands. Trucking operators, service station, sleeping accommodations for truck drivers. Auto graveyard. Overpasses. Cafes and roadhouses. Farms and countryside.

DATE: June 1940

PHOTOGRAPHERS: Jack Delano.

SOURCE: Farm Security Administration.

LOT 1365 (microfilm)

COLLECTION NAME: FSA-OWI Collection

SUBJECTS: Beltsville, Maryland. Activities at the Research Center of the U.S. Department of Agriculture. Livestock, breeding experiments. Laboratory work on bovine tuberculosis. Food testers. Civilian Conservation Corps engaged in construction work.

DATE: November 1935

PHOTOGRAPHERS: Carl Mydans.

SOURCE: Resettlement Administration.

LOT 1377 (microfilm)

COLLECTION NAME: FSA-OWI Collection

SUBJECTS: Montgomery County, Maryland. Winter in farming country. Snow-covered roads, fields, and barns; snow fences. Feeding livestock.

DATE: January 1940

PHOTOGRAPHERS: Arthur Rothstein.

SOURCE: Farm Security Administration.

LOT 1383 (microfilm)

COLLECTION NAME: FSA-OWI Collection

SUBJECTS: Rockville, Maryland, and vicinity. A series of photographs that show dangerous practices and hazards on a farm. Bad electric wiring. Scattered farm tools. Unsafe stairs and ladders. Hazards in operating ensilage cutter and repairing mowing machine. Leading a bull without a pole. Oil and kerosene fire hazards.

DATE: May 1940

PHOTOGRAPHERS: Jack Delano.

SOURCE: Farm Security Administration.

LOT 1393 (microfilm)

COLLECTION NAME: FSA-OWI Collection

SUBJECTS: Rockville, Maryland. Students at the Congressional School of Aeronautics. Learning to fly under the Civilian Pilot Training Program. Students with planes on the ground; listening to instructor. Portraits.

DATE: September 1941

PHOTOGRAPHERS: John Vachon.

SOURCE: Farm Security Administration.

Jack Delano. Souvenir stand along U.S. Highway 1 in the vicinity of Berwyn, Maryland. June 1940. FSA-OWI Collection, Lot 1363.

LC-USF34-40749-D

Jack Delano. Diner along U.S. Highway 1 in the vicinity of Berwyn, Maryland. June 1940. FSA-OWI Collection, Lot 1363.

LC-USF34-40730-D

Carl Mydans. "Children who live in Georgetown. Poor white children at play." November 1935. FSA-OWI Collection, Lot 1395.

LC-USF33-117-M-4 (RA)

Carl Mydans. ''Washington, D.C. Outside water supply. Only source of water supply winter and summer for many houses in slum area. In some places drainage is so poor that surplus water backs up in huge puddles.'' July 1935. FSA-OWI Collection, Lot 1395.

LC-USF33-173-M4 (RA)

LOT 1395 (microfilm)

COLLECTION NAME: FSA-OWI Collection

SUBJECTS: Washington, D.C. Poor housing conditions contrasted with well-built homes. Children playing in slum backyards and on street. Unsanitary conditions. Former residences now used as rooming houses. General views over rooftops. Interiors and details of substandard dwellings.

DATE: September 1935–January 1936

PHOTOGRAPHERS: Carl Mydans.

SOURCE: Resettlement Administration.

LOT 1396 (microfilm)

COLLECTION NAME: FSA-OWI Collection

SUBJECTS: Washington, D.C. Slum area near the U.S. Capitol. Row houses, alleyways, views over rooftops, interiors of substandard dwellings. Portraits of residents, who are black.

DATE: April–November 1937

PHOTOGRAPHERS: John Vachon.

SOURCE: Farm Security Administration.

Carl Mydans. ''Alley behind North Capitol Street with Blake School in background.'' 1935. FSA-OWI Collection, Lot 1395.

LC-USF34-266-D

LOT 1397 (microfilm)

COLLECTION NAME: FSA-OWI Collection

SUBJECTS: Washington, D.C. Slum area near the U.S. Capitol. Alleyways, row houses. Backyards and dilapidated dwellings. Children playing in streets.

DATE: September–October 1941

PHOTOGRAPHERS: Marion Post Wolcott.

SOURCE: Farm Security Administration.

LOT 1398 (microfilm)

COLLECTION NAME: FSA-OWI Collection

SUBJECTS: Washington, D.C. Scenes in slum area. Groups of black residents on front doorsteps. Crates and boxes to be used as firewood. Dead rats in alley. Exteriors and details of substandard dwellings.

DATE: July 1941

PHOTOGRAPHERS: Edwin Rosskam.

SOURCE: Farm Security Administration.

LOT 1399 (microfilm)

COLLECTION NAME: FSA-OWI Collection

SUBJECTS: Washington, D.C. Miscellaneous street scenes. General views over rooftops, row houses, advertising displays, shop windows, residences, automobile parking facilities.

DATE: July 1939

PHOTOGRAPHERS: David Myers.

SOURCE: Farm Security Administration.

LOT 1400 (microfilm)

COLLECTION NAME: FSA-OWI Collection

SUBJECTS: Washington, D.C. The Palace mobile home and expansible trailer, furnished to the U.S. government for use as emergency defense housing. A demonstration conducted by the Farm Security Administration. Step-by-step photographs showing rapid conversion of mobile trailer into a small house with foundation. Interior diagram of four rooms.

DATE: November 1941

PHOTOGRAPHERS: Marion Post Wolcott.

SOURCE: Farm Security Administration.

LOT 1401 (microfilm)

COLLECTION NAME: FSA-OWI Collection

SUBJECTS: Washington, D.C. Government buildings, semipublic buildings, and monuments. General and pictorial views. Details of sculpture.

DATE: 1936–41

SOURCE: Farm Security Administration.

David Myers. Theater on Ninth Street, Washington, D.C. 1939. FSA-OWI Collection, Lot 1399.

LC-USF34-15943-C

John Collier. "Emergency office construction." December 1941. FSA-OWI Collection, Lot 1402.
LC-USF34-82031-C

LOT 1402 (microfilm)

COLLECTION NAME: FSA-OWI Collection

SUBJECTS: Washington, D.C. Construction of emergency office space. Workmen building scaffolding, laying sewer, preparing tar roofing, finishing exterior panels. Workmen waiting to go on the job, and at lunch. Apartment house turned into federal office space. Government clerical and white-collar workers crowded in emergency quarters.

DATE: December 1941

PHOTOGRAPHERS: John Collier, Jr.

SOURCE: Farm Security Administration.

LOT 1403 (microfilm)

COLLECTION NAME: FSA-OWI Collection

SUBJECTS: Washington, D.C. The Cherry Blossom Festival around the Tidal Basin. Groups strolling through the park and taking pictures; servicemen in the park; family picnics.

DATE: May 1941

PHOTOGRAPHERS: Martha McMillan.

SOURCE: Farm Security Administration.

LOT 1404 (microfilm)

COLLECTION NAME: FSA-OWI Collection

SUBJECTS: Washington, D.C. Patrons of a Hot Shoppe restaurant at midnight. Groups around tables and at the counter.

Patrons receiving curb service in automobiles. Cooks at work in the kitchen.

DATE: December 1941

PHOTOGRAPHERS: John Collier, Jr.

SOURCE: Farm Security Administration.

LOT 1405 (microfilm)

COLLECTION NAME: FSA-OWI Collection

SUBJECTS: Washington, D.C. A group of uniformed Boy Scouts inspecting artillery pieces and tanks displayed in Commerce Square. Scouts saluting the flag. Boys sighting machine gun and climbing over larger equipment.

DATE: December 1941

PHOTOGRAPHERS: Marion Post Wolcott.

SOURCE: Farm Security Administration.

LOT 1406 (microfilm)

COLLECTION NAME: FSA-OWI Collection

SUBJECTS: Washington, D.C. National Airport. Main waiting room. Ground crews servicing planes. Portraits of dispatchers, hostesses, stewards. Communications system and the controls. Flight information. Visitors' observation platform. Planes arriving and taking off. Weather Bureau activities. Details of planes.

DATE: July 1941

PHOTOGRAPHERS: Jack Delano.

SOURCE: Farm Security Administration.

John Vachon. "Rosslyn, Virginia. An ice house."
September 1937. FSA-OWI Collection, Lot 1423.
LC-USF34-15619-D

LOT 1423 (microfilm)

COLLECTION NAME: FSA-OWI Collection

SUBJECTS: Rosslyn, and other places in Virginia. Street scenes, backyards, and black homes in Rosslyn. Mountain couple who beg along Skyline Drive in the Shenandoah National Park. Dead trees. Hymn-singing at the Helping Hand Mission in Portsmouth. General store at Diascond. Hilly farmland in the Blue Ridge Mountains. Street scenes in Newport News. Black woman carrying box of groceries on her head.

DATE: September 1937

PHOTOGRAPHERS: John Vachon.

SOURCE: Resettlement Administration.

LOT 1435 (microfilm)

COLLECTION NAME: FSA-OWI Collection

SUBJECTS: Fairfax County, Virginia. Officers, members, and meeting of the Grange, held in the schoolhouse. One of the lodges of the National Grange of the Patrons of Husbandry, a secret, nonpolitical association of farmers to further their interests, and to bring producers and consumers, farmers and manufacturers into direct commercial relationship.

DATE: January 1940

PHOTOGRAPHERS: Arthur Rothstein.

SOURCE: Farm Security Administration.

LOT 1449 (microfilm)

COLLECTION NAME: FSA-OWI Collection

SUBJECTS: Alexandria, Virginia, and vicinity. Trailer camps on U.S. Highway No. 1. The Good Humor ice cream man. Children playing. Electric meter for each trailer. Shower, toilet facilities, and laundry building. Wife of a defense worker hanging clothes on the line to dry. Trailers offered for sale on an open lot.

DATE: March 1941

PHOTOGRAPHERS: Martha McMillan.

SOURCE: Farm Security Administration.

LOT 1755

COLLECTION NAME: FSA-OWI Collection

SUBJECTS: Beltsville, Maryland. National Agricultural Research Center. General statement and description in pictures and text of the U.S. Department of Agriculture's 16,000-acre farm. New strains of plants and livestock, inventing and improving farm machinery, fighting animal parasites and diseases, improving marketing methods, studying nutrition problems, finding new uses for farm products.

DATE: 1937

SOURCE: Resettlement Administration.

LOT 1756

COLLECTION NAME: FSA-OWI Collection

SUBJECTS: Washington, D.C. A Christmas Eve party given by Local 203 of the United Federal Workers of America, Congress of Industrial Organizations (CIO). Crowd, dancers, Christmas tree, punch bowl. Opening of the Washington Labor Canteen, sponsored by the CIO. Hostesses, refreshment bar, entertainers performing. Eleanor Roosevelt. A dance and entertainment at the Washington Labor Canteen. Checker game, magician, dancers, singers, orchestra.

DATE: December 1943–March 1944

PHOTOGRAPHERS: J. A. Horne and Eugene Tourville.

SOURCE: Office of War Information.

LOT 1758

COLLECTION NAME: FSA-OWI Collection

SUBJECTS: Washington, D.C. Combined U.S. and Canada Conservation Committee exhibit, held by the U.S. War Production Board in Room 1625A of the Social Security Building. Identification photographs of exhibit signs and vertical panels with a wide variety of product samples mounted on them. Plywood, protective coatings, plastics, resins, wood substituted for metal, brushes, plumbing and electrical fixtures, tools, war materials.

DATE: December 1943

PHOTOGRAPHERS: Esther Bubley.

SOURCE: Office of War Information.

LOT 1783

COLLECTION NAME: FSA-OWI Collection

SUBJECTS: Washington, D.C. Delegates (identified) to a conference of the International Labor Office arriving at the White House.

DATE: May 1944

SOURCE: U.S. Office of Strategic Services and Office of War Information.

LOT 1791 (microfilm)

COLLECTION NAME: FSA-OWI Collection

SUBJECTS: Washington, D.C., and other locations. Miscellaneous civilian defense activities. Salvage and rationing. Demonstration of gas masks and destruction of bombs. Message and control centers. Stirrup pump and other equipment. Air raid wardens. Victory garden. Utah State Defense Council. Girl Scouts. Ulysses S. Grant III, brigadier general, U.S. Army, and chief of the Protection Division, and Hon. James M. Landis, director of the Office of Civilian Defense. Groups and portraits.

DATE: 1942–43

SOURCE: Office of War Information.

LOT 1793

COLLECTION NAME: FSA-OWI Collection

SUBJECTS: "Art in War," a group of paintings, prints, and drawings purchased by the U.S. Office for Emergency Management from a competition conducted by the Section of Fine Arts, Public Buildings Administration, Works Progress Administration. Also, "Soldiers of Production," an exhibit of painting and drawings by eight American artists appointed by the Office for Emergency Management to record activities in specific defense areas.

DATE: 1941–43

SOURCE: Office of War Information.

LOT 1796

COLLECTION NAME: FSA-OWI Collection

SUBJECTS: Washington, D.C., and Nebraska. Public buildings, victory gardens, speakers in parks, signs relating to the war. Farms, street scenes.

DATE: 1938–44

PHOTOGRAPHERS: J. A. Horne.

SOURCE: Office of War Information.

LOT 1798 (microfilm)

COLLECTION NAME: FSA-OWI Collection

SUBJECTS: Washington, D.C. U.S. Bureau of the Census. Punch card operators, various operations and groups.

DATE: 1939

LOT 1816 (microfilm)

COLLECTION NAME: FSA-OWI Collection

SUBJECTS: Hon. Cordell Hull, secretary of state (1898–1942). Biographical photographs of Hull as a Spanish-American War volunteer; as a member of Congress in 1907; as chairman, National Democratic Convention in 1924; with President Franklin D. Roosevelt in 1933; and at the Pan-American Conference in 1940. Log cabin birthplace; section of the Cordell Hull Highway; portraits and pictures of relatives.

NOTE: Published in the *Portrait of America* series, no. 30.

DATE: 1907–42

SOURCE: Office of War Information.

LOT 1826

COLLECTION NAME: FSA-OWI Collection

SUBJECTS: Washington, D.C. Radio station WOL (Mutual Broadcasting System) presenting a "My People" program devoted to blacks. Special guest, Eleanor Roosevelt, wife of the president of the United States. Groups and portraits.

DATE: February 13, 1943

PHOTOGRAPHERS: Roger Smith.

SOURCE: Office of War Information.

LOT 1829 (microfilm)

COLLECTON NAME: FSA-OWI Collection

SUBJECTS: Washington, D.C., and vicinity. Trucks of various sizes and usage, all pledged to the U.S. Truck Conservation Corps. Tire with worn treads. Hauling lumber and sand. Delivering groceries, bread, and milk. Moving van and oil tank truck. Cement mixer. Checking engine.

DATE: October 1942

PHOTOGRAPHERS: Howard Liberman.

SOURCE: Office of War Information.

LOT 1832 (microfilm)

COLLECTION NAME: FSA-OWI Collection

SUBJECTS: Washington, D.C. Auction sale of household goods and kitchen utensils at Adam A. Wechsler and Sons. Crowds of people, auctioneer, furniture.

DATE: June 1942

PHOTOGRAPHERS: Howard Liberman.

SOURCE: Office of War Information.

LOT 1833 (microfilm)

COLLECTION NAME: FSA-OWI Collection

SUBJECTS: Silver Spring, Maryland, and New York, New York. High School Victory Corps training program. Members of the Victory Corps of Montgomery Blair High School in Silver Spring, Flushing High School in Queens, and Benjamin Franklin High School in New York City, in physical education classes. Wrestling, riding a bike, doing push-ups, and running an obstacle course. Building model planes and welding. Girls in home economics classes serving in cafeteria.

DATE: October 1942

PHOTOGRAPHERS: William Perlitch.

SOURCE: Office of War Information.

LOT 1839

COLLECTION NAME: FSA-OWI Collection

SUBJECTS: Edgewood Arsenal, Maryland. Black men and women working on gas masks and 75-mm shells. Sewing harness tabs on gas masks. Putting bottoms on incendiary bomb cases. Spray painting identification marks and metal stencils on 75-mm shells.

DATE: May 1942

PHOTOGRAPHERS: Howard Liberman.

SOURCE: Office of War Information.

LOT 1841

COLLECTION NAME: FSA-OWI Collection

SUBJECTS: Washington, D.C. Construction of the million-dollar bridge across the Tidal Basin by the firm of Alexander and Repass of Des Moines, Iowa. Archie A. Alexander, senior partner, is black. Derrick, heavy machinery, and piers, in early stages of construction. Hoisting and setting stone. Views of the Washington Monument, Jefferson Memorial, and Japanese cherry trees. Portraits.

DATE: March 23, 1943

PHOTOGRAPHERS: Roger Smith.

SOURCE: Office of War Information.

LOT 1842

COLLECTION NAME: FSA-OWI Collection

SUBJECTS: Washington, D.C. National Youth Administration War Production and Training Center. Black women receiving training under the National Youth Administration program. Juanita E. Gray, formerly a domestic servant, registering for training. Learning to operate a lathe, and later reporting to the Washington Navy Yard.

DATE: January 1943

PHOTOGRAPHERS: Roger Smith.

SOURCE: Office of War Information.

LOT 1857

COLLECTION NAME: FSA-OWI Collection

SUBJECTS: Washington, D.C. Miscellaneous pictures of public buildings and statues. A street in Georgetown, a suburb. Episcopal Cathedral of Sts. Peter and Paul. Tomb of Pierre L'Enfant. Mount Vernon. National Airport and the Easter Monday egg roll on the White House lawn.

NOTE: Used in the *Portrait of America* series, no. 85.

DATE: 1944

SOURCE: Office of War Information.

LOT 1867

COLLECTION NAME: FSA-OWI Collection

SUBJECTS: Washington, D.C. The personal and professional life of Dr. Anita Figueredo, a woman surgeon at St. Elizabeth's Hospital. Cooking, typing for her mother, in a beauty shop. On duty, scrubbing for an operation, reading X rays, and with child patients.

NOTE: Used in the *Portrait of America* series, no. 91.

DATE: 1944

PHOTOGRAPHERS: Three Lions agency.

SOURCE: Office of War Information.

LOT 1869

COLLECTION NAME: FSA-OWI Collection

SUBJECTS: Washington, D.C. Filipino Women's Club. Meeting of the Red Cross surgical dressing unit of the club. Cutting, folding, and packing bandages. Making dresses for war refugees and people in occupied territories.

DATE: September 1944

PHOTOGRAPHERS: Harris & Ewing.

SOURCE: Office of War Information.

LOT 1872

COLLECTION NAME: FSA-OWI Collection

SUBJECTS: Motion picture stills from the film *Bits and Pieces,* produced in 1941 by the U.S. Office for Emergency Management. Machine shops in Washington, D.C., and New York City manufacturing precision parts for airplane engines and other small parts.

DATE: Ca. 1941

SOURCE: Office for Emergency Management.

LOT 1883

COLLECTION NAME: FSA-OWI Collection

SUBJECTS: Washington, D.C. Civilian defense program in the capital. Blacks organized in various activities. Communications center. Sector meeting of air raid wardens. Auxiliary firemen. Medical unit at Howard University.

DATE: April 1943

PHOTOGRAPHERS: Roger Smith.

SOURCE: Office of War Information.

LOT 1887

COLLECTION NAME: FSA-OWI Collection

SUBJECTS: Washington, D.C., and New York City. "Four Freedoms" and "Arsenal of Democracy" exhibits. Jean Carlu, artist, constructing the huge photographic display panels used in the National and Civilian Defense exhibit by the U.S. Office for Emergency Management. Photograph illustrating the four freedoms (of speech, of worship, from want, from fear) from which panels were assembled. Installation at Fourteenth Street and Pennsylvania Avenue NW, and opening ceremonies in Washington, D.C. Display at Times Square, New York City.

DATE: November 1941 and February 1942

PHOTOGRAPHERS: Alfred T. Palmer.

SOURCE: Office for Emergency Management.

LOT 1890

COLLECTION NAME: FSA-OWI Collection

SUBJECTS: Washington, D.C. Trial of Nazi saboteurs before a special seven-man military commission in a U.S. Department of Justice courtroom. Portraits of the prisoners. Exhibits introduced. Transferring prisoners under armed guard.

DATE: July 1942

PHOTOGRAPHERS: U.S. Army Signal Corps.

SOURCE: Office of War Information.

LOT 1893

COLLECTION NAME: FSA-OWI Collection

SUBJECTS: Washington, D.C. Volunteer student nurse's aides at Freedmen's Hospital for Negroes. Feeding bed patients, changing beds, packing surgical kits, and assisting during emergency medical care.

DATE: February 1943

PHOTOGRAPHERS: Roger Smith.

SOURCE: Office of War Information.

LOT 1904

COLLECTION NAME: FSA-OWI Collection

SUBJECTS: Washington, D.C. Black public schools in the war program of Civilian Defense. Vocational education classes in machine shop, aircraft maintenance, and welding. Boys preparing soil for victory gardens. High school boys and girls drilling, making model airplanes, and in gymnasium. Home preserving demonstration. Recruits for the Women's Army Auxiliary Corps (WAAC) and reviewing officers.

DATE: April 1943

PHOTOGRAPHERS: Roger Smith.

SOURCE: Office of War Information.

LOT 1907

COLLECTION NAME: FSA-OWI Collection

SUBJECTS: Washington, D.C. Processing V-mail at the Pentagon building. Armed courier delivering sack of letters to be microfilmed. Letters being registered, sorted, and photographed. Negative being inspected for flaws on an enlarging reader (Recodak). Enlarged reproduction from V-mail microfilm. Paper enlargements being developed, fixed, washed, and dried before inspection. Cutting individual letters from paper rolls and mailing them.

DATE: February 1943

PHOTOGRAPHERS: U.S. Army Signal Corps.

SOURCE: Office of War Information.

LOT 1908

COLLECTION NAME: FSA-OWI Collection

SUBJECTS: Washington, D.C. Social activities of government war workers. Dancing at Scott's Hotel, a high quality boardinghouse. A "lover's lane" roomette; girls putting their names in a "date box" for invitations to nearby camp dances. Horseback riders in Rock Creek Park. A girl and her soldier boyfriend feeding the pigeons in Lafayette Park. Activities at service centers sponsored by the United Service Organizations.

DATE: March 1943

PHOTOGRAPHERS: Roger Smith.

SOURCE: Office of War Information.

LOT 1914

COLLECTION NAME: FSA-OWI Collection

SUBJECTS: Washington, D.C. Construction of Wake and Midway Halls, under the auspices of the Federal Works Agency, by Samuel Plato, a black contractor. Lucy D. Slowe Residence Hall, the first government-constructed hotel for black women war workers. Interior and exterior photographs. Girls in their rooms, playing cards, and visiting. Clara Camille Carroll, recently arrived, with a soldier date.

DATE: Fall 1942 and March 1943

PHOTOGRAPHERS: Roger Smith.

SOURCE: Office of War Information.

LOT 1916

COLLECTION NAME: FSA-OWI Collection

SUBJECTS: Washington, D.C. War wagon trailer, made of noncritical materials with "stand-sit" seats for war industry traffic, sponsored by the Office of Defense Transportation (ODT). The ODT express trailer, an oversize bus trailer, designed by the Office of Defense Transportation and War Production Board. War workers' coach, for fifteen passengers, made from a standard five-passenger light sedan.

DATE: July 1942 and January 1943

PHOTOGRAPHERS: Albert Freeman.

SOURCE: Office of War Information.

LOT 1924

COLLECTION NAME: FSA-OWI Collection

SUBJECTS: Greenbelt, Maryland, and Hollywood, California. Office of Defense Transportation "I'll carry mine" campaign to conserve delivery equipment. Young boys, with wagons, outside a grocery store in Greenbelt, Maryland. Motion picture "stars" in Hollywood, California, carrying their packages. A carryall basket, on wheels, and shopping bags to facilitate carrying.

DATE: November 1942 and June 1943

PHOTOGRAPHERS: Ann Rosener.

SOURCE: Office of War Information.

LOT 1930

COLLECTION NAME: FSA-OWI Collection

SUBJECTS: Washington, D.C., New York, New York, and Rutherford, New Jersey. Publicity and collection drive, under the direction of the U.S. Office of Civilian Defense, in various sections of the country. New York City and Washington, D.C., collections. Store window display in Rutherford, New Jersey. Boy Scouts of America and members of the American Legion assisting.

DATE: July 1941

PHOTOGRAPHERS: Alfred Palmer.

SOURCE: Office for Emergency Management.

LOT 1943

COLLECTION NAME: FSA-OWI Collection

SUBJECTS: Washington, D.C. Office of War Information and Office for Emergency Management newsrooms. Black women operators using teletype machines in the OWI to disseminate war news to all parts of the country. News Bureau rooms of the OWI and the OEM, similar to the city room of a daily newspaper.

DATE: 1942–43

PHOTOGRAPHERS: Roger Smith.

SOURCE: Office of War Information.

LOT 1945

COLLECTION NAME: FSA-OWI Collection

SUBJECTS: War production committees and boards. Meetings of various committees and boards of the War Production Board, War Labor Board, War Manpower Commission, Combined Production and Resources Board, Consultant Board of Smaller War Plants Division, Motor Transport Labor-Management Committee, representatives of U.S. Office of Defense Transportation, and others.

DATE: 1941–42

SOURCE: Office for Emergency Management and Office of War Information.

LOT 1950

COLLECTION NAME: FSA-OWI Collection

SUBJECTS: Washington, D.C. Individual citation winners in the War Production Drive being awarded certificates by President Franklin D. Roosevelt at a White House ceremony. Luncheon given by Donald M. Nelson, chairman of the War Production Board. Frances Perkins, secretary of labor, with citation winners.

DATE: 1942

PHOTOGRAPHERS: Alfred Palmer.

SOURCE: Office of War Information.

LOT 1951

COLLECTION NAME: FSA-OWI Collection

SUBJECTS: Washington, D.C. Office equipment used in Printing and Duplicating Section of the War Production Board. Addressograph and card-punching machine. Graphotype and automatic typewriters. Vari-typers and automatic check-signing machines. Mimeograph. Drafting room. Training pool classroom.

DATE: February 1942

PHOTOGRAPHERS: Howard Liberman.

SOURCE: Office of War Information.

LOT 1952

COLLECTION NAME: FSA-OWI Collection

SUBJECTS: Washington, D.C. Lend-Lease hearings before U.S. House of Representatives Foreign Affairs Committee. Witnesses in support of the continuance of the Lend-Lease Act appearing before the committee. Lend-Lease administrator Edward R. Stettinius, Jr., Secretaries Stimson and Wickard, and war shipping administrator Emory S. Land.

DATE: February 1943

PHOTOGRAPHERS: Alfred Palmer.

SOURCE: Office of War Information.

LOT 1954

COLLECTION NAME: FSA-OWI Collection

SUBJECTS: Washington, D.C. Luncheon of dehydrated foods, served at the Statler Hotel, to mark second anniversary of Lend-Lease. Members of the Diplomatic Corps of the United Nations, and U.S. government officials among guests. Chefs preparing food. War Agency officials at dehydrated food luncheon, in Social Security Building, November 1942.

DATE: 1942–43

PHOTOGRAPHERS: Alfred Palmer.

SOURCE: Office of War Information.

LOT 1955

COLLECTION NAME: FSA-OWI Collection

SUBJECTS: Washington, D.C. Luncheon of dehydrated foods served at the U.S. Senate restaurant. Chefs preparing food in the kitchen. Senators eating.

DATE: December 1942

PHOTOGRAPHERS: George Danor.

SOURCE: Office of War Information.

LOT 1956

COLLECTION NAME: FSA-OWI Collection

SUBJECTS: Washington, D.C. Combined Munitions Assignments Board, at a weekly meeting, presided over by Harry Hopkins, chairman. Members in attendance.

DATE: February 1943

PHOTOGRAPHERS: Alfred Palmer.

SOURCE: Office of War Information.

LOT 1961

COLLECTION NAME: FSA-OWI Collection

SUBJECTS: Washington, D.C. Victory Book Campaign. Bundles of books, contributed by members of Congress, stacked in the Statuary Hall of the Capitol, being received by volunteer workers of the American Red Cross, and soldiers from Fort Myer, Virginia. Hon. James M. Landis, director, U.S. Office of Civilian Defense, giving bundles of books to members of the American Women Volunteer Services.

DATE: 1943

PHOTOGRAPHERS: Alfred Palmer and Roger Smith.

SOURCE: Office of War Information.

LOT 1976

COLLECTION NAME: FSA-OWI Collection

SUBJECTS: Washington, D. C. Work Projects Administration vocational training school. Day and night classes in airplane mechanics, welding, lathe operation, and repairing of automobile engines. Black men and women trainees.

DATE: July 1942

PHOTOGRAPHERS: Howard Liberman.

SOURCE: Office of War Information.

LOT 1978

COLLECTION NAME: FSA-OWI Collection

SUBJECTS: Montgomery County, Maryland. High school boys registering with the U. S. Employment Service for training at nearby farms. Boys learning how well-shocked barley should look, how to pitch hay, and how to operate a tractor. Eating lunch and time-out for lemonade. Boys tying lunches on branches of a tree, away from ants and dogs.

DATE: June 1942

PHOTOGRAPHERS: Howard Liberman.

SOURCE: Office for Emergency Management.

LOT 1981

COLLECTION NAME: FSA-OWI Collection

SUBJECTS: Washington D.C. Women workers at the Washington National Airport. Supervisor of reservations posting data on the flight information board. Welding in the Pennsylvania Central Airlines shop. Operating a motorized, three-wheel "scooter," which hauls a truckload of baggage from plane to baggage room.

DATE: August 1942

PHOTOGRAPHERS: Howard Liberman.

SOURCE: Office of War Information.

LOT 2064

COLLECTION NAME: FSA-OWI Collection

SUBJECTS: Washington, D.C. District of Columbia policemen testing reclaimed rubber heels under actual wearing conditions, at the request of the Office of Price Administration. Policemen leaving the precinct headquarters and walking their beat. Close-ups of a pair of soles and heels.

DATE: May 1942

PHOTOGRAPHERS: Ann Rosener.

SOURCE: Office for Emergency Management.

LOT 2070

COLLECTION NAME: FSA-OWI Collection

SUBJECTS: U.S.S. *Booker T. Washington,* liberty ship. Construction work at the California Shipbuilding Corporation in Wilmington, California. Black workmen. Louise Washington, a federal government employee and granddaughter of Booker T. Washington, leaving Washington D.C., to attend the launching of the ship. Marian Anderson, black contralto, sponsor. Black leaders.

DATE: September-October 1942

PHOTOGRAPHERS: Alfred Palmer and Gordon Parks.

SOURCE: Office of War Information.

LOT 2105

COLLECTION NAME: FSA-OWI Collection

SUBJECTS: Washington, D.C. F.S. Gichner Iron Works, Inc. Iron and steel work. Large machines. Rotary saw, threading machine, and metal strip cutter.

DATE: 1941

PHOTOGRAPHERS: Baker.

SOURCE: Office for Emergency Management.

LOT 2123

COLLECTION NAME: FSA-OWI Collection

SUBJECTS: Washington, D.C. Opening of the Walsh Club, sponsored and supervised by the District of Columbia Municipal Recreation Association, for civilian war workers. Portraits of club officers. A shower held to furnish the kitchen, used for preparing refreshments for social activities. Dramatics group.

DATE: March 1943

PHOTOGRAPHERS: Alfred T. Palmer.

SOURCE: Office of War Information.

LOT 2126

COLLECTION NAME: FSA-OWI Collection

SUBJECTS: Washington, D.C. Officers of the United Nations, attending a garden party at Dumbarton Oaks.

DATE: September 6, 1942

SOURCE: Office of War Information.

LOT 2129

COLLECTION NAME: FSA-OWI Collection

SUBJECT: Washington D.C. Conversion of the Shoreham Hotel furnace from an oil- to a coal-burning system. Oil tank valve; oil burner head. Workmen inside furnace, on scaffold, installing coal grate. Detail of control dial panel. Outdoor coal bins.

DATE: September 1942

PHOTOGRAPHERS: Howard Liberman.

SOURCE: Office for Emergency Management.

LOT 2131

COLLECTION NAME: FSA-OWI Collection

SUBJECTS: Washington, D.C., Baltimore, Maryland, and vicinity. Car pooling as a means of conserving gas, tires, and automobiles. Workers at the Glenn L. Martin Company plant, Baltimore, Maryland, arranging transportation to and from work to conserve critical materials. Effect of gasoline shortage in Washington, D.C.

DATE: June 1942

PHOTOGRAPHERS: Alfred Freeman, Howard Hollem, and Howard Liberman.

SOURCE: Office for Emergency Management.

LOT 2132

COLLECTION NAME: FSA-OWI Collection

SUBJECTS: Washington, D.C. Office of Defense Transportation (ODT) system of port control and its traffic channel control. Method used by ODT to keep a daily map record of freight movement to port areas. International Business Machines used to compile the data. Joseph B. Eastman, director of the ODT, and other officials.

DATE: June 1942

PHOTOGRAPHERS: Alfred Freeman.

SOURCE: Office for Emergency Management.

LOT 2152

COLLECTION NAME: FSA-OWI Collection

SUBJECTS: Washington, D.C. Black laborers carrying and laying railroad ties for a spur line into a coal storage space for the federal government.

DATE: August 1942

PHOTOGRAPHERS: Howard Liberman.

SOURCE: Office of War Information.

LOT 2170

COLLECTION NAME: FSA-OWI Collection

SUBJECTS: Washington, D.C. U.S. Army Air Force demonstration of new equipment. C-82 transport, designed for hauling and landing heavy military cargo on rough fields near battle points. Cargo gliders used to carry utility and service units. Portable refrigeration units for meat and medical supplies. Field baking unit and a laundry unit capable of serving up to six hundred men.

DATE: October 1944

PHOTOGRAPHERS: Pauline Ehrlich and Lewis Walker.

SOURCE: Office of War Information.

LOT 2174

COLLECTION NAME: FSA-OWI Collection

SUBJECT: Montgomery County, Maryland, and Arlington County, Virginia. General election day. Men and women waiting outside polling places, standing in line to receive ballots, and having names checked by election judges. Ballot boxes. Douglas collapsible booths used for marking ballots, in secret, in Virginia. Automatic voting machines used to cast a vote, in secret, in Maryland.

DATE: November 7, 1944

PHOTOGRAPHERS: Lewis Walker, Maria Ealand.

SOURCE: Office of War Information.

LOT 2175

COLLECTION NAME: FSA-OWI Collection

SUBJECTS: Washington, D.C. Ceremonies held in the auditorium of the Department of the Interior at the dedication of a mural painting commemorating a free public concert Marian Anderson gave on the steps of the Lincoln Memorial, Easter Sunday, 1939. Public and other officials present.

DATE: January 1943

PHOTOGRAPHERS: Roger Smith.

SOURCE: Office of War Information.

LOT 2176

COLLECTION NAME: FSA-OWI Collection

SUBJECTS: Washington, D.C. Conservation of gasoline. Attendant at service station filling tank of motorist's car. Ration book of gasoline coupons.

DATE: July 1942

PHOTOGRAPHERS: Albert Freeman.

SOURCE: Office of War Information.

LOT 2177

COLLECTION NAME: FSA-OWI Collection

SUBJECTS: Washington, D.C. Office of War Information employees receiving free inoculation against smallpox, diptheria, and typhoid.

DATE: January 1943

PHOTOGRAPHERS: Roger Smith.

SOURCE: Office of War Information.

LOT 2178

COLLECTION NAME: FSA-OWI Collection

SUBJECTS: College Park, Maryland. Chinese technical experts at the University of Maryland. Discussion groups in the training course attended by the agricultural, social welfare, and water conservancy experts.

DATE: October 1944

PHOTOGRAPHERS: Riedon Tillery

SOURCE: Office of War Information.

LOT 2189

COLLECTION NAME: FSA-OWI Collection

SUBJECTS: Washington, D.C. Stanley Forman Reed, associate justice of the U.S. Supreme Court, administering the oaths of office to Joseph C. Grew, undersecretary of state; and Messrs. Clayton, Acheson, MacLeish, Rockefeller and Dunn, assistant secretaries of state. Secretary of State Edward R. Stettinius, Jr., introducing the group to the press representatives.

DATE: December 20, 1944

PHOTOGRAPHERS: J. Sherrel Lakey.

SOURCE: Office of War Information.

LOT 2191

COLLECTION NAME: FSA-OWI Collection

SUBJECTS: Washington, D.C. First public showing of the army's B-29 "super fortress" bombing plane. Ten-ton bomb load on display. To fill the fuel tanks, 160 fifty-five-gallon drums of gasoline are required. Tailgun assembly and gunner's compartment. Pattern pictures of belts of machine gun ammunition. Portraits of Gen. George C. Marshall and Henry H. Arnold and Col. T. Harmon, pilot of a B-29 that recently raided Japan.

DATE: November 29, 1944

PHOTOGRAPHERS: J. Sherrel Lakey.

SOURCE: Office of War Information.

LOT 2192

COLLECTION NAME: FSA-OWI Collection

SUBJECTS: Washington, D.C. Rural Arts exhibition, held under the auspices of the Farm Security Administration in the patio of the U.S. Department of Agriculture Building. Hand-carved figures and animals. Pewter, glass, and leather work. Hand-woven rugs and baskets.

DATE: 1937

PHOTOGRAPHERS: Theodor Horydczak.

SOURCE: Office of War Information.

LOT 2193

COLLECTION NAME: FSA-OWI Collection

SUBJECTS: Washington, D.C. Restricted display of publications and other materials issued by the Overseas Branch of the Office of War Information, as well as by Allied and enemy countries.

DATE: 1944

PHOTOGRAPHERS: J. Sherrel Lakey.

SOURCE: Office of War Information.

LOT 2206

COLLECTION NAME: FSA-OWI Collection

SUBJECTS: Washington, D.C. Installation of the Office of War Information exhibit of original drawings and paintings by artists serving in the armed forces. Preview, before shipping to Australia, held at the office of the Overseas Picture Division in the Auditor's Building. Visitors to the exhibit.

DATE: January 1945

PHOTOGRAPHERS: J. Sherrel Lakey.

SOURCE: Office of War Information.

LOT 2207

COLLECTION NAME: FSA-OWI Collection

SUBJECTS: Photoreproductions of pages from a unique display book, prepared in 1936 by the U.S. Resettlement Administration, on the housing situation in Washington and vicinity. Plans, poster effects, slums compared with planned communities.

DATE: 1936

SOURCE: Farm Security Administration.

LOT 2210

COLLECTION NAME: FSA-OWI Collection

SUBJECTS: Washington D.C. Defense Train exhibit. Samples of essential articles for the war effort displayed in "Defense Special" railroad trains, which toured the country to acquaint manufacturers with the needs of the war effort.

DATE: November 10, 1941

PHOTOGRAPHERS: U.S. Army Signal Corps.

SOURCE: Office for Emergency Management.

LOT 2211

COLLECTION NAME: FSA-OWI Collection

SUBJECTS: Washington D.C. Close-ups of Joseph C. Grew, U.S. undersecretary of state, and foreign officials and representatives signing the United Nations Declaration and Lend-Lease agreements.

DATE: March 1945

PHOTOGRAPHERS: J. Sherrel Lakey.

SOURCE: Office of War Information.

LOT 2212

COLLECTION NAME: FSA-OWI Collection

SUBJECTS: Washington, D.C. Photographic laboratory of the Farm Security Administration, located in the Auditor's Building (Treasury Department), Fourteenth Street and Independence Avenue, SW. Record photographs of equipment and installation. Enlargers, contact printer, and copying camera. Chemical mixing, film developing, enlarging and drying rooms.

DATE: January 1941

PHOTOGRAPHERS: Reginald Hotchkiss.

SOURCE: Farm Security Administration.

LOT 2213

COLLECTION NAME: FSA-OWI Collection

SUBJECTS: Production of the motion picture *Black Marketing* by the Office of War Information. Scenes being photographed in a wholesale meat market, probably in Washington, D.C. Sides of meat hanging on hooks. Retail grocery store. Woman customer using ration points. Courtroom reconstruction of a hearing on the illegal sale of meat, a black market activity. Actors and motion picture equipment.

DATE: July 1943

PHOTOGRAPHERS: Roger Smith.

SOURCE: Office of War Information.

U.S. Army Signal Corps. "Washington, D.C. 'Defense Special' train." November 1941. FSA-OWI Collection, Lot 2210.

LC-USZ62-89228

LOT 2215

COLLECTION NAME: FSA-OWI Collection

SUBJECTS: Washington, D.C. Reception at the residence of Joseph Davies, former ambassador to the Soviet Union. Small informal groups in conversation, and at the table.

DATE: March 1945

PHOTOGRAPHERS: J. Sherrel Lakey.

SOURCE: Office of War Information.

LOT 2216

COLLECTION NAME: FSA-OWI Collection

SUBJECTS: Washington D.C. French journalists with Gen. George C. Marshall. Group in conference and on steps.

DATE: March 1945

PHOTOGRAPHERS: J. Sherrel Lakey.

SOURCE: Office of War Information.

LOT 2217

COLLECTION NAME: FSA-OWI Collection

SUBJECTS: Washington, D.C. Foreign officials and guests at the fourth inauguration of President Franklin D. Roosevelt. Ceremony at the south portico of the White House. Small groups, portraits, crowd, band.

DATE: January 20, 1945

PHOTOGRAPHERS: J. Sherrel Lakey.

SOURCE: Office of War Information.

LOT 2218

COLLECTION NAME: FSA-OWI Collection

SUBJECTS: Washington, D.C. Officials of the Philippine Commonwealth. Portraits.

DATE: January 1945

PHOTOGRAPHERS: J. Sherrel Lakey.

SOURCE: Office of War Information.

LOT 2219

COLLECTION NAME: FSA-OWI Collection

SUBJECTS: Washington, D.C. Workmen erecting a sample prefabricated house, as a public demonstration of Lend-Lease materials, in Scott Circle, a public park area. Thirty thousand similar housing units (two bedrooms, kitchen, bath) were intended for shipment to Great Britain. Interiors, showing construction and facilities, before furnishing.

DATE: February–March 1945

PHOTOGRAPHERS: J. Sherrel Lakey.

SOURCE: Office of War Information.

LOT 2234

COLLECTION NAME: FSA-OWI Collection

SUBJECTS: Washington, D.C. Celebration of the thirty-third anniversary of the founding of the Girl Scouts of America, at the Norwegian Embassy.

DATE: March 1945

PHOTOGRAPHERS: J. Sherrel Lakey.

SOURCE: Office of War Information.

LOT 2236

COLLECTION NAME: FSA-OWI Collection

SUBJECTS: Washington, D.C. "Aerial Photography Maps Our Farmlands" exhibit for the U.S. Agricultural Adjustment Administration (USAAA), displayed at the meeting of the American Society of Photogrammetry in the Pan American Union. Individual panels and wall installations.

DATE: January 1938

PHOTOGRAPHERS: Aerial Photographic Laboratory, USAAA.

SOURCE: U.S. Agricultural Adjustment Administration.

LOT 2238

COLLECTION NAME: FSA-OWI Collection

SUBJECTS: Washington, D.C. President Franklin D. Roosevelt's funeral cortege. Procession moving along Constitution Avenue. Motorized and marching troops. Band. Soldiers standing at ease before the White House. Catafalque. Crowds of people waiting and watching. Office of War Information overseas radio crew broadcasting in five foreign languages.

DATE: April 14, 1945

PHOTOGRAPHERS: J. Sherrel Lakey.

SOURCE: Office of War Information.

LOT 2239

COLLECTION NAME: FSA-OWI Collection

SUBJECTS: Washington, D.C. Army Air Forces Air Transport Command Headquarters at the Washington National Airport. Terminal building, baggage inspection, operations and overwater briefing rooms. Waiting rooms.

DATE: January 1945

PHOTOGRAPHERS: J. Sherrel Lakey.

SOURCE: Office of War Information.

LOT 2242

COLLECTION NAME: FSA-OWI Collection

SUBJECTS: Washington, D.C. United Nations Committee of Jurists in session at the Interdepartmental Auditorium. Secretary of State Edward Stettinius addressing the delegates. Representatives, alternates, and advisers signing the report.

DATE: April 1945

PHOTOGRAPHERS: J. Sherrel Lakey.

SOURCE: Office of War Information.

LOT 2247

COLLECTION NAME: FSA-OWI Collection

SUBJECTS: Washington, D.C. Springtime. Public parks, government buildings, foreign embassy and legation buildings, apartments, hotels, and private residences. Monuments, animal cages in the National Zoological Park, sailboats. Street scenes and aerial views.

DATE: April–May 1945

PHOTOGRAPHERS: J. Sherrel Lakey, Lewis Walker, and Reginald Hotchkiss.

SOURCE: Office of War Information.

LOT 2281

COLLECTION NAME: FSA-OWI Collection

SUBJECTS: Greenbelt, Maryland. Row houses, shopping center, store interiors, play areas, child-care center, school, highway underpass, and other views of this planned community.

DATE: July 1946

PHOTOGRAPHERS: Gretchen Van Tassel.

SOURCE: Federal Public Housing Authority.

LOT 2288

COLLECTION NAME: FSA-OWI Collection

SUBJECTS: Washington, D.C. Library of Congress. Motion picture stills from a film on the Library of Congress, produced by the Office of War Information. Interiors of the building. A musical concert in the Coolidge Auditorium, close-ups of musicals. Declaration of Independence. Manuscript signatures. Reading braille. Employees at work. Bookstacks.

DATE: 1944

SOURCE: Office of War Information.

LOT 2312 (microfilm)

COLLECTION NAME: FSA-OWI Collection

SUBJECTS: "Negro achievements." Blacks in positions of distinction. Bethune-Cookman College, advanced educational opportunities. President of Howard University, Washington, D.C. Good housing conditions and home life. Churches and libraries. Farmers who have been helped. Military groups, review. Dormitory for office workers. Aircraft production workers.

NOTE: Photographs selected in March 1945 by Louis Reynolds of the Southern

Publishing Association (Seventh Day Adventists) for future use in periodical publications.

DATE: 1940-42

LOT 3075

COLLECTION NAME: FSA-OWI Collection

SUBJECTS: Washington, D.C. Operations in the Photographic Laboratory and Washington office of the Overseas Branch of the Office of War Information. Employees operating photographic equipment, including a specially built enlarger, glossy print dryer, copy camera, and densitometer. Special picture file in use. Processing of photos.

DATE: 1945

SOURCE: Office of War Information.

LOT 3423

COLLECTION NAME: FSA-OWI Collection

SUBJECTS: Miscellaneous group of photographs taken on trips throughout the United States. Views of cities, towns, farms, and people, including scenes from Washington, D.C. Some National Youth Administration projects.

DATE: 1936-42

PHOTOGRAPHERS: Barbara Wright.

SOURCE: Office of War Information.

LOT 3474

COLLECTION NAME: FSA-OWI Collection

SUBJECTS: Miscellaneous publicity photographs dealing with the Second World War and the home front. War production, rent control, blackout in Washington, D.C., interiors of Hechts Department Store in Washington, portraits of typical soldiers and sailors.

DATE: 1941-45

SOURCE: Office for Emergency Management.

Gretchen Van Tassel. "Greenbelt, Maryland, school." July 1946. FSA-OWI Collection, Lot 2281. LC-USZ62-88864

Gretchen Van Tassel. "Greenbelt, Maryland, grocery store." July 1946. FSA-OWI Collection, Lot 2281. LC-USZ62-88863

Ann Rosener. "Within the Jefferson Memorial rotunda in Washington, D.C., stands this nineteen-foot statue of America's third president. A Marine Honor Guard stands watch at its base where the original Declaration of Independence has been placed to commemorate Jefferson's bi-centennial anniversary April 12, 1943. The plaster of paris statue, made by sculptor Rudolph Evans, will be cast in bronze after the war." April 12, 1943. FSA-OWI Collection, Lot 3474.

LC-USE6-D-10111

George Danor. "Sightseeing bus used when gasoline was scarce." November 1942. FSA-OWI Collection, Lot 3474.

LC-USE6-D-7021

LOT 3915

COLLECTION NAME: FSA-OWI Collection

SUBJECTS: Washington, D.C. Sir Carl Berenson and staff of the New Zealand Legation. Portraits at desk, groups.

DATE: 1945

SOURCE: Office of War Information.

LOT 5324

COLLECTION NAME: FSA-OWI Collection

SUBJECTS: Washington, D.C. V-J Day evening at the Chinese Embassy. Informal group portraits; officials cheering from second-story windows. Jubilant crowds of Americans on the White House lawn and at Fourteenth and F Streets NW.

DATE: 1945

SOURCE: Office of War Information.

LOT 7849

COLLECTION NAME: FSA-OWI Collection

SUBJECTS: Greenbelt, Maryland. Planned communities in the United States. Shopping center, apartment house, typical rooms, nursery school classroom, elementary school, swimming pool, gasoline station, community band.

NOTE: Photos used in *Portrait of America*, series no. 44.

DATE: ca. 1940s

SOURCE: Office of War Information.

LOT 9425

COLLECTION NAME: FSA-OWI Collection

SUBJECTS: News pictures selected for information activities abroad. President Franklin D. Roosevelt, war strategists, cabinet officers, men of the armed forces, and other leaders. Civilian defense activities and materiel.

DATE: March 3–11, 1942

SOURCE: Office of War Information.

LOT 9429

COLLECTION NAME: FSA-OWI Collection

SUBJECTS: News pictures selected for information activities abroad. Officers and men of the armed forces. Military aircraft, ship chartered for the return of enemy diplomats. Nuns at work in a marine life laboratory. Temporary building under construction in Washington, D.C.

DATE: May 5–8, 1942

SOURCE: Office of War Information.

LOT 9439

COLLECTION NAME: FSA-OWI Collection

SUBJECTS: News pictures selected for information activities abroad. Cavalry, glider pilots, and other officers and men of the armed forces. Household sawdust furnace. Women at work in an aircraft plant. Air raid siren. War Department typists touring an ordnance plant. Senator Claude Pepper of Florida registering for the draft.

DATE: February 17–March 2, 1942

SOURCE: Office of War Information.

The Washington, D.C., photographer Waldon Fawcett took a special interest in documenting the staff, equipment, activities, and working environments of various government agencies and offices, as well as the White House offices and kitchen areas, embassies, and other organizations. Between about 1900 and 1910, he copyrighted many of these views, which now provide an important record of a young federal bureaucracy, and of the working conditions of clerks and administrators in the capital.

LOT 3261

SUBJECTS: U.S. Naval Medical School, Washington, D.C. Medical cadets in training. Students in laboratories; uniformed students in formation and exercising in front of the Naval Medical School (Old Naval Observatory); and students bearing stretchers. Includes several views of the Old Naval Observatory compound.

DATE: Ca. 1908

PHOTOGRAPHERS: Waldon Fawcett.

PHYSICAL DESCRIPTION: 14 silver gelatin photoprints, 20 × 25 cm, mounted.

ARRANGEMENT: Numbered set of photographs.

SOURCE: Copyright deposit by Waldon Fawcett, 1908.

LOT 4152

SUBJECTS: Exterior and interior views of the old House of Representatives Office Building (Cannon House Office Building). Building shown from the Capitol grounds. Interior views include photographs of desks, chairs, tables, filing cabinets, sinks, mirrors, ice-water taps, and telephones in congressmen's offices.

DATE: Ca. 1908

PHOTOGRAPHERS: Waldon Fawcett.

PHYSICAL DESCRIPTION: 10 silver gelatin photoprints, 20 x 25 cm, mounted.

ARRANGEMENT: Numbered set of photographs.

SOURCE: Copyright deposit by Waldon Fawcett, 1908.

LOT 4154

SUBJECTS: Interior views of the German Embassy in Washington, D.C. Includes photographs of ornate furniture, wall decorations, vases, chandeliers, and other interior subjects.

DATE: Ca. 1906

PHOTOGRAPHERS: Waldon Fawcett.

PHYSICAL DESCRIPTION: 5 silver gelatin photoprints, 20 x 25 cm.

ARRANGEMENT: Numbered set of photographs.

SOURCE: Copyright deposit by Waldon Fawcett, March 1906.

LOT 5002

SUBJECTS: Candid informal photographs of Samuel Gompers at his desk and with his family. Mr. and Mrs. T. L. Woodruff with their guests and pet animals outdoors before a chalet-like lodge. The John W. Kern family; photographs of the Joseph G. Cannon home; "the Shermans and their garden." Portraits of Capt. Charles S. Wallace and other men.

NOTE: Photographs were transferred to the Biographical File. A list of the items remains under this lot number.

DATE: Ca. 1908

PHOTOGRAPHERS: Waldon Fawcett.

PHYSICAL DESCRIPTION: Ca. 40 silver gelatin photoprints, 20 x 25 cm.

SOURCE: Copyright deposit by Waldon Fawcett, 1908.

LOT 8226

SUBJECTS: The White House, Washington, D.C. Interior views include the East Room, main corridor, State Dining Room, president's private office, Cabinet Room, and general office areas.

DATE: Ca. 1903

PHOTOGRAPHERS: Waldon Fawcett.

PHYSICAL DESCRIPTION: 8 silver gelatin photoprints, 20 x 25 cm.

SOURCE: Copyright deposit by Waldon Fawcett, 1903.

Waldon Fawcett. U.S. Naval Medical School, Washington, D.C. Copyright 1908. Lot 3261.
LC-USZ62-91647

Waldon Fawcett. German Embassy interior, Washington, D.C. Copyright 1906. Lot 4154.
LC-USZ62-91644

Waldon Fawcett. U.S. Census Bureau machine (Hollerith Electrical Tabulator). Copyright 1908. Lot 10568.

LC-USZ62-45687

Waldon Fawcett. Stamp-perforating machine operators, Bureau of Engraving and Printing, Washington, D.C. Copyright 1904. Lot 10589.

LC-USZ62-41764

Waldon Fawcett. U.S. Treasury employees. Copyright 1907. Lot 10801.

LC-USZ62-91643

Waldon Fawcett. Congressional reporter using dictaphone. Copyright 1908. Lot 10802.

LC-USZ62-70786

LOT 10568

SUBJECTS: Bureau of the Census tabulating machines. Men and women operating machines. Includes one view of the Hollerith electrical tabulator.

DATE: Ca. 1908

PHOTOGRAPHERS: Waldon Fawcett.

PHYSICAL DESCRIPTION: 6 silver gelatin photoprints, 12 x 18 cm or smaller.

SOURCE: Copyright deposit by Waldon Fawcett, 1908.

LOT 10589

SUBJECTS: U.S. Bureau of Engraving and Printing. Printers with their machines; gumming and perforating postage stamps; preparing uncut bills for shipment. Storage vault; serial numbering machines; women and men at work inspecting printed currency.

DATE: Ca. 1903-7

PHOTOGRAPHERS: Waldon Fawcett.

PHYSICAL DESCRIPTION: 19 silver gelatin photoprints, 20 x 25 cm or smaller.

SOURCE: Copyright deposit by Waldon Fawcett, 1903-7.

LOT 10801

SUBJECTS: U.S. Treasury Department. Handling money; cutting, counting, wrapping, bagging money. Worker inspecting nickels and silver certificates; men and women inspecting currency and operating machinery; money-weighing scales.

DATE: Ca. 1907

PHOTOGRAPHERS: Waldon Fawcett.

PHYSICAL DESCRIPTION: 12 silver gelatin photoprints, 19 x 25 cm or smaller.

SOURCE: Copyright deposit by Waldon Fawcett, 1907.

LOT 10802

SUBJECTS: Congressional reporters. Men using the Edison Business Phonograph, an early dictating machine, and transcribing from it.

DATE: Ca. 1908

PHOTOGRAPHERS: Waldon Fawcett.

PHYSICAL DESCRIPTION: 6 silver gelatin photoprints, 20 x 25 cm or smaller.

SOURCE: Copyright deposit by Waldon Fawcett, 1908.

LOT 10803

SUBJECTS: Early postal delivery automobiles. The dead letter office in Washington, D.C. Views of the inner and outer mechanisms in stamp-vending machines.

DATE: Ca. 1904–7

PHOTOGRAPHERS: Waldon Fawcett.

PHYSICAL DESCRIPTION: 7 silver gelatin photoprints, 19 x 25 cm or smaller.

SOURCE: Copyright deposit by Waldon Fawcett, 1904–7.

LOT 10804

SUBJECTS: U.S Naval Observatory, Washington, D.C. Men operating large telescopes and other astronomical equipment. Clocks and other measuring instruments.

DATE: Ca. 1904

PHOTOGRAPHERS: Waldon Fawcett.

PHYSICAL DESCRIPTION: 4 silver gelatin photoprints, 25 x 19 cm or smaller.

SOURCE: Copyright deposit by Waldon Fawcett, 1904.

LOT 10805

SUBJECTS: The White House kitchen, Washington, D.C. Interior views showing a delivery wagon at the entrance, stoves, tables, sink, boiler, dish cupboards, and cooking implements.

DATE: Ca. 1904

PHOTOGRAPHERS: Waldon Fawcett.

PHYSICAL DESCRIPTION: 6 silver gelatin photoprints, 19 x 25 cm or smaller.

SOURCE: Copyright deposit by Waldon Fawcett, 1904.

LOT 10806

SUBJECTS: The White House business office. Officials, clerks, and messengers at work. Interior views with desks, chairs, lamps, and stacks of papers.

DATE: Ca. 1906

PHOTOGRAPHERS: Waldon Fawcett.

PHYSICAL DESCRIPTION: 6 silver gelatin photoprints, 21 x 25 cm.

SOURCE: Copyright deposit by Waldon Fawcett, 1906.

LOT 10807

SUBJECTS: U.S. Secret Service. Chief John E. Wilkie in his office, sitting at his desk, opening a cabinet of photographs, and examining wall maps. Other employees at work at desks in large office area.

DATE: Ca. 1906

PHOTOGRAPHERS: Waldon Fawcett.

PHYSICAL DESCRIPTION: 4 silver gelatin photoprints, 19 x 26 cm.

SOURCE: Copyright deposit by Waldon Fawcett, 1906.

Waldon Fawcett. U.S. Naval Observatory, Washington, D.C. Copyright 1904. Lot 10804.
LC-USZ62-91645

LOT 11940

SUBJECTS: Printing telegraph. Uniformed operator using a Burry's System telegraph printer in an office. Operator cutting off message with scissors and punching alphabetical keyboard. Close-up view of keyboard and printer.

DATE: Ca. 1908

PHOTOGRAPHERS: Waldon Fawcett.

PHYSICAL DESCRIPTION: 4 silver gelatin photoprints, 19 x 25 cm or smaller.

SOURCE: Copyright deposit by Waldon Fawcett, 1908.

LOT 12514

SUBJECTS: Interior view of the Bolivian Legation, 1904; interior view of the Longworth residence, 1905.

DATE: 1904–5

PHOTOGRAPHERS: Waldon Fawcett.

PHYSICAL DESCRIPTION: 4 silver gelatin photoprints, 19 x 25 cm.

SOURCE: Copyright deposit by Waldon Fawcett, 1904–5.

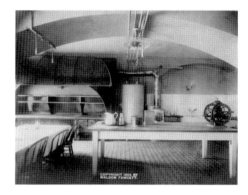

Waldon Fawcett. White House kitchen. Copyright 1904. Lot 10805.
LC-USZ62-91646

Waldon Fawcett. U.S. Secret Service Chief J. E. Wilkie in his office, showing cabinet of photographs of Secret Service Division officers. Copyright 1906. Lot 10807.
LC-USZ62-53526

George Fayer's New York and London portrait studios produced elegant images of public figures in the mid-twentieth century. In the mid-1940s, the Library of Congress exhibited George Fayer's work and acquired from him a collection of portraits of prominent people. During the 1940s, he regularly attended professional meetings and events to photograph the leading members of such groups as the International Bank for Reconstruction, the United Nations Assembly and Security Council, the Monetary Conference at Bretton Woods, and the Civil Aviation Conference in Chicago. He photographed State Department officials, delegates to the International Aeronautical Congress, and delegates to the Centennial of the Academy of Medicine. Cataloged Fayer Collection photographs of people and events in Washington, D.C., are described below.

LOT 2407

COLLECTION NAME: George Fayer Collection

SUBJECTS: Portraits of diplomats, industrialists, and other notable people, American and foreign, and delegates to the United Nations.

DATE: Ca. 1945

PHOTOGRAPHERS: George Fayer Camera Portraits (New York and London).

PHYSICAL DESCRIPTION: 78 silver gelatin photoprints, 20 x 25 cm or smaller.

ARRANGEMENT: Alphabetical. Finding aid available in the Prints and Photographs Reading Room.

SOURCE: Gift of George Fayer, 1945-46.

LOT 11824

COLLECTION NAME: George Fayer Collection

SUBJECTS: Studio portraits of public figures, including military and political leaders, musicians, scholars, public officials, and celebrities. Includes Dean Acheson, Sarah Churchill, Charles DeGaulle, Thomas Dewey, Anthony Eden, Jascha Heifetz, John Maynard Keynes, Louis Krasner, Vivian Leigh, Archibald MacLeish, John Pierpont Morgan, Herbert Putnam, Edward R. Stettinius, Arturo Toscanini, and Wendell Willkie.

DATE: Ca. 1940s

PHOTOGRAPHERS: George Fayer Camera Portraits (New York and London).

PHYSICAL DESCRIPTION: 54 silver gelatin photoprints, 41 x 51 cm or smaller.

ARRANGEMENT: Alphabetical. Finding aid available in the Prints and Photographs Reading Room.

SOURCE: Gift of George Fayer, 1945-46.

George Fayer. Archibald MacLeish, ca. 1940s. George Fayer Collection, Lot 11824.
                                   LC-USZ62-92742

George Fayer. Portrait of William Kapell, pianist, ca. 1945. George Fayer Collection, Lot 2407.
                                   LC-USZ62-92744

George Fayer. Dean Acheson, ca. 1940s. George Fayer Collection, Lot 11824.
                                   LC-USZ62-80188

George Fayer. Herbert Putnam, ca. 1940s. George Fayer Collection, Lot 11824.
                                   LC-USZ62-92743

Benjamin Brown French (1800-1870) held many important positions in Washington from 1833 until his death. He was assistant clerk and later clerk of the House (1833–47), commissioner of public buildings (1853–56 and 1861–67), and chief marshal of the District of Columbia at Lincoln's inauguration. The Manuscript Division holds eleven volumes of his journals, covering the years 1831–70. In 1972, S. LeRoy French presented to the Library an album primarily devoted to photographs of Washington scenes and sites, consisting of salted paper and albumen photographs and photographic copies of architectural drawings and sketches, collected and annotated by Benjamin Brown French. Most images in the album relate to buildings and structures constructed and events that occurred during his tenure as commissioner of public buildings, including the dome and extension wings of the U.S. Capitol, the U.S. General Post Office, the Washington Aqueduct, the Lincoln inauguration, and the Civil War. Many show surrounding buildings, laborers, and actual working methods and conditions. The Executive Mansion is pictured in 1859, and photographs of the troops quartered in the Capitol are included. Many architectural drawings of statuary, decorations, frescoes, and models and portraits of Thomas U. Walter and Constantino Brumidi complement the coverage of Capitol construction projects. Also included are depictions of Civil War armaments, ships, and scenes in Washington State.

"Cast iron column for peristyle of Dome" of the U.S. Capitol. 1863. Benjamin Brown French Album, p. 15. Lot 12251.

LC-USZ62-86286

LOT 12251 (microfilm)

COLLECTION NAME: Benjamin Brown French Album

SUBJECTS: U.S. Capitol construction, including construction of Capitol dome. Statuary, decorations, frescoes, architectural drawings and models. Government buildings in Washington, D.C., including the Executive Mansion, General Post Office, Patent Office, and others. Portraits of Thomas U. Walter and Constantino Brumidi. Washington city views, Civil War troops and armaments. U.S. Sloop *Pensacola.* Spokane River, Walla Walla Indians.

NOTE: Benjamin Brown French, commissioner of public buildings, assembled the album and captioned each image. Album inscribed by Benjamin Brown French to F. O. French.

DATE: Ca. 1853–ca. 1878

PHYSICAL DESCRIPTION: 1 album (141 salted paper and albumen photoprints and engravings), 46 x 33 cm. Images range in size from 6 x 5 cm to 37 x 44 cm. Page numbering added by the Library.

SOURCE: Gift of S. Leroy French, 1972.

RESTRICTIONS: Use of album is restricted because of its extremely fragile condition. Copy prints (arranged by subject) and microfilm (in original album order) are available for reference consultation.

"West Front of Capitol, July 1860 . . . Peristyle complete . . . 'Goose Creek once is Tiber now' . . . Botanical Gardens." July 1860. Benjamin Brown French Album, p. 39, Lot 12251.

LC-USZ62-86299

"View, looking N.W. from roof of Capitol: 27 June 1861." Benjamin Brown French Album, p. 129, Lot 12251.

LC-USZ62-78348

"Raising a monolithic column. Genl. P.O. Building; North facade." Benjamin Brown French Album, p. 73, Lot 12251.

LC-USZ62-86325

"Washington Aqueduct N, Bridge No. 6, Connecting Washington [on right] & Georgetown [on left]." February 18, 1860. Benjamin Brown French Album, p. 101, Lot 12251.

LC-USZ62-86344

"The Capitol a barrack, 'National Guard' D.C. Militia, Capt. Tate." May 1861. Benjamin Brown French Album, p. 55, Lot 12251.

LC-USZ62-86311

Toni Frissell Collection

Nearly forty years of work by commercial photographer Toni Frissell is represented in the collection of tens of thousands of negatives, contact sheets, and prints that she gave to the Library in 1971. Toni Frissell (b. 1907), who lived on Long Island with her husband, financier Francis McNeill Bacon III, is the sister of documentary filmmaker Varick Frissell, who was killed in the Arctic while on location and whose films and papers are held in the Motion Picture, Broadcasting, and Recorded Sound Division and the Manuscript Division of the Library. Toni Frissell photographed the famous and powerful in the United States and in Europe, including Churchill, Adenauer, and Pope Pius XII, and was overseas on assignment during World War II. Washington, D.C., subjects are found primarily in her fashion photographs, for which she often placed models in monumental contexts, against such backdrops as the U.S. Capitol and the Lincoln Memorial. Other subjects include prominent visitors to Washington, leading residents, and important officials.

The Frissell Collection requires the payment of a special fee for use of the images.

Toni Frissell. Model facing the Jefferson Memorial, November 1948. Toni Frissell Collection, Lot 12439.
LC-F9-02-4811-33-3

LOT 12432

COLLECTION NAME: Toni Frissell Collection

SUBJECTS: British military officers Sir John Dill and Sir Alan Brooke, Washington, D.C. Dill with his wife and daughter at the Jefferson Memorial. Brooke with Dill and wife. Brooke succeeded Dill as commander-in-chief of the Imperial General Staff in December 1941. Dill was in the United States as a member of the Joint Anglo-American Board of Strategy.

NOTE: Corresponding negatives are found in series LC-F9-02.

DATE: May 1943

PHOTOGRAPHERS: Toni Frissell.

PHYSICAL DESCRIPTION: 55 silver gelatin photoprints (5 contact sheets), images 6 × 6 cm, on sheets 20 × 25 cm.

Toni Frissell. Fashion model in front of the Capitol, December 1950. Toni Frissell Collection, Lot 12440.
LC-F9-02-5012-05-11

SOURCE: Gift of Toni Frissell, 1971.

RESTRICTIONS: Special reproduction procedures and fees.

LOT 12433

COLLECTION NAME: Toni Frissell Collection

SUBJECTS: Washington, D.C. Jefferson and Washington Monuments, Capitol, and White House in daytime and at night. These are possibly test shots for new cameras or film or for use as backdrops. Also, historian O. H. Van Zee and family in the Lincoln Memorial. Unidentified blacks, informal portraits at the Tidal Basin, a picket line at an unidentified location, possibly Sixteenth and K Streets NW.

NOTE: Corresponding negatives are found in series LC-F9-02.

DATE: 1946−61

PHOTOGRAPHERS: Toni Frissell.

PHYSICAL DESCRIPTION: 348 silver gelatin photoprints (29 contact sheets), images 6 × 6 cm, on sheets 20 × 25 cm.

SOURCE: Gift of Toni Frissell, 1971.

RESTRICTIONS: Special reproduction procedures and fees.

LOT 12434

COLLECTION NAME: Toni Frissell Collection

SUBJECTS: Portraits of Stuart Symington, Washington, D.C. Informal portraits of Symington on a golf course, posing with a golf club.

NOTE: Corresponding negatives are found in series LC-F9-02.

DATE: June 1951

PHOTOGRAPHERS: Toni Frissell.

PHYSICAL DESCRIPTION: 36 silver gelatin photoprints (3 contact sheets), images 6 × 6 cm, on sheets 20 × 25 cm.

SOURCE: Gift of Toni Frissell, 1971.

RESTRICTIONS: Special reproduction procedures and fees.

LOT 12435

COLLECTION NAME: Toni Frissell Collection

SUBJECTS: Brazilian Embassy ball, Washington, D.C. Unidentified people dancing and in conversation; informal portraits.

NOTE: Possibly taken for *Vogue* magazine. Corresponding negatives are found in series LC-F9-02.

DATE: June 1951

PHOTOGRAPHERS: Toni Frissell.

PHYSICAL DESCRIPTION: 27 silver gelatin photoprints (3 contact sheets), images 6 × 6 cm, on sheets 20 × 25 cm.

SOURCE: Gift of Toni Frissell, 1971.

RESTRICTIONS: Special reproduction procedures and fees.

LOT 12436

COLLECTION NAME: Toni Frissell Collection

SUBJECTS: American National Red Cross chairman Norman Davis, Washington, D.C. Portraits of Davis at his desk and with Red Cross staff or volunteers in uniform.

NOTE: Taken for the American Red Cross. Corresponding negatives are found in series LC-F9-02 and LC-F9-53.

DATE: January 1943

PHOTOGRAPHERS: Toni Frissell.

PHYSICAL DESCRIPTION: 38 silver gelatin photoprints (4 contact sheets), images 6 × 6 cm, on sheets 20 × 25 cm.

SOURCE: Gift of Toni Frissell, 1971

RESTRICTIONS: Special reproduction procedures and fees.

LOT 12437

COLLECTION NAME: Toni Frissell Collection

SUBJECTS: Oveta Culp Hobby inspecting Women's Army Auxiliary Corps (WAAC) at Fort Meade, Maryland, and Bolling Air Force Base, Washington, D.C. Hobby, director of the Women's Army Corps, is shown inspecting and conversing with the corps, and posing with other military officers. Also includes such activities of the corps as eating, attending church, hairdressing, polishing shoes, and leisure pastimes.

NOTE: Corresponding negatives are found in series LC-F9-02.

DATE: April 1943

PHOTOGRAPHERS: Toni Frissell.

PUBLISHER: Taken for *Vogue*. One image was published in the article "The WAACs Take Over," *Vogue* 7, no. 5 (July 1, 1943).

PHYSICAL DESCRIPTION: 285 silver gelatin photoprints (27 contact sheets), images 6 × 6 cm, on sheets 20 × 25 cm.

SOURCE: Gift of Toni Frissell, 1971.

RESTRICTIONS: Special reproduction procedures and fees. Particular photographs taken for hire may be protected by copyright.

LOT 12438

COLLECTION NAME: Toni Frissell Collection

SUBJECTS: Gail Whitney and her mother Mrs. Josiah Marvel, Washington, D.C. Gail Whitney looking at paintings in the National Gallery of Art and with her mother (formerly Mrs. Gwladys Hopkins Whitney) at the Lincoln Memorial. Probably taken for a story about busy mothers and their children, possibly for *Vogue* magazine.

NOTE: Corresponding negatives are found in series LC-F9-02.

DATE: May 1944

PHOTOGRAPHERS: Toni Frissell.

PHYSICAL DESCRIPTION: 76 silver gelatin photoprints (7 contact sheets), images 6 × 6 cm, on sheets 20 × 25 cm.

SOURCE: Gift of Toni Frissell, 1971.

RESTRICTIONS: Special reproduction procedures and fees.

LOT 12439

COLLECTION NAME: Toni Frissell Collection

SUBJECTS: Garfinckel's advertisements for *Vogue* magazine, Washington, D.C., region. Suits and street dresses, cocktail and evening gowns modeled against famous Washington backgrounds such as the Jefferson Memorial, Library of Congress, Washington Monument, and U.S. Capitol. Some in front of George Washington Masonic National Memorial Temple in Alexandria. Some models identified. Includes images of Frissell at work taken by A. Wickes and by an unidentified photographer. Frissell, New York fashion and advertising personnel, and models relaxing at Greenbrier Resort, Virginia.

NOTE: Taken for hire for Sterling Advertising Agency. Selected images published in *Vogue* approximately one to six months after each job. Corresponding negatives in series LC-F9-01 and LC-F9-02

DATE: 1943–49

PHOTOGRAPHERS: Toni Frissell and A. Wickes.

PHYSICAL DESCRIPTION: 2,160 silver gelatin photoprints (180 contact sheets), images 6 × 6 cm, on sheets 20 × 25 cm.

ARRANGEMENT: Finding aid available in the Prints and Photographs Reading Room.

Toni Frissell. Model at the Lincoln Memorial, December 1950. Toni Frissell Collection, Lot 12440.
LC-F9-02-5012-52-2

SOURCE: Gift of Toni Frissell, 1971.

RESTRICTIONS: Special reproduction procedures and fees.

LOT 12440

COLLECTION NAME: Toni Frissell Collection

SUBJECTS: Garfinckel's advertisements for *Vogue* magazine, Washington, D.C. Suits and street dresses, cocktail and evening gowns modeled against famous Washington, D.C., backgrounds, mostly the Jefferson Memorial, Reflecting Pool, Tidal Basin, and U.S. Capitol; some at Mount Vernon. Includes night shots possibly made with infrared film. Model often with dogs. Some models identified.

NOTE: Selected images published in *Vogue* approximately one to six months after each job. Corresponding negatives are found in series LC-F9-02.

DATE: 1950–62

PHOTOGRAPHERS: Toni Frissell.

PHYSICAL DESCRIPTION: 4,992 silver gelatin photoprints (416 contact sheets), images 6 × 6 cm, on sheets 20 × 25 cm.

ARRANGEMENT: Finding aid available in the Prints and Photographs Reading Room.

SOURCE: Gift of Toni Frissell, 1971.

RESTRICTIONS: Special reproduction procedures and fees.

Alexander Gardner, Photographer

Alexander Gardner (1821–1882) was a Scot who arrived in New York in 1856, his fare having been paid by Mathew Brady. An expert in the wet collodion process, he worked as studio manager of Brady's Washington establishment from 1858 until he parted company with Brady during the Civil War, to work as official photographer for the Army of the Potomac under Gen. George B. McClellan. In that capacity, he photographed the Union camps, soldiers, and the aftermath of battles and he copied maps for the Army Secret Service. After General McClellan was relieved of his command, Gardner returned to Washington, where he opened his own studio at 511 Seventh Street NW. Working with his brothers James and John and employing Timothy O'Sullivan and Egbert Guy Fox, Gardner became one of Mathew Brady's chief competitors, but in 1867 he closed his Washington studio to pursue photography on the frontier, as a field photographer for the Union Pacific Railroad. The Prints and Photographs Division holds stereographs Gardner made during his travels in the West (see Lot 2775). In 1870, with his son Lawrence he reestablished his Washington photographic operation at 921 Pennsylvania Avenue NW.

Many of the Civil War photographs to which Brady attached his name were in fact made by Alexander Gardner and other photographers who followed the battles in Brady's employ (see "Mathew B. Brady and Brady-Handy Collections" and "Civil War Views"). When Gardner parted company with Brady, he took with him the glass plate negatives he had made for Brady. In compiling the two volumes of *Gardner's Photographic Sketch Book of the War* (Washington: Philip and Solomons, 1865–66), Alexander Gardner made a concerted effort to identify both the photographer who produced each negative and the person who made the print from it.

Alexander Gardner. Marshall House, Alexandria, Virginia, August 1862. Lot 3859.
LC-USZ62-92583

Alexander Gardner (negative by William R. Pywell). "Old Capitol Prison, Washington, D.C." From Gardner's Photographic Sketch Book of the War, volume 2, plate 90, ca. 1865. Master Photographs Collection.
LC-B8184-4159

LOT 3859

SUBJECTS: Civil War-era photographs, most used in *Gardner's Photographic Sketch Book of the War*. These examples bear on the versos descriptive captions that have been attributed to Gardner, after comparison with Gardner's handwriting. Views include camp architecture at Brandy Station, Yorktown, and Dutch Gap; the ruins of Petersburg; the Richmond Railroad on the James River; Harper's Ferry at Manassas Junction; the Mathews House, Bull Run; Gettysburg views; and Marshall House in Alexandria. The lot also includes one reproduction of a cartoon depicting Benjamin Butler and "Harry Gringo" arguing about Sawyer rifles at the Washington Navy Yard, with the Capitol in the background.

DATE: Ca. 1861–ca. 1865

PHOTOGRAPHERS: Alexander Gardner.

PHYSICAL DESCRIPTION: 15 albumen photoprints, 19 × 25 cm.

SOURCE: Gift of the Chester County Historical Society of Westchester, Pennsylvania, 1949.

LOT 4344

SUBJECTS: Scenes of battlefields, camps and forts, soldiers, weapons, hospitals, military field headquarters, and other Civil War views in Virginia, Maryland, Pennsylvania, Washington, D.C., West Virginia, and North Carolina. Washington-area subjects include the Marshall House and a slave pen in Alexandria; Fairfax Courthouse; and the Old Capitol Prison.

NOTE: Some photographs were deposited for copyright in 1865 in the D.C. District Court. All images are captioned and dated.

DATE: Ca. 1862–ca. 1866

PHOTOGRAPHERS: Alexander Gardner, Timothy H. O'Sullivan, George N. Barnard, William Pywell, and James F. Gibson.

PUBLISHER: *Gardner's Photographic Sketch Book of the War*, 2 vols. (Washington: Philip and Solomons, 1865–66; reprint, New York: Dover Publications, 1959). Title page bears the name of A. R. Ward, Del.

PHYSICAL DESCRIPTION: 2 albums (100 albumen photoprints).

SOURCE: Transfer from the U.S. Treasury Department.

LOT 10483

SUBJECTS: Sketches show a full railroad train in the park and on the road, a section-train on the road, and lines in operation.

NOTE: Copy photographs bear the address of Gardner's Washington studio, 511 Seventh Street NW. They were formerly owned by the U.S. Signal Service, Field Telegraph Train, Washington, Office of the Chief Signal Officer (1870).

DATE: Ca. 1860s–ca. 1870

PHOTOGRAPHERS: Copy photographs by Alexander Gardner of sketches by Private Wohlberg.

PHYSICAL DESCRIPTION: 4 albumen photoprints, 44 × 56 cm.

LOT 11790

COLLECTION NAME: James Garfield Papers, Manuscript Division

SUBJECTS: "Photographs of Red Cloud and Principal Chiefs of Dacotah Indians Taken on their Visit to Washington, D.C., May, 1872, by Alex. Gardner, for Trustees of Blackmore Museum, Salisbury, England." Includes studio portraits of fifteen chiefs and two of their squaws. Red Cloud shaking hands with William Blackmore.

NOTE: Portfolio; printed by Gibson Bros., Washington.

Alexander Gardner. "Tchan-Gm-Ani-To-I-Sh-Na-Lah (Lone Wolf)." May 1872. Lot 11790.
LC-USZ62-92582

Alexander Gardner. "Va-How-A-Pah (Ear of Corn), Squaw of Lone Wolf." May 1872. Lot 11790.
LC-USZ62-92581

DATE: May 1872

PHOTOGRAPHERS: Alexander Gardner.

PHYSICAL DESCRIPTION: 35 albumen photoprints, 14 × 10 cm, on original paper mounts, 31 × 26 cm.

SOURCE: Transfer from the Manuscript Division, 1970.

LOT 12658

SUBJECTS: Buildings in Washington, D.C. U.S. Capitol under construction, with unfinished dome; Department of Agriculture Building on the Mall; Executive Mansion; Patent Office, from the southwest; Treasury Building, from the southeast.

NOTE: Photographs bear original printed captions.

DATE: Ca. 1860s

PHOTOGRAPHERS: Alexander Gardner

PHYSICAL DESCRIPTION: 5 albumen photoprints, 48 × 33 cm or smaller.

Alexander Gardner. "Red Cloud [with] Wm. Blackmore." May 1872. Lot 11790.
LC-USZ62-92580

After the publication of his book *Capital Losses: A Cultural History of Washington's Destroyed Buildings* (Washington: Smithsonian Institution Press, 1979), which dealt with the subject of Washington's destroyed and altered buildings, James M. Goode presented to the Library of Congress his collection of research photographs and related notes. The photographs, gathered from repositories and museums throughout the Washington area, include documentary and architectural photographs of buildings and some pictures of events and portraits of people associated with those buildings. Other kinds of structures such as street furniture and architectural oddities are included as well. His collection of research photographs is divided into two cataloged groups: those pictures relating to structures discussed in *Capital Losses*; and those pictures relating to destroyed or altered buildings that were not discussed in the book because of space limitations. Both groups are organized according to the structure of the book, that is, by type of building or building function. All photographs are indexed, and most have corresponding copy negatives.

From time to time, James Goode has presented the Library with photographs and negatives gathered during various other architectural research projects, including photographs from an exhibit about the sculptor Daniel Chester French, photographs of rowhouse architectural details, and photographs of Federal Triangle architectural elements and murals. He is also the author of the book *Outdoor Sculpture in Washington, D.C.* (1974), and of a study of Washington's early twentieth-century apartment building architecture.

Blair House, Silver Spring, Maryland, ca. 1926. James Goode Collection, Lot 12013–CC–1.
LC-G7-117

Tunnicliff's Tavern at Pennsylvania Avenue and Ninth Street SE, ca. 1890. James Goode Collection, Lot 11800–G1 (picture no. G-1671X).
LC-USZ62-92092

Walter Oates, Washington Star. Christian Heurich Brewery, located on the square bounded by Twenty-fifth, Twenty-sixth, D, and Water Streets NW, January 9, 1956. James Goode Collection, Lot 11800–J5.
LC-G7-1774

LOT 11800

COLLECTION NAME: James M. Goode Collection

SUBJECTS: Structures included in James Goode's *Capital Losses: A Cultural History of Washington's Destroyed Buildings* (Washington: Smithsonian Institution Press, 1979). Demolished, altered, or threatened buildings and landmarks in Washington, D.C., including dwellings, hotels, churches, fire stations, and theaters, as well as commercial, government, transportation, school, and other organizations' buildings. Includes architectural elements. Some area businesses, such as the Christian Heurich Brewery and the U.S. Electric Lighting Company, with interior views of plant and workers. Streets and street fixtures, including pumps, watering troughs, traffic signals, and lamps. Photographs of prints, maps, and architectural plans; some portraits of people associated with particular structures.

NOTE: Corresponding negatives in series LC–G7, –G72, and –G73. A few negatives are unprinted. These structures were all discussed in *Capital Losses* and many, but not all, of the images in this collection were published in the book. Images collected by James Goode but not discussed in *Capital Losses* are in Lot 12013.

DATE: Ca. 1850–ca. 1980

PHYSICAL DESCRIPTION: Ca. 2,500 silver gelatin copy photoprints, 21 × 26 cm or smaller.

ARRANGEMENTS: Arranged in groups *A* to *S* by architectural style (e.g., Georgian, Federal), type of structure (e.g., Churches, Theaters, Street Furniture), or date of structure. Finding aids and indexes to building names, addresses, subjects, and image numbers are available in the Prints and Photographs Reading Room. Supplementary textual materials regarding some buildings are also available upon request.

SOURCE: Gift of James M. Goode, 1979.

RESTRICTIONS: Permission to reproduce images bearing credit lines noting institutions other than Library of Congress should be obtained from the custodial institution indicated.

LOT 12013

COLLECTION NAME: James M. Goode Collection

SUBJECTS: Demolished and altered buildings in the Washington, D.C., area. Buildings showing a wide range of architectural styles and building types. Also includes a few portraits of residents or architects, vehicles, bridges, and street scenes.

NOTE: Goode collected these copy photographs while researching his book *Capital Losses*. Most of them represent more obscure buildings that could not be included in the book for lack of space. Images of buildings featured in *Capital Losses* are in Lot 11800. Corresponding negatives in series LC–G7, –G72, and –G73. A few negatives are unprinted.

DATE: Ca. 1870–ca. 1983

PHYSICAL DESCRIPTION: 1,481 silver gelatin photoprints, 20 × 25 cm or smaller.

ARRANGEMENT: Arranged in groups *AA* to *WW* by style (e. g., Georgian, Federal) or type (e. g., Churches, Theaters). Finding aid and indexes to building names, subjects, addresses, and image numbers are available in the Prints and Photographs Reading Room. Supplementary textual materials regarding some buildings are also available upon request.

SOURCE: Gift of James Goode, 1983, 1984.

RESTRICTIONS: Permission to reproduce images with credit lines noting institutions other than Library of Congress should be obtained from the custodial institution indicated.

LOT 12279

SUBJECTS: Row houses and commercial buildings in Washington, D.C. Late nineteenth- and early twentieth-century structures. Facades, architectural details. Includes houses on the following streets: Eighteenth, Nineteenth, Twentieth, Twenty-first, Twenty-second, M, N, Q, R, S, Corcoran, Florida, Swann, Riggs Place, Connecticut Avenue, New Hampshire Avenue. Address and other caption information appears on the verso of most images.

NOTE: Photographs taken for hire for Goode. Corresponding negatives in series LC–G73 for approximately one-third of the prints.

DATE: 1974

PHOTOGRAPHERS: Judy Burr and B. R. (identity unknown).

PHYSICAL DESCRIPTION: 343 silver gelatin photoprints, 28 × 13 cm or smaller.

ARRANGEMENT: *Lot 12279–1*: Numbered streets; *Lot 12279–2*: Lettered streets; *Lot 12279–3*: Named streets; *Lot 12279–4*: Unidentified structures.

SOURCE: Gift of James M. Goode, 1983–84.

Maynard Owen Williams, National Geographic Society. Tidal Basin Bathing Beach, ca. 1922. James Goode Collection, Lot 12013–KK–1 (picture no. G-1000). Reproduced with permission.

LOT 12280

SUBJECTS: Sculptures by Daniel Chester French in Washington, D.C. Compiled for the exhibit "The Nineteen Known Pieces of Sculpture by Daniel Chester French in Washington, D.C.," prepared by James Goode for the National Trust for Historic Preservation, March-April 1971. Statues of Abraham Lincoln, James Garfield, Henry Wilson, Lewis Cass, Thomas Hopkins Gallaudet, Herodotus, and allegorical figures. Fountains, monuments, relief marbles, medals. Portrait of French.

NOTE: Accompanied by a brief biography of French and descriptions of each work; additional descriptions without corresponding images.

DATE: Ca. 1963–70

PHOTOGRAPHERS: J. E. Purdy.

PHYSICAL DESCRIPTION: 16 silver gelatin copy photoprints, 20 × 25 cm.

SOURCE: Gift of James Goode, 1983.

RESTRICTIONS: Permission to reproduce images from collections other than the Library of Congress should be obtained from the custodial institution.

Acme Photo from Washington Daily News. *Concert on the Watergate Barge, moored on the Potomac River below the Lincoln Memorial. At the opening of the season, canoeists raise their paddles in salute as the National Anthem is played. June 16, 1946. James Goode Collection, Lot 12013–RR–1. Reproduced with the permission of UPI/Bettmann Newsphotos.*

United States College of Veterinary Surgeons, 222 C Street NW. An animal ambulance, pulled by "Nippo" the pony, stands in front of the lower stable. The boys, Joseph F. and Charles J. Robinson, are the sons of the college's founder. Ca. 1900. James Goode Collection, Lot 12013–00–1.

LC-G7-2941

"The Sight Seeing Automobile Coach of Washington." Ca. 1905. James Goode Collection, Lot 12013–PP–1.

LC-G7-807

LOT 12563

SUBJECTS: Architectural details from federal buildings, Washington, D.C. Includes photographs of pedimental and other sculptures, paintings, statues and maquettes of statues, and exterior and interior views of artwork in the Commerce Department Building, the National Archives, and the Supreme Court Building. Art work includes "Fisheries," "Foreign and Domestic Commerce," "Declaration of Independence" (by Barry Faulkner); "Contemplation of Justice" and "Executor of the Law" (by J. E. Fraser).

NOTE: Includes one copy of an architectural rendering of the Federal Trade Commission Building.

DATE: Ca. 1930s

PHOTOGRAPHERS: Theodor Horydczak.

PHYSICAL DESCRIPTION: 15 silver gelatin photoprints, 25 × 41 cm or smaller.

SOURCE: Gift of James M. Goode, 1985.

Upon Anson Conger Goodyear's death in April 1964, his collection of photographic images of Abraham Lincoln was bequeathed to the Library of Congress. The collection consists of twelve images, all of which are important portraits but only one of which is a photograph from life. The remaining eleven are copy photographs. Some of these copy photographs are in the form of ambrotypes, and others are salted paper, albumen, and silver gelatin photoprints. One is a tintype, one a glass negative, and one a glass transparency. There is also one daguerreotype that is something of an oddity, it being a copy of a portrait dated 1861 or later showing a bearded Lincoln. The daguerreotype process had been largely abandoned by that time, and the daguerreotype, a nonreproducible medium, was impractical to use as a copy medium.

The truly rare item in this collection is an ambrotype by Preston Butler of Springfield, Illinois, made on August 13, 1860, and still in its original frame of gilt-and-black wood. The portrait shows Lincoln as he appeared about six months before he grew his beard. (This particular image is listed by Meserve as no. 29.) Butler had a studio in Springfield and made four photographs of Lincoln for the use of sculptor Leonard W. Volk. The ambrotype was owned by a Mr. Brown of Philadelphia, possibly a relative of the portrait painter John Henry Brown (1818–1891), who was commissioned to paint Lincoln's portrait. William H. Lambert, the noted Lincoln collector, purchased it from Brown, and it remained in Lambert's collection until his library and pictures were auctioned in 1914. Anson Conger Goodyear purchased the ambrotype at that auction for $450, an exceedingly high price at that time for a historical photograph.

The Manuscript Division holds a small collection of Anson Goodyear's notes, acquired in 1957.

REFERENCES:

Fern, Alan, and Hirst D. Milhollen, "A Preston Butler Ambrotype of Lincoln." In Shaw, *A Century*, pp. 28–29.
Meserve, Frederick Hill. *The Photographs of Abraham Lincoln.* New York, 1911.

Earles' Gallerie (Philadelphia[?]). Framed ambrotype portrait of Abraham Lincoln, ca. 1855–60. Anson Conger Goodyear Collection of Lincoln Images, Lot 12559.

LC-USZ62-7728A

Half-plate daguerreotype copy of post-1860 albumen photograph of Abraham Lincoln, ca. 1864. Anson Conger Goodyear Collection of Lincoln Images, Lot 12559.

LC-USZ62-11178B

LOT 12559

COLLECTION NAME: Anson Conger Goodyear Collection of Lincoln Images

SUBJECTS: Portraits of Abraham Lincoln with and without a beard; most are half-length, some are in profile. Most images are copy photographs. Some photographs are annotated with a Meserve or a Goodyear number. Daguerreotype copy of an 1860s portrait of Lincoln, dated on the basis of his having grown a beard only after his election as president. Includes one ambrotype attributed to Preston Butler, August 13, 1860, and a photograph by Alexander Gardner.

NOTE: Some photographs are faded or have damaged areas; some cases are worn. Related nonpictorial material is filed in the Supplementary Archives.

DATE: Ca. 1856–ca. 1865

PHOTOGRAPHERS: Preston Butler, Alexander Gardner, Hesler, Earles' Gallerie, and Philip & Solomons.

PHYSICAL DESCRIPTION: 12 items (including ambrotypes, albumen photoprints, 1 silver gelatin photoprint, 1 salted paper print, 1 tintype, 1 daguerreotype, 1 transparency, and 1 glass negative), 40 × 30 cm or smaller. Some photographs in leather, lacquer, or brass cases or frames, 20 × 17 cm or smaller; two albumen prints are cabinet cards; one albumen print and the salted paper print are mounted on cardboard.

ARRANGEMENT: A finding aid is available in the Prints and Photographs Reading Room.

SOURCE: Gift of A. Conger Goodyear, 1965.

The Library of Congress acquired a large portion of the photographic negatives and photographic proof prints produced by the architectural photography firm Gottscho-Schleisner, Inc., of New York. The two partners, Samuel H. Gottscho (ca. 1875–1971) and William H. Schleisner (1896–1971), produced fine architectural records on commission for architects and commercial businesses. Most of the early work (pre-1945) and late work (post-1961) is by Gottscho, with most work from the period 1945–61 by Schleisner. The team photographed the interiors and exteriors of homes, stores, factories, gardens, historic buildings, and other structures in the Northeast and elsewhere in the United States. Their work documents important design achievements of clients and architects.

The Prints and Photographs Division holds about 25,000 original negatives (13 × 18 cm or 5 × 7 inch and 11 × 16 cm or 4 × 6 inch format, in series LC-G6), about 16,700 contact prints, about 2,000 prints in albums, about 1,670 modern contact prints produced by the Library from original negatives, about 40 enlargements made by the photographers themselves, and about 280 color film transparencies (35 mm, 11 × 13 cm or 4 × 5 inch and 13 × 18 cm or 5 × 7 inch formats). Original logbooks provide an index of clients and chronological lists of negatives.

The Library does not own the complete Gottscho-Schleisner negative collection. Other negatives are held by the Avery Architectural Library, the Museum of the City of New York, and the Brooklyn Public Library. The Library's purchase of these negatives was supported in part by a gift from Mrs. Jean Flagler Matthews of Rye, New York, 1979–85. The collection is restricted; commercial use requires the written permission of Mrs. Doris Schleisner of Jamaica, New York, during her lifetime. (Doris Schleisner is the daughter of Samuel Gottscho and widow of William Schleisner.) At this time, only the Washington, D.C., portion of the collection is processed and available for research use; proof prints are cataloged and described below.

REFERENCES:

Deschin, Jacob. "Viewpoint." *Popular Photography,* June 1980, pp. 12, 54, 56, and 58.

LOT 12036

COLLECTION NAME: Gottscho-Schleisner Collection

SUBJECTS: Washington, D.C., and vicinity. Building interiors and exteriors. Photographs commissioned by both clients and architects to record important design achievements. Includes College Park, Maryland, and Arlington, Virginia, views.

NOTE: Images have been captioned by the Library. All prints are from original negatives in series LC–G6; a few modern prints were made by the Library. Accompanied by copies of original logbooks and index of clients.

DATE: 1932–50, chiefly 1940–44

PHOTOGRAPHERS: Samuel H. Gottscho and William H. Schleisner.

PHYSICAL DESCRIPTION: 233 silver gelatin photoprints, 13 × 18 cm.

ARRANGEMENT: By original negative numbers, with index to building names and architects.

SOURCE: Purchase from Gottscho-Schleisner, Inc., 1979–83.

RESTRICTIONS: Commercial use requires written permission of Mrs. Doris Schleisner, Jamaica, New York, in her lifetime.

Samuel Gottscho or William Schleisner. Franklin Simon Company store on Connecticut Avenue, October 7, 1948. Gottscho-Schleisner Collection, Lot 12036.

LC-G612-53965

Samuel Gottscho or William Schleisner. Ballroom in the British Embassy, 3100 Massachusetts Avenue NW, February 16, 1945. Gottscho-Schleisner Collection, Lot 12036.

LC-G612-46860

Samuel Gottscho or William Schleisner. Frederick Douglass Homes, rear of typical building, April 28, 1944. Gottscho-Schleisner Collection, Lot 12036.

LC-G612-45256

Samuel Gottscho or William Schleisner. The American Institute of Pharmacy, Constitution Avenue NW, March 8, 1944. Gottscho-Schleisner Collection, Lot 12036.

LC-G612-44961

Samuel Gottscho or William Schleisner. National Gallery of Art, west central gallery, December 12, 1940. Gottscho-Schleisner Collection, Lot 12036.

LC-G612-38974

Gilbert H. Grosvenor Collection of Alexander Graham Bell Photographs

The photographs of Alexander Graham Bell (1847–1922) and his family, activities, and scientific investigations are held in the Prints and Photographs Division and consist of daguerreotypes and other cased images, photographs, glass negatives, and photograph albums, numbering about 28,000 items. The coverage includes family portraits of the Bell, Fairchild, Grosvenor, and other families. Snapshots and family scenes taken during travels in the United States, Canada, Europe, and Australia and at homes in Washington, D.C., New York, New Hampshire, Nova Scotia, and Scotland are included, as are photographs relating to Bell's experimental work with deafness and "Visible Speech," the invention of the telephone, genetics and sheep breeding, experimental kites and aviation, and the hydrofoil. Washington subjects have been cataloged and are described below.

The Manuscript Division holds the Alexander Graham Bell Papers, which were donated by his heirs in 1975. The papers number 140,000 items (accompanied by a container list) and include diaries, correspondence, printed matter, financial and legal records, and several hundred volumes of laboratory notebooks which record his daily work from 1865 to 1922. The papers deal with diverse subjects, including patent disputes and early marketing of the telephone, Bell's scientific research in aeronautics, eugenics, and physics, his financial support of *Science* magazine, and his participation in the National Geographic Society and the Smithsonian Institution. This family archive includes materials relating to Alexander Melville Bell, the inventor's father, Mabel Hubbard Bell, his wife, and Gilbert H. Grosvenor, his son-in-law, as well as correspondence among the various relatives by marriage. Some musical compositions, sound records, and maps have been transferred to the Music Division, the Motion Picture, Broadcasting, and Recorded Sound Division, and the Geography and Map Division. Related material may be found in the Grosvenor Family Papers (65,600 items) and Hubbard Family Papers (8,000 items), which the Manuscript Division acquired in 1977.

Harris & Ewing. Portrait of Alexander Graham Bell, 1902. Gilbert Grosvenor Collection, Lot 11533–B–3–20.

LC-G9-Z4-116776-T

REFERENCES:

Melville, no. 26, pp. 38–39.
Brannan, Beverly W., and Patricia T. Thompson. "Alexander Graham Bell: A Photograph Album." In Shaw, *A Century*, pp. 163–81.

Alexander Graham Bell with his wife Mabel and daughters Elsie (left) *and Marian (Daisy), December 1885. Gilbert Grosvenor Collection, Lot 11533–B–7–4.*

LC-G9-Z4-116794-T

LOT 11533: Collection-Level Description

COLLECTION NAME: Grosvenor Collection of Alexander Graham Bell Photographs

SUBJECTS: Visual archives (primarily photoprints, some prints and charts) of A. G. Bell's family line, documenting scientific endeavors and family and personal relationships.

NOTE: Photographs collected by A. G. Bell and his descendants.

DATE: 1796–ca. 1965

PHYSICAL DESCRIPTION: Ca. 28,000 photographs, negatives, lantern slides, photomechanical prints, and other reproductions.

ARRANGEMENT: Photographs cataloged and stored in lots according to subject, as indicated. Cataloged material arranged in two series: (1) thirty-one groups of original materials in numbered subunits, kept in the order in which they arrived; (2) three groups of vintage and recently made photoprints arranged alphabetically by subject in lettered subunits.

SOURCE: Gift of Alexander Graham Bell's descendants. Transfer from the Manuscript Division, 1975.

RESTRICTIONS: Negative shelflist cards indicate restrictions on use of particular images, when known.

LOT 11533–A

COLLECTION NAME: Grosvenor Collection of Alexander Graham Bell Photographs.

SUBJECTS: Subject albums, compiled by the Library of Congress: Airplanes (vols. 1–13); Animals (vol. 14); Awards (vol. 15); Birdhouses (vol. 16); Boats (vols. 17–26); Buildings (vol. 27); Camping (vol. 28); Deafness (vol. 29); Eclipse of the sun in 1900 (vol. 30); Floats (vol. 31); Gardens (vol. 32); Hydrofoils (vols. 33–34); Kites (vols. 35–57); Museums (vols. 58–59); Phonautograph and photophone (vol. 60); Propellers (vol. 61); Sheep experiments (vol. 62); Telephone (vol. 63); Tetrahedral structures (vols. 64–66); Volta Bureau (vol. 67); Water distillation (vol. 68); X Rays (vol. 69); Miscellany, including written matter (vol. 70). Not all albums contain Washington subjects.

NOTE: Each photograph is captioned, based on National Geographic Society captions, internal evidence, and research. Volumes were arranged chronologically by the Library. Negative numbers used by the National Geographic Society were retained with a Library of Congress prefix.

DATE: Ca. 1885–1955

PHOTOGRAPHERS: Individual photographers are cited when known, based on National Geographic Society records, internal evidence, and deed of gift.

PHYSICAL DESCRIPTION: 70 albums (ca. 1,885 modern and vintage photoprints, some color), 30 × 26 cm.

RESTRICTIONS: Some images restricted. Copyright status noted on negative shelflist cards, when known.

LOT 11533-B

COLLECTION NAME: Grosvenor Collection of Alexander Graham Bell Photographs

SUBJECTS: Albums of subject-related photographs, compiled by the Library of Congress. Frederick W. "Casey" Baldwin and family, Caroline Ballachey and family, Alexander Bell (vol. 1); Alexander Graham Bell, ca. 1850–1922 (vols. 2–6); Alexander Graham Bell family (vols. 7–8); Alexander Graham Bell homes (vols. 9–10); Alexander Melville Bell, ca. 1840–1905 (vols. 11–13); Alexander Melville Bell family (vols. 14–15); Alexander Melville Bell homes (vol. 16); David Charles Bell and family (vol. 17); Edward Charles Bell, Eliza Grace Symonds Bell, Melville James Bell (vol. 18); Mabel Hubbard Bell, ca. 1850–1923 (vols. 19–20); David Fairchild and family (vol. 21); Grossman and Pillot families (vol. 22); Alexander Grosvenor, Carol Grosvenor, Gertrude Grosvenor (vol. 23); Elsie Bell Grosvenor (vol. 24); Gilbert H. Grosvenor (vol. 25); Gloria Grosvenor, Lillian Grosvenor, Mabel Grosvenor (vol. 26); Melville Bell Grosvenor (vol. 27); Gardiner Greene Hubbard (vol. 28); Gertrude McCurdy Hubbard (vol. 29); Gardiner Greene Hubbard homes (vols. 30–31); Samuel Hubbard family (vol. 32); Helen Keller (vol. 33); James Maclaren, Robert McCurdy, Arthur McCurdy, J. A. Douglas McCurdy (vol. 34); Marsh family (vol. 35); Scudder family (vol. 36); Symonds family (vol. 37); Miscellaneous relatives and associates (vols. 38–39); Portraits, unidentified females alone (vol. 40); Portraits, unidentified females in groups (vol. 41); Portraits, unidentified males, sil-

houette of young boy, possibly Alexander Graham Bell or one of his brothers (vol. 42). Not all albums contain Washington subjects.

NOTE: Each photograph is captioned, based on National Geographic Society captions, internal evidence, and research. Negative numbers used by the National Geographic Society were retained with a Library of Congress prefix.

DATE: Ca. 1840–ca. 1940

PHOTOGRAPHERS: Individual photographers are cited when known, based on National Geographic Society records, internal evidence, and deed of gift.

PHYSICAL DESCRIPTION: 44 albums (ca. 1,300 photoprints and photographic copies of vintage photographs and watercolors).

FINDING AID: Cards filed in the Biographical Index identify individual subjects.

LOT 11533-3 (microfilm)

COLLECTION NAME: Grosvenor Collection of Alexander Graham Bell Photographs

SUBJECTS: Portraits and genealogy of Alexander Graham Bell and his ancestors.

DATE: 1837–1916

PHYSICAL DESCRIPTION: 3 albums (125 items), 31 × 21 cm or smaller, and 35 albumen and silver gelatin photoprints, 27 × 21 cm or smaller.

RESTRICTIONS: Use of original albums restricted. Microfilm serves as reference copy.

LOT 11533-17

COLLECTION NAME: Grosvenor Collection of Alexander Graham Bell Photographs

SUBJECTS: Portraits of Mabel Hubbard Bell, some with a child, probably granddaughter Nancy Bell Fairchild.

DATE: Ca. 1910

PHOTOGRAPHERS: Harris & Ewing.

PHYSICAL DESCRIPTION: 1 album (14 silver gelatin photoprints), 35 × 25 cm.

Helen Keller seated among the group that attended the ground-breaking for the Volta Bureau building. From left to right in the foreground are Elsie May Bell, Annie N. Sullivan, and Helen Keller. 1893. Gilbert Grosvenor Collection, Lot 11533–A–67–1.
LC-G9-Z2-14551-B

LOT 11533-26

COLLECTION NAME: Grosvenor Collection of Alexander Graham Bell Photographs

SUBJECTS: Alexander Graham Bell and Gilbert Grosvenor overseeing transfer of James Smithson's tomb from Italy to Washington, D.C.

DATE: 1904

PHYSICAL DESCRIPTION: 2 albums (66 photoprints), 12 × 15 cm, 42 lantern slides, 9 × 11 cm, and 34 photoprints, 11 × 8 cm.

LOT 11533–29

COLLECTION NAME: Grosvenor Collection of Alexander Graham Bell Photographs.

SUBJECTS: Portraits of Alexander Graham Bell, Mabel Hubbard Bell, the family, and colleagues; miscellaneous aeronautical scenes. Includes photograph of A. G. Bell and Theodor N. Vail, among others, on the steps of the National Geographic Society Building, April 4, 1916.

DATE: Ca. 1871–ca. 1917

PHYSICAL DESCRIPTION: 44 albumen and silver gelatin photoprints, 28 × 36 cm or smaller.

In 1955, Harris & Ewing, Inc., Photographers, of Washington, D.C., gave the Library of Congress their collection of an estimated 700,000 glass plate and film negatives in 11 × 13 cm (4 × 5 inch), 13 × 18 cm (5 × 7 inch), and 20 × 25 cm (8 × 10 inch) formats, covering the period from 1905 through 1945. Through deaccessioning—some portraits were transferred to the National Portrait Gallery—the Harris & Ewing Collection was reduced to about 50,000 news pictures and 20,000 studio portraits. At the present time, the negatives are being processed, arranged, and prepared for microfilming, which will provide research access to the Harris & Ewing Collection. The collection will therefore be closed and unavailable for research use until 1995, at which time a microfilm record of the entire collection, incorporating existing caption information, will be available to researchers.

George Harris (d. 1964) founded his company in 1905 with a staff of four people. At the height of its success it had over one hundred people on staff and produced over ten thousand negatives a year. The company had a reputation for elegant and finely finished portraits. The studio's location was first in the vicinity of Thirteenth and F Streets NW, and later at Thirteenth and G Streets. Martha Ewing was George Harris's business partner—and his photo colorist and receptionist—until 1915, when she sold out her interest in the studio and moved to California. Some of Harris's professional achievements include accompanying President Wilson to the Peace Conference in Paris; photographing Presidents Theodore Roosevelt, William Howard Taft, Woodrow Wilson, Warren Harding, Calvin Coolidge, Herbert Hoover, Franklin D. Roosevelt, and Harry Truman; and making portraits of King Albert of Belgium, Marshal Foch, General Pershing, T. B. Shaw (Lawrence of Arabia), Queen Marie of Romania, the Prince of Wales, the poet Edwin Markham, Alexander Graham Bell, Cordell Hull, and the British prime minister David Lloyd George.

The Harris & Ewing Collection provides excellent coverage of Washington people, events, and architecture over a forty-year period. In addition, it covers international events during the period, particularly World War I and World War II. Subjects photographed are too numerous to list fully, but include U.S. presidents from Theodore Roosevelt to Harry Truman in both candid and studio portraits, with heavy coverage of Theodore Roosevelt and Franklin and Eleanor Roosevelt (for the couple there are more than 1,200 images in one series alone), and prepresidential pictures of Harding, Coolidge, Hoover, and Franklin D. Roosevelt. The collection includes photographs of Depression-era activities and programs; U.S. Signal Corps copy photographs from World War II; military leaders and war heroes; defense activities in Washington, including war preparedness, war bond and victory parades and rallies, victory gardens, Red Cross activities, advisory boards for industry, transportation, and other needs, and munitions work in the Washington Navy Yard; and temporary wartime buildings and housing for war workers and construction of the Federal Triangle, various monuments, and the Lincoln Memorial. It covers visits of American Indian delegations to Washington for various treaty negotiations; woman suffrage and activities of the National Women's Party; Republican and Democratic National Committees; senators and congressmen; members of congressional committees and various commissions; public officials who lived or worked in Washington, including cabinet members, Supreme Court justices, and congressional staff members; presidential inaugurations; openings of Congress; special joint sessions; committee hearings; visitors to Washington, including foreign dignitaries and political figures, and American personalities and public figures; movie and radio stars; socialites; extensive coverage of the White House exterior and interior, White House events, and New Year's receptions at the White House and the Capitol.

The collection contains photographs of social events, including horse shows, dog shows, charitable events, and debutante balls; local schools and universities and their activities; local and national church activities and leaders and visits by evangelists; sports events and activities, particularly baseball and professional football; portraits of athletes; views of the downtown Washington business district, including commercial buildings, shoppers and pedestrians, horse-drawn vehicles, trolley cars, and early automobiles and buses; naval events and ships; aviation subjects, including Wright brothers' flights and World War I and II aircraft; the C&O Canal; Union Station, including the arrival of notables; inventions and technological developments; local and national disasters, including floods and fires; Smithsonian Institution buildings and activities, including museum interiors and items from its collections; National Geographic Society explorers and expedition leaders; National Press

Harris & Ewing. Portrait of Theodore Roosevelt. Harris & Ewing Collection.

LC-H25-5450-A

Harris & Ewing. Wireless apparatus at the Post Office Department. Harris & Ewing Collection.

LC-H25-3527

Club activities; the Library of Congress, events held there and subjects related to its collections and buildings, including construction of the Adams Building; government buildings, both exteriors and interiors; government offices and departments, showing people at work, for example, at the Bureau of the Census and Bureau of Engraving and Printing; monuments and memorials in Washington, including Statuary Hall in Congress; monument dedications and the laying of cornerstones; funerals; parades and political demonstrations; the Grand Army of the Republic parades and other military reviews; labor organizations, leaders, demonstrations, and activities; activities of numerous social, fraternal, charitable, political, professional, and service organizations based in Washington or gathered in the city for conventions; Boy Scouts and Girl Scouts; and parks, gardens, and other public and private properties, including private residences, embassies, and hotels; and aerial views of Washington, Virginia, and Maryland.

Negatives retain original studio numbers, preceded by Library-assigned series codes, from LC–H2 through –H278, depending on the type and size of negative and the Harris & Ewing-assigned letter series.

The Harris & Ewing Collection itself consists of negatives without corresponding prints. Over the years, the Library has acquired Harris & Ewing photoprints as copyright deposits and through other sources. These photoprints have been cataloged and are described below.

REFERENCES

Harris, George W. "Forty Years of History in Pictures." *Records of the Columbia Historical Society* (1947), pp. 96–119.
——. "Time Exposure." *Rotarian*, April 1955.

Harris & Ewing. Capt. Clark Gable. Harris & Ewing Collection.

LC-H231N-E-6366

LOT 2395

SUBJECTS: Studio portraits of twenty-four members of Congress, mostly senators. Includes Hiram Johnson, Hattie W. Caraway, Arthur Wash, Francis Mahoney, and Samuel Jackson.

DATE: Ca. 1943

PHOTOGRAPHERS: Harris & Ewing.

PHYSICAL DESCRIPTION: 24 silver gelatin photoprints and halftone photomechanical prints, 20 × 25 cm.

LOT 2482

SUBJECTS: Formal and group portraits of Victor S. Clark, his family, and his associates. He was commissioner of immigration, labor, and statistics for the Territory of Hawaii until 1915. Clark at the Library of Congress.

DATE: 1915–45

PHOTOGRAPHERS: Harris & Ewing

PHYSICAL DESCRIPTION: 17 silver gelatin photoprints, 19 × 25 cm or smaller.

SOURCE: Gift of Victor S. Clark estate, 1946.

Harris & Ewing. General and Mrs. Eisenhower. Harris & Ewing Collection.

LC-H231N-E-9482

LOT 4316

SUBJECTS: Formal portraits and news photographs of President Warren G. Harding, members of his cabinet, their wives, and other public figures. Includes Mrs. Herbert Hoover; Senator and Mrs. Warren Harding; President Harding with Grantland Rice, Ring Lardner, and Henry Fletcher; Surgeon General M. W. Ireland with Maj. Julia C. Stimson; George B. Christian playing tennis; Navy Secretary and Mrs. Edwin Denby; Mrs. Henry C. Wallace and Secretary of Agriculture Wallace; Secretary of War J. W. Weeks; Secretary of the Treasury Andrew W. Mellon; Col. Theodore Roosevelt; Mrs. Calvin Coolidge; Secretary of the Interior Albert B. Fall, and others.

DATE: Ca. 1922

PHOTOGRAPHERS: Harris & Ewing

PHYSICAL DESCRIPTION: 37 silver gelatin photoprints, 20 × 25 cm.

SOURCE: Copyright deposit by Harris & Ewing, 1922.

Harris & Ewing. Mary Bethune, chief of the Negro Section, National Youth Administration. Harris & Ewing Collection.

LC-H22-D-3607

LOT 7623

SUBJECTS: U.S. Supreme Court Building, Washington, D.C. Aerial views, exterior views, architectural details, courtroom, offices, and other interior areas. Also includes portraits of some Supreme Court justices, and views of other structures in which U.S. Supreme Court sessions have been held. Includes views of the U.S. Capitol; the buildings at 204 B Street SE, where the Supreme Court convened after the 1814 burning of the Capitol; the Library of Congress Law Library; the Marshal's Office in the Capitol (ca. 1865); Carroll Row (present site of the Library of Congress Jefferson Building), site of Stele's Hotel and Long's Tavern. Also includes views of the Old State House and Old City Hall, Philadelphia; and the Old Royal Exchange Building on Broad Street in New York City.

NOTE: Photographs are accompanied by a title card, "United States Supreme Court Display." They were apparently used for an exhibit or book.

DATE: Ca. 1920s–1950s

PHOTOGRAPHERS: Harris & Ewing.

PHYSICAL DESCRIPTION: 57 items (silver gelatin photoprints, some colored, and drawings, etchings, lithographs, and photomechanical reproductions), 20 × 25 cm or smaller.

SOURCE: Transfer from the Library of Congress Law Library, 1956.

Harris & Ewing. Harris & Ewing studio photographer taking a picture of Clifford A. Berryman, Washington Star cartoonist. Harris & Ewing Collection.

LC-H25-23400-A

LOT 9709

SUBJECTS: The U.S. Capitol and events therein. Openings of Seventy-third and Seventy-ninth Congresses (1934, 1945); reconvening of Seventy-eighth Congress (1944); new members taking oath (1949); new and old members of Eighty-second Congress taking oath (1951); special session of Congress on housing problems and high prices, held at Truman's request (1948); Congress applauding president's State of the Union address (1943); Truman's State of the Union address (1952); crowds on the steps of the East Front of the Capitol; group of WACs (Women's Army Corps) on the Capitol steps (1943); Mrs. Franklin D. Roosevelt with Vice President Truman; Winifred C. Stanley (of New York) and Clare Booth Luce (of Connecticut) on arrival at the Capitol (1943); Flag Day tribute in the House of Representatives (1955). View of Freedom statue on the Capitol dome; view of House of Representatives chamber (1949); architectural details of the House chamber, and its roof under construction. Japanese submarine captured at Pearl Harbor, displayed at Capitol (1943); Operation Alert, Civil Defense drill in Capitol (1955).

DATE: Ca. 1940s–ca. 1950s

PHOTOGRAPHERS: Harris & Ewing and International News Photo.

PHYSICAL DESCRIPTION: Ca. 25 silver gelatin photoprints, 20 × 25 cm.

Harris & Ewing. "Children's Crusade, composed of seventy-seven wives and children of men still imprisoned for war-law violations, in front of the White House, where they attempted to lobby President Harding for general amnesty." May 2, 1922. Harris & Ewing Collection.

LC-H234-A4380

Harris & Ewing. Harris & Ewing studio waiting room. Harris & Ewing Collection.

LC-H25-23400-B

LOT 10304

COLLECTION NAME: Oliver Wendell Holmes Papers, Manuscript Division

SUBJECTS: Residence of U.S. Supreme Court Justice Oliver Wendell Holmes, 1720 I Street NW, Washington, D.C. Facade and Packard automobile, entrance hall, front and mid-parlors, dining room, bedroom, several studies and libraries. One image shows Jimmy Rowe, his last law clerk, in the first study on the second floor.

BIOGRAPHICAL NOTE: Oliver Wendell Holmes was a jurist and author. A collection of his letters and notes is held by the Manuscript Division. The Library also holds his book and print collection (approximately 1,700 volumes), in the Rare Book and Special Collections Division, representing the combined libraries of several generations of the Holmes family, on a wide variety of subjects.

Harris & Ewing. Street scene, taken from Southern Railway Building, Washington, D.C. Harris & Ewing Collection.

LC-H234-A3719

Harris & Ewing. Harris & Ewing studio exterior, before renovation. Harris & Ewing Collection.

LC-H25-23400-C

DATE: 1935

PHOTOGRAPHERS: Harris & Ewing.

PHYSICAL DESCRIPTION: 14 silver gelatin photoprints, 20 × 25 cm.

SOURCE: Transfer from the Manuscript Division, 1965.

Harris & Ewing. U.S. Marine Band in front of the Commandant's House, Marine Barracks, Washington, D.C. Harris & Ewing Collection.

LC-H2-B941

Harris & Ewing. William O. Douglas, commissioner of the Securities and Exchange Commission, and his assistant commissioner, Abe Fortas. Harris & Ewing Collection.

LC-H22-D767

Harris & Ewing. ''Plenty of Basehits in these Bats. A million dollars of baseball flesh is represented in these sluggers of the two all-star teams which met in the 1937 game at Griffith Stadium today. Left to right: Lou Gehrig, Joe Cronin, Bill Dickey, Joe Di Maggio, F. Gehringer, Jimmie Foxx, and Hank Greenberg.'' July 7, 1937. Harris & Ewing Collection.

LC-H22-D1887

Harris & Ewing. Congressional baseball team. Harris & Ewing Collection.

LC-H261-509

Harris & Ewing. U.S. House of Representatives voting machine. Harris & Ewing Collection.

LC-H261-3537

LOT 12504

SUBJECTS: Library of Congress Jefferson and Adams Buildings, exteriors and interiors. Includes views of the Coolidge Auditorium, the House of Representatives Reading Room, the Card Division, and the exterior of the newly completed Adams Building.

NOTE: Some used in Library of Congress exhibit at the Chicago World's Fair, 1933.

DATE: Ca. 1933–39

PHOTOGRAPHERS: Harris & Ewing.

PHYSICAL DESCRIPTION: 8 silver gelatin photoprints, 57 × 94 cm or smaller.

LOT 12505

SUBJECTS: Portraits of men and women, most identified. View of the French Embassy. Includes portraits of Hoover's literary secretary, French Strother (1929); portraits of Drs. W. Rucker and E. Morales; Judge E. Campbell; Lt. J. Edgerton; Senator H. Lane; Mrs. J. H. Lewis; and Congressmen Temple, Vaughn, Brockson, Woodruff, Carr, Shreve, Kettner, Engle, Stephens, Shackleford, Hill, Garo, Kress, Johnston, and Keys.

DATE: Ca. 1913–29

PHOTOGRAPHERS: Harris & Ewing.

PHYSICAL DESCRIPTION: 25 silver gelatin photoprints, 21 × 26 cm or smaller.

SOURCE: Copyright deposit by Harris & Ewing, 1913–29.

Harris & Ewing. ''After the burning of the Capitol in 1814, Supreme Court sessions were held in nearby quarters generally believed to have been in this old structure at 204 B Street SE, Washington, D.C.'' Ca. 1920s. Lot 7623.

LC-USZ62-88702

Harris & Ewing. William Jennings Bryan. Harris & Ewing Collection.

LC-H261-2888

Harris & Ewing. Photographers on the White House lawn, 1918. Harris & Ewing Collection.
LC-H261-24394

LOT 12506

SUBJECTS: Scenes and events in Washington, D.C. Aerial view of the capital, showing the Washington Monument and government buildings on the Mall; parade welcoming the troops home, on Pennsylvania Avenue (August 27, 1919); the Marine Band on the Capitol steps (1905); a Sylvan Play on the White House grounds (October 1908); unidentified slums in Washington (1912).

DATE: Ca. 1905–19

PHOTOGRAPHERS: Harris & Ewing.

PHYSICAL DESCRIPTION: 5 items, silver gelatin photoprints, 28 × 36 cm or smaller.

SOURCE: Copyright deposit by Harris & Ewing, 1905–19, and other sources.

Harris & Ewing. Mrs. Taft watching Boy Scouts start a fire on the White House steps. Harris & Ewing Collection.
LC-H261-727

Harris & Ewing. Lauren Bacall and Vice President Truman. Harris & Ewing Collection.
LC-H231N-E-8511

Harris & Ewing. ''Mrs. Garner receives cheese bust of husband. Wisconsin, at present celebrating its Diamond Jubilee Cheese Week, sent to Washington a 2,200 lb. cheese and a bust of the Vice President done in cheddar cheese. . . .'' April 15, 1939. Harris & Ewing Collection.
LC-H22-6414

Harris & Ewing. President Harding, Grantland Rice, Ring Lardner, and Henry Fletcher at the White House, 1922. Harris & Ewing Collection, Lot 4316.
LC-USZ62-92898

The Historic American Buildings Survey (HABS) began as a relatively small New Deal public works project during the Depression. Beginning in November 1933, 772 unemployed architects were hired to record and otherwise document significant structures around the country. By March 1934, they had produced 5,000 sheets of measured drawings for 880 sites and structures. Funding of the HABS program ceased during World War II and was not resumed until 1957. To date, more than 45,534 measured drawings, 120,549 photographs, and 65,673 data pages produced by the survey document about 21,805 American buildings of all types, from monumental government structures to gasoline stations, providing information ranging from elevations to photographs of doorknobs.

These documents make up the most important architectural collection in the Prints and Photographs Division, one shaped by its companion projects, the Carnegie Survey of Architecture of the South and the Pictorial Archives of Early American Architecture, and complemented by the Library's numerous and richly varied documentary holdings relating to architectural and monumental sites around the world. The HABS collection covers the fifty states, the District of Columbia, Puerto Rico, the Canal Zone, and the Virgin Islands.

The work of the survey continues today under the joint sponsorship and supervision of the National Park Service, the Library of Congress, and the American Institute of Architects, with funding by Congress, supplemented by individual and institutional contributions. The collection is housed in the Prints and Photographs Division of the Library of Congress, where researchers can obtain copies of any of these unrestricted materials. Extensive indexes provide access by location, building type, and architect. National catalogs and state and local catalogs offer published descriptions. The most up-to-date record of processed holdings is available in the Prints and Photographs Reading Room, which also maintains a listing of HABS publications. The collection of measured drawings through 1974 was microfilmed by the Library (on 63 reels) and is available for purchase in that form. The British firm of Chadwyck-Healey has published a microfiche collection of the HABS photographs and data sheets through 1979 entitled *The Historic American Buildings Survey: The Microfiche Edition* (Teaneck, N. J.: Chadwyck-Healey, Inc., 1979). Over one hundred libraries in the United States hold parts of the HABS collection on microfilm and microfiche. The 1983 publication *Historic America* includes a checklist of documentation through 1981.

Washington, D.C., and vicinity is covered extensively in the Historic American Buildings Survey. Although by 1941 only sixty-one structures had been documented in the city, to date in Washington alone over five hundred buildings are documented in about 500 draw-

Russell Jones. Abner Cloud House, located between Canal Road and C&O Canal NW, June 1963. Historic American Buildings Survey, HABS D.C. 9.
HABS D.C. WASH 167-1

John Brostrup. The Octagon House, located at 1741 New York Avenue NW, November 11, 1936. Historic American Buildings Survey, HABS D.C. 25.
HABS D.C. WASH 8-28

Ronald Comedy. Capital Garage, 1320 New York Avenue NW, Washington, D.C., 1974. Historic American Buildings Survey.
HABS D.C. WASH 279-2; 1983 (HABS):71

Jack Boucher. Georgetown University, Healy Building, located near Thirty-seventh and O Streets NW; Gaston Hall, looking west toward stage, third floor, north wing, September 1969. Historic American Buildings Survey, HABS D.C. 248.
HABS D.C. GEO 118-21

ings, 3,500 photographs, and 2,500 data pages. One of the first buildings to be documented was the Francis Scott Key house in 1933, followed by the Hamburgh Village House, the Maury House, and the Capt. Joseph Johnson House, all of which were demolished soon thereafter. Georgetown structures and street furniture are heavily represented in the collection. Architectural photogrammetry was used to produce drawings of some Washington buildings, including the U.S. Court of Claims (now the Renwick Gallery) and the Smithsonian Institution Building. Other buildings of interest to local architectural history researchers may be found by searching the holdings for Virginia and Maryland for coverage of Alexandria, Arlington, Silver Spring, Takoma Park, and many other historic communities.

A checklist of Washington buildings documented by the survey is given below, and the most currently updated version of the checklist is available in the Prints and Photographs Reading Room. Information about the number of photographs, drawings, and data pages available for a particular structure may be obtained in the reading room, by referring to the HABS number provided below for each building. Uncataloged material is not available for public use.

REFERENCES

Beaty, Laura. "The Historic American Buildings Survey: For Fifty Years, HABS Has Traced the Shape of the Nation's Architecture." *National Parks*, March–April 1983.

District of Columbia Catalog, 1974. Historic American Buildings Survey, National Park Service, Department of the Interior. Compiled by Nancy B. Schwartz. Charlottesville, Va.: Published for the Columbia Historical Society, Washington, D.C., by the University Press of Virginia, 1974.

Forgey, Benjamin. "Record of Greatness: The Historic Buildings Survey Turns 50." *Washington Post*, November 12, 1983, pp. C1, C3.

Historic America: Buildings, Structures, and Sites Recorded by the Historic American Buildings Survey and the Historic American Engineering Record. Checklist compiled by Alicia Stamm and essays edited by C. Ford Peatross. Washington: Library of Congress, 1983.

Melville, no. 117, pp. 171–73.

Peatross, C. Ford. "Architectural Collections of the Library of Congress." *QJLC* 34, no. 3 (July 1977), pp. 249–84.

Vanderbilt, no. 346, pp. 77–78.

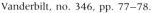

Ronald Comedy. Cairo Hotel, 1615 Q Street NW, Washington, D.C., October 1970. Historic American Buildings Survey.
HABS D.C. WASH 307-1; 1983 (HABS):48

HABS No.	Building or Structure Name
DC–214	Adams Building
DC–469	Adams house
DC–280	Adams Memorial ("Grief")
DC–161	Adams-Mason house
DC–173	Adas Israel Synagogue
DC–542	All Souls Church
DC–371	Ambassador Hotel
DC–305	American Bank Building
DC–387	American Mosaic Company Building
DC–458	American University, Ohio Hall of Government (McKinley-Ohio Hall of Government)
DC–399	American University, The College of History (Hurst Hall)
DC–255	Anderson, Larz, house (Society of the Cincinnati Headquarters)
DC–425	Apartment building (Chinese Legation)
DC–306	Army Medical Museum and Library
DC–277	Army War College (National War College)
DC–448	Ascension and St. Agnes Church
DC–394	Atlantic Coastline Building
DC–524–B	Auditors Complex, Annex Building 2

HABS No.	Building or Structure Name
DC–524	Auditors Complex, Annex Buildings
DC–524–A	Auditors Complex, Annex Buildings 1 and 1–A
DC–15	1000 B Street SW (house)
DC–403	Babcock, Orville E., house (2024–2026 G Street NW, row house)
DC–379	Baker Building
DC–119	Bank of Columbia (Georgetown Town Hall)
DC–121	Barber Shop
DC–504	Barney's Restaurant
DC–256	Barney, Alice Pike, Studio House
DC–180	Barrett, James I., house
DC–533	Bartholdi fountain
DC–257	Beale, Joseph, house (Embassy of the Arab Republic of Egypt)
DC–80	Beall's Express Building
DC–13	Bebb House (Octagonal house)
DC–253	Berry, Philip T., house
DC–142	Birch Funeral Home
DC–187	Birch, W. Taylor, house
DC–45	Blair House (Joseph Lovell house)
DC–398	Bliss, Dr. A. C., house
DC–174	Bodisco house (Clement Smith house)

HABS No.	Building or Structure Name
DC–143	Bomford's Mill (Wilkins-Rogers Milling Company)
DC–60	Bowie house (Sevier house)
DC–295	Brady, Mathew B., Studio
DC–158	Brickyard Hill house
DC–480	Brodt's Hat Factory
DC–209	Bronaugh-Bibb-Libby house (Bibb house)
DC–191	Brown house
DC–322	Brown's Marble Hotel (Indian Queen Hotel)
DC–381	Brownley Building
DC–370	Bruce, Blanche K., house
DC–360	Bunche, Ralph J., house
DC–465	Burling, Edward Jr., house
DC–196	Bussard-Newman house
DC–515	607–609 C Street (commercial building) (McDonald's)
DC–374	458 C Street NW
DC–307	Cairo Hotel
DC–137	Caldwell, Elias B., house, doorway, and archway
DC–84	Caldwell, Timothy, house (Arts Club of Washington)
DC–144	Canal warehouse
DC–2	Cannon House Office Building
DC–279	Capital Garage
DC–145	Capital Traction Company Powerhouse

HABS No.	Building or Structure Name	HABS No.	Building or Structure Name	HABS No.	Building or Structure Name
DC–125	Capital Traction Company Union Station	DC–308	629 D Street NW (commercial building)	DC–518	410 Eighth Street (livery)
DC–146	Carleton, Joseph, house	DC–17	22 D Street SE (house)	DC–499	322 Eighth Street NW (commercial building) (Piccolo's)
DC–250	Carriage house	DC–372	D. C. Central Public Library, old		
DC–368	Cary, Mary Ann Shadd, house			DC–498	320 Eighth Street NW (commercial building) (Capital Souvenirs)
DC–229	Central National Bank Building (Apex Liquor Store)	DC–205	Daly, Carroll, house		
		DC–432	Dashiell, George W., Building	DC–237	320 Eighth Street NW (commercial building)
DC–457	Central Public Library	DC–102	Davidson, John, house	DC–477	409 Eleventh Street (commercial building) (Tanen's)
DC–511	Central Union Mission	DC–312	Davis, James Y., Sons Building		
DC–147	Chesapeake & Ohio Canal, Georgetown section (Chesapeake & Ohio Canal National Historic Park)	DC–179	De La Roche-Jewell tenant house	DC–475	405 Eleventh Street (commercial building) (Universal Newsstand)
		DC–16	Decatur House (National Trust for Historic Preservation)	DC–476	407 Eleventh Street (commercial building) (Kung Fu Restaurant)
DC–456	Chinatown				
DC–281	Chinese Community Church	DC–29	Decatur-Gunther house (John S. Williams house)	DC–481	425–429 Eleventh Street (commercial building) (Alla-Scala Restaurant)
DC–405	Chinese Embassy	DC–419	Delano, Frederic, house (Residence of the Ambassador of Ireland)		
DC–48	Christ Church			DC–479	421 Eleventh Street (commercial building) (Am-Chi Restaurant)
DC–243	Christ Church (Episcopal)				
DC–140	Church of the Covenant (National Presbyterian Church)	DC–288	Devore-Chase house		
		DC–314	District Building	DC–478	415–417 Eleventh Street (commercial buildings) (Staley's Hong Kong Exchange and Regency Liquors)
DC–81	City Tavern	DC–41	District of Columbia City Hall (old City Hall)		
DC–99	Cloud, Abner, house				
DC–450	Cole, Annie A., house	DC–373	Dix, General John A., house		
DC–297	Columbia Railway Company Car Barns (Trinidad Cable Car Barns)	DC–436	Dodge, Francis, warehouse	DC–56	304–306 Eleventh Street SW (double house)
		DC–246	Dodge, Robert P., house		
		DC–97	Douglass, Frederick, house (Cedar Hill)	DC–92	Engine Company Number Fifteen, Firehouse
DC–396	Concordia United Church of Christ (Concordia German Evangelical Church)	DC–8	Duddington Mansion (Carroll House)	DC–87	Engine Company Number Four, Firehouse
				DC–89	Engine Company Number Nine, Firehouse
DC–424	Congressional Cemetery (Latrobe Cenotaphs)	DC–183	3015 Dumbarton Avenue NW (house)	DC–86	Engine Company Number One, Firehouse
DC–384	Convention Center Site, District of Columbia (H Street, 900 and 1000 block)	DC–434	Dumbarton House (Bellevue)	DC–93	Engine Company Number Seventeen, Firehouse
		DC–460	Dunbar, Elizabeth A., house	DC–88	Engine Company Number Six, Firehouse
DC–182	Cocke's Row, Villa No. 3	DC–128	Duncanson-Cranch house (Barney Neighborhood House)	DC–90	Engine Company Number Ten, Firehouse
DC–49	Corcoran Art Gallery (U.S. Court of Claims)				
DC–34	Corcoran, Thomas, house	DC–154	Duvall Foundry	DC–91	Engine Company Number Twelve, Firehouse
DC–422	Cordova Apartments (President Madison Apartments)	DC–520	816 E Street NW and 437 Ninth Street NW (commercial buildings)	DC–95	Engine Company Number Twenty-two, Firehouse
DC–473	Cowing, John C., house			DC–94	Engine Company Number Twenty-one, Firehouse
DC–150	Cox, Col. John, house	DC–354	1216 E Street NW (commercial building and garage)		
DC–118	Cramphin, Thomas, Building			DC–350	Engine Company Number Two, Firehouse
DC–224	Crandell, Germond, Building	DC–519	800 E Street NW (commercial building)	DC–40	Estes Mill (ruins)
DC–184	Crawford-Cassin house	DC–228	625 E Street NW (commercial building)	DC–316	Evening Star Building
DC–220	Culver, Fredrick B., house			DC–258	Everett, Edward H., house (Turkish Embassy)
DC–58	Cuits, Richard, house (Dolley Madison house)	DC–420	1200 E Street NW (commercial building) (service station and garage)		
				DC–61	Evermay
DC–488	1001 D Street (commercial building) (Carpel's Liquor Store)	DC–426	1208–1214 E Street NW (garage)	DC–131	Eye Street NW (house)
		DC–236	514 E Street NW (house)	DC–124	Eynon Building
DC–489	1003 D Street (commercial building) (Souvenir World)	DC–136	2029 E Street NW (house)	DC–213	814 F Street NW (commercial building)
		DC–7	Easby house		
DC–492	1015 D Street (commercial building) (Price Is Right Store)	DC–331	500 East Capitol Street (house)	DC–377	1310 F Street NW (commercial building) (Raleigh's Haberdasher)
		DC–291	Eastern Market		
DC–490	1005–1007 D Street (commercial building) (D. J. Kaufman Store and Blimpie Restaurant)	DC–309	308–310 Eighth Street NW (commercial building)	DC–376	1314 F Street NW (commercial building) (Becker's Leather Goods Store)
		DC–517	408 Eighth Street (commercial building)		

HABS No.	Building or Structure Name
DC–380	1308 F Street NW (commercial building) (Dash's Designer)
DC–215	818 F Street NW (commercial building)
DC–327	1901 F Street NW (row house)
DC–328	1901–1911 F Street NW (row houses)
DC–444	F Street NW, 600 block
DC–335	F Street NW, 600 block (commercial buildings)
DC–259	Fahnestock, Gibson, house (Republic of China Chancery)
DC–500	Federal Triangle Building
DC–105	Female Union Benevolent Society (John Lutz house)
DC–83	Fenwick, Teresa, house (Thomas Parrot house)
DC–537	Field, Mrs. Marshall, house (Inter-American Defense Board Headquarters)
DC–510	Fields Building
DC–192	Findley House
DC–461	Finley, David E., house
DC–235	Firemen's Insurance Company Building
DC–241	First Baptist Church of Georgetown
DC–260	Fitzhugh, Emma S., house (Philippine Embassy)
DC–375	Ford Motor Company Building
DC–82	Ford's Theater (Ford's Theater National Historic Park)
DC–68	Forest-Marbury House
DC–356	501–511 Fourteenth Street NW (commercial building) (The Locker Room)
DC–66	Foxhall, Henry, house (McKenny house)
DC–289	Franklin School
DC–318	Fraser, George, house (Scott-Thorpe house)
DC–467	French, Benjamin Brown, School
DC–404	1908–1916 G Street NW (row houses)
DC–333–A	G Street NW, 1200 block (commercial buildings), no. 1201
DC–333–B	G Street NW, 1200 block (commercial buildings), no. 1204
DC–333–C	G Street NW, 1200 block (commercial buildings), no. 1239
DC–304	Gallaudet College, Gate House (Columbia Institute for the Deaf and Dumb, Gate House)
DC–303	Gallaudet College, President's House (Columbia Institute for the Deaf and Dumb, President's House)
DC–300	Gallaudet College (Columbia Institute for the Deaf and Dumb)

HABS No.	Building or Structure Name
DC–301	Gallaudet College, Chapel Hall
DC–302	Gallaudet College, College Hall (Columbia Institute for the Deaf and Dumb, College Hall)
DC–155	Gazebo
DC–123	Georgetown Market, The
DC–248	Georgetown University, Healy Building
DC–170	Georgetown University, North Building, old
DC–211	Georgetown Visitation Convent
DC–129	Gilman's, Z. D., Drug Store (Mark Weiss Camera Store)
DC–411	Godey Lime Kilns (ruins)
DC–514	Golden Bull Restaurant
DC–193	Goszler-Manogue House
DC–204	Goszler-Meem-Brown House (Brown House)
DC–440	Grace Protestant Episcopal Church
DC–79	Gray, Justice Horace, house (Christian Science Building)
DC–402	Greyhound Bus Terminal
DC–366	Grimke, Charlotte Forten, house
DC–416	Gunston Hall School for Girls
DC–117	Gutman-Wise Building
DC–132	1003 H Street NW (house)
DC–69	Halcyon House (Benjamin Stoddert house)
DC–156	Hall, John Stoddert, house
DC–261	Halliday, Henrietta M., house (Irish Chancery)
DC–10–6	Hamburgh House
DC–485	Hammel's Restaurant
DC–206	Harnedy row houses
DC–429	Harrison, Jane Stone, Building
DC–262	Hauge, Christian, house (Czechoslovakian Embassy)
DC–534	Hay-Adams Hotel (Carleton Chambers, apartment hotel)
DC–160	Hedges, Nicholas, house
DC–195	Herron-Moxley house
DC–292	Heurich, Christian, Mansion (Columbia Historical Society)
DC–30	High Street Bridge (Wisconsin Avenue Bridge)
DC–294	Hillyer Place
DC–201	Holy Trinity Parish
DC–263	Hooe, James C., house
DC–317	Hotel Washington
DC–395	Howard Road Historic District
DC–395–F	Howard Road Historic District (Minnie B. Smoot apartment building)
DC–395–H	Howard Road Historic District (Samuel H. Lucas house no. 1)
DC–395–J	Howard Road Historic District (Henry F. Miller apartment building)

Ronald Comedy. Christ Church, 620 G Street SE, June 1974. Historic American Buildings Survey.
HABS D.C. WASH 48-3; 1983 (HABS):152

Ronald Comedy. Le Droit Park, houses at 603-605 U Street NW, October 1970. Historic American Buildings Survey.
HABS D.C. WASH 287-F-1; 1983 (HABS):97

Ronald Comedy. Gallaudet College, Chapel Hall, Seventh Street and Florida Avenue NE, October 1970. Historic American Buildings Survey.
HABS D.C. WASH 301-3; 1984 (HABS):117

Walter Smalling. Blanche K. Bruce house, 909 M Street NW, November 1979. Historic American Buildings Survey.
HABS D.C. WASH 370-4; 1983 (HABS):48

Ronald Comedy. Commercial building at 1239 G Street NW, October 1970. Historic American Buildings Survey.
HABS D.C. WASH 333-C-1; 1983 (HABS):97

HABS No.	Building or Structure Name
DC–395–I	Howard Road Historic District (Samuel Smith house)
DC–395–A	Howard Road Historic District (Thomas Sparks house)
DC–395–C	Howard Road Historic District (Sylvia L. Phillips house)
DC–395–D	Howard Road Historic District (Lloyd Sharp house)
DC–395–B	Howard Road Historic District (Isaaz Boston house)
DC–395–K	Howard Road Historic District (William E. Willis house)
DC–395–E	Howard Road Historic District (Samuel H. Lucas house no. 3)
DC–395–G	Howard Road Historic District (Samuel H. Lucas house no. 2)
DC–364	Howard University, Founders Library
DC–284	Howard, Gen. Oliver O., house (Howard University, Howard Hall)
DC–278	Hughes, Charles Evans, house (A. Clifford Barney house)
DC–319	Humble Service Station
DC–452	Hume Building (German Hi-Fi)
DC–200	Hurley, John, house
DC–411	2000–2042 I Street NW (commercial buildings) (Red Lion Row)
DC–400–A	2000–2042 I Street NW (commercial buildings), no. 2030 (Red Lion Row)
DC–337	I Street NW, 1900 block (houses)
DC–285	Immaculate Conception Church
DC–509	612 Indiana Avenue NW (commercial building)
DC–508	610 Indiana Avenue NW (commercial building)
DC–230	625 Indiana Avenue NW (commercial building) (David Hayman & Company)
DC–506	600 Indiana Avenue NW (commercial building)
DC–507	608 Indiana Avenue NW (commercial building)
DC–502	Ingleside (T. B. A. Hewlings villa)
DC–244	Jackson (Public) School
DC–21	Jackson Hill (Dr. Henry C. Holt house)
DC–181	Jackson, Albert, house
DC–264	Japanese Embassy
DC–4	Jefferson Memorial
DC–159	1063 Jefferson Street NW (house)
DC–417	Jewell, Capt. Theodore, house

HABS No.	Building or Structure Name
DC–10–3	Johnson, Capt. Joseph, house
DC–197	Kane, Daniel, house
DC–365	Kann, S., & Sons (Kann's Department Store)
DC–320	Keep Building
DC–423	Keith-Albee Building
DC–203	Kelly House
DC–23	Key, Francis Scott, house
DC–57	King House
DC–163	Knowles, William, house
DC–283	Kraemer, Charles, house
DC–355	Lansburgh's Department Store
DC–20	Law, Thomas, house (Honeymoon House)
DC–212	Le Droit Building
DC–287	Le Droit Park
DC–287–G	Le Droit Park (201 T Street NW, house)
DC–287–E	Le Droit Park (316 U Street NW, house)
DC–287–A	Le Droit Park (1901 Sixth Street NW, house)
DC–287–B	Le Droit Park (1908 Third Street NW, house)
DC–287–F	Le Droit Park (603–605 L Street NW, houses)
DC–287–D	Le Droit Park (314 U Street NW, carriage house)
DC–287–C	Le Droit Park (1922 Third Street NW, house)
DC–338	Lemon Building
DC–438	Lenthall houses
DC–26	Lewis, Edward Simon, house (Washington-Lewis house)
DC–351	Library of Congress
DC–207	Lihault House (Simms House)
DC–3	Lincoln Memorial
MA–2–33	Lindens, The (Robert King Hooper house)
DC–168	Linnean Hill (Joshua Fierce house)
DC–321	Litchfield, Grace Denio, house
DC–36	Lock Keeper's House (Toll Keeper's Lodge)
DC–378	Loew's Palace Theatre
DC–339	Logan Circle (Logan Circle Area Survey)
DC–194	Longden House
DC–389	Loughran Building (Bassin's Restaurant)
DC–446	Luther Place Memorial Church
DC–33	3115–3117 M Street NW (house)
DC–112	2922 M Street NW (house)
DC–32	3111–3113 M Street NW (house)
DC–64	2919 M Street NW (house)
DC–65	3001–3009 M Street NW (row houses) (Thomas Simm Lee house)
DC–164	Mackall Square (old Mackall House)

HABS No.	Building or Structure Name	HABS No.	Building or Structure Name	HABS No.	Building or Structure Name
DC–188	Mahorney-Harrington House	DC–275	Miller House (Argyle Terrace)	DC–249	Oak Hill Cemetery, Gatehouse
DC–198	Mahorney-O'Brien House	DC–247	Miller, Benjamin, house	DC–325	Occidental Hotel and Restaurant
DC–190	Mankins, William, house	DC–267	Moore, Clarence, house (Canadian Chancery)	DC–382	Occidental Restaurant (Owen House)
DC–330	Manning, Edwin C., house (Florida House)	DC–464	Moore, Frederick L., house	DC–25	Octagon House (Col. John Tayloe house)
DC–10–5	Maples, The (William Duncanson house)	DC–268	Moran, Francis B., house (Pakistani Chancery)	DC–336	Octagon House, stable (John Tayloe house and stable)
DC–107	Marceron, William, Building	DC–491	Morrison Paper Company (Stein's Dry Cleaning and Shoe Repair)	DC–315	Old Ebbitt Grill
DC–106	Marcey-Payne Building			DC–512	Orienta Coffee Building (La Touraine)
DC–232	811 Market Space NW (commercial building) (Souvenirs)	DC–286	Mosque (The Islamic Center)	DC–62	Owens, Isaac, house (doorway) (Gantt-Williams House)
DC–453	813–815 Market Space NW (commercial building) (National Permanent Federal Savings)	DC–385	Mount Vernon Apartments		
		DC–254	Mount Vernon Theatre	DC–523	P.M.I. Parking Garage
		DC–242	Mount Zion United Methodist Church	DC–388	Pepco Power Station
DC–222	809 Market Space NW (commercial building)	DC–18	Mountz, John, house (Eagle House)	DC–130	Patent Office Building (U.S. Civil Service Commission)
DC–454	817 Market Space NW (commercial building) (old Antique House)	DC–390	Mulliken-Spragins tenant house	DC–269	Patterson House (Washington Club)
DC–541	Marlatt, Dr. Charles L., house	DC–358	Munsey Building	DC–177	Patterson, Edgar, house
		DC–157	2817 N Street NW (house)	DC–513	Pendleton & Robinson law offices
DC–28	Mason, Gen. John, house	DC–296	National Archives		
DC–167	Mason, John Thomson, house (Quality Hill)	DC–223	National Bank of Washington (National Bank of Washington, Washington Branch)	DC–486	Penn Camera Exchange
DC–218	Masonic Temple (Masonic Hall)			DC–334	1922–1932 Pennsylvania Avenue NW (commercial building)
DC–437	Masonic Temple, old (Naval Lodge Number Four)	DC–431	National Metropolitan Bank Building	DC–334–A	1922 Pennsylvania Avenue NW (commercial building)
DC–238	1780 Massachusetts Avenue NW (house)	DC–463	National Union Building	DC–334–B	1924–1926 Pennsylvania Avenue NW (commercial building)
DC–462	1730 Massachusetts Avenue NW (house)	DC–468	Naval Hospital, old		
		DC–341	Naval Observatory, old (U.S. Navy Bureau of Medicine and Surgery, Potomac Annex)	DC–334–C	1928–1932 Pennsylvania Avenue NW (commercial building)
DC–10–4	Maury, John, house				
DC–439	Mayor-Smallwood House	DC–442	Navy Yard	DC–27	2411 Pennsylvania Avenue NW (house)
DC–199	McCarthy-Sullivan House	DC–100	Navy Yard Main Gate		
DC–162	McCleery House	DC–101	Navy Yard Quarters B (Second Officer's House)	DC–204	Pennsylvania Avenue NW, 900 block
DC–265	McCormick Apartments (National Trust for Historic Preservation Headquarters)	DC–442–B	Navy Yard, Boilermaker's Shop (Building 167)	DC–466	1002 Pennsylvania Avenue SE (house)
DC–413	McCutcheon Building (L. Litwin & Son)	DC–12	Navy Yard, Commandant's House (Quarters A)	DC–76	Pension Building
DC–24	McLean, John R., house	DC–442–A	Navy Yard, General Foundry (Building 137)	DC–221	Perry Building (Hickory House)
DC–50	Meigs, Gen. Montgomery, house	DC–417	1810–1820 Nineteenth Street NW (row houses)	DC–70	Peter Houses
DC–282	Memorial Continental Hall (National Society of the Car Headquarters and Museum)	DC–357	Nineteenth Street Baptist Church	DC–165	Peterson House (House Where Lincoln Died)
		DC–521	417 Ninth Street NW (commercial building)	DC–447	Phillips, Duncan, house (The Phillips Collection)
DC–239	Merchants & Mechanics Saving Bank (Loeb Company Store)	DC–522	413–415 Ninth Street NW (commercial building)	DC–14	Pierce, Isaac, house
DC–532	Meridian Hill Park	DC–234	616 Ninth Street NW (commercial building)	DC–22	Pierce, Isaac, Mill
DC–540	Meridian House (Ambassador and Mrs. Irwin Boyle Laughlin house)	DC–455	305 Ninth Street NW (commercial building) (Louis Cocktail Lounge)	DC–538	Embassy of Poland (Polish Embassy)
				DC–166	Potomac Aqueduct
DC–451	Methodist Episcopal Church, South (Mount Vernon Place United Methodist Church)	DC–231	618 Ninth Street NW (commercial building)	DC–153	Potomac Lodge Number Five
		DC–445	Ninth Street NW, 500 block (commercial buildings)	DC–535	Potomac Realty Company, house number 10
DC–176	Methodist Episcopal Parsonage House	DC–116	Nordlinger Building	DC–323	Potomac Savings Bank (National Bank of Washington, Georgetown Branch)
DC–352	Metropolitan A. M. E. Church	DC–342	Northern Market (O Street Market)	DC–152	1061–1063 Potomac Street NW, double house
DC–340	Michler Place	DC–42	Oak Hill (French House)	DC–545	Powhatan Hotel (Roger Smith Hotel)
		DC–172	Oak Hill Cemetery, Chapel		

HABS No.	Building or Structure Name	HABS No.	Building or Structure Name	HABS No.	Building or Structure Name
DC–270	Pullman House (Embassy of the Union of Soviet Socialist Republics)	DC–151	1218 Sixteenth Street NW (house)	DC–19	St. John's Church
		DC–54	Sixth and G Streets SW (house)	DC–19–A	St. John's Church, Ashburton House (St. John's Church, Buckingham House)
DC–345	Q Street NW, 1700 block (row houses)				
DC–148	Ray's Warehouse and Offices (Corson & Gruman Company)	DC–227	507 Sixth Street NW (apartment house)	DC–359	St. Luke's Episcopal Church
		DC–226	513 Sixth Street NW (house)	DC–47	St. Paul's Episcopal Church
DC–120	Reckert House	DC–55	601–603 Sixth Street SW (row houses)	DC–271	Stanley, Arthur C., house
DC–347	Red Cross Building (American National Red Cross National Headquarters)			DC–483	Star Parking Garage
		DC–67	Smith Row (Col. James Smith row houses)	DC–290	State, War and Navy Building (Old Executive Office Building)
DC–122	Reintzel, Anthony, Building	DC–185	Smith-Morton row house		
DC–126	4437 Reservoir Road NW (house)	DC–298	Smithsonian Institution, Arts and Industries Museum Building	DC–44	Steedman-Ray House (Alexander Ray house)
DC–470	1115 Rhode Island Avenue NW (house)			DC–272	Stewart, Alexander, house (Embassy of Luxembourg)
DC–526	1205–1215 Rhode Island Avenue NW (houses) (Logan Circle Area Survey)	DC–525	Smithsonian Institution, Virginia Room	DC–104	Stohlman's Confectionary
		DC–141	Smithsonian Institution Building, The Old Castle	DC–10–2	Stone House, Old (Christopher Layhman house)
DC–527	1300–1322 Rhode Island Avenue NW (houses) (Logan Circle Area Survey)	DC–74	Southeast Area Survey (132–144 and 900–905 Eleventh Street, row houses)	DC–430	Stone, William J., Building (Frisco's)
DC–528	1301–1313 Rhode Island Avenue NW (houses) (Logan Circle Area Survey)			DC–252	Street furniture, Georgetown
		DC–73	Southeast Area Survey (600–602 and 1100 G Street, house)	DC–189	Sullivan House (Buehler House)
DC–326	Rhodes Tavern			DC–202	Sullivan, Jeremiah, Building
DC–343	Richards, Zalmon, house	DC–72	Southeast Area Survey (330 and 706–708 Virginia Avenue, houses)	DC–51	Tayloe, Benjamin Ogle, house (Cameron House)
DC–496	Riggs National Bank, Seventh and D Street Office			DC–240	Temperance Fountain
DC–46	Riggs-Riley House	DC–71	Southeast Area Survey (101 and 122–124 Carroll Street, house)	DC–487	410–412 Tenth Street (commercial building) (Fantasy Books)
DC–391	Ringgold-Carroll House (Bacon House)				
DC–115	Robertson, Thomas, house	DC–474	Square 226 and Reservations 32 and 33 (Pershing Square and National Square)	DC–367	Terrell, Mary Church, house
DC–113	Ross & Getty Building			DC–529–B	1502 Thirteenth Street NW (house) (Logan Circle Area Survey)
DC–435	Ross, Andrew, tenant house I				
DC–175	Ross, Andrew, tenant house II	DC–493	Square 348 (commercial buildings)	DC–529–A	1500 Thirteenth Street NW (house) (Logan Circle Area Survey)
DC–6	Ruppert, Anton, house	DC–516	Square 407		
DC–346	Scottish Rite Temple, Prince Hall Affiliation	DC–484	Square 432 (commercial buildings)	DC–529	1500–1514 Thirteenth Street NW (houses) (Logan Circle Area Survey)
DC–59	Seven Buildings	DC–505	Square 459 (commercial building)		
DC–233	Seventh and C Streets NW (commercial building)	DC–501	Square 460 (commercial buildings)	DC–299	2618 Thirtieth Street NW (house)
DC–495	314–316 Seventh Street NW (commercial building) (Morton's)	DC–349–A	St. Elizabeth's Hospital, B Building (No. 75)	DC–449	Thomas Building
		DC–349–B	St. Elizabeth's Hospital, C Building (No. 73)	DC–459	Thomas Circle (houses)
DC–494	312 Seventh Street NW (commercial building)	DC–349–C	St. Elizabeth's Hospital, I Building (No. 95)	DC–414	Thomson, Strong John, Elementary School
DC–225	415 Seventh Street NW (commercial building) (Cullinan Building)	DC–349–D	St. Elizabeth's Hospital, J Building (No. 60)	DC–471	Thorn Building (Irving's Camera Shop)
		DC–349–E	St. Elizabeth's Hospital, K Building (No. 66)	DC–273	Townsend House (Cosmos Club)
DC–497	437–441 Seventh Street NW (commercial building) (Boyce & Lewis Shoes)	DC–349–F	St. Elizabeth's Hospital, L Building (No. 64)	DC–393	Trans-Lux Theatre
DC–443	700 Seventh Street NW (commercial building)	DC–349–G	St. Elizabeth's Hospital, M Building (No. 72)	DC–96	Truck Company Number Four, Firehouse
DC–85	1005–1023 Seventh Street NW (commercial buildings)	DC–349–H	St. Elizabeth's Hospital, N Building (No. 94)	DC–362	True Reformer Building
DC–313	Seventh Street NW, 500 block (commercial buildings)	DC–349–I	St. Elizabeth's Hospital, P Building (No. 100)	DC–78	Tuckerman, Lucius, house (Motion Picture Association)
DC–418	Sheridan, Irene, house (Embassy of Greece Annex)	DC–349–J	St. Elizabeth's Hospital, G Building (No. 68)	DC–171	Tudor Place
DC–536	Shields, Susan Hart, house	DC–349–K	St. Elizabeth's Hospital, R Building (No. 89)	DC–361	Twelfth Street YMCA Building (Anthony Bowen YMCA Building)
DC–111	Sims House			DC–127	723–725 Twentieth Street (house)

Jack Boucher. Georgetown street furniture at Twenty-eighth and P Streets NW; traffic light, with street lamp and sign, September 1969. Historic American Building Survey, HABS DC 252.
HABS D.C. GEO 120-4

Ronald Comedy. Engine Company No. 2, firehouse at 719 Twelfth Street NW, October 1970. Historic American Buildings Survey.
LC-HABS D.C. WASH 350-1; 1983 (HABS): 71

Historic American Engineering Record

The Historic American Engineering Record (HAER) was established in 1969, as a companion project to the Historic American Buildings Survey, to document significant examples of American engineering. The project documents structures associated with various production or service industries and records landmark engineering structures, such as dams, windmills, pumping stations, and grain elevators. Over five hundred sites surveyed by HAER since 1969 are listed in the national HAER catalog published in 1976. The original drawings, photographs, and data pages are housed in the Prints and Photographs Division of the Library of Congress and, like the HABS materials, are unrestricted in their use and available for reproduction.

Only four Washington, D.C., structures have been documented to date, and they are listed below. Information about the number of photographs, drawings, and data pages for these structures is available from the Prints and Photographs Reading Room, where researchers may consult the most recent checklist of holdings. Uncataloged material is not available for public use.

REFERENCES

Historic America: Buildings, Structures, and Sites Recorded by the Historic American Buildings Survey and the Historic American Engineering Record. Checklist compiled by Alicia Stamm and essays edited by C. Ford Peatross. Washington: Library of Congress, 1983.
The Historic American Engineering Record Catalog, 1976. Compiled by Donald E. Sackheim. Washington: National Park Service, U.S. Department of the Interior, 1976.
Melville, no. 118, p. 174.

HAER No.	Structure Name
DC–1	Washington Terminal Company Power Plant
DC–2	United Clay Products Company, New York Avenue
DC–3	Northeast Railroad Corridor
DC–4	Potomac Aqueduct

William E. Barrett. United Clay Products Company brickworks, 2801 New York Avenue NE, 1973. Historic American Engineering Record.
    HAER D.C. WASH 2-3; 1983 (HAER):84

Herman Hollerith, an inventor and businessman, developed the IBM computer, as well as the earlier Hollerith tabulating machines used in census-taking from 1890 to 1910. He was associated with the Tabulating Machine Company before and after the company's merger with the Computer-Tabulating-Recording Company in 1911 and later moved to the International Business Machines Corporation. Herman Hollerith's Papers, 10,300 items spanning the years 1871–1929 and accompanied by a finding aid, are held in the Manuscript Division. They were a gift of Hollerith's heirs and others, 1972–78.

LOT 11558

COLLECTION NAME: Herman Hollerith Papers, Manuscript Division

SUBJECTS: Normanstone, home of inventor Herman Hollerith, at 3100 Massachusetts Avenue NW, Washington, D.C. Built ca. 1830 on the present site of the British Embassy. Views of the house and outbuildings, some showing servants and groundskeepers. Plans and handwritten specifications by the general contractor, Gilbert White, and by the stonework contractor, Morgan Kavanaugh; bills for building materials.

DATE: Ca. 1870s–ca. 1920s

PHYSICAL DESCRIPTION: 15 items (albumen photoprints, drawings, and manuscripts), 28 × 36 cm or smaller.

SOURCE: Gift of Miss Virginia Hollerith, 1975.

LOT 12259

COLLECTION NAME: Herman Hollerith Papers, Manuscript Division

SUBJECTS: Snapshots (most probably taken by Herman Hollerith) of subjects in Washington, D.C., Virginia, and Gettysburg, Pennsylvania. Washington area subjects include Union Station, the Washington Monument, ice-skaters on the Mall, the Capitol, the White House, the Patent Office, the Post Office Department Building (now the Old Post Office Building), street scenes in Washington, including Pennsylvania Avenue, Great Falls, the Inn at Great Falls, the C&O Canal and barge, the Cabin John Bridge, and Arlington Cemetery. Some photos show Hollerith.

NOTE: Some photographs are badly faded.

DATE: Ca. 1890s–ca. 1915

PHOTOGRAPHERS: Herman Hollerith.

PHYSICAL DESCRIPTION: 41 silver gelatin photoprints, 11 × 14 cm or smaller.

SOURCE: Gift of Miss Virginia Hollerith, 1978.

LOT 12565

SUBJECTS: Casual group portraits of Herman Hollerith, his son (Herman Hollerith, Jr.), grandson (Herman Hollerith III), and granddaughter, taken at Riverton, New Jersey.

DATE: 1924

PHYSICAL DESCRIPTION: 2 silver gelatin photoprints, 8 × 10 inch.

SOURCE: Gift of Mrs. Lucia B. Lefferts, 1979.

Normanstone (north front), the home of Herman Hollerith, now the site of the British Embassy, Washington, D.C. Herman Hollerith Papers, Lot 11558.
LC-USZ62-92541

Theodor Horydczak Collection

The Washington commercial photographer Theodor Horydczak produced about thirty thousand negatives, corresponding photoprints, and color transparencies documenting the architecture and social life of the capital over a thirty-year period, beginning in the early 1920s. In 1973, his daughter and son-in-law, Norma Horydczak Reeves and Francis Reeves, presented the Library of Congress with Theodor Horydczak's collection of work.

Part of this material has been processed and cataloged and is available for research use. Cataloged material related to Washington, D.C., is described below. The photographer's logbooks, with entries arranged by job number and an incomplete name and subject index, have been microfilmed (Lot 11504), and the microfilm is available in the Prints and Photographs Reading Room. Color transparencies are stored in a separate Library of Congress preservation facility and are currently uncataloged and therefore not available for use. Commercial use of material copyrighted by Horydczak's clients may be restricted. All other photographs in this collection are unrestricted.

The Horydczak Collection provides an important record of Art Deco architecture and furnishings in Washington, D.C. Most photographs document the exteriors and interiors of commercial, residential, and government buildings, including the U.S. Capitol, Library of Congress, and Smithsonian Institution, with some additional coverage of street scenes and neighborhoods. Architectural subjects include Georgetown and the southwest waterfront, the C&O Canal and Potomac River bridges, the National Cathedral and other religious buildings, educational and training institutions, social activities and organizations, hotels and restaurants, embassies, museums, and libraries, outdoor sculptures and monuments, the White House and public functions held there, and the residences and activities of several U.S. presidents. Other subjects include transportation and aviation developments, Washington events, including the Bonus Army encampment, World War II preparedness activities, including prefabricated housing, and studies of mechanization and the use of electrical power, with special attention given to Washington's public utilities. The collection also includes some photographs of buildings and activities in Maryland and Virginia.

A few Theodor Horydczak photographs may be found among other cataloged collections in the Prints and Photographs Division. Horydczak photographs acquired as copyright deposits have been dispersed into the appropriate browsing files.

REFERENCES

Brannan, Beverly W. "Discovering Theodor Horydczak's Washington." In Shaw, *A Century*, pp. 182–209.
Melville, no. 20, p. 176.

Theodor Horydczak. A mural inside the Mexican Embassy, Washington, D.C. Horydczak Collection, Lot 12098-12.

LC-H8-E1-12

Theodor Horydczak. The French Embassy, Washington, D.C. Horydczak Collection, Lot 12098-3.

LC-H8-E1-1

Theodor Horydczak. The Majestic apartment building, Washington, D.C. Horydczak Collection, Lot 12097-92.

LC-H8-2391-23

COLLECTION-LEVEL DESCRIPTION

COLLECTION NAME: Theodor Horydczak Collection

NOTE: Corresponding negatives for most of these photographs are found in series LC-H8.

DATE: Ca. 1920–ca. 1950

PHOTOGRAPHERS: Theodor Horydczak.

PHYSICAL DESCRIPTION: Ca. 30,000 items (17,000 photoprints, 14,450 negatives, and 1,500 transparencies). Some modern photoprints have been made by the Library of Congress from original negatives.

ARRANGEMENT: Processed portion of the collection consists of photoprints in lots 12090–12119. A logbook, arranged by job number, and an incomplete name and subject index are available on microfilm in the Prints and Photographs Reading Room.

SOURCE: Gift of Norma Horydczak Reeves and Francis Reeves, 1973.

RESTRICTIONS: Particular photographs taken for hire may be protected by copyright.

LOT 12090

COLLECTION NAME: Theodor Horydczak Collection

SUBJECTS: Commercial and industrial buildings in Washington, D.C. Buildings, including banks, and the construction and dedication of the Acacia Mutual Life Insurance Company. Office interiors, equipment, machinery, employees, store windows. Some street scenes with people; factory workers, cars, airplanes, furniture.

NOTE: Corresponding negatives for most of these photographs are found in series LC-H8.

DATE: Ca. 1920–ca. 1950

PHOTOGRAPHERS: Theodor Horydczak.

PHYSICAL DESCRIPTION: 304 silver gelatin photoprints, 20 × 26 cm or smaller.

ARRANGEMENT: *Lot 12090–1*: Banks; *Lot 12090–2*: Business enterprises; *Lot 12090–3*: Industries and mills.

SOURCE: Gift of Norma Horydczak Reeves and Francis Reeves, 1973.

LOT 12091

COLLECTION NAME: Theodor Horydczak Collection

SUBJECTS: Views of Washington, D.C. The Washington Monument, White House, Jefferson Memorial, and Capitol; includes cityscape and night views. Rock Creek Park; waterfronts, including Tidal Basin with cherry trees, Potomac River; piers and sailboats. Neighborhoods include Georgetown and Southwest marina; dwellings, street scenes, shops.

NOTE: Corresponding negatives for most of these photographs are found in series LC-H8.

DATE: Ca. 1920–ca. 1950

PHOTOGRAPHERS: Theodor Horydczak.

PHYSICAL DESCRIPTION: 229 silver gelatin photoprints, 20 × 26 cm or smaller.

ARRANGEMENT: *Lot 12091–1*: General and aerial views; *Lot 12091–2*: Parks and gardens; *Lot 12091–3*: Neighborhoods; *Lot 12091–4*: Streets, circles, and squares; *Lot 12091–5*: Mall and Tidal Basin.

SOURCE: Gift of Norma Horydczak Reeves and Francis Reeves, 1973.

LOT 12092

COLLECTION NAME: Theodor Horydczak Collection

SUBJECTS: Bridges and Chesapeake and Ohio (C&O) Canal in Washington. Includes Arlington Memorial Bridge, with views of construction, machinery, sculptural details; Dumbarton, Key, and Taft bridges and bridges in Rock Creek Park. C&O Canal, including construction work, houses along banks, people; one image of dedication stone. A few images of Theodore Roosevelt Island.

NOTE: Corresponding negatives for most of these photographs are found in series LC-H8.

DATE: Ca. 1920–ca. 1950

PHOTOGRAPHERS: Theodor Horydczak.

PHYSICAL DESCRIPTION: 106 silver gelatin photoprints, 26 × 21 cm.

SOURCE: Gift of Norma Horydczak Reeves and Francis Reeves, 1973.

LOT 12093

COLLECTION NAME: Theodor Horydczak Collection

SUBJECTS: Religious buildings and charitable institutions in Washington, D.C. National Cathedral grounds, construction work, offices, and people, including portraits of clergy, stone carvers at work, a Boy Scout troop, people at services, one image from rear of men and women in uniform kneeling in prayer. Architectural details, sculpture and sepulchral monuments, stained-glass windows, and other artworks. Franciscan monastery (Mount Saint Sepulchre); Walter Reed Hospital, including interiors and chapel.

NOTE: Corresponding negatives for most of these photographs are found in series LC–H8.

DATE: Ca. 1920–ca. 1950

PHOTOGRAPHERS: Theodor Horydczak.

PHYSICAL DESCRIPTION: 202 silver gelatin photoprints, 21 × 26 cm.

ARRANGEMENT: *Lot 12093–1*: Churches, cathedrals, and monastery; *Lot 12093–2*: National Cathedral interior; *Lot 12093–3*: Hospitals and nursing homes.

SOURCE: Gift of Norma Horydczak Reeves and Francis Reeves, 1973.

LOT 12094

COLLECTION NAME: Theodor Horydczak Collection

SUBJECTS: Washington, D.C., architectural models and plans of government buildings. Includes architectural models and reproductions of bird's-eye view drawings, photo layouts with multiple small images and date ranges printed on them, probably intended to illustrate architecture characteristic of the period cited.

NOTE: Corresponding negatives for most of these photographs are found in series LC-H8.

DATE: Ca. 1920–ca. 1950

PHOTOGRAPHERS: Theodor Horydczak.

PHYSICAL DESCRIPTION: 13 silver gelatin photoprints, 26 × 21 cm.

SOURCE: Gift of Norma Horydczak Reeves and Francis Reeves, 1973.

LOT 12095

COLLECTION NAME: Theodor Horydczak Collection

SUBJECTS: Educational and research institutions in the Washington area. Includes students, offices, and men using broadcasting equipment at Capitol Radio and Electronic (Engineering?) Institute. Buildings, classes, athletic activities, graduation ceremonies, and residential life of women students at Dunbarton College, Trinity College, Holton-Arms School, and the Washington School for Secretaries. Male students, activities, buildings at Georgetown Preparatory School in Garrett Park, Maryland. Georgetown University buildings; a few elementary and high school buildings with students; one image of Convent of the Visitation (Georgetown Visitation Convent).

NOTE: Corresponding negatives for most of these photographs are found in series LC-H8.

DATE: Ca. 1920–ca. 1950

PHOTOGRAPHERS: Theodor Horydczak.

PHYSICAL DESCRIPTION: 191 silver gelatin photoprints, 21 × 26 cm.

SOURCE: Gift of Norma Horydczak Reeves and Francis Reeves, 1973.

LOT 12096

COLLECTION NAME: Theodor Horydczak Collection

SUBJECTS: Events in Washington, D.C. Bonus Army camp with men outside tents and sheds bearing protest messages; men in food lines; demonstration at Capitol. Flood waters and damage. Rural Arts Exhibition hall and close-ups of displays including crafts such as carving, dolls, and textiles. Men in uniform drilling and using electronic equipment; air raid and first aid drills; male and female emergency workers. Window displays about war bonds, rationing, and Red Cross donations.

NOTE: Corresponding negatives for most of these photographs are found in series LC–H8.

DATE: Ca. 1932–ca. 1950

PHOTOGRAPHERS: Theodor Horydczak.

PHYSICAL DESCRIPTION: 183 silver gelatin photoprints, 26 × 21 cm or smaller.

ARRANGEMENT: *Lot 12096–1*: 1932 and 1933; *Lot 12096–2*: 1937 Rural Arts Exhi-

bition; *Lot 12096-3*: World War II preparedness; *Lot 12096–4*: World War II propaganda.

SOURCE: Gift of Norma Horydczak Reeves and Francis Reeves, 1973.

LOT 12097

COLLECTION NAME: Theodor Horydczak Collection

SUBJECTS: Hotels, inns, restaurants, and theaters in Washington, D.C. Hotels with views of surrounding streets, including the Continental Hotel with the Capitol in the background. Lobbies, dining areas, kitchens, guests' rooms, ballrooms, gardens and terraces. People on dance floors, including some photographed from above at the Mayflower Hotel. Shops and men working on the roof of the Mayflower; women working in a laundry room of the Dodge Hotel; sculpture and murals at the Carlton (now Sheraton-Carlton) Hotel. Restaurant entrances, kitchens, lunch counters, and seating areas—some showing cooks, waitresses, and customers; includes bakeries, doughnut shops, cafeterias.

NOTE: Corresponding negatives for most of these photographs are found in series LC–H8.

DATE: Ca. 1920–ca. 1950

PHOTOGRAPHERS: Theodor Horydczak.

PHYSICAL DESCRIPTION: 284 silver gelatin photoprints, 21 × 26 cm.

ARRANGEMENT: *Lot 12097–1*: Hotels and inns; *Lot 12097–2*: Restaurants and theaters.

SOURCE: Gift of Norma Horydczak Reeves and Francis Reeves, 1973.

LOT 12098

COLLECTION NAME: Theodor Horydczak Collection

SUBJECTS: Embassies and chanceries in Washington, D.C., and other locations. Includes entrances, grounds, some interiors; murals at Mexican Embassy. Five reproductions of illustrations of buildings, including U.S. consulate in Tokyo, Japan, most with identifying information inscribed on image.

NOTE: Corresponding negatives for most of these photographs are found in series LC–H8.

DATE: Ca. 1920–ca. 1950

PHOTOGRAPHERS: Theodor Horydczak.

PHYSICAL DESCRIPTION: 30 silver gelatin photoprints, 21 × 26 cm.

SOURCE: Gift of Norma Horydczak Reeves and Francis Reeves, 1973.

LOT 12099

COLLECTION NAME: Theodor Horydczak Collection

SUBJECTS: Galleries, museums, and libraries in Washington, D.C. Includes architectural details and exhibits at National Gallery of Art. Smithsonian Institution exhibits, including early airplanes. Folger Library interiors and architectural details. A few images of the National Zoo; one of the Washington Public Library (Central Library).

NOTE: Corresponding negatives for most of these photographs are found in series LC–H8.

DATE: Ca. 1920–ca. 1950

PHOTOGRAPHERS: Theodor Horydczak.

PHYSICAL DESCRIPTION: 115 silver gelatin photoprints, 21 × 26 cm or smaller.

ARRANGEMENT: *Lot 12099–1*: Galleries and museums; *Lot 12099–2*: Libraries.

SOURCE: Gift of Norma Horydczak Reeves and Francis Reeves, 1973.

LOT 12100

COLLECTION NAME: Theodor Horydczak Collection

SUBJECTS: Library of Congress, Washington, D.C. Cityscapes and architectural details, including doorways, art, reading rooms, and grounds of Library of Congress Jefferson and Adams Buildings. Neptune Fountain; man viewing Declaration of Independence and U.S. Constitution on exhibit at the Library.

NOTE: Corresponding negatives for most of these photographs are found in series LC–H8.

DATE: Ca. 1920–ca. 1950

PHOTOGRAPHERS: Theodor Horydczak.

PHYSICAL DESCRIPTION: 52 silver gelatin photoprints, 26 × 21 cm or smaller.

SOURCE: Gift of Norma Horydczak Reeves and Francis Reeves, 1973.

LOT 12101

COLLECTION NAME: Theodor Horydczak Collection

SUBJECTS: Outdoor sculpture in Washington, D.C., and vicinity. Includes Jefferson Memorial, Lincoln Memorial, and Washington Monument at night and in different seasons, seen from various angles including from above. Airship flying over Jefferson Memorial; Washington Monument with scaffolding and the tip of the monument; one image of Andrew Jackson statue with fireworks exploding in the background; other monuments seen in silhouette. Fountains include a hand pump on Pennsylvania Avenue and one image of a drinking fountain. Arlington Cemetery monuments and structures, including amphitheater.

NOTE: Corresponding negatives for most of these photographs are found in series LC–H8.

DATE: Ca. 1920–ca. 1950

PHOTOGRAPHERS: Theodor Horydczak.

PHYSICAL DESCRIPTION: 226 silver gelatin photoprints, 26 × 21 cm or smaller.

ARRANGEMENT: *Lot 12101–1*: Monuments, memorials, and statues; *Lot 12101–2*: Cemeteries; *Lot 12101–3*: Fountains.

SOURCE: Gift of Norma Horydczak Reeves and Francis Reeves, 1973.

LOT 12102

COLLECTION NAME: Theodor Horydczak Collection

SUBJECTS: Organizations and clubs in Washington, D.C. Includes buildings, interiors, and grounds of the Daughters of the American Revolution (DAR) Memorial Continental Hall, United States Chamber of Commerce Building, Pan American Union Building. Doorways and other architectural details displayed by the National Lumber Manufacturers Association. Masons' convention with views of parade, street decorations, and the city at night; American Photoengravers' booths with firms exhibiting equipment and people conferring. Electric Institute displays advertising the benefits of electricity; kitchen, cleaning, lighting, radio, and heating and cooling appliances; cooking and laundering demonstrations attended by groups of men and women; one image of Nelson Eddy at a microphone labeled "CBS." Some group portraits.

NOTE: Corresponding negatives for most of these photographs are found in series LC–H8.

DATE: Ca. 1920–ca. 1950

PHOTOGRAPHERS: Theodor Horydczak.

PHYSICAL DESCRIPTION: 278 silver gelatin photoprints, 21 × 26 cm or smaller.

ARRANGEMENT: *Lot 12102–1*: Organizations; *Lot 12102–2*: Electric Institute.

SOURCE: Gift of Norma Horydczak Reeves and Francis Reeves, 1973.

LOT 12103

COLLECTION NAME: Theodor Horydczak Collection

SUBJECTS: Social and cultural life and work in Washington, D.C. Recreation and sports, including the 1933 World Series, equestrian and water sports, children playing; parades, eating and drinking occasions, and holiday decorations and activities such as fireworks displays. Portraits of Washington-area residents and government officials, including Vice President John Nance Garner (some are reproductions). Machinery, some horse-drawn; men working, mostly at industrial pursuits; foundry and construction sites; street vendors.

NOTE: Corresponding negatives for most of these photographs are found in series LC–H8.

DATE: Ca. 1920–ca. 1950

PHOTOGRAPHERS: Theodor Horydczak.

PHYSICAL DESCRIPTION: 174 silver gelatin photoprints, 26 × 21 cm or smaller.

ARRANGEMENT: *Lot 12103–1*: Social and cultural life, ca. 1920–ca. 1945; *Lot 12103–2*: Portraits; *Lot 12103–3*: Work and workplaces.

SOURCE: Gift of Norma Horydczak Reeves and Francis Reeves, 1973.

Theodor Horydczak. Bonus Army encampment, across the Anacostia River from the Capitol, 1932. Horydczak Collection, Lot 12096-2.

LC-H8-1459

LOT 12104

COLLECTION NAME: Theodor Horydczak Collection

SUBJECTS: White House, Washington, D.C. Includes interiors, grounds, and architectural details such as entrances, stairways, and chandeliers. Crowds on the lawn for the Easter egg roll. One aerial photograph.

NOTE: Corresponding negatives for most of these photographs are found in series LC–H8.

DATE: Ca. 1920–ca. 1950

PHOTOGRAPHERS: Theodor Horydczak.

PHYSICAL DESCRIPTION: 59 silver gelatin photoprints, 26 × 21 cm.

SOURCE: Gift of Norma Horydczak Reeves and Francis Reeves, 1973.

LOT 12105

COLLECTION NAME: Theodor Horydczak Collection

SUBJECTS: Public utilities in the Washington, D.C., region. Buildings with vehicles parked outside, machinery, offices, and employees at work and posed for portraits. Includes PEPCO plant in Alexandria, Virginia, aerial photos of Benning plant; men working on power lines; railroad cars and tracks at Buzzard Point; copies of photographs of PEPCO equipment and workers taken 1904–5; reproductions of illustrations of appliances. C&P telephone equipment and offices, Washington Gas Company with one photo of men at a gas pump; unidentified water company.

NOTE: Corresponding negatives for most of these photographs are found in series LC–H8.

DATE: Ca. 1920–ca. 1950

PHOTOGRAPHERS: Theodor Horydczak and Fairchild Aerial Surveys, Inc. (New York).

PHYSICAL DESCRIPTION: 177 silver gelatin photoprints, 21 × 26 cm.

SOURCE: Gift of Norma Horydczak Reeves and Francis Reeves, 1973.

LOT 12106

COLLECTION NAME: Theodor Horydczak Collection

SUBJECTS: Residential buildings in Washington, D.C. Includes grounds and interiors showing furniture and architectural details such as ceilings, stairs, doors, and wall decorations. Apartment house lobbies; roof and dining area of the Westchester Apartments; construction of Greenway Apartments; grounds of Sedgewick Gardens viewed from above. Mansions and unidentified houses.

NOTE: Corresponding negatives for most of these photographs are found in series LC–H8.

DATE: Ca. 1920–ca. 1950

PHOTOGRAPHERS: Theodor Horydczak.

PHYSICAL DESCRIPTION: 208 silver gelatin photoprints, 21 × 26 cm or smaller.

ARRANGEMENT: Arranged alphabetically by name of building or owner.

SOURCE: Gift of Norma Horydczak Reeves and Francis Reeves, 1973.

LOT 12107

COLLECTION NAME: Theodor Horydczak Collection

SUBJECTS: Transportation in Washington, D.C. Includes airfield, Mrs. Guy Despart Goff in aviator suit and in airplane cockpit at Washington Hoover Airport. Loading, ticketing, observation, and dining areas, control tower, and hangars at National Airport. Union Station, including views of tracks, sculpture, and inscriptions over doorways. Automobiles, buses, streetcars, railroad car interiors, parking lots, and trucks and trucking activities.

NOTE: Corresponding negatives for most of these photographs are found in series LC–H8.

DATE: Ca. 1920–ca. 1950

PHOTOGRAPHERS: Theodor Horydczak.

PHYSICAL DESCRIPTION: 84 silver gelatin photoprints, 21 × 26 cm or smaller.

SOURCE: Gift of Norma Horydczak Reeves and Francis Reeves, 1973.

LOT 12108

COLLECTION NAME: Theodor Horydczak Collection

SUBJECTS: U.S. Capitol, Washington, D.C. Night, snow, rain, and one aerial view of the Capitol; construction work and activities on the Capitol grounds, including tree planting and a procession of people dressed in eighteenth-century costume. Interiors, including Statuary Hall, art, and architectural details; construction work on House and Senate chambers; House of Representatives kitchens; people riding an underground tram. One photo of an architectural model and one of George F. Thompson restoring a wall in the Senate chamber, ca. 1933.

NOTE: Corresponding negatives for most of these photographs are found in series LC–H8.

DATE: Ca. 1920–ca. 1950

PHOTOGRAPHERS: Theodor Horydczak

PHYSICAL DESCRIPTION: 246 silver gelatin photoprints, 21 × 26 cm or smaller.

SOURCE: Gift of Norma Horydczak Reeves and Francis Reeves, 1973.

LOT 12109

COLLECTION NAME: Theodor Horydczak Collection

SUBJECTS: U.S. government buildings in Washington, D.C. Includes offices, employees, some aerial views, and cityscapes. Many photographs focus on architectural details such as sculpture groups before and after their placement over entrances to the Commerce Department, Federal Trade Commision, Department of Justice, and National Archives buildings; Interstate Commerce Commission floors, ceilings, gates, and light fixtures; a stairwell in the Supreme Court building. National Archives, Post Office Department, and Federal Triangle buildings under construction; some architectural models. A few photos of the Army War College (Fort McNair), Botanic Garden, men working with machinery at the Washington Navy Yard, the Naval Observatory, and House of Representatives office buildings.

NOTE: Corresponding negatives for most of these photographs are found in series LC–H8.

DATE: Ca. 1920–ca. 1950

PHOTOGRAPHERS: Theodor Horydczak.

PHYSICAL DESCRIPTION: 243 silver gelatin photoprints, 21 × 26 cm.

ARRANGEMENT: Alphabetical by name of building.

SOURCE: Gift of Norma Horydczak Reeves and Francis Reeves, 1973.

LOT 12110

COLLECTION NAME: Theodor Horydczak Collection

SUBJECTS: U.S. presidents' dwellings, activities, and portraits. Includes Mount Vernon with outbuildings, Monticello, and Wakefield in Virginia. Franklin D. Roosevelt's inauguration. Woodrow Wilson at an outdoor party. Includes reproductions of illustrations.

NOTE: Corresponding negatives for most of these photographs are found in series LC–H8.

DATE: Ca. 1920–ca. 1950

PHOTOGRAPHERS: Theodor Horydczak.

PHYSICAL DESCRIPTION: 41 silver gelatin photoprints, 21 × 26 cm or smaller.

SOURCE: Gift of Norma Horydczak Reeves and Francis Reeves, 1973.

LOT 12111

COLLECTION NAME: Theodor Horydczak Collection

SUBJECTS: Buildings and activities in Maryland. Primarily dwellings, commercial buildings, public utilities, and churches; transportation; recreation. Includes Glen Echo amusement park, its ballroom, and people at the bathing beach. State Capitol in Annapolis; a grocery store interior, cannons beside Baltimore harbor; Conowingo Hydroelectric Plant.

NOTE: Corresponding negatives for most of these photographs are found in series LC–H8.

DATE: Ca. 1920–ca. 1950

PHOTOGRAPHERS: Theodor Horydczak.

PHYSICAL DESCRIPTION: 159 silver gelatin photoprints, 21 × 26 cm or smaller.

ARRANGEMENT: Alphabetical by place name.

SOURCE: Gift of Norma Horydczak Reeves and Francis Reeves, 1973.

LOT 12112

COLLECTION NAME: Theodor Horydczak Collection

SUBJECTS: Virginia scenes. Includes streets, roads, buildings, and the train yard

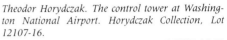

Theodor Horydczak. The control tower at Washington National Airport. Horydczak Collection, Lot 12107-16.

LC-H8-A2-21

in Alexandria; churches and dwellings in Arlington; estates and historic sites such as Stratford Hall, Williamsburg, and Yorktown; the Potomac River at Great Falls; Fairfax quarries; Foxcroft School in Middleburg.

NOTE: Corresponding negatives for most of these photographs are found in series LC–H8.

DATE: Ca. 1920–ca. 1950

PHOTOGRAPHERS: Theodor Horydczak.

PHYSICAL DESCRIPTION: 217 silver gelatin photoprints, 21 × 26 cm or smaller.

SOURCE: Gift of Norma Horydczak Reeves and Francis Reeves, 1973.

LOT 12117

COLLECTION NAME: Theodor Horydczak Collection

SUBJECTS: Dwellings and furnishings at various locations. Includes sequence showing the erection of a prefabricated house and a woman inhabiting it after completion; "PEPCO model home" interiors displaying furnishings and appliances; log houses, brick houses. Individual pieces of furniture such as lamps and chairs.

NOTE: Corresponding negatives for most of these photographs are found in series LC–H8.

DATE: Ca. 1920–ca. 1950

PHOTOGRAPHERS: Theodor Horydczak.

PHYSICAL DESCRIPTION: 89 silver gelatin photoprints, 21 × 26 cm or smaller.

SOURCE: Gift of Norma Horydczak Reeves and Francis Reeves, 1973.

Theodor Horydczak. Carl and Dave's Restaurant on Connecticut Avenue, Washington, D.C. Horydczak Collection, Lot 12097-212.

LC-H8-2451-16

LOT 12118

COLLECTION NAME: Theodor Horydczak Collection

SUBJECTS: Mechanization, at various locations. Machinery and men working in a glass factory and a dairy; people making clocks in a factory and clock-making instruments; electrical power lines; window displays of stores selling electrical appliances, including hardware stores; people using appliances. One image of telephones arrayed in a pattern, photographed from above.

NOTE: Corresponding negatives for most of these photographs are found in series LC–H8.

DATE: Ca. 1920–ca. 1950

PHOTOGRAPHERS: Theodor Horydczak.

PHYSICAL DESCRIPTION: 57 silver gelatin photoprints, 21 × 26 cm.

SOURCE: Gift of Norma Horydczak Reeves and Francis Reeves, 1973.

The Papers of Harold LeClaire Ickes (1874–1952) in the Manuscript Division number 150,000 items and span the years 1815 to 1969. Harold Ickes, a lawyer, was secretary of the interior under Franklin D. Roosevelt and as such was active in the formulation and implementation of many New Deal programs. His papers, described by a finding aid, include correspondence, diaries (1933–51), family papers, legal and financial records, subject files, speeches and writings, and scrapbooks and miscellany. They date mainly from 1933 to 1951 and deal with such questions as conservation, Indian affairs, the problems of Japanese-Americans during World War II, segregation, and other social and political issues of the period. Correspondents include James A. Farley, James Garfield, Will Hays, Charles Evans Hughes, Hiram Johnson, Lyndon Johnson, Frank Knox, Henry Morgenthau, Gifford Pinchot, Franklin D. Roosevelt, Theodore Roosevelt, Harry S. Truman, Henry A. Wallace, and William Allen White. The papers were acquired through gifts of Jane Dahlman Ickes and other Ickes family members, 1952–72. The photographs were transferred to the Prints and Photographs Division.

LOT 12363

COLLECTION NAME: Harold L. Ickes Papers, Manuscript Division

SUBJECTS: Includes tours Ickes took to Puerto Rico, Cuba, Alaska, and Olympic National Park; participation in activities such as dedications, conferences, and speeches. Political figures photographed include Franklin D. Roosevelt, Harry Truman, cabinet members, diplomats, and senators and congressmen; celebrities include Marian Anderson and Katherine Hepburn.

NOTE: Some photos are autographed; some have identification.

DATE: 1874–1962

PHOTOGRAPHERS: Philippe Halsman, Jessie Tarbox Beals, Walter Wilcox, and Thomas D. McAvoy.

PHYSICAL DESCRIPTION: 703 albumen and silver gelatin photoprints, some in 3 albums; postcards; a charcoal drawing; and glass-mounted color transparencies, 35 × 36 cm or smaller.

ARRANGEMENT: *Lot 12363–1*: Ickes' political career; *Lot 12363–2*: Portraits of Ickes; *Lot 12363–3*: Ickes political contemporaries; *Lot 12363–4*: Ickes with celebrities; *Lot 12363–5*: Family pictures and personal portraits; *Lot 12363–6*: Ickes' homes; *Lot 12363–7*: Ickes' childhood; *Lot 12363–8*: Ickes' personal friends. A finding aid is available in the Prints and Photographs Reading Room.

SOURCE: Gift of Jane Dahlman Ickes and other Ickes family members. Transfer from the Manuscript Division, 1971–76.

LOT 12558

COLLECTION NAME: Harold L. Ickes Papers, Manuscript Division.

SUBJECTS: Portraits of Ickes, Franklin D. Roosevelt, and Harry Truman; some autographed. Other political figures and events.

DATE: 1900–1950

PHYSICAL DESCRIPTION: 75 items (silver gelatin photoprints and cyanotypes, some in an album; charcoal and ink drawings; and a photomechanical print), 47 × 34 cm or smaller.

ARRANGEMENT: A finding aid is available in the Prints and Photographs Reading Room.

SOURCE: Gift from Jane Dahlman Ickes and other Ickes family members. Transfer from the Manuscript Division, 1971–76.

Floyd McCarty, Warner Brothers. Katherine Hepburn with Harold Ickes. Harold Ickes Papers, Lot 12363-4-B.

LC-USZ62-90449

Marian Anderson singing in a concert at the Lincoln Memorial, Washington, D.C., April 9, 1939. Harold Ickes Papers, Lot 12363-4-A.

LC-USZ62-90448

Frances Benjamin Johnston (1863–1952) was one of the first women to achieve prominence as a photographer. Born in 1864, Johnston lived in Ohio, in Rochester, New York, and in Washington, D.C., before studying art at Notre Dame Convent in Govanston, Maryland. After continuing her art studies in Europe, she enrolled in the Art Students League in Washington, D.C. Johnston's interests then turned from art to journalism, and she began experimenting with photography in 1889, intending to use the images to illustrate her articles.

She received formal training in photography from Thomas William Smillie of the Division of Photography of the Smithsonian Institution. By 1890, she had opened her own professional studio in Washington and during the next decade she established a reputation as America's "court photographer," with her images of national celebrities and prominent members of Washington's political and social circles. At the same time, she took on photojournalistic assignments, documenting industrial workers and the benefits of education, and publishing in magazines such as the *Ladies' Home Journal,* in which, in 1897, she discussed the opportunities for women in photography ("What a Woman Can Do with a Camera," *Ladies' Home Journal,* September 1897).

Johnston's work was influenced by her conviction that photography is not "purely mechanical"; rather, it is also an art form. Her first precept, expressed in her September 1897 article (p. 6), was "Learn early the immense difference between the photograph that is merely a photograph, and that which is also a picture." She was on the jury of the Philadelphia Photographic Society exhibit in 1899, and she became active in the Photo Secession in 1904. Nevertheless, Johnston did not shy away from the mechanical aspects of the medium, and she was among the first photographers to experiment with the autochrome process for making color photographs, beginning around 1906.

In 1909, Johnston undertook what was probably her first architectural photography commission, documenting the New Theater in New York City for architect John Carrère. Architectural photography became the specialty of the New York City studio she operated in partnership with Mattie Edwards Hewitt from 1913 to 1917. After 1917 Johnston concentrated on photographing gardens and estates, and she traveled extensively, giving lantern slide lectures with the images she made.

Upon the completion of a foreign tour during 1925–26, Johnston embarked on the first of her many contributions to the documentation of historic buildings. A photographic commission for Mrs. Daniel Devore documenting the Virginia estate Chatham developed into a proposal for a more extensive survey of historic structures in Fredericksburg. An exhibit of the resulting photographs at the Library of Congress in 1929 attracted the interest of the Librarian of Congress, Herbert Putnam, and of members of Congress, and a proposal to document historic structures throughout Virginia was put into action. In 1930, the Pictorial Archives of Early American Architecture (PAEAA) was founded, and Johnston was one of the earliest and most regular contributors. With funding from the Carnegie Corporation of New York, Johnston undertook a systematic photographic survey of early southern architecture, which covered nine states; the project lasted until 1940 and resulted in 7,248 negatives. Prints from the negatives were acquired by several institutions, including the Library of Congress. The Library of Congress, which administered some of the grants Johnston received, was also the recipient of the negatives from the Carnegie Survey of the Architecture of the South upon Johnston's death in 1952.

Johnston's work entered the collections of the Library of Congress through copyright deposit, but Johnston also early assumed the role of donor. In 1905 she offered the Library a photograph of Andrew Carnegie, and throughout her long and productive career she continued to send her work to the Library, either for copyright deposit, as a legal deposit, or as a gift. The bulk of her papers and pictorial materials were acquired by the Library through gift and purchase from the Johnston estate in 1953. It is the latter material that primarily makes up the Frances Benjamin Johnston Collection in the Prints and Photographs Division.

The collection consists primarily of photographs made by Johnston in the course of her studio and commission work; some exhibit photographs and personal snapshots are also included. The material spans the period 1864–1940, with the bulk of the material dating from between 1897 and 1927. Among the photographic materials are about 20,000 photoprints (including silver gelatin and cyanotype proofs), 7,000 glass and film negatives, and

Frances Benjamin Johnston. Self-portrait of the photographer with her eight-by-ten-inch format camera at the Arts Club door in Washington, D.C., ca. 1936. Frances Benjamin Johnston Collection, Lot 11734-1.
LC-USZ62-47560

Frances Benjamin Johnston. Johnston's studio in Washington, D.C. Frances Benjamin Johnston Collection, Lot 11738.

LC-J698-8751

800 lantern slides. To preserve evidence of Johnston's photographic techniques and working habits, unretouched and uncropped photoprints and multiple proofs from a single negative have in many cases been included in groups of cataloged images. Johnston's notes, as well as identification supplied later by others, can be found on many of the photoprints. Also included in the collection are photographs and pictorial ephemera Johnston collected throughout her lifetime.

Associated nonpictorial ephemera (for instance, business cards, diaries, clippings, a typewriter, and some photographic equipment) that were not retained in the Manuscript Division's collection of Johnston's papers are housed in the Prints and Photographs Supplementary Archives.

The Johnston Collection has been divided into cohesive units, either according to the nature or provenance of the material or by the subject matter it covers. Each unit has been cataloged and in some cases a finding aid describing in greater detail the contents of a group of images is available. The existence of such a finding aid is indicated by the note, "Finding aid available in the Prints and Photographs Reading Room."

A logbook and a card file listing a selection of Johnston's images are stored in the Supplementary Archives but are of limited use in identifying or documenting Johnston images because of their sporadic coverage and idiosyncratic filing and notation methods.

Except where there are limitations on handling because of the fragility of the material, there are no restrictions on the use of materials in the Johnston Collection.

Negatives from the Frances Benjamin Johnston Collection are found in series LC–J68 through LC–J716. Most are original glass negatives grouped by size and subject matter. Some of Johnston's nitrate film negatives were reproduced on safety film, and in some cases the hazardous nitrate film was subsequently destroyed. Reproductions are made on request.

Also in the collections of the Library of Congress are the Papers of Frances Benjamin Johnston, housed in the Manuscript Division. They span the years 1855–1954 and include extensive correspondence with George Eastman, Frances Folsom Cleveland, Phoebe Apperson Hearst, Ida M. Tarbell, Alfred Stieglitz, Edward W. Bok, Ray Stannard Baker, Theodore Dreiser, George Grantham Bain, and Leicester B. Holland as well as some travel diaries (from 1890 to 1942) and scrapbooks. The papers (about 19,000 items) are also available on 37 reels of microfilm (Photoduplication Service, no. C–378).

Other collections in the Prints and Photographs Division that contain photographs by Frances Benjamin Johnston are the Carnegie Survey of the Architecture of the South, and the Pictorial Archives of Early American Architecture. Art and advertising posters collected by Johnston (about seven hundred items from about 1890 to 1910) are found in the Poster Collection.

Frances Benjamin Johnston. Johnston (sixth from right) and her tintype studio at the Country Fair at Friendship, Washington, D.C., May 1906. Frances Benjamin Johnston Collection, Lot 11500-2.
LC-J713-4931

Frances Benjamin Johnston. Archie Roosevelt photographing Quentin Roosevelt at the White House with Frances Benjamin Johnston's camera, 1902. Frances Benjamin Johnston Collection, Lot 11735.
LC-USZ62-83134

REFERENCES

Daniel, Pete, and Raymond Smock. *A Talent for Detail: The Photographs of Miss Frances Benjamin Johnston, 1889–1910.* New York: Harmony Books, 1974.

Doherty, Amy S. "Frances Benjamin Johnson, 1864–1952." *History of Photography* 4, no. 2 (April 1980), 97–111.

Melville, no. 131, pp. 192–93.

Quitslund, Toby. "Her Feminine Colleagues; Photographs and Letters Collected by Frances Benjamin Johnston." In *Women Artists in Washington Collections,* by Josephine Withers. Catalog for an exhibit, University of Maryland Art Gallery and Women's Caucus for Art, January 18 to February 25, 1979. College Park, Maryland: The Gallery, 1979.

Tucker, Anne, ed. *The Woman's Eye.* New York: Knopf, 1973.

Vanderbilt, no. 391, p. 88.

Vanderbilt, Paul. "Frances Benjamin Johnston, 1864–1952." Unpublished manuscript, 1953. Library of Congress Archives, Manuscript Division.

Frances Benjamin Johnston. Physical education class with weight-lifting equipment at Western High School, Washington, D.C., 1899. Frances Benjamin Johnston Collection, Lot 2749, Box 1.
LC-USZ62-45888

LOT 2749

COLLECTION NAME: Frances Benjamin Johnston Collection

SUBJECTS: Washington, D.C., school survey. Includes high schools, junior high schools, elementary schools, and vocational schools in Washington, D.C. School activities include chemistry, cooking, drawing, physical education classes, and excursions to museums, the zoo, and the Library of Congress.

NOTE: These photographs were displayed at the Paris Exposition, 1900.

DATE: 1899

PHOTOGRAPHERS: Frances Benjamin Johnston.

PHYSICAL DESCRIPTION: 361 cyanotype proofs, 19 × 24 cm or smaller.

ARRANGEMENT: Arranged by photographer's number, 1–416B, in groups pertaining to each of several schools. The groups were mounted and bound together by the Library.

SOURCE: Gift of Frances Benjamin Johnston, 1948.

Frances Benjamin Johnston. Children in First Division School classroom; a map of the City of Washington is on the blackboard, 1899. Frances Benjamin Johnston Collection, Lot 2749, Box 1.
LC-USZ62-90211

LOT 2763

COLLECTION NAME: Frances Benjamin Johnston Collection

SUBJECTS: "Pinkey's blue book, or, The indigo agonies of a photographic amateur." Portraits of members of the Art Students League, including Miss Perrie in "empire costume"; government officials in their offices, including Dr. John Scott of the Pension Office; two images of Johnston ("Pinkey"), one with camera. Women office workers in the Internal Revenue Service. Gypsy encampment, with views of wagons, on Glenwood Road (probably Bethesda, Maryland). Buildings in Washington, including Riggs Bank and the Department of Justice; interiors and exteriors of residences; interior of the Art Students League decorated for a reception. One image of a bronze statuette.

NOTE: Photographs are captioned, dated, and numbered. Title page inscribed, "Lovingly dedicated to Boo."

DATE: November 1–December 6, 1888

PHOTOGRAPHERS: Frances Benjamin Johnston.

PHYSICAL DESCRIPTION: 1 album (44 cyanotypes), 21 × 27 cm.

SOURCE: Gift of Frances Benjamin Johnston, 1948.

LOT 2909

COLLECTION NAME: Frances Benjamin Johnston Collection

SUBJECTS: National Training School for Boys, Bladensburg Road, Washington, D.C. Includes dormitories, workshop, classroom. Boys playing baseball and group portrait of staff.

DATE: Ca. 1908

PHOTOGRAPHERS: Frances Benjamin Johnston.

PHYSICAL DESCRIPTION: 12 cyanotype photoprints, 13 × 18 cm.

SOURCE: Gift of Frances Benjamin Johnston, 1948.

LOT 2910

COLLECTION NAME: Frances Benjamin Johnston Collection

SUBJECTS: Daughters of the American Revolution. Ceremonies at laying of cornerstone and dedication of DAR Memorial Continental Hall. Interiors showing decorations and DAR convention activities, including women making speeches and male dignitaries attending.

NOTE: Corresponding negatives are found in series LC–J698. Accompanied by pamphlets: "History of the Organization of the Society of the Daughters of the American Revolution," prepared by Eugenia Washington (Daughters of the American Revolution, 1895?); and program for dedication ceremony, dated April 7, 1905.

DATE: 1904–8

PHOTOGRAPHERS: Frances Benjamin Johnston.

PHYSICAL DESCRIPTION: 53 items (albumen, cyanotype, and salted paper photoprints; modern silver gelatin photoprints; postcards; and 1 circular image), 24 × 30 cm or smaller.

SOURCE: Gift of Frances Benjamin Johnston, 1948.

LOT 8861

COLLECTION NAME: Frances Benjamin Johnston Collection

SUBJECTS: U.S. Mint in Philadelphia, Pennsylvania; and U.S. Bureau of Engraving in Washington, D.C. Buildings and interiors. Employees, including blacks and women, eating in dining facilities and performing tasks such as sorting sacks and operating presses; portraits of officials in offices. Machinery and equipment including scales, assay equipment, presses, ovens.

NOTE: Identifying information is written in ink on some photos; some have numbers.

DATE: 1889–90

PHOTOGRAPHERS: Frances Benjamin Johnston.

PHYSICAL DESCRIPTION: 53 items (original cyanotype proofs and modern silver gelatin prints made by the Library of Congress from original negatives), 25 × 31 cm or smaller.

SOURCE: Gift of the Frances Benjamin Johnston estate, 1953.

LOT 9214

COLLECTION NAME: Frances Benjamin Johnston Collection

SUBJECTS: President McKinley's inauguration and administration. Portraits of McKinley, some with his cabinet, signers of the peace treaty with Spain, and his first and second Philippine commissions.

NOTE: Corresponding negatives are found in series LC–J698. Some photographs have captions written and signed by Johnston. Accompanied by magazines, clippings, and pamphlets commemorating McKinley and his inauguration, administration, elections, and dedications, many of which feature reproductions of Johnston's photos.

DATE: 1898–1900

PHOTOGRAPHERS: Frances Benjamin Johnston.

PHYSICAL DESCRIPTION: 26 items (original albumen photoprints and modern silver gelatin photoprints made by the Library of Congress), 48 × 40 cm or smaller.

SOURCE: Gift of the Frances Benjamin Johnston estate, 1953.

LOT 9791

COLLECTION NAME: Frances Benjamin Johnston Collection

SUBJECTS: Opening of the sixtieth Congress. House chamber during swearing in of Speaker Cannon; enlargements showing small groups of congressmen at their desks reading and conferring. Includes a young Charles Lindbergh with his father.

NOTE: Corresponding negatives are found in series LC–J689, LC–J698, and LC–J691. Accompanied by a three-page list of members of Congress shown in one image and a board with members' autographs. Some images bear photographer's captions on versos.

DATE: 1907

PHOTOGRAPHERS: Frances Benjamin Johnston.

PHYSICAL DESCRIPTION: 27 silver gelatin photoprints, 36 × 43 cm or smaller.

SOURCE: Gift of the Frances Benjamin Johnston estate, 1953.

LOT 9795

COLLECTION NAME: Frances Benjamin Johnston Collection

SUBJECTS: U.S. Gun Shops. Washington Gun Factory at the Washington Navy Yard. Interiors of gun factory showing men working with machinery, packing ammunition in boxes, and working at desks. Grounds of plant with piles of manufacturing materials. Firing of guns. Close-ups of metal castings, with annotation "Prof. Munroe's experiments."

NOTE: Identification and numbers appear on most photographs or versos; marks for printing on versos of some. Accompanied by a set of galley proofs for an article on the Washington Gun Factory and a rejection slip.

DATE: 1903

PHOTOGRAPHERS: Frances Benjamin Johnston.

PHYSICAL DESCRIPTION: 98 cyanotype proofs and silver gelatin photoprints, 19 × 24 cm or smaller.

SOURCE: Gift of the Frances Benjamin Johnston estate, 1953.

Frances Benjamin Johnston. The Auditor's Building, Washington, D.C. Frances Benjamin Johnston Collection, Lot 8861.

LC-USZ62-92542

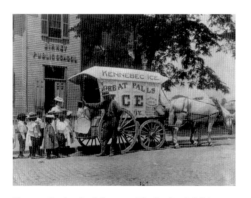

Frances Benjamin Johnston. Black school children at the ice wagon, Birney School, Washington, D.C., 1899. Frances Benjamin Johnston Collection, Lot 2749, Box 2.

LC-USZ62-4553

Frances Benjamin Johnston. Black school children at the Greenough statue of George Washington on the Capitol grounds, 1899. Frances Benjamin Johnston Collection, Lot 2749, Box 2.

LC-USZ62-23939

LOT 9799

COLLECTION NAME: Frances Benjamin Johnston Collection

SUBJECTS: Artistic photographs. Figures, nude or in classical garb, dancing in an outdoor setting and posed beside the water's edge; some identified as Isadora Duncan's dancers. Outdoor theatrical production on Long Island (1915?). Sculpture in the Halls of the Ancients, Washington, D.C., shown on an invitation to an "exhibition of Blue Prints" held on that site. One combination photoprint of a man's face and hand superimposed over stuffed and mounted animals.

NOTE: Some images are stamped "Frances Benjamin Johnston, Mattie Edwards Hewitt" or copyrighted by Johnston and Hewitt. Some have identifying information penciled on versos. Accompanied by a news clipping and an envelope with notes.

DATE: 1900–1915

PHOTOGRAPHERS: Frances Benjamin Johnston.

PHYSICAL DESCRIPTION: 32 cyanotype proofs and silver gelatin photoprints, 42 × 30 cm or smaller.

SOURCE: Copyright deposit by Frances Benjamin Johnston.

LOT 9808

COLLECTION NAME: Frances Benjamin Johnston Collection

SUBJECTS: Ceremonies for Pan American Union Building cornerstone laying. Includes Theodore Roosevelt, John Barrett, Andrew Carnegie, Elihu Root, and other dignitaries at or near speakers' rostrum.

NOTE: Corresponding negatives are found in series LC–J681. Johnston stamp appears on the versos of some photos. Some have written identification on versos or labels.

DATE: May 11, 1908

PHOTOGRAPHERS: Frances Benjamin Johnston.

PHYSICAL DESCRIPTION: 43 cyanotype, albumen, and silver gelatin photoprints, 23 × 30 cm or smaller.

SOURCE: Gift of the Frances Benjamin Johnston estate, 1953.

LOT 10130

COLLECTION NAME: Frances Benjamin Johnston Collection

SUBJECTS: Easter egg roll on the White House lawn. Includes crowds, children playing on lawn, vendors, police, and the presidential party observing from the White House portico.

Frances Benjamin Johnston. The Telegraph Room in the White House, set up to receive news of the Spanish-American War, 1898. Frances Benjamin Johnston Collection, Lot 11350-12.

LC-USZ62-90805

Frances Benjamin Johnston. Center Market, Washington, D.C. Frances Benjamin Johnston Collection, Lot 11727.

LC-J698-81420

NOTE: Corresponding negatives are found in series LC–J682. Photoprints are labeled.

DATE: 1899

PHOTOGRAPHERS: Frances Benjamin Johnston.

PHYSICAL DESCRIPTION: 28 items (original albumen photoprints and modern silver gelatin photoprints), 24 × 30 cm or smaller.

SOURCE: Gift of Frances Benjamin Johnston, 1948.

Frances Benjamin Johnston. The Corcoran house dining room. Frances Benjamin Johnston Collection, Lot 11727.

LC-J698-81391

Frances Benjamin Johnston. The U.S. Navy Gun Shops, Washington Navy Yard. Frances Benjamin Johnston Collection, Lot 9795.

LC-USZ62-92404

Frances Benjamin Johnston. Easter egg roll at the White House, 1898. Frances Benjamin Johnston Collection, Lot 10130.

LC-USZ62-46453

brochures listing members and committees and handwritten and typed lists identifying members shown in group photos.

DATE: 1905–6

PHOTOGRAPHERS: Frances Benjamin Johnston.

PHYSICAL DESCRIPTION: 37 cyanotype and silver gelatin photoprints, 40 × 51 cm or smaller.

SOURCE: Copyright deposit by Frances Benjamin Johnston, February 8, 1906, and gift of the Frances Benjamin Johnston estate, 1953.

Frances Benjamin Johnston. Alice Roosevelt Longworth, 1902. Frances Benjamin Johnston Collection, Lot 11735.

LC-USZ62-70154

Frances Benjamin Johnston. President Taft golfing at the Chevy Chase links. Frances Benjamin Johnston Collection, Lot 11735.

LC-USZ62-87829

LOT 11350

COLLECTION NAME: Frances Benjamin Johnston Collection

SUBJECTS: The White House. Includes interior and exterior views. Unidentified staff and groups attending social functions appear in some photos.

NOTE: Corresponding negatives are found in series LC–J698.

DATE: 1889–1906

PHOTOGRAPHERS: Frances Benjamin Johnston.

PHYSICAL DESCRIPTION: 512 cyanotype, albumen, and silver gelatin photoprints, 25 × 30 cm or smaller.

ARRANGEMENT: *Lot 11350–1:* Exterior views and floor plans; *Lot 11350–2:* Paintings, decorative pieces, sculpture; *Lot 11350–3:* East Room; *Lot 11350–4:* Green Room; *Lot 11350–5:* Blue Room; *Lot 11350–6:* Red Room; *Lot 11350–7:* Dining rooms, unidentified formal rooms; *Lot 11350–8:* Corridors and vestibules; *Lot 11350–9:* President's office and library; *Lot 11350–10:* Bedrooms and nursery; *Lot 11350–11:* Cabinet room; *Lot 11350–12:* Staff, offices, and work areas; *Lot 11350–13:* Conservatory; *Lot 11350–14:* Gardens, grounds, and outbuildings; *Lot 11350–15:* Outdoor events, receptions, etc.; *Lot 11350–16:* Published materials; *Lot 11350–17:* Wedding decorations.

SOURCE: Gift of Frances Benjamin Johnston, 1948.

LOT 11500

COLLECTION NAME: Frances Benjamin Johnston Collection

SUBJECTS: Pastoral play and country fair in Washington, D.C. Includes actors and actresses portraying the seasons, shepherdesses, milkmaids, etc., outdoors; dancing a minuet; posed for individual and group portraits. People at country fair booths, including Johnston's tintype gallery; fortune-tellers.

NOTE: The event was held at Friendship estate on May 4, 1906, sponsored by local charity organizations, and proceeds were used for the relief of victims of the San Francisco fire. Identification, including "The Oaks" and "Friendship," and Johnston numbers appear on some photos. Some bear a copyright statement dated 1906. Corresponding negatives are found in series LC–J698.

DATE: May 4, 1906

PHOTOGRAPHERS: Frances Benjamin Johnston.

PHYSICAL DESCRIPTION: 153 cyanotype, albumen, and silver gelatin photoprints, 30 × 23 cm or smaller.

SOURCE: Gift of the Frances Benjamin Johnston estate, 1953.

LOT 10810

COLLECTION NAME: Frances Benjamin Johnston Collection

SUBJECTS: Opening of the Fifty-ninth Congress. First session of the House, with opening ceremonies, swearing in of state delegations, and Speaker Joseph G. Cannon presiding.

NOTE: Corresponding negatives are found in series LC–J698. Accompanied by two

LOT 11528

COLLECTION NAME: Frances Benjamin Johnston Collection

SUBJECTS: Naval Academy, Annapolis, Maryland. Includes buildings, grounds, midshipmen's activities, visitors, including Theodore Roosevelt; street scenes in Annapolis.

DATE: Ca. 1902

PHOTOGRAPHERS: Frances Benjamin Johnston.

PHYSICAL DESCRIPTION: 91 cyanotype and silver gelatin photoprints, 24 × 30 cm or smaller, 27 photomechanical prints, halftone images, 14 × 20 cm or smaller.

SOURCE: Gift of the Frances Benjamin Johnston estate, 1953.

LOT 11727

COLLECTION NAME: Frances Benjamin Johnston Collection

SUBJECTS: Washington, D.C., architectural views. Buildings, including government buildings, museums, residences, commercial buildings; views of interiors, furnishings, architectural elements. Monuments, gardens. Some portraits included with views of sites.

NOTE: Accompanied by four periodical clippings featuring Johnston photographs.

DATE: 1890–1940s

PHOTOGRAPHERS: Frances Benjamin Johnston.

PHYSICAL DESCRIPTION: 1,969 cyanotype, albumen, and silver gelatin photoprints, 41 × 51 cm or smaller.

ARRANGEMENT: Arranged alphabetically by name of site, surname of building owner, or surname of sitter. A finding aid is available in the Prints and Photographs Reading Room.

SOURCE: Gift of Frances Benjamin Johnston, 1948.

LOT 11734

COLLECTION NAME: Frances Benjamin Johnston Collection

SUBJECTS: Johnston's family, friends, and career. Career-related images include Johnston's studios, the Academie Julian in Paris, the Art Students League, and the Washington Camera Club. Sites include Washington, D.C.; Innisfail, Alberta, Canada; Morgantown, North Carolina; and Johnston's New Orleans, Louisiana, home.

NOTE: Corresponding negatives are found in series LC–J68, –J685, –J691, –J698, and –J713. Includes painting and reproduction of poster by Mills Thompson.

DATE: 1880–1952

PHOTOGRAPHERS: Frances Benjamin Johnston, Mathew Brady Gallery, Gertrude Käsebier, and Bachrach Bros.

PHYSICAL DESCRIPTION: 634 items (cyanotype, albumen—including carte-de-visite, cabinet card, and boudoir images—platinum, silver gelatin, and tintype photoprints; and drawings), 36 × 29 cm or smaller.

ARRANGEMENT: *Lot 11734–1:* Portraits of Johnston; *Lot 11734–2:* Johnston's family; *Lot 11734–3:* Johnston and friends; *Lot 11734–4:* Family genealogy; *Lot 11734–5:* Pets; *Lot 11734–6:* Johnston's career. A finding aid is available in the Prints and Photographs Reading Room.

SOURCE: Gift of the Frances Benjamin Johnston estate, 1953.

Frances Benjamin Johnston. Portrait of John Philip Sousa. Frances Benjamin Johnston Collection, Lot 11735.

LC-USZ62-47071

LOT 11735

COLLECTION NAME: Frances Benjamin Johnston Collection

SUBJECTS: Portraits. Includes politicians, presidents and members of their families, cabinet officers, diplomats, and artists. Some group photos, including family portraits.

DATE: Ca. 1890–1910

PHOTOGRAPHERS: Frances Benjamin Johnston.

PHYSICAL DESCRIPTION: 5,001 cyanotype, albumen, platinum, tintype, and silver gelatin photoprints, 51 × 41 cm or smaller.

ARRANGEMENT: Arranged alphabetically by sitter's surname, followed by unidentified sitters. A finding aid is available in the Prints and Photographs Reading Room.

SOURCE: Gift of the Frances Benjamin Johnston estate, 1953.

Frances Benjamin Johnston. Oliver Wendell Holmes, 1902. Frances Benjamin Johnston Collection, Lot 11735.

LC-USZ62-58677

LOT 11736

COLLECTION NAME: Frances Benjamin Johnston Collection

SUBJECTS: Arts Club of Washington. Activities of the Arts Club, including setting up for "La Foire aux Croûtes" (a white elephant fund-raising sale), window displays, and men and women dressed in costume of artists and peasants for performance. Arts Club garden. Mrs. Grace Rice posed in front of building.

NOTE: Corresponding negatives are found in series LC−J682, −J691, and −J699. Accompanied by programs, announcements, invitations, and newspaper clippings related to activities of the Arts Club.

DATE: 1927−47

PHOTOGRAPHERS: Frances Benjamin Johnston, H. H. Rideout, Tenschert & Flack, and Schütz.

Frances Benjamin Johnston. Portrait of Alice Pike Barney. Frances Benjamin Johnston Collection, Lot 11735.
LC-USZ62-77339

PHYSICAL DESCRIPTION: 66 silver gelatin photoprints, 30 × 26 cm or smaller.

SOURCE: Gift of the Frances Benjamin Johnston estate, 1953.

Frances Benjamin Johnston. Frances Hodgson Burnett (Mrs. Stephen Townsend), author. Frances Benjamin Johnston Collection, Lot 11735.
LC-J698-6215

LOT 11738

COLLECTION NAME: Frances Benjamin Johnston Collection

SUBJECTS: Frances Benjamin Johnston's photographic studio, Washington, D.C. Includes interiors of studio located at 1332 V Street NW, showing furnishings, art objects, photographic equipment, architectural details, and Johnston with friends; garden.

DATE: Ca. 1890-ca. 1913. Dates conjectured as being prior to Johnston's opening a studio in New York City in 1913.

PHOTOGRAPHERS: Frances Benjamin Johnston.

PHYSICAL DESCRIPTION: 156 cyanotype and silver gelatin photoprints, a watercolor drawing, and a photomechanical print, 41 × 51 cm or smaller.

SOURCE: Gift of the Frances Benjamin Johnston estate, 1953.

Frances Benjamin Johnston. Portrait of Ida Tarbell. Frances Benjamin Johnston Collection, Lot 11735.
LC-USZ62-53912

LOT 12373

COLLECTION NAME: Frances Benjamin Johnston Collection

SUBJECTS: Potomac River views. Waterscapes, landscapes, boats; Frances Benjamin Johnston standing on shore; Dr. Egbert A. Clark in a canoe and cooking outdoors.

NOTE: Corresponding negatives in series LC−J698.

DATE: Ca. 1898

PHOTOGRAPHERS: Frances Benjamin Johnston.

Frances Benjamin Johnston. Charlotte Perkins Stetson Gilman, ca. 1900. Frances Benjamin Johnston Collection, Lot 11735.
LC-USZ62-49035

PHYSICAL DESCRIPTION: 20 cyanotype and silver gelatin photoprints, 16 × 20 cm or smaller.

SOURCE: Gift of Frances Benjamin Johnston, 1948.

LOT 12512

COLLECTION NAME: Frances Benjamin Johnston Collection

SUBJECTS: Portraits of Theodore Roosevelt in uniform (1898); George H. Brown (1899); and a group attending the signing of the Peace Protocol in Washington on August 12, 1898.

DATE: 1898–99

PHOTOGRAPHERS: Frances Benjamin Johnston.

PHYSICAL DESCRIPTION: 3 silver gelatin photoprints, 26 × 34 cm or smaller.

SOURCE: Copyright deposit by Frances Benjamin Johnston, 1898–99.

LOT 12551

COLLECTION NAME: Frances Benjamin Johnston Collection

SUBJECTS: Architectural drawings. Floor plans for Arts Club of Washington and for alterations for Greentree House. Elevation for unidentified building.

NOTE: Identifying information appears on most drawings. Four drawings are bound together with a cover sheet bearing the title "Greentree House" and Johnston's stamp.

DATE: 1937

PHOTOGRAPHERS: Frances Benjamin Johnston.

PHYSICAL DESCRIPTION: 8 pencil and graphite drawings on tracing paper, 36 × 67 cm or smaller.

SOURCE: Gift of the Frances Benjamin Johnston estate, 1953.

Frances Benjamin Johnston. Herbert Putnam, Librarian of Congress, ca. 1900. Frances Benjamin Johnston Collection, Lot 11735.

LC-USZ62-92405

Frances Benjamin Johnston. Jacob Riis, journalist and photographer, ca. 1900. Frances Benjamin Johnston Collection, Lot 11735.

LC-USZ62-47078

Frances Benjamin Johnston. Portrait of Eadweard Muybridge, photographer. Frances Benjamin Johnston Collection, Lot 11735.

LC-USZ62-33083

133

The Records of the League of Women Voters, spanning the years 1919–63 and accompanied by a finding aid, are housed in the Library's Manuscript Division. Subjects range from the earliest history of the women's suffrage movement to recent activities of the league. The photographs were transferred to the Prints and Photographs Division.

LOT 5539

COLLECTION NAME: Records of the League of Women Voters, Manuscript Division

SUBJECTS: Material gathered for publication in 1927 under the title, "The National League of Women Voters: What It Is and How It Came to Be." Copy photographs and news pictures, some retouched, with hand-lettered captions. Washington subjects include the league's headquarters at 532 Seventeenth Street NW, the 1913 suffrage parade on Pennsylvania Avenue, a group photograph with President Coolidge at the White House in 1927, a view of the Capitol at night, and portraits of officers. Other subjects include Mrs. Harriet Stanton Blatch addressing a crowd of men on Wall Street in New York; eight women posed with a poster listing planks to be presented to the 1920 Democratic Platform Committee; and a delegation of members visiting the President of Cuba to urge suffrage for women of that country.

DATE: Ca. 1900–ca. 1927

PHOTOGRAPHERS: Underwood & Underwood and Edmonston.

PHYSICAL DESCRIPTION: 76 silver gelatin photoprints, reproductions, and hand-lettered captions, 11 × 14 inch or smaller.

SOURCE: Gift of the League of Women Voters, 1933–40. Transfer from the Manuscript Division.

LOT 5540

COLLECTION NAME: Records of the League of Women Voters, Manuscript Division

SUBJECTS: Illustrated newspaper clippings and copy photographs related to the activities of the women's suffrage movement. Women's suffrage headquarters in Cleveland, Ohio; members of the Minnesota League of Women Voters with a half-mile long petition, at the national headquarters in Washington; portraits of Susan B. Anthony, Elizabeth Cady Stanton, Carrie Chapman Catt, and Anna Howard Shaw, delegates to the 1880 National Suffrage Convention held in Washington, D.C. Photographs of posters.

DATE: Ca. 1920–ca. 1925

PHYSICAL DESCRIPTION: 13 items (silver gelatin copy photoprints of posters, newspaper illustrations, and newspaper clippings), 28 × 36 cm or smaller.

SOURCE: Gift of the League of Women Voters, 1933–40. Transfer from the Manuscript Division.

LOT 5541

COLLECTION NAME: Records of the League of Women Voters, Manuscript Division

SUBJECTS: Women's suffrage processions held in Washington, D.C., on March 3 and April 7, 1913. Milling crowds on Pennsylvania Avenue, and dense crowds preventing parade from passing (March 3); a crowd breaking up the parade at Ninth Street NW; parade float representing women of the Bible lands; a delegation from Bryn Mawr College; a contingent of trained nurses; spectators standing atop streetcars and carriages. Includes views of the April 7 parade, with police escorts.

W. R. Ross. "Suffragists' March to the Capitol," April 7, 1913. Records of the League of Women Voters, Lot 5541.

LC-USZ62-10843

NOTE: Accompanied by the official parade program.

DATE: 1913

PHOTOGRAPHERS: G. V. Buck, Taylor Studio, Leet Bros, W. R. Ross, and I.&M. Ottenheimer (Baltimore).

PHYSICAL DESCRIPTION: 27 silver gelatin photoprints and postcards, 20 × 25 cm or smaller.

SOURCE: Gift of the League of Women Voters, 1933–40. Transfer from the Manuscript Division.

The General Council of the League of Women Voters with President Coolidge at the White House, April 30, 1927. Records of the League of Women Voters, Lot 5539.

LC-USZ62-46765

LOT 5542

COLLECTION NAME: Records of the League of Women Voters, Manuscript Division

SUBJECTS: Scenes from a tableau held on the Treasury Building steps in Washington, in conjunction with the women's suffrage procession on March 3, 1913. Costumed women representing Columbia, Justice, Charity, Peace, Liberty, Hope, and other figures. Includes photographs of a group of costumed young girls with balloons.

DATE: March 1913

PHOTOGRAPHERS: Taylor Studio and Little Art Shop Publishers.

PHYSICAL DESCRIPTION: 17 silver gelatin photoprints (postcards), 9 × 13 cm or smaller.

SOURCE: Gift of the League of Women Voters, 1933–40. Transfer from the Manuscript Division.

LOT 5543

COLLECTION NAME: Records of the League of Women Voters, Manuscript Division

SUBJECTS: News photographs relating to women's suffrage. Governors of various states signing resolutions ratifying the Nineteenth Amendment; the Women's Political Union of New York "delivering the suffrage torch" to women of New Jersey aboard the tug *Holbrook*; a suffrage march in New York City (1917); Mrs. Guilford Dudley of Nashville at a convention costumed as a Democratic donkey; a 1917 victory garden. Includes group portraits of the "Suffrage Campaign of 1896" (Mmes Spring, Severance, Anthony, and Wills). Washington subjects include suffrage mementoes in the Smithsonian Institution; a suffrage group from Illinois lobbying at the Capitol; House Speaker Gillette signing suffrage bill with a group of suffrage leaders; and Judge Florence E. Allen and Miss Bertha marching in the pilgrimage from New York to Washington (winter of 1913).

DATE: Ca. 1912-ca. 1920

PHOTOGRAPHERS: Harris & Ewing and International (New York).

PHYSICAL DESCRIPTION: 22 items (silver gelatin photoprints and newspaper clippings), 28 × 26 cm or smaller.

SOURCE: Gift of the League of Women Voters, 1933–40. Transfer from the Manuscript Division.

Harris & Ewing. Julia Lathrop, Jane Addams, and Mary McDowell on a lobbying trip to Capitol Hill, 1913. Records of the League of Women Voters, Lot 5543.

LC-USZ62-50050

LOT 5544

COLLECTION NAME: Records of the League of Women Voters, Manuscript Division

SUBJECTS: Portraits and copies of portraits of women active in the women's suffrage movement and as members of the League of Women Voters. Subjects include Grace Abbott, Jane Addams, Mrs. Newton D. Baker, Sophonisba P. Breckinridge, Mrs. Raymond Brown, Carrie Chapman Catt, Abigail Scott Duniway, Agnes K. Hanna, Harriet Laidlaw, Katharine Ludington, Maria Sanford, Belle Sherwin, Arminia S. White, and many others.

NOTE: Accompanied by biographical data.

DATE: Ca. 1890-ca. 1930

PHOTOGRAPHERS: Bachrach, Underwood & Underwood, National Photo Company, and Clinedinst.

PHYSICAL DESCRIPTION: 112 silver gelatin photoprints, 20 × 25 cm or smaller.

SOURCE: Gift of the League of Women Voters, 1933–40. Transfer from the Manuscript Division.

Carrie Chapman Catt. Records of the League of Women Voters, Lot 5544.

LC-USZ62-46405

LOT 5545

COLLECTION NAME: Records of the League of Women Voters, Manuscript Division

SUBJECTS: Portraits of men associated with the women's suffrage movement and the League of Women Voters. Includes portraits of Louis Brownlow, James Mullenbach, William A. Neilson, Charles C. Isely, Thomas H. Reed, Charles P. Taft II, and Lent D. Upson.

DATE: Ca. 1925-ca. 1935

PHYSICAL DESCRIPTION: 7 silver gelatin photoprints, 21 × 26 cm or smaller.

SOURCE: Gift of the League of Women Voters, 1933–40. Transfer from the Manuscript Division.

Taylor Studio. Suffragette tableau on the Treasury Building steps, March 3, 1913. Records of the League of Women Voters, Lot 5542.

LC-USZ62-53227

Between 1880 and 1896, the photographer Levin C. Handy was hired on contract to document the construction of the first Library of Congress building, now called the Thomas Jefferson Building. He produced more than nine hundred glass plate negatives that showed every stage of the construction process, including building materials and their ox-drawn transportation, stone-setting cranes and pulleys, work methods, and laborers and artisans on the job. The progress of the building is shown from various angles in all seasons. There are pictures of the cleared site before construction began that document the character of the surrounding neighborhood. The collection of glass negatives includes views of the interior areas of the building, the digging of a tunnel between the Library and Capitol, and the stone carvers at work producing the numerous decorative ornaments used throughout the building. Some plates, when joined, produce panoramic views of the construction work.

The glass negatives, which until recently were unavailable for research use, may now be consulted on microfilm. Images on microfilm are arranged chronologically, within each negative format, and within broad subject categories. In addition, cyanotype proof prints from these negatives were gathered into albums under a roughly chronological arrangement and are cataloged. Some panoramic views of the Library of Congress construction were produced by mounting cyanotype proofs side-by-side; these images are also cataloged and available for research use. These cataloged materials are described below.

LOT 12042

COLLECTION NAME: Library of Congress Construction Photographs

SUBJECTS: Panoramic photographs of the construction of the Library of Congress Jefferson Building. Most photographs in this lot are mounted side-by-side to form panoramic views of the Jefferson Building site at various stages, including initial excavation and interior construction. Workmen, machinery, and horse-drawn carts.

NOTE: Dates and identifying information are inscribed on most images. Corresponding glass negatives are found in series LC–USL5, –USL51, and –USL52; prints and negatives have not been matched. Prints from this negative series also appear as cyanotype proofs mounted in bound volumes in Lot 12335, and the negatives themselves may be viewed on microfilm in Lot 12365.

DATE: 1887–94

PHOTOGRAPHERS: Levin C. Handy.

PHYSICAL DESCRIPTION: 62 cyanotype

and albumen photoprints, 24 × 103 cm or smaller.

ARRANGEMENT: *Lot 12042–1:* April 8, 1888, to December 30, 1891; *Lot 12042–2:* April 23, 1892, to May 15, 1894.

LOT 12335

COLLECTION NAME: Library of Congress Construction Photographs

SUBJECTS: Construction of the Library of Congress building. Some photos are mounted side-by-side to form panoramic views of the Jefferson Building construction site, the Capitol, and surrounding neighborhoods, showing stages of construction from site excavation to the completed structure. Includes horse-drawn carts with building materials, masons and stone carvers at work, details of stonework, including sculptured heads and faces, and other architectural details; interior construction. Includes some architectural plans.

NOTE: Dates and identifying information are inscribed on most images. Corresponding glass negatives are found in series LC–USL5, –USL51, and –USL52. Prints from this negative series also appear mounted as panoramas in Lot 12042. Negatives may be viewed on the microfilm Lot 12365.

DATE: April 1885–December 1895

PHOTOGRAPHERS: Levin C. Handy.

PHYSICAL DESCRIPTION: 3 albums (717 cyanotype proofs), 86 × 26 cm.

ARRANGEMENT: *Vol. 1:* April 1888 to June 1891; *Vol. 2:* May 1891 to November 1893; *Vol. 3:* January 1894 to December 1895.

RESTRICTIONS: Cyanotype proofs are brittle; albums must be handled with great care.

LOT 12365 (microfilm)

COLLECTION NAME: Library of Congress Construction Photographs

SUBJECTS: Construction of the Library of Congress Jefferson Building. Photographs documenting progress of construction, taken at regular intervals and from various angles. Includes buildings on and near the Capitol Hill site that were cleared for the construction; workmen, machinery, tools, oxen, and wagons; interior and exterior architectural details, artwork, and sculpture; copies of drawings, plans, and models.

NOTE: Dates and identifying information are inscribed on most images. Corresponding glass negatives are found in series LC–USL5, –USL51, and –USL52. Prints from this negative series also appear mounted as panoramas in Lot 12042 and as cyanotype proofs mounted in bound volumes in Lot 12335.

DATE: 1880–96

PHOTOGRAPHERS: Levin C. Handy.

PHYSICAL DESCRIPTION: 2 microfilm reels (975 dry plate glass negatives, reproduced as positive images).

ARRANGEMENT: Images in sequence by size of negative and subject of image. Library-assigned negative numbers appear on each image but have not been matched with photoprints in Lots 12042 and 12335.

Levin C. Handy. View of Library of Congress (Jefferson Building) under construction, taken from the northeast, September 16, 1891. Library of Congress Construction Photographs, Lot 12042-1.

LC-USZ62-92849

The Library of Congress Manuscript Division holds a collection of Abraham Lincoln Papers and the papers of his son, Robert Todd Lincoln. The Abraham Lincoln material (42,100 items) spans the years 1833–1916, and is accompanied by a published finding aid. The papers deal with his roles as U.S. president, congressman, and abolitionist, and they include two drafts of the Gettysburg Address, correspondence, and other papers, mainly letters addressed to Lincoln during his presidency. The Robert Todd Lincoln Papers (38 items) cover the period 1861–1909 and are accompanied by an item index. Both groups of papers were acquired by gift or purchase, 1923–72. The photographs from both groups of papers were transferred to the Prints and Photographs Division.

Mathew Brady. Carte-de-visite portrait of Tad Lincoln, ca. 1860s. Abraham Lincoln Papers and Robert Todd Lincoln Papers, Lot 12254.
LC-USZ62-92575

LOT 12253

COLLECTION NAME: Abraham Lincoln Papers and Robert Todd Lincoln Papers, Manuscript Division

SUBJECTS: Portrait photographs of Abraham Lincoln, Stephen A. Douglas, and Robert H. Milroy. Lincoln at his inauguration and with his cabinet. Lincoln's summer home in Washington, D.C. Three cartoons: "Honest Old Abe on the stump, Springfield, 1858"; "The Little Giant in the character of the gladiator"; and one untitled, showing Lincoln in an Indian headdress.

DATE: 1863-ca. 1947

PHOTOGRAPHERS: Mathew Brady, A. H. Ritchie, W. G. Jackman, and F. F. Okley.

PHYSICAL DESCRIPTION: 17 photoprints, engravings, and photomechanical prints, 54 × 46 cm or smaller.

SOURCE: Miscellaneous gifts relating to Lincoln. Transfer from the Manuscript Division, 1973.

LOT 12254

COLLECTION NAME: Abraham Lincoln Papers and Robert Todd Lincoln Papers, Manuscript Division

SUBJECTS: Portraits from the Robert Todd Lincoln Papers. Robert Todd Lincoln, Thomas "Tad" Lincoln, Abraham Lincoln, and William McKinley.

DATE: 1860-ca. 1890

PHOTOGRAPHERS: Mathew Brady, John Goldin & Co., C. D. Mosher, and Thomas Johnson.

PHYSICAL DESCRIPTION: 8 items (photoprints, an engraving, and photomechanical prints), 30 × 23 cm or smaller.

SOURCE: Gift of Parke-Bernet Galleries. Transfer from the Manuscript Division, 1980.

Lincoln's summer home at the Old Soldiers' Home in Washington, D.C., 1863. Abraham Lincoln Papers and Robert Todd Lincoln Papers, Lot 12253.
LC-USZ62-87597

John Goldin. Carte-de-visite portrait of Robert Lincoln, ca. 1860s. Abraham Lincoln Papers and Robert Todd Lincoln Papers, Lot 12254.
LC-USZ62-92576

Gen. John Alexander Logan (1826–1886) began as a volunteer soldier and eventually became commander of the Army of the Tennessee and president of the Grand Army of the Republic. Logan served as a member of Congress and U.S. senator from Illinois, both as a Democrat and a Republican, and originated Memorial Day. He was a candidate for vice president in 1884.

The Manuscript Division holds the papers of the John Alexander Logan family, including material by John Logan's wife, Mary Simmerson (Cunningham) Logan (1838–1923), an author. The collection spans the years 1826–1923, numbers 48,000 items, and is accompanied by a finding aid. The material relates to the military, political, and social history of the Civil War and postwar period, including Reconstruction, the impeachment of Andrew Johnson, the presidential campaigns of 1880–84, Memorial Day, the Grand Army of the Republic, the Society of the Army of the Tennessee, the Belgian Relief Fund, the World's Columbian Exposition, the American Red Cross, and women's suffrage. Photographs from among these papers were transferred to the Prints and Photographs Division and are described below.

Rockwood Studio, New York. Portrait of John A. Logan. John Logan Papers, Lot 9777.
LC-USZ62-92532

LOT 9624

COLLECTION NAME: John Alexander Logan Collection

SUBJECTS: Portraits of U.S. Army officers, including Generals Sherman and Burnside. Portraits of relatives, friends, babies, children, and famous people, including Simon Cameron. Includes a group of carte-de-visite photographs of New York City and vicinity churches, and views of Minnehaha Falls in Minneapolis, Minnesota.

NOTE: Album embossed with the title, "Mr. & Mrs. Genl. John A. Logan."

DATE: Ca. 1865

PHOTOGRAPHERS: C. M. Bell, John Goldin, J. Carbutt, and F. Gutekunst.

PHYSICAL DESCRIPTION: 1 album (ca. 100 carte-de-visite photographs, tintypes, and gem tintypes, some hand-colored), 29 × 23 cm.

SOURCE: Gift of John A. Logan III, 1962.

LOT 9625

COLLECTION NAME: John Alexander Logan Collection

SUBJECTS: Portraits of men, mainly Protestant clergy, members of Congress, and U.S. Army officers in mufti. Includes portraits of Brigham Young and Apostle Lorenzo Snow of Salt Lake City, the Japanese minister Mr. Zoshida (1868), George B. McCreary (secretary of war under President Hayes), Rev. Dr. Sunderland ("Mr. Lincoln's pastor") of Washington, D.C., and Rev. Teunis S. Hamlin (Church of the Covenant, Washington, D.C.).

DATE: Ca. 1870

PHOTOGRAPHERS: Bachrach Bros., C. M. Bell, and A. Bogardus.

PHYSICAL DESCRIPTION: 1 album (33 albumen cabinet card photographs), 22 × 30 cm.

SOURCE: Gift of John A. Logan III, 1962.

LOT 9626

COLLECTION NAME: John Alexander Logan Collection

SUBJECTS: Portraits of U.S. presidents, members of Congress, cabinet officers, and other notables. Includes portraits of John A. Logan, James G. Blaine, U. S. Grant, Rutherford Hayes, Schuyler Colfax, Hannibal Hamlin, Robert Todd Lincoln (secretary of war under Presidents Garfield and Arthur), House Speaker Joseph G. Cannon, the Rev. F. M. Bristol (pastor of the Metropolitan Memorial Methodist Episcopal Church in Washington, D.C.), James Garfield, Chester Arthur, Mrs. William McKinley, a postcard portrait of McKinley delivering his last address (from a Frances Benjamin Johnston photograph), and a cabinet card copy (by A. R. Campbell of Beatrice, Nebraska) of an 1857 ambrotype portrait of Lincoln.

DATE: Ca. 1870

PHOTOGRAPHERS: Mathew Brady studio, F. Thorp, A. Bogardus, and A. R. Campbell.

PHYSICAL DESCRIPTION: 1 album (38 albumen cabinet card photographs), 22 × 30 cm.

SOURCE: Gift of John A. Logan III, 1962.

T. A. and F. W. Mullett. General Logan's tomb, Rock Creek Cemetery, Washington, D.C., ca. 1886. John Logan Papers, Lot 9776.
LC-USZ62-92533

LOT 9627

COLLECTION NAME: John Alexander Logan Collection

SUBJECTS: Portraits of men, mainly U.S. Army officers in uniform, many of whom served on Logan's staff.

DATE: Ca. 1870

PHOTOGRAPHERS: Mathew Brady studio and various other studios.

PHYSICAL DESCRIPTION: 1 album (32 albumen cabinet card and carte-de-visite photographs), 22 × 30 cm.

SOURCE: Gift of John A. Logan III, 1962.

LOT 9628

COLLECTION NAME: John Alexander Logan Collection

SUBJECTS: Portraits of men, mainly U.S. Army officers in uniform. Includes a portrait of Theodore Davis, *Harper's Weekly* artist.

DATE: Ca. 1870

PHOTOGRAPHERS: Various studios.

PHYSICAL DESCRIPTION: 1 album (38 albumen cabinet card and carte-de-visite photographs and reproductions), 15 × 11 cm.

SOURCE: Gift of John A. Logan III, 1962.

LOT 9629

COLLECTION NAME: John Alexander Logan Collection

SUBJECTS: Portraits of men, mainly U.S. Army officers in uniform.

DATE: Ca. 1870

PHYSICAL DESCRIPTION: 1 album (43 carte-de-visite photographs), 15 × 11 cm.

SOURCE: Gift of John A. Logan III, 1962.

LOT 9776

COLLECTION NAME: John Alexander Logan Family Papers, Manuscript Division

SUBJECTS: Funeral ceremonies for Senator John A. Logan and floral tributes. Includes images of his draped chair in the Senate chamber, flowers displayed in the Senate, the draped casket in the Capitol Rotunda, the procession and wreaths at the mausoleum in Rock Creek Cemetery, funeral group gathered at the cemetery, his temporary resting place in the Hutchinson tomb, and the interior of the Logan tomb at Rock Creek Cemetery. Also includes a copy of a sketch for the Logan Monument at Logan Circle in Washington, D.C.

DATE: Ca. 1886

PHOTOGRAPHERS: C. M. Bell, Chas. S. Cudlip, Nephen, and T.A. & F.W. Mullett.

PHYSICAL DESCRIPTION: 22 albumen, cyanotype, and silver gelatin photoprints, 28 × 36 cm or smaller.

SOURCE: Transfer from the Manuscript Division, 1962.

LOT 9777

COLLECTION NAME: John Alexander Logan Family Papers, Manuscript Division

SUBJECTS: Portraits of Senator and Mrs. Logan. Interior views of the Logan home, military units in the United States and in Cuba, President McKinley at the unveiling of the Logan Circle statue in Washington, and portraits of Logan's son, Maj. John A. Logan, Jr. Also includes a group portrait by Brady of the Andrew Johnson impeachment committee, of which Logan was a member, and a group photograph at Zuni, New Mexico, that includes two "artists of the Geological Survey."

DATE: Ca. 1870s–1900

PHOTOGRAPHERS: Mathew Brady studio, Clinedinst, Chas. A. Cudlip, Merritt & Van Wagner, C. M. Gilbert, Rockwood (New York), and Mosher (Chicago).

PHYSICAL DESCRIPTION: 45 items (cartes de visite, albumen and silver gelatin photoprints, and engravings), 28 × 36 cm or smaller.

SOURCE: Transfer from the Manuscript Division, 1962.

Senator John A. Logan's seat in the Senate Chamber, draped at the time of his funeral, 1886. John Logan Papers, Lot 9776.

LC-USZ62-51453

The Master Photographs Collection of the Prints and Photographs Division consists of photographs that document and illustrate significant aspects of the development of the art of photography. The collection covers the entire history of photography, illustrating its beginnings with calotypes by Henry Fox Talbot, David Octavius Hill and Robert Adamson. The division also holds a large number of daguerreotypes, including hundreds by Mathew Brady, examples of the work of John Plumbe, and ambrotypes by Platt Babbitt (see the Daguerreotype Collection).

Work from the collodion wet-plate era is extensive, with outstanding albumen prints by the Civil War photographers Mathew Brady, George N. Barnard, Andrew J. Russell, and Alexander Gardner. The exploration of the western United States is documented in original photographs by William Henry Jackson and Timothy O'Sullivan.

Early efforts at creative and artistic photography are well represented in prints by Julia Margaret Cameron, O. G. Rejlander, and Peter Henry Emerson. Other images represent the work of members and associates of the Photo-Secession group: Alfred Stieglitz, Edward Steichen, Clarence H. White, Gertrude Käsebier, and Frances Benjamin Johnston, as well as those working in the same period, such as F. Holland Day and the English photographer Frederick Evans.

The period from 1910 to 1930 is represented by a large collection of work by Arnold Genthe and materials by Doris Ulmann, James Van Der Zee, Edward Weston, and several other photographers. The Farm Security Administration's best photographers are represented as well, with fine examples by Dorothea Lange and Walker Evans.

Photographs of the present and recent past are collected on a continuing basis by the Prints and Photographs Division. Among the more contemporary photographers represented in the Master Photographs Collection are Ansel Adams, Diane Arbus, Lewis Baltz, Brassaï, Harry Callahan, Paul Caponigro, Judy Dater, Emmett Gowin, Chauncey Hare, George Krause, Ralph Eugene Meatyard, Aaron Siskind, Jerry Uelsmann, and Brett Weston.

Mathew Brady. Portrait of Peter Force, ca. 1865. Master Photographs Collection, MPh B798 B1.
LC-USZ62-91814

ARRANGEMENT

The collection is arranged and cataloged by photographer.

RESTRICTIONS

Some of the earlier photographs can be freely copied, but much of the material is subject to restrictions and can be copied only with the permission of the photographer or his or her agent.

Alexander Gardner. "Post Office, Washington. From North-East." ca. 1860s. Master Photographs Collection, MPh G226 C1.
LC-USZ62-58822

Master Photographs Relating to Washington, D.C.

David Allison. "Antique Store, Washington, D.C." 1976. 19 × 14 cm (MPh A438/A1). Permission of photographer required for reproduction.

Robert Asman. "Street Scenes in Washington, D.C." 1976. (MPh A836/A1, A2). Permission of photographer required for reproduction.

Mathew Brady. "Portrait of Peter Force." Ca. 1865. 34 × 18 cm (MPh B798/B1). No restrictions. LC-USZ62-91814.

Alexander Gardner. "Post Office, Washington. From North-East." Ca. 1860s. 34 × 48 cm (MPh G226/C1). No restrictions. LC-USZ62-58822.

John Gossage. "Alley off of 'S' St., Washington, D.C." 1974. 41 × 51 cm (MPh G677/B1). Permission of photographer required for reproduction.

John Gossage. "The Capitol, Washington, D.C." February 1974. 41 × 51 cm (MPh G677/B2). Permission of photographer required for reproduction.

John Gossage. "Common Gray Squirrel, Washington, D.C." 1974. 41 × 51 cm (MPh G677/B3). Permission of photographer required for reproduction.

John Gossage. "Kenilworth Aquatic Gardens, Washington, D.C." February 1973. 41 × 51 cm. Permission of photographer required for reproduction.

Steve Szabo. "Street Scene, Washington, D.C." 1978. 28 × 36 cm (MPh S996/B3). Permission of photographer required for reproduction.

Steve Szabo. "U.S. Capitol." 1978. 28 × 36 cm (MPh S996/B4). Permission of photographer required for reproduction.

Steve Szabo. "Farragut Square, Washington, D.C." 1978. 28 × 36 cm (MPh S996/B5). Permission of photographer required for reproduction.

Montgomery Cunningham Meigs Papers

The Papers of Montgomery Cunningham Meigs (1816–1892) held in the Manuscript Division consist of correspondence, diaries and journals (1836–91), notebooks, family papers, military papers, drawings and plans, and scrapbooks. The papers number 11,000 items, spanning the years 1799–1968 (chiefly 1849–92), and are accompanied by a finding aid. Quartermaster general during the Civil War, Montgomery Meigs was an engineer, architect, and scientist. He supervised the Corps of Engineers in the construction of the Washington Aqueduct, the Cabin John and Rock Creek bridges, the Capitol dome and extension wings, and the Pension Building. His papers include materials relating to these projects and to his Civil War activities, as well as correspondence with his wife, Louisa Rodgers Meigs, and his father, Charles D. Meigs. Other correspondents include James Buchanan, Ambrose E. Burnside, Simon Cameron, Adolf Cluss, Jefferson Davis, Horace Greeley, Joseph Henry, Joseph Holt, George B. McClellan, William H. Seward, William T. Sherman, Edwin Stanton, and Joseph G. Totten. The papers were acquired through various gifts, purchases, and transfers, 1920–84. The photographs were transferred to the Prints and Photographs Division.

LOT 8544

SUBJECTS: Construction of the Pension Building in Washington, D.C., under the direction of Montgomery C. Meigs, supervising engineer and architect. Partially completed foundation and columns. Copies of panels of the bas-relief terra cotta frieze depicting Civil War scenes designed by C. Buberl. Laborers at work. Views of the complete building.

NOTE: Some images are dated. All photographs are badly faded.

DATE: Ca. 1883–ca. 1885

PHYSICAL DESCRIPTION: 19 albumen photoprints, 28 × 36 cm or smaller.

SOURCE: Gift of Louise Alger, 1959.

Mathew Brady. Portrait of Montgomery C. Meigs. Montgomery Meigs Papers, Lot 9493.

LC-USZ62-56489

Workmen around vaulting rims of Pension Building, November 3, 1883. Montgomery Meigs Papers, Lot 8544.

LC-USZ62-59413

Brick columns in the interior of the Pension Building, November 1, 1883. Montgomery Meigs Papers, Lot 8544.

LC-USZ62-56364

LOT 9493

COLLECTION NAME: Montgomery C. Meigs Papers, Manuscript Division

SUBJECTS: Montgomery C. Meigs family and home, miscellaneous portraits and views. West Point Class of 1864; members of the Meigs family; drawing room of a house built by Meigs; nineteenth-century views of Washington, D.C. Includes a portrait, possibly a hand-painted salted paper print, of M. C. Meigs's oldest son, John Rodgers Meigs, who was killed in the Civil War.

DATE: Ca. 1850s–ca. 1890s

PHOTOGRAPHERS: Mathew Brady studio, Gutekunst (Philadelphia), and The Phillips Studio.

PHYSICAL DESCRIPTION: 14 salted paper, albumen cabinet card, carte-de-visite, and silver gelatin photoprints, 28 × 36 cm or smaller.

SOURCE: Gift of Louisa R. Alger, 1962. Transfer from the Manuscript Division.

LOT 11830

COLLECTION NAME: Montgomery C. Meigs Papers, Manuscript Division

SUBJECTS: Buildings and views of Washington, D.C. Includes views of the Botanic Garden (1859), the Capitol with the old dome (1851), the construction shop south of the Capitol, twenty-inch pipes lying on New Jersey Avenue near the Capitol, the roof structure over the House of Representatives chamber, the plaster model of Crawford's Freedom statue in the old Hall of Representatives, the Tiber Creek and canal looking east toward the Capitol, the interior of the Capitol, views on Capitol Hill, and the north portico of the White House.

NOTE: Copies of original photoprints in the Montgomery C. Meigs Papers, box 14, Manuscript Division. All photographs are mounted and labeled with original captions and album locations.

DATE: Ca. 1851–61

PHYSICAL DESCRIPTION: 11 silver gelatin photoprints, 20 × 25 cm.

LOT 12332 (microfilm)

SUBJECTS: Projects directed by U.S. Army engineer Montgomery Meigs, 1851–60. Primarily photographs of architectural drawings and designs for interior details of the U.S. Capitol and General Post Office (now the U.S. International Trade Commission Building). Models of sculpture used for the U.S. Capitol. Construction photographs of the Capitol dome and extensions, General Post Office, Washington Aqueduct, Washington Canal, Botanic Garden, and one of the Bulfinch gatehouses. One view of London, England.

DATE: Ca. 1851–ca. 1860

PHYSICAL DESCRIPTION: 1 album (325 salted paper and albumen photoprints, 9 × 14 cm or smaller), 42 × 32 cm.

SOURCE: Gift of William H. Boswell, 1981.

RESTRICTIONS: The album is extremely fragile and may not be handled. Microfilm serves as a reference copy. Copy photoprints (arranged by subject) are also available in Lot 12599.

LOT 12599

SUBJECTS: Projects directed by U.S. Army engineer Montgomery Meigs, 1852–60. Primarily photographs of architectural drawings and designs for interior details of the U.S. Capitol and General Post Office (now the U.S. International Trade Commission Building). Models of sculpture used for the Capitol building. Construction photographs of the Capitol dome and extensions, General Post Office, Washington Aqueduct, Washington Canal, Botanic Garden, and one of the Bullfinch gatehouses. One view of London, England.

NOTE: The original album was the gift of William H. Boswell, 1981. Copy photoprints were made by the Library of Congress.

DATE: Ca. 1852–ca. 1860

PHYSICAL DESCRIPTION: 325 silver gelatin photoprints, 20 × 25 cm.

ARRANGEMENT: By subject.

RESTRICTIONS: The original album from which these copy prints were made is extremely fragile and may not be handled. These photographs (and a microfilm copy of the original album in Lot 12332) serve as reference copies.

Construction of the General Post Office (now the Tariff Commission Building). Montgomery Meigs Papers, Lot 12332 and 12599.

LC-USZ62-88268

Corinthian capital (Acanthus leaf), probably at the U.S. Capitol. Montgomery Meigs Papers, Lot 12332 and 12599.

LC-USZ62-88873

Construction of the Washington Aqueduct at Cabin John (Union Arch). Montgomery Meigs Papers, Lot 12332 and 12599.

LC-USZ62-88263

Dr. Albert R. Miller, a physician, practiced medicine in Detroit. In 1917, he established his own investment banking firm on Wall Street in New York. In 1932, he founded a banking firm. And, at the age of sixty, he took up portrait photography. In the 1950s he made a gift to the Library of his portraits of mid-twentieth-century notables, taken in his Washington, D.C., studio.

LOT 11821

COLLECTION NAME: Miller of Washington Collection of Photographic Portraits of Notables

SUBJECTS: Studio portraits of prominent Washingtonians and visitors to Washington. Includes cabinet members, congressmen, U.S. Supreme Court justices, diplomats, lawyers, university presidents, professors, scientists, physicians and surgeons, editors and journalists, corporate officers, directors and administrators of federal agencies, bankers, and labor leaders. Sitters include Carl Albert, Robert Woods Bliss, Hale Boggs, Ellsworth Bunker, Edward S. Bunn, S. J., John Foster Dulles, Leonard Elstad, Luther Evans, David Finley, William Green, Clark Griffith, Mrs. William Randolph Hearst, Hubert Humphrey, Mordecai Johnson, Estes Kefauver, Boris Kroyt, Margaret Landon, William D. Leahy, Eugene McCarthy, George Meany, Agnes Meyer, Howard Mitchell, Ruth Montgomery, Drew Pearson, Mischa Schneider, Harold Stassen, Gloria Swanson, Strom Thurmond, and Gertrude Clarke Whittall.

DATE: Ca. 1950–ca. 1956

PHOTOGRAPHERS: Albert R. Miller.

PHYSICAL DESCRIPTION: 383 silver gelatin photoprints, 44 × 33 cm or smaller.

ARRANGEMENT: Arranged alphabetically. A finding aid is available in the Prints and Photographs Reading Room.

SOURCE: Gift of Albert R. Miller, 1954–56.

Albert Miller. John L. Lewis, president of the United Mine Workers of America. Miller of Washington Collection, Lot 11821.

LC-USZ62-93291

Albert Miller. Agnes Meyer, member of the Library of Congress Trust Fund Board. Miller of Washington Collection, Lot 11821.

LC-USZ62-93292

Albert Miller. Mischa Schneider, cellist with the Budapest String Quartet. Miller of Washington Collection, Lot 11821.

LC-USZ62-93294

Albert Miller. Drew Pearson, syndicated columnist, 1954. Miller of Washington Collection, Lot 11821.

LC-USZ62-93290

On its fiftieth anniversary, in 1954, the National Child Labor Committee presented its official records to the Library of Congress. The gift included about 5,000 photographs and about 350 original glass negatives produced by Lewis Wickes Hine to document the exploitation of children in American mills, mines, canneries, street trades, glass factories, and tenement sweatshops. Hine paid special attention to the plight of immigrant children in the United States. Many of his photographs were reproduced in the committee's publications in the campaign for child welfare legislation in the early part of the twentieth century.

The photographs are grouped in albums compiled by the Library of Congress according to type of employment and geographical location, and they are cataloged. Numbering in the albums refers to Hine's original caption cards. The caption cards, which usually include the name, address, age, and occupation of the child, the date and time the picture was taken, and Hine's additional comments about the child's appearance and working conditions, are available on microfilm. They are stamped to indicate the existence of original negatives.

The Papers of the National Child Labor Committee are held in the Manuscript Division. The papers number 7,000 items, spanning the years 1904–53, and are accompanied by a finding aid. Included in them are correspondence, speeches, reports, press releases, and clippings, as well as field notes and unpublished studies on child labor conditions in various industries. Sixty scrapbooks document the organization's campaign for child welfare legislation, as do the minutes of the board of trustees and of the National Aid to Education Committee (1916–18) and proceedings of the annual conferences (1905–16). The National Child Labor Committee Papers are supplemented by the correspondence of Dr. Alexander J. McKelway, secretary for the southern states of the committee. The McKelway material was acquired by the Library in 1947.

Washington, D.C., subjects include the ubiquitous newsboys and messengers as well as vegetable sellers and peddlers. Across the river in Alexandria, Lewis Hine photographed black and white children at work in a glass factory. The collection documents other Maryland and Virginia subjects at locations too distant from the capital to be included here.

REFERENCES

Gutman, Judith M. *Lewis W. Hine and the American Social Conscience.* New York: Walker, 1967. (Reproduces many Hine photographs made for the National Child Labor Committee and held by the Library of Congress.)
Melville, no. 169, pp. 249–51.
Viewpoints, no. 131, p. 129.

Lewis Hine. "7 yr. old newsboy, without a badge, who tried to 'short-change' me when he sold me a paper. 'He can rustle de poipers' another boy said. William Parralla, 313 Second Street S.W." April 1912. National Child Labor Committee Collection, Lot 7480 (image number 2945).

LC-USZ62-92163

Lewis Hine. "Group of newsies selling on Capitol steps . . . Tony Passaro (8 yrs. old). Dan Mercurio (9 yrs. old). Joseph Tucci (10 yrs. old). John Carlino (11 yrs. old)." April 1912. National Child Labor Committee Collection, Lot 7480 (image number 2904).

LC-USZ62-30472

Lewis Hine. "'Carrying-in' boy [Rob Kidd] in Alexandria Glass Factory, Alexandria, Va. Works on day shift one week and night shift next week." June 1911. National Child Labor Committee Collection, Lot 7478 (image number 2260).

LC-USZ62-10960

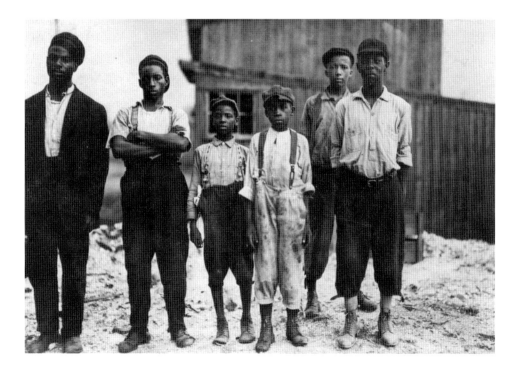

Lewis Hine. "In the Alexandria glass factories, negroes work side by side with the white workers." June 1911. National Child Labor Committee Collection, Lot 7478 (image number 2270).

LC-USZ62-92162

Lewis Hine. "After midnight . . . and still selling extras. There were many of these groups of young news-boys selling very late these nights. Youngest boy in the group is Israel April (9 yrs. old) 314 I Street N.E. . . . The rest were a little older. 12th St. near G." April 17, 1912. National Child Labor Committee Collection, Lot 7480 (image number 2938).

LC-USZ62-60726

Lewis Hine. "At Center Market. 11 yr. old celery vendor Gus Strateges, 212 Jackson Hall Alley. He sold until 11 p.m. and was out again Sunday morning selling papers and gum. Has been in this country only a year and a half." April 1912. National Child Labor Committee Collection, Lot 7480 (image number 2928).

LC-H5-2928

LOT 7478 (microfilm)

COLLECTION NAME: National Child Labor Committee Collection

SUBJECTS: Glass factories. Boys at the ovens, operating machinery. Girls packing tumblers. Includes several pictures of black and white children working at an Alexandria, Virginia, glass factory (image numbers 2260–2271).

NOTE: Some corresponding negatives are found in series LC–H5.

DATE: 1908–24

PHOTOGRAPHERS: Lewis Wickes Hine.

PHYSICAL DESCRIPTION: 156 silver gelatin photoprints, 13 × 18 cm or smaller.

ARRANGEMENT: Photographs are mounted in Library-assembled albums, grouped by broad subjects such as types of work and industries. Original Lewis Hine caption cards are available on microfilm for each numbered image in the albums. Caption cards provide date and hour of day when each photograph was taken, name and address of child pictured, and additional comments. A supplementary Hine Index gives corresponding lot numbers for image numbers found on the caption cards.

SOURCE: Gift of the National Child Labor Committee and Mrs. Gertrude Folks Zimand, 1954. Transfer from the Manuscript Division.

LOT 7480 (microfilm)

COLLECTION NAME: National Child Labor Committee Collection

SUBJECTS: Street trades. Children, mainly boys working as newsboys, messengers, peddlers, bootblacks, and pinsetters, in New York City, Washington, D.C., and elsewhere. Washington subjects include news vendors in front of the U.S. Capitol; group of news vendors holding the *Washington Post*; vendors selling cigars and chewing gum; bicycle messengers; young vendors at the Center Market selling vegetables; shoe-shine boys; boys in a red-light district (image numbers 2896–35).

NOTE: Some corresponding negatives are available in series LC–H5.

DATE: Ca. 1908–24

PHOTOGRAPHERS: Lewis Wickes Hine.

PHYSICAL DESCRIPTION: 861 silver gelatin photoprints, 13 × 18 cm or smaller.

ARRANGEMENT: Photographs are mounted in Library-assembled albums, grouped by broad subjects such as types of work and industries. Original Lewis Hine caption cards are available on microfilm for each numbered image in albums. Caption cards provide date and hour of day when each photograph was taken, name and address of child pictured, and additional comments. A supplementary Hine Index gives corresponding lot numbers for the image numbers found on original caption cards.

SOURCE: Gift of the National Child Labor Committee and Mrs. Gertrude Folks Zimand, 1954. Transfer from the Manuscript Division.

Lewis Hine. "Wilbur H. Woodward, 428 Third St., N.W., Washington, D.C., Western Union messenger 236, one of the youngsters on the border-line (15 yrs. old) works until 8 p.m. only." April 1912. National Child Labor Committee Collection, Lot 7480 (image number 2914).

LC-H5-2914

Herbert E. French (1883-ca. 1950) was a reporter for Bradstreet Company when he bought the National Photo Company in 1912, adding to the company's resources his own stock of negatives dating back to about 1909. The National Photo Company operated as a news service to newspapers, news distributors, and other photo agencies, including Acme, Wide World, the Newspaper Enterprise Association (NEA), the Central Press Association (Cleveland, Ohio), the *Washington Star*, the *New York Times*, and the *U.S. Daily*. In addition, the National Photo Company provided advertising services to various clients, including the local Chamber of Commerce, and prepared photographically illustrated promotional brochures for commercial, fraternal, and service organizations. Herbert French's business correspondence indicates that he instructed his photographers to go after exclusives, that is, subjects not covered by crowds of other news photographers. He supplemented their output by purchasing photographs from other photographers and news agencies on a regular basis.

The company's offices were located at 815 H Street NW in its earliest years, then moved to 1212 G Street NW, and finally to 923 F Street NW. The Library of Congress acquired the collection of about eighty thousand photographs and corresponding glass plate negatives (ranging in size from 11 × 13 cm or 4 × 5 inch to 21 × 26 cm or 8 × 10 inch format) in 1947. Herbert French presented the negatives as a gift, and the Library purchased photographs. The collection was accompanied by albums of fully captioned photographs arranged in chronological or subject order (for instance, photographs of Calvin Coolidge or of horse shows) for use by the company in their day-to-day operations, and a large card index to negative numbers, arranged by subject.

The National Photo Company Collection documents virtually all aspects of Washington, D.C., life from 1909 to 1932, when the company fell victim to the Depression. The company's letterhead listed their services:

News Photographs. Photographs of National Events and Prominent People. Photographic Illustrations of Historical Places, Foreign Countries, and Miscellaneous Special Features. An Endless Variety of Washington's Public Buildings, Parks, Statues, Etc. Interiors of the Government Buildings and Historical Paintings. Lantern Slides of Various Departments, Executive, Legislative, Judicial. The making and handling of United States Currency, and other features illustrating the actual workings of the Federal Government. OUR COMMERCIAL DEPARTMENT. Expert operators capable of handling the most difficult assignments. Banquets. Smokeless Flashlights. Interiors and Exteriors. Real Estate and Construction Work. Automobiles. Pictorial Advertising. Post Cards. Lantern Slides. Enlargements of any size. Amateur Developing. Printing, Copying and Enlarging.

Herbert French was a member of the White House News Photographers at the time of its founding. He covered the administrations of Presidents Taft, Wilson, Harding, Coolidge, and Hoover. His collection of portraits includes many prominent officials and social figures. Visitors to the capital, protests and parades, conventions and meetings, events in Congress, inaugurations and White House events, and to a limited extent, world events in general are represented in the collection. The local social scene in Washington, tourist activities, and residential, commercial, and government buildings are represented as well, as are parks and monuments. Herbert French was particularly fond of baseball, and the Washington Senators are documented thoroughly, especially in years when they were the contenders for the pennant. Similarly, he covered horse shows and automobile racing.

Loose photographs and bound albums are indexed in the Prints and Photographs Division Catalog under the major subjects represented in cataloged groups of photographs. Material once dispersed into browsing files has been retrieved and cataloged, but some images produced by the National Photo Company may still be found in the Biographical and Geographical Files.

Many photographs are annotated with the number of the corresponding glass negative. Some of the original negatives have deteriorated over the years, however, and cannot be successfully printed. Herbert French's subject index uses idiosyncratic terms and is of limited use insofar as it pertains to original negatives. The Library may not hold items for all negative numbers mentioned in the card index.

The Washington photographs are described below. Other National Photo Company materials are available by searching under the company name in the Division Catalog.

National Photo Company. Herbert E. French, proprietor of the National Photo Company, posing in his Washington studio. National Photo Company Collection, Lot 12362.

LC-USZ62-92410

REFERENCES
Melville, no. 170, p. 252.
Vanderbilt, no. 534, pp. 113–14.

National Photo Company. Helen Keller reading Mrs. Coolidge's lips, January 11, 1926. National Photo Company Collection, Lot 12283, vol. 3, p. 23.
LC-F81-38917

National Photo Company. Crowds at the Washington Star scoreboard during the World Series, 1925. National Photo Company Collection, Lot 12287, vol. 1.
LC-F8-37763

LOT 12281

COLLECTION NAME: National Photo Company Collection

SUBJECTS: Woodrow Wilson. Scenes and activities in Washington, D.C. Wilson's inaugurations in 1913 and 1917, addressing Congress, opening baseball seasons between 1913 and 1919, and his first and last cabinet meetings. Preparedness Day Parade; Flag Day, 1914 and 1915; Armistice Day, 1921 and 1922; high school cadets; American Red Cross Building cornerstone and dedication ceremonies, 1915. Wilson's funeral, 1924.

NOTE: Most images are captioned. Corresponding negatives are found in series LC–F8, –F81, and –F82. Some are badly deteriorated.

DATE: 1913–24

PHYSICAL DESCRIPTION: 1 album (ca. 250 silver gelatin photoprints), 39 × 52 cm.

ARRANGEMENT: Roughly chronological.

SOURCE: Purchase from Herbert E. French, 1947.

LOT 12282

COLLECTION NAME: National Photo Company Collection

SUBJECTS: Warren G. Harding. Scenes and activities in Washington, D.C. Portraits of Harding, Vice-President Coolidge, and cabinet. The White House; the Capitol; Pennsylvania Avenue; Walter Reed Hospital; Tomb of the Unknown Soldier; Shrine Convention; Ford-Edison Camp; and Harding at disarmament conference in 1922. Mrs. Harding; Washington clubs, including Girl Scouts; American Indians; American League baseball park; Harding with Albert Einstein; Harding funeral.

NOTE: Most images are captioned. Corresponding negatives are found in series LC–F8, –F81, and –F82. Some are badly deteriorated.

DATE: 1921–23

PHYSICAL DESCRIPTION: 2 albums (ca. 760 silver gelatin photoprints), 39 × 52 cm.

ARRANGEMENT: Roughly chronological.

SOURCE: Purchase from Herbert E. French, 1947.

LOT 12283

COLLECTION NAME: National Photo Company Collection

SUBJECTS: Calvin Coolidge. Scenes and activities in Washington, D.C. Portraits of Coolidge, Mrs. Coolidge, Coolidge cabinet, and Helen Keller. The White House, including Easter egg roll; Navy Yard; funeral of Woodrow Wilson; Warren Harding memorial ceremony; Capitol pages; Coolidge addressing Georgetown University graduates; Memorial Day, 1925; World Series, 1925.

NOTE: Most photos are captioned. Corresponding negatives are found in series LC–F8, –F81, and –F82. Some are badly deteriorated.

DATE: 1921–27

PHYSICAL DESCRIPTION: 3 albums (ca. 1,100 silver gelatin photoprints), 39 × 52 cm.

ARRANGEMENT: Roughly chronological. *Vols. 1–2:* First administration; *Vol. 3:* Second administration.

SOURCE: Purchase from Herbert E. French, 1947.

LOT 12284

COLLECTION NAME: National Photo Company Collection

SUBJECTS: Herbert Hoover. Portraits of Hoover and Mrs. Hoover. Hoover as secretary of commerce, receiving Georgetown University degree in 1926, receiving White House visitors, and with government officials.

NOTE: Most photos are captioned. Corresponding negatives are found in series LC–F8, –F81, and –F82. Some are badly deteriorated.

DATE: 1920–30

PHYSICAL DESCRIPTION: 1 album (ca. 260 silver gelatin photoprints), 39 × 52 cm.

ARRANGEMENT: Roughly chronological.

SOURCE: Purchase from Herbert E. French, 1947.

LOT 12285

COLLECTION NAME: National Photo Company Collection

SUBJECTS: Inaugurations of McKinley, Taft, Wilson, Harding, Coolidge, and Hoover in Washington, D.C. Parades, ceremonies at the Capitol.

NOTE: Most photos are captioned. Corresponding negatives are found in series LC–F8, –F81, and –F82. Some are badly deteriorated.

DATE: 1909–29

PHYSICAL DESCRIPTION: 1 album (ca. 215 silver gelatin photoprints), 39 × 52 cm.

ARRANGEMENT: Roughly chronological.

SOURCE: Purchase from Herbert E. French, 1947.

LOT 12286

COLLECTION NAME: National Photo Company Collection

SUBJECTS: Disarmament conference, November 1922, and burial of the Unknown Soldier (World War I). Scenes and activities in Washington, D.C. American and foreign delegates to the conference and their advisers; treaty ceremony in 1922. President Harding, General Pershing, and military personnel at burial ceremony in Arlington Cemetery. American Indians visiting the president.

NOTE: Most photos are captioned. Corresponding negatives are found in series LC–F8, –F81, and –F82. Some are badly deteriorated.

DATE: 1921–22

PHYSICAL DESCRIPTION: 1 album (ca. 380 silver gelatin photoprints), 33 × 43 cm.

SOURCE: Purchase from Herbert E. French, 1947.

LOT 12287

COLLECTION NAME: National Photo Company Collection

SUBJECTS: Washington Nationals baseball club. President Coolidge at World Series game, 1924. World Series games in Washington, 1924, and Pittsburgh, 1925; individual players and team portraits.

NOTE: Most photos are captioned. Corresponding negatives are found in series LC–F8, –F81, and –F82. Some are badly deteriorated.

DATE: 1924–25

PHYSICAL DESCRIPTION: 6 albums (ca. 620 silver gelatin photoprints), 33 × 43 cm or smaller.

ARRANGEMENT: Roughly chronological. *Vols. 1–3:* Washington Base Ball Club, World Champions, 1924; *Vols. 4–6:* Baseball, Washington Nationals.

SOURCE: Purchase from Herbert E. French, 1947.

LOT 12288

COLLECTION NAME: National Photo Company Collection

SUBJECTS: Grand Army of the Republic. Scenes in Washington, D.C. Parade on Pennsylvania Avenue; boats on the Potomac River; Civil War monuments.

NOTE: Images are not captioned.

DATE: Ca. 1921

PHYSICAL DESCRIPTION: 1 album (ca. 80 silver gelatin photoprints), 28 × 46 cm.

SOURCE: Purchase from Herbert E. French, 1947.

National Photo Company. Walter Johnson and Tye Cobb, baseball players, 1925. National Photo Company Collection, Lot 12287, vol. 2.

LC-F8-36931

National Photo Company. The Navy C-7 circling the Washington Monument before landing after a successful trip from Hampton Roads, Virginia. The C-7 was the first lighter-than-air helium airship in the world. December 5, 1921. National Photo Company Collection, Lot 12293, vol. 3, p. 7.

LC-F8-17031

LOT 12289

COLLECTION NAME: National Photo Company Collection

SUBJECTS: Horse shows. Scenes in Washington, D.C. Horseback riders; horse jumping; spectators, including U.S. and foreign dignitaries and society women.

NOTE: Images are captioned. Corresponding negatives are found in series LC–F8, –F81, and –F82. Some are badly deteriorated.

DATE: 1922–26

PHYSICAL DESCRIPTION: 1 album (166 silver gelatin photoprints), 33 × 43 cm.

ARRANGEMENT: Chronological.

SOURCE: Purchase from Herbert E. French, 1947.

LOT 12290

COLLECTION NAME: National Photo Company Collection

SUBJECTS: White House photographers. Individual and group portraits of White House News Photographers' Association members; humorous snapshot portraits; banquets in 1925 and 1926; World Series baseball photographers in 1924.

NOTE: Some photos are captioned. Some corresponding negatives are found in series LC–F8, –F81, and –F82. Some are badly deteriorated.

DATE: 1922–26

PHYSICAL DESCRIPTION: 1 album (ca. 170 silver gelatin photoprints), 33 × 43 cm.

SOURCE: Purchase from Herbert E. French, 1947.

LOT 12291

COLLECTION NAME: National Photo Company Collection

SUBJECTS: Shrine convention, June 5–7, 1923. Convention in Washington, D.C. Shriners; Wild West show and rodeo; parade; model homes; American Indians in "Indian village."

NOTE: Images are captioned. Corresponding negatives are found in series LC–F8, –F81, and –F82. Some are badly deteriorated.

DATE: 1923

PHYSICAL DESCRIPTION: 1 album (ca. 340 silver gelatin photoprints), 33 × 43 cm.

SOURCE: Purchase from Herbert E. French, 1947.

LOT 12292

COLLECTION NAME: National Photo Company Collection

SUBJECTS: Layouts, 1924–25. Groups of photographs, each with a common theme or subject relating to government or social activities in Washington, D.C.

NOTE: Images are captioned. A list of specific titles is stored with the album. Corresponding negatives are found in series LC–F8, –F81, and –F82. Some are badly deteriorated.

DATE: 1924–25

PHYSICAL DESCRIPTION: 1 album (ca. 375 silver gelatin photoprints), 33 × 43 cm.

SOURCE: Purchase from Herbert E. French, 1947.

LOT 12293

COLLECTION NAME: National Photo Company Collection

SUBJECTS: Washington, D.C., September 1919 to December 1921. Portraits of President Harding, General Pershing, senators and congressmen, foreign dignitaries, Catholic Church dignitaries, women in politics, government officials, debutantes, and celebrities. Events include Pershing Parade, suffrage movement, American Indians visiting Washington, first helium flight, arms conference, horse show, chrys-anthemum show, and Christmas. Pennsylvania Avenue, Washington Navy Yard, Georgetown University, Walter Reed Hospital, and other sites.

NOTE: Most photos are captioned. Corresponding negatives are found in series LC–F8, –F81, and –F82. Some are badly deteriorated.

DATE: 1919–21

PHYSICAL DESCRIPTION: 3 albums (ca. 570 silver gelatin photoprints), 39 × 52 cm.

ARRANGEMENT: Chronological. *Vol. 1:* September–October 1919; *Vol. 2:* November 1921; *Vol. 3:* December 1921.

SOURCE: Purchase from Herbert E. French, 1947.

LOT 12294

COLLECTION NAME: National Photo Company Collection

SUBJECTS: Washington, D.C., 1922. Portraits of President Harding, foreign dignitaries, debutantes, society women, children, National Women's Party, and the Ku Klux Klan. The zoo, the White House, the U.S. Congress, Arlington Cemetery, Mount Vernon, Glen Echo, a bathing beach, citizens' military training camp, and other sites. Events include fires at the Knickerbocker Theatre and U.S. Treasury, a tennis tournament, antiwar demonstrations, a Shriners' barbecue, sports events, parades, the dedication of the Lincoln Memorial and other sites, the Clara Barton centennial, first beauty pageant, Prohibition enforcement, and a Neighborhood House spring pageant.

NOTE: Most photos are captioned. Corresponding negatives are found in series LC–F8, –F81, and –F82. Some are badly deteriorated.

DATE: 1922

PHYSICAL DESCRIPTION: 10 albums (ca. 3,046 silver gelatin photoprints), 39 × 52 cm.

ARRANGEMENT: Roughly chronological. *Vol. 1:* January; *Vol. 2:* February; *Vol. 3:* March; *Vol. 4:* April; *Vol. 5:* May; *Vol. 6:* June; *Vol. 7:* July–August 15; *Vol. 8:* August 16–September; *Vol. 9:* October–November 15; *Vol. 10:* November 16–December.

SOURCE: Purchase from Herbert E. French, 1947.

LOT 12295

COLLECTION NAME: National Photo Company Collection

SUBJECTS: Washington, D.C., January 1923 to January 1924. Portraits of President Coolidge and his cabinet, senators and congressmen, prominent Washingtonians, military personnel, foreign visitors, women in politics, government officials, American Indians, debutantes, war veterans, religious dignitaries, U.S. justices, celebrities, Girl Scouts and Boy Scouts, and the Ku Klux Klan. Rock Creek Park, White House, Capitol, Willard Hotel, Tomb of the Unknown Soldier, Children's Hospital, and a citizens' military training camp. Events include parades, Washington Monument cornerstone-laying ceremony, holiday celebrations, Daughters of the American Revolution convention, a diplomatic wedding, Red Cross activities, Christmas seal campaign, sports, and Neighborhood House spring pageant.

NOTE: Most photos are captioned. Corresponding negatives are found in series LC–F8, –F81, and –F82. Some are badly deteriorated.

DATE: 1923–24

PHYSICAL DESCRIPTION: 9 albums (ca. 2,535 silver gelatin photoprints), 39 × 52 cm.

ARRANGEMENT: Chronological. *Vol. 1:* January–February; *Vol. 2:* March; *Vol. 3:* April; *Vol. 4:* May; *Vol. 5:* June; *Vol. 6:* July–August; *Vol. 7:* September–October; *Vol. 8:* November; *Vol. 9:* December–January.

SOURCE: Purchase from Herbert E. French, 1947.

LOT 12296

COLLECTION NAME: National Photo Company Collection

SUBJECTS: Washington, D.C., 1924. Portraits of President Coolidge, Teapot Dome Committee, senators and congressmen, government officials and ambassadors, foreign dignitaries, prominent women, Catholic Church dignitaries, sculptors, sports celebrities, Socialist National Party, Romany gypsies, and American Indians. The U.S. Congress and Capitol, Navy Yard, Naval Observatory, Arlington Cemetery, Woodrow Wilson home, zoo, Rock Creek Park, and other sites. Events include parades, a football game, the Veterans Monument dedication, the National American Ballet, weddings, a dog show, a flower show, cherry blossoms, holidays, and a Neighborhood House spring pageant.

NOTE: Most photos are captioned. Corresponding negatives are found in series LC–F8, –F81, and –F82. Some are badly deteriorated.

DATE: 1924

PHYSICAL DESCRIPTION: 7 albums (ca. 2,110 silver gelatin photoprints), 39 × 52 cm.

ARRANGEMENT: Chronological. *Vol. 1:* January–February; *Vol. 2:* March–April; *Vol. 3* May–July; *Vol. 4:* August; *Vol. 5:* September; *Vol. 6:* October; *Vol. 7:* November–December.

SOURCE: Purchase from Herbert E. French, 1947.

LOT 12297

COLLECTION NAME: National Photo Company Collection

SUBJECTS: Washington, D.C., January 1925–January 1926. Portraits of Coolidge cabinet, senators and congressmen, U.S. justices, government officials, military personnel, foreign dignitaries, women in politics, feminists, society women, American Indians, Capitol pages, police and firemen, celebrities, artists, and war veterans. Mayflower Hotel, Mount Vernon, U.S. Post Office, Gallaudet College, Georgetown University, churches, Laurel race track, C&O Canal, Potomac River, Boy Scouts at Camp Roosevelt, Naval Observatory, and other sites. Events include holiday activities, Naval Academy graduation, funeral of William Jennings Bryan, Ku Klux Klan parade, gypsy funeral, court-martial of Col. Billy Mitchell, Red Cross activities, sports, Gettysburg Monument unveiling, Bureau of Standards activities, city fires, Admiral Dewey's funeral, National American Ballet, and a dog show, chrysanthemum show, and Neighborhood House spring festival.

NOTE: Most photos are captioned. Corresponding negatives are found in series LC–F8, –F81, and –F82. Some are badly deteriorated.

DATE: 1925–26

PHYSICAL DESCRIPTION: 6 albums (ca. 2,290 silver gelatin photoprints), 39 × 52 cm.

ARRANGEMENT: Chronological. *Vol. 1:* January–February; *Vol. 2:* March–April; *Vol. 3:* May–June; *Vol. 4:* July–August; *Vol. 5:* September–November; *Vol. 6:* December–January.

SOURCE: Purchase from Herbert E. French, 1947.

LOT 12298

COLLECTION NAME: National Photo Company Collection

SUBJECTS: Washington, D.C., 1926. Portraits of congressmen and senators, government officials, Capitol pages, foreign dignitaries, artists, debutantes, children, celebrities, military personnel, religious personnel, and American Indians. Wardman Park swimming pool, zoo, Arlington Cemetery, U.S. Post Office, Capitol, Mount Vernon, and other sites. Events include Indians dancing, University of Maryland activities, Ku Klux Klan parade, Potomac boat races, sports, and Neighborhood House garden party.

NOTE: Most photos are captioned. Corresponding negatives are found in series LC–F8, –F81, and –F82. Some are badly deteriorated.

DATE: 1926

PHYSICAL DESCRIPTION: 3 albums (ca. 1,010 silver gelatin photoprints), 39 × 52 cm.

ARRANGEMENT: Chronological. *Vol. 1:* January–February; *Vol. 2:* March–July; *Vol. 3:* August–December.

SOURCE: Purchase from Herbert E. French, 1947.

National Photo Company. "Division of Paleontology of the National Museum." National Photo Company Collection, Lot 12339.

LC-F81-37513

National Photo Company. Eugene Debs leaving the White House after his interview with the president, two days after his sentence was commuted, and the day after he was released from the Atlanta Penitentiary. December 26, 1921. National Photo Company Collection, Lot 12293, vol. 3, p. 34.

LC-F801-17191

National Photo Company. "President Harding has gone in for horseback riding as a regular form of exercise, usually riding early in the morning. Photographed this morning returning to the White House with his Secty George Christian." November 25, 1921. National Photo Company, Lot 12293, vol. 2, p. 21.

LC-F81-16969

National Photo Company. Bathing beauties, Washington, D.C., 1920. National Photo Company Collection, Lot 12342-5.

LC-USZ62-58272

LOT 12299

COLLECTION NAME: National Photo Company Collection

SUBJECTS: Washington, D.C., January 1927 to February 1930. Portraits of senators, congressmen, foreign dignitaries, government officials, society women, military personnel, Hoover appointees, women in government, celebrities, debutantes, policewomen, artists, disabled veterans, news photographers, Boy Scouts and Girl Scouts, American Indians, Charles Lindbergh and the *Spirit of St. Louis*. Presidential yacht *Mayflower*, Bureau of Engraving and Printing, presidential camp on the Rapidan, and other sites. Events include Naval Academy graduation, White House New Year's party, White House and Capitol fires, and Davis Cup tennis match.

NOTE: Most photos are captioned. Corresponding negatives are found in series LC–F8, –F81, and –F82. Some are badly deteriorated.

DATE: 1927–30

PHYSICAL DESCRIPTION: 4 albums (ca. 1,640 silver gelatin photoprints), 39 × 52 cm.

ARRANGEMENT: Chronological. *Vol. 1:* January–May; *Vol. 2:* June 1927–May 1929; *Vol. 3:* June–September 27, 1929; *Vol. 4:* September 27, 1929–February 1930.

SOURCE: Purchase from Herbert E. French, 1947.

LOT 12337

COLLECTION NAME: National Photo Company Collection

SUBJECTS: American Indians and Eskimos. Includes Osage, Cheyenne, and Hopi delegations in Washington, D.C.; Hopi religious dances at the U.S. Capitol. Portraits of Wolf Robe and Running Antelope, whose faces appear on U.S. currency. Scenes of Indian life, including Navahos and Apaches weaving; dwellings of Pueblo Indians in New Mexico, agricultural activities; and Indian schools. Eskimos with reindeer in Alaska.

NOTE: Most photos are captioned; some have dates. Corresponding negatives in series LC–F8, –F81, and –F82. Some are in poor condition.

DATE: 1909–32

PHYSICAL DESCRIPTION: Ca. 153 silver gelatin photoprints, 20 × 25 cm or smaller. Some are copy photographs and some are from the Smithsonian Institution, Bureau of American Ethnology.

ARRANGEMENT: *Lot 12337–1:* Indians visiting Washington, D.C.; *Lot 12337–2:* Indian chiefs; *Lot 12337–3:* Eskimos; *Lot 12337–4:* Indian life. A finding aid is available in the Prints and Photographs Reading Room.

SOURCE: Negatives: gift of Herbert E. French, 1947. Prints: purchase.

LOT 12338

COLLECTION NAME: National Photo Company Collection

SUBJECTS: Autographed portraits of dignitaries and celebrities. Portraits of presidents, First Ladies, congressmen, diplomats, explorers, athletes, actors, and other public figures, including Taft, Wilson, Hoover, President and Mrs. Coolidge, President and Mrs. Harding, Senator Boies Penrose, Harriet Chalmers Adams, Walter Johnson, and Amos and Andy. Group portrait with General Pershing. Charles Evans Hughes addressing a joint session of Congress during memorial ceremonies for President Harding; in the front row are President Calvin Coolidge and Supreme Court justices.

NOTE: Images autographed by sitters; many addressed to H. E. French.

DATE: 1909–32

PHOTOGRAPHERS: Bruneh, Edmonston, and Harris & Ewing.

PHYSICAL DESCRIPTION: 31 silver gelatin photoprints, 49 × 55 cm or smaller.

SOURCE: Purchase from Herbert E. French, 1947.

National Photo Company. Flag Day at the Post Office Department, 1916. National Photo Company Collection, Lot 12342-9.

LC-F82-1656

LOT 12339

COLLECTION NAME: National Photo Company Collection

SUBJECTS: Museum objects and activities. Includes exhibits and objects in the Smithsonian Institution, Corcoran Gallery, and Alexandria Washington Lodge. Smithsonian staff, including members of the Division of Paleontology at work. First Ladies' gowns; one image of Emile Berliner with early phonograph.

NOTE: Most images are captioned; a few have dates. Corresponding negatives are found in series LC–F8, –F81, and –F82. Some are in poor condition.

DATE: 1909–32

PHYSICAL DESCRIPTION: Ca. 115 silver gelatin photoprints, 20 × 25 cm or smaller.

SOURCE: Negatives: gift from Herbert E. French, 1947. Prints: purchase.

LOT 12340

COLLECTION NAME: National Photo Company Collection

SUBJECTS: United States presidents and First Ladies. Includes inaugural parades and presidential addresses. Presidents Wilson, Harding, and Coolidge with their cabinets; the Coolidges, the Hardings, Theodore Roosevelt, and Franklin D. Roosevelt attending events. Reproductions of illustrations of inaugurations of Washington, Lincoln, Cleveland, Garfield, Grant, and Harrison.

NOTE: Some images are captioned; some have dates. Corresponding negatives are found in series LC–F8, –F81, and –F82. Some are in poor condition.

DATE: 1909–32

PHYSICAL DESCRIPTION: Ca. 185 silver gelatin photoprints, 20 × 25 cm or smaller.

ARRANGEMENT: *Lot 12340–1:* U.S. presidential inaugurations; *Lot 12340–2:* U.S. presidents and First Ladies; *Lot 12340–3:* Presidential yacht–the *Mayflower.*

SOURCE: Negatives: gift of Herbert E. French, 1947. Prints: purchase.

LOT 12341

COLLECTION NAME: National Photo Company Collection

SUBJECTS: People in Washington, D.C., and New York. Includes children working, playing, posed with adults and with animals, and a series titled "Life on the Canal Boat." Immigrants at Ellis Island and engaged in naturalization activities. Portraits of families, blacks, and gypsies in Washington, D.C., and unidentified locations. One jigsaw puzzle made from a woman's portrait.

NOTE: Some photos are captioned; a few have dates. Corresponding negatives are found in series LC–F8, –F81, and –F82. Some are in poor condition.

DATE: 1909–32

PHYSICAL DESCRIPTION: Ca. 240 silver gelatin photoprints, 20 × 25 cm or smaller.

ARRANGEMENT: *Lot 12341–1:* Children, miscellaneous; *Lot 12341–2:* Cabinet and diplomatic corps children; *Lot 12341–3:* Boy Scouts; *12341–4:* Girl Scouts; *Lot 12341–5:* Immigrants; *Lot 12341–6:* People, miscellaneous. A finding aid is available in the Prints and Photographs Reading Room.

SOURCE: Negatives: gift of Herbert E. French, 1947. Prints: purchase.

National Photo Company. Prisoners with their Christmas tree at the District Jail. National Photo Company Collection, Lot 12342-9.

LC-USZ62-92401

LOT 12342

COLLECTION NAME: National Photo Company Collection

SUBJECTS: Social life and recreation in the Washington, D.C., area. Includes portraits and activities of fraternal and patriotic organizations; dignitaries and prominent citizens engaged in domestic, social, and charitable activities; tourists. Some Maryland and Virginia locations.

NOTE: Most photos are captioned; some have dates. Corresponding negatives are found in series LC–F8, –F81, and –F82. Some are in poor condition.

DATE: 1909–32

PHYSICAL DESCRIPTION: Ca. 1,015 silver gelatin photoprints, 20 × 25 cm or smaller.

ARRANGEMENT: *Lot 12342–1:* Clubs and groups; *Lot 12342–2:* Recreation; *Lot 12342–3:* Camps and camping; *Lot 12342–4:* Amusement arcades and parks; *Lot 12342–5:* Clothing and dress; *Lot 12342–6:* Horse shows; *Lot 12342–7:* Social life and customs; *Lot 12342–8:* Pets and owners; *Lot 12342–9:* Holiday activities; *Lot 12342–10:* Performing arts. A finding aid is available in the Prints and Photographs Reading Room.

SOURCE: Negatives: gift of Herbert E. French, 1947. Prints: purchase.

LOT 12343

COLLECTION NAME: National Photo Company Collection

SUBJECTS: The *Fuzzy Focus,* a burlesque newspaper published by the White House News Photographers Association. Contains satiric news stories about members of the association, news photography, and Washington events and comic portraits, some composites, including some of Herbert E. French.

NOTE: French was a founding member of the White House News Photographers Association. The Prints and Photographs Division holds the *Fuzzy Focus,* vol. 1, no. 1 (incomplete?), vol. 2, no. 2 (incomplete?), and undated pages.

DATE: Ca. 1923–ca. 1924

PHYSICAL DESCRIPTION: 12 pages (newspaper), 27 × 44 cm.

SOURCE: Purchase from Herbert E. French, 1947.

LOT 12344

COLLECTION NAME: National Photo Company Collection

SUBJECTS: Sports activities in the Washington, D.C., area. Includes individual and group portraits of members of athletic clubs; action photos of lacrosse, motorcycle racing, hunting in Virginia, ice skating on the Mall, women engaged in various sports, and government officials playing golf at Maryland country clubs. Some locations outside of the Washington, D.C., area.

NOTE: Some photos are captioned; some have dates. Corresponding negatives are found in series LC–F8, –F81, and –F82. Some are in poor condition.

DATE: 1909–32

PHYSICAL DESCRIPTION: Ca. 765 silver gelatin photoprints, 26 × 36 cm or smaller.

ARRANGEMENT: *Lot 12344–1:* Baseball; *Lot 12344–2:* Basketball; *Lot 12344–3:* Boating and rowing; *Lot 12344–4:* Horses; *Lot 12344–5:* Football; *Lot 12344–6:* Golf; *Lot 12344–7:* Auto racing; *Lot 12344–8:* Winter sports; *Lot 12344–9:* Sports, miscellaneous. A finding aid is available in the Prints and Photographs Reading Room.

SOURCE: Negatives: gift of Herbert E. French, 1947. Prints: purchase.

LOT 12347

COLLECTION NAME: National Photo Company Collection

SUBJECTS: "Independence story." Objects and sites relating to U.S. independence, including manuscripts of the "Star Spangled Banner" and Declaration of Independence; furnishings associated with drafting and signing of the Declaration, and painting depicting the signing. Flag that flew over Fort McHenry.

NOTE: Some photos are captioned. Includes some copy photographs. Title from cover of French's original folder.

DATE: 1909–32

PHYSICAL DESCRIPTION: 10 silver gelatin photoprints, 13 × 18 cm.

SOURCE: Purchase from Herbert E. French, 1947.

National Photo Company. *Women's rowing team, Potomac Boat Club, ca. 1919. National Photo Company Collection, Lot 12344-3.*

LC-USZ62-92402

National Photo Company. *Capitol pages in a Democrat-Republican snowball fight. National Photo Company Collection, Lot 12351-3.*

LC-F801-27912

LOT 12350

COLLECTION NAME: National Photo Company Collection

SUBJECTS: Transportation. Includes people posed with cars and trucks, some painted with advertisements, parked in front of Washington landmarks and commercial buildings. Transit buses and military vehicles; aircraft on the ground and in flight; pilots and spectators, including Capt. Roald Amundsen and Congressman O. D. Bleakley. Railroad cars, railway personnel, and railway accidents. Includes reproductions of illustrations and pamphlets on railroads; one pamphlet issued by Baltimore and Ohio Railroad.

NOTE: Most photos are captioned; most have dates. Corresponding negatives are found in series LC–F8, –F81, and –F82. Some are in poor condition.

DATE: 1909–32

PHYSICAL DESCRIPTION: Ca. 430 silver gelatin photoprints, 20 × 25 cm or smaller.

ARRANGEMENT: *Lot 12350–1:* Automobiles; *Lot 12350–2:* Commercial automobiles; *Lot 12350–3:* Auto accidents; *Lot 12350–4:* Aeronautics; *Lot 12350–5:* Railroad and street railroad. A finding aid is available in the Prints and Photographs Reading Room.

SOURCE: Negatives: gift of Herbert E. French, 1947. Prints: purchase.

LOT 12351

COLLECTION NAME: National Photo Company Collection

SUBJECTS: Government and politics. Congress in session and members at work and recreation. Portraits, some silhouette, include Franklin D. Roosevelt with Governor Cox, Vice President Marshall, Bainbridge Colby, the Prince of Wales, Belgian and Swedish royalty, Alexander Mitchell Palmer, and Samuel Gompers. Conferences and groups include the Disarmament Conference, International Labor Conference, Pan American Financial Conference, and British, French, and Japanese Commissions visiting Washington, 1917; congressional pages playing in the snow in front of the U.S. Capitol.

NOTE: Some photos are captioned; some are dated. Corresponding negatives are found in series LC–F8, –F81, and –F82. Some are in poor condition.

DATE: 1909–32

PHYSICAL DESCRIPTION: Ca. 715 silver gelatin photoprints, 1 engraving, 28 × 36 cm or smaller.

ARRANGEMENT: *Lot 12351–1:* Foreign dignitaries and visitors; *Lot 12351–2:* International conferences; *Lot 12351–3:* U.S. Congress and cabinet; *Lot 12351–4:* Public figures and groups; *Lot 12351–5:* Prohibition; *Lot 12351–6:* Reproductions of documents; *Lot 12351–7:* Reproductions of political cartoons; *Lot 12351–8:* Flags; *Lot 12351–9:* Voting; *Lot 12351–10:* Women—politics and suffrage; *Lot 12351–11:* Anarchists. A finding aid is available in the Prints and Photographs Reading Room.

SOURCE: Negatives: gift of Herbert E. French, 1947. Prints: purchase.

LOT 12353

COLLECTION NAME: National Photo Company Collection

SUBJECTS: Business and industry. Includes Virginia Ship Building Corporation in Alexandria, Virginia. Trial trip of the ship *Leviathan*. People listening to the radio; cartoon diagrams of radio transmission process; telephone operators. International First-Aid and Mine Rescue contests. American export activities; Washington business buildings and employees; Center Market in Washington, D.C.

NOTE: Some images are captioned; a few have dates. Corresponding negatives are found in series LC–F8, –F81, and –F82. Some are in poor condition.

DATE: 1909–32

PHYSICAL DESCRIPTION: Ca. 1,042 silver gelatin photoprints and photomechanical prints, 20 × 25 cm or smaller.

ARRANGEMENT: *Lot 12353–1:* Ship industry; *Lot 12353–2:* Patent models; *Lot 12353–3:* Radio and telephone; *Lot 12353–4:* Fishing; *Lot 12353–5:* Mining and drilling; *Lot 12353–6:* Farming; *Lot 12353–7:* Industry; *Lot 12353–8:* Advertisements on postcards; *Lot 12353–9:* Business activities; *Lot 12353–10:* Food business. A finding aid is available in the Prints and Photographs Reading Room.

SOURCE: Negatives: gift of Herbert E. French, 1947. Prints: purchase.

National Photo Company. Ku Klux Klan parade down Pennsylvania Avenue, September 13, 1926. National Photo Company Collection, Lot 12354-4.
LC-USZ62-59666

LOT 12354

COLLECTION NAME: National Photo Company Collection

SUBJECTS: Events in the Washington, D.C., area. Includes aftermath of fires, floods, and storms in Washington, D.C.; Red Cross relief work in flooded Mississippi Valley. Picketers, strikers, peace demonstrations; Ku Klux Klan; Disarmament Conference; Preparedness Day, and labor union parades. Ceremonies marking construction and completion of Washington buildings and monuments; burial of the Unknown Soldier at Arlington National Cemetery. Funerals and weddings. Receptions for public figures, including the king and queen of Belgium, Governor Cox, and Charles Lindbergh, attended by President and Mrs. Coolidge and Franklin D. Roosevelt. Reunion of the Grand Army of the Republic, conventions of the Daughters of the American Revolution, and political, health, and labor organizations. Virginia Ship Building Corporation in Alexandria, Virginia. Some locations other than Washington, D.C. Includes reproductions of illustrations.

NOTE: Some photos are captioned; a few have dates. Corresponding negatives are found in series LC–F8, –F81, and –F82. Some are in poor condition.

DATE: 1909–32

PHYSICAL DESCRIPTION: Ca. 865 silver gelatin photoprints, 20 × 25 cm or smaller.

ARRANGEMENT: *Lot 12354–1:* Demonstrations; *Lot 12354–2:* Disasters; *Lot 12354–3:* Rites and ceremonies; *Lot 12354–4:* Parades and processions; *Lot 12354–5:* Conferences and conventions; *Lot 12354–6:* Ship launchings.

SOURCE: Negatives: gift of Herbert E. French, 1947. Prints: purchase.

LOT 12355

COLLECTION NAME: National Photo Company Collection

SUBJECTS: Occupations and services. Includes public health service employees at work; students from primary grades through university in classes and extracurricular activities; graduations; and conferring of honorary degree on the queen of Belgium. Red Cross posters; montages used in White House News Photographers' publication, the *Fuzzy Focus*. Training of policewomen. Artists and models with paintings and sculpture; labor union members; reporters with President Harding;

National Photo Company. Ice floes on the Potomac River wrecked Dempsey's Boat House and the Washington Canoe Club, February 1918. National Photo Company Collection, Lot 12354-2.
LC-USZ62-92403

industrial vehicles; snow removal in Washington streets; a man with a hurdy-gurdy. Religious groups, services, and pageants; clergy and evangelists, including Cardinal Mercier and Aimee Semple McPherson. Laboratories; astronomical equipment at the U.S. Naval Observatory; members of scientific expeditions, including Dr. R. L. Shantz with South African natives.

NOTE: Some photo are captioned; some have dates. Includes some copy photographs. Corresponding negatives are found in series LC–F8, –F81, and –F82. Some are in poor condition.

DATE: 1909–32

PHYSICAL DESCRIPTION: Ca. 760 silver gelatin photoprints, 28 × 36 cm or smaller.

ARRANGEMENT: *Lot 12355–1:* Health care; *Lot 12355–2:* Education; *Lot 12355–3:* Fire department; *Lot 12355–4:* American Red Cross; *Lot 12355–5:* Photography and photographers; *Lot 12355–6:* Forest Service; *Lot 12355–7:* Police and corrections; *Lot 12355–8:* Art and artists; *Lot 12355–9:* Laborers and trades; *Lot 12355–10:* Religion; *Lot 12355–11:* Office employees; *Lot 12355–12:* Science. A finding aid is available in the Prints and Photographs Reading Room.

SOURCE: Negatives: gift of Herbert E. French, 1947. Prints: purchase.

LOT 12356

COLLECTION NAME: National Photo Company Collection

SUBJECTS: U.S. government departments and the Civil Service. Employees, officials, building interiors, machinery, and activities. Includes agricultural and scientific experiments; laboratories; livestock; motion picture filming at the Department of Agriculture; Bureau of Public Roads, Weather Bureau, office, and assembly line work. Mail delivery by truck, rail, and airplane; Post Office Christmas parade float. Library of Congress units and activities, including Reading Room for the Blind, Main Reading Room, preservation efforts, and Herbert Putnam with the Declaration of of Independence and the U.S. Constitution. Accompanied by a photostat text description of the Bureau of Biological Survey.

NOTE: Some photos are captioned; some have dates. Some images are discolored. Corresponding negatives are found in series LC–F8, –F81, and –F82. Some are in poor condition.

DATE: 1909–32

PHYSICAL DESCRIPTION: Ca. 650 silver gelatin photoprints, 20 × 25 cm or smaller.

ARRANGEMENT: *Lot 12356–1:* Department of Agriculture; *Lot 12356–2:* Treasury Department; *Lot 12356–3:* Bureau of Standards; *Lot 12356–4:* Postal Service; *Lot 12356–5:* Library of Congress; *Lot 12356–6:* Department of the Interior; *Lot 12356–7:* Department of Commerce; *Lot 12356–8:* Government Printing Office; *Lot 12356–9:* Department of Labor; *Lot 12356–10:* Patent Office; *Lot 12356–11:* Veterans Bureau; *Lot 12356–12:* White House; *Lot 12356–13:* General Supply Committee; *Lot 12356–14:* Government departments and Civil Service, miscellaneous. A finding aid is available in the Prints and Photographs Reading Room.

SOURCE: Negatives: gift of Herbert E. French, 1947. Prints: purchase.

LOT 12357

COLLECTION NAME: National Photo Company Collection

SUBJECTS: Washington, D.C., views and outdoor sites. Includes Cedar Hill Cemetery, Arlington National Cemetery, and Tomb of the Unknown Soldier. Buildings and recreational activities along C&O Canal. White House sheep; cows outside Soldiers' Home. Aerial and waterfront views of Washington; Washington Monument; structures in Alexandria and Fairfax, Virginia; and Rock Creek Park. Street scenes, including a parade in Anacostia. Botanical gardens and specimens. Includes reproductions of illustrations.

NOTE: Some photos are captioned; some have dates. Corresponding negatives are found in series LC–F8, –F81, and –F82. Some are in poor condition.

DATE: 1909–32

PHYSICAL DESCRIPTION: Ca. 1,060 silver gelatin photoprints, 20 × 25 cm or smaller.

ARRANGEMENT: *Lot 12357–1:* Cemeteries; *Lot 12357–2:* Bridges; *Lot 12357–3:* C&O Canal; *Lot 12357–4:* Animals, miscellaneous; *Lot 12357–5:* National Zoo; *Lot 12357–6:* Views and outdoor sites; *Lot 12357–7:* Street scenes; *Lot 12357–8:* Parks; *Lot 12357–9:* Monuments and statues; *Lot 12357–10:* Washington, D.C., and environs. A finding aid is available in the Prints and Photographs Reading Room.

SOURCE: Negatives: gift of Herbert E. French, 1947. Prints: purchase.

LOT 12358

COLLECTION NAME: National Photo Company Collection

SUBJECTS: U.S. military and World War I. Includes military training camps; servicemen at drill, work, and recreation; portraits of officers. Women recruiters; draft activities; home defense training; war work in Washington, D.C. Military hospitals, Red Cross and Salvation Army workers; German prisoners of war; Belgian refugees. American, French, Polish, and Italian soldiers; trenches and battlefields in France. Disabled veterans being greeted by public figures including General Pershing; veterans' organizations. Includes reproductions of illustrations; one booklet, "The Hospital Corps of the Navy," illustrated with photographs in the National Photo Company Collection.

NOTE: Some images are captioned; a few have dates. Includes some copy photographs. Corresponding negatives are found in series LC–F8, –F81, and –F82. Some are in poor condition.

DATE: 1909–32

PHYSICAL DESCRIPTION: Ca. 2,600 silver gelatin photoprints, 20 × 25 cm or smaller.

ARRANGEMENT: *Lot 12358–1:* U.S. Army; *Lot 12358–2:* U.S. Army Artillery;

National Photo Company. A local coal yard, Washington, D.C. National Photo Company Collection, Lot 12355-9.

LC-F8-21653

Lot 12358–3: U.S. Army Cavalry; *Lot 12358–4:* U.S. Coast Guard; *Lot 12358–5:* U.S. Military Air Service; *Lot 12358–6:* U.S. Marines; *Lot 12358–7:* U.S. Military Mascots; *Lot 12358–8:* U.S. military medical care; *Lot 12358–9:* Military personnel; *Lot 12358–10:* Recruiting; *Lot 12358–11:* Uniforms; *Lot 12358–12:* Veterans; *Lot 12358–13:* U.S. military women; *Lot 12358–14:* U.S. Navy; *Lot 12358–15:* U.S. ships and U.S. Navy ships; *Lot 12358–16:* World War I, war work; *Lot 12358–17:* World War I abroad; *Lot 12358–18:* Foreign naval vessels. A finding aid is available in the Prints and Photographs Reading Room.

SOURCE: Negatives: gift of Herbert E. French, 1947. Prints: purchase.

LOT 12359–1

COLLECTION NAME: National Photo Company Collection

SUBJECTS: Architecture in the Washington, D.C., region: *local and federal government buildings.* Includes interiors, architectural details. Construction work on the Lincoln Memorial, the White House, and the Treasury Department Building. U.S. Capitol; Union Station; Library of Congress, including the Main Reading Room and bookstacks. Washington Navy Yard, Annapolis Naval Academy, and Fort Myer, Virginia. Post offices and District of Columbia government buildings. Includes reproductions of illustrations.

NOTE: Most images are captioned; some have dates. Includes some copy photographs. Corresponding negatives are found in series LC–F8, –F81, and –F82. Some are in poor condition.

DATE: 1909–32

PHYSICAL DESCRIPTION: 742 silver gelatin photoprints, 20 × 25 cm or smaller.

ARRANGEMENT: By name of building. A finding aid is available in the Prints and Photographs Reading Room.

SOURCE: Negatives: gift of Herbert E. French, 1947. Prints: purchase.

LOT 12359–2

COLLECTION NAME: National Photo Company Collection

SUBJECTS: Architecture in the Washington, D.C., region: *foreign and international government buildings.* Pan American Union, including interiors, architectural details, grounds with fountains and plants. Chan-

ceries and embassies, including Mexican Embassy interiors, murals, and Mexican ambassador and his family.

NOTE: Most photos are captioned; some have dates. Corresponding negatives are found in series LC–F8, –F81, and –F82. Some are in poor condition.

DATE: 1909–32

PHYSICAL DESCRIPTION: 128 silver gelatin photoprints, 20 × 25 cm or smaller.

ARRANGEMENT: A finding aid is available in the Prints and Photographs Reading Room.

SOURCE: Negatives: gift of Herbert E. French, 1947. Prints: purchase.

LOT 12359–3

COLLECTION NAME: National Photo Company Collection

SUBJECTS: Architecture in the Washington, D.C., region: *residential buildings.* Includes homes in Chevy Chase, Maryland. Model home interiors with appliances and furniture. Apartment houses, mansions, row houses, hotels, YMCA. Architectural details. One image of a parking garage and one of a home built out of two streetcars. One aerial photograph.

NOTE: Most images are captioned; some have dates. Includes some copy photographs. Corresponding negatives are found in series LC–F8, –F81, and –F82. Some are in poor condition.

DATE: 1909–32

PHOTOGRAPHERS: Underwood & Underwood and U.S. Army Air Service.

PHYSICAL DESCRIPTION: 287 silver gelatin photoprints, 20 × 25 cm or smaller.

ARRANGEMENT: A finding aid is available in the Prints and Photographs Reading Room.

SOURCE: Negatives: gift of Herbert E. French, 1947. Prints: purchase.

LOT 12359–4

COLLECTION NAME: National Photo Company Collection

SUBJECTS: Architecture in the Washington, D.C., region: *historic buildings.* Residences of historic figures, including William Jennings Bryan. Eighteenth- and nineteenth-century buildings, including churches and hotels. Includes some reproductions of illustrations.

NOTE: Most photos are captioned; some have dates. Includes some copy photographs. Corresponding negatives are found in series LC–F8, –F81, and –F82. Some are in poor condition.

DATE: 1909–32

PHYSICAL DESCRIPTION: 175 silver gelatin photoprints, 20 × 25 cm or smaller.

ARRANGEMENT: A finding aid is available in the Prints and Photographs Reading Room.

SOURCE: Negatives: gift of Herbert E. French, 1947. Prints: purchase.

National Photo Company. The Shoreham Hotel, located at Fifteenth and H Streets NW, Washington, D.C. National Photo Company Collection, Lot 12359-3A.
LC-F82-1775

National Photo Company. Librarian of Congress Herbert Putnam (left) with the U.S. Constitution. National Photo Company Collection, Lot 12356-5.
LC-USZ62-92407

LOT 12359-5

COLLECTION NAME: National Photo Company Collection

SUBJECTS: Architecture in the Washington, D.C., region: *historic homes and buildings in Maryland and Virginia.* Includes interiors, outbuildings, gardens of Monticello and Mount Vernon; Lee Mansion (Arlington House); Gunston Hall; Colvin Run Mill. Some reproductions of illustrations.

NOTE: Most images are captioned; some have dates. Includes some copy photographs. Corresponding negatives are found in series LC-F8, -F81, and -F82. Some are in poor condition.

DATE: 1909-32

PHYSICAL DESCRIPTION: 196 silver gelatin photoprints, 20 × 25 cm or smaller.

ARRANGEMENT: A finding aid is available in the Prints and Photographs Reading Room.

SOURCE: Negatives: gift of Herbert E. French, 1947. Prints: purchase.

LOT 12359-6

COLLECTION NAME: National Photo Company Collection

SUBJECTS: Architecture in the Washington, D.C., region: *business establishments and office buildings.* Includes storefronts with vehicles parked outside, food enterprises, banks, and theaters.

NOTE: Most images are captioned; some have dates. Corresponding negatives are found in series LC-F8, -F81, and -F82. Some are in poor condition.

DATE: 1909-32

PHYSICAL DESCRIPTION: 150 silver gelatin photoprints, 20 × 25 cm or smaller.

ARRANGEMENT: A finding aid is available in the Prints and Photographs Reading Room.

SOURCE: Negatives: gift of Herbert E. French, 1947. Prints: purchase.

LOT 12359-7

COLLECTION NAME: National Photo Company Collection

SUBJECTS: Architecture in the Washington, D.C., region: *religious buildings.* Includes gardens, procession at Washington Cathedral; monks at Franciscan monastery; interiors, including altars decorated for holidays. Some postcards and reproductions of illustrations.

NOTE: Most images are captioned; some have dates. Includes copy photographs. Corresponding negatives are found in series LC-F8, -F81, and -F82. Some are in poor condition.

DATE: 1909-32

PHOTOGRAPHERS: Wide World Photos (1 item).

PHYSICAL DESCRIPTION: 147 silver gelatin photoprints, 20 × 25 cm or smaller.

ARRANGEMENT: A finding aid is available in the Prints and Photographs Reading Room.

SOURCE: Negatives: gift of Herbert E. French, 1947. Prints: purchase.

LOT 12359-8

COLLECTION NAME: National Photo Company Collection

SUBJECTS: Architecture in the Washington, D.C., region: *clubs and organizations.* Includes Daughters of the American Revolution Memorial Continental Hall, Columbia Country Club, Congressional Country Club, and Scottish Rite Temple. Some interiors, one aerial view.

NOTE: Most photos are captioned; some have dates. Corresponding negatives are found in LC-F8, -F81, and -F82. Some are in poor condition.

DATE: 1909-32

PHYSICAL DESCRIPTION: 98 silver gelatin photoprints, 20 × 25 cm or smaller.

ARRANGEMENT: A finding aid is available in the Prints and Photographs Reading Room.

SOURCE: Negatives: gift of Herbert E. French, 1947. Prints: purchase.

National Photo Company. The Affleck Drug Company, on the site of Rhodes Tavern at Fifteenth and F Streets NW, being closed out by Peoples Drug Stores, ca. 1921. National Photo Company Collection, Lot 12359-6A.

LC-F82-6411

National Photo Company. St. Elizabeth's Hospital, ca. 1920. National Photo Company Collection, Lot 12359-10A.

LC-F82-835

National Photo Company. "Famous capital landmark being dismantled to make way for modern business. The Capitol Hotel, famous . . . as the home of many early statesmen and in its day one of the most prominent hotels in the city . . . and on Pennsylvania Avenue." National Photo Company Collection, Lot 12359-3A.

LC-USZ62-92406

LOT 12359–9

COLLECTION NAME: National Photo Company Collection

SUBJECTS: Architecture in the Washington, D.C., region: *educational institutions.* Includes schools, universities, seminaries, trade schools, and correctional institutions; some interiors. Carnegie Library (Central Library) and Carnegie Institution; museums, including Corcoran Gallery and Smithsonian; National Academy of Sciences. Some postcards and reproductions of illustrations.

NOTE: Most images are captioned; some have dates. Includes copy photographs. Corresponding negatives are found in series LC–F8, –F81, and –F82. Some are in poor condition.

DATE: 1909–32

PHYSICAL DESCRIPTION: 172 silver gelatin photoprints, 20 × 25 cm or smaller.

ARRANGEMENT: A finding aid is available in the Prints and Photographs Reading Room.

SOURCE: Negatives: gift of Herbert E. French, 1947. Prints: purchase.

LOT 12359–10

COLLECTION NAME: National Photo Company Collection

SUBJECTS: Architecture in the Washington, D.C., region: *health institutions.* Hospitals and nursing homes, including Saint Elizabeth's and Soldiers' Home; American Red Cross building.

NOTE: Some images are captioned; some have dates. Corresponding negatives are found in series FC–F8, –F81, and –F82. Some are in poor condition.

DATE: 1909–32

PHYSICAL DESCRIPTION: 98 silver gelatin photoprints, 20 × 25 cm or smaller.

ARRANGEMENT: A finding aid is available in the Prints and Photographs Reading Room.

SOURCE: Negatives: gift of Herbert E. French, 1947. Prints: purchase.

National Photo Company. F.B.I. Director J. Edgar Hoover, December 22, 1924. National Photo Company Collection, Lot 12362.

LC-USZ62-92411

LOT 12362

COLLECTION NAME: National Photo Company Collection

SUBJECTS: Portraits. Includes portraits and candid photos of U.S. congressmen, government officials, and cabinet members, and their families; diplomats and U.S. and foreign military personnel; national and local celebrities; and reproductions of illustrations of historical figures.

NOTE: Typed and handwritten identification on versos or attached to some photos. Includes some copy photographs.

DATE: 1909–32

PHYSICAL DESCRIPTION: 1,460 silver gelatin photoprints, 20 × 25 cm or smaller.

ARRANGEMENT: Alphabetical by sitter's surname. A finding aid is available in the Prints and Photographs Reading Room.

SOURCE: Purchase from Herbert E. French, 1947.

LOT 12367

COLLECTION NAME: National Photo Company Collection

SUBJECTS: Abraham Lincoln, miscellaneous. Includes photos of portraits and sculptures of Lincoln, individuals associated with his administration, and John Wilkes Booth. Depictions of Lincoln's inauguration and funeral; memorials to him. Sites in Washington, D.C., Illinois, and Kentucky, as well as photos of documents, objects, and illustrations relating to Lincoln's life and career.

National Photo Company. Douglas Fairbanks and Mary Pickford, newly married, on the occasion of their visit to the White House, June 8, 1920. National Photo Company Collection, Lot 12362.

LC-USZ62-92412

NOTE: Herbert French's original album entitled "Abraham Lincoln, miscelaneous." Includes copy photographs.

DATE: 1909–32

PHYSICAL DESCRIPTION: 59 silver gelatin photoprints and engravings, 22 × 32 cm or smaller.

SOURCE: Purchase from Herbert E. French, 1947.

LOT 12368

COLLECTION NAME: National Photo Company Collection

SUBJECTS: George Washington in engravings and paintings. Portraits of Washington and his family. Monuments to Washington; photos of documents, objects, and buildings in Virginia associated with his life and career, including the Washington Lodge of Masons in Alexandria.

NOTE: Includes copy photographs. Accompanied by newspaper clippings.

DATE: 1909–32

PHYSICAL DESCRIPTION: 101 silver gelatin photoprints and halftone photomechanical prints, 21 × 30 cm or smaller.

SOURCE: Purchase from Herbert E. French, 1947.

National Women's Trade Union League of America Records

The records of the National Women's Trade Union League of America (NWTULA) held in the Manuscript Division span the years 1903-50 and number 7,400 items. The records are accompanied by a finding aid. They include correspondence, reports, speeches, notes, and printed matter concerning the league's formation and activities. The records concern the proceedings of the International Congresses of Working Women (1919, 1921, and 1923), the league's relationship to the American Federation of Labor, its support of strikes (especially in the garment industry), and its legislative efforts toward the eight-hour day, a minimum wage, federal aid to education, civil rights, price control, and social security. The photographs were transferred to the Prints and Photographs Division.

Margaret Dreier Robins, 1907. Records of the National Women's Trade Union League of America, Lot 5793.

LC-USZ62-56516

LOT 5793

COLLECTION NAME: National Women's Trade Union League of America Records, Manuscript Division

SUBJECTS: Portraits of executive board members and officers of the National Women's Trade Union League. Subjects include Elizabeth Christman, Margaret Dreier Robins, Mary E. Dreier, Sarah Green, Alice Henry (Australia), Lillian Herstein, Agnes Nestor, Pauline Newman, Rose Schneiderman, Maud Swartz, and Mary N. Winslow. Washington subjects include a portrait of Mary Van Kleeck, chief of the Women's Division in the Department of Labor, delegates to the First International Congress of Working Women in Washington, 1919, and a halftone reproduction of a montage of portraits of officers elected at the 1919 convention.

DATE: Ca. 1900–ca. 1950

PHOTOGRAPHERS: Moffett, Underwood & Underwood, Clinedinst, Hessler, and Associated News (New York).

PHYSICAL DESCRIPTION: 35 silver gelatin photoprints and halftone photomechanical prints, 28 × 36 cm or smaller.

SOURCE: Gift of the National Women's Trade Union League, 1950. Transfer from the Manuscript Division.

LOT 5794

COLLECTION NAME: Records of the National Women's Trade Union League of America, Manuscript Division

SUBJECTS: Group portraits made at various meetings attended by members of the National Women's Trade Union League of America (NWTULA). Women delegates to the 1886 convention of the Knights of Labor; trade union representatives attending the Conference of Employment Problems of Women, held by the Women's Bureau, U.S. Department of Labor, 1946; eight women who attended the first con-

vention of the NWTULA; and the National War Labor Board, 1919.

DATE: Ca. 1886–1950

PHOTOGRAPHERS: Del Ankers, Clinedinst, Federal Security Agency, and U.S. Department of Labor (Lindley, photographer).

PHYSICAL DESCRIPTION: 12 silver gelatin photoprints and halftone photomechanical prints, 28 × 36 cm or smaller.

SOURCE: Gift of the National Women's Trade Union League of America, 1950. Transfer from the Manuscript Division.

LOT 5796

COLLECTION NAME: Records of the National Women's Trade Union League of America, Manuscript Division

SUBJECTS: Group portraits of delegates to three international congresses of working women. Members of the First International Congress of Working Women, Washington, D.C., 1919, posed on the lawn at Mount Vernon; groups of French, German, Belgian, Polish, Czech, British, and Italian delegates. A session of the second congress, Geneva, Switzerland; delegates to the third congress, Vienna, Austria.

DATE: Ca. 1919–ca. 1923

Clinedinst. Rose Schneiderman, president of the National Women's Trade Union League of America. Records of the National Women's Trade Union League, Lot 5793.

LC-USZ62-30358

Clinedinst. National War Labor Board members, Washington, D.C., 1919. Records of the National Women's Trade Union League of America, Lot 5794.

LC-USZ62-46767

PHOTOGRAPHERS: Underwood & Underwood.

PHYSICAL DESCRIPTION: 16 silver gelatin photoprints, 20 × 25 cm or smaller.

SOURCE: Gift of the National Women's Trade Union League of America, 1950. Transfer from the Manuscript Division.

LOT 5798

COLLECTION NAME: Records of the National Women's Trade Union League of America, Manuscript Division

SUBJECTS: Pictorial material relating to working women and the National Women's Trade Union League of America (NWTULA). Subjects include President Harding's unemployment conference; the NWTULA house in Philadelphia; women staff members working in a league office; a commissary set up during the Chicago garment workers' strike in 1911; a club room at the New York Women's Trade Union League House; department store employees walking to work; and a portrait of Margaret Robins.

DATE: Ca. 1900–ca. 1950

PHOTOGRAPHERS: Underwood & Underwood.

PHYSICAL DESCRIPTION: 24 silver gelatin photoprints, as well as pen-and-ink sketches, 20 × 25 cm or smaller.

SOURCE: Gift of the National Women's Trade Union League of America, 1950. Transfer from the Manuscript Division.

LOT 5799

COLLECTION NAME: Records of the National Women's Trade Union League of America, Manuscript Division

SUBJECTS: Banquet camera portraits of delegates to various labor conventions, hearings, and meetings. Washington subjects include U.S. Department of Labor administrative personnel gathered on the Mall, 1919; portraits of representatives to the Unemployment Council called by President Harding, September 26, 1921; league members with President Hoover at the White House, May 6, 1929; the Women's Industrial Conference in Washington, January 1926; the Glove Manufacturer's code hearing in the Willard Hotel, May 23, 1934. Other subjects include conventions and congresses held in Kansas City (1911), and in St. Louis (1919); the First National Labor Party Convention in Chicago (1919); meetings in Waukegan, Illinois (1922), and New York City (1924); the 1924 league meeting in New York City; the 1924 American Federation of Labor meeting in El Paso; the 1926 meeting of the league in Kansas City; a meeting in Chicago (1939); and a meeting of the Trades and Labor Congress of Canada, possibly in Hamilton, Ontario, date unknown.

DATE: Ca. 1914–ca. 1940

PHOTOGRAPHERS: Tenschert, Scherer, Post, and R. S. Clements.

PHYSICAL DESCRIPTION: 25 silver gelatin photoprints, 26 × 92 cm or smaller.

SOURCE: Gift of the National Women's Trade Union League of America, 1950. Transfer from the Manuscript Division.

"Delegates & visitors to the 1st International Congress of Working Women. Guests of Federal Employees Union No. 2, Washington, D.C., at Mt. Vernon, Nov. 3, 1919." Records of the National Women's Trade Union League of America, Lot 5796.
LC-USZ62-92818

"French, German, Belgian, Polish, Czech, British, and Italian delegates to the First International Congress of Working Women, Washington, D.C." 1919. Records of the National Women's Trade Union League of America, Lot 5796.

LC-USZ62-92817

Scherer. "National Women's Trade Union League of America. Received by President Hoover at the White House, May 6, 1929." Records of the National Women's Trade Union League of America, Lot 5799.
LC-USZ62-63375

Joseph C. O'Mahoney Papers

Joseph C. O'Mahoney (1884–1962) was a Democratic senator from Wyoming for twenty-four years. He espoused the New Deal philosophy of the Roosevelt Administration and was considered an implacable foe of big business. He served as vice-chairman of the Democratic National Committee with James A. Farley for the 1932 and 1936 presidential campaigns. He served in the leadership of the Temporary National Economic Committee in 1938 and became known as one of the most articulate members of the Senate. His papers are held in the Manuscript Division. His collection of photographs was transferred to the Prints and Photographs Division.

LOT 8949

COLLECTION NAME: Joseph C. O'Mahoney Papers, Manuscript Division

SUBJECTS: Portraits of O'Mahoney's acquaintances and colleagues. Includes portraits of Franklin D. Roosevelt, James Farley, President Wilson giving a speech; Platform Committee Subcommittee of the Democratic National Convention in Chicago, 1932; commencement exercises at the Columbia University Library in 1938; Franklin D. Roosevelt addressing the Seventy-sixth Congress, January 4, 1939; and the Prayer Room in the Capitol. Also includes a photograph of the sculpting of Mt. Rushmore, signed by Gutzon Borglum; and a print, signed by the photographer, Joe Rosenthal, of the famous (restaged) "Planting of the Flag on Iwo Jima." Portraits include Alben Barkley, Bernard Baruch, Richard E. Byrd, Clarence D. Clark, Tom Connolly, Homer Cummings, Gen. George C. Marshall, President and Mrs. Roosevelt, W. A. Stanfill, Edward R. Stettinius, Brehon Somervell, and President and Mrs. Truman.

NOTE: Includes original political cartoons and a sketch of Ashland, Pennsylvania.

DATE: Ca. 1932–ca. 1957

PHOTOGRAPHERS: Bachrach, Underwood & Underwood, Harris & Ewing, Schutz, U.S. Army Signal Corps, ACME, and Joe Rosenthal.

PHYSICAL DESCRIPTION: 53 silver gelatin photoprints, 41 × 51 cm or smaller.

SOURCE: Gift of Mrs. Joseph C. O'Mahoney, 1961.

LOT 9564

COLLECTION NAME: Joseph C. O'Mahoney Papers, Manuscript Division

SUBJECTS: Events in Washington, D.C. Joseph C. O'Mahoney speaking at the Post Office Department Building dedication, June 11, 1934; Winston Churchill addressing the Senate in 1941; President Roosevelt taking the oath of office at his inaugu-

ration and delivering his first State of the Union message; spectators reacting to the President Franklin D. Roosevelt funeral parade; marines marching on the Capitol grounds; group portrait of the Senate Appropriations Committee, ca. 1940.

DATE: Ca. 1934–ca. 1942

PHYSICAL DESCRIPTION: 10 silver gelatin photoprints, 41 × 51 cm or smaller.

SOURCE: Transfer from the Manuscript Division, 1961.

LOT 9770

COLLECTION NAME: Joseph C. O'Mahoney Papers, Manuscript Division

SUBJECTS: News pictures made while Joseph C. O'Mahoney was a senator from Wyoming. Committee meetings and hearings held in rooms of the U.S. Capitol. The senator speaking at banquets, award-granting ceremonies, and other events, mainly in Washington, D.C. Includes O'Mahoney attending the funeral of Franklin D. Roosevelt in 1945; O'Mahoney's Irish Fellowship activities; the Democratic Convention in Philadelphia, June 23, 1936; and the Columbia University Library building.

DATE: Ca. 1938–1957

PHOTOGRAPHERS: Harris & Ewing, Ankers, F. Clyde Wilkinson (Arlington, Va.), Curtis Publishing Company, New York Times, Air Force Photos, and ACME.

PHYSICAL DESCRIPTION: 291 silver gelatin photoprints, 20 × 25 cm or smaller.

SOURCE: Gift of Mrs. Joseph C. O'Mahoney, 1963.

LOT 9830

COLLECTION NAME: Joseph C. O'Mahoney Papers, Manuscript Division

SUBJECTS: Senator Joseph C. O'Mahoney's visit to an unidentified army

Portrait of Joseph C. O'Mahoney, ca. 1946. Joseph O'Mahoney Papers, Lot 8949.

LC-USZ62-92820

U.S. Senate Committee on Appropriations, ca. 1940. Joseph O'Mahoney Papers, Lot 9564.

LC-USZ62-51497

ordnance installation, probably near Washington, D.C. The inspection party posed with a railroad gun, watching indoor and outdoor demonstrations and listening to explanations.

NOTE: Includes a letter from Maj. Gen. L. H. Campbell, Jr., chief of ordnance.

DATE: 1943

PHYSICAL DESCRIPTION: 6 silver gelatin photoprints, 22 × 36 cm or smaller.

SOURCE: Gift of Mrs. Joseph C. O'Mahoney, 1963.

Panoramic views of the capital in the Library of Congress collections date from about 1874 and were made from various vantage points, most often the Capitol dome, the Washington Monument, and the Smithsonian Institution Building. These all-encompassing views, at least one of which offers a complete 360-degree view of Washington, provide a rich source of information about the development of various Washington commercial districts and neighborhoods in the context of the city as a whole. Of particular interest is the changing design of the Mall, reflecting the McMillan Commission's recommendations and construction of temporary wartime buildings and various encampments. Supplemented by aerial views, these panoramas offer a record of Washington's growth upward and outward over the decades since the 1870s, with particularly heavy coverage in the early twentieth century after the invention of panoramic cameras and flexible roll film for use in them. Many of the Library's panoramic views were acquired between 1900 and 1930 as copyright deposits from U.S. photographers who had discovered a market for these dramatic images of the nation's capital. The Library's earliest such photographic record is a rare view from about 1874 that consists of five large albumen prints, which when joined together form a panorama.

Panoramic view of Sheridan Circle. Copyright 1911. Panoramic Photographs of Washington, Lot 12333-1.

LC-USZ62-92797
LC-USZ62-92798

LOT 12333

COLLECTION NAME: Panoramic photographs

SUBJECTS: Panoramic and aerial photographs of Washington, D.C., and environs. Includes a tiny panoramic view taken from the State, War, and Navy Building, 1906; a view of northwest Washington, downtown area; a view of Pennsylvania Avenue looking west from the Capitol dome, showing the northwest, southwest, and Mall areas, 1901; Pennsylvania Avenue looking east from the Hotel Washington, showing the northwest area, 1909; a view looking south, featuring the District Building, the Mall, and northwest Washington between the Old Post Office and Washington Monument; a retouched view entitled "Our Future Capitol," showing the Federal Triangle buildings sketched in, 1930; a 360-degree panorama in two parts, taken from the Washington Monument, providing

views of all areas of the capital and the Potomac River; and other views, some of which show all or some of southwest Washington. Also includes one aerial view of Washington and Virginia, ca. 1932.

DATE: 1891–1932

PHOTOGRAPHERS: Rideout, Leet Bros., Haines Photo Company, Shultz Photo, and William Rau (Philadelphia).

PHYSICAL DESCRIPTION: 12 silver gelatin photoprints, 46 × 221 cm or smaller.

SOURCE: Copyright deposit, gift, and transfer.

LOT 12361

COLLECTION NAME: Panoramic photographs

SUBJECTS: Panoramic view of Washington, D.C., from the Smithsonian Institution Building (now the "Castle"). Includes the old Agriculture Department building, incomplete Washington Monument, B Street (now Constitution Avenue) side of Mall, with building trades structures, Center Market, Baltimore and Potomac Railroad Station and tracks, the Capitol, and Independence Avenue area of Capitol Hill. Georgetown visible in the distance.

DATE: 1874

PHYSICAL DESCRIPTION: 5 albumen photoprints, 41 × 56 cm.

ARRANGEMENT: Five separate images provide a panoramic view when placed side-by-side. Photos are numbered to indicate arrangement.

SOURCE: Transfer from the Geography and Map Division.

John Joseph Pershing (1860–1948) was a U.S. Army officer and commander in chief of the American Expeditionary Forces in World War I. The Manuscript Division holds his papers, numbering 127,000 items and spanning the years 1882–1949. The papers, accompanied by a finding aid, include correspondence, diaries, notebooks, speeches, orders, maps, scrapbooks, clippings, picture albums, posters, miscellaneous printed matter, and memorabilia. They relate to Pershing's career in the Indian campaigns, in Cuba and the Philippines, as military attaché in Tokyo and Manchuria during the Russo-Japanese War, and as commander of the expedition to Mexico in 1916. The papers cover his World War I activities and responsibilities and include preparatory drafts for his book *My Experiences in the World War* and his unpublished memoirs. The papers were acquired through gifts, 1945–55, and the photographs they contained were transferred to the Prints and Photographs Division.

LOT 7712

COLLECTION NAME: John J. Pershing Papers, Manuscript Division

SUBJECTS: "Photographs of Review of 1st Division, U.S. Army at Washington, D.C., September 17, 1919," a presentation album of photographs taken by the U.S. Army Air Service from an observation balloon. Includes aerial views of the Capitol; the Pennsylvania Avenue parade in front of P.F. Keith's Vaudeville Theater; the Post Office Department (now the Old Post Office Building); the Occidental Hotel and Willard Hotel; the New York Avenue, Fifteenth Street, and F Street NW area; the Hotel Washington; Riggs Bank; Renwick Gallery; State, War, and Navy Building (now the Old Executive Office Building);

Balloon aerial view of Pennsylvania Avenue, during Welcome Home Parade for the First Division, 1919. John Pershing Papers, Lot 7712.
— *LC-USZ62-88102*

Triumphal Arch; views of troops and horses in parade; Hotel Powhatan; various shops and hotel on Pennsylvania Avenue; Union Station, showing the temporary wartime buildings; the Treasury Building; and Rhodes Tavern.

NOTE: Corresponding negatives are in the custody of the National Archives.

DATE: September 17, 1919

PHOTOGRAPHERS: U.S. Army Air Service.

PHYSICAL DESCRIPTION: 1 album (17 silver gelatin photoprints), 22 × 28 cm.

SOURCE: Transfer from the Manuscript Division, 1953.

LOT 7713

COLLECTION NAME: John J. Pershing Papers, Manuscript Division

SUBJECTS: Pershing's departure from France, 1919. Arrival at Brest, farewell ceremonies, party boarding the *Leviathan*, shipboard scenes. Parades in New York City and Washington, D.C. Includes President Wilson's review stand in Washington, the parade passing in front of the Hotel Occidental and Riggs Bank; views of the Hotel Washington, Rhodes Tavern, the Treasury Building, and other Pennsylvania Avenue buildings; the Triumphal Arch.

DATE: 1919

PHOTOGRAPHERS: Mann & Landry (Baltimore).

PHYSICAL DESCRIPTION: 1 album (55 silver gelatin photoprints, 13 × 18 cm).

SOURCE: Gift of the John J. Pershing estate, 1952. Transfer from the Manuscript Division.

RESTRICTIONS: Requires permission for use.

LOT 8836

COLLECTION NAME: John J. Pershing Papers, Manuscript Division

SUBJECTS: Parades, reviews, and other military ceremonies in Europe and the United States. Includes review of the First Division victory parade in Washington, D.C., September 17, 1919, including views of hotels, businesses, and crowds on Pennsylvania Avenue, the Treasury Building, and the Triumphal Arch. Pershing addressing a joint session of Congress on September 19, 1919.

NOTE: Includes one silhouette of Pershing cut by Beatrix Sherman at the Pan-Pacific Exposition in San Francisco, 1915.

DATE: Ca. 1917–ca. 1928

PHOTOGRAPHERS: Underwood & Underwood, George W. Stephenson, International Film Service (New York), and Press Illustrating Service/Keystone View Co.

PHYSICAL DESCRIPTION: Ca. 150 silver gelatin and platinum photoprints and a silhouette, 28 × 36 cm or smaller.

SOURCE: Gift of the John J. Pershing estate, 1952. Transfer from the Manuscript Division.

RESTRICTIONS: Requires permission for use.

LOT 8839

COLLECTION NAME: John J. Pershing Papers, Manuscript Division

SUBJECTS: Photographs related to the career and activities of General Pershing. Pershing on his eightieth birthday receiving the Distinguished Service Cross from President Roosevelt; Armistice Day ceremonies at Arlington Cemetery in 1942; meeting with Gen. Charles de Gaulle in 1944;

Pershing's office in the Pentagon, 1948; horses of the Front Royal, Virginia, remount station. Includes portrait of Pershing in his room at Walter Reed Hospital.

DATE: Ca. 1940–ca. 1948

PHOTOGRAPHERS: U.S. Army Signal Corps and Associated Press.

PHYSICAL DESCRIPTION: 27 silver gelatin photoprints, 28 × 36 cm or smaller.

SOURCE: Gift of the John J. Pershing estate, 1952. Transfer from the Manuscript Division.

RESTRICTIONS: Requires permission for use.

LOT 8840

COLLECTION NAME: John J. Pershing Papers, Manuscript Division

SUBJECTS: Funeral of Gen. John J. Pershing, who died July 15, 1948, at the age of eighty-seven. Ceremonies at the U.S. Capitol; procession crossing Memorial Bridge; final services in amphitheater at Arlington Cemetery with caparisoned horse and other traditional military rites. Includes photographs of Gen. Dwight D. Eisenhower, Gen. Omar Bradley, and other high-ranking military officers; and views of crowds lined up waiting to view the casket in the Capitol Rotunda.

DATE: July 1948

PHOTOGRAPHERS: U.S. Army photographs.

PHYSICAL DESCRIPTION: 36 silver gelatin photoprints, 20 × 25 cm or smaller.

SOURCE: Gift of the John J. Pershing estate, 1952. Transfer from the Manuscript Division.

RESTRICTIONS: Requires permission for use.

LOT 8841

COLLECTION NAME: John J. Pershing Papers, Manuscript Division

SUBJECTS: Autographed portraits presented to John Joseph Pershing by his friends and colleagues. Includes portraits of William Howard Taft; President Theodore Roosevelt (1904); Calvin Coolidge (signed 1920); and a view of Marshal Henri P. Pétain with Pershing at Mount Vernon (signed 1931). Other subjects include

Newton D. Baker, C. H. Brent, Winston S. Churchill, James L. Collins, Josephus Daniels, Roland Davison, Charles G. Dawes, Hugh A. Drum, W. C. Forbes, Gouraud, Douglas Haig, George C. Marshall, and William G. Sharp. Also includes a photograph of the French cruiser *Duquesne*.

DATE: Ca. 1900–ca. 1940s

PHOTOGRAPHERS: George Prince, Harris & Ewing, Edmonston, Elliott & Fry (London), U.S. Army Signal Corps, and photographers in San Francisco, Rome, Paris, Nice, and Havana.

PHYSICAL DESCRIPTION: 49 items (platinum, palladium, and silver gelatin photoprints, some colored, and halftone photomechanical prints), 28 × 36 cm or smaller.

SOURCE: Gift of the John J. Pershing estate, 1952. Transfer from the Manuscript Division.

RESTRICTIONS: Requires permission for use.

LOT 8844

COLLECTION NAME: John J. Pershing Papers, Manuscript Division

SUBJECTS: Portraits of General Pershing, mainly in uniform. Includes photographic copies of paintings by several artists.

DATE: Ca. 1920–ca. 1925

PHOTOGRAPHERS: Harris & Ewing, Clinedinst, Underwood & Underwood, George Prince, Pach Bros. (New York), U.S. Army Signal Corps, Brentano's (Paris and New York), and Harcourt (Paris).

Welcome Home Parade for the First Division passing under the Triumphal Arch on Pennsylvania Avenue, Washington, D.C., 1919. John Pershing Papers, Lot 8836.

LC-USZ62-92815

PHYSICAL DESCRIPTION: 93 platinum, palladium, and silver gelatin photoprints, photomechanical prints, and postcards, 28 × 36 cm or smaller.

SOURCE: Gift of the John J. Pershing estate, 1952. Transfer from the Manuscript Division.

RESTRICTIONS: Requires permission for use.

LOT 8845

COLLECTION NAME: John J. Pershing Papers, Manuscript Division

SUBJECTS: Informal portraits and snapshots of John J. Pershing. Pershing in uniform laying a wreath, delivering an address, working at a desk, riding a horse.

DATE: Ca. 1918–ca. 1930

PHOTOGRAPHERS: Harris & Ewing, U.S. Army Signal Corps, ACME, and Fotograms Newservice (New York).

PHYSICAL DESCRIPTION: 30 silver gelatin and platinum photoprints, 28 × 36 cm or smaller.

SOURCE: Gift of the John J. Pershing estate, 1952. Transfer from the Manuscript Division.

RESTRICTIONS: Requires permission for use.

Hugh Miller. Ceremony at the Lafayette Monument, Washington, D.C., with Marshal Foch, French Ambassador Jusserand, and General Pershing, ca. 1919. John Pershing Papers, Lot 8841.

LC-USZ62-92814

Signal Corps. Charles de Gaulle visiting with Gen. John Pershing at Walter Reed Hospital, July 1944. John Pershing Papers, Lot 8839.

LC-USZ62-92813

Funeral services for Gen. John Pershing, held in the amphitheater at Arlington National Cemetery, July 19, 1948. John Pershing Papers, Lot 8840.

LC-USZ62-92812

LOT 8846

COLLECTION NAME: John J. Pershing Papers, Manuscript Division

SUBJECTS: Informal portraits, mainly snapshots or news pictures, of General Pershing in mufti. Includes a photograph taken at the White House, and a portrait of Pershing in his room at Walter Reed Hospital.

DATE: Ca. 1925–ca. 1948

PHYSICAL DESCRIPTION: 21 silver gelatin photoprints, 28 × 36 cm or smaller.

SOURCE: Gift of the John J. Pershing estate, 1952. Transfer from the Manuscript Division.

RESTRICTIONS: Requires permission for use.

Harris & Ewing. General Pershing with Marshal Henri Pétain at Mount Vernon, ca. 1941. John Pershing Papers, Lot 8841.

LC-USZ62-92816

LOT 8848

COLLECTION NAME: John J. Pershing Papers, Manuscript Division

SUBJECTS: Ceremonies at the Lafayette Monument in Lafayette Park, Washington, D.C. Marshal Foch posed with young girls costumed in French and U.S. flags; group of dignitaries, including Ambassador Jusserand of France and General Pershing, posed at the base of the statue.

DATE: Ca. 1925

PHOTOGRAPHERS: National Photo Company, Underwood & Underwood, and Hugh Miller.

PHYSICAL DESCRIPTION: 6 silver gelatin photoprints, 20 × 25 cm or smaller.

SOURCE: Gift of the John J. Pershing estate, 1952. Transfer from the Manuscript Division.

RESTRICTIONS: Requires permission for use.

LOT 8853

COLLECTION NAME: John J. Pershing Papers, Manuscript Division

SUBJECTS: News pictures collected by General Pershing. Group portraits of U.S. Army officers; a military parade in Washington, D.C.; Pershing photographing a group of uniformed women on the U.S. Capitol steps; General Pershing's horse at Fort Monroe, Virginia; monuments in Boston and elsewhere; prizewinning Sons of the American Legion Drum and Bugle Corps; portrait of Pershing with Marshal Foch. Many photographs taken in Europe.

DATE: Ca. 1918–ca. 1930

PHOTOGRAPHERS: Underwood & Underwood and Harris & Ewing.

PHYSICAL DESCRIPTION: 88 silver gelatin photoprints, 20 × 25 cm or smaller.

SOURCE: Gift of the John J. Pershing estate, 1952. Transfer from the Manuscript Division.

RESTRICTIONS: Requires permission for use.

LOT 8854

COLLECTION NAME: John J. Pershing Papers, Manuscript Division

SUBJECTS: Photographs presented to General Pershing by admirers, friends, and associates. Includes one aerial view of the Pershing residence in Chevy Chase, Maryland. Also includes views of the Philippines; group portraits of army officers, statesmen, and others; monuments; and artists' portraits of American soldiers.

NOTE: Most items are uncaptioned and unidentified. Includes enlargement prints of photos from other lots.

DATE: Ca. 1885–ca. 1930

PHOTOGRAPHERS: Studios in the United States, France, and Japan.

PHYSICAL DESCRIPTION: Ca. 75 albumen, platinum, and silver gelatin photoprints and photomechanical prints, 36 × 44 cm or smaller.

SOURCE: Gift of the John J. Pershing estate, 1952. Transfer from the Manuscript Division.

RESTRICTIONS: Requires permission for use.

The Pictorial Archives of Early American Architecture (PAEAA) was the first photographic collection for the study of American architecture to be assembled at the Library of Congress. Operating with funding from the Carnegie Corporation, the project ran from 1930 to 1940, although the most active collecting period ended in 1938. Potential contributors of photographs of seventeenth-, eighteenth-, and nineteenth-century American architecture were asked to pool their negatives in the interest of establishing a centralized record for research. The collection includes approximately 10,000 negatives and some corresponding photoprints given by amateur and professional photographers, or in a few cases, purchased from them. It includes work by Frances Benjamin Johnston, John Mead Howells, Delos Smith, Thomas T. Waterman, and Francis M. Wigmore. Photoprints from the contributed negatives were made by professional printers, including Thomas F. Scott and the W. F. Roberts Company. Not all the negatives were printed.

The images document exteriors and interior details. Buildings in New Hampshire, Massachusetts, Connecticut, New York, New Jersey, Pennsylvania, Delaware, Maryland, the District of Columbia, Virginia, and South Carolina are especially well-represented in the collection. Most of the images were made during the 1930s, but a few depict nineteenth-century street scenes, particularly in Boston.

ARRANGEMENT AND DESCRIPTION

Most of the collection is currently housed in boxes with the Architecture, Design, and Engineering (ADE) Collection, organized by state, county, and city. Photoprints of sites in Washington, D.C., and Georgetown, however, have been separately processed and described in Lots 12553 and 12554. Items in the PAEAA Collection are listed in the PAEAA card index (with other ADE card indexes) in the Prints and Photographs Reading Room, and the sites represented in the collection are also listed in the master card catalog for the architectural collections.

A list of photographers who participated in the PAEAA project, the regions they covered, and the range of accession numbers for the images they contributed (listed in accession number sequence) is available in the reading room. A shelflist citing images by accession number is available in the Prints and Photographs Supplementary Archives.

RESTRICTIONS

Except where handling is restricted because of the fragility of the material, there are no restrictions on access to materials in PAEEA.

Water's Row, 1918-1922 Pennsylvania Avenue NW.
Pictorial Archives of Early American Architecture,
Lot 12553-1.

LC-P52-4507

REPRODUCTIONS

Corresponding negatives are filed in series LC–P5, –P51, –P52, –P53, and –P54. The bulk of the negatives, with the exception of the Washington, D.C., and Georgetown images, have no series code; these are filed by shelflist number as they await processing.

REFERENCES

Melville, no. 186, p. 275.
"Pictorial Archives at Washington, D.C.: Records of Early American Architecture to Be Preserved." *The Architect* 14 (July 1930), pp. 361–62, 428.
Peatross, C. Ford. "Architectural Collections of the Library of Congress." *QJLC* 34, no. 3 (July 1977), pp. 249–84.
Vanderbilt, no. 583, pp. 126–27.

LOT 12553

COLLECTION NAME: Pictorial Archives of Early American Architecture

SUBJECTS: Washington, D.C., architecture. Examples of eighteenth- and nineteenth-century architecture in Washington, D.C., exclusive of Georgetown. Includes residential buildings (some abandoned and some occupied by businesses or organizations), St. John's Church on Lafayette Square and St. Paul's Church in Rock Creek Cemetery, and the Pan American Union Building. Some architectural elements such as entrances, brickwork, wrought-iron work, and sculpture; a few structures photographed from above. Also documents activities on neighboring streets, including black street cleaners at work, automobiles, and pedestrians.

NOTE: Photographs are captioned. Most are copy prints from copy negatives in series LC–P52 and nitrate negatives in series LC–P54.

DATE: 1929–40

PHOTOGRAPHERS: Various photographers, including Frances Benjamin Johnston and William Van Benschoten.

PHYSICAL DESCRIPTION: 272 silver gelatin photoprints, 21 × 25 cm or smaller.

ARRANGEMENT: *Lot 12553–1*: Named structures; *Lot 12553–2*: Structures identified by address; *Lot 12553–3*: Unidentified structures. A finding aid listing buildings and photographers is available in the Prints and Photographs Reading Room.

SOURCE: Gift, various sources, including the photographers, 1929–40.

LOT 12554

COLLECTION NAME: Pictorial Archives of Early American Architecture

SUBJECTS: Georgetown architecture. Examples of eighteenth- and nineteenth-century architecture. Emphasis on dwellings and estates, including Dumbarton House, Montrose (now Montrose Park), and Tudor Place. C&O Canal, Washington Aqueduct Bridge.

NOTE: Photographs are captioned. Corresponding negatives are found in series LC–P5. A finding aid is available in the Prints and Photographs Reading Room.

DATE: 1929–40

PHOTOGRAPHERS: Various photographers, including Frances Benjamin Johnston.

PHYSICAL DESCRIPTION: 56 silver gelatin photoprints, 21 × 25 cm or smaller.

SOURCE: Gift of various sources, including the photographers, 1929–40.

Van Ness Mansion, Washington, D.C. Pictorial Archives of Early American Architecture, Lot 12553-1.
LC-P52-5953

Aqueduct Bridge, Georgetown. Pictorial Archives of Early American Architecture, Lot 12554.
LC-P52-731N

Washington's first daguerreotypist and first professional photographer, the Welshman John Plumbe, Jr., made the earliest existing photographic views of buildings in the capital in 1846 or thereabout. Plumbe (1809–1857) had come to Washington in 1845, just six years after the announcement of Daguerre's invention, with the purpose of making daguerreotype portraits of presidents, First Ladies, members of congress, actors, clergymen, and other people of distinction. These portraits he intended to sell in his New York gallery. By all accounts, he succeeded famously and was rewarded with sittings by President-elect James K. Polk, former presidents John Quincy Adams and Martin Van Buren, Supreme Court Justice Levi Woodbury, and many others. An 1846 letter from John Plumbe to Dolley Madison (found among the Dolley Madison Papers in the Manuscript Division) seeks her permission to use her portrait as a "Plumbeotype" illustration in an illustrated publication. Plumbe's invention, the "Plumbeotype" was not a method for directly reproducing daguerreotype images, as was suggested at the time, but was a way of making hand-produced lithographic images based on daguerreotypes. Through the existence of a nearly identical "Plumbeotype" image of the Capitol, daguerreotypes dating from about 1846 were attributed to John Plumbe.

The Library purchased the six rare images described here from Michael Kessler, a California collector of early photographica, who found them in the Alameda flea market in San Francisco in 1972. Identification of the daguerreotypes was aided by their having been described in the Washington *Daily Times* of February 1846. The daguerreotypes show the Patent Office, the General Post Office, a winter view of the President's House (as it was then called), and the U.S. Capitol before the construction of the large cast-iron dome and extension wings. One daguerreotype shows the Battle of North Point Monument on Calvert and Fayette Streets in Baltimore.

In 1846, John Plumbe, Jr., had daguerreotype studios or "depots" in New York; Philadelphia; Boston; Cincinnati; Louisville, Kentucky; Harrisburg, Pennsylvania; Dubuque, Iowa; Saratoga Springs, New York; Petersburg, Virginia; Baltimore; Washington, D.C. (on Pennsylvania Avenue); Alexandria (in Lyceum Hall); and other American locations. He also had studios in Paris and Liverpool. He was the proprietor of the National Plumbeotype Gallery, the National Publishing Company, and Plumbe's National Daguerrian Gallery. His fortunes diminished in 1847, however, when financial difficulties forced the sale of his establishments to his employees. Some of his studios were carried on in his name, but

John Plumbe, Jr. U.S. Capitol from the east, ca. 1846. Plumbe Daguerreotypes, Lot 11338.
LC-USZ62-46801

Plumbe returned to his hometown of Dubuque, Iowa, and later attempted to recoup his fortune in the California gold rush and in the railroad business, in which he had always had an active interest. His brother and nephew lived in San Francisco in the 1890s, which perhaps explains how Plumbe's daguerreotypes found their way to the West Coast. His proposal for a southern railroad route across the continent was rejected in favor of a northern route, dashing Plumbe's hopes for success in this new venture. He returned to Dubuque and committed suicide there in 1857.

These half-plate and quarter-plate daguerreotypes are remarkably well preserved despite their having been transported back and forth across the country. The Library's only other early photographic views of the capital were salted paper prints made in 1850 by Frederick and William Langenheim, of which the Prints and Photographs Division has copy photographs (see Lot 4823 in "Other Sources").

John Plumbe, Jr. The President's House (White House), Washington, D.C., ca. 1846. Plumbe Daguerreotypes, Lot 11338.

LC-USZ62-46804

REFERENCES

Busey, Samuel C. "Early History of Daguerreotypy in the City of Washington." *Records of the Columbia Historical Society,* vol. 3 (1900), pp. 81–95. (Written in 1898.)

Fern, Alan, and Milton Kaplan. "John Plumbe, Jr., and the First Architectural Photographs of the Nation's Capital." In Shaw, *A Century,* pp. 5–17. Contains a checklist of daguerreotype images by John Plumbe, Jr., and reproductions in collections throughout the United States.

Heissenbuttel, Orva. "Early Daguerreotypes of Historic Merit Purchased by Library of Congress." *Mid-Atlantic Antique Journal* 3, no. 10 (October 1971), pp. 1, 10–11.

King, John. "John Plumbe, Originator of the Pacific Railroad." *Annals of Iowa,* 3d series, vol. 6, no. 4 (January 1904), pp. 188–96.

Taft, Robert. "John Plumbe, America's First Nationally Known Photographer." *American Photography* 30, no. 1 (January 1936), pp. 1–12.

LOT 11338

SUBJECTS: The earliest known photographic views of Washington, D.C. Includes a view of the White House, the U.S. Capitol, and the Patent Office and two views of the General Post Office (now International Trade Commission Building). Also includes a view of Battle Monument in Baltimore.

NOTE: Daguerreotypes stored in Prints and Photographs Division safe. Copy photoprints serve for reference.

DATE: Ca. 1846

PHOTOGRAPHERS: John Plumbe, Jr.

PHYSICAL DESCRIPTION: 6 silver gelatin copy photoprints of daguerreotypes.

SOURCE: Purchase, 1972.

John Plumbe, Jr. The General Post Office, taken from the corner of Eighth and E Streets NW, ca. 1846. Plumbe Daguerreotypes, Lot 11338.

LC-USZ62-46802

John Plumbe, Jr. Patent Office, Washington, D.C., ca. 1846. Plumbe Daguerreotypes, Lot 11338.

LC-USZ62-46805

George Prince was a Washington photographer who was most active from the 1890s until about 1910. His platinum portraits of Washington's public officials and personalities are memorable for their elegance. Senators and congressmen, the McKinley cabinet, and President Theodore Roosevelt are among those who sat for their portraits. Prince also photographed some events in Washington in this period, including the Admiral Dewey sword presentation at the Capitol, inaugural ball decorations in the Pension Building, and the Grand Army of the Republic parade in 1892. George Prince copyrighted many of his photographs and it is from this source that the Library acquired representative samples of his work.

LOT 3791

SUBJECTS: Formal portraits of several U.S. senators and attorneys general. Includes Elihu Root (secretary of war); Senators O. H. Platt, T. C. Platt, John Kean, Boies Penrose, Matthew S. Quay, Joseph B. Foraker, William A. Clark, and Henry M. Teller; Attorney General Philander Chase Knox, and former Attorney General John William Griggs.

DATE: 1902

PHOTOGRAPHERS: George Prince.

PHYSICAL DESCRIPTION: 11 platinum photoprints, 23 × 18 cm or smaller.

SOURCE: Copyright deposit by George Prince, 1902.

LOT 6604

SUBJECTS: "Members of the 58th Congress, 3d Session, 1904."

NOTE: Reproductions submitted on disassembled sheets of a publication. Some bear the note, "Photographed for Boston Budget by Prince." The publication carries biographical data.

DATE: 1904

PHOTOGRAPHERS: George Prince.

PUBLISHER: Boston Budget, December 17, 1904.

PHYSICAL DESCRIPTION: 88 photomechanical prints on sheets, 41 × 30 cm.

SOURCE: Copyright deposit by the Budget Company, 1904.

LOT 11921

SUBJECTS: Cabinet and Senate of the McKinley administration, March 1901. Includes portraits of William McKinley, President Theodore Roosevelt, Cabinet members John Hay (secretary of war), Lyman Gage (secretary of the treasury), Elihu Root (secretary of war), and senators from each state.

PHOTOGRAPHERS: George Prince.

PHYSICAL DESCRIPTION: 1 album (106 platinum photoprints, 22 × 17 cm).

ARRANGEMENT: Presidents, followed by cabinet members and alphabetically arranged portraits of senators from each state.

SOURCE: Copyright deposit by George Prince, 1901–2.

LOT 12507

SUBJECTS: Events in Washington, D.C. Views of the McKinley inaugural ballroom at the Pension Building, March 1897; Admiral Dewey sword presentation at the Capitol, October 7, 1899; and christening of the U.S.S. Illinois, possibly in Washington, Ocotober 1898.

DATE: 1897–99

PHOTOGRAPHERS: George Prince.

PHYSICAL DESCRIPTION: 6 albumen and silver gelatin photoprints, 29 × 42 cm or smaller.

SOURCE: Copyright deposit by George Prince, 1897–99.

LOT 12508

SUBJECTS: Group portraits and sites in Washington and elsewhere. Includes the "Ancient & Honorable Artillery Co. of Boston, Mass." on the Capitol steps, October 1894, and "The Lambs' Star Gambol" on an unidentified theater stage. One view of George Washington's Tomb at Mount Vernon, and a view of "The Chamberlin" resort hotel, unidentified location, mounted on the verso of another image.

DATE: 1894–98

PHOTOGRAPHERS: George Prince.

PHYSICAL DESCRIPTION: 4 albumen and platinum photoprints, 44 × 52 cm.

George Prince. Elihu Root, secretary of war. Copyright 1902. Lot 3791.

LC-USZ62-92819

SOURCE: Copyright deposit by George Prince, 1894–98.

LOT 12509

SUBJECTS: Parade of the Grand Army of the Republic, Twenty-sixth Annual Encampment, Washington, D.C., September 20, 1892. Various posts and divisions are shown marching in the parade down Pennsylvania Avenue.

NOTE: All photographs are captioned as to army post or division.

DATE: 1892

PHOTOGRAPHERS: George Prince.

PHYSICAL DESCRIPTION: 18 albumen photoprints, 28 × 41 cm.

SOURCE: Copyright deposit by George Prince, 1892.

A. J. Russell, Photographer, and the Herman Haupt Collection

Capt. Andrew Joseph Russell (1830–1902) was probably the first official U.S. Army photographer. Gen. Herman Haupt hired him in 1863 to document the work of the Construction Corps of the U.S. Army Military Railroad. During the Civil War, Russell photographed such things as the construction and repair of railroad bridges.

Russell was a teacher and a painter before becoming a photographer. Before Haupt hired him, he worked for Mathew Brady. After the Civil War, from 1867 to 1870, he was an official photographer for the Union Pacific Railroad as it worked its way west toward Promontory Point, Utah. In 1869, he also carried out photographic work for Clarence King for the Fortieth Parallel Survey of the U.S. Geological Survey. He worked as an illustrator for *Frank Leslie's Illustrated Newspaper* and as a studio photographer in New York City.

Herman Haupt collected many of what are presumed to be A. J. Russell photographs in albums for official use. The Library's Russell photographs provide some of the earliest and best views of nineteenth-century Washington, D.C., and Alexandria, Virginia.

A. J. Russell. *Smithsonian Institution, north front, June 1862. Lot 4336.*

LC-USZ62-12780

REFERENCES

Anthony's Photographic Bulletin 13 (1882), pp. 212–13. Contains Russell's remarks about the role of photography in documenting the Civil War.
Cobb, Josephine. "Photographs of the Civil War." *Military Affairs* 26 (1962).
Fels, Thomas W. *Destruction and Destiny: The Photographs of A. J. Russell, Directing American Energy in War and Peace, 1862–1869.* Pittsfield, Mass.: The Berkshire Museum, 1987.
Gladstone, William. "Capt. Andrew J. Russell: First Army Photographer." *Photographica* 10, no. 2 (1978), pp. 7–9.
Haupt, Herman. *Photographs Illustrative of Operations in Construction and Transportation . . . .* Boston: Wright and Potter, 1863.
Russell, Andrew J. *Russell's Civil War Photographs: 116 Historic Prints.* With a preface by Joe Buberger and Matthew Isenberg. New York: Dover, 1982.

A. J. Russell. *"Potomac River, Looking down from Georgetown. Showing Mason's Island, Long Bridge, & c."* Lot 4336.

LC-B8184-10598

LOT 4336 (microfilm available)

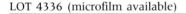

SUBJECTS: Documentary survey of the U.S. military railroad construction corps activities in the Washington area during the Civil War, including military installations, views of the construction of the U.S. Capitol dome and extensions, Georgetown, and the battle of Fredericksburg. Photographs are boxed by subject, as follows. *Railroads*: views on the Orange & Alexandria Railroad, including the roundhouse with a steam engine, and Union Mills Station; the Potomac Creek Bridge on the Acquia Creek; and the Fredericksburgh Railroad. *Washington, D.C.*: views of the Capitol dome under construction, June-July 1863, close-ups of pedimental sculpture; the south front of the Treasury Building; the Maryland Avenue railroad depot with the Capitol in the distance, June 1863; views from Georgetown, K and M Streets, and wharf areas, showing Mason's (Roosevelt) Island; guns stored at the Washington Arsenal, August 1863, north front of the arsenal buildings, and a view in the arsenal yard. *Alexandria and Arlington, Virginia*: Arlington House, June 1864; barns and soldiers' barracks; views along the Orange & Alexandria Railroad lines; convalescent camp near Alexandria; government hay barns in Alexandria; views of Battery Rodgers, Alexandria; Gen. Slough's headquarters, St. Asaph Street, Alexandria; Fort Ellsworth, near Alexandria; view of railway engine house with the town of Alexandria in the background;

City Hotel in Alexandria; Fire Department in Alexandria, with steam fire engines; general view of the city of Alexandria, from a distance, 1864. *Landscapes, Washington, D.C., and vicinity*: Great Falls on the Potomac River; view on Pope's Head, near Burnt Bridge, on the Orange & Alexandria Railroad; looking up the Potomac River from Fort Sumner; Bull Run, near a railroad bridge. *Bridges, Washington, D.C., and vicinity*: Aqueduct Bridge in Georgetown; Union Arch, Washington Aqueduct; Long Bridge and Washington, viewed from the Virginia shore; Cabin John Bridge, looking upstream; a bridge over the Washington Aqueduct near the Union Arch; General Benham's pontoon bridge across the Anacostia River near the Washington Navy Yard, 1863; Aqueduct Bridge in Georgetown, looking toward Washington, show-

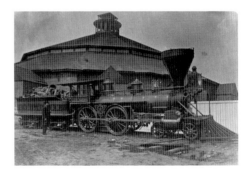

A. J. Russell. *"Engine 'Gen. Haupt,' Alexandria, 1863."* Lot 4336.

LC-B8184-10162

A. J. Russell. *"Front of Arlington House."* June 28, 1864. Lot 4336.

LC-B8184-10265

ing the C&O Canal. *General Civil War views*: no Washington, D.C., images.

NOTE: Photographs are captioned with details about railroad construction, where relevant. Some photographs are on printed mounts; some have printed captions attached to the mounts.

DATE: Ca. 1861–ca. 1865

PHOTOGRAPHERS: Andrew J. Russell

PHYSICAL DESCRIPTION: 72 albumen photoprints, 31 × 41 cm or smaller.

ARRANGEMENT: By subject.

SOURCE: Gift of Marion Haley, 1939.

RESTRICTIONS: Use of original prints is restricted. Microfilm provides initial reference access.

A. J. Russell. Cabin John Bridge, looking upstream. Lot 4336.

LC-B8184-10437

A. J. Russell. Aqueduct Bridge, Georgetown. Lot 4336.

LC-B8184-10436

A. J. Russell. Gen. Herman Haupt in a portable pontoon boat on the Potomac River. "Expedients for Crossing Streams . . . a pair of small pontoons, designed to facilitate scouting operations. . . . They can be carried by a strap around the waist, and concealed by an overcoat. A boat can be made of these by running poles through the loops, and then placing sticks across." Lot 9209.

LC-B8184-10488

LOT 9209 (microfilm available)

SUBJECTS: "Civil War Photos: Military Construction and Transportation in Northern Virginia and Elsewhere. United States Military Railway Department." Bridges, arks, and barges under construction; barges loaded with railway cars; tracks under construction; experimental means of crossing water; railway construction workers. Many views made in the Washington area, and in Alexandria, Virginia. Includes photographs of a shed at a carpenter shop in Alexandria, where the Construction Corps built portable bridge trusses; soldiers and crew members crossing the Potomac in rubber "blanket boat" rafts. Includes many photographs of black laborers.

NOTE: Title from spine of library binding of an album, disassembled by the Library, produced at the time Andrew J. Russell worked for the U.S. Army Military Railroad Construction Corps. Some images are unidentified. Album carried the handwritten label, "War Department Library photographs, vol. 32, Quarter Master General, Construction and Transportation."

DATE: Ca. 1862–ca. 1863

PHOTOGRAPHERS: Probably Andrew J. Russell.

PHYSICAL DESCRIPTION: 1 album (82 albumen photoprints), 28 × 20 cm.

ARRANGEMENT: Images numbered with original album pages.

SOURCE: Transfer from the Army War College, 1933.

RESTRICTIONS: Use of original album images restricted. Microfilm serves for initial reference access.

LOT 11486

COLLECTION NAME: Herman Haupt Collection

SUBJECT: *Lot 11486-A:* Richmond, Fredericksburg, Petersburg. Includes views of Castle Thunder Prison in Petersburg; the Custom House, Washington statue, Libby Prison, and scenes of rubble and burned ruins in Richmond; and Marie's House in Fredericksburg, Virginia. *Lot 11486-B:* Washington, D.C.; Arlington and Alexandria, Virginia; and vicinity. Includes views in Alexandria of the government coal wharf, looking up the wharf from Pioneer Mill, Soldiers' Cemetery, the government bakery, and the headquarters of Capt. J. G. C. Lee, A.Q.M. Also includes Arlington House, the corral on the Arlington National Cemetery grounds, Long Bridge and the hotel at its entrance and the Treasury Building, Washington, D.C.; Great Falls and the Washington Water Works on the Potomac River. Includes views in City Point, Virginia, such as the railroad depot,

A. J. Russell. "View from Pioneer Mill, looking up the wharf," Alexandria, Virginia. Lot 11486-B. LC-B8184-10213

A. J. Russell. "Hotel entrance to Long Bridge, Washington, D.C." Lot 11486-B. LC-B8184-10208

A. J. Russell. "Soldiers' Cemetery, Alexandria, Virginia." Lot 11486-B. LC-B8184-10211

post office, hospital, and headquarters of the Quartermaster's Department. *Lot 11486-C:* Railroads. Includes a train wreck near Brandy; a railroad mortar at Petersburg; train wreckage, ready for transport to Alexandria; roundhouse and depot of the Orange & Alexandria Railroad at Alexandria; the Engine "W.H. Whiton" and the President's Car in Alexandria, January 1865 (later used as Lincoln's funeral car); machine shops on the Orange & Alexandria Railroad in Alexandria; railroad depot and turntable in Petersburg; engine house at City Point; trestle work on the City Point & Army Railroad; the first train across Bull Run Bridge (Spring 1863); Cedar Level Station; and Stoneman's Station. *Lot 11486-D:* Artillery wagons, Giesboro, Maryland. Includes views taken at the cavalry depot, including photographs of horses in corrals, baggage trucks, and artillery wagons; the Potomac River at Giesboro; the Washington Arsenal, batteries of field pieces; and captured guns at Richmond, ready for transportation to Washington. *Lot 11486-E:* Hospitals and bridges. Includes views of the "New Bridge over the Potomac River on the Washington, Alexandria, & Georgetown Railroad"; Aqueduct Bridge in Georgetown; Union Arch, Washington Aqueduct (Cabin John Bridge); Potomac Creek Bridge, Acquia Creek & Fredericksburgh Railroad; Sickel Hospital in Alexandria; scenes showing repair work on the Bull Run Bridge; temporary bridge over the James River; a Confederate hospital near Richmond, Virginia,

April 1865; hospitals of the Army of the Potomac, January 1865; and the upper wharf at Belle Plain. *Lot 11486-F:* River views, landings, and ships. Includes a view down the Potomac from Union Arch; the Orange & Alexandria Railroad tracks and wharf; sailors on the Russian frigate *Osliaba* in Alexandria harbor; the "landing where they exchanged prisoners" on the James River (April 1865); the *Monitor* off Akin's Landing on the James River; Point of Rocks, Appomattox River; the *Connecticut* and the wharf, Acquia Creek; a view of the Appomattox River; view of the James River from Dutch Gap; the lower wharf at Belle Plain; and parrot gun on board the *Mendota. Lot 11486-G:* Forts, camps, headquarters, unidentified buildings, and miscellaneous views. Includes views of Battery Rodgers in Alexandria, April 1864; the barracks and guns at Fort Carroll, Washington, D.C.; General Patrick's headquarters at Brandy; Fort Sedgwick, near Petersburg; Confederate guns in front of Fort Hell; Fort Brady interior; a dead Confederate soldier in Petersburg, April 1865; the artillery camp at City Point, January 1865, and U.S. Military Academy cadets. (Collection includes four commercially produced albumen travel photos of buildings in Rome, which were part of Herman Haupt's album.) *Lot 11486-H:* Oversize photographs. Some of these images are mounted with original letters explaining the photographs, signed by Herman Haupt. Washington Arsenal, interior court and scene from roof, showing the weapons and transports stored there; the U.S. Capitol, showing the unfinished dome, with Horatio Greenough's statue of George Washington on the East Front grounds, July 1863; northeast front of the Capitol, showing construction work, June 1863; a slave pen in Alexandria; Gen. John Pope's headquarters in the field; Bull Run; Potomac Creek Bridge on the Acquia Creek & Fredericksburgh Railroad; view on Pope's Head, near Burnt Bridge, on the Orange & Alexandria Railroad; excavating for "Y" at Devereux Station, showing the Engine "Herman Haupt" and Superintendent J.H. Devereux, on the Orange & Alexandria Railroad; an embankment near Union Mills Station, Orange & Alexandria Railroad, military railroad bridge over Potomac Creek, Acquia Creek & Fredericksburgh Railroad; stone wall, rear of Fredericksburg, with Confederate dead, May 3, 1863; Bull Run, showing the scene of General Taylor's death, May 1863.

DATE: Ca. 1861–ca. 1865

PHOTOGRAPHERS: Andrew J. Russell.

PHYSICAL DESCRIPTION: Ca. 250 albumen photoprints, removed from large album, 27 × 31 cm or smaller.

SOURCE: Gift of Alma C. Haupt, 1955.

Predecessors of the souvenir postcard, made for travelers as visual reminders of places they had visited, were first the albumen photograph, sold unmounted or in albums by bookshops, and then booklets offering an array of lithographed or engraved scenes, which were often based on photographic views. Later methods of photomechanical reproduction, too, including photolithographic, photogravure, and halftone processes, were used for souvenir viewbooks. Today, such souvenirs take new forms like the fanfold string of postcards or the color brochure.

The Library of Congress has acquired souvenir viewbooks primarily as copyright deposits from the 1870s on, although some fine examples have been presented as gifts. Such outstanding names in this medium as Ph. Frey and Co., Louis Glaser, and the Albertype Company are represented in the Library's collections of Washington souvenir viewbooks. Washington photographers such as J. F. Jarvis and Edward Fitzki published their photographs in this form, and booklets were sold at all tourist sites in the city. One booklet of views of Washington and Mount Vernon, published in 1896 for Jos. S. Topham of 1231–1233 Pennsylvania Avenue, was sold at Topham's store for "Trunks, Travelers and Leather-Goods." Major Washington buildings, sites, and institutions were represented in viewbooks, as were Mount Vernon and Arlington Cemetery. Some events were featured as well. Viewbooks were used as promotional material by Catholic University, Trinity College, the U.S. Soldiers' Home, and the Government Printing Office Mutual Relief Association.

Souvenir viewbooks contain pictures of buildings and street scenes that may not be available in their original photographic versions. Because their subjects are sharply delineated, researchers may find in souvenir viewbooks information, albeit in a mediated form, that is unavailable elsewhere.

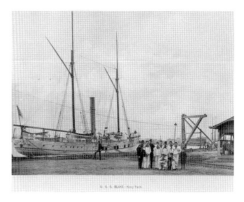

"U.S.S. Blake—Navy Yard." From The City of Washington: Photographs . . . ,*" published by the Albertype Company, 1892. Souvenir Viewbooks, Lot 12043-1.*

LC-USZ62-92482

"National Bank of Washington. Louisiana Avenue. Central National Bank." From The City of Washington: Photographs . . . ,*" published by the Albertype Company and A. Wittemann, New York, 1892. Souvenir Viewbooks, Lot 12043-1.*

LC-USZ62-92481

J. F. Jarvis. Composite layout showing hotels in Washington, D.C. From Washington Album, *published by Jarvis, Washington, D.C. Souvenir Viewbooks, Glaser-Frey Collection, Lot 12039.*

LC-USZ62-92480

LOT 12039

COLLECTION NAME: Glaser-Frey Viewbooks

SUBJECTS: Washington, D.C., buildings, monuments, street scenes, and other attractions.

NOTE: Titles include "Paintings in U.S. Capitol at Washington," "The Capitol at Washington," "The White House at Washington," "Washington" (two booklets), and "Washington Album" (J. F. Jarvis).

PUBLISHER: Ph. Frey, L. Glaser, and J. F. Jarvis.

PHYSICAL DESCRIPTION: 6 lithographic and photomechanical prints, 17 × 25 cm or smaller.

ARRANGEMENT: Alphabetical by state. Washington, D.C., section is in Box 11.

SOURCE: Copyright deposit and various gifts.

Lot 12043

COLLECTION NAME: Souvenir Viewbooks

SUBJECTS: Washington, D.C., and environs. (1) General views; (2) Catholic University; (3) U.S. Government Printing Office Mutual Relief Association; (4) Inauguration of President McKinley; (5) Library of Congress; (6) Mount Vernon; (7) U.S. Soldiers' Home; (8) Trinity College; (9) White House.

NOTE: Some are in very poor condition. A finding list is filed with the collection.

DATE: Ca. 1873–ca. 1953

PUBLISHERS: American Security and Trust, Avil Publishing, J. W. Carnahan, Catholic University, E. Fitzki, Ph. Frey, W. B. Garrison, L. Glaser, U.S. Government Printing Office, I. K. Hunter, Inter-State Medicine, J. F. Jarvis, T. G. McCrory, J. W. McKitrick, W. H. Morrison, L. H. Nelson, Sudwarth Printing, J. S. Topham, H.E. Wilkins Printing, and Wittemann Bros. (Albertype Co., printer).

PHYSICAL DESCRIPTION: 50 viewbooks, 23 × 31 cm or smaller.

ARRANGEMENT: By subject.

SOURCE: Some by copyright deposit; source of others is unknown.

Carl Andrew Spaatz Papers

Carl Andrew Spaatz (1891–1974), an army and air force officer, served as commanding general and chief of staff of the U.S. Air Force. The Manuscript Division holds his correspondence, diaries, reports, notes, flight records, and miscellaneous papers, numbering 115,150 items and spanning the years 1915–53 (chiefly 1942–48). The papers are accompanied by a finding aid. They relate to Spaatz's military career, and in particular to his role as commander in chief of the U.S. Strategic Air Forces in Europe and Japan, as commanding general, and as chief of staff. The papers were acquired through gifts, 1948–60. The photographs were transferred to the Prints and Photographs Division in 1961.

Margaret Bourke-White. Portrait of Carl Andrew Spaatz. Carl Spaatz Papers, Lot 8985.
LC-USZ62-92807

LOT 8982

COLLECTION NAME: Carl Andrew Spaatz Papers, Manuscript Division

SUBJECTS: Autographed portraits of President Truman, U.S. Air Force officers, statesmen, and other leaders, including Dwight D. Eisenhower, George S. Patton, Stuart Symington, John L. Sullivan, James Forrestal, Omar N. Bradley, Charles Lindbergh, and Fleet Adm. Chester Nimitz.

DATE: Ca. 1938–ca. 1947

PHOTOGRAPHERS: Chase-Statler, Hessler, U.S. Army, and U.S. Air Force.

PHYSICAL DESCRIPTION: 52 silver gelatin photoprints and 1 lithograph, 28 × 36 cm or smaller.

SOURCE: Transfer from the Manuscript Division, 1961.

LOT 8985

COLLECTION NAME: Carl Andrew Spaatz Papers, Manuscript Division

SUBJECTS: Portraits of Gen. Carl Spaatz. Includes one photographic copy of a caricature.

DATE: Ca. 1940–ca. 1948

PHOTOGRAPHERS: Harris & Ewing, U.S. Army, U.S. Air Force, and Margaret Bourke-White

PHYSICAL DESCRIPTION: 40 silver gelatin photoprints, 28 × 36 cm or smaller.

SOURCE: Transfer from the Manuscript Division, 1961.

LOT 8990

COLLECTION NAME: Carl Andrew Spaatz Papers, Manuscript Division

SUBJECTS: Gen. Henry Harley ("Hap") Arnold's annual Wild Game Dinner at Bolling Field, Washington, D.C., 1945. Gen. Carl Spaatz, General Eisenhower, Admiral Leahy, and others at the buffet.

Buffet decorations, including nooses, a wishing well, trees, and other humorous decorations. Includes a photographic copy of caricatures presented to each person in attendance.

DATE: Ca. 1945

PHOTOGRAPHERS: U.S. Army photographers.

PHYSICAL DESCRIPTION: 29 silver gelatin photoprints, 20 × 25 cm.

SOURCE: Transfer from the Manuscript Division, 1961.

LOT 8992

COLLECTION NAME: Carl Andrew Spaatz Papers, Manuscript Division

SUBJECTS: Events in the United States and England attended by Carl Spaatz during his military career. Spaatz at the Pentagon, 1947. Spaatz's B-17 landing at Andrews Field in one-eighth-mile visibility, February 1948. Gen. Hoyt Vandenberg, Spaatz's successor, taking his oath (from Chief Justice Fred M. Vinson) as chief of staff, U.S. Air Force. Also includes Spaatz receiving an honorary degree at Oxford; a party held to celebrate the eightieth birthday of Henry L. Stimson; a meeting with British dignitaries in London; group portrait made at the Key West Conference.

DATE: Ca. 1946–ca. 1948

PHOTOGRAPHERS: Francis Templeton, U.S. Signal Corps, British Air Ministry.

PHYSICAL DESCRIPTION: 23 silver gelatin photoprints, 20 × 25 cm or smaller.

SOURCE: Transfer from the Manuscript Division, 1961.

LOT 9325

COLLECTION NAME: Carl Andrew Spaatz Papers, Manuscript Division

SUBJECTS: Portraits of Gen. Henry Harley ("Hap") Arnold. Studio portraits, and casual photographs in uniform, some made

while Arnold was at his desk. Includes photographs of the 1945 Wild Game Dinner at Fort Myer, Virginia. Also includes photographs with Generals Patton and Clark, taken while Arnold was in North Africa, and with Generals Spaatz and Vandenberg in France.

DATE: Ca. 1942–ca. 1949

PHOTOGRAPHERS: U.S. Army, U.S. Air Force, and U.S. Signal Corps.

PHYSICAL DESCRIPTION: 30 silver gelatin photoprints and 1 color photoprint, 28 × 36 cm or smaller.

SOURCE: Transfer from the Manuscript Division, 1962.

LOT 9326

COLLECTION NAME: Carl Andrew Spaatz Papers, Manuscript Division

SUBJECTS: Funeral of Gen. Henry Harley ("Hap") Arnold. Honor guards at the airport and at the National Cathedral, Washington, D.C. Arnold's body lying in state in the Chapel of St. Joseph of Arimathea. Procession with caisson and caparisoned horse. Services in Arlington Cemetery amphitheater. Floral tributes.

DATE: Ca. January 1950

PHOTOGRAPHERS: U.S. Air Force.

PHYSICAL DESCRIPTION: 19 silver gelatin photoprints, 20 × 25 cm or smaller.

SOURCE: Transfer from the Manuscript Division, 1962.

Plans for the construction of a new building that would combine the War and Navy Departments in a single fireproof complex, comparable in design to the Treasury Building, were proposed as early as 1838 by Robert Mills. Various competitions were held over the next decades, until Alfred B. Mullett's design was accepted in 1870. Construction of the various wings of the $10 million building at Seventeenth Street and Pennsylvania Avenue NW was carried out in stages: first the south wing (1871–75), then the east wing (1872–79), the north wing (1879–82), and, finally, the west and center wings (1884–88). As architectural tastes changed, Mullett's lavish Second Empire design was subjected to increasing ridicule for its excessive ornamentation and this rejection and various financial problems led to Mullett's suicide in 1890.

The post-World War I Commission of Fine Arts asked John Russell Pope to remodel the exterior in classical style. The architect Waddy Wood was awarded a contract for a remodeling project in 1930, the funds for which were withdrawn as the Great Depression changed funding priorities. By 1957, the original State, War, and Navy Department occupants had vacated the building, and its demolition was recommended. In 1962, however, its restoration for use as an executive office building was proposed as part of the plan for the restoration of Lafayette Square.

The Library's collection of albumen photographs of the construction of the north, west, and center wings is thought to be the most complete documentation of the subject in existence. Most views were dated on the negative. They show construction methods, building materials, early methods for transporting heavy materials, and laborers and supervisors at work on the site.

REFERENCES

Lowry, Bates, ed. *The Architecture of Washington, D.C.* 2 vols. Washington: The Dunlap Society, 1976. Vol. 1, chap. 6.

LOT 10574

SUBJECTS: Official progress photographs documenting the various stages of construction of the State, War, and Navy Building (now the Old Executive Office Building) from the early stages of the construction of the north wing (1879) to the near completion of the west and center wings (1886). Includes a view of the interior of the "Indian Treaty Room," and a view of the Navy Department Library.

NOTE: Dates were inscribed on glass negatives. Thought to be the most complete documentation in existence. A note in the *G.S.A. Historical Study,* no. 3 (1964) indicates that at that time "only seven . . . of the surviving construction photographs . . . have been found."

DATE: August 23, 1879–February 24, 1886

PHYSICAL DESCRIPTION: 17 albumen and cyanotype photoprints, 41 × 57 cm or smaller.

View of the State, War, and Navy Building under construction, looking out on Seventeenth Street toward the Potomac River, January 3, 1885. Lot 10574.

LC-USZ62-56745

View of the stone-setting cranes in use during construction of the State, War, and Navy Building, October 20, 1884. Lot 10574.

LC-USZ62-59169

Construction of the State, War, and Navy Building, July 25, 1884. Lot 10574.

LC-USZ62-60467

Street Survey of Washington, D.C.

One of the most popular collections of photographs of the capital is the result of a turn-of-the-century project to systematically document Washington's neighborhoods in photographs. The glass plate negatives from which the Library made photoprints were originally unlabeled, but the locations they depict have been determined through the work of researchers and reference staff. Many of the photographs were taken from street corners, and thus include a view of two cross streets. Some high views were taken to present panoramic pictures of neighborhoods. These photographs provide a rare look at houses, vehicles, street furniture, stores, residents, and pedestrians in Washington's residential and semicommercial neighborhoods. The photographer or photographers are unknown.

52 Canal Street SW (or E Street SW and Maine Avenue), ca. 1900–1905. Street Survey of Washington, D.C., Lot 11516-D.

LC-Z7-4

LOT 11516

SUBJECTS: Washington streets and neighborhoods around the turn of the century. Residents of neighborhoods near their houses, people shopping and walking on the downtown sidewalks, typical clothing styles, and modes of transportation. Some high views, when adjoined, form panoramas. Includes a few building interiors and portraits.

NOTE: Most views have been tentatively identified. Corresponding negatives are found in series LC–Z7 and –Z71. Some negatives are badly deteriorated.

DATE: Ca. 1900–ca. 1905

PHYSICAL DESCRIPTION: 207 modern silver gelatin photoprints from original glass negatives, 20 × 25 cm or smaller.

ARRANGEMENT: Arranged in five sections: *NW, NE, SE, SW,* and *Unidentified.*

Tenth and I Streets NW, ca. 1900–1905. Street Survey of Washington, D.C., Lot 11516-A.

LC-Z7-5

View of the Library of Congress from Southwest Washington, ca. 1900–1905. Street Survey of Washington, D.C., Lot 11516-D.

LC-Z71-10

Pennsylvania Avenue SE (200 block) viewed from the Library of Congress roof, showing Trinity M.E. Church. Ca. 1900–1905. Street Survey of Washington, D.C., Lot 11516-C.

LC-Z7-72

The Treasury Building that stands today at Fifteenth Street and Pennsylvania Avenue NW was constructed following Robert Mills's design between 1836 and 1842. Thomas U. Walter proposed an extension in 1855, and his south and west wings were completed in 1860 and 1864, respectively. The Civil War halted construction from 1864 to 1867, when Alfred B. Mullett was hired to construct the north wing, completed in 1869. Construction of the entire building cost $6.6 million.

In 1869, the architect A. B. Mullett presented a collection of albumen construction photographs to the Library of Congress, which had them bound as an album. Dates inscribed on the glass plate negatives range from September 23, 1857, to November 6, 1867.

The photographs show laborers at work, ox-drawn transportation of heavy stones and columns, and construction machinery, methods, and materials, including the setting into place of the columns on the north side of the building.

A microfilm copy of the album serves for reference use.

REFERENCES

Lowry, Bates, ed. *The Architecture of Washington, D.C.* 2 vols. Washington: The Dunlap Society, 1976. Vol. 1, chap. 3.

LOT 12364 (microfilm)

COLLECTION NAME: Treasury Building Construction Photographs

SUBJECTS: Construction of the U.S. Treasury building. Includes views of laborers, machinery, and horse- and ox-drawn carts hauling building materials.

NOTE: A. B. Mullett was the architect for the north side of the Treasury Building.

DATE: September 23, 1857–November 6, 1867 (none bear dates for the period 1864–66)

PHYSICAL DESCRIPTION: 1 album (75 albumen photoprints), 47 × 38 cm.

SOURCE: Gift of A. B. Mullett, 1869.

Oxen in front of the south side of the Treasury Building during construction, May 4, 1860. Treasury Building Construction Photographs, Lot 12364 (microfilm).

LC-USZ62-90245

A column being raised into position at the Treasury Building, September 16, 1861. Treasury Building Construction Photographs, Lot 12364 (microfilm).
LC-USZ62-90244

Underwood & Underwood Collection

Many of the news and documentary photographs of Washington, D.C., from the early 1900s to 1932, received either as gifts or as copyright deposits, came to the Library of Congress from the Washington branch of Underwood & Underwood. This news agency was founded in the 1880s by Elmer and Bert Underwood and was reorganized in the early 1930s into four distinct companies, with branches in New York, Chicago, Detroit, Philadelphia, Cleveland, and Washington, D.C.

Coverage of subjects is as varied as were events of the period and as broad as the market for news topics demanded. Cataloged photographs pertaining to Washington document aviation subjects, including the 1909 Wright airplane trials, the "Bonus Expeditionary Force" and the "Hunger Army" march, the 1932 Supreme Court hearing of the Scottsboro boys' case, suffragette marchers and headquarters, and activities in such government offices as the Bureau of Engraving and Printing, White House, and National Bureau of Standards. Transportation in the city, the U.S. Mail Service, and the U.S. Capitol and other buildings and construction projects were documented.

Most Underwood & Underwood photographs acquired by gift, exchange, or other sources are described here; some of the agency's Washington photographs have, however, been incorporated into the Biographical, Presidential, Geographical, or Specific Subject Files. Some Underwood & Underwood photographs may carry restrictions on commercial use. Information about restrictions may be obtained in the Prints and Photographs Reading Room.

REFERENCES

Vanderbilt, no. 717, pp. 152–53.

Lot 2550

COLLECTION NAME: Underwood & Underwood Collection

SUBJECTS: Development of aviation. Airplanes of all types in flight and on the ground, including dirigibles, blimps, and autogiros. Pilots, engineers, U.S. officials, and stunt fliers. Groups of spectators witnessing daring new flights, cross-country and around the world. Experimental engines and aircraft. Washington images include test craft arriving at the Naval Air Station and Bolling Field; an antiprohibition aviator landing after setting speed records, 1931; events at Washington Hoover Airport; a speed record set by Hugh Nicholson at College Park Airport, May 3, 1932; the New York-to-Miami Air Races flight stopover, 1932; the first diesel engine presented to the Smithsonian Institution, August 1931; the dirigible U.S.S. *Akron* over the White House; a children's model aircraft tournament at Constitution Hall and the White House, 1931; the first autogiro flown in the United States aloft near the Capitol on the way to the Smithsonian Institution; the dirigible C-71 at the foot of the Washington Monument, February 1932; the inauguration of the world's fastest commercial airline, July 1931; Mrs. Herbert Hoover christening the 45-passenger Pan American Airways American Clipper, 1931; an autogiro landing on the East Plaza of the U.S. Capitol, July 1931; high-altitude flight pilots at Bolling Field, November 1931; an airmail pickup device, September 1931; and Col. Charles Lindbergh and his wife on the first leg of a 7,100-mile flight to Tokyo.

NOTE: Most photographs are accompanied by original news captions.

DATE: Ca. 1931–ca. 1932

PHOTOGRAPHERS: Underwood & Underwood.

PHYSICAL DESCRIPTION: 62 silver gelatin photoprints, 20 × 25 cm.

SOURCE: Gift of Underwood & Underwood, Washington, D.C., 1920s–1930s.

RESTRICTIONS: Permission for publication or commercial use may be required.

LOT 3739

COLLECTION NAME: Underwood & Underwood Collection

SUBJECTS: The "Bonus Expeditionary Force," veterans of World War I, marching on Washington. Encampment on Anacostia flats, tent homes and makeshift shelters; U.S. Army troops receiving orders from Generals MacArthur and Eisenhower to march on the veterans. Includes marchers inside the Capitol; demonstrations; Communist contingents; families accompanying marchers; boxcars carrying veterans arriving in Washington; donated food and soap; bathing, laundry, and cooking activities; the Salvation Army library and recreational activities; fingerprinting of marchers; issuing of railroad tickets to marchers for passage home; Congressman Wright Patman, sponsor of the Bonus Bill, speaking to marchers; funeral procession for

Underwood & Underwood. "Western Bonus Army lays siege to Capitol, spends night on plaza lawns. Filled with the idea of more agressive lobbying in favor of the enactment of the Bonus law, 700 veterans from the far West have [vowed] . . . that they will remain in sight of the legislators until favorable action is taken on their bill or Congress adjourns." July 13, 1932. Underwood & Underwood Collection, Lot 3739. Reproduced with the permission of Joseph Rotwein.

Underwood & Underwood. "Red Veterans parade past Capitol in Bonus demonstration. Despite threats from other veterans' organizations and efforts of the police to discourage them, approximately 200 veterans, said to be Communists, paraded down Pennsylvania Avenue in Washington . . . and gathered on the steps of the Library of Congress." July 15, 1932. Underwood & Underwood Collection, Lot 3739. Reproduced with the permission of Joseph Rotwein.

Congressman Eslick of Tennessee, who dropped dead on the floor of the House while delivering a plea for support for the Bonus Bill. Also, includes the "Hunger Army" march on Washington, December 1931; the Scottsboro boys' Supreme Court hearing, May 31, 1932; and Memorial Day services at Catholic University stadium, May 30, 1932.

NOTE: Photographs are accompanied by original news agency captions.

DATE: June–July 1932

PHOTOGRAPHERS: Keystone-Underwood.

PHYSICAL DESCRIPTION: 74 silver gelatin photoprints, 20 × 25 cm.

SOURCE: Gift of Underwood & Underwood, Washington, D.C., 1920s–1930s.

RESTRICTIONS: Permission may be required for publication or commercial use of photographs.

LOT 5480

COLLECTION NAME: Underwood & Underwood Collection

SUBJECTS: Communist picketers and rioters in Washington, D.C., and New York City. Police battling rioters at the Japanese Embassy; men and women bearing signs protesting against Japanese activities in Manchuria; Communists at the White House waiting for police patrol wagons; protestors fighting in Battery Park, New York City.

NOTE: Photographs accompanied by original news captions.

DATE: Ca. 1931–ca. 1932

PHOTOGRAPHERS: Underwood & Underwood.

PHYSICAL DESCRIPTION: 4 silver gelatin photoprints, 20 × 25 cm.

SOURCE: Gift of Underwood & Underwood, Washington, D.C., 1920s–1930s.

RESTRICTIONS: Permission may be required for publication or commercial use of photographs.

LOT 7292

SUBJECTS: Women inspecting currency, surprinting, and checking currency in drying trays, at the U.S. Bureau of Engraving and Printing, Washington, D.C.

DATE: Ca. 1906–8

PHOTOGRAPHERS: Underwood & Underwood.

PHYSICAL DESCRIPTIONS: 6 silver gelatin photoprints (stereograph), 12 × 9 cm.

SOURCE: Copyright deposit by Underwood & Underwood, January 18, 1908.

LOT 8064

SUBJECTS: Cornerstone-laying ceremonies at the George Washington Masonic Memorial, Alexandria, Virginia. Parade, spectators, and dignitaries in Masonic regalia around a rostrum. Construction machinery in place near monument base.

DATE: November 1, 1923

PHOTOGRAPHERS: Underwood & Underwood.

PHYSICAL DESCRIPTION: 7 silver gelatin photoprints, 16 × 22 cm.

SOURCE: Copyright deposit by Underwood & Underwood.

LOT 8720

SUBJECTS: Preparations for a U.S. Signal Corps balloon ascension at Fort Myer, Arlington, Virginia. Crew adjusting ballast, inflating the balloon; balloon in flight.

DATE: 1907

Underwood & Underwood. "Bonus Army receives new supplies at Washington camp. Members of the Bonus Expeditionary Force . . . continue to carry on with the aid of supplies donated by sympathizers. . . . At Camp Camden . . . a group of the veterans [are] cutting and wrapping a shipment of soap, contributed by a local merchant; the boys will be clean for some time on this gift." June 7, 1932. Underwood & Underwood Collection, Lot 3739. Reproduced with the permission of Joseph Rotwein.

PHOTOGRAPHERS: Underwood & Underwood.

PHYSICAL DESCRIPTION: 11 silver gelatin photoprints (stereograph), 12 × 10 cm.

SOURCE: Copyright deposit by Underwood & Underwood, September 27, 1907.

LOT 8721

SUBJECTS: The Wright airplane at Fort Myer, Arlington, Virginia, during U.S. Army acceptance trials, 1909. Shown on the ground.

NOTE: This Wright airplane, sometimes known as Signal Corps No. 1, was the first airplane purchased by any government and was the world's first military airplane. In restored form, this airplane is preserved in the National Air and Space Museum, Smithsonian Institution, a gift of the War Department in 1911.

DATE: 1909

PHOTOGRAPHERS: Underwood & Underwood.

PHYSICAL DESCRIPTION: 2 silver gelatin photoprints (stereograph), 12 × 10 cm.

SOURCE: Copyright deposit by Underwood & Underwood, July 23, 1909.

Underwood & Underwood. "Continuing with their 'siege' of Washington, members of the Bonus Expeditionary Forces are moving into the Capital City from their camps in the suburbs and a number of them have established a billet within a few blocks and within plain sight of the Capitol building." June 21, 1932. Underwood & Underwood Collection, Lot 3739.

LC-USZ62-22705

Underwood & Underwood. "Bonus Army stages huge demonstration at empty Capitol. Unaware that Congress had adjourned for the holidays, members of the Bonus Army, led by their newly reelected National Commander, Walter W. Waters, marched to the Capitol plaza. . . . " July 2, 1932. Underwood & Underwood Collection, Lot 3739. Reproduced with the permission of Joseph Rotwein.

LOT 8798

SUBJECTS: One Washington image captioned, "Navy Tests Models of all New Ships. An exact hull model of each new Naval vessel is tested in this 450-foot basin in Washington, towed behind a fast-running electric carriage, or under its own power, to secure perfect 'lines'. Insert shows Naval Constructor McEntee, in charge of the test basin, inspecting a model destroyer." Also includes a jack rabbit drive; radio station apparatus invented by L. W. Elias, in Chicago; Georges Carpentier, in Paris; Charles Jewtraw skating at Lake Placid; band aboard the *Celtic*; ice harvesting; free night school for workers; stop-motion photograph; navy divers; Census Bureau clerks; weight lifter; midair acrobat; fake freaks for sideshows; ski tournament.

NOTE: News pictures for use in window displays.

DATE: Ca. 1919–ca. 1920

PHOTOGRAPHERS: Underwood & Underwood.

PHYSICAL DESCRIPTION: 14 silver gelatin photoprints, 36 × 44 cm.

SOURCE: Exchange, 1960.

LOT 8802

SUBJECTS: World War I soldiers who died in France being interred in Arlington Cemetery; British Maj. Evelyn Wrench presenting to Navy Secretary Daniels funds to be used to erect a memorial to the U.S. Navy's World War I Dover Patrol; and presidentially appointed Labor Board meeting with Railroad Brotherhood leaders about outlaw strikes. Also includes Gene Walker and his motorcycle; a parade protesting the high cost of clothes; champion runner Tommy Milton; seaplane after a record-breaking flight; steeple jack; yacht owned by Marcone; herring catch; "Lost Battalion" veterans in a Zionist parade; Mexican troops in Juarez; Wilson Dam construction.

NOTE: News pictures for use in window displays.

DATE: Ca. 1920

PHOTOGRAPHERS: Underwood & Underwood.

PHYSICAL DESCRIPTION: 16 silver gelatin photoprints, 36 × 44 cm.

SOURCE: Exchange, 1960.

LOT 8806

SUBJECTS: Alice Paul raising the Suffrage Flag at the Washington headquarters, on the occasion of the ratification of the Nineteenth Amendment; Census Bureau office, showing automatic record-sorting machines, 1920; and the raising of a two-hundred-ton steel span for Key Bridge, Washington, 1923. Also includes housewives in a public school canning class; a Texas oil field; champion high jumper R. W. Landon; Polish women defending Warsaw; water bicycles; blasting; hammer thrower; leather chemist Fred A. Howard at work; fish dealers; auto race; cars for Alaskan railroad; anniversary of the Pilgrim landing; raising the *Vindictive*; submarine crews; Royal S. Copeland at a pure milk station; death of an aerial acrobat.

NOTE: News pictures for use in window displays.

DATE: Ca. 1920s

PHOTOGRAPHERS: Underwood & Underwood.

PHYSICAL DESCRIPTION: 24 silver gelatin photoprints, 36 × 44 cm.

SOURCE: Exchange, 1960.

LOT 8807

SUBJECTS: Washington Monument, viewed from an army plane. Cardinal Gibbons during cornerstone-laying ceremonies at the Shrine of the Immaculate Conception, Washington. Also includes a Wall Street explosion in New York; a man walking a greased pole; a streetcar-locomotive collision; American Legion members traveling in boxcars; victorious U.S. athletes; oil ship explosion damage; lacrosse; conveyor at a Great Lakes port; and an aerial view of West Point.

NOTE: News photos for use in window displays.

DATE: Ca. 1920s

PHOTOGRAPHERS: Underwood & Underwood.

PHYSICAL DESCRIPTION: 15 silver gelatin photoprints, 36 × 44 cm.

SOURCE: Exchange, 1960.

LOT 12652

SUBJECTS: Arlington Cemetery. Tomb of the Unknown Soldier, April 12, 1932; aerial view of Easter Sunday ceremonies conducted by the capital area Knights Templar in the amphitheater, March 27, 1932; Mother's Day ceremonies in amphitheater and at the Tomb of the Unknown Soldier, May 8, 1932.

DATE: 1932

Underwood & Underwood. "Army's highest officer directs troops in routing Bonus seekers. . . . General Douglas MacArthur, Chief of Staff of the Army, personally directed the evacuation of the Bonus Army by United States Army troopers, after the veterans had violently resisted efforts of the Washington police to remove them peaceably." (Dwight D. Eisenhower stands at the far right edge of the picture.) July 29, 1923. Underwood & Underwood Collection, Lot 3739. Reproduced with the permission of Joseph Rotwein.

PHOTOGRAPHERS: Underwood & Underwood.

PHYSICAL DESCRIPTION: 6 silver gelatin photoprints, 20 × 25 cm or smaller.

LOT 12653

SUBJECTS: U.S. government agencies and offices. White House office workers at desks, September 27, 1929. Testing the load-bearing strength of brick columns at the National Bureau of Standards, September 21, 1931. U.S. Mail Service; collecting mail, sewing mail bags, and marines guarding bags of mail.

DATE: Ca. 1929–31

PHOTOGRAPHERS: Underwood & Underwood.

PHYSICAL DESCRIPTION: 7 silver gelatin photoprints, 20 × 25 cm.

LOT 12654

SUBJECTS: Washington, D.C., buildings, monuments, and sites. C&O Canal; Pan American Union water lily pond; Meridian Hill Park fountain; Rock Creek Park and Taft Bridge; National Women's Party Headquarters near the Capitol, 1929; home of Gaston B. Means, a Secret Service agent charged in the theft of Evalyn Walsh McLean's $100,000 reward for return of the Lindbergh baby, 1932; National Cathedral interior, 1932; White House with scaffolding for painting, 1931; Brazilian Embassy; residence of Walter E. Edge, ambassador to France, Eighteenth Street NW; night view of Washington Monument and cherry blossoms; Arlington Memorial Bridge; proposed Theodore Roosevelt Memorial, 1925; John R. Pope's design for the National Archives, 1931.

DATE: 1925–32

PHOTOGRAPHERS: Underwood & Underwood.

PHYSICAL DESCRIPTIONS: 16 silver gelatin photoprints, 19 × 24 cm or smaller.

LOT 12655

SUBJECTS: Transportation in Washington, D.C. Sightseeing bus at the White House; Washington Rapid Transit Company motor bus on F Street NW; Cadillac parked near Lincoln Memorial, 1931; automobiles in blizzard of March 7, 1932, near Dupont Circle; cleaning the streets after the blizzard; St. Peter's Chapel Car, a Catholic shrine built in a railroad car for travel to remote areas of the West and South, 1931; automobiles on the old Klingle Bridge over Rock Creek Park, during bridge repair work, 1931; Connecticut Avenue bridge under construction, 1931; traffic signs and signals with automobiles at New Hampshire Avenue and Eighteenth Street NW; Red Top cabs near the Pan American Union Building.

DATE: Ca. 1925–ca. 1932

PHOTOGRAPHERS: Underwood & Underwood.

PHYSICAL DESCRIPTION: 11 silver gelatin photoprints, 20 × 25 cm or smaller.

SOURCE: Copyright deposit by Underwood & Underwood.

LOT 12656

SUBJECTS: Events in Washington, D.C. The world's largest radio exhibited in Washington, 1931; Easter Monday egg roll at the Capitol and White House, 1932; bicentennial celebrations of George Washington's birth, including a speech by President Hoover at the Capitol, a memorial tree-planting, and a ball at the Mayflower Hotel, 1932; the unemployed, led by Father James R. Cox from Pittsburgh, Pennsylvania, marching on the Capitol, 1932; Vesper Flag Services, with the world's largest flag, 1929; Pan American Day flag-raising on the White House Ellipse, 1932; 4-H Clubs' "tent city" on the Department of Agriculture grounds, 1929; U.S. Army Band at the White House, playing Christmas carols for President Hoover, 1930; army polo match at Potomac Park; firemen and trucks outside Dulin & Martin store in downtown Washington, 1929; fire at Bolling Field; portraits of Congressmen H. T. Rainey and Bertrand H. Snell; Governor's Conference attendees at President Hoover's White House dinner in their honor; Budget Chief J. C. Roop explaining the furlough system, 1932; Democratic party leaders at Jefferson Day dinner at the Willard Hotel, April 13, 1932; Maj.-Gen. Frederick W. Coleman taking oath of office as chief of finance, with Douglas MacArthur, 1932; socialites at the Davis Cup tennis matches, 1932; F. M. Feeker taking oath of office as chief of Bureau of Foreign and Domestic Commerce; Geneva Arms Conference delegation, 1932; officers of the Reconstruction Finance Corporation, 1932; women protesting at the Capitol against the proposed repeal of the Eighteenth Amendment, 1932; congressmen presenting a petition signed by five million citizens supporting the repeal of prohibition, 1932; senators on the committee to investigate the Stock Exchange, 1932; group of automobile industry leaders in Washington, 1932; Bishop James Cannon, Jr., at a Prohibition "bar."

DATE: Ca. 1929–ca. 1932

PHOTOGRAPHERS: Underwood & Underwood.

PHYSICAL DESCRIPTION: 39 silver gelatin photoprints, 20 × 25 cm or smaller.

LOT 12657

SUBJECTS: U.S. Capitol, grounds, and related buildings. Library of Congress getting a new copper roof, 1931; painting the flag pole above the House Chamber, 1930; installing heating system in the Capitol, 1931; replacing the West Front steps of the Capitol, 1931; the Capitol reflected in an automobile headlight; Capitol dome at night with an advertisement projected against it; Statuary Hall; steel skeleton of the Botanic Garden under construction, 1932; remodeling of the exterior of the Old Senate Office Building, 1932; the Capitol seen through a blizzard, March 7, 1932, and unemployed men recruited to clean snow from the Capitol grounds; digging the Capitol subway to the Senate Office Building, 1931; construction of the North Capitol Plaza Park and reflecting pool, 1932.

DATE: 1930–32

PHOTOGRAPHERS: Underwood & Underwood.

PHYSICAL DESCRIPTION: 15 silver gelatin photoprints, 20 × 25 cm.

Underwood & Underwood. "A small party of alleged Communists, who were arrested today for picketing the White House, had a good joke on their captors when a balky patrol wagon kept the party waiting in the rain in front of the Executive Mansion for almost half an hour." November 27, 1931. Underwood & Underwood Collection, Lot 5480. Reproduced with the permission of Joseph Rotwein.

Union Station Construction Photographs

As part of the beautification and redesign of the Mall, the McMillan Commission—Daniel Burnham, Charles Follen McKim, Frederick Law Olmsted, Jr., and Augustus Saint-Gaudens—proposed that the B&O and other railroad terminals and tracks be removed from the Mall and city streets to be replaced by a single railroad terminal that would serve as a "gateway to Washington." Daniel Burnham designed the building, construction began in 1903, and Union Station opened in 1907. Lorado Taft's Columbus fountain and statue were dedicated in 1912.

In 1968, with the declining demand for railroad passenger service, work began to convert Union Station into a National Visitors' Center under the direction of the National Park Service. This center opened in 1976 for the American Revolution Bicentennial celebration but closed shortly thereafter for lack of use. Recently, plans were laid to reconvert the terminal to its original use, that of a railway station of grand design befitting the nation's capital. Original construction photographs and drawings document the building and its furnishings.

Copyright deposit materials show Union Station at the time of its opening in 1907, and photographs taken on the arrival in Washington of distinguished visitors, before the advent of airline travel, picture the building as well.

REFERENCES

Lowry, Bates, ed. *The Architecture of Washington, D. C.* 2 vols. Washington: The Dunlap Society, 1976. Vol. 1, chap. 8.

LOT 12334

COLLECTION NAME: Union Station Construction Photographs

SUBJECTS: Union Station, Washington, D. C. Construction photographs of Burnham & Company. Later interior and exterior views. Drawings of wicker furniture. One blueprint.

DATE: Ca. 1903–ca. 1950

PHOTOGRAPHERS: Leet Bros., Tenschert, and Underwood & Underwood.

PHYSICAL DESCRIPTION: 139 silver gelatin photoprints, halftone photomechanical prints, and pencil and blueprint drawings, 31 × 61 cm or smaller.

SOURCE: Transfer from the National Park Service, 1984.

Gate in the train fence at Union Station. The sign shows the departure time of the B&O "Royal Limited" between Baltimore and New York, ca. 1907. Union Station Construction, Lot 12334.

LC-USZ62-91605

Union Station dining room, ca. 1907. Union Station Construction, Lot 12334.

LC-USZ62-89230

The completed Union Station, with trolley cars in front, ca. 1907. Union Station Construction, Lot 12334.

LC-USZ62-92472

The general waiting room in Union Station, looking west; the ticket lobby is in the back. Ca. 1907. Union Station Construction, Lot 12334.

LC-USZ62-92471

In 1983, the publishers of *U.S. News & World Report* presented to the Library of Congress the magazine's archive of photographs, covering the years 1952–73. The archive includes about 900,000 black-and-white negative exposures (35-mm) and accompanying contact sheets arranged in chronological sequence and bearing the original assignment numbers provided by the magazine. Photographs of U.S. presidents in office have not yet been transferred from the archive to the Library. Access is provided through a card index, arranged alphabetically by subject. Bound copies of *U.S. News & World Report* provide researchers with subjects and date ranges.

Washington social, cultural, and political events, neighborhoods, and architecture are well covered in this collection, which provides the most thorough documentation in the Prints and Photographs Division's collections of recent events in the capital.

SUBJECTS: 1968 riots and aftermath; Nazi party marches and counter-pickets during the Vietnam War; school integration in Washington; documentation of slums and evidence of segregation in Washington; crime in the capital; demolition of temporary wartime buildings; redevelopment of Southwest Washington; closing of the Willard Hotel; House Committee on Un-American Activities hearings; 1967 march on the Pentagon in protest of the Vietnam War; 1966 Poverty March on Washington; 1968 Poor Peoples' March on Washington; the 1963 Civil Rights March, with Robert Kennedy addressing marchers at the Justice Department; civil rights and Vietnam War protests at the Capitol; President John F. Kennedy meeting with leaders of black civil rights organizations; Mrs. Kennedy unveiling plans for Lafayette Park; St. Matthew's and Holy Trinity churches, attended by the Kennedy family; the John F. Kennedy funeral and his body lying in state in the Capitol Rotunda; tourists at Jacqueline Kennedy's home in Georgetown, after President Kennedy's assassination; the White House mailroom with letters received after the Kennedy assassination; stone carvers at work on the National Cathedral; Africans protesting against the South African government's shooting of blacks in 1960; the inauguration of new jet flights from National Airport to Los Angeles in 1959; aerial views of Washington and Virginia and Maryland suburbs; high views taken from the Old Post Office Building; photographs of Blair House; digging the new subway between the Senate offices and the Capitol in 1958; paintings in the Capitol slashed by a vandal; Gen. Douglas MacArthur's body lying in state in the Capitol Rotunda in 1964; construction of the Kennedy Center; views of the Watergate Apartments, Foggy Bottom, and the Washington Circle area; concerts on the Watergate barge; Walter Reed Hospital; Howard University; the cleaning of the Washington Monument; views of the Potomac River; smog and traffic jams on Washington-area freeways; street scenes in Georgetown; Union Station; visits of American and foreign dignitaries to the capital; completion of construction of the Federal Triangle; White House events; and tourist activities.

Attorney General Robert Kennedy at the Department of Justice, addressing the civil rights march on Washington, June 14, 1963. U.S. News & World Report *Collection.*

LC-U9-9954-18

Troops guarding the Capitol during the riots in Washington, April 7–8, 1968. U.S. News & World Report *Collection.*

LC-U9-18951-33

The Poor People's March on Washington, near Lafayette Park on Connecticut Avenue NW, June 18, 1968. U.S. News & World Report *Collection.*

LC-U9-19271-19

Military police frisking black citizens in Northwest Washington during the riots, April 7–8, 1968. U.S. News & World Report *Collection.*

LC-U9-18943-22

Africans demonstrating in front of the White House in protest against the South African government's shooting of black protestors, March 28, 1960. U.S. News & World Report *Collection.*

LC-U9-4124-10

Washington Monument Construction Photographs

Strengthening the foundation of the Washington Monument, May 28, 1880. Washington Monument Construction Photographs, Lot 7468.
LC-USZ62-15294

L'Enfant's plan for Washington specified a site due west of the Capitol and due south of the White House for an equestrian statue of George Washington, which was proposed instead as the site for a pyramid-shaped mausoleum. In 1833, the Washington National Monument Society was founded to raise funds for a monument. In 1836 Robert Mills's design for a 600-foot obelisk on a colonnaded base was chosen in competition and the monument cornerstone was laid in 1848 at a site slightly removed from L'Enfant's that provided a more secure footing. (The original 1810 marker for the intersection of L'Enfant's north-south and east-west axes, called the "Jefferson Pier," may be found slightly downhill to the northwest of the present Washington Monument site.) Funds for its erection ran out in 1854, when construction was halted at about 150 feet. The growing threat of civil war and political controversies involving the control of the Washington Monument Society impeded progress as well.

Inside the Washington Monument, memorial stones lined the walls, visible to anyone climbing the stairs to the top. One memorial stone, sent by Pope Pius IX from the Temple of Concord at Rome, with the inscription, "Rome to America," was stolen on the night of March 15, 1854. The culprits were thought to be supporters of the Know-Nothing party, whose antipapist sentiments made them prime suspects.

In 1876, Congress appropriated $200,000 for the completion of the monument. The foundation was strengthened and a simple obelisk design adopted. Construction resumed on August 7, 1880, and the capstone was set on December 6, 1884. The Washington Monument opened to the public on October 9, 1888, having cost about $1.5 million. The structure is a little more than 555 feet in height, with walls 15 feet thick at the base graduating to 18 inches thick at the top.

The McMillan Commission's proposal to shift the axis of the Mall southward to compensate for the off-center placement of the Washington Monument was adopted in 1901–2. A proposal to compensate on the north-south axis called for the construction of terraced and sunken gardens and a pool, but it was rejected as a threat to the foundation of the monument.

Original construction photographs made during 1879–80, when work resumed on the partially completed stump that had been an eyesore for over twenty years, show the area to the west and north of the monument, marshy tidal flats eventually built up by landfill for the Lincoln Memorial and Reflecting Pool, and the building trade and commercial structures existing along what is now called Constitution Avenue. These rare albumen photographs also document early engineering feats, showing the elevator used in the Washington Monument when it first opened and the stone-setting cranes used for the project. The strengthening of the foundation is documented as well. All photographs carry original inscriptions on their mounts.

Stone-setting cranes used for the construction of the Washington Monument, ca. 1880. Washington Monument Construction Photographs, Lot 7468.
LC-USZ62-15293

REFERENCES

Lowry, Bates, ed. *The Architecture of Washington, D.C.* 2 vols. Washington: The Dunlap Society, 1976. Vol. 1, chap. 5.

LOT 7468

SUBJECTS: Washington Monument construction. Views of the uncompleted monument, strengthening of the foundations, excavations for buttresses, the elevator engine, stone-setting cranes, workmen, and horse-drawn carriages. Tiber Creek, Washington Canal, and the Potomac River are visible near the monument (before landfill was deposited).

NOTE: Photographs are stamped, "Engineer Office Washington Monument 693 received Feby 16 1880," and mounted on captioned boards.

DATE: 1879–80

PHYSICAL DESCRIPTION: 13 albumen photoprints, 42 × 32 cm or smaller.

SOURCE: Transfer, 1947.

The elevator engine used in the Washington Monument, May 25, 1880. Washington Monument Construction Photographs, Lot 7468.
LC-USZ62-26190

A collection of portraits of men and women prominent in Washington during the late 1930s and early 1940s was purchased by the Library in 1952 from the General Photographic Corporation of Washington, D.C. Washington residents, members of the Seventy-sixth Congress, cabinet members, federal and city government officials, diplomats, military officers and personnel, doctors, religious leaders and church officials, lawyers and judges, labor leaders, scientists, and corporate executives are pictured in these portraits. Assembled as a picture resource file for newspapers and information agencies, the Washington Press-Photo Bureau Collection includes 9,000 sets of negatives, each set consisting of several exposures made during one portrait session. Corresponding portrait photoprints have been integrated into the Biographical File.

A card index to the collection provides alphabetical access by name; there is no separate shelflist for negatives. The index provides the sitter's name, title or occupation, address, and phone number, the date of the portrait, and the names of the studio photographers who carried out the work. The index includes some subjects for which the Library received no negatives. Corresponding negatives are found in series LC−W25 and −W26.

REFERENCES

Melville, no. 260, p. 376.
Milhollen, Hirst D. "Saved from the Silver Mines." *LCIB* 11 (June 23, 1952), p. 2.
Vanderbilt, no. 752, pp. 159−60.

Washington Press-Photo Bureau. Canon Stokes, Washington Cathedral. Ca. 1935−45. Washington Press-Photo Bureau Collection.

LC-W26-110-1

Washington Press-Photo Bureau. Father Fred W. Sohon, S.J., director of the Seismic Observatory, Georgetown University. Ca. 1935−45. Washington Press-Photo Bureau.

LC-W26-1437

Washington Press-Photo Bureau. Dr. Samuel Silk, clinical director, St. Elizabeth's Hospital, Washington, D.C. Ca. 1935−45. Washington Press-Photo Bureau.

LC-W26-1243

Washington Press-Photo Bureau. Dean W. B. West, Miner Hall, Howard University, Washington, D.C. Ca. 1935−45. Washington Press-Photo Bureau.

LC-W26-151-1

Werner E. Weber of Fredericksburg, Texas, gave his extensive collection of postcards of churches in the United States and various foreign countries to the Smithsonian Institution, and it was subsequently transferred to the Library of Congress in 1980, through the efforts of James M. Goode. The collection not only provides important documentation of well-known churches, cathedrals, and synagogues but, perhaps more importantly, provides what is in many cases the only existing photographic record of small-town and inner-city churches. Washington, D.C., churches are included in Lot 12336, described below. (For 2,511 postcards in the Weber Collection documenting church and religious buildings outside the United States, see Lot 12360.)

LOT 12336

COLLECTION NAME: Weber Collection of Postcards of Churches

SUBJECTS: Churches in the United States. Primarily exteriors; some interiors with views of altars, organs, and architectural elements such as stained glass windows. Includes some missions.

NOTE: Most postcards are captioned. "Collection of Werner E. Weber, Fredericksburg, Texas" is stamped on versos of most. Messages penned on some items.

DATE: 1908–69

PHYSICAL DESCRIPTION: 6,351 items, primarily postcards; also includes notecards and a few snapshots, photomechanical prints (some color), and silver gelatin photoprints, 12 × 17 cm or smaller.

ARRANGEMENT: Alphabetical by state; larger items in separate folders, also arranged alphabetically by state. Finding aid available in Prints and Photographs Reading Room.

SOURCE: Gift of Werner E. Weber to the Smithsonian Institution. Transfer from the Smithsonian Institution, 1980.

The National Tabernacle, Washington, D.C. Weber Collection, Lot 12336.

LC-USZ62-9175A

Calvary Baptist Church (Eighth and H Streets NW), Washington, D.C. Weber Collection, Lot 12336.
LC-USZ62-91755

Harvey Washington Wiley (1844–1930) was a chemist, teacher, author, and lecturer. He is remembered especially for his role in establishing standards for food purity, which led to the passage of the Food and Drugs Act of 1906, while he was chief of the Bureau of Chemistry of the U.S. Department of Agriculture (1883–1912). During his retirement years, he lectured on the Chautauqua circuit and directed the Good Housekeeping Magazine's Bureau of Food, Sanitation, and Health. His papers are held in the Manuscript Division. They number 70,000 items, spanning the years 1854–1944, and are accompanied by a finding aid. The papers include correspondence, diaries, legal papers, clippings, memoranda, printed matter, articles, speeches, essays, maps, blueprints, charts, and memorabilia. They were acquired through a gift from Mrs. Harvey W. Wiley, 1952–56. The photographs were transferred to the Prints and Photographs Division.

LOT 6793

COLLECTION NAME: Harvey Washington Wiley Papers, Manuscript Division

SUBJECTS: Studio portraits of Harvey W. Wiley.

DATE: Ca. 1863–ca. 1929

PHOTOGRAPHERS: Paine Studio, Bachrach, Underwood & Underwood, Harris & Ewing, Taylor's studio, Elliott & Fry (London), Notman (Boston), and National Cyclopedia of American Biography.

PHYSICAL DESCRIPTION: 37 albumen, platinum, and silver gelatin photoprints (including cartes de visite and cabinet cards), 1 silhouette, and 1 photogravure print, 20 × 25 cm or smaller.

SOURCE: Gift of Mrs. Harvey W. Wiley, 1952. Transfer from the Manuscript Division, 1955.

LOT 6794

COLLECTION NAME: Harvey Washington Wiley Papers, Manuscript Division

SUBJECTS: Photographs of Gutzon Borglum sculpting a bust of Harvey W. Wiley.

DATE: Ca. 1925–30

PHOTOGRAPHERS: Harris & Ewing and Henry Miller.

PHYSICAL DESCRIPTION: 6 silver gelatin photoprints and 1 newspaper clipping, 20 × 25 cm or smaller.

SOURCE: Transfer from the Manuscript Division, 1955.

LOT 6795

COLLECTION NAME: Harvey Washington Wiley Papers, Manuscript Division

SUBJECTS: Informal portraits and snapshots of Harvey W. Wiley. Includes one photograph of his first car, a steam automobile, captioned, "the 3rd one in Washington."

DATE: Ca. 1890–ca. 1929

PHYSICAL DESCRIPTION: 42 silver gelatin and albumen photoprints, 20 × 25 cm or smaller.

SOURCE: Transfer from the Manuscript Division, 1955.

"U.S. Marshal destroying worm-infested currants and raisins seized in possession of Washington, D.C., bakeries." November 20, 1909. Harvey W. Wiley Papers, Lot 6798.

LC-USZ62-68363

Dr. Harvey Wiley in his laboratory, ca. 1910. Harvey W. Wiley Papers, Lot 6798.

LC-USZ62-55461

"Salt fish and stock food seized in Washington, D.C., and condemned under the Pure Food Law. Loaded on wagons to be taken to crematory for destruction." January 25, 1910. Harvey W. Wiley Papers, Lot 6798.

LC-USZ62-55771

SUBJECTS: Photographs of Harvey W. Wiley's friends, teachers, colleagues, and contemporaries, some unidentified. Includes portraits of Charles Eliot, president of Harvard University; Asa Gray; Henry Lawrence Eustis; Josiah Parsons Cooke, and several Harvard chemistry professors.

DATE: Ca. 1865–ca. 1929

PHOTOGRAPHERS: Stalee, George Prince, C. M. Bell, Gilbert studio, Edmonston, Harris & Ewing, Buchanan, Pach Bros. (New York), and Notman (Boston).

PHYSICAL DESCRIPTION: Ca. 200 albumen, platinum, and silver gelatin photoprints (including cartes de visite and cabinet cards), 20 × 25 cm or smaller.

SOURCE: Transfer from the Manuscript Division, 1955.

LOT 6796

COLLECTION NAME: Harvey Washington Wiley Papers, Manuscript Division

SUBJECTS: Harvey W. Wiley with his children, and at his home in Washington.

DATE: Ca. 1908–ca. 1925

PHOTOGRAPHERS: Harris & Ewing and Underwood & Underwood.

PHYSICAL DESCRIPTION: 2 silver gelatin photoprints and 1 newspaper clipping, 20 × 25 cm or smaller.

SOURCE: Transfer from the Manuscript Division, 1955.

LOT 6798

COLLECTION NAME: Harvey Washington Wiley Papers, Manuscript Division

SUBJECTS: U.S. Department of Agriculture Bureau of Chemistry activities. Office buildings, laboratory and clerical workers, wagons of condemned food. Harvey W. Wiley at work. Includes clerical staff and office, ca. 1907; the old laboratory at Fourteenth and B Streets NW, which was torn down in July 1898; early photomicrographic equipment; experiments feeding rats, ca. 1910; experimental apparatus in a research lab in the Bureau of Chemistry. Officials seizing contaminated salt fish and stock food January 25, 1910; and U.S. marshal destroying worm-infested currants and raisins seized at Washington, D.C., bakeries, November 20, 1909.

DATE: Ca. 1883–ca. 1912

PHOTOGRAPHERS: Harris & Ewing, Scherer, C. M. Bell, Bachrach, and Clinedinst.

PHYSICAL DESCRIPTION: 97 albumen and silver gelatin photoprints, 20 × 25 cm or smaller.

SOURCE: Transfer from the Manuscript Division, 1955.

LOT 6799

COLLECTION NAME: Harvey Washington Wiley Papers, Manuscript Division

LOT 6802

COLLECTION NAME: Harvey Washington Wiley Papers, Manuscript Division

SUBJECTS: Rock formations in and around Washington, D.C. Cut on the Great Falls electric railroad; bank on the east side of Connecticut Avenue north of the zoo; excavation near Somerset Heights; and cut on the Chevy Chase and Glen Echo Railroad, near Somerset Heights.

DATE: Ca. 1885

PHYSICAL DESCRIPTION: 11 silver gelatin photoprints, 16 × 21 cm.

SOURCE: Transfer from the Manuscript Division, 1955.

LOT 6810

COLLECTION NAME: Harvey Washington Wiley Papers, Manuscript Division

SUBJECTS: Snapshot photographs taken by Harvey W. Wiley and his family and friends. Some made at or near Wiley's home in Washington. Some show Rock Creek Park and the Chevy Chase Club in Washington, D.C. Other subjects include a visit to Indiana relatives; the Tuileries and Versailles; and Florence, Rome, and Venice.

DATE: Ca. 1902

PHYSICAL DESCRIPTION: Ca. 100 silver gelatin photoprints, 11 × 13 cm or smaller.

SOURCE: Transfer from the Manuscript Division, 1955.

LOT 6820

COLLECTION NAME: Harvey Washington Wiley Papers, Manuscript Division

SUBJECTS: Tuberculosis Association activities. Presidents Coolidge and Hoover buying Christmas seals; Harvey W. Wiley eating with children in a health school; boys and girls demonstrating handicrafts.

DATE: Ca. 1924–ca. 1929

PHOTOGRAPHERS: National Photo Company, Henry Miller, Underwood & Underwood, and Wide World Photos.

PHYSICAL DESCRIPTION: 7 silver gelatin photoprints and newspaper clippings, 20 × 25 cm or smaller.

SOURCE: Transfer from the Manuscript Division, 1955.

LOT 6827

COLLECTION NAME: Harvey Washington Wiley Papers, Manuscript Division

SUBJECTS: Meetings attended by Harvey W. Wiley, including a meeting of agricultural chemists at the Jamestown Exposition, 1907; group portrait of "Official Agricultural Chemists," from the A.O.A.C. meetings held in 1906, 1908, and 1910 (one meeting held at the Raleigh Hotel in Washington, D.C.); Wiley with Milton Garrigus in front of the Pension Building in Washington, on the occasion of the Grand Army of the Republic meeting, 1915; a group portrait of the board of directors of the Washington Loan and Trust, of which Wiley was a member, 1919; and a photograph made during the peanut hearings, June 1911. Also includes large portraits of Wiley made on his wedding day; portraits of him in academic robes; and photographs made after cataract surgery. Includes photographs of Mrs. Wiley.

DATE: Ca. 1890–ca. 1925

PHOTOGRAPHERS: Harris & Ewing and National Press Association.

PHYSICAL DESCRIPTION: 27 silver gelatin photoprints, 28 × 45 cm or smaller.

SOURCE: Transfer from the Manuscript Division, 1955.

LOT 6831

COLLECTION NAME: Harvey Washington Wiley Papers, Manuscript Division

SUBJECTS: Various subjects related to Harvey W. Wiley's life and career, many unidentified snapshot photographs. Includes views of a Washington trolley car; women suffrage marchers on their way to Washington in 1915; a building at Mount Weather, and the International Weather Laboratory in the Loudoun Valley, proposed as the summer White House. Also includes subjects in England and commercial travel views; picnics and family outings; agricultural subjects, including fields, farmers, canneries, and beehives; and chemical apparatus.

DATE: Ca. 1880–ca. 1920

PHYSICAL DESCRIPTION: Ca. 200 silver gelatin and albumen photoprints, 20 × 25 cm or smaller.

SOURCE: Transfer from the Manuscript Division, 1955.

Division of Chemistry clerical staff, Department of Agriculture, ca. 1907. Harvey W. Wiley Papers, Lot 6798.

LC-USZ62-55449

LOT 6832

COLLECTION NAME: Harvey Washington Wiley Papers, Manuscript Division

SUBJECTS: Group portraits made at banquets, conventions, and other meetings and events. Includes the trustees of the U.S. Pharmacopoeial Convention held in Washington, 1918; A.A.A.B. group at Mt. Vernon, 1891; Wiley in the Grand Army of the Republic parade, 1915; Cosmos Club contingent in a parade, marching past the Treasury Building; officers of the Thirty-Ninth Annual Convention of the A.O.A.C. in Washington, 1923.

DATE: Ca. 1880–ca. 1920

PHOTOGRAPHERS: Tenschert & Flack, Harris & Ewing, and Clinedinst.

PHYSICAL DESCRIPTION: 85 silver gelatin and albumen photoprints, 25 × 30 cm or smaller.

SOURCE: Transfer from the Manuscript Division, 1955.

Division of Chemistry personnel, ca. 1899. Harvey W. Wiley Papers, Lot 6798.

LC-USZ62-46435

Willard Family Papers

The Willard Family Papers, spanning the years 1800–1955 and numbering 80,000 items, are held by the Manuscript Division. An accompanying finding aid describes the correspondence, letterbooks, notebooks, diaries, subject files, financial records, and other papers. The papers relate chiefly to the career of Joseph E. Willard (1865–1924), lawyer and diplomat, his wife Belle (Wyatt) Willard (1873–1954), and Confederate spy Antonia Ford (1838–1871), who was arrested by Maj. Joseph C. Willard and later married him. Some papers relating to the Willard Hotel (called Willard's Hotel in its early years) in Washington, D.C., are included. The papers were acquired as a gift from Belle Willard Roosevelt and Elizabeth Willard Herbert, 1954–64. Photographs were transferred to the Prints and Photographs Division.

Levin C. Handy. Willard Hotel, Pennsylvania Avenue NW, Washington, D.C. Ca. 1870s. Willard Family Papers, Lot 7395.

LC-USZ62-35231

LOT 7395

COLLECTION NAME: Willard Family Papers, Manuscript Division

SUBJECTS: Willard's Hotel, Washington, D.C., and events that took place there. Napier Ball, 1859, New York Fire Zouaves saving the burning hotel, 1861, Hanlan-Courtney boat race party, 1880. Willard's Hall, built in the rear of the hotel. Views of the rotunda of the hotel, politicians in front of it, and other subjects related to the White House, the Willard concert hall, and various inaugurations and parades. Most images are wood engravings, many of which are clippings from illustrated newspapers of the period.

DATE: Ca. 1853–ca. 1920s

PHOTOGRAPHERS: L. C. Handy, Harris & Ewing, and Lowell.

PHYSICAL DESCRIPTION: 21 wood engravings, etchings, and albumen and silver gelatin photoprints, 20 × 33 cm or smaller.

SOURCE: Transfer from the Manuscript Division, 1956.

LOT 7396

COLLECTION NAME: Willard Family Papers, Manuscript Division

SUBJECTS: The first Japanese diplomatic delegation to the United States at Willard's Hotel, Washington, D.C., 1860. Shinmi Masaoki returning to the hotel after a visit with President Buchanan; servants unpacking eighty tons of luggage in the ballroom; Japanese officers playing a game similar to checkers. Includes one wood engraving of Mathew Brady taking photographs of Japanese gifts in the reception room of the hotel.

NOTE: Wood engravings published in *Harper's Weekly, Frank Leslie's Illustrated Magazine,* and *New York Illustrierte Zeit.*

DATE: Ca. 1860

PHYSICAL DESCRIPTION: 11 wood engravings, 20 × 25 cm or smaller.

SOURCE: Transfer from the Manuscript Division, 1956.

LOT 7397

COLLECTION NAME: Willard Family Papers, Manuscript Division

SUBJECTS: Military and political subjects related to the Willard family and the Willard Hotel. Willard's Hotel, Washington, D.C., in 1888 and ca. 1924. Army encampment near Alexandria, Virginia; fire at the Willard, 1861; Union Army on the Potomac; Grand Review of 1865 in Washington, showing the Second Regiment of the National Guard of New Jersey on Pennsylvania Avenue; group portrait with Joseph E. Willard; various military groups; portrait of Fitzhugh Lee in Cuba, with Capt. Joseph Willard; review of troops at the State Capitol in Richmond; group montage photographs of the Virginia House of Delegates and the Virginia Senate Sessions, 1895–96 and 1897–98. One photograph shows the Hon. Joseph E. Willard speaking to a crowd and is titled, "Our Governor, a Look into the Future." Includes wood engravings of the Hanlan-Courtney rowing contest.

DATE: Ca. 1860–ca. 1924

PHOTOGRAPHERS: George Prince, Stalee, and D. H. Naramore (Alexandria).

PHYSICAL DESCRIPTION: 22 items (wood engravings and silver gelatin, albumen, and platinum photoprints), 41 × 51 cm or smaller.

SOURCE: Transfer from the Manuscript Division, 1956.

Lowell. Willard Hall, next door to the Willard Hotel. Willard Family Papers, Lot 7395.

LC-USZ62-35229

Tenschert. Willard Hotel, Washington, D.C., ca. 1920s. Willard Family Papers, Lot 7397.

LC-USZ62-35230

Edith (Bolling) Galt Wilson (1872–1961) was the second wife of President Woodrow Wilson. The Manuscript Division holds her papers, which number 19,000 items and span the years 1833–1961. They are accompanied by a finding aid. The papers include family and general correspondence, diary notes, drafts and correspondence concerning Edith Wilson's manuscript entitled "My Memoir" (1938), financial and legal papers, genealogical material, memorabilia, and printed matter. Correspondents include Ray Stannard Baker, Bernard M. Baruch, Josephus Daniels, Norman Davis, Cleveland Dodge, Charles Hamlin, Jesse Jones, William McAdoo, Cyrus McCormick, Adlai Stevenson, Henry White, and other leading political and social figures. Also included is correspondence with presidents and wives of presidents, including Calvin Coolidge, Grace Coolidge, Dwight D. Eisenhower, Mamie D. Eisenhower, Florence Harding, Herbert Hoover, Lou Hoover, Lyndon B. Johnson, Jacqueline Kennedy, John F. Kennedy, Eleanor Roosevelt, Franklin D. Roosevelt, and William Howard Taft. The papers were acquired through gifts of Edith Galt Wilson, 1957–60, and the Woodrow Wilson House, Washington, D.C., 1962–65. The photographs were transferred to the Prints and Photographs Division.

LOT 11138

COLLECTION NAME: Edith (Bolling) Galt Wilson Papers, Manuscript Division

SUBJECTS: *Lot 11138–1:* Interiors of Edith (Bolling) Galt residence on wedding evening, December 15, 1915; Edith in first electric car to be driven by a woman in Washington, D.C., 1904; at Charity House Show in Fort Myer; at opening of Democratic Women's Home in Washington, 1927; laying the cornerstone of the new Red Cross Building with President Calvin Coolidge; at the unveiling of the Wilson plaque; at a fashion show; at the Jackson Day Dinner in the Mayflower Hotel Ballroom; with family members and friends; at banquets. Includes baby photos and travel photos. *Lot 11138–2:* Wilson inauguration, 1917; landing from the presidential yacht *Mayflower*; in a reviewing stand at Camp Meade, 1918; tossing a ball at the opening of baseball games, 1916, 1918; at Flag Day exercises at the Sylvan Theatre in Washington, 1918. Wilson leaving funeral services for Yuan Shi Kai, president of China; at the Daughters of the American Revolution (D.A.R.) Continental Hall, 1916; at the D.A.R. Convention, 1916; buying Christmas seals; group portraits of Wilson's cabinet members. Wilson leading Preparedness Day Parade at the entry of the United States into World War I, ad-

Portrait of Edith Bolling Galt, ca. 1899. Edith Wilson Papers, Lot 11138–1.

LC-USZ62-78051

International News Photo. President Wilson signing the Child Labor Bill, September 2, 1916. Edith Wilson Papers, Lot 11138–2. Reproduced with the permission of UPI/Bettmann Newsphotos.

Harris & Ewing. Edith Bolling Galt, ca. 1913. Edith Wilson Papers, Lot 11144.

LC-USZ62-92811

International News Photo. President Wilson speaking to Congress on the occasion of the entry of the United States into World War I. April 1917. Edith Wilson Papers, Lot 11138–2. Reproduced with the permission of UPI/Bettmann Newsphotos.

dressing the closing session of the Sixty-third Congress, signing the Child Labor Bill, September 2, 1916, addressing Congress on Germany's conduct of the "U-boat War," 1916, and on the U.S. entry into World War I. President Wilson with the War Relief Committee, 1917; at Memorial Day Exercises in Arlington Cemetery, 1917; in a Liberty Loan Parade, 1918; purchasing Liberty Bonds. Wilson in public after months of illness; delivering speeches; with Navy Secretary Josephus Daniels at the inauguration of Air Mail, May 1918. Wilson at home in Washington, 1922; Wilson and wife riding in automobiles in Washington; Wilson in President Harding's funeral procession, August 8, 1923. Citizens kneeling on sidewalks in Washington, upon hearing the news that Wilson was near death. Armistice Day Commemoration of President Wilson at the Washington Cathedral, November 11, 1930. Also includes photographs of Wilson's reception in Paris, and other events outside Washington, D.C. *Lot 11138–5:* includes one view of Wilson residence in Washington, D.C.

DATE: Ca. 1870s–ca. 1961

PHOTOGRAPHERS: Underwood & Underwood, Tenschert, Harris & Ewing, C. M. Bell, Clinedinst, Hessler, Chase-Statler, Washington Post, Coller, WPIX (Alexandria), Bain News Service (New York), Pach (New York), Acme, and International News Photo.

PHYSICAL DESCRIPTION: Ca. 750 albumen, cyanotype, and silver gelatin photoprints; postcards; watercolors; and an oil sketch; 20 × 25 cm or smaller.

ARRANGEMENT: *Lot 11138–1:* Portraits of Mrs. Wilson; *Lot 11138–2:* President Wilson; *Lot 11138–3:* Postcards (Europe, United States); *Lot 11138–4:* Unidentified individuals: family, friends, colleagues; *Lot 11138–5:* Photographs of residences in the United States and other places, many taken during travels abroad. *Lot 11138–6:* Identified portraits of family and friends, many autographed. *Lot 11138–7:* Four watercolors and one oil sketch.

SOURCE: Transfer from the Manuscript Division.

LOT 11144

COLLECTION NAME: Edith (Bolling) Galt Wilson Papers, Manuscript Division

SUBJECTS: Edith Galt Wilson's life and career. Includes family pictures, portraits of Edith Wilson, photographs of unidentified places, and autographed portraits of leading political figures, including Presidents Taft, Coolidge, Hoover, and Truman. Also includes banquet camera group portraits taken at various events, including the Woodrow Wilson Birthday Commemorative Dinner at the Mayflower Hotel, 1933.

DATE: Ca. 1890s–ca. 1950s

PHOTOGRAPHERS: Harris & Ewing, George Tames, G. V. Buck, and Tenschert.

PHYSICAL DESCRIPTION: 26 silver gelatin photoprints and etchings, 45 × 115 cm or smaller.

SOURCE: Transfer from the Manuscript Division.

After the Civil War, Adolph Wittemann and his brother founded Wittemann Brothers, a view and souvenir viewbook publishing business, which Adolph's son Hermann L. Wittemann carried on until his death in 1952. After buying the rights to a special printing process from Joseph Albert, the Wittemanns began calling their Brooklyn, New York, business the Albertype Company. It became one of the major publishers of souvenir postcards and viewbooks.

The process Joseph Albert developed used negatives as the basis for printing views. For use in their business, the Wittemanns acquired prints from local photographers and also made photographs themselves, traveling throughout the United States. After her husband's death, Mrs. Hermann L. Wittemann presented the Library with tens of thousands of retouched photographs and reproductions produced by the Wittemann and Albertype Companies. Washington, D.C., views are described below. Other Albertype publications are described under "Souvenir Viewbooks."

Aerial view of the Army War College and Fort McNair, ca. 1920. Wittemann Collection, Lot 10181. LC-USZ62-58714

REFERENCES

Vanderbilt, no. 782, p. 166.

LOT 6712

COLLECTION NAME: Wittemann Collection

SUBJECTS: Mount Vernon, Virginia. Interior hallway and stairway, family kitchen, New Jersey Room, New York Room (with life-size painting of George Washington on horseback), bedroom, old brick barn, east and west views of mansion. Washington's Tomb and old Washington family tomb.

DATE: Ca. 1890

PHOTOGRAPHERS: Luke C. Dillon (Pullman's Gallery, "Photographer to Mount Vernon"), C. S. Cudlip & Co., and Mount Vernon Association.

PUBLISHER: Albertype Company.

PHYSICAL DESCRIPTION: 11 albumen cabinet card photographs, 12 × 27 cm.

SOURCE: Gift of Mrs. Gladys G. Wittemann, 1954, and copyright deposit.

LOT 7034

COLLECTION NAME: Wittemann Collection

SUBJECTS: Mount Vernon, Virginia. Wharf with passengers disembarking from a ferry; walkway from the mansion to the Potomac River; gardens; north, west, and east views of the mansion; interior views of the house, including bedrooms, parlor, and music room; outbuildings; Washington's Tomb; souvenir shop and restaurant.

NOTE: Most photographs have been retouched for reproduction.

DATE: Ca. 1936

PHOTOGRAPHERS: G. Tebbs.

PUBLISHER: Albertype Company.

PHYSICAL DESCRIPTION: 18 silver gelatin photoprints, 15 × 19 cm.

SOURCE: Gift of Mrs. Gladys G. Wittemann, 1953, and copyright deposit.

LOT 10181

COLLECTION NAME: Wittemann Collection

SUBJECTS: Aerial views of Washington, D.C. Includes photos of the Smithsonian Institution Building and the Museum of Natural History; the Cannon House Office Building, showing the future sites of the Library of Congress Adams and Madison Buildings; the Library of Congress Jefferson Building and Southeast Capitol Hill neighborhood; Georgetown University; the Navy Department Munitions Building; the Mall at Constitution Avenue between Seventeenth and Nineteenth Streets NW (now Constitution Park); Patent Office; Washington Navy Yard and Anacostia River; Mount Vernon; Bolling Field; Senate Office Building; Bureau of Engraving and Printing; White House; National Bureau of Standards; Union Station; Pension Building; State, War, and Navy Building (now the Old Executive Office Building); Arlington Cemetery and amphitheater; Army War College; Naval Air Station; Central High School; McMillan Reservoir.

DATE: Ca. 1920

PUBLISHER: Albertype Company.

PHYSICAL DESCRIPTION: 21 silver gelatin aerial photoprints, 17 × 23 cm or smaller.

SOURCE: Gift of Mrs. Gladys E. Wittemann, 1953.

LOT 10456

COLLECTION NAME: Wittemann Collection

SUBJECTS: Howard University, Washington, D.C. Exterior views of the Andrew Rankin Chapel; Carnegie Library; Thirkield Science Hall; Clark Hall (men's dormitory), Miner Hall (women's dormitory); sports stadium and gymnasium; interior views of the cooperative bookstore.

DATE: Ca. 1927

PHOTOGRAPHERS: Scurlock Studio.

PUBLISHER: Albertype Company.

PHYSICAL DESCRIPTION: 7 silver gelatin photoprints, 20 × 25 cm.

SOURCE: Gift of Mrs. Gladys G. Wittemann, 1953.

LOT 12524

COLLECTION NAME: Wittemann Collection

SUBJECTS: Strayer's Business College library and music room, Washington, D.C.; Grand Army of the Republic Monument near Seventh Street and Pennsylvania Avenue NW.

PUBLISHER: Albertype Company.

PHYSICAL DESCRIPTION: 2 silver gelatin photoprints, 17 × 24 cm or smaller.

SOURCE: Gift of Mrs. Gladys G. Wittemann, 1953.

Other Sources

Miscellaneous single lots of photographs in the collections of the Prints and Photographs Division that contain items having to do with Washington, D.C., are listed here in numerical order. For large and well-defined groups of materials that have been described here as collections, see "Major Sources" above, where they are listed in alphabetical order by collection name. See also "Browsing Files," below, for other items.

Levin C. Handy. Workers and young assistants at work on the attic octagon during construction of the Library of Congress (Jefferson Building), August 6, 1892. Library of Congress Construction Photographs, Lot 12365.

LC-USL5-404

ATTIC OCTAGON AUG 6TH 1902

LOT 2290

SUBJECTS: Historical material concerning Samuel F. B. Morse and the invention and development of the telegraph. Assembled in connection with an observance on May 24, 1944, of the centennial with a reenactment of the sending of the first message from the Capitol to Baltimore. Washington subjects include joint congressional committee members in the old Supreme Court chamber on the centennial anniversary and Washington telegraph employees and switchboard messengers.

NOTE: All photographs are captioned.

DATE: May 24, 1944

PHOTOGRAPHERS: N.W. Ayer & Son, Inc. (New York).

PHYSICAL DESCRIPTION: 44 silver gelatin photoprints, 20 × 25 cm or smaller.

SOURCE: N.W. Ayer & Son, Inc., New York, New York.

LOT 2350

SUBJECTS: Nurses aides of the local American Red Cross receiving caps and pins; classes; service in hospitals. All are interior views, some taken inside Georgetown University Hospital.

NOTE: All photos are captioned. Produced for the American Red Cross for use in press releases.

DATE: 1941

PHYSICAL DESCRIPTION: 7 silver gelatin photoprints, 20 × 25 cm.

SOURCE: U.S. Office of Civilian Defense.

John Carlyle House, Alexandria, Virginia. Lot 2552.
LC-USZ62-88835

LOT 2351

SUBJECTS: George Washington family homes and birthplaces in Virginia and West Virginia. Includes one view of Mount Vernon.

NOTE: Produced for the U.S. George Washington Bicentennial Commission, Washington, D.C.

DATE: Ca. 1932

PHOTOGRAPHERS: Sol Bloom.

PHYSICAL DESCRIPTION: 11 silver gelatin photoprints, 20 × 25 cm or smaller.

LOT 2423

SUBJECTS: Views of the Capitol; Botanic Garden; White House; Washington Monument; State, War, and Navy Building; Army War College, Tidal Basin; Rock Creek Park; and Mount Vernon. Street scenes during a military parade.

DATE: Ca. 1919

PHYSICAL DESCRIPTION: 1 album (50 silver gelatin photoprints, 11 × 18 cm or smaller).

LOT 2437

SUBJECTS: Portrait photographs of members of the Seventy-eighth Congress.

NOTE: Includes a typescript list of 302 senators and representatives.

DATE: 1943

PHOTOGRAPHERS: Naiman Studios and Chase.

PHYSICAL DESCRIPTION: 19 silver gelatin photoprints, 20 × 25 cm or smaller.

SOURCE: Gift of Senator J. C. Scrugham.

LOT 2438

SUBJECTS: "Living Leaders." Portraits of President Truman and cabinet members.

DATE: 1941–45

PUBLISHER: Living Leaders, Cambridge, Massachusetts.

PHYSICAL DESCRIPTION: 11 halftone photomechanical prints, 20 × 25 cm.

SOURCE: Copyright deposit.

RESTRICTIONS: Copyright by Catherine Howard, 1946.

LOT 2552

SUBJECTS: Capitol Rotunda, Botanic Garden, National Gallery, Pan American Union Building, Daughters of the American Revolution Building, Freer Gallery, new Corcoran Gallery, Renwick Gallery, D.C. City Hall, Taft Bridge on Connecticut Avenue, Rock Creek Park, Aqueduct Bridge in Georgetown, Army War College, interiors of the Northern Liberty Market, Braddock House, Christ Church in Alexandria, an unidentified library, and street scenes.

DATE: 1910–42

PHYSICAL DESCRIPTION: 43 silver gelatin photoprints, 20 × 25 cm.

SOURCE: Gift of the Washingtoniana Division, D.C. Public Library.

The Gen. George McClellan statue, in front of the Highland Apartments at Connecticut Avenue and Columbia Road NW, Washington, D.C. Lot 2553.
LC-USZ62-88834

Northern Liberty Market, Washington, D.C. Lot 2552.
LC-USZ62-88831

LOT 2553

SUBJECTS: Treasury Building, Tomb of the Unknown Soldier of the Civil War, Joseph Wheeler Monument, Daughters of the Confederacy Memorial, Monument to Confederate Dead in Alexandria, and a Connecticut Avenue scene. War memorials, military cemeteries, a military funeral, and a public gathering to dedicate war memorials.

DATE: 1910

PHYSICAL DESCRIPTION: 30 silver gelatin photoprints, 20 × 25 cm.

SOURCE: Gift of the Washingtoniana Division, D.C. Public Library.

LOT 2614

SUBJECTS: Portraits of scientists, collected by C. A. Browne, chief of the U.S. Department of Agriculture. Agricultural chemists and scientists in related fields of general chemistry and pharmacy. Earlier scientists, Archimedes to Priestley. Intermixed with portraits of U.S. and European scientists are portraits and group photos of many who served in some capacity in the Department of Agriculture in Washington, D.C. Some photos show individuals in laboratories; a few show Department of Agriculture interiors.

NOTE: Some images are accompanied by detailed biographical information.

PHYSICAL DESCRIPTION: Ca. 500 vintage and copy photoprints, engravings, and photomechanical prints, 20 × 25 cm or smaller.

ARRANGEMENT: Roughly alphabetical.

SOURCE: Gift of Louise McDaniell Browne, in 1948.

LOT 2858 (stereographs)

SUBJECTS: The Review of the Grand Army of the Republic. A parade down Pennsylvania Avenue shows the army band, black soldiers, mounted military units, and spectators lining the streets.

DATE: September 1892

PUBLISHER: Griffith and Griffith.

PHYSICAL DESCRIPTION: 10 stereographs.

SOURCE: Copyright deposit, October 8, 1892.

Griffith and Griffith (Philadelphia). "Grand Review G.A.R." Grand Army of the Republic parade down Pennsylvania Avenue NW, September 20, 1892. Lot 2858.
LC-USZ62-89123

LOT 2896 (stereographs)

SUBJECTS: Coxey's Army marching to Washington, D.C. Scenes in camp in Washington.

DATE: 1894

PHOTOGRAPHERS: J. F. Jarvis.

PHYSICAL DESCRIPTION: 11 stereographs.

SOURCE: Copyright deposit, May 11, 1894.

LOT 2941

SUBJECTS: Portraits of well-known public and military figures from the Civil War period, including Abraham Lincoln, Jefferson Davis, Ulysses S. Grant, Stonewall Jackson, and other officers in the Union and Confederate armies.

DATE: Ca. 1860–70

PHYSICAL DESCRIPTION: 1 album (ca. 50 carte-de-visite photographs).

SOURCE: Gift of Eleanor Wyllys Allen, 1938.

LOT 2971

SUBJECTS: Photographs of a variety of signs and signposts, public, commercial, and residential, from Washington, D.C., and elsewhere. Sign advertising the Dumbarton community in Washington, D.C.

J. F. Jarvis and Underwood & Underwood. "Gen. Coxey and his Secretary nearing Washington." 1894. Lot 2896.
LC-USZ62-9362

DATE: Ca. 1940s

PHYSICAL DESCRIPTION: 28 silver gelatin photoprints, 20 × 25 cm.

SOURCE: Gift, 1944.

LOT 3017

SUBJECTS: Formal group portraits of American professional baseball teams of 1946. Includes one photograph of the Washington Senators.

NOTE: All photographs captioned.

DATE: 1946

PUBLISHER: Sporting News Publishing Company.

PHYSICAL DESCRIPTION: 15 silver gelatin photoprints.

SOURCE: Copyright deposit, 1947.

Sporting News Publishing Company. Washington Senators baseball team, 1947. Lot 3017.

LC-USZ62-88865

LOT 3177

SUBJECTS: "Burnside Post No. 8, Department of the Potomac, Grand Army of the Republic." Portrait photographs of aged members of the Grand Army of the Republic. Only eleven members of the Burnside Post No. 8 were living in 1914, and the oldest was 101 years of age.

DATE: 1914

PHOTOGRAPHERS: Clinedinst Studio.

PHYSICAL DESCRIPTION: 1 album (181 silver gelatin photoprints, 13 × 18 cm).

SOURCE: Gift of Francis J. Young, 1930.

LOT 3189 (stereographs)

SUBJECTS: Baltimore & Ohio Railroad Centenary Exhibition pageant, Baltimore (Halethorpe), Maryland. Pictures of crowds, ceremonies, Transportation Hall, and exhibits and floats passing on a track before the grandstand. One float shows "Abraham Lincoln, Martyred President"

George Barrie. Commandant's Residence, Washington Navy Yard, 1888. Lot 3259.

LC-USZ62-90015

arriving in Washington in 1861 on the B&O Railroad. A canal boat float depicts the towpath, mule, and driver. A double float shows S. F. B. Morse sending the first telegraph message in 1844, and includes a painting of the Capitol. Included are images of the Capitol Limited (the all-Pullman daily service), and the "No. 1310" (a high-speed passenger locomotive of 1896), both of which ran between Washington and major cities. In addition, one image shows the Thomas Jefferson, the first train to run in Virginia.

NOTE: Descriptive and historical information is found on the verso of each stereograph.

DATE: September 24–October 16, 1927

PHYSICAL DESCRIPTION: 108 silver gelatin stereographs.

LOT 3239

SUBJECTS: White House rooms during Theodore Roosevelt's administration: his bedroom, the rooms of Alice and Ethel Roosevelt, the state dining rooms, the telegraph office, bathrooms, the Red Room, Green Room, Grand Corridor wing, kitchen, gardens, and terrace. Includes views of the Cabinet Room in the Executive Office Building and other interiors, as well as a view down Sixteenth Street from the White House.

DATE: 1902

PHOTOGRAPHERS: Clinedinst.

PHYSICAL DESCRIPTION: 18 silver gelatin photoprints, 20 × 25 cm.

SOURCE: Copyright deposit by Clinedinst, Washington, D.C.

LOT 3259

SUBJECTS: Miscellaneous naval photographs. Washington images include one view of the Commandant's Residence at the Washington Navy Yard, three pictures of captured guns, and George Washington's and General Jackson's uniforms.

NOTE: Some images are captioned.

DATE: 1888

PHOTOGRAPHERS: George Barrie.

PHYSICAL DESCRIPTION: 31 albumen photoprints, 20 × 25 cm.

SOURCE: Copyright deposit by George Barrie, 1888.

Post Office Department (Old Post Office), Pennsylvania Avenue NW. Lot 3402.

LC-USZ62-90016

LOT 3329

SUBJECTS: Funeral of Dr. Thomas De Witt Talmage, clergyman. Coffin being carried from home to hearse, then to church; Washington notables attending funeral. Includes view of Talmage residence, funeral parlor, and church.

DATE: 1902

PHOTOGRAPHERS: Abby G. Baker.

PHYSICAL DESCRIPTION: 13 silver gelatin photoprints, 13 × 18 cm.

SOURCE: Copyright deposit by Abby G. Baker, 1902.

LOT 3402

SUBJECTS: Copy photographs of portraits and historical material relating to the U.S. Post Office. Portraits of postmasters general, early departmental buildings, mail ships, mail coach, crowds receiving mail in San Francisco, army camp delivery, Washington Post Office officials. Copy of August Köllner lithograph of Old Post Office in Washington.

DATE: Ca. 1860–1940s

PHOTOGRAPHERS: Harris & Ewing, Scherer, and American Press Association (New York).

PHYSICAL DESCRIPTION: 22 silver gelatin photoprints, 20 × 25 cm.

SOURCE: Gift of George F. Grayson, 1946.

LOT 3425

SUBJECTS: "Washington Walkbook." Rustic, undeveloped scenic areas in and around Washington, particularly on the Potomac River. Views of Great Falls, C&O Canal, canal barges, Canal Road and trolley, lock tavern at Great Falls, Little Falls, Pennyfield Lock, Stubblefield Falls, Mather Gorge, Chain Bridge, Cabin John Bridge, Cleft Island, stone gate at Scott's Run, Prospect Rock, Harper's Ferry, Burnt Mills (Maryland), Potomac River near Glen Echo; "Spring in Rock Creek Park," bridges in Rock Creek Park, Fairfax (Virginia) Court House, Sugarloaf Mountain, Fort Barnard trenches, summits of the Blue Ridge, Riggs Mill (Maryland), Rock Creek Cemetery, the Pan American Union Building gardens, Aqueduct Bridge, Mount Vernon, St. Paul's Church, Smithsonian Institution, St. John's Church, Franklin Park, apse of the Washington Cathedral, Arlington Cemetery, Old Soldiers' Home, view of Washington from the Virginia side of the Potomac, and Georgetown.

NOTE: This notebook, titled "Washington Walkbook," was apparently intended for publication by the American Geographical Society, New York, in 1922. Includes sketches, watercolors, photographic views, and a typed introduction by Robert Latou Dickinson. The Manuscript Division holds a typewritten literary manuscript by Robert Latou Dickinson, a gift of the author in 1942.

DATE: Ca. 1918

PHOTOGRAPHERS: Harris & Ewing, F. L. Scribner, Ernest L. Crandall, and Charles Martin.

PHYSICAL DESCRIPTION: 1 notebook (ca. 85 original pen, pencil, and pastel drawings, 23 silver gelatin photoprints, and 5 reproductions, 20 × 25 cm or smaller).

SOURCE: Gift of Robert Latou Dickinson, 1941.

LOT 3585

SUBJECTS: "Library Planning." Reproductions of architectural plans, engravings, and photographs of well-known libraries all over the world. Seven of the images and drawings pertain to the Library of Congress.

DATE: Ca. 1895–1910

PHYSICAL DESCRIPTION: 2 albums (ca. 150 halftone photomechanical prints).

SOURCE: Gift of Herbert G. Putnam, Librarian Emeritus of Congress.

LOT 3723

SUBJECTS: Japanese social and diplomatic activities in New York City and Washington, D.C., before the attack on Pearl Harbor. Fewer than 50 images are identifiable as having been made in Washington; these include pictures taken inside the Japanese Embassy in February 1941 and photo-graphs of the Cherry Blossom Festival, April 1941.

NOTE: Photographs are captioned in English.

DATE: 1938–41

PHYSICAL DESCRIPTION: Albums (ca. 400 silver gelatin photoprints).

SOURCE: Transfer from the U.S. Coordinator of Information Library.

LOT 3860

SUBJECTS: Informal snapshot views of people on a holiday, and on the White House grounds, young boys gathered around a waffle-vendor, and a bearded young man in a top hat carrying an early Kodak camera. Street scenes show Pennsylvania Avenue flooded, a horse car in the snow-covered streets, Franklin Park around a home at 900 Fourteenth Street NW, and on downtown F Street NW. Includes pictures of a boiler factory explosion and the Evening Star Building fire.

DATE: Ca. 1885–ca. 1895

PHYSICAL DESCRIPTION: 100 albumen photoprints, 20 × 25 cm or smaller, most 8 cm or 12 cm circular images on 11 × 13 cm mounts, taken with early models of Kodak cameras.

SOURCE: Gift of the Chester County Historical Society of Westchester, Pennsylvania, 1949.

"Panorama of Great Falls," from "Washington Walkbook," ca. 1918. Lot 3425.
LC-USZ62-92540

The Old Ebbitt Hotel, Washington, D.C., ca. 1885–95. Lot 3860.
LC-USZ62-46464

Cushings & Bailey and Hagadorn Brothers (Baltimore). "Washington Depot with U.S. Capitol in the distance." From Photographic Views of the Baltimore and Ohio Rail Road and Its Branches from the Lakes to the Sea. Ca. 1860s–72. Lot 3864.
LC-USZ62-28100

LOT 3864

SUBJECTS: "Photographic Views of the Baltimore and Ohio Rail Road and Its Branches from the Lakes to the Sea." Scenes along the B&O Railway route of mountain and river scenery, cities and towns, hotels, railroad stations, mills, cement works, coke furnaces, railroad repair shops and rolling mills, and bridges and tunnels. Views taken in the Washington area include the Bladensburg station, the Arlington Hotel, the Washington Depot with the U.S. Capitol in the background, the Relay House, Washington Junctions, and the Potomac River. Includes Baltimore scenes. Harpers Ferry and bridge photographs show C&O Canal.

NOTE: Photographs captioned.

DATE: Ca. 1860s–1872

PUBLISHER: Cushings & Bailey and Hagadorn Brothers (Baltimore, 1872).

PHYSICAL DESCRIPTION: 1 album (128 albumen photoprints, 18 × 25 cm or smaller).

SOURCE: Purchase, 1949.

LOT 3896

SUBJECTS: Construction and other public works projects in various parts of the United States, executed by the U.S. Works Progress Administration, the U.S. Public Works Administration, and the U.S. Public Roads Administration, including schools,

Fairchild Aerial Surveys (New York). Smithsonian Institution Museum of Natural History and Pennsylvania Avenue NW area of downtown Washington. Ca. 1930s. Lot 3903.
LC-USZ62-90011

playgrounds, craft shops, bridges, roads, and parks. Washington views include Rosedale playground and Washington National Airport Administration Building. Also includes a plan for a garage, store, and office development for the central retail district in the city.

NOTE: Photographs produced as part of the "1944 Transportation Survey and Plan for the General Area of Washington, D.C."

DATE: 1934–40

PHYSICAL DESCRIPTION: 56 silver gelatin photoprints, 20 × 25 cm.

SOURCE: Transfer from the U.S. Bureau of Public Roads.

LOT 3903

SUBJECTS: Aerial views of the capital and metropolitan area, including the Southwest waterfront area, the Tidal Basin before Jefferson Memorial construction, the Federal Triangle, Foggy Bottom area, Smithsonian Institution buildings and the Mall, Union Station and Capitol Hill, the White House, downtown business district, and temporary World War II buildings on the Mall.

NOTE: Album title: "Aerial Views of Washington."

DATE: Ca. 1930–40

PHOTOGRAPHERS: Fairchild Aerial Surveys, Inc. (New York).

PHYSICAL DESCRIPTION: 1 album (27 silver gelatin photoprints, 41 × 41 cm and 21 × 21 cm).

SOURCE: Transfer from the U.S. Treasury Department, 1944.

LOT 3923

SUBJECTS: Scenic views of Washington and its environs, used in an exhibit. Includes Civil War scenes, the Capitol dome under construction, Post Office Building, Jefferson Memorial and Tidal Basin, White House interiors and exteriors, including the Easter egg roll and peanut vendors on the White House grounds, Washington Monument, Lincoln Memorial, C&O Canal boats, fisherman's boat docked at wharf in Southwest Washington, the Brazilian and Japanese Embassies, Chain Bridge, Stoddert House in Georgetown, and the Elephant House at the National Zoo.

DATE: Ca. 1940–45

PHYSICAL DESCRIPTION: 17 silver gelatin photoprints, 41 × 51 cm.

SOURCE: Transfer from the Federal Works Agency, 1943.

LOT 4000

SUBJECTS: Equestrian statues. American and European national heroes, mythological and allegorical figures. Includes some commercially distributed nineteenth-century travel views.

NOTE: Accompanied by voluminous articles, notes, and correspondence.

DATE: Ca. 1890–1910

PHYSICAL DESCRIPTION: Ca. 2,000 albumen and silver gelatin photographs and photographic reproductions and original engravings and drawings; newspaper and magazine clippings, souvenir viewbooks, 28 × 36 cm or smaller. Assembled in 4 volumes.

ARRANGEMENT: Two volumes contain clippings; two volumes contain photographs and other visual materials. Within each volume, items are arranged roughly alphabetically by statue name.

SOURCE: Gift of S. H. and R. Kauffman, 1906 and 1924.

LOT 4021

SUBJECTS: Construction of the Coolidge Auditorium in the Jefferson Building of the Library of Congress. Hoisting beams, bricklaying, and other views of construction work in the inner courtyard of the Jefferson Building.

NOTE: Photographs stamped on verso: "U.S. Capitol, a pictorial history by John Crane."

DATE: 1925

PHYSICAL DESCRIPTION: 6 silver gelatin photoprints, 20 × 25 cm.

LOT 4071

SUBJECTS: The White House, Washington, D.C. Photographic reproductions of architectural drawings. Floor plans and elevations of proposed additions by F. A. Owen and others. Rendered drawings by Jules Guérin. Interior views by Alfred Brennan. Includes Jarvis photographs of later model proposed by Theodore Bingham.

NOTE: Album cover titled "Photos and Text suggestions of Mrs. Benjamin Harrison for the Betterment of the Executive Mansion 1891. Presented to The White House Library by Mr. Fred D. Owen, Archt."

DATE: Ca. 1890–ca. 1900

PHOTOGRAPHERS: J. F. Jarvis.

PHYSICAL DESCRIPTION: 23 photostats, halftone photomechanical prints, drawings, and albumen and silver gelatin photoprints, 28 × 36 cm or smaller.

SOURCE: Gift of Mrs. H. S. Owen of Stonington, Connecticut, 1932.

LOT 4150

SUBJECTS: U.S. Capitol, White House, and government buildings in Washington, D.C. Includes Capitol grounds, unoccupied House and Senate chambers, and Statuary Hall. State, War, and Navy Building (now the Old Executive Office Building); White House facade and driveway; Treasury Building and Pennsylvania Avenue with streetcar and horse-drawn wagon; and views overlooking city and Washington Monument.

NOTE: Series has Bonine numbers, 240–62. Nine numbers wanting.

DATE: Ca. 1891

PHOTOGRAPHERS: R. K. Bonine (Tyrone, Pennsylvania).

PUBLISHER: R. K. Bonine.

PHYSICAL DESCRIPTION: 13 stereographs, 9 × 18 cm.

SOURCE: Copyright deposit by Bonine, 1891.

Lt. Comdr. Edward Steichen, USN, Bureau of Aeronautics. Secretary of the Navy Frank Knox. Lot 4263.

LC-USZ62-92897

LOT 4263

SUBJECTS: Photographs of Secretary of the U.S. Navy Frank Knox (1874–1944), documenting his travels around the world, speeches, receptions, dinners, and military reviews. Includes inspection tours of North Africa, Sicily, Hawaii, and the Southwest Pacific, trips to England and Brazil; victory loan speeches, naval inspection tour with President Roosevelt, and his funeral, attended by notables. Includes portraits of Knox with cabinet members and Franklin D. Roosevelt; Secretary Knox's press conferences at the Navy Department in 1942; the Navy Department staff; presentation of medals and awards in the Navy Department; Knox with President Hoover and with General Eisenhower; the Knox funeral procession passing near the Navy Department; and a portrait of Knox by Lt. Comdr. Edward Steichen (1942).

DATE: Most ca. 1930–44

PHYSICAL DESCRIPTION: 8 albums (ca. 800 silver gelatin photoprints and newspaper clippings), 28 × 36 cm or smaller.

SOURCE: Gift of Mrs. Frank Knox, 1950.

LOT 4299

SUBJECTS: Portraits of members of the Senate and House of Representatives, the president, vice president, cabinet members, and U.S. Supreme Court justices.

Plew. Interior of the Knickerbocker Theatre, Washington, D.C., after the weight of accumulated snow on the roof caused its collapse. Police and firemen are looking for bodies under the rubble, January 28, 1922. Lot 4317.

LC-USZ62-10975

DATE: 1921

PUBLISHER: Consolidated Publishing Company.

PHYSICAL DESCRIPTION: Booklet of photomechanical prints.

LOT 4317

SUBJECTS: Knickerbocker Theatre after the roof collapsed under the weight of a heavy accumulation of snow. Interior and exterior views showing firemen and policemen looking for bodies; twisted steel beams, views of the stage and interior.

DATE: 1922

PHOTOGRAPHERS: Plew.

PHYSICAL DESCRIPTION: 7 silver gelatin photoprints, 11 × 13 cm.

SOURCE: Copyright deposit by Plew, 1922.

LOT 4380

SUBJECTS: Library of Congress. Interior views of the Jefferson Building, including the Great Hall and reading rooms. Interior and exterior views of the Adams Building.

PHYSICAL DESCRIPTION: 4 silver gelatin photoprints.

LOT 4505

SUBJECTS: Construction of the Cabin John Bridge and Washington Aqueduct. The bridge at different stages of construction; workmen and building materials, including blocks of roughly cut stone.

NOTE: One photograph dated "June 8, 1859."

DATE: 1859

PHYSICAL DESCRIPTION: 2 albumen photoprints, 20 × 25 cm.

SOURCE: Transfer from the U.S. War Department, 1919.

LOT 4541

SUBJECTS: Buildings in Washington, D.C., and scenes in the country. Includes views of the British Legation in Washington, D.C., homes on Connecticut Avenue NW, unidentified groups of people, family outings in horse carriages, graveyards, lake resorts, home interiors. Also includes identified scenes in Appomattox, City Point, and Hampton, Virginia, and Glen Cove (Long Island), New York.

NOTE: Some photographs are dated 1886. Some are badly faded.

DATE: Ca. 1886

PHYSICAL DESCRIPTION: 1 album (ca. 85 albumen photoprints, 13 × 18 cm or smaller).

LOT 4546

SUBJECTS: Clara Barton tree-planting ceremony, 1922. Unidentified elderly men and women, Red Cross nurses, and spectators.

Cabin John Bridge under construction, 1859. Lot 4505.

LC-USZ62-78665

DATE: 1922

PHOTOGRAPHERS: R.J. Bonde and Sons.

PHYSICAL DESCRIPTION: 7 silver gelatin photoprints.

SOURCE: Copyright deposit by R.J. Bonde and Sons, 1922.

LOT 4582

SUBJECTS: Martha Carr, geologist of the U.S. Geological Survey, examining rocks along the banks of the Potomac River, and walking through the gateposts of the National Zoological Park, with two young companions. Includes views of the cornerstone of the District of Columbia (Federal Territory) at Jones Point, Alexandria, Virginia; photographs of a dinosaur bone and of a drawing of a brontosaurus.

NOTE: Photographs are fully captioned. Martha Carr is the author of *The District of Columbia: Its Rocks and Their Geologic History.*

DATE: Ca. 1948–49

PHOTOGRAPHERS: U.S. Geological Survey.

PHYSICAL DESCRIPTION: 8 silver gelatin photoprints, 20 × 25 cm or smaller.

SOURCE: Transfer from the U.S. Geological Survey, 1949.

LOT 4586

SUBJECTS: Dedication of the shrine of the Declaration of Independence and the Constitution at the Library of Congress, in the presence of President Calvin Coolidge, Secretary of State Charles Evans Hughes, Librarian of Congress Herbert Putnam, and other high officials. Includes photographs of Herbert Putnam carrying the Constitution and placing it in the shrine in the Jefferson Building of the Library of Congress; children visiting the shrine; and Arline Brook, "Columbia," at the dedication, standing with navy, army, and marine guards.

DATE: 1925

PHOTOGRAPHERS: Underwood & Underwood and Leet Bros.

PHYSICAL DESCRIPTION: 10 silver gelatin photoprints, 23 × 33 cm or smaller.

SOURCE: Purchase and gift, 1929.

RESTRICTIONS: Permission may be required for publication or commercial use of Underwood & Underwood images.

LOT 4632

SUBJECTS: Library of Congress Jefferson Building exterior and interior views. Main Reading Room, gallery, and details of murals, sculpture, lighting fixtures, arches, doors, and fireplaces.

NOTE: Collotypes are by the Heliotype Printing Company, Boston.

DATE: 1897–98

PUBLISHER: American Architect and Building News Company

PHYSICAL DESCRIPTION: 19 collotypes, 26 × 35 cm.

SOURCE: Copyright deposit by the American Architect and Building News Company, 1898.

LOT 4719

SUBJECTS: National Capital Parks amusement and recreational facilities. Tennis courts on the Mall, golf links, children's sandbox in Lincoln Park, and horseshoe courts. Includes views of the President's Cup Regatta, C&O Canal hike, ice-skating on the Lincoln Memorial reflecting pool, archery, canal barge rides, Watergate floating symphony concerts, horseback riding and picnicking in Rock Creek Park, rose

American Architect and Building News Company. The mantle in the House of Representatives Reading Room in the Library of Congress (Jefferson Building), ca. 1897–98. Lot 4632.

LC-USZ62-90207

gardens, cherry blossoms, *Times-Herald* Art Fair, Fourth of July celebrations, Washington Monument relighted on V-E Day, bicycling, soccer, and softball on the Mall.

NOTE: Produced by the U.S. National Capital Parks.

DATE: 1938–45

PHYSICAL DESCRIPTION: 25 silver gelatin photoprints, 20 × 25 cm.

SOURCE: Gift of George Galloway, 1950.

LOT 4804

SUBJECTS: Aerial and high views of Washington, D.C., from various sources, all featuring Union Station and plaza, and the Senate Office Building.

NOTE: Most photographs are dated. Some reproductions are from the *Washington Star.*

DATE: Ca. 1907–39

PHYSICAL DESCRIPTION: 6 silver gelatin photoprints, 20 × 25 cm.

SOURCE: Gift of George Schwegmann.

U.S. National Capital Parks. C&O Canal hike, 1943. Lot 4719.

LC-USZ62-90447

Barr-Farnham Picture Postcard Company. "Washington Base Ball Club. 1909." Lot 4927.

LC-USZ62-90434

LOT 4806

SUBJECTS: "New York and Washington Views." Washington views (7) include photographs of the Capitol, U.S. Treasury Building, Washington Monument, Library of Congress, and Pennsylvania Avenue. Also includes street scenes, public buildings, and country scenes in New York and Arkansas.

NOTE: Manuscript cover dated July 1906.

DATE: Ca. 1906

PHOTOGRAPHERS: Paul C. Lange (Little Rock, Arkansas).

PHYSICAL DESCRIPTION: 1 album (35 silver gelatin photoprints, 13 × 16 cm or smaller), 19 × 26 cm.

LOT 4807

SUBJECTS: Washington, D.C., landmarks and buildings. Capitol exterior and interior, Smithsonian Institution, White House exterior and interior, U.S. Treasury Building, Agriculture Department, Washington Monument, Potomac River. Arlington Cemetery, Lee Mansion, Arlington Hotel, and the David Burnes cottage. Thomas and Scott statues, Horatio Greenough's statue *The Rescue,* and the Emancipation statue.

NOTE: Photographs are faded.

DATE: Ca. 1890–1900

PHYSICAL DESCRIPTION: 1 album (25 albumen photoprints, 10 × 12 cm), 16 × 19 cm.

LOT 4823

SUBJECTS: Views in Philadelphia, Niagara Falls, and Washington, D.C. Washington subjects include the U.S. Capitol before construction of the dome or extensions (July 1850); the East Front and northeast

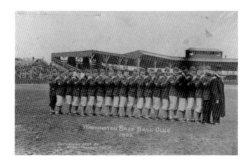

views of the Capitol (July 1850); the State Department Building and Treasury Building (July 1850); the White House (July 1850); the City Hall (July 1850); Mount Vernon and Washington's Tomb (July 1850); Washington Navy Yard (July 1850). Also includes portraits of President Millard Fillmore, Zachary Taylor, and Winfield Scott.

NOTE: Album titled "Views in North America." Frederick Langenheim and his brother William were the first to produce stereographs commercially in America. They were instrumental in forming the American Stereoscopic Company.

DATE: Ca. 1840–ca. 1860

PHOTOGRAPHERS: W.&F. Langenheim.

PHYSICAL DESCRIPTION: 49 silver gelatin copy photoprints of original salted paper prints in stereo-half format, 28 × 36 cm or smaller.

SOURCE: Original album from the Eduard Robyn Collection, Missouri Historical Society, lent to the Library for copying, 1951.

LOT 4927

SUBJECTS: "The Washington Base Ball Club of 1909." Informal portraits of each player, all made in a ballpark with stands in the background. One group portrait of the entire team. Portraits of the trainer, manager, and "rubber."

NOTE: Photographs are captioned.

DATE: 1909

PUBLISHER: Barr-Farnham Picture Post Card Company.

PHYSICAL DESCRIPTION: 21 silver gelatin photoprints, 16 × 11 cm.

SOURCE: Copyright deposit by Barr-Farnham Picture Post Card Company, 1909.

LOT 4942

SUBJECTS: Monuments, tombs, burial places, and gravestones erected in memory of U.S. presidents from George Washington through William McKinley. Includes one photograph of George Washington's Tomb at Mount Vernon.

DATE: Ca. 1908

PHYSICAL DESCRIPTION: 24 silver gelatin photoprints, 14 × 9 cm.

SOURCE: Copyright deposit, 1908.

LOT 5016

SUBJECTS: Diplomatic representatives and members of their staffs from China, Chile, Japan, and Korea, posed in open automobiles in Washington. Portraits of Mr. and Mrs. Henderson, Countess Cassini, and others.

NOTE: Photographs are captioned and dated.

DATE: Ca. 1904

PHOTOGRAPHERS: B. M. Clinedinst.

PHYSICAL DESCRIPTION: 15 silver gelatin photoprints, 11 × 13 cm.

SOURCE: Copyright deposit by B. M. Clinedinst, 1904.

LOT 5042

SUBJECTS: Photographs of a series of 7 mural paintings, executed by Frederick Dielman for the Evening Star Building in Washington, some of which show well-known Washington structures in the background. Includes "Typography," "Newsgathering," "The Diffusion of Intelligence," "Steam and Electricity," "Commerce, Manufacture and Advertising," "Art, History, and Literature," and "Justice, Instruction, and Moderation."

NOTE: Includes copy of newspaper descriptions of the murals.

DATE: Ca. 1901

PHYSICAL DESCRIPTION: 7 albumen photoprints, 19 × 34 cm.

SOURCE: Copyright deposit by Frederick Dielman, 1901.

LOT 5045

SUBJECTS: Jefferson and Adams Buildings of the Library of Congress. Photographic copies of various floor plans, book collection growth charts, the will of Joseph Pennell (a donor), letters and drawings by Thomas Jefferson, and the Magna Carta. Photographs of the Declaration of Independence and Constitution shrine, Main Reading Room, and Adams Building reading room.

NOTE: Includes press releases and explanatory notes.

DATE: Ca. 1897–1945

PHOTOGRAPHERS: Haines Photo Company and Pix.

Clinedinst. The Chilean minister and his secretary. Copyright 1904. Lot 5016.

LC-USZ62-90454

PHYSICAL DESCRIPTION: 51 silver gelatin photoprints, architectural drawings, and thermographic copies, 51 × 61 cm or smaller.

SOURCE: Transfer from the Information Office, 1951.

LOT 5087

SUBJECTS: Tourist attractions in Washington, D.C., New Mexico, France, Germany, Italy, and Vienna. Washington images include 7 carte-de-visite photographs by Bell & Bro. studio of the Brumidi fresco inside the Capitol dome.

DATE: Ca. 1860–90

PHOTOGRAPHERS: Bell & Bro.

PHYSICAL DESCRIPTION: 25 carte-de-visite and cabinet card photographs and a postcard.

SOURCE: Gift of Edith Allen, 1951.

LOT 5102

SUBJECTS: Herb Garden Shop at the Washington Cathedral, Washington, D.C. Shop interior, jars of herbs, pinecones, and booklets, arranged on shelves and on the floor of the shop. A nearby section of the garden with beehives and the "dipping" pool.

NOTE: Photographs are captioned.

DATE: Ca. 1935

PHYSICAL DESCRIPTION: 4 silver gelatin photoprints and 1 explanatory chart, 20 × 25 cm.

SOURCE: Copyright deposit, 1935.

*Alfred Eisenstaedt for Pix Incorporated (New York). Library of Congress reading room (Adams Building), ca. 1940s. Lot 5045. Copyright © Alfred Eisenstaedt–*Life *Magazine. Used with permission.*

LOT 5183

SUBJECTS: Portfolio of photographs of architectural details and murals of the Library of Congress Jefferson Building. View of the exterior front elevation, Grand Entrance, Grand Staircase, gallery of the rotunda (Herodotus and Beethoven statues), Main Reading Room, Representatives Reading Room, bookstacks, corridor of the main entrance hall, and corridor of the Congressional Reading Room. Includes photographic copies of mosaic "Minerva" (designed by E. Vedder), and murals by E. Vedder ("Anarchy" and "Corrupt Legislation"), H. O. Walker ("Comus," "The Boy of Winander," "Adonis," "Uriel," "Ganymede," "Endymion," and "Lyric Poetry"), J. W. Alexander ("Manuscript Book," "Printing Press," "Picture Writing," and "Hieroglyphics"), Gari Melchers ("War" and "Peace"), and E. H. Blashfield (rotunda dome and "Evolution of Civilization").

NOTE: Portfolio may have been prepared to illustrate Herbert Small, *Handbook of the New Library of Congress* (Boston: Curtis & Cameron, 1897). Cover page reads, "Library of Congress, Washington D.C. National Library Founded 1800, Building Erected 1897, [Number of] Volumes 1899, 957,056."

DATE: Ca. 1897–1900

PHOTOGRAPHERS: Some images bear "Copley Print" label.

PHYSICAL DESCRIPTION: 24 silver gelatin photoprints, 36 × 44 cm or smaller, mounted.

SOURCE: Copyright deposit by Curtis & Cameron, 1897.

LOT 5200

SUBJECTS: White House china used by Woodrow Wilson and other U.S. presidents. Gold-bordered service plates, the Dolley Madison fruit bowl with large pedestal and classic figurines, an oyster dish and cocktail cup from the State dining set, decanters and wine glasses.

NOTE: Photographs are captioned.

DATE: Ca. 1918

PHYSICAL DESCRIPTION: 8 silver gelatin photoprints, 20 × 25 cm.

SOURCE: Copyright deposit, 1918.

LOT 5305

SUBJECTS: Panoramic views of a Grand Army of the Republic parade in Washington, D.C., in 1902. Marching men, some in uniform; mounted policemen, crowds, hawkers of souvenirs. Views of the U.S. Treasury Building, Rhodes Tavern, Post Office, and Pennsylvania Avenue buildings.

DATE: 1902

PHOTOGRAPHERS: Falk (New York).

PHYSICAL DESCRIPTION: 3 palladium photoprints, 25 × 74 cm.

SOURCE: Copyright deposit by Falk, 1902.

LOT 5313

COLLECTION NAME: Benjamin Harrison Papers, Manuscript Division

SUBJECTS: White House collection of formal portraits of babies and small children, many of whom were named for President Benjamin Harrison, presented to the president. Many portraits of twins and triplets, including one C. M. Bell portrait of triplets ''born December 17, 1890, photo June 11, 1890 [sic]. Children of Mr. and Mrs. Patrick Brennan, 1818 L St. NW, Washington, D.C.'' Includes one portrait of Henry Irving. Also includes a few portraits of adults, views of the Dolsen homestead, Tecumseh Park, the battlefield at Thames, Ontario, and the pipe of peace smoked after the battle of Tippecanoe.

BIOGRAPHICAL NOTE: The Manuscript Division holds the papers of U.S. president

''The Dipping Pool in the Cottage Herb Garden, Mount Saint Albans, Washington, D.C.'' National Cathedral. Copyright 1935. Lot 5102.
LC-USZ62-90441

and army officer Benjamin Harrison. The correspondence, notebooks, speeches, scrapbooks, and memorabilia span the years 1787–1938, number 69,600 items, and are accompanied by a finding aid. The papers include material related to the Civil War, Harrison's presidency, Indiana politics, and the Venezuela boundary dispute. They were acquired through gift and purchase, 1901–60. The photographs were transferred to the Prints and Photographs Division.

DATE: Ca. 1889–ca. 1892

PHOTOGRAPHERS: C. M. Bell and various other studios.

PHYSICAL DESCRIPTION: Ca. 100 albumen carte-de-visite, cabinet card, and silver gelatin photoprints, tintypes, and silhouettes, 20 × 25 cm or smaller.

Herodotus and Beethoven statues in the gallery of the rotunda, Library of Congress (Jefferson Building), ca. 1897–1900. Lot 5183.
LC-USZ62-92215

SOURCE: Transfer from the Manuscript Division.

LOT 5336

SUBJECTS: Informal portraits of the envoy extraordinary and minister plenipotentiary of Ireland with family at home. Father and son playing chess, and views of the Irish Legation in Washington.

DATE: Ca. 1941–42

PHYSICAL DESCRIPTION: 10 silver gelatin photoprints, 20 × 25 cm.

LOT 5338

SUBJECTS: Young children in open-air schools. Facilities for normal, tubercular, anemic, and myopic children in the United States and several foreign countries. Montessori methods, furniture, and toys in use. Some old one-room schoolhouses. Washington-area materials include open-air education at Mackin playground in Georgetown; and black students at Miner Normal School learning to brush their teeth.

DATE: Ca. 1900–1925

PHOTOGRAPHERS: Underwood & Underwood.

PHYSICAL DESCRIPTION: Ca. 2,500 silver gelatin photoprints and photomechanical prints, 36 × 44 cm or smaller.

ARRANGEMENT: Alphabetical by geographical location.

SOURCE: Purchase from Mrs. L. D. Goldsberry, Tacoma Park, Maryland, 1926, and other sources.

Charles K. Stellwagen. View of the Capitol showing an undeveloped Independence Avenue SW, ca. 1866. Lot 5341.
LC-USZ62-56556

LOT 5341

SUBJECTS: Souvenir set of photographs of the Capitol (Senate wing and East Front portico, and a view from Pennsylvania Avenue), White House, U.S. Treasury Building, Washington Monument, State Department, General Post Office, Patent Office, Interior Department, "Quartermaster General's Office" (Corcoran's Art Gallery, now the Renwick Gallery), Old Soldiers' Home, Blair House, Lee House, Smithsonian Institution Building, equestrian statues by Clark Mills (Andrew Jackson and George Washington), and Horatio Greenough's statue of George Washington.

DATE: Ca. 1866

PHOTOGRAPHERS: Attributed to Charles K. Stellwagen.

PHYSICAL DESCRIPTION: 16 albumen photoprints, 13 × 21 cm.

SOURCE: Gift of Louis M. Rabinowitz, 1952.

LOT 5458

SUBJECTS: Snapshots showing the Mellon Memorial Fountain under construction at Sixth Street and Pennsylvania Avenue NW, Washington, D.C.

NOTE: Photographs are captioned.

DATE: 1950

PHYSICAL DESCRIPTION: 32 silver gelatin photoprints, 12 × 9 cm.

SOURCE: Gift of Everett B. Anderson, 1951.

LOT 5462

SUBJECTS: Record photographs of bas-relief marble portrait plaques installed over the House of Representatives Gallery doors, U.S. Capitol, Washington. Subjects include Alfonso the Wise, Blackstone, Colbert, Edward I, Gaius, Gregory IX, Grotius, Hammurabi, Innocent III, Thomas Jefferson, Justinian, St. Louis, Lycurgus, Maimonides, George Mason, Simon de Montfort, Moses, Napoleon, Papinian, Pothier, Solon, Suleyman the Magnificent, and Tribonian.

NOTE: Photographs are captioned.

DATE: 1950–51

PHOTOGRAPHERS: Architect of the Capitol staff photographers.

PHYSICAL DESCRIPTION: 23 silver gelatin photoprints, 20 × 25 cm.

SOURCE: Printed from negatives in the custody of the Architect of the Capitol.

LOT 5510

SUBJECTS: Progress photographs made during construction of the new Department of Interior Building. Photographs show workers leveling the site, excavating, and laying the foundation. View of the limestone and granite storage yard, typical under-floor ducts, and roofing. Aerial views of the completed building.

NOTE: Photographs captioned, dated, and numbered. Produced for George A. Fuller Company, builders.

DATE: 1935–37

PHOTOGRAPHERS: Commercial Photo Company.

PHYSICAL DESCRIPTION: 83 silver gelatin photoprints, 20 × 25 cm.

SOURCE: Transfer from the Department of the Interior, 1951.

LOT 5713

SUBJECTS: Color transparencies under the general title "Miscellaneous Travelog." Forty-six Washington-area views include the U.S. Capitol, Lincoln Memorial, Jefferson Memorial, Washington Monument, Treasury Building and Alexander Hamilton statue, Supreme Court building, National Gallery, Rock Creek Park, Arlington Memorial Bridge, General Meade statue, Lafayette statue, and Arlington Cemetery and the Tomb of the Unknown Soldier. Also scenes in Alexandria, including Prince Street and Gadsby's Tavern. Other subjects include Wakefield and Manassas, Virginia; dams, mountains, and lakes in Washington State; erosion patterns, and wheat fields in Montana; mines in Idaho; orange groves and dams in California; range stock in Montana; Fort Ticonderoga, New York; Caledonia State Park in Pennsylvania; and the 1951 Missouri River flood.

NOTE: Accompanied by card index.

DATE: Ca. 1951

PHOTOGRAPHERS: William E. Warne.

PHYSICAL DESCRIPTION: 194 color transparencies (35 mm), in 5 × 5 cm mounts.

SOURCE: Gift of William E. Warne, 1952.

Commercial Photo Company. Newly constructed Interior Department Building, January 9, 1937. Lot 5510.

LC-USZ62-90436

LOT 5732

SUBJECTS: American colonial buildings restored by Thomas T. Waterman for the National Park Service and others. Exhibit photographs and floor plans of buildings in Washington, Virginia, Maryland, West Virginia, and New Jersey. Projects in the city of Washington include Decatur House, the museum building at Dumbarton Oaks, and Pierce Mill. Also Gadsby's Tavern and Leadbeater's Apothecary Shop in Alexandria, Virginia.

NOTE: Photographs produced by Thomas T. Waterman. Used in a 1947 Richmond Museum exhibit.

DATE: Ca. 1947

PHYSICAL DESCRIPTION: 42 silver gelatin photoprints, 28 × 36 cm or smaller.

SOURCE: Gift of Janet S. Reed, Thomas T. Waterman's niece, 1952.

LOT 5760

SUBJECTS: Views of the Library of Congress. Aerial views of the Adams Building site, and views made during and after construction of the Adams Building, architectural details, views of the Main Reading Room, and other reading rooms, bookstacks, permanent and temporary exhibits, and photographic copies of important manuscripts. Includes views of a branch of the U.S. Government Printing Office in the Library of Congress; copies of drawings by Paul Cret of the proposed Hispanic Room, designs by Lee Lawrie for the Adams Building doors, and drawings and floor plans for the Library of Congress Jefferson and Adams buildings; empty bookstacks in the Adams Building; murals, mosaics, statues, and the Gutenberg Bible; musical instruments in the Archive of American Folk Song; the Coolidge Auditorium; the shrine of the Declaration of Independence and Constitution; heads of various Library of Congress divisions and staff members at work; portraits of several Librarians of Congress. Also includes views of the Senate Chamber, the Marble Room in the U.S. Senate, and the President's Room in the Senate wing of the Capitol, the Supreme Court building and the library of the Department of State (1931).

NOTE: Volumes variously titled "Library of Congress: A Photographic Representation," "Library of Congress: A Collection of Miscellaneous Photographs," and "Library of Congress: Photographs 1939." Title page of one volume reads, "Photographs of the Library of Congress, its buildings, exhibits, activities, and personnel, as well as of certain other governmental buildings in Washington. Chiefly from negatives in the possession of Messrs. Harris & Ewing, Horydczak, and Underwood & Underwood of Washington, D.C. Office of the Superintendent of the Reading Rooms, 1939."

DATE: Ca. 1930–ca. 1940

PHOTOGRAPHERS: Harris & Ewing, Architect of the Capitol, L. C. Handy, Horydczak, Louden, Louis H. Dreyer, Underwood & Underwood, Hessler Studio, Leet Bros. Buckingham Studio, and W. E. Mair (U.S. Army Air Corps).

PHYSICAL DESCRIPTION: 4 volumes (390 silver gelatin photoprints, 20 × 25 cm or smaller).

SOURCE: Transfer from the Information Office, 1952.

LOT 5778

SUBJECTS: Portraits of U.S. senators. Includes a carte-de-visite portrait of President Arthur and cabinet card portraits of Schuy-

Buckingham Studio. "Line waiting admittance to the main reading room on a Sunday." Library of Congress (Jefferson Building). January 1938. Lot 5760.

LC-USZ62-88815

ler Colfax, Charles Sumner, Simon Cameron, Justin Morrill, and James A. Garfield and his wife.

NOTE: Most album pages bear the sitters' autographs. The album was apparently owned by John S. Harris, former senator from Louisiana, who was appointed surveyor general for Montana by President Arthur in 1881.

DATE: Ca. 1868–71

PHOTOGRAPHERS: Mathew Brady studio.

PHYSICAL DESCRIPTION: 1 album (50 albumen cabinet card and carte-de-visite photographs).

SOURCE: Gift of C. A. Rasmusson, 1933.

LOT 5898

SUBJECTS: Portraits of Arthur Spooner, Theodore Marsh, Charles W. Richards, Levi C. Hubbard, and other military men; a few children in military costume; and the Murays Midgets.

DATE: Ca. 1860–70s

PHOTOGRAPHERS: R. W. Addis, G. F. Child, Slagle, Jno. Holyland, Bell & Bro., McClees Gallery, Hugo Bartels, and Mathew Brady.

PHYSICAL DESCRIPTION: 20 items (cartes de visite and tintypes), 6 × 11 cm or smaller.

SOURCE: Gift of Jacques Schurre, 1952.

LOT 5909

SUBJECTS: Photographs relating to William E. Warne's activities in the U.S. Department of the Interior and Democratic party. Washington material consists of three photographs of a Democratic party dinner, with Harry Truman seated at the head table; undated. Other subjects include informal portraits of Warne; men pitching horseshoes and running a three-legged race; blasting near Boise, Idaho; exhibit panels and window displays.

NOTE: Some photos marked, "Bureau of Reclamation Region 1 Boise Idaho."

DATE: Ca. 1940s–ca. 1950

PHOTOGRAPHERS: Abbie Rowe (National Park Service).

PHYSICAL DESCRIPTION: 34 silver gelatin photoprints, 20 × 25 cm or smaller.

SOURCE: Gift of William E. Warne, 1952.

LOT 5933

SUBJECT: Mount Vernon. The entrance hall and stairway, the library, a bedroom, Washington's Tomb, the gardens.

DATE: Ca. 1952

PHOTOGRAPHERS: Mount Vernon Ladies' Association.

PHYSICAL DESCRIPTION: 5 color postcards, 9 × 13 cm.

SOURCE: Copyright deposit by the Mount Vernon Ladies' Association, 1952.

LOT 5963

SUBJECTS: *Guide to the Franciscan Monastery, Washington, D.C.* Views of the Franciscan Monastery in Washington, D.C., including consecration ceremonies, general exterior and interior views, and architectural details. Also includes pictures of Roman catacombs, grotto at Lourdes, and other well-known places of pilgrimage.

DATE: Ca. 1929

PUBLISHER: Commissariat of the Holy Land, 1929 (4th edition).

PHYSICAL DESCRIPTION: Paperbound booklet of 50 photomechanical prints of photographs, drawings, and maps, 18 × 12 cm.

SOURCE: Copyright deposit, 1929.

LOT 6039

SUBJECTS: Photographs made in Washington, D.C., and New York relating to airmail service and its twenty-fifth anniversary, June 16, 1943. Postmaster Merritt O. Chance with the first sack of airmail, group portrait of six pilots, takeoff for first New York-Washington airmail trip, and President Wilson waiting for the plane's arrival. Curtiss "Jenny" airplanes used for first flights in 1918, leaving from Potomac Park in Washington. Ceremonies held twenty-five years later at the Washington National Airport, showing helicopter and autogiro, and an airmail pickup demonstration.

DATE: Ca. 1918–43

PHYSICAL DESCRIPTION: 17 silver gelatin photoprints, 20 × 25 cm or smaller.

SOURCE: Transfer from the Aeronautics Division, 1953.

LOT 6046

SUBJECTS: Aeronautics photographs distributed for public relations by the Civil Aeronautics Administration. Washington subjects include a group portrait of the 1928 staff of the Regulation Division, Aeronautical Branch, Department of Commerce; and an autogiro being driven on a downtown Washington street.

DATE: Ca. 1926–45

PHOTOGRAPHERS: Scherer.

PHYSICAL DESCRIPTION: 14 silver gelatin photoprints, 21 × 26 cm.

SOURCE: Transfer from the Aeronautics Division, 1953.

LOT 6087

SUBJECTS: Aerial views of Pennsylvania Avenue, from the Capitol to Washington Circle, during a parade welcoming General Pershing and the First Division. Other subjects include pilots posed with their airplanes and Captain Gallop's horse.

NOTE: Photographs collected by William ("Billy") Mitchell.

DATE: Ca. 1919

PHYSICAL DESCRIPTION: 72 silver gelatin photoprints, 26 × 26 cm or smaller.

SOURCE: Transfer from the Aeronautics Divison, 1953.

LOT 6131

SUBJECTS: Airplanes, lighter-than-air craft, gliders, airships, and balloons, mainly American. Portraits of aviators. Washington subjects include acceptance trials for Baldwin's airship by the army, Fort Myer, Virginia, 1908; the Smidley monoplane at College Park, Maryland, October 1910; George Oakley Totten of Washington, with his glider at the base of the Washington Monument, 1909; and Claude Graham White flying his Farman biplane along West Executive Avenue, near the State, War, and Navy Building, October 1910. Also includes Alexander Graham Bell and Thomas E. Selfridge with their tetrahedral kite; and Miss E. L. Todd's airship, built by Witteman Brothers, 1906.

NOTE: Most images are uncaptioned.
DATE: Ca. 1906–ca. 1916

PHOTOGRAPHERS: G. V. Buck, D. B. Edmonston, and the U.S. Army Signal Corps.

PHYSICAL DESCRIPTION: Ca. 250 silver gelatin photoprints, 20 × 25 cm or smaller.

SOURCE: Transfer from the Aeronautics Division, 1954.

LOT 6274

SUBJECTS: Celebration of Adm. George Dewey's arrival in Washington in 1899. President McKinley and Admiral Dewey descending the steps at the East Front of the Capitol, Dewey receiving and displaying his sword, and benediction being delivered by Cardinal Gibbon.

DATE: 1899

PHOTOGRAPHERS: William H. Rau.

PHYSICAL DESCRIPTION: 6 silver gelatin photoprints, 33 × 27 cm.

SOURCE: Copyright deposit by William Rau, 1899.

LOT 6282

SUBJECTS: "Souvenir of the Reception in Honor of the President of the U.S. and Mrs. Coolidge. Tendered by the Ambassadors, Ministers, and Chargés d'Affaires of the Republics of America on the Evening of Friday, May 29, 1925." Presentation album of photographs of the Pan American Union, Washington, D.C. Interior and exterior views of the building, some with night lighting. Banquet table set for Coolidge reception.

DATE: 1925

PHYSICAL DESCRIPTION: 1 album (12 silver gelatin photoprints, 19 × 25 cm).

The first airplane leaving Potomac Park, Washington, D.C., on the inauguration of air mail service between Washington and New York City, 1918. Lot 6039.

LC-USZ62-32227

SOURCE: International exchange, 1953.

LOT 6286

SUBJECTS: Portraits of men and women, some in uniform, from the Civil War period. Includes portraits of Edwin Sumner, and Generals Burnside, Stonewall Jackson, Fitz John Porter, Hooker, Martindale, and John Henry.

NOTE: Album inscribed to Eugenia Berry, 1863, by a group of nurses who served under her in Washington, D.C.

DATE: Ca. 1860s

PHOTOGRAPHERS: Bell & Bro., Mathew Brady studio, and Johnson's Union Photograph Gallery.

PHYSICAL DESCRIPTION: 1 album (93 cartes de visite, tintypes, and gem tintypes).

SOURCE: Gift of Mrs. Charles P. Lyon, 1953.

LOT 6376

SUBJECTS: The Wright-Selfridge experimental flight at Fort Myer, Virginia, September 17, 1908. Lt. Thomas Selfridge and Orville Wright in their plane before takeoff; the collapsed plane; the broken propeller; doctors tending to Selfridge, who was killed in the crash; men carrying Wright on a stretcher after his injury.

An autogiro on a downtown Washington street, ca. 1947. Lot 6046.

LC-USZ62-90446

NOTE: All photographs captioned.

DATE: September 17, 1908

PHYSICAL DESCRIPTION: 8 silver gelatin photoprints, 13 × 18 cm.

SOURCE: Copyright deposit, 1908.

LOT 6399

COLLECTION NAME: Arthur Stanley Riggs Papers, Manuscript Division

SUBJECTS: Nurses at Walter Reed General Hospital. Anesthetist explaining her work; nurses' quarters; army nurses in front of Delano Hall; and interior of Assembly Hall at Delano Hall, Army Medical Center, Walter Reed General Hospital. Group of nurses at a monument erected at the nurses' plot in Arlington National Cemetery.

NOTE: Accompanied by a 2,500-word typescript on the history of the military medical corps by Arthur Stanley Riggs titled "Army Nurse."

BIOGRAPHICAL NOTE: The Manuscript Division holds the papers of Arthur Stanley Riggs (1879–1952), consisting of 900 items with a finding aid, spanning the years 1929–52. The Riggs Papers form part of the Library's Naval Historical Foundation Collection. Riggs was a Naval Reserve officer and the author of numerous books and articles, as well as a fellow of the Royal Geographic Society, lecturer, teacher of art history, member of the editorial staff of *Art and Archaeology,* and secretary of the Archaeological Society of Washington. Man-

uscript Division holdings relate to Riggs's unpublished book ("Drake of the Seven Seas") and include notes, correspondence, clippings, maps, and articles, dating chiefly from 1949–51. Acquired by deposit, 1955.

DATE: Ca. 1930–ca. 1945

PHOTOGRAPHERS: U.S. Army Medical Museum.

PHYSICAL DESCRIPTION: 13 silver gelatin photoprints, 20 × 25 cm or smaller.

SOURCE: Gift of the Arthur Stanley Riggs estate, 1953.

LOT 6477

SUBJECTS: Photographs showing free elections in the United States, produced for the U.S. Information Agency. One Washington photograph of the Truman inauguration on the East Front of the Capitol, January 1945; typical voters, campaigns, and national political conventions in New Hampshire, Tennessee, Maryland, Texas, and South Dakota.

DATE: Ca. 1952

PHYSICAL DESCRIPTION: 16 silver gelatin photoprints, 28 × 36 cm or smaller.

SOURCE: Transfer from the Senate Foreign Relations Committee, 1953.

The General Pershing (First Division) parade down Pennsylvania Avenue NW, under the Triumphal Arch, 1919. Lot 6087.

LC-USZ62-90442

William Rau. Cardinal Gibbons delivering the benediction during the celebration of Adm. George Dewey's arrival in Washington. President McKinley stands on the platform with Admiral Dewey, at the East Front of the Capitol, 1899. Lot 6274.

LC-USZ62-90459

Claude Graham White flying his Farman biplane along West Executive Avenue, Washington, October 14, 1910. Lot 6131.

LC-USZ62-10900

Orville Wright and Lt. Thomas E. Selfridge preparing to take off at Fort Myer, Virginia, September 17, 1908. Lot 6376.

LC-USZ61-470

The collapsed Wright airplane just after it struck the ground, injuring Wright and killing Selfridge, September 17, 1908. Lot 6376.

LC-USZ61-473

LOT 6517

SUBJECTS: Washington, D.C. Includes the Capitol, Supreme Court, Lincoln Memorial, Pentagon, Jefferson Memorial, Pennsylvania Avenue, National Gallery, White House, Tomb of the Unknown Soldier in Arlington Cemetery, Washington Monument, Library of Congress, and Declaration of Independence. Also includes views of Mt. Vernon, Virginia.

NOTE: Mounts labeled "Another True Vue Scenic Adventure."

DATE: Ca. 1953

PUBLISHER: True-Vue Company (Beaverton, Oregon).

PHYSICAL DESCRIPTION: 38 pairs of "three-dimensional" View Master film transparencies, 16 mm on 14 × 10 cm mounts.

SOURCE: Copyright deposit by True-Vue Company, 1953.

LOT 6592

SUBJECTS: U.S. Army officers and others from the Civil War period. Regimental banners carried by black troops. Views of Murfreesboro, Tennessee, and Lookout Mountain. One image shows "Lincoln cane at home." One carte de visite shows the Washington Monument.

NOTE: Photographs collected by John White Geary.

DATE: Ca. 1861–ca. 1865

PHOTOGRAPHERS: Mathew Brady, Slagle, R. W. Addis, Bell & Bro., J. Gurney & Son (New York), Gutekunst (Philadelphia), Bryant (Charleston, West Virginia), Butler, Bonsall & Co., "Army Photographers, General Rousseau's Division," Abdullah Frères (Constantinople), and Pera (Constantinople).

PHYSICAL DESCRIPTION: 1 album (160 albumen cartes de visite).

SOURCE: Gift of Edward Hamilton Geary, 1954.

LOT 6650

SUBJECTS: Senator Thomas Terry (Tom) Connally, his family, and associates, shown in news photographs, political cartoons, and studio portraits. Includes pictures of senators with architectural model of the extended East Front of the Capitol, President Franklin D. Roosevelt tossing the ball to begin the Washington baseball season, meetings of the Committee on Foreign Affairs of the Sixty-seventh Congress, 1930 group portrait on the steps of the Capitol, Winston Churchill addressing a joint session of Congress, May 19, 1943, Connally speaking at Arlington National Cemetery in 1934, and a Roosevelt-Wallace inauguration program.

DATE: Ca. 1890–1950

PHOTOGRAPHERS: Tenschert & Flack, Harris & Ewing, David Edmonston, National Photo Company, Margaret Bourke-White, David Sherman (Life Magazine), Bachrach, and International News Photo Company.

PHYSICAL DESCRIPTION: Ca. 150 silver gelatin photoprints, 46 × 56 cm or smaller.

SOURCE: Gift of Thomas Connally, 1953.

LOT 6657

SUBJECTS: Library of Congress Jefferson Building Main Reading Room pictured on a color photolithograph postcard, among a collection of postcards of public and other libraries in the United States and Europe.

NOTE: Many postcards are addressed to Mrs. Nettie K. Gravette, who was probably the collector.

DATE: Ca. 1908–23

PHYSICAL DESCRIPTION: 101 postcards, some colored.

SOURCE: Transfer.

LOT 6880

SUBJECTS: Gardens at the Cathedral of Saints Peter and Paul, Washington, D.C. Lilies, iris, and perennial border. Pool, wayside cross, thirteenth-century capital, shadow house, and other structures.

DATE: Ca. 1928

PHOTOGRAPHERS: R.J. Bonde & Sons.

PHYSICAL DESCRIPTION: 13 silver gelatin photoprints, 20 × 25 cm.

SOURCE: Copyright deposit by the National Cathedral Association, 1928.

LOT 6923

SUBJECTS: U.S. National Archives in Washington, D.C. General exterior views and architectural details, reading rooms, stacks, men unloading government records from trucks, records of various agencies stored in White House garage (Twenty-first Street wing), dehumidifier and other machinery, fumigation vault, photographic laboratory, manuscript lamination, and other operations.

DATE: Ca. 1936–38

PHYSICAL DESCRIPTION: 179 silver gelatin photoprints, 20 × 25 cm.

SOURCE: Gift of Dorsey W. Hyde, Jr., 1955.

LOT 6945

SUBJECTS: Military and political subjects in Washington, D.C., Missouri, and cemeteries in France. Washington subjects include the Dumbarton Oaks Conference

Winston Churchill addressing a joint session of Congress, May 19, 1943. Lot 6650.
LC-USZ62-90452

Thomas D. McAvoy, Life Magazine. President Franklin D. Roosevelt signing the Declaration of War against Japan, December 8, 1941. Lot 6650. Reproduced with the permission of Life Picture Service, Time Inc.

Dusting Veterans Bureau records at the National Archives, Washington, D.C., June 12, 1936. Lot 6923.
LC-USZ62-90438

participants and the laying of the cornerstone by Stansbury Lodge No. 24.

DATE: Ca. 1918–44

PHOTOGRAPHERS: Schutz.

PHYSICAL DESCRIPTION: 7 silver gelatin photoprints (banquet camera), 21 × 115 cm or smaller.

SOURCE: Gift of Breckenridge Long, 1953.

LOT 7022 (glass lantern slides)

SUBJECTS: Library of Congress Jefferson Building. Views of architectural details, reading rooms, catalogs, employees at work, and U.S. Government Printing Office branch. Reproductions of pages from rare books and reports of the Librarian of Congress.

NOTE: Accompanied by a caption list.

DATE: Ca. 1895–1937

PHYSICAL DESCRIPTION: 100 lantern slides, 9 × 11 cm.

LOT 7055

COLLECTION NAME: Ellery C. Stowell Papers, Manuscript Division

SUBJECTS: Ellery C. Stowell, executive secretary of the Hall of Nations, American University, Washington, D.C. Meeting of the Stowell Association. Includes portraits of some students from a group from twelve foreign countries who attended American University as members of the "Hall of Nations," pictured with their respective foreign ministers.

BIOGRAPHICAL NOTE: Ellery Cory Stowell (1875–1958) was an author, jurist, and professor of international law. The Stowell Papers in the Manuscript Division span the years 1802–1952, number 14,000 items, and are accompanied by a finding aid. The material relates to Stowell's activities at Harvard University and the Universities of Paris and Berlin, his studies in international law, civic enterprise, armament limitation, the Hague Conferences, and World Wars I and II. The photographs were transferred to the Prints and Photographs Division.

DATE: Ca. 1918–38

PHOTOGRAPHERS: Underwood & Underwood.

PHYSICAL DESCRIPTION: 5 silver gelatin photoprints and a newspaper clipping, 20 × 25 cm or smaller.

SOURCE: Gift of Ellery C. Stowell, 1949. Transfer from the Manuscript Division, 1955.

LOT 7074

SUBJECTS: The Wingfoot prefabricated home. Model erected in Washington, D.C. Also includes interiors of typical homes and a housing development near Phoenix, Arizona.

NOTE: Photographs captioned. Produced for Goodyear Tire and Rubber Company. Collection includes a pamphlet, press release, and clipping.

DATE: 1946

PHYSICAL DESCRIPTION: 22 silver gelatin photoprints, 21 × 26 cm.

Schutz. Group portrait of the Dumbarton Oaks Conference participants, Washington, D.C., August 1944. Lot 6945.
LC-USZ62-90119

LOT 7207

SUBJECTS: "World Photo Review No. 16; Brotherhood for Peace and Freedom." Includes pictures of Harry S. Truman conferring with Winston Churchill during Churchill's visit to the United States; Mary C. Welch of the National Education Association discussing books on audiovisual aids with Indonesian teachers in the Library of Congress; and Admiral Spruance, U.S. ambassador to Philippines, conferring in Washington with former Ambassador Cowen.

NOTE: Photographs captioned. Includes poster produced from 7 of the pictures.

DATE: 1952

PHYSICAL DESCRIPTION: 14 silver gelatin photoprints, 20 × 25 cm.

SOURCE: U.S. Information Service, Bombay.

LOT 7285 (stereographs)

SUBJECTS: "Metropolitan and suburban scenery, Washington, D.C." Includes views of Pennsylvania Avenue; U.S. Treasury Building and New York Avenue; the White House; and Capitol exteriors, interiors, and statuary.

DATE: Ca. 1885

PHOTOGRAPHERS: W. M. Chase.

PHYSICAL DESCRIPTION: 10 albumen photoprints (stereograph), 9 × 18 cm.

LOT 7312

SUBJECTS: Adjutant General's Office (AGO) exhibit: "Back the Attack." Washington Monument grounds, general high views, Women's Army Corps contingent,

Reni Newsphoto Service. A model of the Wingfoot prefabricated home, erected in Washington, D.C., and ready for occupancy. 1946. Lot 7074.
LC-USZ62-90433

President Harry S. Truman meeting with Winston Churchill, 1952. Lot 7207.
LC-USZ62-90445

adjutant general's department tent, typical field post office, and V-mail exhibit.

NOTE: Accompanied by layout of grounds and list of personnel.

DATE: September 9–26, 1943.

PHYSICAL DESCRIPTION: 1 album (31 silver gelatin photoprints), 20 × 25 cm.

SOURCE: U.S. Army Signal Corps.

LOT 7387

SUBJECTS: Portraits, most unidentified, by photographers in Washington, D.C., and Richmond and other Virginia cities.

NOTE: Possibly collected by a member of the Hatcher family.

DATE: Ca. 1860–75

PHOTOGRAPHERS: Mathew Brady, John Goldin, Agustus M. Hall (Alexandria, Virginia), and E. Schuler (Alexandria, Virginia).

PHYSICAL DESCRIPTION: 35 cartes de visite and tintypes.

SOURCE: Gift of Caroline L. Heironimus, 1956.

LOT 7428 (glass lantern slides)

SUBJECTS: One copy of a newspaper reproduction featuring the Sherman monument with the U.S. Treasury Building in the background, among miscellaneous images (including Houdini jumping off a Boston bridge and "the only photograph of a cannibal feast ever taken").

NOTE: Possibly used during lectures by Oscar S. Teale.

DATE: Ca. 1860–1920

PUBLISHER: "W. S. Davis (publ.)" appears on some slides.

PHYSICAL DESCRIPTION: 12 lantern slides, some hand-colored, 8 × 10 cm.

SOURCE: Gift of John J. and Hanna M. McManus and Morris N. and Chesley V. Young, 1955.

LOT 7589

COLLECTION NAME: William ("Billy") Mitchell collection

SUBJECTS: U.S. forces in or near Manila. Signal corpsmen building telegraph lines; headquarters of MacArthur. Washington subjects limited to one view of officers of the U.S. Volunteer Signal Corps, Washington Barracks, July 1898. Also includes group portraits of officers in Florida.

DATE: Ca. 1898

PHYSICAL DESCRIPTION: 8 silver gelatin photoprints, 20 × 25 cm.

SOURCE: Transfer from the Aeronautics Division, 1954.

LOT 7630

SUBJECTS: Views, landmarks, industries, and people in Washington, D.C., Argentina, Bolivia, Brazil, Chile, Hawaii, Jordan, Lebanon, and Turkey. Washington subjects (3 items) include the U.S. Marine Corps Memorial (1955) and the White House.

NOTE: Accompanied by a list of captions.

DATE: Ca. 1954–ca. 1956

PHOTOGRAPHERS: William E. Warne.

PHYSICAL DESCRIPTION: 123 color transparencies (35mm), in 5 × 5 cm mounts.

SOURCE: Gift of William E. Warne, 1956.

LOT 7800

SUBJECTS: Post Office buildings in forty-five states and the District of Columbia, as well as in several foreign countries. Washington views include two colored postcards of the "New Post Office," ca. 1935.

NOTE: Collected by Henry B. Myers.

DATE: Ca. 1900–1945

PHYSICAL DESCRIPTION: 344 postcards, some colored photomechanical and photolithographic reproductions.

SOURCE: Gift of Buford M. Myers, 1957.

LOT 7801

SUBJECTS: U.S. postmasters general, 1776–1929. Includes portraits, early airmail planes and trucks, snow plow equipment, mail trains, Overland Mail wagons, and mail boats.

NOTE: Collected by Henry B. Myers.

DATE: Before 1929

PHYSICAL DESCRIPTION: 1 album (60 photomechanical prints of paintings and photographs).

SOURCE: Gift of Buford M. Myers, 1947.

LOT 7864

SUBJECTS: Portraits of the Beebe, Conkling, Dwight, Hooper, Motley, Reed, Thornton, and other Washington and Boston families. Includes portraits of members of the foreign diplomatic service stationed in Washington.

NOTE: Collected by Mary Elizabeth Lee (Mrs. Charles Addison Mann), mother of the donor.

DATE: Ca. 1870–74

PHOTOGRAPHERS: Henry Ulke, Julius Ulke, Henry Ulke & Bro., Alexander Gardner, and Mathew Brady.

PHYSICAL DESCRIPTION: 1 album (76 carte-de-visite and cabinet card albumen photoprints), 25 × 22 cm.

SOURCE: Gift of Mary Lee Mann, 1957.

LOT 7881

SUBJECTS: Portraits, most unidentified. Family groups, men in uniform, young children, youths, young women, and married couples.

DATE: Ca. 1860–90

PHOTOGRAPHERS: Tintypes by J. E. Spencer and Spencer & Downs; cartes de visite by Henry Ulke, Mathew Brady, Whitehurst Gallery, Jno. Holyland, The Addis Gallery (P. B. Marvin, photographer), R. W. Addis (photographer in McClee's Gallery), J. Goldin, and Bell & Bro.; cabinet cards by Smith and Buck, C. M. Bell, M. Kers Kemethy, Ulke Bros., G. W. Davis, and W. L. Spedden.

PHYSICAL DESCRIPTION: 189 cartes de visite, cabinet cards, and tintypes, and some larger mounted portraits.

LOT 7897

SUBJECTS: "Views of Washington City." The Capitol, Pennsylvania Avenue, Department of Agriculture, White House, Corcoran Art Gallery, City Hall, State, War and Navy Department Building, Metropolitan Memorial M. E. Church, Four-and-a-half Street SW, General Post Office, Smithsonian Institution, Patent Office, Soldiers' Home, and Mount Vernon.

NOTE: Includes 16 pages of text.

DATE: Ca. 1873

PUBLISHER: Edward Fitzki.

PHYSICAL DESCRIPTION: 16 lithographs, in a folder 8 × 12 cm.

SOURCE: Exchange, 1944.

LOT 7901

COLLECTION NAME: Henry Laurens Dawes Papers, Manuscript Division

SUBJECTS: Portraits of Henry Laurens Dawes, representative and senator from Massachusetts, and Mrs. Dawes.

DATE: Ca. 1862–90

PHOTOGRAPHERS: Charles Parker, Mathew Brady Studio, and C. M. Bell.

PHYSICAL DESCRIPTION: 21 cartes de visite and cabinet cards and a silhouette, 21 × 12 cm or smaller.

SOURCE: Transfer from the Manuscript Division, 1958.

LOT 7940

SUBJECTS: Autographed portraits of government officials in Washington, D.C. Also includes employees of the Post Office and Treasury Departments at work and a money-washing machine at the Treasury Department. Firemen and telephone operators, horse-drawn truck no. 1, Washington Fire Department. U.S. Redemption Bureau. Flag-unfurling exercises and singing at ceremonies in the Post Office Court, June 14, 1912. Unidentified soda fountain or bar.

DATE: Ca. 1912–29

PHOTOGRAPHERS: Frank R. Scherer.

PHYSICAL DESCRIPTION: 26 silver gelatin photoprints, 20 × 25 cm or smaller.

SOURCE: Gift of Frank R. Scherer, 1958.

LOT 7963

SUBJECTS: State visit of Carlos Arroyo del Rio, president of Ecuador. Includes his arrival in Washington, attending banquets and meetings, addressing a joint session of Congress, receiving an honorary degree from George Washington University, watching a parade at the Army War College at Fort McNair, visiting the National Cathedral, riding with Franklin D. Roosevelt in an automobile, visiting the Tomb of the Unknown Soldier at Arlington Cemetery and Mount Vernon, and laying a wreath at Washington's Tomb.

NOTE: Presentation album titled "Mi Viaje a los Estados Unidas."

DATE: November 24–December 5, 1942

PHOTOGRAPHERS: Acme Newspictures.

PHYSICAL DESCRIPTION: 28 silver gelatin photoprints, 31 × 48 cm or smaller.

Frank R. Scherer. Money-washing machine at the Treasury Department. Copyright 1912. Lot 7940. LC-USZ62-90450

LOT 8016

SUBJECTS: Funeral of Secretary of the Navy Frank Knox. Guard of honor at flag-draped coffin in Mt. Pleasant Congregational Church, artillery caisson drawn by white horses bearing the body down Constitution Avenue, procession crossing Memorial Bridge, and graveside ceremonies at Arlington National Cemetery. Includes portraits of Eleanor Roosevelt, Vice President Henry Wallace, Secretary of State Cordell Hull, and Acting Secretary of the Navy James Forrestal.

DATE: May 1, 1944

PHOTOGRAPHERS: U.S. Navy photographers.

PHYSICAL DESCRIPTION: 7 silver gelatin photoprints, 20 × 25 cm.

LOT 8032

SUBJECTS: Wooden signs erected by real estate companies and others, some in the Washington area. Local examples include signs for the Waverly Taylor, Inc., Exhibit Home and Dumbarton Real Estate Development; a sign for the Clara Barton House; and a sign for Shady Grove Road.

DATE: Ca. 1944

PHYSICAL DESCRIPTION: 20 silver gelatin photoprints, 20 × 25 cm.

SOURCE: Transfer, 1944.

LOT 8033

SUBJECTS: Railway tunnel construction in Washington, D.C. Views of excavations and timbering for the First Street tunnel from the south portal to the station; old Navy Yard tunnel; and Virginia Avenue tunnel.

NOTE: Most photographs are captioned.

DATE: Ca. 1904–5

PHOTOGRAPHERS: J. F. Jarvis.

PHYSICAL DESCRIPTION: 34 silver gelatin photoprints, 20 × 25 cm or smaller.

SOURCE: Gift of Covington K. Allen, 1958.

J. F. Jarvis. Construction work on a railway tunnel, Washington, D.C., ca. 1904–5. Lot 8033.
LC-USZ62-90439

LOT 8227

SUBJECTS: Interior views of the White House. Entrance hall; corridor; East, Green, and Red Rooms; library; and State Dining Room.

DATE: 1902

PHOTOGRAPHERS: J. F. Jarvis.

PHYSICAL DESCRIPTION: 10 silver gelatin printing-out paper photoprints, 18 × 23 cm or smaller.

SOURCE: Copyright deposit by J. F. Jarvis, 1902.

LOT 8241

SUBJECTS: Photographic copies of paintings of the presidents of the United States (Washington through Truman) on display at the White House.

PHOTOGRAPHERS: Abbie Rowe.

PHYSICAL DESCRIPTION: 32 silver gelatin photoprints, 20 × 25 cm.

SOURCE: Transfer from the National Park Service, 1958.

LOT 8268

SUBJECTS: Fort Washington, Maryland. U.S. Army Quartermaster Corps. Opera-

tions of the Mobile Laundry Unit No. 3 and other activities at Fort Washington. Includes interior and exterior views of the three-truck laundry unit; tractor to furnish hot water and steam for the laundry; warehouse; post garage; storehouses; historic manor house and quarters; and a general panoramic view of Fort Washington.

NOTE: Photographs are captioned.

DATE: Ca. 1918

PHYSICAL DESCRIPTION: 1 album (25 silver gelatin photoprints, 15 × 22 cm or smaller).

SOURCE: Transfer, 1942.

LOT 8270

SUBJECTS: Washington Barracks, Washington, D.C. U.S. Army Quartermaster Corps. Operations at the barracks, including the mobile machine, electricians', carpenter, and plumbing shops; farriers' shop and blacksmith's tool chests; saddlers' tools and chest; old and new haversacks; storehouses, warehouses, and offices; commissary and sales rooms; Field Medical Supply Depot; and portable field kitchen, with cooking utensils. Includes photographs of Quartermaster's Clothing and Grocery Department (1130 Connecticut Avenue), Salvage Plant (Third and Randolph Streets NE), Zone Supply Office Buildings (Seventeenth and F Streets and Nineteenth Street and Virginia Avenue, NW), and Quartermaster Storehouses

Henri Cartier-Bresson for Magnum. "Prayer Pilgrimage for Freedom" at the Lincoln Memorial, 1957. Lot 8718. Copyright © Henri Cartier-Bresson/ Magnum Photos. Used with permission.

American Library Association Library War Service Headquarters in the Library of Congress (Jefferson Building), Washington, D.C., January 5, 1918. Lot 8871.

LC-USZ62-90451

(First and Q Streets, First and K Streets, and 510 Eckington Place, NE).

NOTE: Photographs are captioned.

DATE: Ca. 1918

PHYSICAL DESCRIPTION: 1 album (30 silver gelatin photoprints, 17 × 22 cm or smaller).

SOURCE: Transfer, 1942.

LOT 8271

SUBJECTS: Fort Myer, Virginia; and Baltimore, Maryland. U.S. Army Quartermaster Corps. Views of various quartermaster buildings. Warehouses and piers for handling of overseas freight in Baltimore. Stables, blacksmith shop at Fort Myer. Includes views of building used by quartermaster for main sales rooms and personnel, Washington, D.C.; Quartermaster warehouse and storehouse; laborers and office personnel headquarters, and record storehouse.

DATE: Ca. 1918

PHYSICAL DESCRIPTION: 1 album (25 silver gelatin photoprints, 17 × 22 cm or smaller).

SOURCE: Transfer, 1942.

LOT 8354

SUBJECTS: World's Columbian Exposition exhibits erected by U.S. government agencies. Includes typical Weather Bureau installations, a scale model of Arlington Cemetery and Fort Myer, and veterinary supplies used by the Quartermaster Corps.

DATE: Ca. 1893

PHYSICAL DESCRIPTION: 1 album (36 silver gelatin photoprints, 21 × 30 cm).

SOURCE: Transfer from the Treasury Department, 1910.

LOT 8448

SUBJECTS: Snapshot and travel photographs taken in Washington, D.C., New Jersey, New York City and New York State, and Salem, Massachusetts. Washington photographs (8 items, all taken in May 1898) include the White House, Soldiers' Home, Mount Vernon, and George Washington's Tomb.

DATE: July 1897–July 1902

PHOTOGRAPHERS: Albert G. Havens.

PHYSICAL DESCRIPTION: 1 album (55 platinum photoprints, 11 × 13 cm).

SOURCE: Gift of Mrs. Lloyd Goodrich, 1959.

LOT 8505

SUBJECTS: Spanish-American War events and locations. Includes the burial at Arlington Cemetery of the soldiers who died in the Spanish-American War (2 photographs).

DATE: Ca. 1898–99

PHOTOGRAPHERS: Ernest C. Rost.

PHYSICAL DESCRIPTION: 24 silver gelatin photoprints, 16 × 21 cm.

SOURCE: Gift of Ernest C. Rost, 1899.

LOT 8718

SUBJECTS: Illustrations for an article on civil rights in the *Encyclopedia Britannica Yearbook* (1958). One Washington photo, by Henri Cartier-Bresson, shows the "Prayer Pilgrimage for Freedom" at the Lincoln Memorial, May 18, 1957.

DATE: Ca. 1957–58

PHOTOGRAPHERS: Henri Cartier-Bresson, other Magnum Photos, Inc., photographers, and United Press.

PUBLISHER: Encyclopedia Britannica, Inc.

PHYSICAL DESCRIPTION: 5 silver gelatin photoprints, 23 × 33 cm or smaller.

SOURCE: Gift, 1960.

LOT 8871

SUBJECTS: Libraries in dozens of army camps and naval installations. Interior views with soldiers reading; facilities under construction. Includes one photograph of the American Library Association Library War Service Headquarters in the Library of Congress.

NOTE: Produced by the American Library Association.

DATE: Ca. 1918–19

PHYSICAL DESCRIPTION: 51 silver gelatin photoprints, 20 × 25 cm.

LOT 8882

SUBJECTS: Photographs related to World War I, taken in Washington, D.C., New York City, Japan, the Soviet Union, and various Eastern European countries. Washington subjects include "reconstruction work" for recuperating soldiers and an influenza ward at Walter Reed Hospital; engineers at Washington Barracks; YMCA rooms at Camp Meade, and Camp Meade under snow; homecoming parade of First Division on Pennsylvania Avenue; "peace crowd" in front of the White House, 1918; Secretary McAdoo and Geraldine Farrar selling Liberty Bonds; and War Camp Community entertainers in a park near the State, War, and Navy Building.

DATE: Ca. 1918

PHOTOGRAPHERS: Harris & Ewing.

PHYSICAL DESCRIPTION: 205 silver gelatin photoprints, 28 × 36 cm.

SOURCE: Copyright deposit.

Other Sources

LOT 8885

SUBJECTS: World War I subjects taken in Europe, Washington, D.C., and elsewhere in the United States. Washington subjects include photographs of the engineers at Washington Barracks, "marinettes" on the White House lawn, a welcome home parade, and a parade of marines on Pennsylvania Avenue.

NOTE: Most photographs are captioned.

DATE: Ca. 1914–20

PHOTOGRAPHERS: Underwood & Underwood and Harris & Ewing.

PHYSICAL DESCRIPTION: Ca. 125 silver gelatin photoprints and copy photographs of drawings, 20 × 25 cm or smaller.

SOURCE: Copyright deposit.

State Department Library in the State, War, and Navy Building, Washington, D.C. Ca. 1900–1905. Lot 8908.
LC-USZ62-90440

Howard Hughes (left) with Jesse H. Jones, chief of the Reconstruction Finance Corporation. Lot 9587.
LC-USZ62-90437

LOT 8908

SUBJECTS: Libraries in twenty-two states and the District of Columbia. Exterior and interior views, including reading rooms, bookstacks, and floor plans. Includes the D.C. Public Library interior, the State Department library, and the Navy Department library (3 items).

NOTE: Most photographs are captioned.

DATE: Ca. 1900–1905

PHYSICAL DESCRIPTION: 410 silver gelatin photoprints and copy photographs of drawings, 33 × 39 cm or smaller.

SOURCE: Purchase, 1905.

LOT 9305

SUBJECTS: Mt. Pleasant trolley funeral, Washington, D.C. Ceremony held in Northwest Washington to mark the end of service on this streetcar line.

NOTE: Corresponding negatives are found in series LC-C7-558-565.

DATE: November 25, 1961.

PHOTOGRAPHERS: Suzanne Cooper.

PHYSICAL DESCRIPTION: 8 silver gelatin photoprints, 9 × 13 cm.

SOURCE: Gift of Suzanne Cooper, 1961.

U.S. Supreme Court justices and Justice Department administrators meeting with President Harry S. Truman, October 16, 1945. Lot 9745.
LC-USZ62-90443

LOT 9326

SUBJECTS: Funeral of Air Force Gen. Henry Harley ("Hap") Arnold in Washington, D.C. Honor guards at the airport and at the National Cathedral (showing the exterior of the cathedral and the St. Joseph of Arimathee and Bethlehem Chapels). Procession with caisson and caparisoned horse. Services in the Arlington National Cemetery amphitheater.

DATE: January 18, 1950.

PHOTOGRAPHERS: U.S. Air Force photographers.

PHYSICAL DESCRIPTION: 19 silver gelatin photoprints, 20 × 25 cm and 11 × 13 cm.

SOURCE: Gift of Edna M. Adkins. Transfer from the Manuscript Division, 1962.

LOT 9587

SUBJECTS: Photographs documenting the career of Jesse Jones (1874–1956), secretary of commerce, treasurer of the Democratic National Committee, and chairman of the Reconstruction Finance Corporation. Jones with Howard Hughes, Pearl Buck, Undersecretary of War Patterson, Generals Knudson and Forrestal, Supreme Court Justice Stanley Reed, Secretary of the Navy Frank Knox, and various labor leaders. Also with President Roosevelt, Nelson Rockefeller, Senator Truman of Missouri, and Gov. Alfred E. Smith, the Democratic nominee in 1928. Includes views of the Reconstruction Finance Corporation Building (811 Vermont Avenue NW), and the Democratic National Convention in Chicago. One photographic copy of a Jim Berryman cartoon.

DATE: Ca. 1918–50

PHOTOGRAPHERS: Harris & Ewing and Pacific & Atlantic Photos.

PHYSICAL DESCRIPTION: 31 silver gelatin photoprints and a copy photograph, 20 × 25 cm or smaller.

SOURCE: Gift of Mrs. Jesse H. Jones, 1962.

LOT 9605

SUBJECTS: Congressman Breeding greeting a high school student band from Morton County, Kansas, after their arrival at Union Station in Washington, D.C., to play in the Inaugural Parade.

DATE: 1960

PHYSICAL DESCRIPTION: 3 silver gelatin photoprints, 20 × 25 cm.

SOURCE: Gift of J. Floyd Breeding, 1962.

LOT 9607

SUBJECTS: World War I naval subjects, taken in Washington, D.C., Virginia, New York, Washington State, and elsewhere. Washington images include the Navy League entertaining wounded soldiers and the Supply Department of the Division Third Naval District.

DATE: Ca. 1914–19

PHOTOGRAPHERS: Harris & Ewing.

PHYSICAL DESCRIPTION: 140 silver gelatin photoprints, 28 × 36 cm or smaller.

SOURCE: Copyright deposit.

LOT 9668

COLLECTION NAME: John Archer Lejeune Papers, Manuscript Division

SUBJECTS: Photographs relating to the career of Maj.-Gen. John Lejeune. Includes one photograph of Lejeune addressing a joint session of Congress. Also includes a photograph on Staten Island, and a group portrait of Chicago veterans who served under Lejeune.

BIOGRAPHICAL NOTE: John Archer Lejeune (1867–1942) was a Marine Corps officer and educator. His correspondence, memoranda, speeches, military papers, and writings held in the Manuscript Division span the years 1815–1950 (chiefly 1900–1942), number 6,000 items, and are accompanied by a finding aid. The Library's holdings relate to Lejeune's military career; his service in Samoa, Vera Cruz, Haiti, Panama, France, and Germany; and his work as superintendent of the Virginia Military Institute. The photographs were transferred to the Prints and Photographs Division.

DATE: 1928–34

PHYSICAL DESCRIPTION: 3 silver gelatin photoprints, 20 × 25 cm or smaller.

SOURCE: Transfer from the Manuscript Division, 1963.

LOT 9675

COLLECTION NAME: Lester Hood Woolsey Papers, Manuscript Division

SUBJECTS: Portraits of Latin-American diplomats and other dignitaries posed in formal groups on several occasions at the Pan American Union, Washington, D.C.

NOTE: Collected by Lester Hood Woolsey. Inscribed to him by Leo Stanton Rowe, Director General of the Pan American Union. All photographs are captioned; some captions are in Spanish.

BIOGRAPHICAL NOTE: Lester Hood Woolsey (1877–1961) was a lawyer, diplomat, and geologist. His papers are held by the Manuscript Division, number 33,000 items, and span the years 1831–1958 (chiefly 1909–20). The papers, accompanied by a finding aid, relate to Woolsey's service in the Department of State and his practice of international law during World War I. They consist of correspondence, diaries, treaty papers, minutes and resolutions of conferences, articles, and annotated printed material. The papers were acquired by gift, 1961. The photographs were transferred to the Prints and Photographs Division.

DATE: Ca. 1931–ca. 1943

PHYSICAL DESCRIPTION: 16 silver gelatin photoprints, 19 × 24 cm or smaller.

SOURCE: Transfer from the Manuscript Division, 1963.

LOT 9715

SUBJECTS: Washington, D.C.; Baltimore; and Mount Vernon, Virginia. Snapshots taken with an amateur camera of the Botanic Garden near the Capitol; Mount Vernon interiors, exteriors, and grounds; George Washington's Tomb at Mount Vernon; Capitol exteriors; and the Washington Monument.

DATE: Ca. 1896

PHYSICAL DESCRIPTION: 17 silver gelatin photoprints, 4 × 5 cm, on original Pocket Kodak mounts.

LOT 9716

SUBJECTS: Motion pictures in the custody of the Library of Congress and in the Library's film vault in Suitland, Maryland. Typical paper prints, shelves of boxed items, and cans of deteriorating nitrate film. Portraits of James H. Culver, head of the Motion Picture Section.

DATE: Ca. 1951–55

PHOTOGRAPHERS: Library of Congress staff.

PHYSICAL DESCRIPTION: 5 silver gelatin photoprints, 20 × 25 cm.

SOURCE: Transfer.

LOT 9723

COLLECTION NAME: Bess Furman Papers, Manuscript Division

SUBJECTS: Material concerning the proposed National Cultural Center to be built in Washington, D.C. Photographs of architect's sketches and copies of newspaper clippings. Portraits of Robert W. Dowling, Arthur S. Flemming, Edward Durell Stone, and L. Corrin Strong.

BIOGRAPHICAL NOTE: Bess Furman was an author and journalist who was active in the Children's Bureau, the American Association of University Women, the League of Women Voters, the Democratic National Committee, and the Department of Health, Education, and Welfare. Her writings cover education, health, Washington's social and political history, the White House, and women in public life. Her correspondence, diaries, family papers, subject files, speeches, writings, and scrapbooks are held in the Manuscript Division, span the years 1728–1967 (chiefly 1900–1966), number 47,000 items, and are accompanied by a finding aid. The Bess Furman Papers were a gift of Bess Furman Armstrong and Robert F. Armstrong, 1954–69. The photographs were transferred to the Prints and Photographs Division.

DATE: 1958–59

PHYSICAL DESCRIPTION: 23 silver gelatin photoprints and newspaper clippings, 20 × 25 cm or smaller.

SOURCE: Transfer from the Manuscript Division, 1963.

LOT 9744

SUBJECTS: News pictures made while Harold Hitz Burton was U.S. senator from Ohio. Group photographs show Burton with various colleagues and notables including Senator Harry Truman, Orville Wright, Basil O'Connor, John Nance Garner, and members of the Truman Committee. Presentation of Gourgas Medal to President Harry Truman, 1945. Most of the photos were taken in Ohio.

DATE: Ca. 1940–1945

PHOTOGRAPHERS: U.S. Army Signal Corps.

PHYSICAL DESCRIPTION: 70 silver gelatin photoprints, 28 × 36 cm or smaller.

SOURCE: Gift of Harold H. Burton, 1963.

Other Sources

LOT 9745

SUBJECTS: News pictures made while Harold Hitz Burton was on the U.S. Supreme Court. Group photographs show Burton with Robert A. Taft, Owen J. Roberts, Sam Rayburn, and other notables. President Harry Truman with newly appointed Associate Justice Burton in 1945. Retiring Justice Owen Roberts. Group portrait of the Supreme Court justices, the clerk, marshal, solicitor, and attorney general with Truman in 1945. Burton with Sam Rayburn at the Mayflower Hotel. Burton with family members.

DATE: Ca. 1940–ca. 1958

PHYSICAL DESCRIPTION: 14 silver gelatin photoprints, 20 × 25 cm.

SOURCE: Gift of Harold H. Burton, 1963.

LOT 9749

SUBJECTS: "A Day with Ohio's New Senator." Harold Hitz Burton (formerly mayor of Cleveland) riding the Capitol subway, at his desk, using a rowing machine, walking back to his hotel, reading a newspaper, using a dictating machine, and being assisted by a Senate page.

DATE: January 15, 1941

PHOTOGRAPHERS: Acme Newspictures, Inc.

PHYSICAL DESCRIPTION: 11 silver gelatin photoprints, 20 × 25 cm.

SOURCE: Gift of Harold H. Burton, 1963.

Central News Photo Service (New York). "Another branch of our Marine Service. U.S.M.C. Telegraph Division at the Marine Barracks, Washington, D.C. . . . Many of those shown are new recruits who are just breaking in on the wire." Ca. 1917. Lot 9834.
LC-USZ62-90455

George Tames, New York Times photo. A view of the Lincoln Memorial from above and behind the statue, for use by the Lincoln Sesquicentennial Commission, 1959. Lot 9900. Reproduced with the permission of NYT Pictures.

LOT 9813

SUBJECTS: The icebreaker and buoy tender *Madrona* on the Potomac River near Washington, D.C., at anchor and freeing ice-bound vessels. Tanker and tug using a channel broken open by the *Madrona*. Crewman hacking ice from a buoy.

NOTE: Produced by the Public Information Division, U.S. Coast Guard Headquarters.

DATE: February 1961

PHYSICAL DESCRIPTION: 7 silver gelatin photoprints, 21 × 26 cm.

SOURCE: Transfer, 1961.

LOT 9834

SUBJECTS: U.S. Marines engaged in various training and military activities. Includes photographs of the Telegraph Division and Marine Barracks in Washington, D.C.

DATE: Ca. 1917

PHOTOGRAPHERS: Central News Photo Service (New York).

PHYSICAL DESCRIPTION: 9 silver gelatin photoprints, 20 × 25 cm.

LOT 9900

SUBJECTS: Photographs produced by the Lincoln Sesquicentennial Commission to commemorate the 150th anniversary of

Harvey. Baltimore & Potomac Railway Depot, Washington, D.C., ca. 1897. Lot 10021.
LC-USZ62-90609

Abraham Lincoln's birth. Among photographs taken in Germany, France, and Tokyo are several Washington images, including the poet Carl Sandburg addressing a joint session of Congress on the occasion; President Dwight Eisenhower, Vice President Richard Nixon, and Senator Everett Dirksen at the Lincoln Sesquicentennial dinner, February 11, 1959; and interior views of the Lincoln Memorial in Washington, D.C.

NOTE: Some photographs published in House Document no. 211, 86th Congress, 1st session.

DATE: 1959

PHOTOGRAPHERS: Capitol Photo Service and New York Times.

PHYSICAL DESCRIPTION: 20 silver gelatin photoprints, 20 × 25 cm or smaller.

SOURCE: Transfer, 1963.

LOT 9934

SUBJECTS: Portraits of U.S. Army officers, children, and others, including James Fenimore Cooper, Garibaldi, Empress Eugenie, Kit Carson, and Louis Agassiz. Portraits of Generals Beauregard (C.S.A.), Fitz John Porter, Dix, Ulysses S. Grant, Robert Anderson, and Burnside; Maj. Gens. George McClellan, Joe Hooker, and Nathaniel Banks; and Admiral Dupont. Also includes one view of the Long Bridge from Fourteenth Street in Washington, D.C., and Civil War battle sites in Virginia.

DATE: Ca. 1865

PHOTOGRAPHERS: Mathew Brady studio and E. & H. T. Anthony.

PHYSICAL DESCRIPTION: 1 album (70 albumen carte-de-visite portraits, some colored), 14 × 19 cm.

SOURCE: Gift of Mrs. Norman P. Mason, 1963.

LOT 10021

SUBJECTS: U.S. Capitol, Library of Congress, Lafayette statue, Washington Monument, White House, Baltimore & Potomac Railway Depot (captioned, "where President Garfield was shot by Charles Guiteau on 2 July 1881"), Ford's Theater, and Peterson house (House Where Lincoln Died).

DATE: Ca. 1897

PHOTOGRAPHERS: Harvey.

PHYSICAL DESCRIPTION: 12 silver gelatin photoprints, 9 × 9 cm.

LOT 10023

SUBJECTS: May Day festivities at Forest Glen, Maryland. Crowning of the queen, and maypole dance.

DATE: 1907

PHOTOGRAPHERS: Leet Brothers.

PHYSICAL DESCRIPTION: 8 cyanotype photoprints, 19 × 23 cm.

SOURCE: Copyright deposit by Leet Brothers, 1907.

LOT 10296 (glass lantern slides)

SUBJECTS: Library of Congress Jefferson Building. Exterior, Neptune Fountain, Great Hall, murals, and permanent exhibits. Main Reading Room, central desk, card catalog. Book conveyor and bookstack area. Special facilities for manuscripts and rare books, for the blind, and for members of Congress. Views of various offices in the Library. Coolidge Auditorium. Copies of rare materials in the collections. Proposed annex.

NOTE: Accompanied by captions in French. Lantern slides document a portion of an exhibit prepared for the Exposition Internationale des Arts et des Techniques, Paris, 1937 (*Report of the Librarian of Congress . . . ending June 30, 1937,* p. 279). Compiled by Martin Arnold Roberts.

DATE: Ca. 1937

PHYSICAL DESCRIPTION: 50 lantern slides, some hand-colored, 9 × 11 cm.

SOURCE: Transfer from the Stack and Reader Division, 1964.

LOT 10301

SUBJECTS: "First World War," a series of rotogravures of the *Sunday Evening Star,* published in 1934. Part 10 (March 18, 1934) shows demonstrations and promotions of Victory and Liberty Loans; Secretary of War Baker drawing the first number in the selective draft; President Wilson in a preparedness parade; cabinet members; Washington soldiers arriving at Camp Meade, Maryland; and the Evening Star Building. Part 15 (April 22, 1934) shows the "war map" on display at the Evening Star Building.

NOTE: Incomplete set: includes sections 1-10, 13-15 only.

DATE: June 28, 1914–November 11, 1918

PHOTOGRAPHERS: Harris & Ewing.

PUBLISHER: *Sunday Evening Star,* Washington, D.C., 1934.

PHYSICAL DESCRIPTION: 13 newspaper sections (ca. 200 rotogravure reproductions of photographs).

LOT 10387

SUBJECTS: Group portraits and news pictures of members of Congress, Senate and House committees, high-ranking members of the military, and government officials, mainly in Washington, D.C.

NOTE: Photographs were used as illustrations in the periodical *Machinist.*

Leet Bros. May Day festivities at Forest Glen, Maryland, ca. 1907. Lot 10023.

LC-USZ62-30339

DATE: Ca. 1938–59

PHOTOGRAPHERS: Harris & Ewing, Acme Photo, and United Press Association.

PHYSICAL DESCRIPTION: 81 silver gelatin photoprints, 20 × 25 cm.

SOURCE: Gift of Gordon Cole, 1965.

LOT 10450

SUBJECTS: Historic buildings and ruins in the Washington vicinity, Maryland, and Virginia. Washington area subjects include the Barnaby Addison House, the Klingle-Pierce House in Rock Creek Park, Holmead (Rock Hill) at Twenty-second and S Streets NW, Glebe House in Arlington, and Woodlawn, near Mount Vernon.

NOTE: Some images are unidentified.

DATE: Ca. 1895–ca. 1905

PHOTOGRAPHERS: William A. Miller.

PHYSICAL DESCRIPTION: 13 modern silver gelatin photoprints, 20 × 25 cm, printed by the Library of Congress from original glass negatives.

LOT 10451

SUBJECTS: Historic sites and buildings in or near Washington, D.C.; Alexandria, Bluemont, and Leesburg, Virginia; and Riverdale, Maryland. Sites and events in the vicinity of Washington include the cornerstone laying on the grounds of American University; the Francis Scott Key House, and an oyster bar in Georgetown; the Confederate Monument and a house in Alexandria, Virginia; a house in Riverdale, Maryland; the village square and Burton-Wade house, the Thomas Stone home (Habre de Venture), and Rose Hill in Port Tobacco, Maryland; Prospect Hill (Pope's Creek), and Causin Manor (near Chapel Point) in Charles County, Maryland; a mill in Shepherdstown, West Virginia; a stable at Ravensworth, Fairfax County, Virginia; Snicker's Gap, near Bluemont, Virginia; Morven Park and other houses in Leesburg, Virginia. Also includes scenes in Savannah, Georgia; St. Augustine, Florida, and Cuba.

DATE: Ca. 1895–ca. 1905

PHOTOGRAPHERS: William A. Miller.

PHYSICAL DESCRIPTION: 33 silver gelatin photoprints, 20 × 25 cm, printed by the Library of Congress from original negatives.

LOT 10452

SUBJECTS: Historic sites, buildings, and ruins in or near Washington, D.C.; Bladensburg and Frederick, Maryland; Shepherdstown, West Virginia; and Camden, South Carolina. Washington area subjects include the Old Stone House in Georgetown; Nourse House on Wisconsin Avenue (now part of Sidwell Friends School); Bellevue-Rittenhouse residence (2715 Q Street NW); the old Supreme Court townhouse buildings in Washington; Clean Drinking Manor in Chevy Chase, Maryland; the Mason House and ruins on Analostan Island (Theodore Roosevelt Island); George Washington House in Bladensburg, Maryland; and a debtors' prison. Other sites include an unidentified old mill; Colton; the William Benning House, Prospect Hill; a house in Fort Pleasant, West Virginia; White Post, Virginia; Coleman's-Sugarland Run; the Shenandoah River; De Kalb Monument, Camden, South Carolina; and the South Carolina State Capitol, Columbia.

DATE: Ca. 1895–ca. 1905

PHOTOGRAPHERS: William A. Miller.

PHYSICAL DESCRIPTION: 46 silver gelatin photoprints, 20 × 25 cm, printed by the Library of Congress from original negatives.

LOT 10481

SUBJECTS: Funeral procession of President Franklin Delano Roosevelt in Washington, D.C. Horse-drawn caisson going to Union Station accompanied by police on motorcycles; railroad car. Close-ups of men, women, and children, both black and white, watching the procession; many openly weeping. Gen. George C. Marshall saluting.

NOTE: A handwritten note on an accompanying envelope states that these were taken for *Time* magazine. The 58 photos were made by the Library of Congress from original negatives, 44 of which are filed in series LC-T2. The other 14 negatives no longer exist.

Additional subjects are found in transparency series LC-T21 (4 35-mm color transparencies of the Franklin D. Roosevelt funeral procession) and LC-T22 (8 color transparencies, 6 × 6 cm and 10 × 13 cm, of Eisenhower administration notables, including Mrs. Richard Nixon, James C. Hagerty, and Charles E. Wilson).

DATE: April 14, 1945

PHOTOGRAPHERS: George Tames.

PHYSICAL DESCRIPTION: 62 silver gela-

William A. Miller. Rear view of the George Washington house, Bladensburg, Maryland, ca. 1900. Lot 10452.

LC-M61-11

tin photoprints (6 contact sheets), images 6 × 6 cm on sheets 20 × 25 cm; 58 silver gelatin photoprints, images 19 × 19 cm, on sheets 20 × 25 cm.

SOURCE: Gift of George Tames, 1966.

LOT 10499

SUBJECTS: Civil rights activities and personalities, in Washington, D.C., Texas, Tennessee, Mississippi, New York, Alabama, and Virginia, preceding and during the John F. Kennedy administration. Washington images may be found in the following five subdivisions: *Lot 10499-4:* President Kennedy arriving at a Washington movie theater; with cabinet and advisers; with visiting foreign student in the White House; with Janet Travell, his personal physician; delivering his first address to a joint session of congress (1961); and with Jacqueline Kennedy, receiving guests at the White House. (Photos by Cornell Capa.) *Lot 10499-5:* Senator Kennedy meeting with President Eisenhower at the White House to arrange for the change in administration (January 1961); and copy of manuscript of Kennedy's inaugural address. (Photos by Elliott Erwitt.) *Lot 10499-7:* Civil Rights March on Washington, August 28, 1963; close-ups of picketers in Washington, D.C.; portrait of Attorney General Robert Kennedy in his office. (Photos by Cornell Capa, Charles Harbutt, and Henri Cartier-Bresson.) *Lot 10499-8:* Pickets in front of the White House at the time of the Cuban missile crisis. (Photos by Dan Budnik.) *Lot 10499-12:* John F. Kennedy funeral. Coming out of St. Matthews Church, Washington, D.C.; Pennsylvania Avenue procession, including President Lyndon Johnson, Charles DeGaulle, John F. Kennedy's children, and Robert and Edward Kennedy; riderless horse in cortege; citizens lined up to file past coffin in Capitol Rotunda; citizens listening to car radios. (Photos by Dan Budnik, Wayne Miller, Charles Harbutt, Cornell Capa, and Elliott Erwitt.)

William A. Miller. Old Supreme Court building on Capitol Hill, ca. 1900. Lot 10452.

LC-M61-9

DATE: Ca. 1950s–1960s

PHOTOGRAPHERS: Magnum Photos, Inc., photographers, including Cornell Capa, Elliott Erwitt, Charles Harbutt, Henri Cartier-Bresson, Dan Budnik, and Wayne Miller.

PHYSICAL DESCRIPTION: Silver gelatin photoprints, 28 × 36 cm or smaller.

ARRANGEMENT: Lot consists of 12 subdivisions, only 5 of which picture events in Washington, D.C.

SOURCE: Gift of Magnum Photos, Inc., 1963.

RESTRICTIONS: Permission to copy must be obtained from Magnum Photos, Inc.

LOT 10535

SUBJECTS: Currency and postage stamp production at the U.S. Bureau of Engraving and Printing, Washington, D.C. Employees at work in the engraving, printing, trimming, wetting, and examining rooms; views of the numbering, sealing, and perforating processes.

DATE: Ca. 1934

PHOTOGRAPHERS: J. J. Campbell.

PHYSICAL DESCRIPTION: 8 silver gelatin photoprints, 21 × 26 cm.

SOURCE: Gift of J. J. Campbell, 1934.

LOT 10594

SUBJECTS: The frigate U.S.S. *Constitution*, which served in the War of 1812, during her visit to Washington, D.C., November 11, 1931, and to Los Angeles, California, in

1933. Also includes views in the Panama Canal and the Delaware River, approaching Philadelphia, Pennsylvania. Exterior and shipboard views, recommissioning ceremonies, July 1, 1931, and views of the ship afloat and tied to the dock; details of bow, stern, and rigging. Washington photographs (6 items) show the ship at anchor in the Anacostia River at the Washington Navy Yard.

NOTE: Photographs are captioned.

DATE: Ca. 1931–33

PHOTOGRAPHERS: Charles M. Hiller (San Francisco) for Associated Oil Co.

PHYSICAL DESCRIPTION: 27 silver gelatin photoprints, 20 × 25 cm or smaller.

SOURCE: Gift of Comdr. Louis J. Gulliver, 1940.

LOT 10647

COLLECTION NAME: Records of the National Association for the Advancement of Colored People (NAACP), Manuscript Division

SUBJECTS: Washington-related subjects include the Stokowski Youth Orchestra, the "All American Youth Orchestra," on the Watergate Barge and portraits of black and white musicians auditioning for the orchestra; Howard University students picketing the National Crime Conference in Washington, December 1934, over the conference's refusal to discuss lynching as a national crime; and interior views of Princess Anne Academy and the Colored State Normal School in Bowie, Maryland. Portraits of black leaders.

J. J. Campbell Photo Service. Currency Examining Room, Bureau of Engraving and Printing, Washington, D.C., ca. 1934. Lot 10535.
LC-USZ62-90610

REFERENCE: Melville, no. 168, pp. 247–48.

BIOGRAPHICAL NOTE: The Manuscript Division holds the records of the National Association for the Advancement of Colored People (NAACP), spanning the years 1909–39 (chiefly 1919–39). The records number 400,000 items and are accompanied by a finding aid. They contain correspondence, clippings, legal briefs, court records, speeches, articles, and printed matter treating such subjects as discrimination and segregation, lynchings, race riots, labor disputes, voting rights violations in the South, politics, and Negro life in urban and rural America, especially in the 1930s. Coverage includes Haiti, the Virgin Islands, and the Pan-African Congress. The records include personal papers of Supreme Court Justice Thurgood Marshall and the Scottsboro Defense Committee records. The photographs from the processed portion of the records were transferred to the [the] Prints and Photographs Division.

DATE: Ca. 1909–39

PHYSICAL DESCRIPTION: Ca. 500 albumen, platinum, and silver gelatin photoprints, reproductions, and newspaper clippings, 28 × 36 cm or smaller.

ARRANGEMENT: Arranged by subject; portraits of black leaders are alphabetically arranged.

SOURCE: Transfer from the Manuscript Division, 1968.

Charles Miller. "U.S. frigate Constitution at anchor off the Washington Navy Yard. . . . President [Hoover] was on board when [the] picture was taken." November 11, 1931. Lot 10594.
LC-USZ62-90611

LOT 10657

SUBJECTS: "The Library of Congress, Washington, D.C. Its Principal Architectural and Decorative Features in the Colors of the Originals," by Howard Grey Douglas (1901). Exterior and interior views of the Library of Congress Jefferson Building, including the Great Hall and many of the murals.

DATE: Ca. 1901

PUBLISHER: Printed by Osgood Art Colortype Co., New York.

PHYSICAL DESCRIPTION: 23 color photomechanical prints in a booklet, 24 × 28 cm.

SOURCE: Gift of Mrs. John Glenn, Jr.

Howard University students picketing the National Crime Conference in Washington, D.C., because the leaders of the conference refused to discuss lynching as a national crime. December 1934. Papers of the National Association for the Advancement of Colored People (NAACP), Lot 10647-1.
LC-USZ62-35363

Clinedinst. White House Office telegraph operator, November 1909. Lot 10809.
LC-USZ62-45952

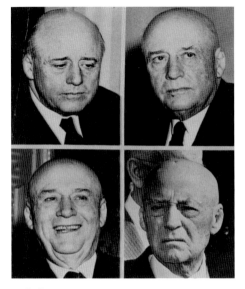

United Press International. Speaker of the House of Representatives, Sam Rayburn, shown (top left to bottom right) in 1937, 1953, 1958, and 1961. November 16, 1961. Lot 10994. Reproduced with the permission of UPI/Bettmann Newsphotos.

LOT 10809

SUBJECTS: New White House Office Building, Washington, D.C. Fred Carpenter in his private office; telegraph operator; congressional waiting room.

DATE: Ca. 1909

PHOTOGRAPHERS: B. M. Clinedinst.

PHYSICAL DESCRIPTION: 4 silver gelatin photoprints, 20 × 25 cm.

SOURCE: Copyright deposit by Clinedinst, 1909.

LOT 10994

SUBJECTS: Portraits of Sam Rayburn; with Joe Martin at House Speaker turnover, 1947 and 1955; with Harry Truman, Eleanor Roosevelt, Earl Warren, and Lyndon Johnson at dedication of Truman Library, 1957; administering oath of office to Dale Alford, 1959. Rayburn's funeral services, 1961.

DATE: ca. 1937–1961

PHOTOGRAPHERS: UPI and Wide World.

PHYSICAL DESCRIPTION: 11 silver gelatin photoprints, 20 × 25 cm or smaller.

RESTRICTIONS: Requires permission for reproduction.

LOT 11015 (stereographs)

SUBJECTS: Funeral of Adm. William T. Sampson, Washington, D.C. Scenes at his home, at an unidentified church, and at the gravesite. Naval cadets marching down Connecticut Avenue.

DATE: Ca. 1902

PHOTOGRAPHERS: William H. Rau.

PHYSICAL DESCRIPTION: 8 silver gelatin stereographs.

SOURCE: Copyright deposit by William H. Rau, May 28, 1902.

LOT 11022 (stereographs)

SUBJECTS: Armistice Day burial services for the Unknown Soldier. Arrival of the U.S.S. *Olympia*; President Harding, General Pershing, and Chief Justice Taft marching in the funeral procession; services at Arlington National Cemetery. Washington views include the Jewelled Arch, Pan American Union Building, and the World Disarmament Conference in Constitution Hall of the Daughters of the American Revolution Building, November 21, 1921.

DATE: November 1921

PHOTOGRAPHERS: Keystone View Company.

PHYSICAL DESCRIPTION: 11 silver gelatin stereographs.

SOURCE: Copyright deposit by Keystone View Company, 1921.

Keystone View Company. ''Jewelled Arch, Washington, D.C.'' November 1921. Lot 11022.
LC-USZ62-64030

LOT 11023 (stereographs)

SUBJECTS: Gen. John Joseph Pershing in Washington, D.C., and Armistice Day Parade. Pershing's arrival at Union Station; Pershing riding in an automobile and riding in the Pennsylvania Avenue parade, with the Victory Arch in the background. Wounded soldiers of First Division viewing the Pershing parade. Pershing with Vice President Marshall and Secretary of War Baker; and with workers at the War Department.

DATE: 1919

PHOTOGRAPHERS: Keystone View Company.

PHYSICAL DESCRIPTION: 8 silver gelatin stereographs.

SOURCE: Copyright deposit by Keystone, October 17, 1919.

LOT 11027 (stereographs)

SUBJECTS: National Service Camp for Girls, Washington, D.C. Classes in wireless, surgical dressing, knitting and sewing, and first aid; drilling under army supervision.

DATE: Ca. 1917

PHOTOGRAPHERS: Keystone View Company.

PHYSICAL DESCRIPTION: 5 silver gelatin stereographs.

SOURCE: Copyright deposit by Keystone View Company, June 22, 1917.

Keystone View Company. ''Welcoming General Pershing upon his arrival at the Union Station, Washington, D.C.'' 1919. Lot 11023.
LC-USZ62-90777

LOT 11039 (stereographs)

SUBJECTS: Scenes at the Capitol, Washington, D.C., during the celebration honoring Adm. George Dewey, October 3, 1899. Dewey with President McKinley and Cardinal Gibbons; White House table prepared for a state dinner. Also includes images of Dewey Day parade in St. Louis.

DATE: Ca. 1899–1900

PHOTOGRAPHERS: J. F. Jarvis, William Rau, C. L. Wasson, Young, C. H. Graves, and Keystone View Company.

PHYSICAL DESCRIPTION: 35 silver gelatin stereographs.

SOURCE: Copyright deposit.

LOT 11112

SUBJECTS: White House weddings and brides. Photographs, engravings, and photographic copies of periodical illustrations. Includes portraits of Mrs. Grover Cleveland (1886); and Jessie Wilson (Sayre) (1913). Some stereographs show flowers and wedding carriages (1906).

DATE: Ca. 1886–ca. 1920s

PHOTOGRAPHERS: Waldon Fawcett, D. B. Edmonston, Harris & Ewing, Clinedinst, C. M. Bell, E. S. Curtis, Keystone Stereoview, C. L. Wasson, C. H. Graves, and Universal Photo Art Co.

PHYSICAL DESCRIPTION: 63 albumen, silver gelatin, and dye gelatin photoprints (including some stereographs), and copies of engravings and photomechanical prints, 20 × 25 cm or smaller.

Keystone View Company. "Class in Wireless— National Service Camp for Girls, Washington, D.C." Copyright 1917. Lot 11027.

LC-USZ62-90778

ARRANGEMENT: Arranged chronologically.

SOURCE: Most by copyright deposit.

LOT 11205

COLLECTION NAME: Hanna-McCormick Family Papers, Manuscript Division

SUBJECTS: *Lot 11205–2*: Joseph Medill McCormick and his wife, Ruth Hanna McCormick, ca. 1890 to 1925. Portraits; their wood frame house in Georgetown; farm in Byron, Illinois. Joseph McCormick on congressional tour of the Western Front, 1917; Ruth McCormick at head table of Republican National Committee banquet, held in the new Willard Hotel, Washington, D.C., December 11, 1923. *Lot 11205–4*: Ruth Hanna McCormick: her political campaigns for U.S. House of Representatives, 1928, and U.S. Senate, 1930. Barbecue; casting ballot in Byron, Illinois; testifying on campaign expenses before Nye Committee, 1930; with local, state, and national political figures, including Gov. Louis Emmerson, Alice Longworth, and a group of seven newly elected congresswomen, in April 1929. One photograph shows Mrs. Medill McCormick with Paulina Longworth (daughter of House Speaker Longworth) at the Capital Society Children's Horse Show in Washington. Another image shows her on the Nye Committee (Senate Slush Fund) with other senators. *Lot 11205–5*: Ruth Hanna McCormick Simms; her political and social activities, 1932–44. Republican National Conventions; seconding speech for Landon; campaigning for Dewey; with Dawes, Wilkie, Dewey, Alice Longworth, and with her husband, Albert Gallatin Simms (former representative from New York). Wedding group, 1932. Special obituary supplement of the *Rockford Register-Republic* and the *Rockford Morning Star*, which she published.

NOTE: Corresponding negatives are found in series LC-H1 and LC-H11.

BIOGRAPHICAL NOTE: The Manuscript Division holds the papers of the Hanna-McCormick family, including diary and notebooks fragments, speeches, financial records, and printed matter. Ruth Hanna McCormick served in the House of Representatives and the Senate. After the death of her husband, Joseph Medill McCormick (senator from Illinois) in 1925, she married Albert Gallatin Simms, whom she had met while both of them were serving in the House of Representatives. She co-managed Thomas E. Dewey's presidential campaign and served on the Republican National Committee.

International Newsreel Corp. "Some of the new Congresswomen who took their seats in the House at the opening of the 71st session of Congress." 1929. Hanna-McCormick Family Papers, Lot 11205–4.

LC-USZ62-92529

Fort Myer, Virginia, 1894. Edgar A. Mearns Papers, Lot 11212.

LC-USZ62-48668

DATE: Ca. 1890s–ca. 1945

PHOTOGRAPHERS: Harris & Ewing, Fletcher's, News Picture Service, Moffett (Chicago), Associated Press, International Newsreel Corporation, and Acme.

PHYSICAL DESCRIPTION: Ca. 200 silver gelatin photoprints, 20 × 25 cm or smaller.

ARRANGEMENT: Lot is subdivided into five parts. Only Washington, D.C., material is described here.

SOURCE: Transfer from the Manuscript Division, 1969.

LOT 11212

COLLECTION NAME: Edgar A. Mearns Papers, Manuscript Division

SUBJECTS: U.S. Army posts. Includes four views of Fort Myer, Virginia, in 1894. Also includes views of Fort Snelling, Minnesota (1888); a hospital at Fort Meade, South Dakota (ca. 1890); and Fort Clark, Texas (1893). Some photos are unidentified.

BIOGRAPHICAL NOTE: The Papers of Edgar Alexander Mearns (1856–1916), naturalist and army surgeon, are held in the Manuscript Division and number 5,850 items. They span the years 1864–1918 and are accompanied by a finding aid. The papers consist of correspondence, reports, printed matter, and newspaper clippings, relating chiefly to Mearns's activities as a collector of data on animal and plant life, to his participation in the Smithsonian African Expedition of 1909, and to his duties as an army surgeon. Correspondents include Theodore Roosevelt. The Mearns Papers were acquired through a gift of Charles W. Richmond in 1924. The photographs were transferred to the Prints and Photographs Division.

DATE: Ca. 1888–ca. 1900

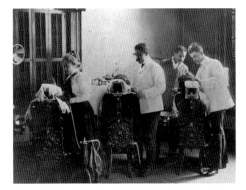

Dentistry students at Howard University, Washington, D.C., ca. 1900. Lot 11294.
LC-USZ62-35751

Law Library at Howard University, ca. 1900. Lot 11294.
LC-USZ62-40468

PHOTOGRAPHERS: D. H. Naramore.

PHYSICAL DESCRIPTION: 14 albumen, cyanotype, and silver gelatin photoprints, 20 × 25 cm or smaller.

SOURCE: Transfer from the Manuscript Division, 1970.

LOT 11294

SUBJECTS: Howard University, Washington D.C. Group portraits, President J. E. Rankin and his home; classroom scenes in sewing, dentistry, bacteriology, chemistry, pharmacy, carpentry, and printing; law library; main university building; Andrew Rankin Memorial Chapel. "Practice school" for young children; group portrait of the practice school teachers.

NOTE: Displayed as part of the American Negro exhibit at the Paris Exposition of 1900.

DATE: Ca. 1899–1900

PHYSICAL DESCRIPTION: 16 silver gelatin photoprints, 19 × 24 cm.

LOT 11303

SUBJECTS: Homes, churches, and businesses of blacks in Washington, D.C. Includes views of the Southern Hotel, "The Bee" (advertising printing), the Odd Fellows Hall, a black man standing in a doorway of a fashionable home, St. Augustine

"Negro hotel, Washington, D.C." Ca. 1900. Lot 11303.
LC-USZ62-51951

Catholic Church, Metropolitan Baptist Church on R Street, Presbyterian Church, Metropolitan African Methodist Episcopal Church, and the Vermont Avenue Baptist Church.

NOTE: Displayed as part of the American Negro exhibit at the Paris Exposition of 1900.

DATE: Ca. 1899–1900

PHYSICAL DESCRIPTION: 9 silver gelatin photoprints, 19 × 14 cm.

LOT 11329

SUBJECTS: U.S. Capitol and White House. Views include the Capitol at night, after a rainstorm, and after a snowstorm; the old Supreme Court Chamber in the Capitol; a joint session of Congress; and the White House after a snowstorm.

NOTE: Collected by John E. Helmus. Corresponding negatives for some images are found in series LC–X2.

DATE: Ca. 1900s–ca. 1930s

PHOTOGRAPHERS: Ernest Crandall and T. Stewart.

PHYSICAL DESCRIPTION: 16 silver gelatin photoprints, 28 × 36 cm or smaller.

SOURCE: Gift of Kennedy C. Watkins, 1970.

LOT 11352

SUBJECTS: Wedding of Patricia Nixon and Edward Cox in the Rose Garden of the White House, June 12, 1971. Documentary coverage of events from the formal announcement on March 16 to the post-reception departure of the bride and groom. Includes portraits of Richard Nixon, Mrs. Nixon, and Julie Nixon; the Cox family; and various wedding guests, including J. Edgar Hoover, Rose Mary Woods, Rev. Billy Graham, Ethel Waters, and cabinet members. Interiors of the White House, including the Blue Room, State Dining Room, East Room, Grand Hall, Lincoln Bedroom, and Map Room. President Nixon announcing Tricia's engagement to Edward Cox. Wedding rehearsal and other preparations, television booths, press stands, and tent. Blair House rehearsal dinner, and wedding cake. Diplomatic reception at Anderson House for Tricia and Ed Cox. Mrs. Agnew's shower for Tricia. Party given for Tricia at the Decatur House by Helen Thomas, UPI, and members of the Washington Press Corps.

DATE: 1971

PHOTOGRAPHERS: White House photographers.

PHYSICAL DESCRIPTION: 68 black-and-white and color photoprints, 20 × 25 cm.

SOURCE: Gift of the White House, 1972.

LOT 11489

COLLECTION NAME: Gutzon Borglum Papers, Manuscript Division

SUBJECTS: Mostly unidentified photographs of sculpture and paintings, portraits, groups, pictures from the Bull Moose Convention (1912), the postcard series "Oregon Train Monument Expedition, 1906–1911," and other postcards and views. Includes one banquet camera group portrait with President Coolidge in front of the White House.

NOTE: John Gutzon de la Mothe Borglum (1867–1941) was a sculptor, artist, and author. His papers are held in the Manuscript Division (71,000 items, spanning the years 1895–1960) and include material relating to his artistic works, chiefly Mount Rushmore and the Stone Mountain Confederate Memorial, and correspondence on a variety of issues with Presidents Theodore Roosevelt, Franklin D. Roosevelt, Warren Harding, Calvin Coolidge, and Woodrow Wilson, as well as with cabinet members, artists, authors, and government leaders. His papers were a gift of Mary Borglum and Lincoln Borglum (1951–53 and 1961–65), and some were transferred from the U.S. National Park Service in 1973. The photographs were transferred to the Prints and Photograph Division.

PHOTOGRAPHERS: Harris & Ewing and Parker.

PHYSICAL DESCRIPTION: Ca. 150 silver gelatin photoprints, 21 × 71 cm or smaller.

SOURCE: Transfer from the Manuscript Division, 1972.

LOT 11490

COLLECTION NAME: Herbert Putnam Papers, Manuscript Division

SUBJECTS: Portraits of Herbert Putnam's family and friends. Includes photos of the sculptor Brenda Putnam and Herbert Putnam.

NOTE: Most images are uncaptioned.

Librarian of Congress Herbert Putnam at his desk, 1912. Herbert Putnam Papers, Lot 11491.
LC-USZ62-90776

BIOGRAPHICAL NOTE: Herbert Putnam was Librarian of Congress from 1899 to 1939. The Manuscript Division holds his papers, which span the years 1783–1958 and number 8,000 items. They are accompanied by a finding aid. These materials, which were a gift of Brenda Putnam and Mrs. Eliot O'Hara, 1956–63, include family diaries, speeches, articles, scrapbooks, genealogical material, and an autograph collection. Putnam's papers relate not only to his position as Librarian of Congress but also to his work as director of the Boston Public Library. The main body of Putnam's archive as Librarian of Congress is in the Library of Congress Archive (Central File) in the Manuscript Division.

DATE: Ca. 1860s–ca. 1950s

PHYSICAL DESCRIPTION: 5 family albums (ca. 350 items) and loose albumen, collodion, and silver gelatin photoprints, including cartes de visite, tintypes, cabinet cards, stereographs, and early snapshot photoprints, 20 × 25 cm or smaller.

SOURCE: Transfer from the Manuscript Division, 1971.

LOT 11491

COLLECTION NAME: Herbert Putnam Papers, Manuscript Division

SUBJECTS: Portraits of Herbert Putnam. Putnam as a child; with his family; as a librarian and as director of the Boston Public Library; as Librarian of Congress, in various Library of Congress settings, and with

the staff; with honorary degree recipients at Princeton University; at class reunions (Harvard 1883); at an American Library Association dinner honoring him (Boston, 1950). Includes photographs of Putnam with the Gutenberg Bible; and with Luther Evans and Milton Lord at a 1950 dinner at the Mayflower Hotel.

BIOGRAPHICAL NOTE: See Lot 11490.

DATE: Ca. 1860s–ca. 1950s

PHOTOGRAPHERS: Harris & Ewing, Bachrach, Underwood & Underwood, Tager, Scherer, Clinedinst, Keystone View Company, M. Thérèse Bonney, Pach Bros., Associated News, and Notman.

PHYSICAL DESCRIPTION: Ca. 65 albumen, platinum, and silver gelatin photoprints, 28 × 36 cm or smaller.

SOURCE: Transfer from the Manuscript Division, 1971.

LOT 11520

SUBJECTS: Group portraits of U.S. Supreme Court Justices. Includes one photomontage composite print of all justices from 1789–1939.

DATE: Ca. 1865–1987

PHOTOGRAPHERS: Mathew Brady studio, A. Gardner, C. M. Bell, Clinedinst, George Prince, Bachrach, Capitol Art & Publishing Co., C. F. Robinson, M. G. Steele, Harris & Ewing, and Sarony (New York).

PHYSICAL DESCRIPTION: 78 albumen, platinum, and silver gelatin photoprints, and photomechanical prints, 41 × 51 cm or smaller, including carte-de-visite format.

C. M. Bell. Group portrait of U.S. Supreme Court justices, 1888. Lot 11520.
LC-USZ62-90608

Model of an unexecuted scheme for the Smithsonian Institution Museum of Natural History, for the facade facing the Mall. Lot 11534.

LC-USZ62-58778

LOT 11534

SUBJECTS: Photographs of models of various Washington, D.C., federal buildings by the architectural sculptor James Parrington Earley, as well as public buildings in Baltimore and Chicago. Includes models for light standards similar to those now in front of the Library of Congress, a model of the Library of Congress Jefferson Building reading room and exterior facades; a full-size model of the Department of Agriculture Building on the Mall; and an unexecuted scheme for the Museum of Natural History on the Mall.

PHYSICAL DESCRIPTION: 21 silver gelatin photoprints form copy negatives, 20 × 25 cm.

SOURCE: Copy negatives lent to the Library for printing in 1976.

LOT 11659

COLLECTION NAME: Albert James Myer Papers, Manuscript Division

SUBJECTS: Photographs relating to the military career of Albert James Myer, who organized the U.S. Army Signal Corps in 1861. Washington-area subjects include the "Balloon Camp" at Gaines Mill, Virginia (May 1862); Professor Lowe preparing to ascend in a reconnaissance balloon (May 1862); a signal tower on Elk Mountain, overlooking Antietam battlefield; a sketch of the Signal Camp of Instruction in Georgetown; a wash drawing of a signal tower at Fort Reno, Washington, D.C.; and a photograph of meteorological instruments. Also includes photographic portraits of Myer, and a photographic copy of a painted portrait of Myer. Other subjects include the grounds of the Centennial Exhibition in Philadelphia and Pike's Peak summit observation station.

Mathew Brady. Portrait of Brig. Gen. Albert J. Myer, chief signal officer, U.S. Army. Myer organized the U.S. Army Signal Corps in 1861. Ca. 1865. Albert James Myer Papers, Lot 11659.

LC-USZ62-92899

BIOGRAPHICAL NOTE: The Manuscript Division holds the Papers of Albert James Myer (1829–1880). They number 300 items, span the years 1851–1933, and are accompanied by a finding aid. Myer was an army officer and surgeon, who organized and commanded the U.S. Army Signal Corps (1856–80). His papers pertain to his army career and to the Signal Corps' contribution to Union military efforts in the Civil War.

DATE: Ca. 1860s–1870s

PHOTOGRAPHERS: Hinton's Gallery, Alexander Gardner, Mathew Brady studio, Rice, and Morris Smith.

PHYSICAL DESCRIPTION: 21 albumen and silver gelatin photoprints (including cabinet cards and cartes de visite) and halftone photomechanical prints, 22 × 26 cm or smaller.

SOURCE: Transfer from the Manuscript Division, 1977.

LOT 11670

SUBJECTS: Pentagon construction photographs and plans. Aerial, panoramic, and close-up views of the building; elevations, grading and planting plans, land maps.

DATE: 1941–43

PHYSICAL DESCRIPTION: 72 silver gela-

tin and Vandyke photoprints and photostats, 74 × 103 cm or smaller.

SOURCE: Gift of the Ohio Historical Society, 1970.

LOT 11807

SUBJECTS: Photographic documentation of crowded work and storage areas in the Library of Congress, Washington, D.C. Photographs were used as exhibits in congressional appropriations hearings in 1966. Includes views of bookstacks; Legislative Reference Service; Great Hall exhibit area; and Orientalia, Exchange and Gift, Science and Technology, Card, and Map Divisions.

DATE: Ca. 1966

PHYSICAL DESCRIPTION: 28 silver gelatin photoprints, 20 × 25 cm.

SOURCE: Transfer from the Information Office, 1970s.

LOT 12044

SUBJECTS: Marine Barracks, Eighth and I Streets SE, Washington, D.C. Parade grounds, drills, inspection, Marine Band, mess hall, main gate, officers' quarters, and Commandant's House.

NOTE: "Passed by the Committee on Public Information, Washington" stamped on verso of each item.

DATE: 1917

PHYSICAL DESCRIPTION: 41 silver gelatin photoprints, 10 × 15 cm.

LOT 12045

COLLECTION: Myrtilla Miner Papers, Manuscript Division

Pentagon construction site, across the Potomac River from Washington, D.C., ca. 1941. Pentagon Construction Photographs, Lot 11670.

LC-USZ62-92751

SUBJECTS: Portraits of Miner; Miner Hall at Howard University; unidentified homes; two unidentified silhouettes; heraldic design. Drawing of Thaddeus Hyatt's cell in the Washington Jail, inscribed by him to Miner.

BIOGRAPHICAL NOTE: Myrtilla Miner (1815–1864) was an educator and feminist. She founded a "school for colored girls" in Washington, D.C., in 1851.

DATE: Ca. 1860–ca. 1940

PHOTOGRAPHERS: Henry Ulke, J. K. Stevens, and the Scurlock Studio.

PHYSICAL DESCRIPTION: 9 photoprints and photomechanical prints, 26 × 30 cm or smaller.

SOURCE: Gift of Sophia M. Albe, 1952. Transfer from the Manuscript Division.

Marine Barracks, Squad Room, Washington, D.C., ca. 1917. Lot 12044.
LC-USZ62-92802

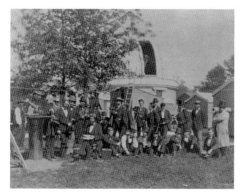

Transit of Venus teams on the U.S. Naval Observatory south lawn, Washington, D.C. Group portrait includes Superintendent Charles Henry Davis, Dr. Henry Draper, Professor of Mathematics Simon Newcomb, and photographer Irvin Stanley. Spring 1874. Asaph Hall Family Papers, Lot 12046.
LC-USZ62-92801

LOT 12046

COLLECTION NAME: Asaph Hall Family Papers, Manuscript Division

SUBJECTS: Portraits of Asaph Hall III, Francis Brunnow, Alvin Clark, Charles H. Davis, Henry Draper, Simon Newcomb, and Irvin Stanley. U.S. Naval Observatory, Washington, D.C. Also includes Cairo, Egypt; Vladivostok, Russia; group at Pike's Peak; observatory buildings and equipment from Transit of Venus Expedition to Russian Station.

BIOGRAPHICAL NOTE: Asaph Hall was an astronomer and professor of mathematics at the U.S. Naval Observatory. The Manuscript Division holds the Hall Family Papers, spanning the years 1837–1980, which number 1,000 items. The papers include Asaph Hall IV's typescript manuscript "Reminiscences of the Naval Observatory" (1929). The papers were acquired by gifts from members of the Hall family, 1969–82.

DATE: Ca. 1870–ca. 1900

PHYSICAL DESCRIPTION: 4 photoprints and 1 collotype, 26 × 31 cm or smaller.

SOURCE: Gift of Mary (Mrs. Wylie) Kilpatrick, granddaughter of Asaph Hall III. Transfer from the Manuscript Division, 1972.

LOT 12252 (stereographs)

SUBJECTS: U.S. Capitol, Washington Monument and the Mall, Library of Congress, Union Station, National Museum of Natural History, Arlington Cemetery amphitheater, and Mount Vernon.

NOTE: "Herbert E. Ives" stamped on recto of some items. Five stereographs have views both back and front.

DATE: Ca. 1935–45

PHOTOGRAPHERS: Herbert Eugene Ives.

PHYSICAL DESCRIPTION: 19 photoprints, 9 × 18 cm and 14 × 19 cm.

SOURCE: Transfer from the Smithsonian Institution's Frederick and Herbert Ives Collection, 1964.

LOT 12255

COLLECTION NAME: Arthur Wallace Dunn Papers, Manuscript Division

SUBJECTS: Arthur Wallace Dunn, James Hall McKenney and family members,

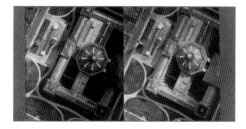

Herbert E. Ives. Aerial view (stereopair) of the Library of Congress (Jefferson Building), ca. 1935–45. Lot 12252.
LC-USZ62-92803

Abraham Lincoln reading to his son. Ca. 1860s. Lot 12255.
LC-USZ62-92539

Abraham Lincoln and son, and others. Some unidentified items.

BIOGRAPHICAL NOTE: Arthur Wallace Dunn was a journalist whose papers in the Manuscript Division span the years 1882–1927 and number 250 items. Dunn corresponded with many important Washington figures, including Presidents Warren G. Harding, Theodore Roosevelt, and Woodrow Wilson.

DATE: Ca. 1860–ca. 1910

PHOTOGRAPHERS: C. M. Bell and B. J. Falk.

PHYSICAL DESCRIPTION: 12 albumen and silver gelatin photoprints, 27 × 20 cm or smaller.

SOURCE: Gift of Mrs. Arthur Dunn and others, 1967. Transfer from the Manuscript Division, 1972.

Dedication of the Washington Monument, Washington, D.C., February 21, 1885. Constance McLaughlin Green Papers, Lot 12258.

LC-USZ62-89199

Harris & Ewing. Portrait of Mary Church Terrell. Mary Church Terrell Papers, Lot 12257.

LC-USZ62-92821

René Bache. Model designed by Theodore Bingham, commissioner of public buildings during the McKinley administration, of the proposed wings to the White House, ca. 1900. Theodore A. Bingham Collection, Lot 12264.

LC-X14-1

LOT 12256

COLLECTION NAME: George Washington Papers, Manuscript Division

SUBJECTS: Gadsby's Tavern, Christ Church, Carlyle House, City Hotel, Hayfield Farm, and Washington's property, in Alexandria and Mount Vernon, Virginia; Gunston Hall; monuments to Washington. Portraits of George and Martha Washington. Silhouette of Washington.

BIOGRAPHICAL NOTE: The Manuscript Division holds the George Washington Papers, which number 77,000 items. The papers span the years 1592–1937 (chiefly 1748–99) and are accompanied by a finding aid. They consist of correspondence, diaries, military papers, and accounts that relate not only to Washington's term as president but to his career as a Continental Army officer and patriot. Acquired through purchase, gift, and exchange, ca. 1867–1962. Photographs were transferred to the Prints and Photographs Division.

DATE: Ca. 1783–ca. 1910

PHOTOGRAPHERS: Jameson (Alexandria, Virginia).

PHYSICAL DESCRIPTION: 22 photoprints, engravings, lithographs, and other reproductions, 20 × 25 cm or smaller.

SOURCE: Gift of E. E. Prussing. Transfer from the Manuscript Division, 1974.

LOT 12257

COLLECTION NAME: Mary Church Terrell Papers, Manuscript Division

SUBJECTS: Portraits of Mary Church Terrell, Terrell's mother, Harriet Beecher Stowe, and Susan B. Anthony.

BIOGRAPHICAL NOTE: Mary Church Terrell (1863–1954) was a black leader, author, lecturer, and educator. The Manuscript Division holds her papers, numbering 13,000 items and spanning the years 1851–1962 (chiefly 1886–1954). They are accompanied by a finding aid. The papers include correspondence, diaries, speeches, clippings, and other materials. The photographs were transferred to the Prints and Photographs Division.

DATE: Ca. 1890–ca. 1940

PHOTOGRAPHERS: Harris & Ewing and Sarony (New York).

PHYSICAL DESCRIPTION: 9 albumen and silver gelatin photoprints and a die stamp, 26 × 18 cm or smaller.

SOURCE: Gift of Phyllis Terrell Langston. Transfer from the Manuscript Division, 1976.

LOT 12258

COLLECTION NAME: Constance McLaughlin Green Papers, Manuscript Division

SUBJECTS: Views, portrait paintings, and engravings of historical figures, Capitol Hill alleys, Potomac River bathers, federal housing projects, temporary army housing on the Mall, construction sites, Franklin D. Roosevelt gravesite, Bonus Army, maps.

NOTE: These are copy prints from originals in the Library of Congress, National Archives, Smithsonian Institution, and the Department of the Army, with credit lines on the verso of each item. Used in preparation of Constance McLaughlin Green's *Washington*, 2 vols. (Princeton: Princeton University Press, 1962–63). Two images in this lot were published in vol. 2 as illustrations 1 and 20.

BIOGRAPHICAL NOTE: Constance McLaughlin Green (1897–1975) was a historian and author. The Manuscript Division holds her papers, which are accompanied by a finding aid. They span the years 1920–69 (chiefly 1953–63) and number 22,000 items. The correspondence, drafts, clippings, and other materials relate primarily to her research on the history of Washington, D.C., and the subsequent publication of her two-volume Pulitzer Prize-winning history of the capitol. Her interests included urban history and the history of blacks in Washington. The photographs from her papers were transferred to the Prints and Photographs Division.

DATE: Ca. 1850–1950

PHYSICAL DESCRIPTION: 61 silver gelatin copy photoprints, 20 × 25 cm or smaller.

SOURCE: Gift of Constance Green, 1966 and 1970. Transfer from the Manuscript Division, 1977.

LOT 12260

COLLECTION NAME: Montgomery Family Papers, Manuscript Division

SUBJECTS: Banquet camera portraits of groups of black and white citizens in Washington, D.C. Republican National Committee meetings and banquet in the Carleton Hotel, presidents of Republican women's clubs, Presidents Coolidge and Hoover in group photos taken in front of the White House, a dinner held by Perry W. Howard in the Whitelaw Hotel, and prominent black citizens such as Mary Church Terrell, Eugene P. Booze, and Mary Montgomery Booze.

BIOGRAPHICAL NOTE: The Manuscript Division holds the Montgomery Family Papers, which number 12 items and span the years 1872–1938. Isaiah Thornton Montgomery (1847–1924) founded a

black community in Mound Bayou, Mississippi, in 1887. The holdings include a master's thesis on Mound Bayou, a transcript entitled "The Montgomery Saga, from Slavery to Black Power," Mary Virginia Montgomery's diary, and biographical sketches of Mary Cordelia Booze (Isaiah's daughter) and her husband Eugene P. Booze. The photographs were transferred to the Prints and Photographs Division.

DATE: 1919–38

PHOTOGRAPHERS: Schutz, Scurlock, and Tenschert.

PHYSICAL DESCRIPTION: 6 silver gelatin photoprints, 31 × 86 cm or smaller.

SOURCE: Gift of Mrs. Eugene Wood. Transfer from the Manuscript Division, 1971.

LOT 12263

COLLECTION NAME: James Garfield Randall Papers, Manuscript Division

SUBJECTS: Portraits and copies of wood engravings from illustrated newspapers of the period, related to the Civil War and Abraham Lincoln. Portrait of President Lincoln, Frederick Douglass, and Postmaster General Montgomery Blair. Includes copy photographs of portraits of congressmen, cabinet members, and Civil War officers, including Generals Butler, Sherman, Banks, Francis Blair, Jr., and Grant. Also includes a view of the Brick Capitol.

NOTE: Copy photographs obtained by Randall from various repositories.

BIOGRAPHICAL NOTE: James Garfield Randall (1881–1953) was a historian who wrote about Abraham Lincoln and the Civil War. The Manuscript Division holds the Papers of James G. and Ruth (Painter) Randall, numbering 7,800 items, which span the years 1850–1952 and are accompanied by a finding aid. The papers consist of correspondence, notes, memoranda, drafts, printed matter and photocopies related to his research, and the manuscript of "Mary Lincoln: Biography of a Marriage," written by Randall's wife, Ruth (Painter) Randall.

DATE: Ca. 1860s–ca. 1870s

PHOTOGRAPHERS: Mathew Brady.

PHYSICAL DESCRIPTION: 38 silver gelatin photoprints and photographic copies of photomechanical prints, 40 × 35 cm or smaller.

SOURCE: Transfer from the Manuscript Division, 1969.

LOT 12264

COLLECTION NAME: Theodore A. Bingham Collection, Manuscript Division

SUBJECTS: Architectural model for side extensions to the White House, designed by Theodore A. Bingham, commissioner of public buildings and grounds during the McKinley administration. The design was never realized.

NOTE: Corresponding negatives are found in series LC-X-14.

BIOGRAPHICAL NOTE: Theodore A. Bingham was commissioner of public buildings and grounds for Washington during the McKinley and Roosevelt administrations and served informally as an aide at the White House for various social and political functions held there during that period. The Manuscript Division holds his papers, including newspaper clippings and other material related to his official functions at the White House from the years 1897–1903.

DATE: Ca. 1900

PHOTOGRAPHERS: René Bache.

PHYSICAL DESCRIPTION: 4 modern silver gelatin photoprints, 20 × 25 cm, made by the Library from original glass plate negatives.

SOURCE: Transfer from the Manuscript Division, 1966

"$1,000,000 in $1 Currency Notes," silver certificates, at the Bureau of Engraving and Printing, ca. 1950–69. Lot 12265.

LC-USZ62-92466

LOT 12265

SUBJECTS: Bureau of Engraving and Printing, Washington, D.C. Engraving processes, machinery, staff at work, stacks of printed money, building exterior.

NOTE: Photographs are captioned.

DATE: Ca. 1950–69

PHYSICAL DESCRIPTION: 16 silver gelatin photoprints, 20 × 25 cm.

LOT 12266

SUBJECTS: Four Chief Assistant Librarians of Congress: Ainsworth R. Spofford, Martin A. Roberts, Luther H. Evans, and Frederick W. Ashley. Ashley is shown receiving the Gutenberg Bible in a trunk.

NOTE: Photographs collected by Verner W. Clapp, Chief Assistant Librarian under Librarian of Congress Luther Evans.

DATE: Ca. 1865–1947

PHOTOGRAPHERS: Underwood & Underwood.

PHYSICAL DESCRIPTION: 4 silver gelatin photoprints, 27 × 22 cm or smaller.

SOURCE: Gift of Mrs. Verner W. Clapp, 1972.

Underwood & Underwood. Frederick W. Ashley, chief of the Order Division and Chief Assistant Librarian of Congress, with the Gutenberg Bible, upon its arrival from Austria at the Library of Congress with the Vollbehr Collection. Lot 12266. Reproduced with the permission of Joseph Rotwein.

LOT 12267

SUBJECTS: Hillcrest Children's Center, Washington, D.C., located at 4123 Nebraska Avenue NW from 1927 to 1966. Interior and exterior views, officials, children playing, Christmas activities, outings. Portrait of Mrs. John P. Van Ness, founder.

NOTE: Corresponding negatives for some photographs are found in series LC-X15.

DATE: Before 1963

PHOTOGRAPHERS: C. M. Bell.

PHYSICAL DESCRIPTION: 140 silver gelatin photoprints and drawings, 37 × 18 cm or smaller.

SOURCE: Gift of the Hillcrest Children's Center. Transfer from the Manuscript Division, 1972.

LOT 12268

SUBJECTS: Presentation of Wide Wide World TV series kinescopes to the Library of Congress. L. Quincy Mumford, Librarian of Congress; S. E. Skinner, General Motors; and Davidson Taylor, NBC Television, at presentation ceremony. NBC TV cameras and crew trucks outside Library of Congress Jefferson Building.

NOTE: Accompanied by newspaper clipping that reproduces one of the photos with caption added.

Ellen Lewis Herndon Arthur, wife of President Chester Alan Arthur. Chester Alan Arthur Papers, Lot 12270.

LC-USZ62-92599

DATE: 1956

PHOTOGRAPHERS: Mark English for Reni Newsphoto Service.

PHYSICAL DESCRIPTION: 8 silver gelatin photoprints, 20 × 25 cm.

LOT 12269

COLLECTION NAME: Louis Freeland Post Papers, Manuscript Division

SUBJECTS: Portrait photographs related to the life and career of Louis Freeland Post. Louis Freeland Post; his wife, Alice Thacher Post; war cabinet of Secretary of Labor William B. Wilson, in 1918; Department of Labor conference participants in San Francisco.

BIOGRAPHICAL NOTE: Louis Freeland Post was a lawyer, editor, and author. The Manuscript Division holds his papers, which span the years 1864–1939 and number 600 items. They are accompanied by a finding aid. Included are his correspondence with William Jennings Bryan (1900–1922), the manuscript of his autobiography (*Living a Long Life Over Again*), book manuscripts (*Delirium of Nineteen Twenty* and *The Prophet of San Francisco*), and many articles written for various national magazines and newspapers. The photographs were transferred to the Prints and Photographs Division.

DATE: Ca. 1877–ca. 1918

PHYSICAL DESCRIPTION: 7 albumen and silver gelatin photoprints, 31 × 36 cm or smaller.

SOURCE: Gift of Mrs. Phyllis B. Post, 1933–36. Transfer from the Manuscript Division, 1973.

LOT 12270

COLLECTION NAME: Chester Alan Arthur Papers, Manuscript Division

SUBJECTS: Ellen Herndon Arthur, wife of President Arthur. Members of Arthur's cabinet: Timothy Howe, Charles Folger, William Chandler, Hugh McCulloch, Robert Todd Lincoln, Frank Hatton, Henry Teller, Benjamin Brewster, Frederick Frelinghuysen.

NOTE: Portrait of Ellen Arthur is a hand-tinted albumen print in an oval silver frame.

BIOGRAPHICAL NOTE: The papers of Chester Alan Arthur (1829–1886), president of the United States, 1881–85, are held in the Manuscript Division. Numbering 4,400 items, the papers span the years 1843–1960 and contain correspondence, financial documents, scrapbooks, clippings, and miscellany, dating chiefly from 1870–88. A finding aid to the papers was published in 1961. The photographs were transferred to the Prints and Photographs Division.

DATE: Ca. 1870–ca. 1885

PHOTOGRAPHERS: C. M. Bell and Sterry (Saratoga Springs, N.Y.).

PHYSICAL DESCRIPTION: 10 albumen and silver gelatin photoprints, 18 × 14 cm or smaller.

SOURCE: Gift of Chester Alan Arthur III. Transfer from the Manuscript Division.

LOT 12271

COLLECTION NAME: Elihu Root photographs from the Emily Stewart collection, Manuscript Division

SUBJECTS: Portrait of Elihu Root; unidentified house and grounds.

BIOGRAPHICAL NOTE: The papers of the statesman Elihu Root (1845–1937) are held in the Manuscript Division. They number 66,000 items, span the years 1863–1937 (chiefly 1899–1937), and are accompanied by a finding aid. The papers include Root's correspondence, speeches, subject files, financial papers, and appointment books and printed matter related to his public service as secretary of war and state, member of the Alaskan Boundary Tribunal, U.S. senator from New York, chairman of the Board of Trustees of the Carnegie Institute of Washington, and head or member of numerous high-level delegations and committees involved with international politics. The papers were acquired through gifts, 1919–72. Related photographs from the Emily A. Stewart collection of Elihu Root material were transferred to the Prints and Photographs Division.

DATE: Ca. 1909–ca. 1920

PHOTOGRAPHER: L. K. Frey.

PHYSICAL DESCRIPTION: 8 silver gelatin photoprints, 25 × 31 cm or smaller.

SOURCE: Gift of Mary Smith. Transfer from the Manuscript Division, 1973.

LOT 12272

COLLECTION NAME: John C. Calhoun Collection, Manuscript Division

SUBJECTS: Portraits, including John C. Calhoun and Stephen A. Douglas.

BIOGRAPHICAL NOTE: John Caldwell Calhoun (1781–1850) was vice president of the United States, secretary of state, secretary of war, and U.S. senator from South Carolina. His collection in the Manuscript Division (67 items) spans the years 1819–1950 and was acquired through gift and purchase, 1901–56. The photographs were transferred to the Prints and Photographs Division.

DATE: Ca. 1825–ca. 1860

PHYSICAL DESCRIPTION: 4 photomechanical reproductions, a photoprint, and an engraving, 17 × 27 cm or smaller.

SOURCE: Transfer from the Manuscript Division, 1975.

LOT 12273

SUBJECTS: William Redish Pywell and family. Portraits of Pywell and his sister, Laura Pywell O'Sullivan, wife of Timothy O'Sullivan.

NOTE: Handwritten captions on versos. Accompanied by copies of a family record, a list of participants in the Transit of Venus Expedition (including Pywell), and other documents.

BIOGRAPHICAL NOTE: Pywell was a photographer employed by both Mathew Brady and Alexander Gardner on western expeditions. He also participated in the Transit of Venus Expedition, directed by the U.S. Naval Observatory in Washington, D.C.

DATE: Ca. 1860–ca. 1880

PHYSICAL DESCRIPTION: 7 albumen photoprints, 20 × 25 cm and 18 × 13 cm.

SOURCE: Gift of E. Marshall Pywell, 1975.

LOT 12275

COLLECTION NAME: Joseph C. Mehaffey Papers, Manuscript Division

SUBJECTS: Construction of the Arlington Memorial Bridge, views behind the Lincoln Memorial, and the Great Terrace in Meridian Hill Park, Washington, D.C. Includes views of the Memorial Bridge drawbridge while open, close-ups of bridge structural elements, and construction of the stairway and terraced grassy areas on the Potomac River bank behind the Lincoln Memorial. Includes aerial view of

U.S. Army Air Service. Aerial view of the Lincoln Memorial Bridge, Washington, D.C. The Boundary Channel Bridge appears in the left background. September 6, 1930. Joseph C. Mehaffey Papers, Lot 12275.

LC-USZ62-92531

Hains Point, Fort McNair, and the Lincoln Memorial area. One photographic copy of an 1824 watercolor of the Capitol by C. Burton. Also includes photographs from Panama, showing various receptions and ceremonies, the Madden Dam project, the Panama Canal model, and various promotional subjects.

BIOGRAPHICAL NOTE: Joseph Cowles Mehaffey (1889–1963) was a U.S. Army engineer and governor of the Panama Canal Zone. His engineering projects included Arlington Memorial Bridge and the renovation of the White House. His papers, held in the Manuscript Division, span the years 1925–59, number 900 items, and are accompanied by a finding aid. The photographs were transferred to the Prints and Photographs Division.

DATE: Ca. 1925–ca. 1948

PHOTOGRAPHERS: U.S. Army Air Service and Commercial Photo.

PHYSICAL DESCRIPTION: 1 album (15 photoprints), 18 × 26 cm, and 105 silver gelatin photoprints, 21 × 29 cm or smaller.

ARRANGEMENT: Panama; Washington, D.C.; and Miscellaneous.

SOURCE: Gift of Harry N. Burgess. Transfer from the Manuscript Division, 1972.

LOT 12500

SUBJECTS: Library of Congress Jefferson Building. High views of the Jefferson Building from the Capitol dome; Main Reading Room and dome; Rare Book Reading Room; courtyard; Great Hall, first and second floors; exhibit areas; the Gutenberg Bible on display; plaster decorative elements; door by Olin L. Warner; the shrine for the Declaration of Independence and Constitution. Includes an aerial view of Capitol, Library of Congress, Capitol Hill, the Mall, and Southwest and Northwest Washington.

NOTE: Corresponding negatives for some views are found in series LC-USL5 (L. C. Handy photographs).

DATE: Ca. 1880s–1940s

PHOTOGRAPHERS: Leet Bros. and L. C. Handy.

PHYSICAL DESCRIPTION: 17 silver gelatin photoprints, 45 × 67 cm or smaller.

LOT 12502

SUBJECTS: Library of Congress in the U.S. Capitol, including copies of wood engravings. Portrait of Ainsworth Rand Spofford. Photograph of Jefferson's book collection stored in Library of Congress vault.

DATE: Ca. 1880s–1900

PHYSICAL DESCRIPTION: 5 silver gelatin copy photoprints, 20 × 25 cm.

LOT 12503

SUBJECTS: Library of Congress, Jefferson Building and Adams Building. Rare Book Reading Room; public card catalog in the Jefferson Building; two architectural renderings for the Adams Building by F. Duckett and David Lynn.

NOTE: Some images carry exhibition captions in French, possibly for the Paris Exhibition of 1900.

DATE: Ca. 1900–ca. 1930s

PHOTOGRAPHERS: Leet Bros.

PHYSICAL DESCRIPTION: 4 silver gelatin photoprints, 62 × 123 cm or smaller.

LOT 12510

SUBJECTS: Model of the proposed extensions to the White House during the McKinley administration.

DATE: 1900

PHOTOGRAPHERS: J. F. Jarvis.

PHYSICAL DESCRIPTION: 2 silver gelatin photoprints, 30 × 42 cm.

SOURCE: Copyright deposit by J. F. Jarvis, 1900.

LOT 12511

SUBJECTS: Catholic University, Washington, D.C. Washington's Tomb at Mount Vernon.

DATE: 1890

PHOTOGRAPHERS: Luke C. Dillon of Pullman's Gallery.

PHYSICAL DESCRIPTION: 2 albumen photoprints, 33 × 47 cm or smaller.

SOURCE: Copyright deposit by Luke C. Dillon, 1890.

LOT 12513

SUBJECTS: Dedication of the Pilgrim Steps at the National Cathedral, Washington, D.C. Service of dedication; unveiling of the dedication tablets; Roland Taylor, benefactor, presenting key to Bishop Freeman.

DATE: May 16, 1930

PHOTOGRAPHERS: R. J. Bonde.

PHYSICAL DESCRIPTION: 5 silver gelatin photoprints, 20 × 25 cm.

SOURCE: Copyright deposit by Bonde, 1930.

LOT 12515

SUBJECTS: "Parade of Peace Jubilee" on Pennsylvania Avenue, Washington, D.C. Images show Post Office Department Building (now the Old Post Office), businesses, and other buildings in the vicinity of Pennsylvania Avenue; trolley cars and horse-drawn carriages; and the neighborhood between Twelfth and Fourteenth Streets on Pennsylvania Avenue NW.

NOTE: All photos are captioned.

DATE: 1899

PHOTOGRAPHERS: J. D. Givens.

PHYSICAL DESCRIPTION: 6 silver gelatin photoprints, 36 × 43 cm or smaller.

Lee Pitchlynn. *The B&P Railway Depot, Pennsylvania Avenue and Sixth Street NW, during a flood, June 2, 1889. Lot 12517.*

LC-USZ62-4508

Clinedinst. *Automobile manufacturers in their automobiles outside of the White House, 1906. Lot 12525.*

LC-USZ62-77948

SOURCE: Copyright deposit by J. D. Givens, 1899.

LOT 12516

SUBJECTS: "Proposed Design of Decorations, Pension Building, Washington, D.C. For Inaugural Ball, March 4, 1893." Photographs are copies of sketches of floral arrangements.

NOTE: Photographs are captioned.

DATE: March 1893

PHYSICAL DESCRIPTION: 3 albumen photoprints, 23 × 35 cm or smaller.

SOURCE: Copyright deposit by The Floral Exchange, 614 Chestnut Street, Philadelphia, Pennsylvania, 1893.

LOT 12517

SUBJECTS: Flood in Washington, D.C., Sunday, June 2, 1889. Flooded Pennsylvania Avenue between Ninth and Tenth Streets, at Sixth Street, at Seventh Street and Center Market, and near the B&P Railroad Depot at Sixth Street NW.

NOTE: Photographs are captioned.

DATE: June 2, 1899

PHOTOGRAPHERS: Lee Pitchlynn.

PHYSICAL DESCRIPTION: 4 albumen photoprints, 11 × 20 cm.

SOURCE: Gift of the Hugo W. Hesselbach estate, 1920, and the Alaska Historical Library, 1979.

LOT 12518

SUBJECTS: Mount Vernon interiors. Sideboard in family dining room; mirror and clock in the banquet hall.

DATE: 1903

PHOTOGRAPHERS: H. H. Dodge.

PHYSICAL DESCRIPTION: 2 silver gelatin photoprints, 21 × 16 cm or smaller.

SOURCE: Copyright deposit by H. H. Dodge, 1903.

LOT 12519

SUBJECTS: White House, north side; Great Falls on the Potomac River.

DATE: 1919

PHOTOGRAPHERS: S. I. Markel.

PHYSICAL DESCRIPTION: 2 silver gelatin photoprints, 30 × 50 cm or smaller.

SOURCE: Copyright deposit by S. I. Markel, 1919.

LOT 12520

SUBJECTS: Opening session of the Fifteenth Congress, showing Speaker Cannon taking the oath of office. Presentation exercises at the Friends School, Washington, D.C., May 24, 1907.

DATE: 1907

PHOTOGRAPHERS: George Lawrence Co.

PHYSICAL DESCRIPTION: 2 silver gelatin photoprints, 33 × 49 cm or smaller.

SOURCE: Copyright deposit by George Lawrence Co., 1907.

LOT 12523

SUBJECTS: Library of Congress, Jefferson Building and Adams Building. Adams Building exterior; views of the public card catalog in the Adams Building Reading Room; view of the north reading room; typical study rooms; Division of Orientalia. Jefferson Building exterior; view of the Division of Hispanic Literature.

NOTE: Photographs are matted, mounted, and captioned for exhibition use.

DATE: Ca. 1930s

PHOTOGRAPHERS: L. C. Handy.

PHYSICAL DESCRIPTION: 7 silver gelatin photoprints, 20 × 25 cm.

LOT 12525

SUBJECTS: Portraits of government officials and socialites; photo montage of President Wilson and his family, 1913; group portrait of automobile manufacturers in automobiles at the White House, 1906; montage portrait of the U.S. Supreme Court justices, 1913.

DATE: Ca. 1906–ca. 1913

PHOTOGRAPHERS: B. M. Clinedinst.

PHYSICAL DESCRIPTION: 9 silver gelatin photoprints, 19 × 24 cm or smaller.

SOURCE: Copyright deposit by Clinedinst, 1906–13.

LOT 12526

SUBJECTS: Interior of the Barney Studio House; interior of Representative Longworth's house (1905); interiors of the

Clinedinst. Interior of the Barney studio house, Washington, D.C., January 13, 1909. Lot 12526.
LC-USZ62-93099

Clinedinst. The U.S. Senate kitchen in the Capitol, December 22, 1911. Lot 12526.
LC-USZ62-93098

Edson Bradley residence, Washington, D.C., showing the reception hall, China Room, and Oratory (1910); black cooks in the U.S. Senate kitchen (1911).

DATE: Ca. 1905–ca. 1911

PHOTOGRAPHERS: B. M. Clinedinst.

PHYSICAL DESCRIPTION: 8 silver gelatin photoprints, 19 × 25 cm or smaller.

SOURCE: Copyright deposit by Clinedinst, 1905–11.

LOT 12575

SUBJECTS: Government buildings in Washington, D.C. General Post Office (1866); War Department (1865); District Court building (1865).

DATE: 1865–66

PHOTOGRAPHERS: G. D. Wakely.

PHYSICAL DESCRIPTION: 3 albumen photoprints, 25 × 34 cm or smaller.

SOURCE: Copyright deposit by G. D. Wakely, 1865–66.

G. D. Wakely. District Court, Washington, D.C., 1865. Lot 12575.
LC-USZ62-14826

LOT 12576

SUBJECTS: Library of Congress staff at work in the Adams Building. Exterior views of the Library of Congress Jefferson and Adams buildings; reading rooms and study rooms; staff at work in the Card Division, Catalog Division, Printing Office, Bindery, Cooperative Cataloging and Classification Service, and Photoduplication Lab. Card catalogs, bookstacks.

DATE: Ca. 1940s

PHYSICAL DESCRIPTION: 23 silver gelatin photoprints, 20 × 25 cm.

LOT 12579

SUBJECTS: Copy photoprints of illustration of Jefferson's scheme of classification, from a catalog of the Library of Congress, 1815, and copy of a letter from Edward Everett to Librarian of Congress George Watterston (Boston, October 31, 1826), discussing acquisition goals and methods for American books and journals.

G. D. Wakely. *Old War Department Building, Washington, D.C., 1865. Lot 12575.*
LC-USZ62-24804

B. W. Kilburn. *"'Showers of Blessings,' Junior Rally, C. E. Washington, D.C." 1896. Lot 12582.*
LC-USZ62-92900

Mathew Brady. *Group portrait of North American Indians in the White House Conservatory, ca. 1865. Lot 12661.*
LC-USZ62-11880

NOTE: Some mounts are stamped, "Johnston's History of the Library."

DATE: 1815–26

PHOTOGRAPHERS: Possibly L. C. Handy.

PHYSICAL DESCRIPTION: 2 silver gelatin photoprints, 20 × 25 cm or smaller.

LOT 12580

SUBJECTS: Library of Congress staff at work in the Music Division and Card Division.

DATE: Ca. 1910

PHOTOGRAPHERS: Possibly L. C. Handy.

PHYSICAL DESCRIPTION: 3 silver gelatin photoprints, 58 × 70 cm or smaller.

LOT 12581 (stereographs)

SUBJECTS: Christian Endeavor Army convention in Washington, D.C. Crowds assembled around the Capitol; Christian Endeavorers visiting Washington Monument and posed for group portraits.

NOTE: Images captioned.

DATE: 1896

PHOTOGRAPHERS: John F. Jarvis.

PUBLISHER: Underwood & Underwood (New York).

PHYSICAL DESCRIPTION: 15 albumen stereographs.

SOURCE: Copyright deposit by Jarvis, 1896.

LOT 12582

SUBJECTS: Meeting of 50,000 Christian Endeavorers at their Fifteenth International Convention, Washington, D.C. Participants at the East Front of the Capitol, with the Library of Congress in the background, at a song service on the Capitol East Front; meeting in tents on the Mall, with the Washington Monument in the background; on the White House grounds, and near the Smithsonian Institution. Includes views of the Junior Rally for young people; separate seating sections for black Endeavorers; news reporters at the convention; members of the Negro Delegation on the Department of Agriculture grounds; the Brennan triplets attending the convention. Also includes general scenes in Washington, D.C., including downtown views, and views of the Capitol.

DATE: 1896

PHOTOGRAPHERS: B. W. Kilburn (Littleton, New Hampshire).

PHYSICAL DESCRIPTION: 52 albumen stereographs, 9 × 18 cm or smaller.

SOURCE: Copyright deposit, 1896.

LOT 12660

SUBJECTS: Buildings, monuments, views, and events in Washington, D.C. President Wilson reading the terms of the Armistice to a joint session of Congress, November 11, 1918; the Bond Building under construction; the Washington Monument (1912); the White House; House of Representatives in session, 1919; opening of the George Washington Bicentennial at the U.S. Capitol, 1932; and a fox hunt in Chevy Chase, 1903. Bird's-eye-view color lithograph of Washington (1916); photographic copy of a painting by John Ross Key, grandson of Francis Scott Key, of the Key house in Georgetown (1908); H. R. Searle's design for the Washington Monument.

DATE: Ca. 1898–ca. 1932

PHOTOGRAPHERS: Leet Bros., H. Clayton Graff, Lyday Photogravure Company, Frank W. Hines, and Burr McIntosh Studios (New York).

PHYSICAL DESCRIPTION: 11 silver gelatin and albumen photoprints and a color lithograph, 66 × 51 cm or smaller.

SOURCE: Transfer, 1919, and copyright deposit.

LOT 12661

SUBJECTS: Portraits of Theodore Roosevelt (1912); Maj. J. H. Russell, USMC (1914). Carte-de-visite portraits of U.S. Grant and Dr. Mary E. Walker. Group portrait by Brady of visiting Indians in the White House Conservatory during the Civil War, accompanied by J. G. Nicolay and others, one of whom may be Mary Lincoln.

DATE: Ca. 1865–ca. 1914

PHOTOGRAPHERS: George Prince, W. H. Towles,——— & Joslyn ("Photographers of the Army of the West"), J. Holyland, and Mathew Brady.

PHYSICAL DESCRIPTION: 5 albumen and silver gelatin photoprints, including cartes de visite, 22 × 16 cm or smaller.

SOURCE: Copyright deposit and other sources.

LOT 12662

SUBJECTS: Postcard and other reproductions of scenes in Washington, D.C. Includes a large postcard of composite views and buildings in the Washington area; the Library of Congress Jefferson Building Main Reading Room, murals, and Neptune Fountain; the Library of Congress Adams Building; the White House State Dining Room (1907); Pennsylvania Avenue from the U.S. Treasury Building; the Mount Vernon steamer *Charles Macalester*; Georgetown University and the Washington Canoe Club in Georgetown. A booklet of reproductions covers areas in Southwest Washington, including aerial views of the Washington Channel; views of the yacht harbor, fish market, Water Street, the U.S. Lighthouse Wharf at O Street, and the Norfolk and Washington Steamboat Company office at Seventh Street.

NOTE: Some halftone reproductions used in "Potomac River, North Side of Washington Channel, D.C.," House Document no. 127, 71st Congress, 2d session, 1929.

DATE: Ca. 1907–ca. 1944

PHOTOGRAPHERS: Leet Bros., R. G. Mattice, W. B. Garrison, Ottenheimer (Baltimore), Capitol Souvenir Company, and National Society of Colonial Dames of America (Albertype Co., Brooklyn New York).

PHYSICAL DESCRIPTION: 35 postcards and halftone reproductions, 18 × 29 cm or smaller.

SOURCE: Copyright deposit and other sources.

LOT 12663

SUBJECTS: U.S. Capitol and Library of Congress. View of the West Front of the Capitol and grounds; pre-1850s copy of a watercolor of the Capitol and Pennsylvania Avenue; East Front of the Capitol, east portico; blizzard of 1888, showing the Capitol grounds. Copies of wood engravings of the Library of Congress in the Capitol, and as rebuilt there after the 1851 fire; the Jefferson Building Neptune Fountain; the shrine of the Declaration of Independence and Constitution in the Jefferson Building.

DATE: Ca. 1850s–ca. 1900

PHOTOGRAPHERS: C. O. Buckingham and L. C. Handy.

PHYSICAL DESCRIPTION: 11 albumen and silver gelatin photoprints, including copy photographs of wood engravings and a watercolor, halftone photomechanical prints, and a lithograph, 25 × 20 cm or smaller.

SOURCE: Gift and other sources.

Burr McIntosh Studio. Fox hunt at Chevy Chase, Maryland, 1903. Lot 12660.

LC-Z62-11349

LOT 12664

SUBJECTS: Aerial and high views of Washington, D.C. Pre-1889 view from the Capitol dome of the Library of Congress construction site and East Capitol Street; Hains Point, Potomac and Anacostia Rivers, and Washington Navy Yard; Bolling Field area; Tidal Basin area, with overview of the capital.

DATE: Ca. 1880s–ca. 1930

PHYSICAL DESCRIPTION: 4 silver gelatin photoprints, 17 × 23 cm.

SOURCE: Transfer from the Geography and Map Division.

LOT 12665

SUBJECTS: C&O Canal, Washington, D.C. Scenes on the canal at various locations; lock houses, showing locks; barges, mules, lock tenders, and barge crews; towpath; and a canal wall in Georgetown.

DATE: Ca. 1905–ca. 1950

PHOTOGRAPHERS: Mildred Mugridge and National Photo Company.

PHYSICAL DESCRIPTION: 5 silver gelatin photoprints, 19 × 25 cm or smaller.

C&O Canal in Georgetown. Lot 12665.

LC-USZ62-19840

W. C. Babcock. Dedication of Grand Army Place during the G.A.R. encampment in Washington, D.C., 1892. Lot 12666.

LC-USZ62-4607

Market Space and Pennsylvania Avenue NW, Washington, D.C., 1901. Lot 12667.

LC-USZ62-55022

Katie Gallaher. The ruins of St. Dominic's Church after a fire, March 12, 1885. Lot 12667.

LC-USZ62-67844

LOT 12666

SUBJECTS: Events in Washington, D.C. Dedication of Grand Army Place during the Grand Army of the Republic Encampment at Washington, 1892, taken while Vice President Levi Parsons Morton unfurled the flag and the U.S. Artillery fired the salute; suffragettes marching up the West Front steps into the Capitol, 1913; the U.S. Navy Band on the West Front of the Capitol and at the White House, with Lt. Charles Brendler, conductor.

DATE: Ca. 1892–ca. 1946

PHOTOGRAPHERS: W. C. Babcock, Evans Lantz, and American Press Association.

PHYSICAL DESCRIPTION: 4 albumen and silver gelatin photoprints, 20 × 25 cm.

SOURCE: Copyright deposit.

LOT 12667

SUBJECTS: Buildings, monuments, and views in Washington, D.C. Includes aerial views of Union Station, 1913; the Capitol, the Mall, Washington area and Virginia, 1952; and wartime buildings on the Mall, 1919. Also includes views of laundry and kitchen facilities, possibly in the White House, 1913; the White House East Room and Red Room, 1909 and 1906; the Washington Monument after completion, ca. 1884; the Washington Monument with an airship flying near it, 1906; the Adams Memorial by Augustus Saint-Gaudens in Rock Creek Cemetery, 1946; the National Gallery of Art rotunda, 1950; a Mount Vernon bedroom, 1904; a mantle in the Banquet Hall, Mount Vernon, 1903; composite photographs of Mount Vernon buildings, interiors, and scenes, 1881; the Marshall House in Alexandria, 1897 and 1903; the C&O Canal, lock no. 3, 1939; Market Space and Pennsylvania Avenue with pedestrians and horse-drawn carriages, 1901; the ruins of St. Dominic's Church after the fire of March 12, 1885; Metropolitan Club Building, 1908; Capitol dome at night, 1955; and the Department of State Building, 1957. Includes copy photograph of a seal design for Washington, D.C. (1900).

DATE: Ca. 1881–ca. 1957

PHOTOGRAPHERS: G. V. Buck, C. S. Cudlip & Co., N. G. Johnson, H. H. Dodge, Katie Gallaher, A. E. Nesbitt, Horace K. Turner Co. (Boston), Lucia Myers, Wide World, Abajian, Kurtis Bros (New York), and Scharlach.

PHYSICAL DESCRIPTION: 23 silver gelatin and albumen photoprints, photolithographs, and halftone photomechanical prints, 28 × 36 cm or smaller.

SOURCE: Copyright deposit, gift, and other sources.

LOT 12668

SUBJECTS: Buildings and views in Washington, D.C. Aqueduct bridge in Georgetown (1859); State, War, and Navy Department; old Winder Building on Seventeenth Street, below Pennsylvania Avenue; the U.S. Patent Office (ca. 1860s–70s); Georgetown University (ca. 1880s–90s); the White House (1886, ca. 1860s–70s, and ca. 1890–1900); cable cars on Seventh Street NW (1892); flooded Pennsylvania Avenue (ca. 1897–98); uncompleted Washington Monument, and a crowd of people on the White House grounds (ca. 1883); St. Matthew's Church at Fifteenth and H Streets NW (ca. 1870s); the Agriculture Department Building on the Mall; view of F Street from the Patent Office; the Arts and Industries Building; Freer Gallery; railroad tracks in Washington; the Cabin John Bridge under construction (1858) and completed; the Capitol Hill home of J. McDonald (chief clerk of the Senate); Queen Street warehouse in Alexandria (ca. 1860s–80s). Completed Washington Monument; Prentice Studio, Music Department, American University (1960s); the U.S. Capitol, Statuary Hall; the Emancipation statue in Lincoln Park; Old Soldiers' Home. Interior of Morgan's Pharmacy (ca. 1940s); Smithsonian Institution Building (ca. 1890–1900, ca. 1940s); Joseph Henry statue (ca. 1940s); National Gallery of Art (ca. 1940s); Colorado Building under construction in Washington; Lincoln Memorial (ca. 1940s); Chinese Embassy (ca. 1940s); rush-hour traffic over Memorial Bridge (ca. 1940s). Includes an aerial view of Washington, Maryland, Virginia, Pennsylvania, Delaware, and New Jersey, showing the Potomac and Anacostia Rivers, taken from a five-mile altitude, using infra-red photography (ca. 1940); and a retouched aerial view of Washington and Maryland, showing the Potomac River, Tidal Basin, Mall, and Southeast, Northwest, Northeast areas (1915). Also includes a wood engraving of the Washington Monument (1885).

DATE: Ca. 1859–ca. 1960s

PHOTOGRAPHERS: L. C. Handy, J. F. Jarvis, Price, Heliotype Printing Company (Boston), Reni Newsphoto Service, S. McMullin (Philadelphia), U.S. Army Air Corps, Federal Works Agency, and H. H. Green for Matthews Northrup Works.

PHYSICAL DESCRIPTION: 45 albumen and silver gelatin photoprints, including cabinet cards, photographic copies of lithographs and wood engravings, and a collotype, 39 × 50 cm or smaller.

SOURCE: Transfer from the Geography and Map Division and the U.S. Naval Academy; gift of Public Affairs Press, 1954; and other sources.

Uncompleted Washington Monument photographed from the White House grounds, ca. 1883. Lot 12668.
LC-USZ62-24664

Interior of Morgan's Pharmacy, Washington, D.C., ca. 1940s–50s. Lot 12668.

LC-USZ62-92956

S. McMullin. Queen Street warehouse, Alexandria, Virginia, ca. 1860s–ca. 1880. Lot 12668.
LC-USZ62-92954

Reddington & Shaffer. Group portrait of U.S. senators, Forty-third Congress. February 12, 1874. Lot 12671.
LC-USZ62-4525

Jno. Bowers. Composite photograph of the D.C. Fire Department, Washington. Includes montage group portrait, portraits of chief and assistants, and photographs of firehouses in the city, 1904. Lot 12670.
LC-USZ62-92952

LOT 12670

SUBJECTS: Photomontages of the Washington, D.C., Fire Department (1904) and Metropolitan Police Department (1904). D.C. Fire Department photo includes captioned, inset portraits of chief, fire marshals, assistant chiefs, foremen, machinists, and clerks and small inset photographs of fire stations. Entire department is shown (in montage) in front of the U.S. Capitol, holding fire equipment. The Metropolitan Police Department photograph includes captioned inset portraits of the chief, high-ranking officers, and sergeants and inset photographs of police stations. The entire department is shown (in montage) in front of the U.S. Capitol, with bicycles.

DATE: 1904

PHOTOGRAPHERS: Jno. Bowers.

PHYSICAL DESCRIPTION: 2 silver gelatin photoprints, 51 × 61 cm or smaller.

SOURCE: Copyright deposit, 1904.

LOT 12671

SUBJECTS: Group portraits, Washington, D.C. "U.S. Senators, 43rd Congress," taken February 12, 1874, on the east Senate portico steps of the U.S. Capitol; portrait includes senators, assistant doorkeepers, clerk, sergeant-at-arms, all identified, and onlookers. "Bishop Hare and the 'Sioux Delegation' at Washington," a heavily retouched photomontage portrait, fully captioned (1875). "Survivors of the 34th Congress, 1888," a group portrait of eleven "survivors," including Justin Morrill and Nathaniel Banks. Composite photolithograph (Albertype Company) of "Representative Washington Correspondents," published by the Public Opinion Company as an advertising poster ("Group No. 4") for the Phoenix Insurance Company, Hartford, Connecticut; includes 61 reduced portraits of newspaper and news service correspondents, including E. G. Dunnell (New York Times), George Grantham Bain (Syndicate Letters), Frank A. Richardson (Baltimore Sun), and A. Maurice Low (Boston Globe). Group portrait of delegates to the First International Labour Conference, Washington, D.C., October 29, 1919; accompanied by a booklet, "Delegates' Official Guide."

DATE: Ca. 1874–ca. 1919

PHOTOGRAPHERS: Brady & Rice, Reddington & Shaffer, Public Opinion Company, and M. E. Mann.

PHYSICAL DESCRIPTION: 5 albumen and silver gelatin photoprints, a photolithograph (Albertype), and a booklet, 56 × 71 cm.

SOURCE: Copyright deposit.

LOT 12672

SUBJECTS: The U.S. Capitol and related buildings. Construction of the Capitol dome (ca. 1860s); construction of Senate wing of U.S. Capitol (ca. 1870s); East Front of Capitol (heavily retouched); U.S. Capitol from the northeast (ca. 1870s); wide-angle view of the Capitol East Front, from the Library of Congress dome; buildings on the future site of the Longworth House Office Building; House of Representatives in session.

DATE: Ca. 1860s–ca. 1930s

PHOTOGRAPHERS: T. Horydczak and Kerston & Fordham (Newark, New Jersey).

PHYSICAL DESCRIPTION: 7 silver gelatin, albumen, and salted paper photoprints and 1 photomechanical print, 47 × 60 cm or smaller.

SOURCE: Transfer, gift, and other sources.

Construction of the U.S. Capitol dome, ca. 1860s. Lot 12672.

LC-USZ62-5634

Construction of the Senate wing of the U.S. Capitol, ca. 1870s. Lot 12672

LC-USZ62-92957

Site of the Longworth House Office Building. Lot 12672.

LC-USZ62-4516

LOT 12673

SUBJECTS: Group portraits and events, Washington, D.C. Most photos made with banquet cameras. Includes governors and mayors after a conference with President Woodrow Wilson at the White House, March 3, 1919; delegates of the Latin American Republics to the Twenty-third Session of the Interparliamentary Union, at the Pan American Union Building, October 6, 1925; a group placing a wreath on a tomb in Arlington Cemetery; inauguration of President Hoover, March 4, 1929; the Washington baseball team (1913); Eighteenth Annual Dixie Ball at the Willard Hotel, March 28, 1921; annual dinner of the American Engineering Council, Mayflower Hotel, January 15, 1937; Thirty-eighth Annual Meeting of the American Ornithologists Union, November 9–11, 1920; Forty-fifth Meeting of the American Ornithologists Union, November 14–17, 1927; inauguration of President Harding, March 4, 1921; female Navy Department yeoman on the White House grounds, February 1919; Twentieth Annual Convention of the Special Libraries Association, May 21–23, 1928; Grand Jury, District of Columbia, October term, 1927; conference of National Park Service superintendents, November 1934; funeral ceremonies for President Harding, U.S. Capitol, August 8, 1923.

DATE: Ca. 1913–ca. 1937

PHOTOGRAPHERS: Schutz, Harris & Ewing, E. DeSouza and DeSouza Bros., Rideout, Tenschert, and Edmonston.

PHYSICAL DESCRIPTION: 15 silver gelatin photoprints, 47 × 117 cm or smaller.

SOURCE: Copyright deposit, transfer, and gift.

LOT 12675

SUBJECTS: Oversize and wide-angle views of Washington-area buildings and sites. Includes the U.S. Capitol, East Front and grounds (1906); Washington Monument (1909, 1912); Library of Congress from the Capitol dome (1906); Mount Vernon (1899); Jackson Monument (ca. 1900–1909); Great Falls, Virginia, on the Potomac River (1909, 1919); Sheridan Circle; inauguration of Theodore Roosevelt on the Capitol East Front grounds, 1905; U.S. Patent Office (1881); White House (1909); Navy Department Building; U.S. Treasury Building (1909); Senate Office Building (1909); Tidal Basin (1921); Patent Office and Warder Building; Pennsylvania Avenue and Fifteenth Street from the Treasury Building (1909).

DATE: 1899–1919

PHOTOGRAPHERS: Schutz, H. L. Ludwig, Post Photo Service, H. A. Fletcher, F. W. Brehm (Rochester, New York), A. W. Elson & Co. (Boston), Haines Photo Co. (Conneaut, Ohio), and Norris Peters Co.

PHYSICAL DESCRIPTION: 9 silver gelatin photoprints, 41 × 126 cm or smaller.

SOURCE: Copyright deposit.

Browsing Files

The Prints and Photographs Division maintains certain files of photographs to which materials can be added without formal cataloging. These self-indexing vertical files, more commonly referred to as "browsing files," provide large numbers of photographs on the most frequently called-for subjects. In many cases, the photographs in these files are modern copy photoprints or duplicate photographs from images in cataloged collections. Browsing files have been organized to provide easy and immediate access by researchers to portraits or photographs having to do with presidents, members of Congress, specific subjects, and geographical locations. With the exception of the Congressional Portrait File, each browsing file has a corresponding stereograph file.

Accompanying indexes provide alphabetical access to subjects from each of these files for which the Library holds a copy negative and to sources of material on particular subjects in other collections in the Prints and Photographs Division or elsewhere in the Library. The various browsing files contain many images for which there is no entry to be found in the indexes, however, and researchers should therefore search both the file itself and the appropriate index. Finally, researchers are advised to consult the Prints and Photographs Division Catalog for other sources of material beyond what may be found in the browsing files.

Levin C. Handy. Setting the keystone in the southwest clerestory arch during construction of the Library of Congress (Jefferson Building), June 28, 1892. Library of Congress Construction Photographs, Lot 12365.

LC-USL5-381

The Washington, D.C., Geographical File and the Washington, D.C., Geographical Stereograph File provide familiar single images of the capital. At present, the Washington, D.C., Geographical File numbers about 7,600 items, organized by subject as outlined below. These Washington materials are modern silver gelatin photoprints, for the most part copies of vintage photographs received through copyright deposit, or copies of popular images found in the cataloged collections. This browsing file represents only about 1 percent of the Washington, D.C., photographs held in the Prints and Photographs Division. The division catalog and this guide provide access to many other sources.

The Washington section of the Geographical and Historical Index begins with useful cross-references from desired Washington subjects to the terms under which photographs of those subjects are filed (for instance, "Old Executive Office Building, search under State, War, and Navy Building"). The entries in this index primarily identify items that have been copied for previous researchers and for which the Library therefore holds a copy negative. The index, however, contains references to copy negatives for Washington images of a geographical nature and pictures of historical events (as opposed to portraits or specific subjects) from sources other than the Washington, D.C., Geographical File. The index therefore provides one kind of access to Washington images in many collections in the Library, including those in the Geography and Map Division and the Rare Book and Special Collections Division, and it should be consulted by researchers looking for particular Washington subjects.

The Washington, D.C., Subject List reflects the current holdings in the Washington, D.C., Geographical File. The list is designed to be easily expanded as material is added in new categories. Cross-references and subcategories have been omitted here, but a much more detailed listing of subjects is displayed in the Prints and Photographs Reading Room near the Washington, D.C., Geographical File. The Washington, D.C., Geographical Stereograph File is organized according to the same scheme, although not all subject categories are represented in that smaller collection.

Clinedinst. *Alice P. Barney studio house. Copyright 1909. Washington, D.C., Geographical File, "Houses."*

LC-USZ62-79904

Levin C. Handy. *First Regiment, D.C. Volunteers, leaving for Camp Alger, May 14, 1898. Washington, D.C., Geographical File, "Historical events— 1898."*

LC-USZ62-34430

Levin C. Handy. *Labor Day parade on Pennsylvania Avenue NW, with the unfinished Post Office Department Building in the background, ca. 1894. Washington, D.C., Geographical File, "Historical events— 1894."*

LC-BH8233-15

Traders National Bank, Tenth Street and Pennsylvania Avenue NW, ca. 1890. Washington, D.C., Geographical File, "Commerce."

LC-USZ62-26496

Underwood & Underwood. Center Market, ca. 1931. Washington, D.C., Geographical File, "Commerce." Reproduced with the permission of Joseph Rotwein.

Levin C. Handy. View of the Potomac River and East Potomac Park from the Washington Monument, ca. 1890. Washington, D.C., Geographical File, "Views—aerial and bird's-eye."

LC-USZ62-4511

Pediment model being placed in position over the U.S. House of Representatives portico in the Capitol. Washington, D.C., Geographical File, "Capitol—exterior."

LC-USZ62-50577

Old Glen Echo car barn, beyond Georgetown, ca. 1890s. Washington, D.C., Geographical File, "Transportation."

LC-USZ62-59722

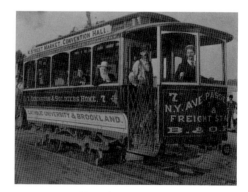

Streetcar owned by Eckington & Soldiers Home Railway Company, ca. 1890s. Washington, D.C., Geographical File, "Transportation."

LC-USZ62-15878

SUBJECT LIST

Airports
Apartment buildings
Aqueducts
Bridges
Canals
Capitol
   Architectural drawings and plans
   Construction
   Exterior
   Interior
Cemeteries
Chanceries and embassies
Churches
Circles and squares

City plans
Commerce
Convents
Correctional institutions
D.C. government buildings
Disasters
Educational institutions
Fire department
Fires
Floods
Fountains
Galleries and museums
Historical events
Hospitals

Hotels and inns
Houses
Industry
Jails and prisons
Libraries
Library of Congress
   Adams Building
   Jefferson Building
   Madison Building
   Seals, emblems, bookplates
   Staff
   Treasures
Monuments and memorials
Neighborhoods and areas

Nursing homes
Organizations
Parks and gardens
Performing arts facilities
Police department
Public utilities
Railroad stations
Reformatories
Religious buildings
Residential buildings
Restaurants and taverns
Rivers and islands
Schools
Smithsonian Institution
Social life and customs
Statues
Streets
Transportation
U.S. government buildings
  Armory
  Botanic Garden
  Bureau of Engraving and Printing
  Bureau of Standards
  Cannon House Office Building
  Department of Agriculture
  Department of Commerce
  Department of Interior
  Department of Justice
  Department of Labor
  Department of Navy
  Department of State
  Department of Treasury
  Dirksen Senate Office Building
  Federal Trade Commission
  Government Printing Office
  Internal Revenue Service
  Longworth House Office Building
  National Archives
  Naval Observatory
  Navy and Munitions Building
  Navy Yard
  Patent Office
  Pension Building
  Post Office Department
  Rayburn House Office Building
  Russell Senate Office Building
  Social Security Administration
  State, War, and Navy Building
  Supreme Court
  Tariff Commission Building
  Union Station
  Veterans Administration
  War Department
Universities and colleges
Views
  Aerial and bird's-eye views
  Panoramic views
Vocational schools
Waterfront
White House
  Animals
  Architectural details
  Architectural drawings and plans
  Construction and restoration
  Events
  Exterior
  Fires and disasters
  Interior
  Staff
Work and workplaces

Harris & Ewing. Harry Atwood taking off from the White House lawn in a Wright Type B airplane, July 1911. Washington, D.C., Geographical File, "White House—views."

LC-USZ62-56945

Harris & Ewing. Government worker housing on Union Station Plaza during and after World War I. February 12, 1919. Washington, D.C., Geographical File, "U.S. government buildings—Union Station."

LC-USZ62-63970

Congressional Cemetery. Washington, D.C., Geographical File, "Cemeteries."

LC-USZ62-83310

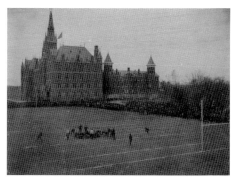

A football game at Georgetown University. Washington, D.C., Geographical File, "Universities and colleges."

LC-USZ62-79417

Titian R. Peale. Bird's-eye view of Southwest Washington, taken from the Smithsonian Institution, August 18, 1863. Washington, D.C., Geographical File, "Views—aerial and bird's-eye."

LC-USZ62-37931

The Army Medical Museum Library, Seventh Street and Independence Avenue SW, ca. 1943. Washington, D.C., Geographical File, "Libraries."

LC-USZ62-92469

R. Douglas (Livingston, New Jersey). Gallaudet College. Copyright 1897. Washington, D.C., Geographical File, "Universities and colleges."

LC-USZ62-92468

Movie stars Mary Pickford and Charlie Chaplin selling Liberty Bonds on the Capitol steps, ca. 1917. Washington, D.C., Geographical File, "Historical events—WWI."

LC-USZ62-67912

Levin C. Handy. The furnaces in the Library of Congress (Jefferson Building), ca. 1900. Washington, D.C., Geographical File, "Library of Congress—Jefferson Building—interior."

LC-USZ62-59275

American Press Association. Carnegie Institution, 1910. Washington, D.C., Geographical File, "Libraries."

LC-USZ62-92470

Stereographic views of Washington, D.C., have been acquired mainly as copyright deposits since 1870. At present this browsing collection numbers about 1,000 items, ranging in date from the 1870s to about 1920, and it is organized by the same subject list as outlined under "Washington, D.C., Geographical File," with fewer categories represented, however. The Washington, D.C., section of the Geographical and Historical Index includes items from this stereograph collection that have been copied.

Kilburn Brothers. "The Anxious Politicians." Copyright 1899. Washington, D.C., Geographical Stereographs, "Historical events—1889."
LC-USZ62-41509

J. F. Jarvis. "The Agriculture Department." Washington, D.C., Geographical Stereographs, "U.S. government buildings—Dept. of Agriculture."
LC-USZ62-16411

C. L. Wasson. McMahon Hall, Catholic University. Copyright 1900. Washington, D.C., Geographical Stereographs, "Universities and colleges."
LC-USZ62-92288

Keystone View Company. "Doing Their Bit—Students of McKinley Manual Training High School . . . With 4-inch Shells They Have Made." Copyright 1917. Washington, D.C., Geographical Stereographs, "Schools."
LC-USZ62-92290

T. W. Ingersoll. The Big Tree on the grounds of the Smithsonian Institution. Copyright 1897. Washington, D.C., Geographical Stereographs, "Smithsonian Institution—Grounds."

LC-USZ62-92292

Underwood & Underwood. "The Inaugural Ballroom—from President Roosevelt's box—Pension Building." Copyright 1905. Washington, D.C., Geographical Stereographs, "U.S. government buildings—Pension Building."

LC-USZ62-92289

The U.S.S. Nipsic in the Washington Navy Yard, October 15, 1874. Washington, D.C., Geographical Stereographs, "D.C. government buildings—Washington Navy Yard."

LC-USZ62-92291

Photographs, lithographs, engravings, copies of paintings, and other kinds of portraits are gathered together under an alphabetical arrangement in the Biographical File. Nearly two hundred file drawers hold over 100,000 portraits of the famous and not-so-famous from around the world and throughout history, including people who played major and minor roles in Washington's political, social, architectural, and commercial history. The portraits have come from a variety of sources, including copyright deposit, gift, and transfer. Many portraits from the Bain Collection and the Underwood & Underwood Collection may be found in this file. Besides portraits, the Biographical File includes pictures of the homes of some famous people and a few images that depict related events. Cross-references guide researchers to the proper form of many names, particularly foreign names. Several drawers at the end of the alphabetical arrangement contain group portraits (such as, "diplomatic corps," "dramatists," "Geneva Conference," or "Methodist Episcopal Church Bishops") in an alphabetical arrangement.

The Biographical Index includes portrait materials from the Biographical File and from other sources for which the division holds a copy negative or an original negative. In some cases, cards have been filed in the Biographical Index for original photoprints or other media where no negative exists, as a reminder to researchers of other sources of particular portrait subjects. Not all images in the Biographical File are listed in the Biographical Index, and the index does not represent all the portrait material to be found in the Prints and Photographs Division. The index includes references to portrait subjects from other divisions in the Library (for instance, the Manuscript Division and the Rare Book and Special Collections Division) that have been copied by researchers and for which the Prints and Photographs Division holds a copy negative.

Separate indexes list portraits of American Indians and Civil War portraits.

Levin C. Handy. Portrait of Mathew B. Brady, ca. 1875. Biographical File.

LC-BH826-2681

Joseph Henry, ca. 1845-50. Biographical File.
LC-USZ62-14760

Rice (Washington D.C.). Portrait of W. W. Corcoran. Biographical File.

LC-USZ62-16521

Frederick Douglass and his grandson Joseph. Biographical File.

LC-USZ62-51528

Mathew Brady or Levin C. Handy. Portrait of Montgomery C. Meigs. Biographical File.
LC-BH832-391

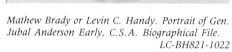

Mathew Brady or Levin C. Handy. Portrait of Gen. Jubal Anderson Early, C.S.A. Biographical File.
LC-BH821-1022

Mathew Brady. Jefferson Davis. Biographical File.
LC-B8184-4146

Alexander Robey Shepherd. Biographical File.
LC-USZ62-4909

Mathew Brady or Levin C. Handy. Prof. Edward H. Gallaudet. Biographical File.
LC-BH826-29808A

Mathew Brady or Levin C. Handy. Benjamin Brown French, commissioner of public buildings, Washington, D.C. Biographical File.
LC-BH82-5077

Mathew Brady. Constantino Brumidi. Biographical File.
LC-USA7-31233

Biographical Stereograph File

Stereograph portraits of prominent people have been collected by the Library in a browsing file, arranged alphabetically. This collection includes about 600 images, which were acquired primarily by copyright deposit and gift.

The Biographical Index includes references to images from the Biographical Stereograph File that have been copied, and for which the Prints and Photographs Division holds a copy negative.

Samuel T. Rayburn, with Lyndon B. Johnson in the background, throwing the baseball to begin the game. Biographical Stereographs.

LC-USZ62-86878

Keystone View Company. "Col. Lindbergh Acknowledging the Nation's Welcome, Washington, D.C." Copyright September 1927. Biographical Stereographs.

LC-USZ62-92420

Strohmeyer & Wyman for Underwood & Underwood. "Hon. Geo. B. Cortelyou, Executive Clerk to the President" (William McKinley). Copyright 1898. Biographical Stereographs.

LC-USZ62-